Trade Marks: Law and Practice

Third Edition

Trade Marks: Law and Practice

Third Edition

Alison Firth
Visiting Professor, CCLS, Queen Mary, University of London
and Newcastle University

Gary Lea
Consultant to Aruna Trade Mark Attorneys

Peter Cornford
Partner, Stevens Hewlett & Perkins
Consulting Editor

JORDANS

Published by Jordan Publishing Limited
21 St Thomas Street
Bristol BS1 6JS

British Library Cataloguing-in-Publication Data

A catalogue record for this book is available from the British Library.

ISBN 978 1 84661 263 3

Typeset by Letterpart Ltd, Reigate, Surrey
Printed and bound in Great Britain by CPI Group (UK) Ltd, Croydon, CR0 4YY

To Will, Anne, Alexander, Catherine, Hannah and Adam

AUTHOR BIOGRAPHIES

Alison Firth

MA, MSc, Barrister

Alison originally read physics. Before commencing her career at the Bar, she conducted postgraduate research in polymer physics, and taught in both London and Lima. She has been a full time academic since 1985, most recently holding chairs in law at Newcastle University (2005–09) and Surrey University (2009–12). She is now visiting professor at Newcastle and at the Centre for Commercial Law Studies, Queen Mary, University of London.

She has taught intellectual property law, competition law and contract law to undergraduate and postgraduate students and supervised a number of doctoral researchers. Her own research centres on the law of intellectual property and its relationship with other areas, including competition law and civil procedure. She is author of a number of books, chapters and articles on these areas. Her practice includes advising in respect of patents, copyright, design right, trade marks, passing off, confidential information and competition law. Alison was Honorary Legal Adviser to the British Copyright Council from 1994–2007. She is an associate member of the Institute of Trade Mark Attorneys.

Gary Lea

LLB (Hons), LLM, MPhil

Gary Lea is a consultant to Aruna Trade Mark Attorneys, a trade mark attorney firm in Canberra, Australian Capital Territory. Previously, he was a Senior Lecturer in Business Law, University of New South Wales (UNSW@ADFA), Canberra, Australia. His teaching covered business law and all allied subjects (including intellectual property) at both undergraduate and postgraduate level. Prior to that, Gary taught and researched in various capacities at Queen Mary, University of London, principally within the Queen Mary Intellectual Property Research Institute (QMIPRI) and IP Unit. Starting as a Herchel Smith Junior Research Fellow (1997–99), he was eventually appointed as Senior Research Fellow and Lecturer in Industrial Property Law (2002–04). His work focused on IP issues affecting the information and communications technology (ICT) sector.

Peter Cornford

BA (Hons) RTMA, ETMA, MITMA

Peter Cornford is a Registered Trade Mark Attorney, European Trade Mark Attorney and Member of the Institute of Trade Mark Attorneys. He has worked in private practice since 1989 and is a Partner at Stevens Hewlett & Perkins.

As a trade mark attorney, Peter is involved continuously in a wide variety of contentious and non-contentious matters. He is responsible for the worldwide trade mark portfolios of many of his practice's major clients in industries as diverse as footwear and clothing, tobacco, homeopathic medicines and publishing.

CONTENTS

TABLE OF CASES

References are to paragraph numbers.

TABLE OF STATUTES

References are to paragraph numbers.

TABLE OF STATUTORY INSTRUMENTS

References are to paragraph numbers.

TABLE OF EUROPEAN AND
INTERNATIONAL MATERIALS

References are to paragraph numbers.

Chapter 1

THE COMMERCIAL FUNCTIONS OF A TRADE MARK

INTRODUCTION

1.1   Human society uses signs, symbols or marks in many ways.[1] Name tags, cattle brands and shipping symbols indicate ownership of chattels. Car registration numbers may be used to trace a person having charge of the vehicle, and 'special' or 'personalised' registration numbers are valued highly.[2] A plant variety name identifies a plant with specific genetic makeup.[3] Indications of geographical origin speak volumes on the characteristics of products, especially foodstuffs.[4] Domain names facilitate navigation of the web.[5] When a commercial undertaking provides goods or services, trade marks or brand names provide important information as to the nature and origin of those products. Such information is essential to the functioning of a competitive market.[6] This book seeks to explain how the indicative value of

---

[1]   For an historical account, see Ida, Maniatis and Sodipo 'Distinctive Signs and Early Markets: Europe, Africa and Islam' in A Firth (ed) *Prehistory and Development of Intellectual Property Systems* (1997) vol 1 (Perspectives on Intellectual Property).

[2]   As recognised in *Naylor v Hutson* [1994] FSR 63 ('1700 MG').

[3]   Council Regulation (EC) 2100/94 on Community Plant Variety Rights OJ [1994] L 227/1, Arts 17, 18, 63 – variety denomination must be approved and used for protected plant varieties; UK Plant Varieties Act 1997, ss 18–20; Piatti and Jouffray 'Plant Variety Names in National and International Law' [1984] EIPR 283 and 311; Sherman 'Taxonomic Property' [2008] CLJ 560. In *Antonio Munoz y Cia SA v Frumar Ltd* Case C253/00 [2002] ECR I-7289, the European Court of Justice held that a grape producer could sue to enforce a Community requirement under marketing regulations that fruit be marketed by reference to their variety names.

[4]   Council Regulation (EEC) 823/87 OJ [1987] L 84/59 (wines); (EEC) 2081/92 OJ [1991] L 208/00 (agricultural products and food). Van Caenegem 'Registered GIs: Intellectual Property, Agricultural Policy and International Trade' [2004] EIPR 170; Ribeiro de Almeida 'Key Differences between Trade Marks and Geographical Indications' [2008] EIPR 406; Evans 'The Comparative Advantages of Geographical Indications and Community Trade Marks for the Marketing of Agricultural Products in the European Union' (2010) IIC 645.

[5]   Maniatis 'Trade Mark Law and Domain Names: Back to Basics' [2002] EIPR 397. Much useful information on domain names may be found on the web pages of the World Intellectual Property Organisation, which offered a domain name dispute resolution service. See www.wipo.int/amc/en/domains.

[6]   On the economic functions of trade marks, see Landes and Posner 'The Economics of Trademark Law' (1988) 78 TMR 267; Economides 'The Economics of Trademark Law' (1988) 78 TMR 523; Cornish and Phillips 'The Economic Function of Trade Marks: An Analysis with Special Reference to Developing Countries' (1982) 13 IIC 41; Korah 'The Interface between Intellectual Property Rights and Competition in Developed Countries' (2005) 24 Script-Ed 430; Rosler 'The Rationale for European Trade Mark Protection' [2007] EIPR 100; Aldred 'The Economic Rationale of Trademarks: An Economist's Critique', in Bently, Davis

trade marks is protected by law in the UK and Europe, and to outline the international systems and influences under which this law operates.

1.2   The UK's Trade Marks Act 1994[7] ('the 1994 Act') made major changes to the UK law of registered marks. It implemented the European Community's First Council Directive[8] ('the Directive') to approximate the trade marks laws of member states. That Directive, in turn, by ironing out differences in national trade mark laws was designed to pave the way for the unitary system of Community trade mark protection.[9] Both these Community instruments were promulgated in the interest of transparent competition and free movement of goods and services in the Community's internal market.[10] The goal of providing uniform protection for intellectual property through the European Union is now enshrined in Art 118 of the Treaty on the Functioning of the European Union (TFEU), which confers specific legislative power in this area. The 1994 Act also enabled the UK to take advantage of developments in the international filing of trade marks provided by the Madrid Protocol.[11] The 1994 Act demonstrates the UK's compliance with its obligations under the venerable Paris Convention for the Protection of Industrial Property[12] and under the Trade-Related Aspects of Intellectual Property Rights (TRIPs) Agreement of 1993.[13]

---

and Ginsburg (eds), *Trade Marks and Brands: an Interdisciplinary Critique* (2008). For a note of scepticism, see Dogan and Lemley 'Trademarks and Consumer Search Costs on the Internet' (2004) Houston LR 777.

[7]   Commencement 31 October 1994: Trade Marks Act 1994 (Commencement) Order 1994, SI 1994/2550.

[8]   First Council Directive (EEC) 89/104, OJ [1988] L 40/1; the texts of EU law in the field of trade marks may be accessed through the website of the Office for Harmonisation in the Internal Market at http://oami.europa.eu/en/mark/aspects/default.htm.

[9]   Council Regulation (EC) 40/94 on the Community trade mark OJ [1994] L 11/1, established that system. Applications for Community trade marks were accepted by the Office for Harmonisation in the Internal Market from January 1996, and processing began in April 1996. See, further, Chapter 13 and http://oami.europa.eu.

[10] See the first preamble or recital to the Directive and the Regulation.

[11] Madrid Protocol Relating to the International Registration of Marks of 27 June 1989. The text is available at www.wipo.int/treaties/en. The UK has ratified the Protocol, implementing it by way of the Trade Marks (International Registration) Order 1996, SI 1996/714, made under s 54 of the 1994 Act. The European Union also became a party to the Madrid Protocol in 2004. See, further, Chapter 16.

[12] Paris Convention for the Protection of Industrial Property of 20 March 1883 and revisions. On 26 February 1969, the UK ratified the 1967 Stockholm text, published in TS 16 (1970) Cmnd 4431. The Paris Convention is administered by the World Intellectual Property Organisation – see www.wipo.int/treaties/en which offers a link to the text of the Convention. See, further, Chapter 14.

[13] Agreement on Trade-Related Aspects of Intellectual Property Rights – negotiated during the GATT Uruguay round – concluded on 15 December 1993 and signed at Marrakesh on 15 April 1994. The text comprises Annex 1C to the Agreement establishing the World Trade Organisation and is available at www.wto.org/English/docs_e/legal_e/27-trips_01_e.htm. See Worthy 'Intellectual Property Protection after GATT' [1994] 5 EIPR 185. Co-operation between the World Trade Organisation and the World Intellectual Property Organisation was established by an agreement of 22 December 1995.

1.3   Interpretation of the 1994 Act by the courts may involve traditional techniques of statutory construction,[14] together with the possibility of referring to parliamentary debates (*'Hansard'*) in cases of ambiguity, obscurity or absurdity as outlined in *Pepper v Hart*.[15] However, as Aldous LJ put it in *Arsenal Football Club plc v Reed*:[16]

> 'The Trade Marks Act 1994 swept away the old law and implemented the Directive. It follows that the provisions of the Act must be construed so as to reflect the terms of the Directive.'

In interpreting the 1994 Act, therefore, UK courts have increasingly turned to the texts[17] of the Community Trade Mark Regulation (EC) 40/94 ('the Regulation') and the Directive and to the rapidly developing case-law of the Court of Justice of the European Union (CJEU, formerly European Court of Justice – ECJ)[18] under the Directive and Regulation. Opinions of the European Court on referred questions of interpretation of the Directive are binding.[19] Because many substantive provisions of the Regulation are identical to corresponding provisions of the Directive, decisions of the Court of First Instance on appeal from the Office for Harmonisation in the Internal Market[20] (OHIM) and of the full ECJ on further appeal are highly persuasive.[21] Preparatory works generated by the European institutions, for example, the Commission and Council's statements for inclusion in the minutes of adoption of the Regulation,[22] were thought to be available to guide the courts as a matter of Community law,[23] but national and European courts[24] and OHIM[25] showed

---

[14]   See, e g Brown 'The Increasing Influence of Intellectual Property Cases on the Principles of Statutory Interpretation' [1996] EIPR 526.

[15]   [1993] 1 All ER 42.

[16]   [2003] RPC 39 at para 11.

[17]   Including the detailed preambles or recitals. See, e g *Procter & Gamble's TM Applications, sub nom Procter & Gamble Ltd v Registrar of Trade Marks* [1999] ETMR 375, [1999] RPC 673, CA.

[18]   The phrase 'Court of Justice' when used below will refer to that court in both its incarnations.

[19]   That is, the ECJ's ruling, read in the light of its reasoning: *Arsenal Football Club plc v Reed* [2003] RPC 39 at para 31, citing *Robert Bosch GmbH v Hauptzollamt Hildesheim* Case C135/77 [1978] ECR 855, ECJ.

[20]   Usually abbreviated to OHIM in English, or OAMI in Spanish. The Office has its seat in Alicante, Spain.

[21]   See Folliard-Monguiral and Rogers 'Significant Case Law from 2004 on the Community Trade Mark from the Court of First Instance, the European Court of Justice and OHIM' [2005] EIPR 133; 'Significant 2005 Case Law on the Community Trade Mark from the Court of First Instance, the European Court of Justice and OHIM' [2006] JIPLP 315; 'Community Trade Mark Case Law Round-up 2006' [2007] JIPLP 215; 'Significant 2007 Case Law on the Community Trade Mark from the ECJ and the CFI' [2008] JIPLP 291; 'Significant 2008 Case Law on the Community Trade Mark from the ECJ and the CFI' [2009] JIPLP 325; 'Significant 2009 Case Law on the Community Trade Mark from the Court of Justice of the European Union and the General Court' [2010] JIPLP 306.

[22]   Conveniently collected together with texts of the Regulation, Directive and TRIPs Agreement in *ECTA Law Book* (European Communities Trade Mark Association, 1994).

[23]   See *Netherlands v The Commission* [1979] ECR 245, cited in Smyth 'Service Mark Registrations in Ireland: a Myth or a Reality?' [1994] 4 EIPR 167 at n 2.

[24]   *Wagamama v City Centre Restaurants* [1995] FSR 713. The Council and the Commission recognised that the European Court was free to disregard the statements: 'Since the following

scant regard for these statements. The UK Trade Marks Registry, part of the UK Intellectual Property Office, inevitably has regard to the decisions and practices of the OHIM and the Court of Justice.[26] Accordingly, in this book we shall refer to all these sources, both in relation to the 1994 Act and to marks protected in the UK through registration under the Regulation or under the Madrid Protocol for the international registration of marks.[27]

TRADE MARK FUNCTIONS AND PLAYERS

1.4   In order to analyse the effects of the 1994 Act and to identify areas of uncertainty or difficulty, it is useful first to examine the functions of trade marks. In previous statutes, one can discern the trade mark acting as a kind of 'golden thread' linking a product to its source – trade marks were said to indicate a 'connection in the course of trade' between the proprietor of the mark and the products for which the mark was used. Section 2 of the Trade Marks Act 1905[28] helpfully spelled out varieties of connection which a trade mark might indicate:

'… manufacture, selection, certification, dealing with or offering for sale.'

No such examples were listed in the Trade Marks Act 1938 ('the 1938 Act'); by then it was recognised that patterns of trade develop and change. In particular, it was accepted that there could be an appropriate connection between a licensor and licensed goods, provided that adequate control was exercised over their quality.[29]

1.5   To indicate a trade connection, the mark must enable someone to distinguish goods or services which enjoy such a connection from those which do not. Section 1(1) of the 1994 Act provides that a 'trade mark' means 'any sign capable of being represented graphically which is capable of distinguishing goods or services of one undertaking[30] from those of other undertakings'.

---

statements of the Council and the Commission are not part of the legal text they are without prejudice to the interpretation of that text by the Court of Justice of the European Communities', cited by that court in *Boehringer Ingelheim KG v Swingward Ltd* Case C143/00 [2002] All ER (EC) 581, [2002] 2 CMLR 26, [2003] Ch 27, [2002] ETMR 78, [2002] FSR 61, [2002] 3 WLR 1697.

25   *Giacomelli Sport SpA's Application* [2000] ETMR 277.

26   In the early days of applying the 1994 Act, until recently, the Registry was reluctant to have regard to the decisions of courts or registries in other member states; they are now prepared to do so, at least in the absence of significant linguistic or cultural differences: see *Manual of trade marks practice*, ch 3, para 1.2, quoting the decision of the ECJ in *Henkel* Case C218/01. The *Trade Marks Registry Work Manual* may be consulted online. See www.ipo.gov.uk/tmmanual-chap3-exam.pdf for this particular point.

27   See **1.2**.

28   Edw 7, c 15.

29   Trade Marks Act 1938, s 28. On the effect of s 28 and decided cases, see Norman 'Trade Mark Licences in the United Kingdom: Time for Bostitch to be Re-evaluated?' [1994] 4 EIPR 155.

30   An 'undertaking' may be a natural person, firm, company or association; in EU law the word connotes economic activity in the market: 'the concept of an undertaking encompasses every

Despite the change of wording from previous statutes, it is submitted that the concept of a trade mark did not change significantly. Affirmation of the trade mark's role as indicating a trade connection between proprietor and product appeared in Advocate-General Jacobs' opinion in *Holterhoff v Freiesleben*:[31]

> 'Use of a trade mark involves identifying the proprietor's goods or services as his own. Although perhaps so self-evident that it may not be specifically set out in trade mark legislation, that is the purpose for which trade marks exist ...'

1.6   A good trade mark will be distinctive, attractive and memorable, generating a frisson of favourable connotations. The information carried by the mark is concentrated in concise, symbolic form. Like a poem, the information content and uses of a trade mark depend not just upon its inherent and perceptible features, but also on the characteristics of the perceiver, especially the extent to which he has been educated in the significance of the mark. A newly coined sign may be highly distinctive, in the sense of very different from previously known images or words, but it becomes a trade mark distinctive *of* an undertaking and its products only when the public has learned to make the appropriate associations. For example, when 'Orange' mobile telephony services were launched, the concept of using a colour in combination with the equivalent word as the trade mark for a service was unusual.[32] It is unlikely that consumers would have known, without being told, that the colour and word 'Orange' denoted a particular supplier's mobile network service. Advertising influences the public's appreciation of a mark but changing social conditions play their part too. The effect of a mark may be altered by current affairs[33] and the activities of third parties,[34] as well as by the activities of its proprietor.[35] An important action is to register the mark for goods or services for which it is used (or intended to be used); this signals the proprietor's interest to the world at large and confers better protection against imitators.

1.7   A trade-marked 'product' may be goods or a service. An undertaking may incorporate its trade mark in a business name, or in a domain name to attract customers navigating the internet. Since a mark takes colour and meaning from its surroundings and from the mind-set of customers, the

---

entity engaged in an economic activity regardless of the legal status of the entity and way in which it is financed', *Hofner and Elser v Macrotron* [1991] ECR I-1979 (a case on EU competition law).

[31]   Case C2/00 [2002] ETMR 7, [2002] FSR 23; for the line of cases engendered by this decision, see Po Jen Yap 'Essential Function of a Trade Mark: from BMW to O2' [2009] EIPR 8.

[32]   See *Libertel Groep BV v Benelux Merkenbureau* Case C104/01 [2003] ECR I-3793, [2003] ETMR 63, [2004] FSR 4 (ECJ) at para 65. That case illustrated the practical difficulties in registering the colour orange as a trade mark.

[33]   Eg, the oil spillage from the tanker Exxon Valdez must have reflected badly on Standard Oil's 'Exxon' mark.

[34]   The action for infringement enables a mark's proprietor to control third party use. See Chapter 7.

[35]   The owner must be particularly careful to avoid using the mark 'generically', as a product description. Thus, marks such as 'Linoleum' and 'Aspirin' have fallen into general and commercial usage to denote a type of product, rather than the product of a particular company. See **6.17** (generic use).

message conveyed by a mark may vary as goods travel along a chain of distribution, or as a service is extended to a wider range of users. At this stage, we will turn to the personalities interested in trade marks and the functions of a trade mark as between the various parties.

Figure 1.1: Personalities interested in trade marks

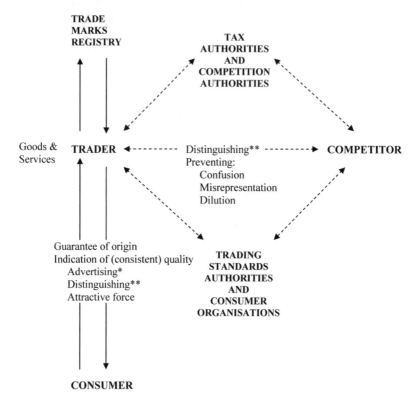

*   Educates customers to recognise mark and stimulates them to buy.
** Distinguishes trader's products from competitor's and distinguishes between trader's own different ranges.

COMPETITORS, DISTRIBUTORS AND CONSUMERS

1.8   At each link in a chain of commercial transactions the trade mark plays its part. Manufacturers, wholesalers, retailers, agents and consumers use marks to identify, order, catalogue, advertise, sell or buy products. The mark may also be used when returning faulty goods, complaining about unsatisfactory services or suggesting improvements. Figure 1.1 shows a single-link chain of commerce and the relationship of relevant parties. For simplicity, it is assumed that the trader is the trade mark proprietor.[36] A middleman would act both as customer and supplier; the trade mark enables him to select which products to stock or which services to recommend. He uses the drawing power of the mark to

---

[36]   The trader could, of course, be a formal licensee, or one who legitimately uses a mark to identify the proprietor's goods.

attract custom. In addition, a retailer's 'own-label' goods[37] may benefit from price comparisons with premium brands.[38]

1.9   A trader uses a mark to educate customers as to the characteristics of the product; recognition of the mark will stimulate purchase. For a product which is bought repeatedly,[39] customer satisfaction associated with the trade mark will encourage repeat purchases. For a major 'one-off' transaction, marks can act as a banner under which the consumer amasses information.[40] Where a product is new, advertising it under its new mark arouses the customer's curiosity.[41] The new mark may be combined with an established mark of the same proprietor, thus inspiring customer confidence.[42] Conversely, an existing product may be given a new image by rebranding or by association with a fictional character.[43]

1.10   The effect of the mark on customers and consumers varies not only with the type of product but also with time. A mark coined to intrigue at a product's launch may build up immense goodwill by virtue of customer satisfaction and eventually be used to launch new products and marks. Initially, that mark denotes a narrow product range, later it becomes a vehicle for diversification (sometimes loosely described as 'brand extension'). At this stage of development, the fact that later products come 'from the same stable' as earlier products will carry much weight; an example of this process was the use of the 'Virgin' mark, used initially for record stores, but later on many kinds of goods and services – Virgin cola, Virgin air services, etc.

TRADERS AND GOVERNMENT AGENCIES

1.11   When a trader applies to register a mark,[44] they may find that the application is refused by the Registry, or that a competing trader opposes registration. Scrutiny by the Registry and objections from watchful competitors

---

37   A supermarket such as Tesco may sell 'Heinz' beans, as well as other recognised independent brands, and its 'own-label' 'Tesco' beans.

38   Legitimate unless the 'own label' product is designed to look too similar to the premium brand. See, eg, Spencer 'Look-alikes and Private Label Competition' in *Trademark World*, September 1994, p 14; Mills 'Own Label Products and the "Lookalike" Phenomenon: a Lack of Trade Dress and Unfair Competition Protection?' [1995] EIPR 116. A legislative attempt to prohibit 'look-alikes' was made but withdrawn: Binns, Everitt 'Intellectual Property – The UK Copyright and Trade Marks Bill' [2000] EIPR N86; Davis 'Why the United Kingdom Should Have a Law Against Misappropriation' [2010] CLJ 561.

39   Eg 'Viennetta' ice-cream dessert.

40   Thus a consumer may consider taking out a mortgage with a major bank.

41   As in the case of many 'designer' soft drinks.

42   Motor manufacturers use a combination of house marks and model marks, thus 'Renault Clio', 'Renault Espace Quadra'. Cohen calls these 'primary' and 'secondary' brands in 'Brands and Valuations' *Managing Intellectual Property*, June 1994, p 23.

43   Eg use of 'Lara Croft' to revitalise the image of 'Lucozade' soft drink among teenage consumers or the use of a 'Bratz' doll image to render a library book bag 'cool'. The mark itself may also be 'refreshed' by alteration or abbreviation, thus 'Hewlett Packard' to 'HP'

44   See Chapter 5.

can serve to encourage the adoption and registration of truly distinctive marks. Even after a mark is accepted on to the register, someone may see fit to apply for cancellation,[45] on the grounds of invalidity or of non-use.[46] Trade Marks Registries can play an important part in reconciling the interests of market players and in sustaining the public interest in eloquent, informative and reliable signs.[47] However, OHIM, the Community Trade Marks Registry tends to take a laxer view and the UK Registry tends to follow suit. Since OHIM does not examine on 'relative grounds' for conflict with earlier marks, and the UK Registry abandoned *ex officio* examination on relative grounds in 2007,[48] one could argue that there is a predisposition to allow the market to regulate itself and for applicants to 'have a go' at registering borderline or, possibly, invalid marks. It is up to the proprietors of earlier marks to be vigilant.

1.12 To protect its proper functions, a trade mark may be litigated as between traders in the civil courts.[49] Weights and measures authorities exercising their powers to enforce local trading standards have a duty to enforce the criminal provisions of the 1994 Act.[50] Other agencies such as the National Consumer Council also oversee the consumer's interest in trade marks.[51] The registration of company names which come too close to protected trade marks may be challenged before the Company Names Adjudicator,[52] while inappropriate use as a domain name may involve taking a dispute to an arbitration service.

TRADE MARK FUNCTIONS

1.13 As seen above, trade marks can function in a number of different ways, as between different actors in the marketplace. The functions and uses appear to fall into three main categories:[53]

---

[45] See Chapter 9.

[46] See Chapter 9.

[47] Davis argues that European legislation has prejudiced this aspect: 'To Protect or Serve? European Trade Mark Law and the Decline of the Public Interest' [2003] EIPR 180. See also, Antill and James 'Registrability and the Scope of Monopoly: Current Trends' [2004] EIPR 157.

[48] The UK Registry conducts a search against earlier marks and notifies their proprietors of a later clashing application, so that opposition may be set in train.

[49] See Chapter 7.

[50] Trade Marks Act 1994, s 93.

[51] The National Consumer Council's Working Paper No 6 'Intellectual Property – the Consumer View of Patents, Copyright, Trade Marks and Allied Rights' (1991) was hostile to most intellectual property but sympathetic to trade marks.

[52] See **7.66** and Johnson 'I Object! The New Company Names Adjudicator in the United Kingdom' [2008] JIPLP 695.

[53] This scheme may be traced back to the influential work of Schechter, see especially, 'The Rational Basis for Trade Mark Protection' (1927) 40 Harv LR 813; Norman 'Schechter's "The Rational Basis of Trade Mark Protection" Revisited' in N Dawson and A Firth, *Trade Marks Retrospective* (2000) vol 7 (*Perspectives on Intellectual Property*); Sharpston notes in *Intel Corp Inc v CPM United Kingdom Ltd* Case C-252/07 [2008] ECR I-8823; [2009] ETMR 13 at para 10 that Schechter himself drew inspiration from a 1924 German decision 'ODOL'.

(a)   advertising;[54]

(b)   quality;[55] and

(c)   origin.[56]

In drawing a line between acceptable and prohibited uses of marks, the legislator or the court will inevitably assess whether the mark's proper functions have been upheld or undermined. Conscious appreciation of the various ways in which trade marks operate can only assist in this process. The following paragraphs explore the extent to which the various functions are recognised in the UK and Europe.

1.14   Thus, only the last, the origin function, is universally recognised as the proper object of protection by registration. Although the origin function is said to be the basis for the legal protection of marks, legislation and the cases do show solicitude for the quality and advertising functions as well.[57] In its explanatory memorandum on the creation of a Community trade mark,[58] the EC Commission refers to a trade mark's function:

'... of providing consumers with a guide to the particular origin of the product and its particular quality and characteristics, although these are not legally guaranteed.'

It then adds firmly:

'Both economically and legally the function of the trade mark as an indication of origin is paramount ... From this basic function of the trade mark are derived all the other functions which the trade mark fulfils in economic life'

before going on to admit that:

'... the quality function predominates in the mind of the consumer and the publicity function predominates in the mind of the producer ...'

---

[54]   See, further, **1.30–1.31**.

[55]   See, **1.27–1.29**; this includes indicating that the 'original quality' of a product has been maintained and not debased – see *Boehringer-Ingelheim v Swingward* Case C143/00 [2002] All ER (EC) 581 at para 12.

[56]   Kamperman Sanders and Maniatis dub the trade mark which fulfils all three functions as the 'consumer trade mark': see 'A Consumer Trade Mark: Protection Based on Origin and Quality' [1993] 11 EIPR 406. This article cites a number of classic analyses of trade mark function; see in particular the work of the US authors Schechter and Diamond.

[57]   Eg, a mark which is deceptive as to quality may not be registered – Trade Marks Act 1994, s 3(3)(b) – whilst use of a mark in relation to debased product may be prohibited – the Directive, Art 7(2). The advertising function is protected by Arts 8(5) and 9(1)(c) of the Regulation (see **5.38, 5.50–5.58**).

[58]   Bulletin of the European Communities, Supplement 8/76, paras 14 and 68.

Advocate-General Ruiz-Jarabo Colomer of the ECJ advocated recognition of all three functions. In *Arsenal Football Club plc v Reed*[59] he went as far as to say:

> 'It seems to me to be simplistic reductionism to limit the function of the trade mark to an indication of trade origin. The Commission, moreover, took the same view in its oral submissions to the Court. Experience teaches that, in most cases, the user is unaware of who produces the goods he consumes. The trademark acquires a life of its own, making a statement, as I have suggested, about quality, reputation and even, in certain cases, a way of seeing life.'

However, in *Arsenal* the ECJ went on to base its decision on protection of the origin function.[60]

1.15 It has been suggested by Trimmer that the UK courts have been less receptive to the wider functions of trade marks than the institutions of the European Union.[61] There is certainly evidence for this in the respective judgments of the CJEU and the English Court of Appeal in *L'Oréal SA v Bellure NV*.[62] Whereas the Court of Justice stated, at para 58:

> 'Those functions include not only the essential function of the trade mark, which is to guarantee to consumers the origin of the goods or services, but also its other functions, in particular that of guaranteeing the quality of the goods or services in question and those of communication, investment or advertising.'

Jacob LJ observed, at para 30:

> 'I am bound to say that I have real difficulty with these functions when divorced from the origin function.'

Ultimately the UK courts are bound by rulings of the CJEU on harmonised law, as conceded by Jacob LJ in *L'Oréal* at para 31. However, the quality and advertising functions are not unknown to English law; as shall be seen, the law of passing off has long recognised that misrepresentations as to quality are actionable.

1.16 A trade mark's operation as between traders, competitors and consumers was recognised by the ECJ in *CNL-Sucal NV SA v Hag GF AG*:[63]

---

[59] [2003] RPC 9 ECJ at para A46.

[60] [2003] RPC 9 ECJ; Kilbey 'The Ironies of *Arsenal v Reed*' [2004] EIPR 479.

[61] Trimmer 'The Power of Attraction: Do Trade Marks Have an 'Image' Problem in the English Courts?' [2009] EIPR 195 at 196. For a considered view from another common law jurisdiction, see Ng-Loy Wee Loon 'Time to Re-think the Ever Expanding Concept of Trade Marks? Re-calibrating Singapore's Trade Mark Law after the Controversial US-Singapore FTA' [2008] EIPR 161.

[62] *L'Oréal SA v Bellure NV* Case C-487/07 [2010] All ER (EC) 28; [2009] ECR I-5185; [2010] RPC 1; [2009] ETMR 987, ECJ; [2010] EWCA Civ 535; [2010] RPC 23; [2010] ETMR 47, CA.

[63] Case C-10/89 [1990] ECR I-3711; [1990] 3 CMLR 571; [1991] FSR 99, (1990) *The Times*, December 7, ECJ; for other cases, see Norman 'Trade Mark Licences in the United Kingdom: Time for Bostitch to be Re-evaluated?' [1994] 4 EIPR 155 at n 23.

'Consequently, as the court has stated on many occasions, the specific subject matter of a trade mark right is to grant the owner the right to use the trade mark for the first marketing of a product and, in this way, to protect him against competitors who would like to abuse the position and reputation of the mark by selling products to which the mark has been improperly affixed. To determine the exact effect of this exclusive right which is granted to the owner of the mark, it is essential to take account of the essential function of the mark, which is to give the consumer or final user the guarantee of the identity of the origin of the marked product by enabling him to distinguish, without any possible confusion, that product from others of a different provenance.'

Recognition that indication of quality is important as between trade mark proprietor and customers can be found in the ECJ's decision in *Merz & Krell v Deutsches Patent-und-Markenamt*:[64]

'Trade mark rights constitute an essential element in the system of undistorted competition which the Treaty is intended to establish. In such a system, undertakings must be able to attract and retain customers by the quality of their products or services, which is made possible only by distinctive signs allowing them to be identified (see, inter alia, Case C-349/95 *Loendersloot* [1997] ECR I-6227, paragraph 22). From that point of view, the essential function of the trade mark is to guarantee the identity of the origin of the marked goods or service to the consumer or end user by enabling him, without any possibility of confusion, to distinguish the goods or service from others which have another origin (see, inter alia, Case C-39/97 *Canon* [1998] ECR I-5507, paragraph 28).'

In para 10 of the preamble to the Directive are the words:

'... the registered trade mark, the function of which is *in particular* to guarantee the trade mark as an indication of origin.' (emphasis added)

Advocate-General Sharpston had this to say in *Intel*[65] of the relationship between the origin function and quality of products:

'A significant function of a trade mark is to link goods or services to a source of supply, whether the original producer or a commercial intermediary. That is in the interest of both supplier and consumer. The supplier can establish a reputation, which is protected from usurpation by competitors, for products bearing the mark, and can thus promote trade in those products. Likewise, the consumer can make purchasing decisions on the basis of the qualities he perceives as attached to the mark. Since those decisions may be negative, suppliers have an incentive to maintain and improve the quality of the goods or services supplied under the mark.'

In the English case of *Colgate*,[66] the quality function of a registered mark was acknowledged and protected by restraining the circulation of different quality

---

[64]   [2002] All ER (EC) 441, [2001] ECR I-6959, [2002] ETMR 21 at paras 21–22.
[65]   *Intel Corp Inc v CPM United Kingdom Ltd* Case C-252/07 [2008] ECR I-8823; [2009] ETMR 13.
[66]   *Colgate-Palmolive v Markwell Finance* [1989] RPC 497 at 527.

toothpaste originally destined for the Brazilian market. It is submitted that *Colgate* remains valid in the light of EC harmonisation.

OTHER PLAYERS

1.17   As the above quotations illustrate, the chief effect of a mark as between a trader and a competitor is that of differentiation in the eyes of customers and consumers. Their respective marks distinguish them as distinct sources of goods or services. Trade journals and market advisers, as well as customers, can use the marks to categorise market shares and track fluctuations in sales. Which?, formerly the Consumers' Association, makes extensive use of marks to identify products which it evaluates.[67] In many spheres of commercial activity, one trader may offer different grades of a product at varying prices; the use of marks enables such products to be distinguished just as effectively as the products of different traders. It is important for the trader and the customers that the lines of demarcation remain clear. There is a public interest[68] in maintaining the integrity of the information carried by trade marks, whether the message relates to origin, quality or the subject matter of advertising. We shall now consider the three main trade mark functions in a little more detail.

GUARANTEES OF ORIGIN

1.18   Several points can be made about the concept of commercial origin. First, early passing-off cases[69] established that it does not matter whether the mark conveys the identity of its proprietor. Rather, it must indicate that a common source exists for the marked goods or services.[70] Secondly, even though 'origin' implies a causal link between an act of the proprietor and the arrival of the products on the market, the link can take many forms. The trade mark's proprietor may manufacture or select goods,[71] license the provision of services under the mark, subject to the provision of know-how and quality control,[72] or choose a licensee to manufacture goods who is competent to exercise quality control itself.[73] Although formal requirements as to quality

---

[67]   See any issue of *Which?* magazine. The Association now also trades as 'Which?'.

[68]   In *Elizabeth Florence Emanuel v Continental Shelf 128 Ltd* Case C-259/04 [2006] ETMR 56, the public interest against registering a deceptive mark had to be balanced against the public interest in assignability of businesses, goodwill and trade marks.

[69]   Eg *Powell v Birmingham Vinegar Brewery* [1897] AC 710 ('Yorkshire Relish').

[70]   The European Commission's explanatory memorandum, at para 68 echoes this: 'If the trade mark guarantees that the commercial origin is the same, the consumer can count on a similarity of composition and quality of goods bearing the trade mark'. See, also, *Bristol-Myers Squibb v Paranova* [1996] ECR I-3457, ECJ; *Arsenal Football Club plc v Reed* [2003] RPC 9 ECJ at para 48.

[71]   See the quotation in **1.4** from the Trade Marks Act 1905.

[72]   See *Bostitch* [1963] RPC 183: provision of designs and know-how for the manufacture of goods.

[73]   *Molyslip* [1978] RPC 211.

control in licences have been dropped from the 1994 Act,[74] the more tenuous the commercial connection, the more emphasis has traditionally been given to control of quality.

1.19 Origin is here used in the sense of commercial origin, rather than geographical origin. Usually, the two are mutually exclusive: s 3(1)(c) of the 1994 Act bars from registration a mark which consists exclusively of an indication of geographical origin. The latter may be protected as a UK certification mark,[75] or as a geographical indication protected under Regulation (EC) No 510/2006, where there is a link between geographical origin and product characteristics.[76] Occasionally, however, the geographical and commercial connotations of 'origin' coincide. In *The Glenlivet*,[77] a case about registration of the mark for mineral water, the court took the view that only someone seeking to trade on the applicant's reputation for whisky was likely to want to extract water from Glenlivet and to use that geographical name. The geographical name had become indicative of a specific commercial source. Conversely, a non-geographical name may carry geographical connotations: it may be assumed that a motor car bearing a French mark is manufactured in France, although this may not be justified.[78] Dixons (DSG Retail), a UK electrical goods retailer, has a long-standing registration of 'Matsui' for consumer electrical goods, presumably to increase consumers' perception of quality by analogy with Sony and other Japanese marks.[79]

INDICATIONS OF QUALITY

1.20 Customers' use of a mark as indicating product quality contributes to the health of the market[80] and has long been recognised at common law. In

---

[74] The parties themselves are responsible for maintaining the integrity of a mark: see 'Reform of Trade Mark Law' (1990) Cm 1203, para 4.36. In practice, de facto quality control is likely to be as important as ever: see Norman 'Trade Mark Licences in the United Kingdom: Time for *Bostitch* to be Re-evaluated?' [1994] 4 EIPR 155 at n 23.

[75] See **1.32** and **12.7–12.18**.

[76] Council Regulation (EC) No 510/2006 of 20 March 2006 on the protection of geographical indications and designations of origin for agricultural products and foodstuffs; Art 19 repealed its predecessor Regulation (EEC) 2081/92 (as amended). See, Dawson 'Locating Geographical Origin – Perspectives From English law' (2000) 90 TMR 590; Knaak 'Caselaw of the ECJ on the Protection of Geographical Indications and Designations of Origin Pursuant to EC Reg No 2081/92' (2001) 32 IIC 375; Ribeiro de Almeida 'Key Differences Between Trade Marks and Geographical Indications' [2008] EIPR 406; Evans 'The Comparative Advantages of Geographical Indications and Community Trade Marks for the Marketing of Agricultural Products in the European Union' (2010) IIC 645.

[77] [1993] RPC 461.

[78] Comment made during the Trade Mark Bill's second reading in the House of Lords: Lord Peston, *Hansard*, vol 550, no 10, col 758 (6 December 1993).

[79] It is possible to search the UK register for specific trade marks online at www.ipo.gov.uk/pro-types/pro-tm/pro-t-os/pro-t-find.htm to reveal the registrations of 'Matsui'. For a search of the international register, see www.wipo.int/ipdl/en/madrid.

[80] See the discussion and citations in Kamperman Sanders and Maniatis 'A Consumer Trade Mark: Protection Based on Origin and Quality' [1993] 11 EIPR 406 at 407–8.

Spalding v Gamage,[81] supply of the plaintiff's obsolete goods, under the mark associated with its improved goods, was held to be passing off. Courts and commentators[82] have been slower to acknowledge such a function in the case of registered marks, although customer perception is hardly dependent on whether a mark is registered or not.

1.21 What has militated against legal recognition of the quality function of a registered mark? One argument is that the concept might be used against a mark's proprietor when, for whatever reason, he introduces quality changes. The 1938 Act[83] made explicitly clear that a mere change in the form of connection between the proprietor and his goods or service would not invalidate a mark. In *Bostitch*,[84] changes in methods and country of manufacture were held not to render the mark deceptive. More recently, when inventor James Dyson moved production of his eponymous vacuum cleaners from England to the Far East, newspapers expressed dismay but did not suggest that the foreign-manufactured cleaners would not be 'Dyson' machines.

1.22 However, it is submitted that this argument should not prevail where anyone uses a mark significantly to mislead customers as to quality. The possibility that a mark may be rendered deceptive by acts of the proprietor or licensees is recognised in a ground for revocation under s 46(1)(d) of the 1994 Act. However, this need not open the floodgates to a deluge of capricious consumer litigation. At least in the context of infringement, the Court of Appeal confirmed long ago that a mark's quality function may be protected by registration. In *Colgate-Palmolive v Markwell Finance*,[85] Slade LJ said:

> 'I accept Mr Hobbs' submission that there is nothing incongruous in holding that a registered trade mark is infringed in relation to goods which do not conform to an identifiable quality which purchasing members of the public in this country ordinarily receive by reference to the mark.'

As long as the quality indications of a mark remain broadly true, its registration will remain valid and confer protection against others using the mark for services or goods of a different quality to the expectations of customers.

VEHICLES FOR ADVERTISING

1.23 A well-chosen mark can play a significant role in the success of a promotional campaign. Some marks are chosen to complement a proposed

---

[81] (1915) 32 RPC 273.
[82] See, eg, Beier 'Territoriality of Trade Mark Law and International Trade' (1970) 1 IIC 48. For the views of the European Commission and Court of Justice, see **1.12–1.13**.
[83] Section 62.
[84] [1963] RPC 183.
[85] [1989] RPC 497 at 527.

advertising theme, others are adopted to echo someone else's effective advertising.[86] Four particular situations may be singled out:

(a) The proprietor of the mark uses it in advertising. There has been considerable debate as to whether the value of identified brands[87] should be entered in their proprietors' trading accounts.[88] Whatever the outcome on that particular issue, it is beyond question that a good mark is of great value to its proprietor as an advertising tool. As indicated above, the meaning attributed to the mark by customers or the content of the advertising message it conveys can vary with time and place. The mark itself may undergo subtle alteration. With investment in advertising and in the quality and distribution of the product it denotes[89] a mark becomes an important asset. This is reflected in the proprietary nature of a registered mark, which is stated to be personal property,[90] which may be assigned, disposed of by will or transmitted by operation of laws.[91]

(b) A third party uses the mark to advertise its own products. In this case the proprietor's investment inures to the advertiser's benefit and the mark is likely to lose its power to denote the proprietor's goods or services. The proprietor may arrest this process by suing for trade mark infringement or passing off.[92]

(c) A third party uses the mark in advertising to refer to the proprietor's products. In this way, retailers or distributors can inform the public of the availability of the proprietor's products. However, if there is a misrepresentation as to their quality or as to the business of the advertiser, the proprietor of the mark may sue as before.

---

[86] As in *Cadbury-Schweppes v Pub Squash* [1981] 1 WLR 193; [1981] RPC 429.

[87] For 'brand', see **1.35**.

[88] For examples of this phenomenon and a summary of valuation methods, see Birkin 'Brand Valuation' in D Cowley (ed) *Understanding Brands* (1991). The papers in Cowley's book provide an excellent overview of trade marks from the advertiser's perspective. For a lawyer's view, see Cohen, 'Brands and Valuations' *Managing Intellectual Property* (June 1994) p 23. It appears that the Accounting Standards Board disapproves of the valuation of individual brands, regarding them as inseparable from goodwill: *Managing Intellectual Property* (March 1994) p 10; see also Kontor and Day 'Corporate Lending in an Intangibles Economy: Approaches and Challenges' [2002] JIBL 125; Tollington 'The Separable Nature of Brands as Assets: The United Kingdom Legal and Accounting Perspective' [2001] EIPR 6; Yelnik 'Commercial Value of Trade Marks: Do Current Laws Provide Brands Sufficient Protection from Infringement?' [2010] EIPR 203.

[89] A campaign will fail if contradicted by customer experience of the product. In 'Brands and the Role of Advertising' in D Cowley (ed) *Understanding Brands* (1991), Duckworth cites as examples 'The wonder of Woolworths' and 'The age of the train'.

[90] Section 22 of the 1994 Act. See Maniatis 'Trade Mark Rights – A Justification Based on Property' [2002] IPQ 123.

[91] See further Chapter 11.

[92] See Chapter 7. In *Specsavers International Healthcare Ltd v Asda Stores Ltd (No 2)* [2010] EWHC 2035 (Ch); [2011] FSR 1, there is fascinating evidence of the defendants' policy of 'poaching', parodying or merely keeping an eye on Specsavers' marks and slogans. The claimants were partly successful in the litigation.

(d)   Alternatively, the advertiser may refer to the proprietor's trade mark, goods or services for the purposes of comparison, commonly to show that its own products are as good, but cheaper.[93] Under the 1938 Act a mark registered in the former Part A of the register could be used to enjoin comparative advertising, even where the advertisement clearly distinguished between the products of the advertiser and the trade mark owner. Under the 1994 Act, comparative advertising in accordance with honest business practices is permitted;[94] its legitimacy will depend upon the necessity, purpose and fairness of the comparison.[95]

GOODS AND SERVICES

1.24   Marks can serve to distinguish goods, services and whole businesses. All these possibilities have been recognised by the common law in passing-off actions.[96] Until 1984, UK legislation provided only for the registration of marks for goods. Service marks could sometimes be protected indirectly by registering for goods used in the supply of the service,[97] but the Trade Marks (Amendment) Act 1984 introduced service mark registration.[98] The Nice classification scheme,[99] which is used to categorise marks by product, is currently in its 8th edition which includes 34 classes for goods, but a mere 11 for services. Service classes include: advertising and business, insurance and financial, construction and repair, telecommunications, transportation and storage, material treatment, education and entertainment, research and development, catering and hotels, medical, personal and social services.

1.25   Where retailers sell a very wide range of products, they have to apply for and administer a huge number of registrations for the same mark in different classes to enjoy the benefits of registration across the product range. It is not surprising that they have tried to register their marks for 'retail services', arguing that by giving advice on prospective purchases and providing facilities such as credit, banking, mother-and-baby rooms, and so on, they offer a

---

[93]   For the competitive advantages of this, see Jacob LJ's remarks in *L'Oréal SA v Bellure NV* [2010] EWCA Civ 535; [2010] RPC 23; [2010] ETMR 47, CA.

[94]   Section 10(6), interpreted successively in the light of Directives (EC) 97/55, 84/450 and 2006/114 on misleading and comparative advertising. See Morcom '*L'Oréal v Bellure* – Who Has Won?' [2009] EIPR 627.

[95]   See Chapter 13; Carty 'Registered Trade Marks and Permissible Comparative Advertising' [2002] EIPR 294.

[96]   *Spalding v Gamage* (1915) 32 RPC: 273; *Harrods* (1924) 41 RPC 74; *Legal and General* [1968] RPC 253.

[97]   As in *VISA TM* [1985] RPC 323.

[98]   The 1984 Act was itself amended before commencement by the Patents, Designs and Trade Marks Act 1986.

[99]   Developed under the Nice Agreement Concerning the International Classification of Goods and Services for the Purposes of the Registration of Marks, 1957 and revisions. See www.wipo.int/classifications/nice/en/index.html. As at 24 December 2010, 83 states were listed as party to Nice, although non-member countries may also use the scheme.

retailing service.[100] Such attempts were unsuccessful under the 1938 Act and Parliament debated whether to introduce specific wording in the 1994 Act to make sure that retail services were registrable.[101] There was some scepticism as to whether 'retail service' existed as a distinct service, a view shared by the European Commission and Council who prepared a statement for entry in the minutes of adoption of the Community Trade Mark Regulation:[102]

'The Council and the Commission consider that the activity of retail trading in goods is not as such a service for which a Community trade mark may be registered under this regulation.'

1.26 However, in *Giacomelli Sport SpA's Application*,[103] the OHIM decided that a Community trade mark could be registered for retail services limited to a particular field, such as 'retail services in the field of sports goods'. The Office remarked in *Giacomelli:*

'That an imprudent applicant for registration of a trade mark for "retail services" alone might have an expectation that it also covers its goods, cannot be a reason why retail sales services should be disallowed.'

Subsequently in *Praktiker*[104] the Court of Justice confirmed that 'services' within the meaning of Directive 89/104 included services provided in connection with retail trade in goods; to register a retail service mark it is not necessary to enumerate the services offered, but it is necessary to detail types of good to which those services relate.

1.27 OHIM practice is now detailed in a Communication from the President.[105] In the light of *Giacomelli*, the UK Patent Office changed its practice to allow registration of marks for 'retail services'.[106]

---

[100] See Olsen 'Cinderella Spurned: a Retailer's Lament' [1987] 9 EIPR 251. For examples of the various suggested components of retail services, see *Dee Corp's Applications* [1989] FSR 266.

[101] See, especially, *Hansard,* HL Deb, vol 550, no 10, cols 766–767 (6 December 1993); Public Bill Committee, cols 3–10 (13 January 1994). In the event, reference to retail services was omitted from the Trade Marks Act 1994.

[102] Council Regulation (EC) 40/94, OJ [1994] L 11/1.

[103] [2000] ETMR 277.

[104] *Praktiker Bau-und Heimwerkermarkte AG v Deutsches Patent-und Markenamt* Case C-418/02 [2005] ECR I-5873; [2005] ETMR 88. For scope of protection, see **5.50–5.58** and Chapter 7; in *Praktiker* the Court of Justice did not answer the referring court's question on scope of protection conferred by registration as a retail service mark; but in Case C-418/02, A-G Leger agreed with OHIM Presidential Communication No 3/01 that 'the risk of confusion between [retail] services and the products, if it cannot be excluded, is nevertheless improbable except in particular circumstances, for example when the respective marks are identical or almost identical and well established on the market'.

[105] Communication No 7/05 of the President of the Office of 31 October 2005 concerning the registration of Community trade marks for retail services, available at http://oami.europa.eu/en/office/aspects/pdf/co05-7.pdf.

[106] PAC 13/00 'Change of Practice on "Retail Services"' [2001] RPC 33; followed by Practice Notices on retail services in the light of *Praktiker* (PAN 6/05), search of the register (PAN 7/06) and shopping centre services (PAN 1/09).

1.28 Whereas goods may be marked physically with the trade mark, services are insufficiently tangible to be stamped or branded. Although one may watch a builder working on a neighbour's land, or admire a friend's haircut, services are usually more difficult to inspect than goods. Thus, the information carried by a service mark will be particularly important. Visual use of a mark in relation to services may be made on business signs and papers and in advertising. Aural use is likely to be important, too, especially as services are often advertised on the radio.

PRODUCTS AND BUSINESSES

1.29 In some countries, business names are registrable, as distinct both from company names and trade marks. Often, of course, all three share a common main element. Thus, Jordan Publishing Limited is one of the companies which carries on business under the trading style 'Jordans', which is used as a trade mark on books, advertising literature and other items. In other cases, names and marks are different. For example, for many years Marks & Spencer plc labelled its goods with the mark 'St Michael'.

1.30 In the UK, Companies House does not permit two or more companies to be registered with identical names,[107] but similarity of company names was no bar to their respective registrations. The practice of registering company names emulating those of well-known but unconnected companies was deplored in *Lease Management Services Ltd v Purnell Secretarial Services Ltd; Canon (South West) Ltd, Third Party*.[108] In response to this type of problem, curative provisions were introduced into the Companies Act 2006; s 67 empowers the Secretary of State to require change of a company names which too closely resembles a prior company name and a company name adjudication service has been introduced to allow objections to be raised to inappropriate company names.[109] Nevertheless, registration of business names is not at present compulsory in the UK. Thus, registration of marks and the action for passing off[110] are also needed to protect business names and trading styles from undue imitation.

1.31 Doubts have been expressed as to whether a company, such as Marks & Spencer, uses its name as a trade mark in relation to its products if the latter are labelled with another mark ('St Michael'). These doubts were implicit in the parliamentary debates on retail service marks.[111] A case which was often quoted in this regard is *Autodrome*,[112] where the sale of used motor cars from premises called 'the Autodrome' was held not to be use of a registered mark.

---

[107] Pursuant to what is now s 66 of the Companies Act 2006.

[108] (1994) *The Times*, April 1, CA.

[109] Companies Act 2006, s 69 et seq.

[110] See **3.5**. Article 8 of the Paris Convention obliges signatories to protect trade names, whether or not they form part of a trade mark.

[111] See **1.23**.

[112] [1969] RPC 564; [1969] FSR 320.

However, it is clear from the judgment that, had proper evidence been forthcoming as to the use of 'Autodrome' on invoices, the case would have been decided differently. More recently, in *Cheetah TM*[113] the court held that use of a mark on invoices and delivery notes was trade mark use. This is confirmed by s 10 of the 1994 Act. It is submitted that the wording of s 10(4)(a) of the 1994 Act, which refers to offering or exposing goods for sale (etc) under the sign, is apt to include use on a shop sign or as a business name.[114] Where a number of retailers carry on business under the umbrella of a shopping mall, the latter is providing services for which the mall name can be registered.[115]

1.32 Related questions arise when a company's trade mark is included as part of its company name or internet domain name: for example, does use of the full company name constitute use of the mark? The European Commission's view was clearly to the contrary:[116]

> 'It should be made clear in the text [of the Community Trade Mark Regulation] that the protection of the EEC trade mark also extends to its use as a part of a business name.'

Thus, the outcome of any case is likely to depend upon the overall impression made by the way in which the name is used. This is echoed by the practice of the UK Trade Marks Registry; a company name is eligible for registration as a trade mark if it meets normal criteria. The addition of a company indicator such as 'Ltd' or 'plc' may, but normally will not, add distinctive character to an otherwise unregistrable word or phrase.[117] Thus a descriptive name such as 'soft and gentle' denoting goods or services for which registration is sought will be refused registration but may be fanciful and therefore distinctive if seen as denoting characteristics of the organisation itself.

SPECIAL CATEGORY MARKS

1.33 Three special categories of mark are examined in Chapter 12: certification marks, collective marks and well-known marks.

Certification marks

1.34 Certification marks are sometimes called 'guarantee marks' because they indicate that products comply with objective criteria as to quality, quantity, materials, geographic origin and so forth. Thus, the 'kitemark' indicates

---

[113] [1993] FSR 263.
[114] See 'Reform of Trade Marks Law' (1990) Cm 1203, paras 3.26 and 3.27.
[115] *Land Securities' TM Application* [2008] EWHC 1744 (Pat); [2009] RPC. 5; [2008] ETMR 67.
[116] Memorandum on the creation of an EEC trade mark, 'Bulletin of the European Communities', Supplement 8/76, para 109.
[117] See 'Company Names' section in ch 3 of the *OK Trade Marks Examination Manual*, available at www.ipo.gov.uk/tmmanual-chap3-exam.pdf.

compliance with the relevant British Standard,[118] the wool mark evidences all-woollen fabric or clothes,[119] and 'Stilton' cheese is made by defined processes in a limited geographic region.[120] Certification marks are owned and administered by independent bodies, which do not themselves trade in the products concerned. This is believed to ensure their impartiality in applying the rules by which products qualify to use the mark. Certification marks have long been registrable for goods and the 1994 Act provides for their registration in respect of services. They are not, however, registrable as Community trade marks, although the Directive allows member states to have certification as well as collective and guarantee marks (Art 15).

Collective marks

1.35 Small and medium-sized enterprises often collaborate to increase their competitiveness. Thus, grocery retailers join purchasing groups and travel agents spread the risks of their trade by joining associations which provide insurance against calamity or failure. To be effective, these organisations must be active in the commercial area concerned. Registration of their marks as collective marks is now possible; the right to use the mark is conferred by membership of the association.

Well-known marks

1.36 Some trade marks gain international recognition. Article 6*bis* of the Paris Convention[121] obliges signatories to protect such marks by preventing third parties from using or registering them in their territories. Article 6*bis* is rather obscurely worded, but it is doubtful whether the UK previously complied with its obligations.[122] Refusal of speculative registrations of famous marks was left to the good sense and discretion of the Registrar. The 1994 Act gives statutory force to Art 6*bis* and to Art 16.2 and 3 of TRIPs, which extended its ambit.[123]

OTHER USES OF MARKS

1.37 Trade marks are powerful symbols, charged with meaning. All the uses discussed so far relate to the distinguishing function of marks in the course of trade: providing information about the goods, services and business of a proprietor or advertiser. These functions are protected by the 1994 Act and by

---

[118] Information on the kitemark and the standards it denotes may be found at www.bsigroup.com/en/Assessment-and-certification-services/Kitemark.

[119] Discussed by Belson, 'Certification marks, guarantees and trust' [2002] EIPR 340 at 344.

[120] See www.stiltoncheese.com.

[121] Properly, the Paris Convention for the Protection of Industrial Property, 1883 as revised.

[122] A foreign plaintiff would fail in a passing-off suit if it did not trade within the jurisdiction, or at least have a good customer base: see **3.5**.

[123] Text available at www.wto.org/english/docs_e/legal_e/27-trips_04_e.htm#article16_2. See, further **15.16ff**.

the common law.[124] Non-commercial uses do not fall within the scope of that protection.[125] If people choose to adorn their houses or themselves with images of famous marks, that is a matter for them. If someone makes up a story for a child in which a cat eats 'Paws' cat food, or a teenager makes disparaging remarks about a friend for wearing a cheap brand of jeans, such decorative, descriptive or social use is not in the course of trade and falls outside the proprietor's exclusive rights.[126] In a number of cases, however, the Court of Justice has grappled with the question as to whether there may be commercial uses of a mark which do not infringe the rights of the registered proprietor. In *Holterhoff v Freiesleben*,[127] the court held that the use of registered terms 'SPIRIT SUN' and 'CONTEXT CUT' merely to indicate the cut of gemstones would not infringe. In *Adam Opel AG v Autec AG*,[128] where a model car bore the relevant marque by way of faithful reproduction, this might not infringe the claimant's rights in the mark registered for toy cars.

WHAT, THEN, ARE 'BRANDS'?

1.38 The terms 'trade mark' and 'brand' are often used interchangeably.[129] For example, the Institute of Trade Mark Attorney's website carries a booklet 'UK Professionals Protecting Brands'.[130]

1.39 The UK Intellectual Property Office's press release of 1 October 2009 quote David Lammy, then Minister responsible for intellectual property, as saying: 'Trade marks enable businesses to protect and profit from the brand identity they have carefully crafted.'[131] What might be the difference between 'trade marks' and 'brands'? The word 'brand' is often used to mean a trade mark plus something. From a strictly legal perspective, it could be a combination of trade marks used on a particular product, the combination of a mark with its underlying goodwill, and related intellectual property rights in industrial design and advertising materials. Beyond this, there is no universally agreed definition of 'brand' as a term of art, but the International Trademark Association has this to say:[132]

---

[124] *Spalding v Gamage* (1915) 32 RPC 273 (goods); *Harrods v Harrod (R) Ltd* (1924) 41 RPC 74 (services); *Legal & General Assurance Society v Daniel* [1968] RPC 253 (businesses).

[125] Section 10 of the Trade Marks Act 1994 makes clear that infringements of registered marks occur only 'in the course of trade'.

[126] See, also, *Arsenal Football Club plc v Reed* [2003] RPC 9 ECJ; [2003] RPC 39 CA.

[127] Case C-2/00 [2002] ECR I-4187; [2002] ETMR 79.

[128] Case C-48/05 [2007] ECR I-1017; [2007] ETMR 33; the question whether the defendant's use affected the essential functions of the mark and in particular its function as an indication of origin was a matter for the national court. See Po-Jen Yap 'Making Sense of Trade Mark Use' [2007] EIPR 420.

[129] A practice commented on unfavourably by Jacob J in *British Sugar plc v James Robertson & Sons Ltd* [1996] RPC 281 at 300 (see references to 'Treat Brand').

[130] See www.itma.org.uk/download/170/Uk_prof_protecting_brands.pdf.

[131] See www.ipo.gov.uk/about/press/press-release/press-release-2009/press-release-20091001.htm.

[132] See 'Brand Valuation' available at www.inta.org.

'What is a brand? A brand is a trademark (or combination of trademarks) that, through promotion and use, has acquired significance in distinguishing the source or origin of the goods or services offered under the trademark from those offered by others in the marketplace.'

1.40 Yelnik puts it thus:[133]

'... trade marks represent only a part of a brand. They may be considered important and, arguably, the most valuable part but there are other issues such as public perception, the mark's goodwill and others to be taken into account when contemplating a brand's protection.'

1.41 Most recently under the aegis of marketing experts, the notion of 'brand' itself has been expanded to encompass the notion of 'lifestyle';[134] in this context, not only are trade marks linked tightly to industrial design and advertising as before, but they are chosen to promote specific aspirations[135] forming part of a notional consumer lifestyle.

---

[133] Yelnick 'Commercial Value of Trade Marks: Do Current Laws Provide Brands Sufficient Protection from Infringement?' [2010] EIPR 203 at 204.

[134] See Kiley 'Not Every Brand is a Lifestyle Brand' at www.businessweek.com/the_thread/ brandnewday/archives/2005/07/not_every_brand.html.

[135] Eg in the case of the Apple iPod music player, iTunes software and iTunes Store download services, creating a personal digital song library which forms 'the soundtrack to one's life': see interview with Dr Michael Bull in Anon, 'iPod Lifestyle Part of New Book' at www.macobserver.com/article/2005/05/23.3.shtml.

Chapter 2

THE MARK ITSELF

IMPACT UPON THE SENSES

2.1   The Trade Marks Act 1994 ('the 1994 Act') provides for the registration of trade marks. But what actually is meant by 'trade mark'? Section 1 of the 1994 Act defines what may be registered as a trade mark:

> '... any sign capable of being represented graphically which is capable of distinguishing goods or services of one undertaking from those of other undertakings.'

The important elements here are a *sign*, which can be *represented graphically* and is *capable of distinguishing*. If a mark does not exhibit these characteristics, it will not be registered.[1] These criteria derive from the trade marks harmonisation Directive (EC) 89/104, now amended and codified as Directive 2008/95/EC[2] ('the Directive') and are shared with the definition for a Community trade mark in Council Regulation (EC) 207/2009[3]('the Regulation'). Some equivalent provisions of all three instruments are set out in Table 2.1, together with a brief indication of what each provision is about. The provisions of s 3 of the 1994 Act, Art 3 of the Directive and Art 9 of the Regulation are the 'absolute' grounds for refusal of registration – they relate to the mark itself, assessed in the light of the goods or services for which registration is sought.[4] It should be noted that often the UK courts refer to the provisions of the Directive, rather than the 1994 Act as the Act must be interpreted in conformity with the Directive. *LTJ Diffusion v Sadas Vertbaudet* stressed the need for uniform interpretation of parallel provisions of the Directive and the Regulation.[5]

---

[1]   Trade Marks Act 1994, s 3(1)(a).
[2]   22 October 2008 [2008] OJ L 299/25, effective from 28 November 2008: see Recital 1 (amendments and codification), Art 17 (repel) and Art 18 (entry into force).
[3]   The original Community Trade Mark Regulation, 40/94 as amended, was codified into and repealed by Reg 207/2009 of 26 February 2009 [2009] OJ L 78/1, with effect from 13 April 2009: see Recital 1 (amendments and codification), Art 166 (repeal) and 167 (entry into force).
[4]   In contrast to 'relative' grounds, which relate to conflict with earlier marks and rights.
[5]   Case C291/00 [2003] ECR I-2799 at paras 41 and 43, in that case the meaning of 'identical' conflicting marks for the purposes of registration and infringement.

Table 2.1: Comparison of various UK and EU provisions defining trade mark subject matter

Trade Marks Act 1994	Directive 2008/95/EC	Regulation (EC) 207/2009	Concerning
S 1(1)	Art 2	Art 4	What may be a trade mark
S 1(2)	Arts 1 and 15 permit but do not require collective marks and guarantee or certification marks	Art 64 (collective marks)	Registration of collective marks and certification marks[6]
S 2(1)	Art 345 of the TFEU (ex Art 295 of the EC Treaty) leaves property rules of member states intact	Art 16ff	Trade marks as objects of property
S 2(2)	Recitals 5 and 7– coexistence with user rights and unfair competition	Recital 5 and Art 14(2) – coexistence with national trade marks, unfair competition	Relationship to other rights incl passing off
S 3(1)(a)	Art 3(1)(a)	Art 7(1)(a)	Marks which do not satisfy s 1(1)/Art 2/Art 4
S 3(1)(b)	Art 3(1)(b)	Art 7(1)(b)	Devoid of distinctive character
S 3(1)(c)	Art 3(1)(c)	Art 7(1)(c)	Variously descriptive
S 3(1)(d)	Art 3(1)(d)	Art 7(1)(d)	Generic
Provisos 3(1) (b)–(d)	Art 3(3)	Art 7(3)	Acquired distinctiveness
S 3(2)	Art 3(1)(e)	Art 7(1)(e)	Shape marks
S 3(3)(a)	Art 3(1)(f)	Art 7(1)(f)	Contra policy or morality
S 3(3)(b)	Art 3(1)(g)	Art 7(1)(g)	Mark deceptive to public
S 3(5), s 4	Art 3(1)(h) (Paris 6ter) Art 3(2)(c) (badges of public interest; optional)	Art 7(1)(h) Art 7(1)(i)	Specially protected emblems*

---

6   See Chapter 12.

Trade Marks Act 1994	Directive 2008/95/EC	Regulation (EC) 207/2009	Concerning
S 3(3)(b)	Art 3(2)(a)(optional)	Art 7(1)(j) (wines and spirits) Art 7(1)(k) (geographical indications Regulation (EEC) 2081/92)	Contra other national or Community law
		Art 7(2)	Non-registrability in only part of Community
S 3(3)(a)	Art 3(2)(b) (optional)	–	Religious, etc symbols
S 3(6)	Art 3(2)(d) (optional)	Not a ground for refusing application but for invalidity under Art 51(1)(b)	Bad faith
Sch 1, paras 10, 11	Art 3(4)	–	Transitional provisions

* Specially protected emblems, such as national flags, the Red Cross and Crescent, are mentioned in Chapter 5. The other provisions will be considered in this chapter.

Signs and signals

2.2 Section 1 and its equivalents give an indicative list of signs which may qualify as trade marks – words (including personal names), designs, letters, numerals or the shapes[7] of goods or their packing. For a sign to get its message through, it must be perceptible to the human senses. A concept cannot be a sign – in *Dyson Ltd v Registrar of Trade Marks*[8] the European Court of Justice (ECJ, now styled Court of Justice of the European Union) took it upon itself to consider whether the subject matter of Dyson's applications, 'a transparent bin or collection chamber forming part of the external surface of a vacuum cleaner' (shown in representations) constituted a sign. The European Commission argued that it was a concept, which appealed to the imagination but was not capable of being perceived by one of the five senses, and consequently not a 'sign'. The ECJ found that the applications could cover all conceivable shapes of transparent bin[9] and so registration would confer unfair competitive advantage. The transparent bin was held not to be a sign. Although information may be received through all five senses, does the list in s 1 implicitly limit trade marks to visual signs? Under the Trade Marks Act 1938 ('the 1938 Act'), the definitions of 'mark'[10] and 'use'[11] ensured that only visual

---

[7] Not all shapes are registrable – see **2.15–2.19**.
[8] Case C-321/03 [2007] ECR I-687; [2007] 2 CMLR 14; [2007] ETMR 34; [2007] RPC 27. See E Smith 'Dyson and the public interest' [2007] EIPR 469.
[9] Dyson had conceded that the representations were illustrative rather than definitive.
[10] Trade Marks Act 1938, s 68(1).

marks were registered and only visual use infringed.[12] All the named types of sign in s 1 are visual, although shapes may also be detected by touch. It was not the intention of those framing the legislation to limit protection to visual marks. For example, the statements prepared for entry in the minutes of adoption of the Regulation admitted the possibility of registering colours and sounds,[13] whilst the UK White Paper 'Reform of Trade Mark Law'[14] referred to colours, sounds, smells and taste.[15] The case-law of the European Court discussed below establishes that, in principle. all signs perceived by the various senses can be protected, although their registration may be limited in practice by difficulties of identification and recordal.

Colours

2.3   The ECJ has ruled definitively on the registration of colour marks in *Libertel*.[16] The applicant applied to register the colour and word 'Orange' in relation to telephony services. The ECJ held that colour per se might be registered, even in the absence of any delineating contours. However, since the range of distinguishable colours is limited, care must be taken to ensure the availability of colours to other traders.[17] In this regard the range of goods and services for which registration is sought would be relevant as well as an adequate indication of precisely which colour or colours are to be used, and how.[18] Colours may be denominative rather than distinctive, as the passing-off

---

[11]   Trade Marks Act 1938, s 68(2).

[12]   Thus where 'Saab' advertised motor cars on television with a voice spelling out the mark in air traffic notation as 'Sierra, Alpha, Alpha, Bravo', the Ford Motor Co could not have relied on any registration of 'Sierra' to stop it.

[13]   'Re Article 4:
        (a) The Council and the Commission consider that Article 4 does not rule out the possibility:
        – of registering as a Community trade mark a combination of colours or a single colour;
        – of registering in the future sounds as Community trade marks,
        provided that they are capable of distinguishing the goods or services of one undertaking from those of other undertakings.'
        The English and European courts have given such statements short shrift as an interpretive tool – see *Libertel Groep BV v Benelux-Merkenbureau* (C-104/01) [2003] ECR I-3793, [2003] ETMR 63, [2004] FSR 4 at para 25; (C-292/89) *Antonissen* [1991] ECR I-745, an employment case; *Wagamama v City Centre Restaurants* [1996] ETMR 23, [1995] FSR 713.

[14]   (1990) Cm 1203, para 2.06.

[15]   Citing and endorsing a statement from the European Commission's Explanatory Memorandum on the Community trade mark:
        'No type of sign is automatically excluded from registration ... Depending on the circumstances, therefore, the trade-marks office, the national courts, or in the last resort the Court of Justice will be responsible for determining whether, for example, solid colours or shades of colours, and signs denoting sound, smell or taste may constitute Community trade marks.' *Bulletin of the European Communities*, Supplement 5/80, p 56.

[16]   *Libertel Groep BV v Benelux-Merkenbureau* (C104/01) [2005] 2 CMLR 45, [2004] Ch 83, [2003] ECR I-3793, [2003] EMR 63, [2004] FSR 4, [2004] 2 WLR 1081. For colour marks in various EC countries, see C Schulze 'Registering Colour Trade Marks In The European Union' [2003] EIPR 55.

[17]   Echoing the 'colour depletion' theory arising from US case-law, and rejected in *Qualitex v Jacobsen* 115 S Ct 1300 (1995). Thus, single colour registrations should be the exception rather than the rule.

[18]   For combinations of colours there must be 'a systematic arrangement associating the colours

case of *Rizla* shows: it seemed that the colours in dispute indicated the qualities of different cigarette papers, rather than origin.[19] Humphreys refers to unsuccessful attempts to register colour codings as Community trade marks and points out that colours may be laudatory or generic.[20]

Sounds

2.4 In *Shield Mark*,[21] the ECJ confirmed that sound marks may, in principle, be registered, subject to distinctiveness and graphical representation.[22] Indeed, the Advocate-General pointed out that a number of EU member states, although not the UK, make express provision for sound marks in their legislation.[23] The *Shield* case involved two groups of sound marks; the first nine notes of Beethoven's *Für Elise*, represented in various ways, the second was the crow of a cockerel, described as such and rendered onomatopoetically in Dutch as 'Kukelekuuuuu'.[24] Such onomatopoetic descriptions were not held adequate to enter on the register (see below); nor were verbal descriptions.

Smells

2.5 Smell marks[25] are recorded both as having been registered, such as 'the smell of fresh cut grass'[26] for tennis balls, and as having been refused registration, such as the 'smell, aroma or essence of cinnamon' in relation to furniture[27] or the smell of raspberries for fuel.[28] However, the ECJ in *Sieckmann*,[29] whilst confirming that smells may act as distinctive signs, appears

---

concerned in a predetermined and uniform way' according to *Heidelberger Bauchemie GmbH* [2004] ETMR 99 ECJ. As the UK Registry point out in Practice Amendment Notice PAN 2/07, this is not wholly clear what this means in practice, but the Notice and the *Manual of Trade Mark Practice* at ch1, para 4.4.2 give examples of stripes in a particular colour order and proportions.

[19] *Rizla Limited v Bryant & May Limited* [1986] RPC 389. See G Kelly 'Protecting the goods: dealing with the lookalike phenomenon through the enforcement of IP rights in the United Kingdom and Ireland' [2011] EIPR 425.

[20] G Humphreys 'Non-conventional trade marks: an overview of some of the leading case law of the Boards of Appeal' [2010] EIPR 437.

[21] *Shield Mark BV v Kist (t/a Memex)* (C-283/01) [2004] All ER (EC) 277, [2005] 1 CMLR 41, [2004] Ch 97, [2004] ETMR 33, [2004] RPC 17, [2004] 2 WLR 1117, ECJ.

[22] See **2.26–2.31**.

[23] *Shield Mark BV v Kist (t/a Memex)* (C-283/01) [2004] All ER (EC) 277, [2005] 1 CMLR 41, [2004] Ch 97, [2004] ETMR 33, [2004] RPC 17, [2004] 2 WLR 1117, ECJ at para AG22.

[24] Footnote 12 to the AG's opinion lists the onomatopoeia of a cock crow in various official languages of the EU: kikiriki, in German; kikeli-ki, in Danish; quiquiriqui, in Spanish; kukkokiekuu, in Finnish; cocorico, in French; kokoriko, in Greek; cock-a-doodle-doo, in English; chichirichi, in Italian; kukeleku, in Dutch; cocorocócó, in Portuguese; and kukeliku, in Swedish.

[25] See S Maniatis 'Scents as Trademarks: Propertisation of Scents and Olfactory Poverty' in L Bently and L Flynn (eds) *Law and the Senses: Sensational Jurisprudence* (1996) pp 217, 224.

[26] *Venootschap onder Firma Senta Aromatic Marketing's Application* [1999] ETMR 429.

[27] *John Lewis of Hungerford's TM* [2002] RPC 28.

[28] *Myles Ltd's Application* [2003] ETMR 56.

[29] *Sieckmann v Deutsches Patent-und-Markenamt* (C-273/00) [2002] ECR I-11737. The 2011 'Study on the Overall Functioning of the European Trade Mark System' by the Max Planck Institute for Intellectual Property and Competition Law Munich endorsed the legal security

to have rejected all current practical methods of representing them graphically.[30] In *Eden SARL v Office for Harmonisation in the Internal Market*,[31] the Court of First Instance of the European Communities (CFI now the 'General Court') did not rule out that the *Sieckmann* criteria could be satisfied for smell marks, but found that 'the smell of ripe strawberries' accompanied by a picture of a strawberry was not sufficient.

Taste

2.6   In the only reported case[32] to date on applications to register taste marks, the Office for Harmonisation in the Internal Market (OHIM) refused to register an artificial strawberry flavour for medicines as a Community trade mark. The OHIM board of appeal upheld this decision, remarking that consumers would not regard the flavour as serving to distinguish the medicines from those of other drug companies, but rather as a means of disguising the unpleasant flavour of the medicine.

Touch

2.7   The Braille system for blind readers is well known. Registration of a distinctive word in Braille notation is conceptually straightforward. But what about less well-defined tactile marks? Could the fluffy texture of a 'Donald Duck' address book be registered? If it is recognised as indicating that the Disney Corporation have licensed production of the address book, the texture can serve to distinguish these from other trader's address books. Again the problem of representation has arisen; the German Supreme Court dismissed an appeal against rejection of an application to register a touch mark by way of drawings.[33]

Movement marks

2.8   This is a non-traditional category contemplated by the UK Trade Mark Registry[34] along with holograms. No UK cases are cited of 'movement marks' but short animated sequences, such as the dancing telephone in television advertisements for Direct Line insurance, seem to be envisaged and the *Manual of Trade Mark Practice* indicates that the movement may be represented

---

provided by *Sieckmann*, although curiously it recommended abolition of the requirement for graphical representation: http://ec.europa.eu/internal_market/indprop/docs/tm/20110308_allensbach-study_en.pdf, Part VII, para 59.

[30]   See **2.26** and **2.31**.

[31]   Case T-305/04 [2006] ETMR 14.

[32]   *Eli Lilly & Co's Community Trade Mark Application* [2004] ETMR 4 OHIM; see S Middlemiss and C Badger 'Nipping Taste Marks in the Bud' [2004] EIPR 152.

[33]   *Haptic Trade Mark Application* Case I ZB 73/05 [2008] ETMR 16 ('Haptic' means tactile, relating to touch).

[34]   See *Manual of Trade Mark Practice*, ch 1, para 4.4.6. The *Manual of Trade Mark Practice* is often also called the 'Work Manual'. It may be consulted at www.ipo.gov.uk/pro-types/pro-tm/t-law/t-manual.htm.

graphically by a series of stills. Kraft Foods UK Ltd has registered a moving mark for chocolate described as a 'three-dimensional shape breaking apart'.[35]

2.9 In *Lamborghini*,[36] OHIM refused the application on the basis that the 'movement mark' was not a distinguishing sign but rather depicted a technical feature of a class of sports car.

Non-traditional trade marks – how might they function?

2.10 From the foregoing, it seems clear that distinctive,[37] tactile,[38] aural,[39] olfactory[40] and taste marks are not excluded from registration, provided they can be represented graphically in a clear and unambiguous way.[41] In *Shield*,[42] the ECJ stated:

> '2. Article 2 of Directive 89/104 must be interpreted as meaning that a trade mark may consist of a sign which is not in itself capable of being perceived visually, provided that it can be represented graphically, particularly by means of images, lines or characters, and that its representation is clear, precise, self-contained, easily accessible, intelligible, durable and objective.'

This position is reinforced by s 103(2) of the 1994 Act, which establishes that use of a mark includes use otherwise than by means of a graphic representation. Word marks are often chosen for their sound as well as their appearance; these sensible provisions mean that the protection conferred by registration of a word mark extends to use on sound radio. If a 'pure' sound mark can be registered, the distinctive 'jingle' by which a broadcaster identifies its programme is less likely to be imitated.[43] Where touch, taste or smell is concerned it may be difficult to say in a particular case that the information conveyed by those senses has trade mark significance. The sounds coming from a discotheque or the smells wafting from a restaurant may draw in custom but are unlikely to be distinctive of a particular establishment. Probably they amount to an eloquent description of the services available inside.[44]

---

35 UK No 2280003, cited by VK Ahuja 'Non-traditional trade marks: new dimension of trade marks law' [2010] EIPR 575.

36 *Automobili Lamborghini Holding SpA's Application* [2005] ETMR 43 OHIM (First Board of Appeal) – the swivel action of the 'gull-wing' doors of the Lamborghini Diablo.

37 See **2.32** (distinctiveness).

38 No cases known to date.

39 *Shield Mark BV v Kist (t/a Memex)* (C283/01) [2004] All ER (EC) 277, [2005] 1 CMLR 41, [2004] Ch 97, [2004] ETMR 33, [2004] RPC 17, [2004] 2 WLR 1117, ECJ – the first nine notes of Beethoven's *Für Elise*.

40 *Sieckmann v Deutsches Patent-und-Markenamt* (C273/00) [2002] ECR I-11737.

41 See **2.26–2.31** (requirements for graphic representation); *Sieckmann v Deutsches Patent-und-Markenamt* (C273/00) [2002] ECR I-11737.

42 *Shield Mark BV v Kist (t/a Memex)* (C283/01) [2004] All ER (EC) 277, [2005] 1 CMLR 41, [2004] Ch 97, [2004] ETMR 33, [2004] RPC 17, [2004] 2 WLR 1117, ECJ, citing *Sieckmann v Deutsches Patent-und-Markenamt* (C273/00) [2002] ECR I-11737.

43 Although a jingle may be protected as a copyright musical work: see *Lawton v Dundas* (1985) *The Times*, June 13.

44 See **2.31** (exclusion for descriptive marks).

Alternatively, they may appear with other more traditional marks and not be perceived by consumers as distinguishing signs. In *Weldebräu v OHIM*,[45] an argument that bottles with helical necks would be confused due to their similar feel was rejected, on the basis that customers would experience this only after having chosen a drink using other indicia. This, together with the problem of representing non-traditional marks adequately for recording on the register,[46] is likely to limit their number in practice.[47] One may imagine signs being regarded as acting as trade marks for some products but not for others: the sound of a lion for films[48] (but not for a zoo); a roughened disc tag for men's luggage (but not for power tools); a scent reminiscent of roses for sewing thread or motor tyres (but not for toilet water);[49] maracuya flavour for lipstick (but not for yoghurt).

Perception of the mark

2.11 Must the perceiver be conscious of the mark?[50] Would subliminal use of a visual cue amount to trade mark use? Since subliminal advertising is not encouraged in the UK, a judge might be moved to enforce a registered mark against a subliminal infringer. However, in *Laura Ashley v Coloroll*,[51] Whitford J gave short shrift to subliminal experiments designed to establish confusion between the plaintiff's and defendant's marks. His remarks suggested that the law would regard marks as operating only at the level of conscious choice. A related question is whether use of a mark in invisible form as a webpage 'metatag' infringes.[52] Here, however, the consumer is consciously using the

---

[45] Case T-24/08, 4 March 2010, General Court.

[46] See **2.26–2.31** (requirements for graphic representation).

[47] Their rarity is noted by G Humphreys 'Non-conventional trade marks: an overview of some of the leading case law of the Boards of Appeal' [2010] EIPR 437: in 2009, 58% of filings concerned word marks, 41% figurative marks, just over 0.5% cent three-dimensional marks with colour and other signs together reaching around 0.4%. OHIM figures for 2010 available at http://oami.europa.eu show a similar picture.

[48] An application to register the MGM 'roaring lion' as a Community trade mark failed on the issue of graphical representation, but the OHIM Fourth Board of Appeal held that it was in principle registrable: *Metro-Goldwyn-Mayer Lion Corp's Application* [2004] ETMR 34.

[49] *The Times*, 1 November 1994, p 7 reported UK applications being filed on 31 October 1994 (the first day of operation of the 1994 Act) to register 'the smell of roses when applied to tyres' and 'the scent of aldehyde-floral fragrance product, with an aldehydic top note from aldehydes, bergamot, lemon and neroli; an elegant floral middle note, from jasmine, rose, lily of the valley, orris and ylang-ylang; and a sensual feminine base note from sandal, cedar, vanilla, amber civet and musk. The scent also being known as Chanel No 5'. In *Re Celia Clarke* 17 USPQ 2d 1238, the scent of plumeria blossom was registered in the USA for sewing thread. However, in Case R-711/1999-3 the smell of raspberries for motor fuel was held to be functional – to disguise the unpleasant smell of the fuel – rather than distinctive. Case R-711/1999-3 (Smell of raspberries) 5 December 2001.

[50] The editors of *Kerly's Law of Trade Marks and Trade Names* (Sweet & Maxwell, 14th edn, 2005), doubted whether a registration would be infringed where the mark was so small as to be visible to the naked eye: para 17–058, but this view has probably been overtaken by *Google France Sarl v Louis Vuitton Malletier SA & ors* (conjoined cases C-236/08 to 238/08) [2011] All ER (EC) 411; [2010] ETMR 30; [2010] RPC 19 ECJ (Grand Chamber).

[51] [1987] RPC 1.

[52] See *Roadtech Computer Systems Ltd v Mandata (Management and Data Services) Ltd* [2000] ETMR 970 Ch D; JR Kuester and PA Nieves 'Hyperlinks, Frames and Meta-tags; an

mark to browse the internet but may be led by the metatag to a site unconnected with the trade mark owner.

2.12 Must the mark be used at point of sale of goods or services, and by whom? The traditional view would have been 'yes', and by the trader.[53] The ECJ has, however, taken post-sale confusion into account in *Arsenal v Reed*.[54] Moreover, McCutcheon[55] points out that although the banana scent of writing paper may not be perceptible at point of sale, the consumer may be 'intellectually' aware of the scent from advertising and ask for the product by reference to its scent. In the context of infringement, Geoffrey Hobbs QC, sitting as a judge of the Community trade mark court, has held that 'initial interest confusion' is actionable, so perception before though not at point of sale can also be regarded as relevant.[56] The relevant perceiver in trade mark law is the 'average consumer' of the products in question,[57] who is reasonably well informed, circumspect and observant.[58]

SUITABILITY FOR MARKING AND THE 'INTEGRAL MARK' PROBLEM

2.13 Where a mark is to be applied to goods, it goes without saying that it must be possible to do so. An embossed crest is suitable for paper goods but not for diamonds. The mark should not interfere with the use of the product: an overly fancy shape would confer a very short working life on a bar of soap. Where services are requested by reference to the mark, it must be easy to pronounce, or bashful customers will make a different choice.

Intellectual Property Analysis' (1998) 38 IDEA: *Journal of Law and Technology* 243. See, also, *Google France Sarl v Louis Vuitton Malletier SA & ors* (conjoined cases C-236/08 to 238/08)) [2011] All ER (EC) 411; [2010] ETMR 30; [2010] RPC 19 ECJ (Grand Chamber)) use of trade marks as keywords or 'Adwords', by which advertisers paid to achieve a higher position in search rankings, would infringe if internet users could not easily ascertain the source of the advertised goods or services.

[53] *Aristoc v Rysta* [1945] AC 68 – post-sale use no longer 'in the course of trade'; *'Blu-tak'* *Bostik Ltd v Sellotape GB Ltd* [1994] RPC 556 Ch D. In the Google Adword scenario (n 50 and 52) the mark is used by the consumer to search and (imperceptibly) by the advertiser to ensure that its advertisement comes high on the list returned by the search engine. For a discussion of earlier cases, see P Prescott 'Trade marks invisible at point of sale' [1990] EIPR 241: 'One of the most important functions of a trader is to seek repeat orders.'

[54] [2003] 1 CMLR 12.

[55] J McCutcheon 'The Registration Of Sounds And Scents As Trade Marks Under Australian Law' [2004] IPQ 138. However, the UK Registry is sceptical that consumers will regard the fragrance of such a product as denoting origin: *Manual of Trade Mark Practice*, ch 3, para 3.2.

[56] *Och-Ziff Management Europe Ltd v Och Capital LLP* [2010] EWHC 2599 (Ch); [2011] ETMR 1; [2011] FSR 11.

[57] *Sabel BV v Puma AG* (C-251/95) [1997] ECR I-6191; [1998] 1 CMLR 445; [1998] ETMR 1; [1998] RPC 199; ECJ at 224. In *Whirlpool Corp v Kenwood Ltd* [2008] EWHC 1930 (Ch); [2009] ETMR 5; [2009] RPC 2 at [69], upheld [2009] EWCA Civ 753 at [23] the importance of identifying the average consumer in a real market was stressed; in that case the consumers were design-conscious.

[58] *Lloyd Schuhfabrik Meyer & Co GmbH v Klijsen Handel BV* (C-342/97) [1999] ECR I-3819; [1999] 2 CMLR 1343; [1999] ETMR 690; [2000] FSR 77 at para 27.

2.14 All these examples suggest that the mark is distinct from the basic product. A more subtle problem arises when the sign alleged to be a trade mark is the product itself, or its most striking feature. This could be the scent of a perfume or the shape of a shaver head. The legislation attempts to govern this difficulty in the case of shape marks, as will be seen in subsequent paragraphs, but the problem may be more general. Where a product is bought for the deliciousness of its scent or the elegance of its shape, the smell or contours may be regarded as 'aesthetically' functional[59] rather than apt to distinguish the product from that of other traders.

SHAPES OF GOODS OR THEIR PACKAGING – FUNCTIONALITY AND SUBSTANTIAL VALUE

2.15 The shape of goods and their packaging are listed as signs which may be registered as trade marks:[60] for example, the 'distinctively triangulated' Toblerone chocolate bar[61] and packaging.[62] This was a welcome development; proving the distinctiveness of product shape or packaging has been an uphill task for claimants in passing-off actions.[63] There is an elaborate regime to allow registration of product and packing shapes whilst preventing monopolisation of some important types of feature.[64] Section 3(2) of the 1994 Act prohibits the registration of signs which consist exclusively of certain shapes.

2.16 First, there is the shape which results from the nature of the goods themselves. Thus, a spherical shape results from the nature of a ball.

2.17 Secondly, shapes which are necessary to obtain a technical result are excluded. Wheels must be round to achieve smooth and efficient locomotion; a sailboard needs a ball joint between hull and mast. What is not clear is the degree of 'necessity' which disqualifies the shape. If a shape is uniquely able to produce the technical result, it is clearly unregistrable. What if it is not a unique solution, but, say, one of two possible solutions? The first applicant may persuade the Registry that another solution is available. But what about the second application? If registered, both possible solutions would be unavailable to competitors for a potentially infinite period.[65] In *Philips v Remington*[66] and

---

[59]   G Dinwoodie 'The death of ontology: a teleological approach to trade mark law' (1999) 84 Iowa LR 611; see below at n 73.

[60]   See A Firth, E Gredley and S Maniatis 'Shapes as Trade Marks: Public Policy, Functional Considerations and Consumer Perception' [2001] EIPR 86.

[61]   J Phillips 'The Thin End of the Wedge' [2005] EIPR 31.

[62]   T Helbling 'Shapes as Trade Marks? The Struggle to Register Three-Dimensional Signs: A Comparative Study of United Kingdom and Swiss Law' [1997] IPQ 413 discusses Toblerone registrations.

[63]   Although many cases have special features which explain the claimant's failure: see B Mills 'Just Pot Luck! The UK Cup Noodles Case' [1994] 7 EIPR 307. See also, JR Jeremiah 'Passing off the "Buzzy Bee": when get-up can be functional' [1994] 8 EIPR 355.

[64]   A Firth, E Gredley and S Maniatis 'Shapes as Trade Marks: Public Policy, Functional Considerations and Consumer Perception' [2001] EIPR 86.

[65]   A similar line of reasoning has been used against the registration of colours in the USA, and the argument has been honoured with the title 'colour depletion theory'. *Re Owens Coming*

Linde,[67] the ECJ has confirmed that the purpose of s 3(2) and its equivalents is to ensure that registration of a shape mark could not be used 'in order to acquire or perpetuate exclusive rights relating to technical solutions'.[68] Thus, both should be refused registration. This was confirmed by the ECJ in *Lego Juris A/S v OHIM*.[69] In a UK Registry example, the bulbous tip of an agricultural tine was held to be unregistrable. Although it differed from others' products, it conferred a practical advantage in being especially hardwearing.[70]

2.18 The third and last limb excludes shapes which give substantial value to the goods. This brings to mind examples such as the cut of a diamond[71] or a very elaborate container holding a token quantity of alcoholic beverage.[72] The principle of excluding such value-adding shapes from registration has been described in the USA as the doctrine of 'aesthetic functionality',[73] applied by some courts in the USA in cases such as such as *Pagliero v Wallace China*[74] where a floral pattern on china was denied protection as a trade mark or *Walmart*,[75] where colour and design of dresses were not regarded as an indication of source. The European Court considered this provision in *Benetton Group SpA v G-Star International BV*, where applications had been filed to register marks consisting in the stitching patterns and cut of jeans.[76] There was evidence of distinctiveness acquired prior to the application to register, but the court held that a shape conferring substantial value could not constitute a 'trade mark' even if it had acquired distinctive character. Section 3(2) and its equivalents do not mean that one can never register product features which are attractive and admired; the DaimlerChrysler Jeep Grille was held registrable by OHIM.[77] Products bearing a highly regarded trade mark are often sold at a

---

774 F 2d 1116 (Fed Cir, 1985). Some courts have been reluctant to follow this ruling and the theory was rejected in the case of *Qualitex Co v Jacobson Products Co* 115 S Ct 1300 (1995).

[66] *Koninklijke Philips v Remington* (C-299/99) [2002] ECR I-5475; [2002] ETMR 81 ECJ.

[67] *Linde, Winward, Rado/DPMA (Motorised Truck, Torch and Wrist Watch)* (Joined Cases C-53–55/01) [2003] RPC 45.

[68] *Koninklijke Philips Electronics NV v Remington Consumer Products Ltd* (C299/99) [2002] All ER (EC) 634, [2002] CEC 525, [2002] 2 CMLR 52, [2003] Ch 159, [2002] ECR I-5475, [2002] ETMR 81, [2003] RPC 2, [2003] 2 WLR 294 at para 82.

[69] (C-48/09) P [2010] ETMR 63.

[70] *Maasland NV's Application for a 3-Dimensional Trade Mark* [2000] RPC 893 AP. In *Ekornes ASA's Trade Mark* [BL O-017-06], the Appointed Person held that the combination of functional features in a chair would not render the shape unregistrable under s 3(2), although there were other valid grounds for refusal in the case. See *Manual of Trade Mark Practice*, ch 3, para 4 under 'Shapes'.

[71] Registering names of such cuts seems to confer very narrow protection: *Hölterhoff v Freiesleben* [2002] FSR 52 ECJ.

[72] As in the *Old Dutch Houses* case [1984] BIE 193, cited by A Kamperman Sanders in 'Some frequently asked questions about the Trade Marks Act 1994' [1995] 2 EIPR 67 at footnote 16.

[73] G Dinwoodie 'The death of ontology: a teleological approach to trade mark law' (1999) 84 Iowa LR 611 has criticised the phrase.

[74] 198 F 2d 339 (9th Cir, 1952). Contrast *Keene v Paraglex* 653 F 2d 822 (3rd Cir, 1981) where the doctrine was rejected.

[75] *Wal-Mart Stores, Inc v Samara Bros Inc* 120 S Ct 1339 (2000) 54 USP Q 2d 1065.

[76] (C-371/06) [2007] ECR I-7709; [2008] ETMR 5, a case decided under Art 3(3) of the Directive and the equivalent provision of Benelux trade mark law.

[77] Confirmed by the CFI in (T-128/01) *DaimlerChrysler v OHIM* [2003] ECR II-701, [2003]

premium as compared with the basic product. This 'trade mark premium' must be distinguished from the 'substantial' value of s 3(2). The Dutch Supreme Court has grappled with the distinction between the premium conferred on a product by the cachet of its mark and the 'substantial value' which renders a shape mark unregistrable. In a case involving 'twirled snacks',[78] it held that the value of the crisp resided in its eating qualities and not in the fancy shape.

2.19 On the issue of 'substantial value' the troubled UK case-law on passing off by get-up[79] may be relevant. The courts have to consider whether the appearance of a product acts as a trade mark in drawing custom, or whether it encourages purchase for other reasons. Thus, in *Jarman & Platt v Barget*,[80] customers bought the plaintiff's 'Louis' chairs because they valued their appearance. This was not regarded as distinctive of the plaintiff's chairs alone. In *Hodgkinson & Corby v Wards Mobility Services*,[81] those ordering 'black egg-box' prosthetic cushions were held not to be 'moved by source' but rather by the technical advantages conferred by the shape. In dismissing *Hodgkinson's* action, however, Jacob J rejected the distinction between capricious additions and integral features of products. It is clear that both may operate as marks. Conversely, even an unusual added shape may not necessarily operate to distinguish a product from those of other traders.[82]

A 'preliminary obstacle'

2.20 The prohibitions of s 3(2) are absolute; they were described as a 'preliminary obstacle' in *Philips v Remington* and in *Linde* and similar conclusions were reached in *Bennetton v G-Star*. No amount of distinctiveness acquired by virtue of use[83] can render these features of shape registrable on their own. After all, the purpose of s 3(2) and its equivalents is to ensure that registration of a shape mark cannot be used 'in order to acquire or perpetuate exclusive[84] rights relating to technical solutions'. But note the word 'exclusively': evidence of distinctiveness may be admissible to show that the

---

ETMR 87. However, the scope of protection may be limited: in *Whirlpool Corp v Kenwood Ltd* [2008] EWHC 1930 (Ch); [2009] ETMR 5; [2009] RPC 2 Ch D, the policy consideration underlying the registration of shape marks were taken into account in assessing infringement in the absence of confusion.

[78] Hoge Raad, 11 November (1983), NJ (1984) 203; BIE (1985) 23. See, further, A Kamperman Sanders 'Some Frequently Asked Questions about the Trade Marks Act 1994' [1995] 2 EIPR 67.

[79] For a fuller selection of cases, see *Kerly's Law of Trade Marks and Trade Names* (Sweet & Maxwell, 15th edn, 2011) paras 18.176–189; C Wadlow *The Law of Passing Off* (Sweet and Maxwell, 4th edn, 2011) pp 727–767.

[80] [1977] FSR 260.

[81] [1995] FSR 169; A Firth 'Cushions and confusion: the RoHo passing off case' (1994) 11 EIPR 494.

[82] In *Bongrain SA's TM* [2005] RPC 14, Jacob J stressed the public interest in freedom of action and healthy competition in holding a flower shape unregistrable for cheese.

[83] See **2.32**.

[84] Note that s 13(1)(a) of the 1994 Act enables the applicant or proprietor to disclaim any right to the exclusive use of any specified element of the mark. Disclaimer is effected by notice in writing to the Registrar, who publishes it (r 24). Disclaimed elements enjoy no exclusivity,

features concerned do have a trade mark significance. Once a shape mark is found to pass the hurdle of s 3(2), it must still pass the normal[85] test of distinctiveness.[86] The ECJ considered this issue in relation to rectangular washing tablets in *Procter & Gamble v OHIM*,[87] and in relation to bottle shapes in *Develey Holding v OHIM*,[88] where the court indicated that, though the principles for ascertaining distinctiveness were the same for three-dimensional as for other marks, consumer perceptions might differ, making it more difficult for the applicant to establish distinctiveness.

COMPOUND MARKS – SHAPES AND GENERALLY

2.21 Even where all individual features are excluded, is it open to an applicant for registration to argue that the particular combination of features is capable of being distinctive? Cases on disclaimers show that a mark composed of commonplace elements may be registrable as a whole. Thus, in *Diamond T*,[89] the letter 'T' and the surrounding device of a diamond were disclaimed, but the mark as a whole was registered. It is submitted that where a combination of shape elements is technically or functionally necessary, it will not be registrable. But where there is freedom to use different combinations, could the whole be capable of registration? This argument was raised in *Procter & Gamble v OHIM*. The applicants complained that OHIM and the Court of First Instance had failed properly to consider the shape of their washing tablets as a whole. The ECJ rejected this plea, remarking that although the average consumer normally perceives a mark as a whole,[90] a trade mark office could and should examine each of the individual features of the mark in turn. However, overall impression is important.[91] This may be more than just the sum of its parts. Sometimes one hears talk of a designer's 'trademark style', suggesting that the designer uses a characteristic combination of features. But *Dyson*[92] shows that a design concept cannot be a 'sign', while *Whirlpool*[93] suggests that even where a combination of features is registered, there is no protection against stylistic imitation. Use of a compound mark may confer distinctiveness on its

---

either in the context of infringement or in the context of blocking later applications: *CIFUENTES TM, General Cigar v Partagas* [2005] EWHC 1729 (Ch). See, further, **5.28**.

[85] In *Linde*, joined cases C-53/01 to 55/01 [2003] ETMR 78 the ECJ stated that the standard of distinctiveness is the same for all marks.

[86] See **2.32ff**.

[87] *Procter & Gamble Co v Office for Harmonisation in the Internal Market (Trade Marks and Designs) (OHIM)* (C-473/01 P) [2004] ECR I-5173, [2004] ETMR 89; a Community trade mark case, following a decision to similar effect under the directive in *Henkel KGaA v OHIM* (C-456/01 P) [2004] ECR I-5089.

[88] (C-238/06) P [2007] ECR I-9375; [2008] ETMR 20.

[89] [1921] 2 Ch 583; (1921) 38 RPC 373.

[90] At paras 44 and 45. It is clear that these remarks apply to trade marks generally, including word marks.

[91] *Medion v Thomson Multimedia* (C-120/04) ECJ ('*Thomson Life*'), 6 October 2005.

[92] *Dyson Ltd v Registrar of Trade Marks* (C-321/03) [2007] ECR I-687; [2007] 2 CMLR 14; [2007] ETMR 34; [2007] RPC 27.

[93] *Whirlpool Corp v Kenwood Ltd* [2008] EWHC 1930 (Ch); [2009] ETMR 5; [2009] RPC 2.

elements.[94] The use of a compound mark by a single trader should be distinguished from the practice of 'co-branding', where the marks of different traders are combined for joint activity.[95]

'SUBSTANTIAL VALUE' GENERALLY

2.22   The registration of shape marks consisting exclusively of signs which confer substantial value in use is expressly prohibited by s 3(2)(c). The same problem may arise, however, in relation to smell, taste or sound marks. The distinctive scent of upmarket toiletries may confer substantial value, as may the smell of instant coffee or the taste of a soft drink. These features are important elements of the products. Likewise, the opening bars of a musical work may be compelling and distinctive but they are usually the most significant part of the work itself. They may operate perfectly well as a trade mark for insurance services, but be less suitable as a 'jingle' for a classical radio station.

2.23   In practice, the question as to whether the distinctive feature is a trade mark will be much affected by the way the goods or service has been advertised. If the feature is promoted as enhancing the functional or aesthetic qualities of the product, then it is unlikely to be accepted as a mark.[96] This can be regarded as a form of estoppel. Promotion of the feature as a distinguishing sign constitutes a self-serving statement, to which little weight would normally attach. However, it may be relevant in educating the public to recognise the feature as distinctive.[97] Such use may be taken into account by the Registry or court in deciding whether the sign is perceived as a trade mark, though *Bennetton v G-Star* shows the limitations of this approach.

SUITABILITY FOR ADVERTISING

2.24   A trader adopting a mark should consider all likely advertising media and in particular those likely to reach the target market. A good mark can be long-lived; in the classic situation the product acts as its own advertisement. This has been overtaken by hoardings, print media, sound broadcasting, television, mobile telephony, web advertising, etc. For some of these, a mark may be physically or morally[98] ill-suited.

2.25   Conversely, an advertising technique may mature into a trade mark. It used to be doubted that advertising slogans were trade marks. UK registration

---

94   *Société des Produits Nestlé SA v Mars UK Ltd* (C-353/03), [2005] 3 CMLR 12, ECJ, [2005] ETMR 96.

95   T Blackett and B Boad 'Co-Branding: the Science of Alliance' [1999].

96   As with the triple headed shaver in *Philips v Remington* (C-299/99) [2002] ECR I-5475, [2002] ETMR 81 ECJ.

97   US case-law stresses the education of the consumer, see, e g *Fabrication Enters v Hygenic Corp* 64 F 3d 53, 35 USPQ2d 1753 (2nd Cir, 1995).

98   See **2.45**.

was refused to the Kit-Kat slogan 'Have a break'.[99] The ECJ has held on a reference in this case that distinctiveness may be acquired by use in a composite phrase, such as 'Have a break – have a Kit-Kat'.[100] So we may expect to find 'Have a break' on the UK register in due course. However, even under the 1938 Act, slogans such as 'I can't believe it's yogurt'[101] were registered in the UK.[102]

SUITABILITY FOR ENTERING ON THE REGISTER

2.26 To be registrable as a mark, a sign must be capable of graphic representation.[103] This requirement ensures that the mark can be entered upon the register. Although 'register' suggests a huge leather-bound book, the register need not be kept in documentary form. The UK Trade Marks Registry (a division of the Intellectual Property Office) has a computerised register.[104] Section 63(1) of the 1994 Act defines 'register' and s 63(3) merely provides that it be kept in such manner as may be prescribed. This is done in r 46 of the Trade Marks Rules 2008,[105] which again states that the register need not be kept in documentary form.

2.27 Words, devices, letters and numerals already have their graphical representation. They may be registered in general or in a specific typeface or colour.[106] Logos can be represented pictorially. Where packaging or product shapes are concerned, the representation may be achieved by drawings or photographs, often multiple views will be needed, and preferably accompanied by an appropriate description.[107] The Registry has indicated that representations up to A4 size can be accepted.[108] It appears that the UK Registry will not accept descriptions of shape signs[109] but not OHIM.[110] The difficulties of using descriptions are illustrated by applications to register the shapes of various

---

99 [1993] RPC 217 (decided in 1983), and again in *Société des Produits Nestlé SA v Mars UK Ltd* [2003] ETMR 101 sub nom *Nestlé SA's Trade Mark Application (Have a break)* at [2004] FSR 2 CA.

100 *Société des Produits Nestlé SA v Mars UK Ltd* (C353/03) [2005] 3 CMLR 12, ECJ, [2005] ETMR 96.

101 [1992] RPC 533. Note that the requirement of distinctiveness will be absent where the slogan refers to the qualities of the service or goods: 'Where People Matter' ITMA Information, April/May 1994, p 1.

102 In enacting the 1994 Act, Parliament rejected as unnecessary an amendment to the Trade Marks Bill which would have added 'slogans' to the list of signs in s 1: House of Lords Public Bill Committee Report, cols 10–11 (13 January 1994).

103 Trade Marks Act 1994, s 1(1). A mark which does not satisfy s 1(1) cannot be registered (s 3(1)(a)).

104 Known as OPTICS, for Office of Patents and Trademarks Integrated Computer Systems. There is also a database facility for devices dubbed TRIMS (Trade Marks Imaging System).

105 SI 2008/1797, as amended by SI 2008/2300 (see Appendix 2 of this book).

106 The UK IPO's *Manual of Trade Mark Practice*, ch 1, para 4.4.2 recommends stating the colour in words and defining by use of an internationally recognised colour identification system, such as 'Pantone', 'Focoltone', 'Munsell Color' or 'Toyo'.

107 *Manual of Trade Mark Practice*, ch 1, para 4.4.4.

108 Guidance notes for Form TM3, section 2.

109 *Manual of Trade Mark Practice*, ch 1, para 4.4.4.

110 *Antoni & Alison's Application* [1998] ETMR 460.

sweets as trade marks by Swizzel Matlow: 'chewy sweet on a stick' was held to be too vague,[111] whilst their attempt to describe their 'love heart' sweets would convey their appearance to those familiar with the products, but not to others.[112] The Appointed Person[113] stressed the need for clarity for third parties.

2.28 The representation of colours, sounds, taste, smells and tactile marks may be more taxing on the applicant's powers of description. Precision could be attained by a highly technical formula but might not be comprehensible to those consulting the register. In *Sieckmann*,[114] it was held that the representation must be 'clear, precise, self-contained, easily accessible, intelligible, durable and objective'. The nature of the mark must be stated, be it a shape, colour, sound, etc.[115]

Colours

2.29 In *Ty-Nant*,[116] an elaborate technical method of identifying the colour cobalt blue was firmly rejected. Conversely, it may be difficult to identify a colour with adequate precision using words. However, there are colour standards which are almost universally recognised. The *Manual of Trade Mark Practice*[117] refers to the 'Pantone', 'Focoltone', 'Munsell Color' or 'Toyo' systems as suitable for reference use in colour mark applications and recommends also including a description of the colour.

Sounds

2.30 Sound marks frequently comprise snatches of music, which can be represented in musical staff notation.[118] This can be reasonably precise and is widely understood. Sound marks might also be represented in a technical or in a descriptive way. The notes 'GEC' played on chimes at a particular pitch and pace could be described as such. In *Shield Mark*,[119] the ECJ having held that sound marks are registrable in principle, went on to rule:

> 'Article 2 of Directive 89/104 must be interpreted as meaning that a trade mark may consist of a sign which is not in itself capable of being perceived visually, provided that it can be represented graphically, particularly by means of images,

[111] *Swizzel Matlow's Application (No 1)* [1998] RPC 244.

[112] *Swizzel Matlow's Application (No 2)* [1999] RPC 879; [2000] ETMR 58.

[113] Simon Thorley, QC.

[114] *Sieckmann v Deutsches Patent-und-Markenamt* (C273/00) [2002] ECR I-11737.

[115] *Shield Mark BV v Kist (t/a Memex)* (C283/01) [2004] All ER (EC) 277, [2005] 1 CMLR 41, [2004] Ch 97, [2004] ETMR 33, [2004] RPC 17, [2004] 2 WLR 1117, ECJ (sounds).

[116] *Ty-Nant* [1999] RPC 392, TMR; [2000] RPC 55, AP.

[117] Chapter 1, para 4.4.2.

[118] Such as the opening note of Beethoven's *Fur Elise* in *Shield Mark BV v Kist (t/a Memex)* (C-283/01) [2004] All ER (EC) 277, [2005] 1 CMLR 41, [2004] Ch 97, [2004] ETMR 33, [2004] RPC 17, [2004] 2 WLR 1117, ECJ.

[119] *Shield Mark BV v Kist (t/a Memex)* (C-283/01) [2004] All ER (EC) 277, [2005] 1 CMLR 41, [2004] Ch 97, [2004] ETMR 33, [2004] RPC 17, [2004] 2 WLR 1117, ECJ.

lines or characters, and that its representation is clear, precise, self-contained, easily accessible, intelligible, durable and objective. In the case of a sound sign, those requirements are not satisfied when the sign is represented graphically by means of a description using the written language, such as an indication that the sign consists of the notes going to make up a musical work, or the indication that it is the cry of an animal, or by means of a simple onomatopoeia, without more, or by means of a sequence of musical notes, without more. On the other hand, those requirements are satisfied where the sign is represented by a stave divided into bars and showing, in particular, a clef, musical notes and rests whose form indicates the relative value and, where necessary, accidentals.'

As outlined in the UK *Manual of trade marks practice*,[120] musical notation provides unambiguous representation, rendering timing and pitch intelligible, unlike a written description of the sound. A musical instrument may be specified. The use of a sonogram or waveform was briefly discussed in *Shield*,[121] but the court did not give a ruling. In *Edgar Rice Burroughs Inc v OHIM*,[122] an application to register Tarzan's yell, accompanied by a spectrogram, was rejected. Subsequently OHIM decided to accept sounds files, in formats such as MP3.[123]

Smells

2.31 In *Sieckmann*,[124] every imaginable method of representing a smell graphically was canvassed but rejected by the ECJ. Dr Sieckmann, as befitted his scientific and legal background as an IP attorney, identified his 'olfactory mark' by the pure chemical substance producing the characteristic smell – methyl cinnamate or cinnamic acid methyl ester, also giving the chemical's formula in symbols. He submitted an odour sample in a container. He stated that the scent was usually described as 'balsamically fruity with a slight hint of

---

[120] At ch 1, para 4.4.5. According to this, the UK registry has not taken a position on sonograms. In *Edgar Rice Burroughs Inc v OHIM* R 708/2006-4, an application to register Tarzan's yell, described in words and accompanied by a spectrogram, was refused for lack of proper graphical representation, but OHIM now accepts sounds files, for example in MP3 format. see S Yavorsky 'Ministry of Sound – OHIM and the Tarzan yell' [2008] Ent LR 63.

[121] The referring court had asked whether, in particular, the requirement of graphical representation would be satisfied if the sound or the noise is registered in one of the following forms:
– musical notes;
– a written description in the form of an onomatopoeia;
– a written description in some other form;
– a graphical representation such as a sonogram;
– a sound recording annexed to the registration form;
– a digital recording accessible via the Internet;
– a combination of those methods;
– some other form and, if so, which?
The UK Registrar 'has not taken a position on sonograms' according to the *Manual of Trade Mark Practice*, ch 1, para 4.4.5.

[122] R-708/2006-4.

[123] Regulation 2868/95 of 13 December 1995 implementing Regulation 40/94 on the Community trade mark (as amended) ('CTMIR') art 3(6). Decision No EX-05-3 of the President of the Office of 10 October 2005, see C Seville 'Trade Marks' [2008] ICLQ 955.

[124] *Sieckmann v Deustches Patent-und-Markenamt* (C-273/00) [2002] ECR I-11737.

cinnamon'. He identified laboratories where samples of the mark could be obtained, all to no effect. It seems that, unless and until there is a further ruling, no more smell marks can validly be registered in the EU.

ABILITY TO DISTINGUISH

2.32 Capability of distinguishing is the fundamental characteristic of a trade mark. Section 1(1) requires it and s 3(1)(a) forbids registration without it. The sign must be capable of identifying the goods or services as originating with a particular undertaking (the proprietor) and distinguishing them from others.[125] A mark may be distinctive by nature, or by 'nurture'.[126] Marks which are incapable of distinguishing, therefore, cannot be registered; ss 3, 4 and 5[127] ensure this. In particular, the absolute grounds for refusal under s 3(1)(c) and its proviso explore different situations in which a sign may lack distinctive character and be denied registration. Conversely, where evidence shows that a sign operates as a distinctive mark, it will generally be possible to register the mark. The spirit of the Directive and the 1994 Act was said to allow registration of marks unless prohibited.[128] However, after a very permissive set of decisions under the equivalent provisions of the Regulation, culminating in *Baby-Dry*,[129] the ECJ seems to have resiled from a presumption of registrability in favour of what Turner-Kerr has called a 'principle of availability'.[130] Without overruling *Baby-Dry*, the court has ruled that *Double-Mint*[131] was unregistrable even though its descriptive connotations were ambiguous and *Post-Kantoor*[132] likewise, notwithstanding the availability of other, perhaps more usual, descriptors. A similar principle underlay the UK Registry's practice of refusing to register common surnames by reference to frequency of appearance in telephone directories. This practice, however, came in for criticism in *Nichols* and is no longer used.[133] The 'absolute grounds' are recognised as overlapping[134] and each protects an aspect of the public

---

[125] *Electrocoin Automatics Ltd v Coinworld Ltd* [2004] EWHC 1498; [2005] ETMR 31.

[126] Ie by virtue of use: AD 2000 [1997] RPC 168, as in *OHIM v Celltech R&D Ltd* (C-273/05 P) [2007] ECR I-2883.

[127] 'Absolute grounds for refusal of registration' (s 3); 'specially protected emblems' (s 4); and 'relative grounds for refusal of registration' (s 5).

[128] White Paper 'Reform of Trade Mark Law' (1990) Cm 1203, paras 2.06 and 3.07–3.09.

[129] For babies' nappies or diapers, *Procter & Gamble v OHIM* [2001] ECR I-6251.

[130] P Turner-Kerr 'Trade Mark Tangles: Recent Twists and Turns in EC Trade Mark Law' [2004] EL Rev 345.

[131] *(OHIM) v Wm Wrigley Jr Co* (C-191/01 P) [2004] 1 WLR 1728; [2004] All ER (EC) 1040; [2003] ECR I-12447; [2005] 3 CMLR 21; [2004] ETMR 9; [2004] RPC 18.

[132] *Koninklijke KPN Nederland NV v Benelux-Merkenbureau* (C-363/99) [2006] Ch 1; [2005] 3 WLR 649; [2005] All ER (EC) 19; [2004] ECR I-1619; [2005] 2 CMLR 10; [2005] CEC 216; [2004] ETMR 57, ruling that: 'The practice of a trade mark registration authority which concentrates solely on refusing to register "manifestly inadmissible" marks is incompatible with article 3 of Directive 89/104.'

[133] *Nichols plc v Registrar of Trade Marks* (C-404/02), [2004] ECR I-8499, [2005] RPC 12; see *Manual of Trade Mark Practice*, ch 3 Examination Guide, heading 'Surnames, Forenames and Full Names'.

[134] Especially in decisions of the UK courts such as *Procter & Gamble Ltd's Trade Mark Applications* [1999] RPC 673; *Electrocoin Automatics Ltd v Coinworld Ltd* [2005] ETMR 31;

interest.[135] The next section analyses reasons why a sign may lack distinctiveness on a temporary or a permanent basis. The mark is always assessed, of course, in relation to the goods or services for which registration is sought.[136]

NON-DISTINCTIVE SIGNS

2.33 Section 3 of the 1994 Act, Art 3 of the Directive and Art 7 of the Regulation, refers to absolute grounds for refusal to register 'signs'. In each of these equivalent provisions, indent (a) refers to signs (signs which do not satisfy the requirements of s 1 in the 1994 Act; 'signs which cannot constitute a trade mark' in the Directive and Regulation). Leaving aside problems of non-sign and capacity for graphical representation, is there a class of 'sign' which cannot be a 'trade mark' in law, even if it otherwise satisfies the requirements of s 1? Such as York for trailers, which was held under the Trade Marks Act 1938 to be incapable of registration in law, albeit 100% distinctive in fact?[137] The ECJ ruled otherwise in *Philips v Remington*,[138] thus leaving s 3(1)(a) and its equivalents with no separate function to perform as regards distinctiveness.[139] In the sections that follow, 'sign' will be used in relation to candidates for registration as trade marks. In the writers' view, non-distinctive signs[140] fall logically into five categories, covering both 'absolute' and 'relative' grounds for refusal of registration.

The sign is incapable of conveying information

2.34 A short, isolated straight line or the single letter (and indefinite article) 'a' simply cannot carry a distinctive message. 'White' noise would be too complex to operate as a sound mark. Section 3(1)(b) prohibits registration of signs which are devoid of any distinctive character. However, this is subject to the proviso that the mark can be registered on proof of distinctiveness acquired through use. In the past, evidence of use has been accepted as evidence of distinctiveness. Does the proviso require proof of recognition of the mark as well? Common sense suggests that for a borderline mark, evidence of actual

---

Bongrain SA's Trade Mark Application [2004] [2005] RPC 14, CA. See, further M Handler 'The Distinctive Problem of European Trade Mark Law' [2005] EIPR 306.

[135] *Linde AG v Deutsches Patent-und-Markenamt* [2003] RPC 45 ECJ.

[136] *Procter & Gamble Co v OHIM* (C-473/01 P) [2004] ECR I-5173, [2004] ETMR 89, citing *Linde*, para 41, and *Koninklijke KPN Nederland* (C-363/99), para 34. See also *Philips v Remington* (C299/99) [2003] 2 WLR 294, [2003] RPC 2.

[137] [1984] RPC 231.

[138] *Koninklijke Philips v Remington* (C-299/99) [2002] ECR I-5475; [2002] ETMR 81 ECJ. Despite the ECJ's holding in Philips that the indents are independent, they clearly address overlapping public interest concerns: M Handler 'The distinctive problem of European trade mark law' [2005] EIPR 306.

[139] On s 3(1)(a) case-law, see C Colston & J Galloway 'Modern Intellectual Property Law' (Routledge, 3rd edn, 2010) at pp 608–609.

[140] Note that in s 3 of the 1994 Act, Art 3 of the Directive and Art 7 of the Regulation, indent (a) refers to relative ground of refusal of 'signs', whereas the remaining indents refer to 'trade marks'. In this chapter, 'signs' shall be used throughout.

distinctiveness is desirable. For a 'stronger' mark, evidence of use may suffice to put its registrability beyond doubt. Secondly, is it necessary to show that the mark has become distinctive in the UK, or will proof of distinctiveness through use abroad be adequate? Evidence of use abroad, especially in another member state of the EU, may be relevant to capability to distinguish, but could never be conclusive. Different linguistic and other conditions will pertain.[141]

2.35 Past refusals to register which may exemplify this category included two- and three-letter combinations other than words.[142] The Registry now takes the view that two- and three-letter non-words may be registered, unless they would not be regarded as a trade mark by the average consumer. Nor is there a bar to registration of a single letter, but its use in combination with other features, such as colour, would assist.[143] Similar practices relate to numbers[144] and combinations of letters and numbers.

The sign is descriptive, ab initio, of the product

2.36 Section 3(1)(c) obliges the Registry to refuse to register marks which consist exclusively of signs which serve, in trade, to designate the kind ('frocks'), quality ('all wool'), quantity ('tonne'), intended purpose ('cat food'), value ('pound'),[145] geographical origin[146] ('Brighton' for rock), the time of production of goods or rendering of services ('24 hours'), or other characteristics of goods and services ('speedy', 'perfect'). This category is again subject to the proviso for acquired distinctiveness.[147] Dealing with the last examples first, UK law has traditionally been strict as to laudatory marks. In a classic case, registration was refused to 'Perfection'.[148] However, where words have been subtly rather than directly laudatory,[149] registration has been allowed.

---

[141] See *Ford-Werke* (1955) 72 RPC 191.

[142] *W&G* (1913) 30 RPL 661; IQ [1993] RPC 379. Monograms and other 'fancy' combinations were often registered, however.

[143] *Manual of Trade Mark Practice*, ch 3, heading 'Letters and Numerals'. *Letter K Trade Mark* [2001] ETMR 102 (Bundesgerichtshof) ('K' not necessarily devoid of distinctive character).

[144] *Caterham Car Sales & Coachwork Ltd's Application* [2000] ETMR 14 (OHIM Third Board of Appeal) ('7').

[145] Although 'Pound Puppies' was registered under the 1938 Act, [1988] RPC 530 (Board of Trade).

[146] The strength of a geographical objection will depend upon the size and importance of the geographical location and whether it does or could have a reputation for the product. The Registry has formulated guidelines, assessing whether the name is liable to be used as designating geographical origin and following the ECJ's ruling in *Windsurfing Chiemsee v Boots and Attenberger* (C-108/97 & 109/97) [2000] Ch 523; [2000] 2 WLR 205; [1999] ECR I-2779; [1999] ETMR 585: *Manual of Trade Mark Practice*, ch 3, heading 'Geographical Names'.

[147] Surprisingly descriptive words have been held to have acquired distinctiveness. Manganin, the name of an alloy, became distinctive of an applicant's products, [1967] RPC 271.

[148] *Crosfield's Application* [1910] 1 Ch 130; 26 RPC 561. In this case the judge recognised that a word could be simultaneously descriptive and distinctive. For a more recent example, see 'Bravo': *Merz & Krell v Deutsches Patent und Markenamt* (C-517/99) [2002] All ER (EC) 441, [2001] ECR I-6959, [2002] ETMR 21 ECJ.

[149] As in Sheen for sewing thread, (1936) 53 RPC 355, or Chunky for dog food, [1978] FSR 322.

2.37 Marketing departments seem extraordinarily fond of descriptive marks.[150] This is understandable in the case of new products, where advertising has to create recognition of the product as well as the mark. Unfortunately, a descriptive mark may be taken as a mere product description, and fail to achieve distinctiveness even through use.[151] Another common ploy is to misspell or combine descriptive words, or to use foreign words.[152] In *Matratzen* the ECJ emphasised that understanding in the member state of registration is the determinant for national marks.[153] To date, the UK Registry has been quick to spot and refuse applications to register marks such as 'Soflens'.[154] Device marks have also been refused as descriptive, as in *Unilever*.[155] However, if it can be shown that the descriptive symbol or word refers to a distinctive feature of the goods or services, then it can be registered.[156] Descriptive words may be combined together in a distinctive way, although this was not the case in 'COLOR EDITION'.[157]

2.38 Marks in this category range from direct and overt descriptions, for example Motor Lodge,[158] which are likely to fall foul of s 3(1)(c) to 'covert and skilful allusions'[159] which will not be caught. The latter type of mark, suggestive rather than descriptive of a product's qualities, can be very effective.

2.39 If a mark in a foreign language or script[160] is descriptive in its own language, its registrability in the UK will depend upon the degree of recognition of the language or script in the relevant UK (residents of the UK are likely to be familiar with French, but not Lithuanian; Non-European languages such as Arabic may be familiar in the market for certain types of goods) and whether the language is customarily used for the products

---

For an interesting and detailed analysis of the registration of laudatory marks in Canada, see RM Colbert and E Manolakis 'Laudatory Words in Trade Marks – are proper considerations being applied?' (1994) 10 CIPR 635.

[150] For cautionary examples from US case-law, see any edition of Diamond *Trade Mark Problems and How to Avoid Them.*

[151] As in 'Oven Chips': *McCain v Country Fair* [1981] RPC 69.

[152] A former requirement that foreign words or symbols be translated or transliterated has not been retained; presumably it is covered by the Registry's powers to call for translation of all or part of any document: Trade Marks Rules 1994, r 66.

[153] *Matratzen Concord AG v Hukla Germany SA* (C-421/04) [2006] ECR I-2303; [2006] CEC 621; [2006] ETMR 48.

[154] For contact lenses, [1976] RPC 694. See also *Orlwoola* [1910] 1 Ch 130; (1909) 26 RPC 683 and 850.

[155] Representation of striped toothpaste, [1984] RPC 155, and see [1987] RPC 13.

[156] *Blue Paraffin* [1977] RPC 473; *Unilever Ltd's (Striped Toothpaste No 2) TM* [1987] RPC 13.

[157] *Lancôme Parfums et Beauté & Cie SNC v OHIM* (C-408/08 P) [2010] ETMR 34, although both SPECIAL EFFECTS and its phonic equivalent SPECIAL FX achieved registration: *Special Effects Ltd v L'Oréal SA* [2007] EWCA Civ 1; [2007] ETMR 51; [2007] RPC 15.

[158] [1965] RPC 35.

[159] *Solio* [1898] AC 571; 15 RPC 476.

[160] See *Manual of Trade Mark Practice*, ch 3, heading 'Non English Words (Registrability of)', following *Matratzen*. Registry examiners may use the internet to ascertain whether there is a descriptive sense in the public domain. *Ruiz-Picasso and Others v OHIM – DaimlerChrysler (PICARO)* Case T-185/02 [2004] ECR II-1739 at paras 28–29 indicating that judicial notice may be taken, including information from generally accessible sources.

(eg French for beauty products). It will also depend upon the degree of descriptiveness of the mark's meaning.[161]

The sign is misdescriptive of the product

2.40 Section 3(3)(b) prohibits registration of marks which are of such a nature as to deceive the public, for instance as to the nature, quality or geographical origin of the product. Thus, 'babycare' would be misdescriptive of rat poison and 'all wool' deceptive if used in relation to synthetic fabrics. In *CFA Institute's Application*,[162] 'Chartered' in applicant's collective mark was held to be misdescriptive of its status, particularly among private investors, contrary to s 3(1)(b). Sometimes, however, a misdescription is so fanciful as to avoid deceptiveness. Thus, 'North Pole' for bananas or 'Sahara' for ice cubes would deceive nobody as to geographical origin.

The sign was distinctive but has become descriptive

2.41 Just as a descriptive sign can become distinctive through use as a trade mark, so a trade mark can lose distinctiveness through misuse as a product description. Such marks are said to have become 'generic'. Where a mark has been registered whilst distinctive, only 'generic' use in the trade is sufficient to invalidate it.[163] What if the mark is not already on the register, or registration is sought for further goods or services? Section 3(1)(d) denies registration to signs which have become customary in the current language or in the bona fide and established practices of the trade.[164] It is submitted that these two limbs are distinct;[165] currency in the language may be established by dictionary entries.[166] In *Matsushita* the UK Registry had found generic use in the trade of the phrase 'combi steam' on the internet; refusal of the application was upheld.[167]

---

[161] See, eg *Kiku* [1978] FSR 246, Japanese for 'Chrysanthemum'.

[162] *CFA Institute's Application; Opposition of the Chartered Insurance Institute*, Case O-315-06 [2007] ETMR 76 UK TM Registry, Allan James. No free-standing objection under s 3(1)(a).

[163] See **9.16**. *Hasbro Inc v 123 Nahrmittel* GmbH [2011] EWHC 199 (Ch); [2011] ETMR 25; [2011] FSR 21.

[164] *Björnekulla Fruktindustrier AB v Procordia Food AB* [2004] RPC 45, ECJ (6th Chamber) (C-371/02), in cases where intermediaries participate in the distribution to the consumer or the end user of a product which is the subject of a registered trade mark, the relevant circles whose views fall to be taken into account in determining whether that trade mark has become the common name in the trade for the product in question comprise all consumers and end users and, depending on the features of the market concerned, all those in the trade who deal with that product commercially.

[165] So that everyday language as well as trade usage counts.

[166] Dictionary editors should always be encouraged to refer to trade marks as such. Specific provision is made for this in Art 10 of the Regulation. A similar provision appeared in earlier drafts of the Directive (see, eg Art 4 of the amended proposal published at OJ [1985] (C-351/4)) but was omitted from the final text.

[167] *Matsushita Electric Industrial Co Ltd's Trade Mark Application* (No 2443998) O-363-09 App Person. And see *Telefon & Buch Verlagsgesellschaft v OHIM* Case T-322/03, [2006] ECR II-835 (weisse seiten ('white pages') customary for telephone directories).

The sign calls to mind the goods or services of others

2.42 Where the sign carries deceptive information as to the origin of the product, s 5 sets out the 'relative' grounds on which registration of a mark is to be refused. Fatal conflict can occur whether the prior mark is registered or not (s 6).

2.43 Confusion with other marks may also lead to deception as to the nature of the product. In some cases, this could pose a danger to consumers. Thus, under the 1938 Act, an application to register 'Jardex' for disinfectant was refused by reason of a prior registration 'Jardox' for meat extract.[168] However, during the passage of the 1994 Act, it was indicated in Parliament that the Registry no longer had a direct consumer protection role.[169] Furthermore, it was noted that refusal to register would not, of itself, prevent use and concomitant deception of the public.[170] Consequently, the Registry no longer searches for or raises such 'danger' citations.[171]

2.44 Also included in this category are cases where use of a sign suggests a connection with the Royal family, or resembles the Red Cross, a national flag or other state or international symbol, or contains an Olympic symbol. In these cases, registration is prohibited by ss 3(5), 4,[172] 57[173] and 58[174] and r 9. The prohibitions may be overcome by authorisation from the appropriate state, organisation or member of the Royal family; in the case of UK and national flags, the Registrar is arbiter (s 4(2)).

INAPPROPRIATE SIGNS

2.45 Where a mark is universally repellent, market forces will prevent its adoption. Sometimes, however, a 'bad' mark[175] will appeal to a target sector of the public. Section 3(3)(a) prohibits the registration of a trade mark which is contrary to public policy or to accepted principles of morality. Bearing in mind both the deregulatory intent behind the 1994 Act and the current social climate, this 'public order' exception is likely to be used sparingly. In the past, registration was refused to 'Hallelujah' for jeans;[176] at the time, it was felt that the mark had a powerful religious significance and was likely to offend but it is unlikely that the same decision would be reached today. However, 'Jesus' has more recently been refused registration,[177] as has 'Tiny Penis'.[178] In *Couture*

---

[168] (1945) 63 RPC 19.

[169] House of Lords, vol 550, no 10, col 752 (6 December 1993).

[170] House of Lords Public Bill Committee, cols 16–17 (13 January 1994).

[171] ITMA Information, January/February 1995, p 3.

[172] Royal arms, crown, flags, likenesses, etc; the union or national flags of the UK.

[173] The national emblems of Paris Convention countries.

[174] The names, abbreviations and emblems of international intergovernmental organisations of which one or more Paris Convention countries are members.

[175] Eg 'Opium' and 'Poison' for toiletries, 'Death' for cigarettes.

[176] [1976] RPC 605.

[177] *Basic Trademark SA's Trade Mark Application* [2005] RPC 25 AP.

Tech Ltd's Application[179] OHIM's Second Board of Appeal upheld a refusal to register the official symbol of the Soviet Communist party, on the basis that it would offend a significant proportion of the population of EU countries formerly under Soviet control. The Board commented that 'the organs of government and public administration should not positively assist people who wish to further their business aims by means of trade marks that offend against certain basic values of civilised society'.[180] A more general exclusion is contained in s 3(4): 'a mark shall not be registered if or to the extent that its use is prohibited in the UK by any enactment, rule of law or provision of Community law'.[181] 'To the extent that' suggests that a mark whose use was wholly prohibited by, say, obscenity laws could not be registered at all. Conversely, an otherwise unobjectionable mark might be refused registration for products where its use was restricted. To take an historical example, assume that deregulation of the financial services sector had not occurred in 1986. Building societies would not be permitted to provide estate agency services. Therefore, in this scenario, use by the 'Nationwide'[182] building society of its mark in relation to estate agency would be prohibited within the meaning of s 3(4), and the mark could not be registered for estate agency services. But this would not prevent its registration for, say, mortgage lending services.

CHOOSING A MARK

2.46 A mark needs to be chosen for its intrinsic and extrinsic qualities. It must convey information but not be descriptive of the product. Keating[183] categorises marks as:

(a)   coined (the most enduring);

(b)   fanciful;

(c)   suggestive; and

(d)   descriptive.

The last should be avoided. Which of the other categories is used depends very much upon the characteristics of product and market. An allusive mark may be

---

[178]   *Ghazilian's Trade Mark Application* [2002] ETMR 57; [2002] RPC 33; Appointed Person.

[179]   Case (R-1509/2008-2) [2010] ETMR 45 OHIM Second Board of Appeal, considering the 'Jesus' and 'Tiny Penis' decisions with approval.

[180]   At para 73, citing from *Screw You* [2007] ETMR 7 OHIM First Board of Appeal.

[181]   Eg a registration of 'Champagne' for a different beverage; its use would contravene Regulation (EEC) 823/87. See *Taittinger v Allbev* [1993] FSR 641 at p 672.

[182]   See *Nationwide* [1987] FSR 579, where the building society sued in passing off shortly before liberalisation to restrain use of 'Nationwide' by estate agents. An interlocutory injunction was refused but undertakings from the defendants not to expand further were accepted.

[183]   Author of *Franchising Adviser* (1987).

popular among young people, but its connotations may be liable to rapid change. A classical mark[184] may prove longer lasting; its allusions may be more obscure but less prone to change.

2.47 Before adoption of a new mark, a search of existing registrations and, if sufficiently far advanced to have been published, applications for marks on the UK or Community registers is essential. With a wider range of relevant prior matter than under the 1938 Act and a wider range of signs which can be protected, it was predicted that, under the 1994 Act regime, trade mark searching would be more significant[185] and become more widespread. Whilst the first prediction was arguably correct, the latter was certainly not. In principle, a trade mark search should help to indicate whether use of a mark is likely to infringe and whether registration is likely to be blocked by earlier marks; however, in practice, a number of limitations exist, in particular, the proper identification of earlier unregistered rights (ie rights arising from other intellectual property rights like copyright or unregistered marks protected under the law of passing off). Whether because of these limitations, the cost of searching, or a simple lack of public knowledge, the fact remains that, even today, trade mark searches are still not as widely conducted as they ought to be.

---

[184] Eg those cited in Gredley 'Is your trade mark classic?' *Managing Intellectual Property*, June 1993, p 31.

[185] For comments on the effect of the 1994 Act provisions on conflicting marks, see Spencer 'European Harmonisation: Harmony – or confusion and conflict?' *Trademark World*, December/January 1993/94, p 23.

Chapter 3

LEGAL MODES OF PROTECTION

HISTORICAL BACKGROUND

3.1   From the Middle Ages the Guild system controlled access to and the conduct of the various trades and professions. The weakening of those controls, together with the opportunities for profit and for cheating in the metal trades,[1] seems to have led to the early enactment of protective statutes, the Cutlers Company Acts. These bolstered the powers of the Company to allot unique marks by prohibiting their unauthorised use. Other trades must have envied this system. In 1862, Parliament considered Bills for the registration of marks and for the protection of the public and traders from deceptive use of marks. The latter prevailed, and the Merchandise Marks Act 1862 passed on to the statute book. This was superseded by the Merchandise Marks Act 1887, which can be regarded as the precursor to the Trade Descriptions Acts 1968 and 1972. These criminal statutes were said in *Advocaat* not to confer any civil rights of action upon competing traders.[2] The same may be true of their legislative successors, the Consumer Protection from Unfair Trading Regulations 2008[3] and the Business Protection from Misleading Marketing Regulations 2008,[4] although in *Tiscali UK Ltd v British Telecommunications plc*,[5] Eady J allowed the claimants to amend their pleadings to introduce allegations of interference with business by unlawful means by way of breaches of the Regulations.

3.2   In 1875 the Trade Marks Registration Act 1875 ('the 1875 Act') created a general Registry, providing for registration of marks for all classes of goods. To be registrable, the mark had to comprise at least one 'essential particular',[6] but any special or distinctive word or combination of figures or letters used as a

---

[1]   The hallmarking system for precious metals appears to have been more secure and remains distinct from the trade mark system. For further historical details, see the website of the British Hallmarking Council at www.britishhallmarkingcouncil.gov.uk/hlaw.htm.

[2]   *Erven Warnink v Townend* [1979] AC 731; [1980] RPC 31.

[3]   SI 2008/1277, which implements Directive 2005/29/EC of the European Parliament and of the Council concerning unfair business-to-consumer commercial practices [2005] OJ L149/22 and largely repeal the Trade Descriptions Act 1968, save as to false assertion of Royal warrant and importation of falsely marked goods.

[4]   SI 2008/1276, implementing Directive 2006/114/EC of the European Parliament and of the Council concerning misleading and comparative advertising [2006] OJ L376/21.

[5]   [2008] EWHC 3129 (QB). In *Rickless v United Artists Corp* [1988] QB 40; [1987] 2 WLR 945; [1987] 1 All ER 679; [1987] FSR 362, the Court of Appeal confirmed that civil remedies could be afforded to the estate of a performer protected by criminal statutes.

[6]   An individual or firm name printed, etc, in some particular or distinctive manner, a written signature, distinctive device, mark, heading label or ticket, plus any letters, words, etc (s 10).

trade mark before commencement was also registrable. Provision was made for coordination with the Cutlers system of allotting metal or 'Sheffield' marks; eventually the Sheffield Register became a limb of the general Register[7] and was abolished as a separate category by the Trade Marks Act 1994 ('the 1994 Act').[8] The 1875 Act stipulated that no action for infringement of an unregistered mark was to be brought. This did not, however, prove fatal to the general action in passing off.[9]

3.3   The Registry appears to have been inundated with applications to register textile marks,[10] because the Acts of 1876 and 1877 extended transitional provisions for applicants of those marks waiting for registration. Amending and consolidating Acts followed fast upon the 1875–1877 Acts, as shown in Table 3.1. The texts of subsequent Acts acknowledge a widening range of registrable marks and permissible transactions. The 1994 Act accelerates this process.

3.4   In parallel with the statutory measures and Guild controls, common law and equity provided redress for consumers and traders injured by the deceptive use of marks. The most important and most 'protean'[11] cause of action is passing off, considered together with other actions.

---

[7]   For a history of the system, see *Kerly's Law of Trade Marks and Trade Names* (13th edn, 2001) ch 6; GE TM [1972] FSR 225, HL.

[8]   Section 105 and Sch 3, para 20. Note also the existence of the Hallmarking Act 1973.

[9]   See **3.5–3.23** (discussion of passing off).

[10]   A distinct office was created in Manchester for the registration of textile marks. In Australia and New Zealand, 'manchester' is still used as the generic term for fabrics and bedding.

[11]   *Advocaat* [1980] RPC 31, per Lord Diplock.

Table 3.1: Trade mark legislation in the UK[12]

Date	Statute	Main effect
1623,1791, 1801, 1814, 1860	Cutlers Company Acts	Empowered the Cutlers Company in Sheffield to allot marks to users for metal goods
1862	Merchandise Marks Act	Created criminal penalties for the deceptive use of marks on merchandise
1875	Trade Marks Registration Act	Introduced general registration system
1876	Trade Marks Registration Amendment Act	Suspended s 1 (no infringement of unregistered mark) to allow more time for registration of textile marks
1877	Trade Marks Registration Extension Act	As above
1883	Patents Designs and Trade Marks Act	Amended and consolidated law of registered marks
1887	Merchandise Marks Act	As above
1888	Patents, Designs and Trade Marks Amendment Act	Amended definition of registrable symbols and introduced disclaimers
1905	Trade Marks Act	Consolidated and amended; defined 'trade mark'; broadened criteria for registration
1914	Trade Marks Act	Amendments
1919	Trade Marks Act	Created Part B of register; provided for removal of generic marks from the register

---

[12] For a fuller account of trade mark history, see S Ricketson *The Law of Intellectual Property* (Law Book, Sydney, 1984) paras 30.1–30.5; FI Schechter *Historical Foundations of the Law Relating to Trade Marks* (Columbia University Press, New York, 1925).

Date	Statute	Main effect
1938	Trade Marks Act	Liberalised licensing and assignment of registered marks; elaborated system for certification marks
1968	Trade Descriptions Act	Replaced Merchandise Marks Act with criminal statute prohibiting false trade descriptions
1984	Trade Marks (Amendment) Act	Provided for registration of service marks
1986	Patents, Designs and Trade Marks Act 1986	Enabled register to be kept in non-documentary (ie computerised) form; consolidated Paris priority provisions into trade marks statute
1994	Trade Marks Act	Implemented EC Harmonisation Directive; with enabling sections for Madrid Protocol, Community Trade Mark
1995	Olympic Symbol etc. (Protection) Act	Conferred wide-ranging protection on symbols associated with Olympic Games
2002	Copyright, etc. and Trade Marks (Offences and Enforcement) Act	Provisions on criminal offences and penalties
2006	Intellectual Property (Enforcement, etc.) Regulations 2006	Introduced certain remedial provisions to comply with European IP enforcement directive and WTO TRIPs

PASSING OFF AND OTHER TORTS

Passing off

3.5   Passing off appears to have developed[13] out of the tort of deceit, in which a customer could sue in respect of deceptive use of a badge of trade, to a

---

[13]   See S Ricketson *The Law of Intellectual Property,* paras 24.1–24.2; C Wadlow *The Law of Passing Off: Unfair Competition by Misrepresentation* (Sweet & Maxwell, 4th edn, 2011) para 1.24ff and comments by Laddie J in *Inter Lotto (UK) Ltd v Camelot Group plc* [2004] RPC 9 at 171–180 (decision upheld at [2004] FSR 186); K Stolte 'How early did

situation where the presence of a deceived customer[14] establishes an important element of the tort alleged by one trader against another. Initially, a claimant had to show actual intention to deceive on the part of the defendant, but by the mid-nineteenth century, equity would intervene without such proof.[15] Objective likelihood of deception or confusion became the benchmark.[16]

3.6   Passing off is said to protect a property right in the goodwill of the business carried on by reference to the mark, and not any property right in the mark as such.[17] Historically, this is not surprising, since the Trade Marks Registration Act 1875 and its successors made clear that there was no right to sue for infringement of an unregistered trade mark. Thus, the continued protection of marks by passing off had to be by way of protection of a different entity. In *Inland Revenue Commissioners v Muller & Co's Margarine Ltd*,[18] Lord Macnaughton said of goodwill:

> 'It is a thing very easy to describe, very difficult to define. It is the benefit and advantage of the good name, reputation and connection of a business. It is the attractive force which brings in custom … It must be attached to a business.'

Actual or likely damage to goodwill is an essential element of passing off.[19] The business to which the goodwill attaches is usually in the UK; the English courts have had difficulty with the standing of a foreign claimant (see **3.12**). The existence of a misrepresentation without goodwill,[20] or mere confusion[21] is not sufficient of itself.

Formulations of passing off

3.7   The courts regularly apply two comparatively recent formulations of the tort of passing off, those of Lord Diplock in *Advocaat*[22] and of Lord Oliver in the *Jif Lemon* case.[23] Lord Diplock identified five factors present in all cases of

---

Anglo-American trademark law begin? An answer to Schechter's conundrum' 88 TMR 564 (1998) (seemingly, in 1584, with *Sandforth's Case* Cory's entries, BL MS Hargrave 123, folio 168 (1584). For other references see note 2 to Stolte's article. Also known as *Samford's* or *Sandford's* case).

[14]   Actual or potential.

[15]   Eg *Millington v Fox* (1838) 3 My & Cr 338, 40 ER 210.

[16]   Eg '*Advocaat*', *Erven Warnink Besloten Vennotschap v Townend & Sons* [1979] AC 731; [1980] RPC 31.

[17]   Eg *Reddaway v Banham* [1896] AC 199; 13 RPC 218; *Spalding (AG) & Bros v Gamage (AW) Ltd* [1914] 2 Ch 405; 32 RPC 273. *Diageo North America Inc. & Anor v Intercontinental Brands (ICB) Ltd. and Ors* [2010] EWCA Civ 920 at [24].

[18]   [1901] AC 217 at 223.

[19]   *Stringfellow v McCain* [1984] RPC 501. Where evidence shows an intention to pass off, the burden of proving damage is lightened. See **3.5–3.8** (basic elements of passing-off action); **3.18–3.19** (damage element).

[20]   Eg *BBC v Talksport* [2001] FSR 6, where the defendant's false representation that its football coverage was live did not amount to passing off – the BBC could not show goodwill in the descriptive term 'live sports broadcasting'.

[21]   Eg *HFC Bank plc v Midland Bank plc* [2000] FSR 176.

[22]   [1979] AC 731; [1980] RPC 31.

[23]   *Reckitt & Colman v Borden* [1990] 1 All ER 873; [1990] RPC 341.

passing off (although he warned that occasionally the factors could be present without amounting to passing off – the mysterious 'undistributed middle').[24] His five factors are:

(a)   a misrepresentation;

(b)   by a trader in the course of trade;

(c)   to then claimant's prospective customers or ultimate consumers of the claimant's products;

(d)   which is calculated (objectively likely) to injure the claimant's goodwill or business; and

(e)   which causes actual damage to business or goodwill, or a serious likelihood of damage in the case of a *quia timet* action (brought to restrain a threatened wrong).[25]

An alternative formulation by Lord Fraser in *Advocaat* has been held to apply in a more limited class of case[26] and is not discussed here.

3.8   In *Jif*, Lord Oliver analysed passing off in terms of the 'classical trinity' often used in pleading:

(a)   goodwill or reputation attached to the goods or services supplied by reference to the distinctive mark;

(b)   a misrepresentation to the relevant public;[27]

(c)   causing actual or likely damage.

Badges of trade, reputation and goodwill

Distinctive marks and badges of trade

3.9   Starting with the question of reputation in a mark, passing off has been founded on all manner of insignia, including names (such as 'Harrods'[28] or 'Annabel's'),[29] words (such as 'Camel Hair Belting'[30] or 'New Orb'),[31] numbers

---

[24]   Their presence might indicate dishonest trading which is nonetheless permitted in the interests of competition – an economic policy exception. However, it is difficult to identify real-life examples.

[25]   In *Numatic International Ltd v Qualtex (UK) Ltd* [2010] EWHC 1237 (Ch); [2010] RPC 25, Floyd J recognised that such a claimant 'is necessarily obliged to prove the elements of its case (other than its reputation) on a somewhat theoretical basis', which presents some difficulty for the court in the absence of actual instances of confusion.

[26]   See *Bristol Conservatories v Conservatories Custom Built* [1989] RPC 455.

[27]   On identifying the relevant public, see *Neutrogena v Golden* [1996] RPC 473.

[28]   *Harrods Ltd v Harrod (R) Ltd* (1924) 41 RPC 74.

[29]   *Annabel's (Berkeley Square) v Schock* [1972] FSR 261; [1972] RPC 838.

(such as '4711'),[32] devices (such as an inlaid white spot[33] or the image of a penguin),[34] colours (such as grey for gas cylinder),[35] the livery and uniforms of a bus company,[36] the design of a restaurant,[37] the style of an advertising campaign,[38] the shape and colour of packaging or containers ('Jif' lemons,[39] 'Coca-Cola' bottles)[40] or a geographical name which denotes the claimant's class of product ('Champagne' for sparkling wine,[41] 'Swiss' for chocolate).[42]

3.10 It must be shown that the badge of trade is in some way distinctive of the claimant's goods or services and not the defendant's; otherwise it will be impossible to demonstrate that the defendant's use amounts to a misrepresentation. Thus, where passing off by get-up (the overall appearance of the product) is alleged, claimants often find it difficult to persuade the courts that their get-up is distinctive (and thus capable of engendering goodwill), and that an operative misrepresentation is being made.[43] In these cases, the totality of the claimant's and the defendant's respective get-up is taken into account; the defendant may avoid a finding of confusion by the use of one or more distinguishing features, or be required by the court to do so. Claimants also tend to have an uphill struggle where a mark is not inherently distinctive, such as 'Oven Chips' for oven-ready chipped potatoes.[44] It is not sufficient to coin a new phrase or arrive first upon the market.[45] Nor is long use and massive advertising enough when others use the mark in question.[46]

---

30   *Reddaway v Banham* [1896] AC 199.

31   *Spalding (AG) & Bros v Gamage (AW) Ltd* [1914] 2 Ch 405; 31 RPC 431.

32   *Reuter v Muhlens* (1953) 70 RPC 735; [1954] Ch 50.

33   *Dunhill v Bartlett* (1922) 39 RPC 426, although the defendant's spot was sufficiently different to avoid passing off.

34   *United Biscuits v Asda Stores* [1997] RPC 513 ('Penguin' and image v 'Puffin' and image).

35   *Sodastream v Thorn Cascade* [1982] RPC 459.

36   *London General Omnibus v Felton* (1896) 12 TLR 213.

37   *My Kinda Town v Soll* [1983] RPC 15.

38   *Cadbury-Schweppes v Pub Squash* suggests this, although there was held to be no passing off in that case. See also, *Elida-Gibbs v Colgate Palmolive* [1983] FSR 95.

39   '*Jif Lemon*' discussed at **3.7–3.8**; injunction granted.

40   *Coca-Cola Co v Barr* [1961] RPC 387.

41   *Bollinger v Costa Brava* [1960] RPC 16; [1961] RPC 116; *Taittinger v Albev* [1994] 4 All ER 75.

42   *Chocosuisse v Cadbury* [1999] RPC 826.

43   See, e g *Jaffa Cakes* [1992] FSR 14; [1994] FSR 504; *Bostik v Sellotape* [1994] RPC 556; *Hodgkinson & Corby v Ward Mobility Services* [1995] FSR 169 and cases cited therein, discussed in A Firth 'Cushions and confusion' [1994] 11 EIPR 494; Cf *Numatic International Ltd v Qualtex (UK) Ltd* [2010] EWHC 1237 (Ch); [2010] RPC 25 – anthropomorphic 'Henry' vacuum cleaner, with black bowler hat.

44   *McCain v Country Fair* [1981] RPC 69. Contrast 'Camel Hair Belting', found to have acquired distinctiveness in *Reddaway v Banham* [1896] AC 199.

45   Although in some cases goodwill can be established in a short time, e g *Stannard v Reay* [1967] RPC 589 (3 weeks).

46   So, in '*Raffles*', *Imperial Group v Philip Morris* [1984] RPC 293, the presence on the market of other black and gold cigarette packs defeated the claimant's claim that 'Raffles' cigarettes were being passed off as 'John Player Specials'.

Shared reputation or goodwill

3.11 The mark may uniquely denote the claimant, or may denote a clearly delineated class to which the claimant belongs, but not the defendant.[47] For example, shared goodwill has been found in class designations such as Champagne, Parma Ham, Swiss Chocolate or Advocaat, and entities wrongfully using such class designations on products or services may be liable in passing off. Whether shared goodwill exists and the extent of protection will depend on evidence as to what the public understand the sign to mean.[48] Note that the claimant's actual identity need not be known to consumers.[49] Nor, it seems, need consumers be able to identify the product's characteristics with precision.[50] In VODKAT[51] the Court of Appeal rejected the defendants' assertion that this so-called 'extended' form of passing off was available only where cachet existed in the sense of a product being a superior or luxury brand.

Locus of goodwill

3.12 In *Inland Revenue Commissioners v Muller*, the House of Lords stated that goodwill must be attached to a business. In *Advocaat*, Lord Fraser referred to the requirement of a business in England. In *Jif Lemon*, the court used the phrase 'reputation or goodwill'. Will reputation alone be sufficient? Because passing off protects goodwill rather than any proprietary interest in the mark itself, a claimant with reputation in a mark may nonetheless fail unless it has business in the UK. Thus, in *Budweiser*,[52] the claimant enjoyed only minimal sales in the UK proper (US airbase and embassy sales were discounted) and failed in its action to restrain a rival 'Budweiser' beer. However, in contrast, a number of decisions, typically relating to services, suggest that a customer base in the UK will suffice;[53] certainly, a fairly slight business activity will do.[54] In

---

[47] Eg, because the defendant has ceased to belong to claimant's group: *Artistic Upholstery v Art Forma (Furniture)* [1999] 4 All ER 277; *Byford v Oliver* [2003] EWHC 295 (Ch); [2003] EMLR 20; [2003] FSR 39.

[48] Eg, that 'sherry' comes from the Jerez district of Spain; *Vine Products v Mackenzie* [1968] FSR 625; [1969] RPC 1. Note that geographical indications are also protected under Community law, including Regulation (EEC) 208/92, as amended by Regulation (EC) 535/97, Regulation (EEC) 2392/89 and Regulation (EEC) 1576/89. See, further, Chapter 12.

[49] Eg, *Powell v Birmingham Vinegar Brewery* [1897] AC 710.

[50] *Chocosuisse & others v Cadbury Ltd* [1998] ETMR 205. For a critique of this aspect of the case, see Jennifer Davis 'Why the United Kingdom should have a law against misappropriation' [2010] CLJ 561 at 570–1.

[51] *Diageo North America Inc v Intercontinental Brands (ICB) Ltd* [2010] EWCA Civ 920; [2011] 1 All ER 242; [2010] ETMR 57; [2011] RPC 2.

[52] *Anheuser-Busch v Budjovicky Budvar* [1984] FSR 413.

[53] Eg *Maxim's v Dye* [1977] FSR 364 (English customer base for French restaurant sufficient); *Sheraton Corp v Sheraton Motels* [1964] RPC 202 (UK bookings for overseas hotel sufficient); *Pete Waterman Ltd v CBS UK Ltd* [1993] EMLR 27 (UK musicians travelled to New York studio); cf *Bernadin v Pavilion Properties* [1967] RPC 581 (advertising in UK for French bar insufficient); *Athletes Foot v Cobra Sports* [1980] RPC 343 (preparations by UK prospective franchisees insufficient without UK sales).

[54] *Bernadin v Pavilion Properties* [1967] RPC 581 at p 584; *Jian Tools v Manhattan* [1995] FSR 924 (one UK customer for specialised system): see, further, D Rose 'Season of goodwill: overseas traders and passing off' [1996] EIPR 356; K Schmit and L Cohen 'Is the English law of passing

Hotel Cipriani, the combination of a 'substantial reputation in England and a substantial body of customers from England' sufficed to establish the claimant's goodwill; conversely the defendant had failed to establish such a combination.[55] However, a local distributor may enjoy goodwill in precedence to an overseas supplier.[56] Where a localised reputation is enjoyed, it may nonetheless be protected by nationwide injunction, as in *Chelsea Man*.[57] The Scots Court granted an interim interdict (injunction) to an English trader with customer, though no outlets, in Scotland in *Flaxcell Ltd v Freedman*.[58] Scots law of passing protects goodwill[59] in a manner broadly similar to that in England and Wales,[60] despite a different juridical basis.[61]

Kind of business

3.13 Passing off is not concerned with non-commercial matters, such as a residential address.[62] However, a claimant may be a professional or other organisation which does not trade in the commonplace sense of the word; the courts will grant relief if use of a similar name by others is likely to tarnish its reputation or to discourage membership.[63]

Temporal factors

3.14 A trader is particularly vulnerable to passing off around the time of a successful launch. The courts recognise this and have come to the aid of passing-off claimants at an early stage.[64] Goodwill may endure after cessation

---

off discriminatory to continental European trade mark owners?' [1999] EIPR 88; and the Commonwealth perspective in Cheng Lim Saw 'Goodwill hunting in passing off: time to jettison the strict "hard line" approach in England?' [2010] JBL 645.

[55] [2010] EWCA Civ 110; [2010] RPC 16. In *Plentyoffish Media Inc v Plenty More LLP* [2011] EWHC 2568 (Ch) Colin Birss QC, applying *Hotel Cipriani*, held that visits to a dating website, with no evidence that English visitors had enjoyed its services, was insufficient to establish goodwill.

[56] *Scandecor Development AB v Scandecor Marketing AB* [1999] FSR 26; applied in *MedGen Inc v Passion for Life Products Ltd* [2001] FSR 30.

[57] [1985] FSR 567; the claimant intended to expand.

[58] 1981 SLT (Notes) 131.

[59] *Haig & Co v Forth Blending Co* 1954 SC 35.

[60] See C Ng 'A common law of passing-off? English and Scottish perspectives' [2009] Edin LR 134; C Colston & J Galloway *Modern Intellectual Property Law* (OUP, 2010) ch 14.

[61] Hector MacQueen 'Intellectual property and the common law in Scotland c1700-c1850' in Catherine W Ng, Lionel Bently, Giuseppina DAgostino (eds) *The Common Law of Intellectual Property: Essays in honour of Professor David Vaver* (Hart Publishing, 2010) pp 21–43.

[62] *Day v Brownrigg* (1878) 10 Ch D 294.

[63] Eg *British Legion v British Legion Club (Street) Ltd* (1931) 48 RPC 555: ex-serviceman's organisation; *British Medical Association v Marsh* (1931) 48 RPC 565; *British Diabetic Association v Diabetic Society* [1996] FSR 1; *National Guild of Removers & Storers Ltd v Silveria (tla CS Movers)* [2011] FSR 9, applying *Irvine v Talksport Ltd (Damages)* [2003] EWCA Civ 423; [2003] 2 All ER 881; [2003] 2 All ER (Comm) 141; [2003] EMLR 26; [2003] FSR 35. Contrast *Kean v McGivan* [1982] FSR 119 ('SDP'); *Oxford Ltd v HS Tank & Sons Ltd* decision O-080–04 available at www.ipo.gov.uk/tm/legal/decisions/2004/o08004.pdf ('OXFORD BLUE', a term reserved by the University as an award for representing the university in inter-varsity matches).

[64] *Stannard v Reay* [1967] FSR 140, Ch D; *Elida Gibbs* [1983] FSR 95.

of a business, at least where there is some intention to resume. This was the case in *Ad Lib Club*[65] where a club had closed because of noise problems. The relevant point in time for establishing goodwill is that at which the defendant starts to use the contested sign.[66]

Misrepresentation

3.15 Many kinds of misrepresentation have been enjoined in passing-off actions. The most common is where a defendant's representation leads the public to believe that that the defendant's goods emanate from the claimant.[67] It may also be passing off to represent that the claimant's goods or services were supplied by the defendant.[68] Many other forms have been recognised; Table 3.2 lists some varieties, together with examples of cases founded upon them. Note that the representation need not be verbal – it can be conveyed by use of the claimant's logo or likeness,[69] or by conduct.[70] Silence does not usually amount to a misrepresentation in passing off; exceptionally if a trader is aware that a customer is under a 'self-induced' misapprehension, failure to disabuse the customer may be actionable.[71]

---

[65]   *Ad-Lib Club v Granville* [1971] FSR 1; [1972] RPC 673; applied in *Sutherland v V2 Music Ltd* [2002] EWHC 14 (Ch); [2002] EMLR 28.

[66]   In *Phones 4U Ltd v Phone4U.co.uk Internet Ltd* [2006] EWCA Civ 244; [2007] RPC 5, in this case a domain name, albeit innocently acquired.

[67]   Thus, in *Reddaway v Banham* it was stated that 'nobody has any right to represent his goods as the goods of somebody else': [1896] AC 199 at 204.

[68]   *Bristol Conservatories v Conservatories Custom Built* [1989] RPC 455. This form is often known as reverse or inverse passing off.

[69]   *Irvine v Talksport* [2003] FSR 619.

[70]   *Bovril Ltd v Bodega Company Ltd* (1916) 33 RPC 153 (supplying 'OXO' hot drinks to customers who had asked for 'BOVRIL', a practice described as 'switch-selling' in *British Sky Broadcasting Group plc v Sky Home Services Ltd* [2006] EWHC 3165 (Ch); [2007] 3 All ER 1066; [2007] FSR 14).

[71]   *British Sky Broadcasting Group plc v Sky Home Services Ltd* [2006] EWHC 3165 (Ch); [2007] 3 All ER 1066; [2007] FSR 14 at paras 83–84.

Table 3.2: Typical forms of misrepresentation

Type of misrepresentation (D = defendant; P =claimant)	Case example
D's products emanate from P	*Reddaway v Banham*[72]
D's goods are of the same class as P's	*Advocaat*[73]
D's goods are in some way connected with the products or business which has the goodwill	*Taittinger v Allbev*[74]
P's products emanate from D	*Bristol Conservatories*[75]
P's goods are actually P's goods but of a different quality	*Spalding v Gamage*[76]
P's altered or deteriorated goods are original quality	*Wilts United Dairies v Robinson*[77]
P has had the opportunity to check the quality of the goods	*Primark v Lollypop*[78]
C endorses D's services	*Irvine v Talksport*[79]
D is P's licensee	*Mirage Studios v Counterfeat Clothing*[80]
D's business is connected with P's, e g a branchor authorised distributor	*Ewing v Buttercup;*[81] *Sony v Saray*[82]
P is in some way responsible for the quality of D's products or D's customers' products	*Associated Newspapers v Insert Media*[83]

3.16 In order to be actionable, the representation must be false and likely to have an effect[84] on customers' or consumers' behaviour or perception, an effect on consumers that is more than momentary or inconsequential. Thus, where

---

[72] [1896] AC 199.

[73] [1979] AC 731; [1980] RPC 31.

[74] [1993] FSR 641 at 668, 673.

[75] [1989] RPC 455 often called 'inverse passing off'.

[76] [1914] 2 Ch 405; claimant's superseded 'ORB'footballs sold as the new and improved product.

[77] [1958] RPC 94; affirming [1957] RPC 220: old stocks of canned milk.

[78] *Primark v Lollypop* [2001] FSR 637.

[79] [2002] EWHC 367; [2003] FSR 619. Note that Laddie J at para 44 distinguished false endorsement cases from character merchandising cases, exemplified by the next category.

[80] [1991] FSR 145; 'Teenage Mutant Ninja Turtles' clothing.

[81] (1917) 34 RPC 232.

[82] [1983] FSR 302.

[83] [1991] FSR 380: suggestion that claimants had approved insertion of additional material into its periodicals, news publishers taking responsible attitude to advertising.

[84] Cf misrepresentation inducing the recipient to enter into a contract, under the Misrepresentation Act 1967 and at common law.

the term 'Gledhill coils' had come to denote paper rolls to fit the claimant's tills, rather than rolls manufactured by the claimant, there was no misrepresentation and hence no passing off. In *Specsavers International Healthcare Ltd v Asda Stores Ltd*[85] neither the defendants' use of individual signs similar to the claimants, nor their combined effect was liable to cause confusion. In the '*RoHo*' cushions case, *Hodgkinson & Corby v Wards Mobility Services*,[86] the resemblance between the defendant's and the claimant's prosthetic cushions was not likely to confuse the careful purchasers. In that case and in '*Blu-tak*',[87] the possibility of post-sale confusion did not assist the claimant. Although evidence of customer confusion is always relevant, it does not necessarily mean that a misrepresentation has been made. Various kinds of customer confusion were canvassed in the *RoHo* case. However, in that case Jacob J reiterated that the misrepresentation must lead to deception:

> 'At the heart of passing off lies deception or its likelihood, deception of the ultimate consumer in particular. Over the years passing off has developed from the classic case of the defendant selling his goods as and for those of the plaintiff to cover other kinds of deception, e g that the defendant's goods are the same as those of the plaintiff when they are not, e g *Combe International Ltd. v. Scholl (U.K.) Ltd.* [1980] R.P.C. 1; or that defendant's goods are the same as goods sold by a class of persons of which the plaintiff is a member when they are not, e g *Erven Warnink Besloten Vennootschap v. J. Townend & Sons* (Hull) Ltd. [1979] A.C. 731 (the Advocaat case). Never has the tort shown even a slight tendency to stray beyond cases of deception. Were it to do so it would enter the field of honest competition, declared unlawful for some reason other than deceptiveness. Why there should be any such reason I cannot imagine. It would serve only to stifle competition.'

Does this mean that the passing-off claimant must show that the defendant has been intentionally dishonest? If this were to occur, passing off would have lost its equitable strand.[88] It is submitted that the courts continue to take the objective approach demonstrated in *Advocaat*; in particular the House of Lords in *JIF* indicated that a misrepresentation to the relevant public can be actionable whether or not it was intentional.[89] It is clear from Jacob J's view of the various scenarios put by the claimants in *RoHo* that the deception of someone who is not an actual or potential customer or consumer is insufficient to found passing off. This is because the misrepresentation must be causative of the final element of the tort – damage to business or goodwill. Before moving on to damage, we consider further couple of questions.

---

[85]   [2010] EWHC 2035 (Ch); [2011] FSR 1.

[86]   [1995] FSR 169; A Firth 'Cushions and confusion: the RoHo passing off case' [1994] 11 EIPR 494.

[87]   *Bostik v Sellotape* [1994] RPC 556. More recent trade mark cases, however, have suggested that post-sale confusion is relevant to infringement: *Arsenal FC v Reed* [2003] RPC 39; [2003] ETMR 73; [2003] 2 CMLR 25 CA.

[88]   In contractual misrepresentation, equity intervened to remedy innocent misrepresentation.

[89]   *Reckitt & Colman Products Ltd v Borden Inc (No 3)* [1990] 1 WLR 491; [1990] RPC 341 (HL) cited, e g by Floyd J in *Hasbro Inc, Hasbro SA and Hasbro UK Ltd v 123 Nahrmittel GmbH and Marketing & Promotional Services Ltd* [2011] EWHC 199 (Ch); [2011] ETMR 25 at para 233.

Is there a difference between confusion and deception, and can there be passing off without them?

3.17 Although these two concepts lie at the core of a passing-off case – proving that the misrepresentation has misled – is there a conceptual difference? What follows is the authors' view – it is difficult to substantiate by reference to case-law, which tends to differentiate between 'mere confusion' – not actionable – and 'deception' in the sense of a successful misrepresentation. Inherent in the idea of confusion may be knowledge on the part of the purchaser that there is something to compare and consider; he is confused because he knows of the other thing. By contrast, with deception, the purchaser believes that he is getting the thing he wants without being aware of other possibilities. In other words, with 'confusion' the purchaser is faced with having to make a decision and may or may not choose wrongly, whereas he is more passive with 'deception'. One can imagine a spectrum – deception (as the most extreme effect of a misrepresentation), confusion (where there is at least the possibility of doubt) and non-confusion (where the customer recognises that there may be more than one trader and is able to discriminate). Of course the latter may still be damaging but not passing off, as illustrated in the first instance decision in *Arsenal v Reed*, where a trader expressly indicated that his merchandise was 'unofficial'.[90] If there is no operative misrepresentation, can passing off remedy the situation where a defendant profits from use of a sign, a situation usually described as 'misappropriation'? In *L'Oréal v Bellure*,[91] Jacob LJ rejected this possibility. Wadlow has argued that although misappropriation had its place in the history of passing off, 'misrepresentation is the overt defining characteristic of passing off as we know it today, whereas misappropriation is no more than a latent and silent one'.[92]

Damage

3.18 Damage is an essential element and comes in a variety of forms.[93] The defendant's misrepresentation may cause diversion of business – sales or members. Thus, customers wishing to buy traditional 'Advocaat' were likely to be diverted to the defendant's non-conforming drink by use of the mark. Conversely, Stringfellow's passing-off action failed[94] because the judge was not persuaded that the defendant's use of 'Stringfellows' on chips had affected attendance at the claimant's nightclub. Less direct damage occurs when the claimant's reputation is tarnished or prejudiced in some way,[95] which diminishes the attractive force of the mark. This often occurs because the

---

[90] *Arsenal FC v Reed* [2003] RPC 39; [2003] ETMR 73; [2003] 2 CMLR 25 (CA); interestingly, although the judge's finding of no passing off had not been appealed, the Court of Appeal expressed doubt as to this decision at paras 70–71.

[91] *L'Oréal v Bellure* [2007] EWCA Civ 968; [2008] RPC 8 at para 160.

[92] C Wadlow 'Passing off at the crossroads again' [2011] EIPR 447 at 450.

[93] H Carty 'Heads of damage in passing off' [1996] EIPR 587.

[94] *Stringfellow v McCain* [1984] RPC 501.

[95] As by the unflattering association of 'Annabels' nightclub with escort agency in *Annabel's (Berkeley Square) v Schock* [1972] FSR 261; [1972] RPC 838.

defendant's product is inferior to the claimant's. The effect of prejudice to reputation is difficult to quantify, which factor may encourage the grant of an interlocutory injunction.

3.19 Damage may also be sustained by a claimant where it is exposed to litigation or complaint. It may be necessary to mollify dissatisfied customers or consumers.[96] Where a mark is popular with customers, the courts recognise that a claimant may wish to exploit goodwill by diversifying its business under the mark. It may wish to expand its product range, or enter into licensing arrangements. Alternatively, it may deliberately refrain from so doing in order to maintain the mark's exclusivity. In recent years, the action for passing off has been used to protect these aspects of goodwill in a mark, with cases like *Lego*,[97] *Mirage Studios*[98] and *Elderflower Champagne*.[99] The last case is significant in referring explicitly to the concept of damage by blurring or erosion of the unique character of a mark, often referred to as 'dilution'.[100] Although rejected as a head of damage in *Harrods v Harrodian School*,[101] at least in the absence of confusion,[102] the indirect damage that loss of exclusivity may cause was recognised long ago in *Buttercup v Ewing*.[103] In *Irvine v Talksport Ltd*[104] at first instance, Laddie J referred to *Elderflower Champagne*[105] and remarked that: 'The law will vindicate the claimant's exclusive right to the reputation or goodwill. It will not allow others to so use goodwill as to reduce, blur or diminish its exclusivity'. Damage to the claimant does not necessarily correlate with gain to the defendant, nor need they be in competition.[106] Cases on quantification of damages by using the concept of a reasonable use fee – endorsement[107] or licensing[108] – where sales are not lost suggest that loss of exclusivity may be transformed into loss of licensing opportunity for remedial purposes.

---

[96] See, e g *Associated Newspapers Ltd v Express Newspapers* [2003] EWHC 1322, [2003] FSR 51, (2003) 100(31) LSG 32, (2003) *The Times*, June 17, Ch D.

[97] *Lego v Lego M Lemelstrich* [1983] FSR 155. 'Lego' was a household name for toy bricks; the defendants were enjoined from using it on garden equipment.

[98] [1991] FSR 145.

[99] *Taittinger v Allbev* [1993] FSR 641 at 678 (use of 'champagne' in name of fizzy non-alcoholic drink); see also *Parfums Givenchy v Designer Alternatives* [1994] RPC 243.

[100] See Chapter 7 (trade mark infringement). The passing-off scholar Christopher Wadlow has described protection against dilution 'of little or no demonstrable public benefit; its grounding in either ethics or economics is shaky': C Wadlow 'Passing off at the crossroads again: a review article for Hazel Carty, An Analysis of the Economic Torts' [2011] EIPR 447. Cf Ilanah Simon Fhima 'Dilution by blurring – a conceptual roadmap' [2010] IPQ 44.

[101] [1996] RPC 697.

[102] H Carty 'Passing off and instruments of deception – the need for clarity' [2003] EIPR 188.

[103] (1917) 34 RPC 232 at p 239; applied in *Sir Robert McAlpine Ltd v Alfred McAlpine plc* [2004] RPC 36; *Associated Newspapers v Express Newspapers* [2003] FSR 909. For a historical survey, see N Dawson 'Famous and well known trade marks – usurping a corner of the giant's robe' [1998] IPQ 350.

[104] [2002] EWHC 367; [2002] FSR 60 at p 957.

[105] Including further reference back in *Taittinger* to dicta of Cross J in *Vine Products Ltd v Mackenzie & Co Ltd* [1969] RPC 1 on 'blurring' or 'diluting' of the plaintiff's goodwill.

[106] *Harrods v Harrodian School* [1996] RPC 697 CA.

[107] *Irvine v Talksport Ltd (Damages)* [2003] EWCA Civ 423, applying the patent damages case of

At what point does passing off occur in the chain of commerce?

3.20 A deceptive mark can cause damage at all stages of the chain of commerce. This was recognised in the *Advocaat* case, where Lord Diplock refers to ultimate consumers as well as prospective customers for the claimant's products. It may amount to a misrepresentation at one stage, but not another. A person who participates in use of a misleading mark may be liable for damage further down the line if they are seen as supplying instruments of fraud or deception. In the most extreme case, a passing-off action may lie where consumers are outside the jurisdiction. In *John Walker v Ost*[109] and in *White Horse v Gregson*,[110] the defendants' activities caused or enabled adulterated Scotch whisky to be passed off abroad as the real thing; injunctions were granted in both cases. However, a defendant will not be held liable if an unobjectionable mark is subsequently misused.[111] In *British Telecommunications plc v One in a Million Ltd*[112] the registration of others' 'household name' marks and business names as domain names by the defendant was seen as having the potential to deceive if the registrant sold them on otherwise than to the claimants. On the basis that 'the defendant is equipped with or is intending to equip another with an instrument of fraud', summary judgment in the claimants' favour was upheld. However, in *L'Oréal SA v Bellure NV*,[113] the Court of Appeal rejected the proposition that 'smell-alike' perfumes should be characterised as instruments of fraud.

Defences to passing off

Concurrent rights and use of own name

3.21 Even if a claimant makes out a case in passing off, the defendant may argue that it has an independent or concurrent right to use the mark.[114] Thus, a defendant may not be enjoined from making proper use of its own name and

General Tire & Rubber Co Ltd v Firestone Tyre & Rubber Co Ltd (No 2) [1975] 1 WLR 819 and increasing damages from £2,000 to the £25,000 that evidence suggested Mr Irvine could have commanded.

[108] *National Guild of Removers & Storers Ltd v Silveria (t/a CS Movers)* [2011] FSR 9; PCC, applying *Irvine v Talksport Ltd (Damages)* [2003] EWCA Civ 423; [2003] 2 All ER 881; [2003] FSR 35.

[109] [1970] RPC 489.

[110] [1984] RPC 61.

[111] *Payton v Snelling* (1901) 17 RPC 628 at 635; see also *Cadbury v Ulmer* [1988] FSR 385 (chocolate bars resembling Cadbury's 'Flake' not enjoined, even though liable to be substituted by ice cream vendors when consumers asked for '99' – a combination of 'Flake' and whipped ice cream).

[112] [1999] 1 WLR 903; [1998] 4 All ER 476; [1999] ETMR 61; [1999] FSR 1 (CA) per Aldous LJ: 'It follows that a court will intervene by way of injunction in passing off cases in three types of case. First, where there is passing off established or it is threatened. Second, where the defendant is a joint tortfeasor with another in passing off either actual or threatened. Third, where the defendant has equipped himself with or intends to equip another with an instrument of fraud. This third type is probably a mere quia timet action.'

[113] [2007] EWCA Civ 968; [2008] ECC 5 (CA (Civ Div)). See Jennifer Davis 'Passing off and joint liability: the rise and fall of "instruments of deception"' [2011] EIPR 204.

[114] *Websphere TM* [2004] FSR 39; *IBM v Web-Sphere* [2004] ETMR 94; [2004] EWHC 529 796. In

address, provided it makes sufficient distinction from the claimant.[115] Wherever the defendant is a company, the court will look carefully at the circumstances of adoption of the company name and how it is used. In *Hotel Cipriani Srl v Cipriani (Grosvenor Street) Ltd*,[116] it was held that a company could use its trading name rather than the precise company name as registered, but only if the claimant's legitimate interests were properly taken into account. If goodwill is sold, the vendor may only use his own name in business if it can distinguish the new business from the old with clarity, so as to 'bring it home to all types of reader (including a reader with imperfect or partial memory) what the position is'.[117] Occasionally it is difficult to see quite what the defendant can do to distinguish itself.[118] A defendant may not use nicknames or abbreviations.[119] Where a defendant has been in breach of an injunction elsewhere, he may exceptionally be restrained from using his own name at all in a particular commercial sphere.[120] As Jacob LJ pointed out in *Reed* and in *Newman*,[121] the defence is very limited – it is always open to a trader to adopt a different trading name. It sometimes happens that two traders with similar names expand their businesses until they come into conflict. In these cases,[122] the courts are not inclined to restrain either trader, even if there is some confusion of customers, although each may restrain third parties.

Parody

3.22 Although a parody has been essayed as a defence in trade mark cases,[123] examples are rare in passing-off cases. Here it would enter into the assessment of misrepresentation, humour perhaps reducing consumer confusion.[124] In *Alan Clark v Associated Newspapers Ltd*, the passing-off claim in relation to

---

IN Newman Ltd v Adlem [2005] EWCA Civ 741; [2006] FSR 16 this situation arose as a result of a transaction purporting to transfer goodwill.

[115] *Reed Executive plc v Reed Business Information Ltd* [2004] RPC 40 summarising earlier cases at para 110.

[116] [2010] EWCA Civ 110; [2010] RPC 16; see also *Och-Ziff Management Europe Ltd v Och Capital LLP* [2010] EWHC 2599 (Ch); [2011] Bus LR 632; [2011] ECC 5; [2011] ETMR 1; [2011] FSR 11.

[117] *IN Newman Ltd v Adlem* [2005] EWCA Civ 741; [2006] FSR 16.

[118] Eg *Boswell-Wilkie Circus (Pty) Ltd v Brian Boswell Circus (Pty) Ltd* [1986] FSR 479; *Parker-Knoll v Knoll International* [1962] RPC 243 at 257ff; *IN Newman Ltd v Adlem* [2005] EWCA Civ 741; [2006] FSR 16.

[119] *BIBA Group v BIBA Boutique* [1980] RPC 413; cf *Bud* [1988] RPC 535, where there was held to be honest concurrent use of the consumers' nickname for Czech Budweiser beer. See also *Kerly's Law of Trade Marks and Trade Names* (14th edn, 2005) para 15–223. Honest concurrent use appears to have been recognised as inherent in European trade mark law by *Budejovicky Budvar v Anheuser-Busch* (C-482/09) [2011] ECR I-0000.

[120] *Gucci v Gucci* [1991] FSR 89.

[121] At para 46.

[122] Such as *Evans v Eradicure* [1972] RPC 808; *Anheuser-Busch v Budjovicky Budvar* [1984] FSR 413 (where there had been an earlier delimitation agreement).

[123] SM Maniatis & E Gredley 'Parody: a fatal attraction? Part 2: Trade mark parodies' [1997] EIPR 412; Ilanah Simon 'Nominative use and honest practices in industrial and commercial matters – a very European history' [2007] IPQ 117.

[124] 'If the defendant employs a successful parody,' it was said, 'the customer would not be confused, but amused.' M Spence 'Intellectual property and the problem of parody' [1998]

spoof diaries 'of' the MP prevailed over the parody defence. There was evidence of confusion in the minds of readers as to authorship of the 'diaries':[125]

> 'A parody which occasions only a momentary and inconsequential deception is both successful and permissible; but a parody which occasions an enduring deception is neither.'

In *Irvine v Talksport*,[126] a witness referred to the humorous nature of the promotional pack containing the doctored photograph of Irvine, but this did not avert a finding of passing off. In *Cowshed Products Limited v Island Origins Limited & others*,[127] the humorous use of 'cow' in relation to beauty products was part of the claimant's goodwill.

Equitable defences

3.23 Equitable defences may be available, at least to the grant of an injunction. Thus, in *Habib Bank*,[128] the defendant bank, which had previously been a branch of the claimant's predecessor, had traded independently after nationalisation of the parent bank. Acquiescence, laches and estoppel were also pleaded; it was held that in each case the question was whether it would be unconscionable for the claimant to succeed. In *Nationwide*,[129] grant of an interlocutory injunction would have conferred an unfair commercial advantage upon the claimant.

Other torts

Injurious or malicious falsehood

3.24 Misuse of another's mark may amount to an injurious or malicious falsehood.[130] In *Wilts United Dairies Ltd v Thomas Robinson Sons & Co Ltd*,[131] old stock which had deteriorated was sold as current stock under the claimant's mark. There was no disclaimer as to its condition. This was held to be both passing off and malicious falsehood. The latter tort is committed when:

(a)   a false statement is made of the claimant's goods, services or business;

LQR 594 citing *Alan Clark v. Associated Newspapers Ltd* [1998] 1 All ER 959; [1998] RPC 261, which in turn cited *Nike Inc v 'Just Did It' Enterprises* 6 F 3d 1225 at 1227–1228.

[125]   *Alan Clark v Associated Newspapers Ltd* [1998] 1 WLR 1558 at 1568; [1998] RPC 261 at 272.

[126]   Referred to by the Court of Appeal: *Irvine v Talksport Ltd (Damages)* [2003] EWCA Civ 423; [2003] 2 All ER 881; [2003] 2 All ER (Comm) 141; [2003] EMLR 26; [2003] FSR 35.

[127]   [2010] EWHC 3357 (Ch), a decision which shows the difficulty of deciding application for an interim injunction in passing-off cases.

[128]   [1982] RPC 1.

[129]   [1987] FSR 579; injunction refused.

[130]   The terms 'trade libel' or 'slander of goods' are also used.

[131]   [1958] RPC 94, affirming [1957] RPC 220.

(b)   a false statement is made maliciously, that is without just cause or excuse; and

(c)   a false statement causes special damage.[132]

Proving the last element was eased by s 3(1) of the Defamation Act 1952[133] which dispenses with proof of special damage if the words in question are calculated to cause pecuniary damage to the claimant and are either in writing or other permanent form or are in respect of the claimant's office, profession, trade, calling or business carried on at the time of publication.

3.25   The meaning of malice was elaborated in *Balden v Shorter*;[134] it involves some dishonest or otherwise improper motive. Malicious falsehood is usually less attractive to a claimant than passing off. This is partly because of the need to show malice, and partly because a defence of justification may lie. A defendant who claims he will justify at trial will be able to avert an interlocutory injunction, as in *Bestobell Paint v Bigg*.[135] Statements which are true in context may amount to falsehood if taken out of context.[136] In some cases, by analogy with personal defamation, the courts have looked for a single meaning of the disputed statement.[137] However, in *Ajinomoto Sweeteners Europe SAS v Asda Stores Ltd*,[138] the Court of Appeal rejected this approach, thus allowing 'the damaging effect of the words to be put in perspective and both malice and (if it comes to it) damage to be more realistically gauged'.[139]

3.26   Malicious falsehood has been used in a number of comparative advertising cases, such as a *British Airways v Ryanair*[140] and it has also stood surrogate for a privacy law in *Kaye v Robertson*, where a disguised reporter purported to have interviewed an injured actor in hospital.[141]

Unfair competition

3.27   In *Advocaat*,[142] Lord Diplock referred to passing off as a form of unfair competition. However, a wider tort of unfair competition has not been

---

[132]   *Royal Baking Powder Co v Wright Crossley & Co* (1900) 18 RPC 95.
[133]   Applied in cases such as *Dorset Flint & Stone Blocks Ltd v Moir* [2004] EWHC 2173; *DSG Retail Ltd v Comet Group plc* [2002] FSR 58 (QBD).
[134]   [1933] Ch 427.
[135]   [1975] FSR 421.
[136]   *Compaq Computer v Dell Computer* [1992] FSR 93.
[137]   *Vodafone v Orange* [1997] FSR 34.
[138]   [2010] EWCA Civ 609; [2011] 2 WLR 91; [2010] 4 All ER 1029; [2010] EMLR 23; [2010] FSR 30.
[139]   Ibid at para 34, per Sedley LJ.
[140]   *British Airways plc v Ryanair Ltd* [2001] FSR 32; [2001] ETMR 24 Ch D, overruled as to the legitimacy of comparisons by the trade mark case *of O2 Holdings Ltd v Hutchison 3G Ltd* [2006] EWCA Civ 1656; [2007] RPC 16.
[141]   [1991] FSR 62; a situation now likely within the scope of privacy law as it has developed from breach of confidence under the influence of the Human Rights Act 1998, see, e g *Campbell v MGN Ltd* [2004] 2 AC 457.
[142]   *Advocaat* [1980] RPC 31.

recognised in English law, despite periodic calls from commentators.[143] In *Arsenal v Reed*,[144] albeit obiter, the Court of Appeal mentioned the breadth of the modern action for passing off and referred to remarks on unfair competition from the earlier drinks cases.[145] However, Jacob LJ took the opportunity in *L'Oréal v Bellure*[146] to reiterate the English courts' opposition to a generalised tort of unfair competition. This was on the basis of difficulty in drawing the line between fair and unfair conduct and in affirming the principle of free competition subject to specific intellectual property rights, each with its own justification and (except for trade marks) specified duration.[147] Reference had been made on the case to unfair competition laws in other EU member states and the dictates of the Paris Convention for the protection of industrial property.

In other member states of the EU,[148] unfair competition law is variously founded upon general provisions of a civil code as to damage[149] or fault[150] or is provided by a specific statute.[151] Article 10*bis* of the Paris Convention obliges members of the Paris Union to give protection[152] against unfair competition in its various forms, in particular:

'1.   all acts of such a nature as to create confusion by any means whatsoever with the establishment, the goods, or the industrial or commercial activities, of a competitor;
2.   false allegations in the course of trade of such a nature as to discredit the establishment, the goods, or the industrial or commercial activities, of a competitor;
3.   indications or allegations the use of which in the course of trade is liable to mislead the public as to the nature, the manufacturing process, the characteristics, the suitability for their purpose, or the quantity, of the goods.'

In the UK, passing off is seen as dealing with 1 and 3, which are also prohibited by the provisions of the Consumer Protection from Unfair Trading

---

[143]   See G Dworkin 'Unfair Competition – is the Common Law Developing a New Tort?' [1979] EIPR 241. The answer to date has been a firm 'no': see also J Adams 'Unfair competition – why a need is unmet' [1992] EIPR 259 and citations therein; A Robertson and A Horton 'Does the UK or the EC need an unfair competition law?' [1995] EIPR 568; see, also, J Davis 'Why the United Kingdom should have a law against misappropriation' [2010] CLJ 561 at paras 570–571.
[144]   *Arsenal FC v Reed* [2003] RPC 39; [2003] ETMR 73; EWCA Civ 696 CA at paras 70–71.
[145]   Citing *Vine Products Ltd v Mackenzie & Co Ltd* [1969] RPC 1, per Cross J. Such a point was argued by counsel for the claimants in *L'Oréal v Bellure* [2007] EWCA Civ 968; [2008] RPC 8.
[146]   [2007] EWCA Civ 968; [2008] RPC 8 at paras 135–142.
[147]   And see M Spence 'Passing off and the misappropriation of valuable intangibles' (1996) 112 LQR 472 at 474 and 476.
[148]   And many other countries throughout the world. For an overview see WIPO 'Protection against Unfair competition – an Analysis of the World Situation' (1994).
[149]   As in France: Art 1382 of the Civil Code.
[150]   As in The Netherlands: Civil Code of 1992, Arts 6.162 and 6.194–6.196. See A Kamperman Sanders *Unfair Competition* (Oxford University Press, 1997) for these and other jurisdictions.
[151]   As in Germany or Belgium.
[152]   Article 10*bis* obliges such states to provide appropriate legal remedies.

Regulations 2008[153] and the Business Protection from Misleading Marketing Regulations 2008.[154] Malicious or injurious falsehood provides an avenue for preventing the second category of unfair conduct. Art 10*bis* does not, however, explicitly require protection against misappropriation of goodwill[155] in the absence of confusion, falsehood or deception of the public. Jacob LJ made clear that the tort passing off has not escaped from the requirement of a misrepresentation.[156]

TRADE MARK REGISTRATION

3.28 Although still providing useful trade mark protection,[157] including protection of forms of a mark different from those registered,[158] and capable of lateral movement into those areas not readily covered by registered trade marks,[159] the causes of action outlined above have considerable disadvantages. A passing-off action can prove very expensive,[160] unless satisfactorily compromised at an early stage. Malicious falsehood has the additional difficulty of establishing malice and the risk that an injunction will be refused. Other torts such as interference with contract or unlawful interference with trade are usually difficult to sustain where trade marks are concerned. One of the greatest advantages of registration[161] lies in the simplification of infringement proceedings.[162] Where an identical mark is used in relation to the

---

[153] SI 2008/1277, which implement Directive 2005/29/EC of the European Parliament and of the Council concerning unfair business-to-consumer commercial practices [2005] OJ L149/22. See S Singleton 'The Consumer Protection from Unfair Trading Regulations' [2009] CTLR 77. A duty of consistent interpretation of the Unfair Commercial Practices Directive was emphasised by the ECJ in *VTB-VAB NV v Total Belgium NV; Galatea BVBA v Sanoma Magazines Belgium NV* (Joined Cases C-261/07 and C-299/07) [2009] 3 CMLR 17.

[154] SI 2008/1276, implementing Directive 2006/114/EC of the European Parliament and of the Council concerning misleading and comparative advertising [2006] OJ L376/21. See J Smith and R Montagnon 'The new consumer and business protection regulations: another string to the brand owner's bow?' [2009] JIPLP 33.

[155] A turn of phrase described by Jacob LJ as 'very unhelpful' in *L'Oréal v Bellure*; see, also, H Carty 'The common law and the quest for the IP effect' [2007] IPQ 237 cited by Jacob LJ; Christopher Wadlow 'Rudolf Callmann and the misappropriation doctrine in the common law of unfair competition' [2011] IPQ 111; J Davis 'Why the United Kingdom should have a law against misappropriation' [2010] CLJ 561 at paras 570–571.

[156] But see the view of Wadlow that protection against misappropriation was present in the early history of passing off: C Wadlow 'Passing off at the crossroads again' [2011] EIPR 447 at para 450, citations therein and **3.17** above at n 91.

[157] See M Ni Shuilleabhain 'Common-law protection of trade marks – the continuing relevance of passing off' (2003) 34 IIC 722.

[158] In *United Biscuits (UK) Ltd v Asda Stores Ltd* [1997] RPC 513.

[159] Eg the (re)emergence of the special form of passing off covering so-called 'instruments of fraud' in cybersquatting cases: see *British Telecommunications plc v One in a Million Ltd* [1999] 1 WLR 903 (CA); A Sims 'Rethinking One in a Million' [2004] EIPR 442.

[160] Although the courts have taken steps to ensure that costs are not wasted by inappropriate consumer surveys in passing off and trade mark cases using case management techniques approved by the court of appeal: *esure Insurance v Direct Line Insurance* [2008] RPC 34 at para 63, per Arden LJ.

[161] See Chapter 5.

[162] See Chapter 7.

goods or services for which a mark is registered, the claimant in an infringement action need prove neither reputation nor confusion. Where the marks or products are merely similar, likelihood of confusion must be established but not reputation. Reputation need only be proved where the goods or services are not similar or it is sought to enjoin non-confusing use. In these cases either damage to distinctiveness/reputation of the claimant's mark or unfair advantage to the defendant must also be proved.

3.29 Other advantages to the proprietor of registering a mark include the enhanced possibility of preventing subsequent registration of the same or similar marks by others.[163] The registration acts as a repellent, since a search will reveal its existence to third parties. A registered mark is an object of property in its own right.[164] Section 22 of the 1994 Act states that it is incorporeal moveable property in Scotland; elsewhere personal property. A registered mark can thus be assigned with or without goodwill, as opposed to a 'common law (unregistered) mark', for which assignment without goodwill is meaningless.[165] A licensee under a registered trade mark may enjoy rights of action for infringement, as well as sharing in the other benefits enjoyed by a proprietor.[166]

3.30 Competitors and others also benefit from registration; where a mark is used but not registered a competitor may risk defending an expensive passing-off action. It is essential to conduct a search of the registers[167] when choosing a new mark and to avoid the possibility of infringement. It is also essential, but more difficult, to identify marks which are used but not registered. Where unjustified threats of infringement proceedings are made, an aggrieved party may sue to restrain the threats and recover damages.[168] This statutory protection is not available for those aggrieved by threats to sue in

---

[163] See Chapter 5 (conflict with earlier marks).

[164] For a theoretical perspective, see S Maniatis 'Trade mark rights – a justification based on property' [2002] IPQ 123; for a philosophical one, see J Wilson 'Could there be a right to own intellectual property?' [2009] *Law and Philosophy* 393.

[165] See S Lane *The Status of Licensing Common Law Marks* (Dareheath, 1991) p 10; S Lane 'Goodwill hunting' [1999] IPQ 264, commenting on *Scandecor v Scandecor* [1999] FSR 26 (CA); that case was subsequently appealed to the House of Lords: [2001] UKHL 21; [2001] 2 CMLR 30 (HL).

[166] See Chapter 10; in certain circumstance a proprietor is empowered to claim damages on behalf of non-party licensees A Firth 'Damages/monetary remedies for trade mark infringement' [2008] 1 *Anuario de la Facultad de Derecho – Universidad de Alcala* 73.

[167] Trade marks protected in the UK may appear on the UK, Community Trade Mark or International Registers: see Chapters 5, 14 and 15.

[168] Unless they relate to marking or importing of goods or the supply of services under the marks (s 21(1)). See **8.2–8.8** (unjustified threats).

passing off.[169] Consumers have a means of identifying the proprietor of the mark and may have redress in case of injury caused by defective goods.[170]

CIVIL PROCEEDINGS FOR INFRINGEMENT

3.31   Infringement of registered trade marks is a tort and may also constitute a criminal offence. Civil proceedings for infringement may be brought in the High Court in England and Wales and Northern Ireland and in the Court of Session in Scotland.[171] County courts and sheriff courts can make orders for the delivery up and destruction of infringing goods, materials or articles,[172] county courts can hear trade mark infringement cases but not consider validity[173] and county courts with Chancery district registries can hear trade mark cases generally, as may the Patents County Court.[174]

CRIMINAL SANCTIONS

3.32   Section 92 of the 1994 Act creates a number of criminal offences.[175] These are triable either way. Conviction may result in imprisonment, with a maximum of 6 months on summary conviction or 10 years on indictment, or a fine, or both. In addition, infringing goods and materials may be forfeit; in fact, forfeiture orders can be made without a conviction, providing the court is satisfied that an offence has been committed. This power will be useful to trading standards officers in possession of goods whose owners understandably do not wish to reappear to claim them. The criminal provisions of the 1994 Act supplemented trading standards officers' powers under the Trade Descriptions Acts 1968 and 1972;[176] these powers have now been expanded by promulgation

---

[169]   Although they may seek to strike out a wholly unmeritorious case under the Civil Procedure Rules, Part 3, r 3.4/Part 24, it is more difficult in that the strike-out applicant must show that to be the case. See, e g *Reality Group Ltd v Chance* [2002] FSR 13 Ch D. Up-to-date versions of the Civil Procedure Rules and practice directions thereunder are maintained on the Ministry of Justice website at www.justice.gov.uk/guidance/courts-and-tribunals/courts/procedure-rules/civil/menus/rules.htm.

[170]   Consumer Protection Act 1987, s 2(1) and (2)(b).

[171]   Trade Marks Act 1994, s 75 (as amended) defines 'court'.

[172]   Sections 16, 19 and 20. See, further, **7.68–7.70** (removal, delivery up and disposal).

[173]   *Minerstone Ltd v Be Modern Ltd* [2002] FSR 53 CC (Central London). Sections 16, 19 and 20. See, further, **7.68–7.70** (removal, delivery up and disposal).

[174]   See **7.1**.

[175]   Considered by the House of Lords in *R v Johnstone* [2003] UKHL 28; [2003] 1 WLR 1736; [2003] 3 All ER 884; [2003] 2 Cr App R 33; [2003] FSR 42; [2004] ETMR 2. See, further, **7.72–7.74** (criminal provisions).

[176]   See A Worsdell and A Clark *Anti-counterfeiting: A Practical Guide* (Jordan Publishing Ltd, 1998).

of the Consumer Protection from Unfair Trading Regulations 2008[177] and the Business Protection from Misleading Marketing Regulations 2008.[178]

PERSONNEL OF TRADE MARK LAW

3.33 As under previous legislation, there are no restrictions on providing trade mark agency services. Anyone can act as a trade mark agent. For several reasons, however, it is desirable to employ a professionally qualified agent. First, registration of trade mark agents depends upon professional qualification; examinations are currently administered by a joint board of the Institute of Trade Mark Attorneys and the Chartered Institute of Patent Attorneys. Secondly, communications with a registered trade mark agent on matters relating to trade marks, passing off and designs are privileged in the same way as communications with a solicitor.[179] This extends to communications with third parties for the purpose of obtaining information for instructing the agent or in response to such a request. Privilege also applies where the trade mark agent is a partnership of registered agents or a company entitled to call itself a registered trade mark agent.[180] A registered trade mark agent may be described as a 'trade mark attorney' without breaching rules otherwise restricting the term 'attorney' to solicitors.[181] Trade mark attorneys may be accredited to litigate in the High Court and can appear in the Patents County Court and other county courts with trade mark jurisdiction.[182]

3.34 To preserve these important advantages, s 84 renders criminal the unjustified use of the terms 'registered trade mark agent' by unqualified persons. Proceedings must be brought within a year. The Registry may refuse to deal with a person who has been convicted of such an offence, as well as anyone whose conduct would render them liable to removal from the register of trade mark agents (s 88). The 1994 Act contains powers to prescribe rules for mixed

---

[177] SI 2008/1277, which implements Directive 2005/29/EC of the European Parliament and of the Council concerning unfair business-to-consumer commercial practices [2005] OJ L149/22. See S Singleton 'The Consumer Protection from Unfair Trading Regulations' [2009] CTLR 77. A duty of consistent interpretation of the Unfair Commercial Practices Directive was emphasised by the ECJ in *VTB-VAB NV v Total Belgium NV; Galatea BVBA v Sanoma Magazines Belgium NV* (Joined Cases C-261/07 and C-299/07) [2009] 3 CMLR 17.

[178] SI 2008/1276, implementing Directive 2006/114/EC of the European Parliament and of the Council concerning misleading and comparative advertising [2006] OJ L376/21. See J Smith and R Montagnon 'The new consumer and business protection regulations: another string to the brand owner's bow?' [2009] JIPLP 33.

[179] This has been considered by the House of Lords in *Three Rivers DC v Bank of England (Disclosure) (No 4)* [2004] UKHL 48; [2004] 3 WLR 1274. For a useful comparative account, see J Copeman and K Hurford 'Practical considerations in maintaining privilege' [2005] JIBLR 360; L Bastin 'Should "independence" of in-house counsel be a condition precedent to a claim of legal professional privilege in respect of communications between them and their employer clients?' [2011] CJQ 33.

[180] In particular because all its directors are registered agents (s 84(4)).

[181] Section 86.

[182] See **7.1.**

partnerships.[183] A number of solicitors also do trade mark work; a recent trend has been the employment of trade mark agents by firms of solicitors in order to provide clients with a 'one-stop shop' for trade mark matters.

ADMINISTRATIVE MECHANISMS CAPABLE OF PROTECTING SIGNS

Advertising Standards Authority (ASA)

3.35 This is an industry self-regulation body dedicated to ensuring that advertising is 'legal, decent, honest and truthful' and thus does not 'mislead, harm or offend'.[184] It adjudicates on complaints where advertising is covered by codes of advertising practice, drawn up by committees for the broadcasting and non-broadcasting sectors. Its conclusions are not binding upon the courts,[185] but have considerable persuasive value if the advertiser subscribes to the code.

Company names adjudicator

3.36 Chapter II of the Companies Act 2006 requires companies to register names. Chapter III introduced a system for adjudication where a company chooses a name which is too similar to a name registered for another company or protected in some other way, for example under the law of passing off or trade mark infringement. Section 68 prohibits registration of a name that is the same as another company's. Sections 67–68 empower the Secretary of State to require a company to change a name which is the same as, or 'too like', another company name, whilst third parties may object to a company name under s 69 by way of application to the company names adjudicator.[186] Standing is shown if the disputed company name is the same as, or sufficiently similar to, a name associated with the applicant in which he has goodwill or reputation, such that its use in the UK would be likely to mislead by suggesting a connection between the company and the applicant. These criteria effectively involve passing-off rights in the name and the company will be ordered to change the registered name unless it can make out one of five defences – that the company name pre-dates the applicant's goodwill, that the company is operating under the name, has done so or has committed substantial startup costs to so doing, that the company is available for purchase from a company formation agent on normal terms, that the name was adopted in good faith or that the applicant's interests are not significantly affected. Sections 70 and 71 of the Act deal with the appointment of adjudicators and procedural rules, while s 72 provides for

---

[183] Patent Agents (Mixed Partnerships and Bodies Corporate) Rules 1994, SI 1994/362; Partnerships (Unrestricted Size) No 11 Regulations 1994, SI 1994/644.
[184] Full details are available on the ASA website at www.asa.org.uk.
[185] *Croydon LBC v Hogarth* [2011] EWHC 1126 (QB).
[186] Details and links are available at www.ipo.gov.uk/cna.htm.

publication of decisions. This is achieved by posting them onto the website of the UK Intellectual Property Office.[187] A considerable majority of cases decided to date are undefended.

Office of Fair Trading and local Trading Standards

3.37 These bodies are responsible for enforcing the Consumer Protection from Unfair Trading Regulations 2008[188] and the Business Protection from Misleading Marketing Regulations 2008.[189] Their powers have been extended over those available under the Trade Descriptions Act 1968 and the Control of Misleading Advertisements Regulations 1988 (both largely repealed by the 2008 Regulations) to include the power to apply to the civil courts for injunctions as well as to bring proceedings in the criminal courts.[190] Published guidelines[191] make clear that the authorities will use proportionate measures, including education, advice and guidance, to combat unfair practices but are prepared to use civil and criminal measures for serious cases. In *Croydon London Borough Council v Hogarth*[192] an injunction was granted to restrain persistent behaviour in sending misleading contractual documents (the defendants' conduct had been previously criticised by the Advertising Standards Authority and the Office of Fair Trading but they had refused to cease their practices) Mackie J recommended that for speed and saving of costs, applications for an injunction under the Business Protection from Misleading Marketing Regulations 2008, reg 15 be brought before a senior circuit judge in the Mercantile Court.

3.38 The Consumer Protection from Unfair Trading Regulations 2008 have a cascade of prohibited practices, from a general prohibition in reg 3 on conduct 'contrary to requirements of professional diligence' which it materially distorts the 'economic behaviour of the average consumer', or is likely to, through a range of specific practices which are prohibited if they produce such effect on

---

[187] For links to practice directions and databases of decisions, see www.ipo.gov.uk/cna.htm.

[188] SI 2008/1277, which implement Directive 2005/29/EC of the European Parliament and of the Council concerning unfair business-to-consumer commercial practices [2005] OJ L149/22. See S Singleton 'The Consumer Protection from Unfair Trading Regulations' [2009] CTLR 77. A duty of consistent interpretation of the Unfair Commercial Practices Directive was emphasised by the ECJ in *VTB-VAB NV v Total Belgium NV; Galatea BVBA v Sanoma Magazines Belgium NV* (Joined Cases C-261/07 and C-299/07) [2009] 3 CMLR 17.

[189] SI 2008/1276, implementing Directive 2006/114/EC of the European Parliament and of the Council concerning misleading and comparative advertising [2006] OJ L376/21. See J Smith and R Montagnon 'The new consumer and business protection regulations: another string to the brand owner's bow?' [2009] JIPLP 33.

[190] A development lamented by G Howells in 'The end of an era – implementing the Unfair Commercial Practices Directive in the United Kingdom: punctual criminal law gives way to a general criminal/civil law standard' [2009] JBL 183.

[191] The OFT and BERR's 'Guidance on the Consumer Protection from Unfair Trading Regulations' may be downloaded from www.oft.gov.uk/shared_oft/business_leaflets/cpregs/oft1008.pdf; the OFT's 'Business to business promotions and comparative advertisements: A quick guide to the Business Protection from Misleading Marketing Regulations 2008' is available at www.oft.gov.uk/shared_oft/business_leaflets/general/oft1056.pdf.

[192] [2011] EWHC 1126 (QB).

consumer behaviour (misleading acts[193] and omissions,[194] aggressive marketing)[195] to 'banned practices' which are presumed to be unfair.[196] Promotion of unfair practices through codes of conduct is also prohibited (reg 4). Glockner has raised questions on the ambit of the underlying Directive, especially regarding post-sale conduct, conduct without market effects and practices with market effect but 'engaged in by science, consumer associations or media'.[197] The requirement of effect on consumers' transactional decision-making has considerable resonance with the notion of an operative misrepresentation in passing off[198] and with the notion that trade mark infringement involves some change in consumers' economic behaviour.[199]

3.39 The Business Protection from Misleading Marketing Regulations 2008 and the Misleading Advertising Directive which they implement are targeted at deceptive advertising which affects the recipient trader's economic behaviour or thereby causes injury to a competitor. They have given rise to a number of cases in the context of passing off, malicious falsehood and trade mark infringement, mainly triggered by comparative advertising. Five principles for such cases and the effect of key decisions of the European Court of Justice[200] on Art 4 of the directive[201] were considered by Kitchin J in *Kingspan Group plc, Kingspan Holdings (IRL) Limited v Rockwool Limited Rockwool Limited v Kingspan Group plc*:[202]

(a)　'the purpose of the various conditions set out in Article 4 (previously Article 3(a)(1) of Directive 84/450) is to achieve a balance between the different interests that may be affected by comparative advertising. The aim is to stimulate competition between suppliers of goods and services to

---

[193]　Regulation 5, including references to 'marketing of a product (including comparative advertising) which creates confusion with any products, trade marks, trade names or other distinguishing marks of a competitor', the use of statements or symbols relating to sponsorship or approval, geographical or commercial origin, approval and the trader's affiliations, connections or ownership of industrial, commercial or intellectual property rights.

[194]　Regulation 6.

[195]　Regulation 7.

[196]　Schedule 1, including product imitation so as to mislead as to manufacturing source.

[197]　J Glockner 'The scope of application of the UCP Directive – "I know what you did last summer"' [2010] IIC 570.

[198]　*The Office of Fair Trading v Purely Creative Limited & ors* [2011] EWHC 106 (Ch, Companies Court) 'the practical difference in the court's approach in passing off cases is not in my view substantial'.

[199]　See, e g *Intel* [2009] ETMR 13 at para 77; *Whirlpool Corp v Kenwood Ltd* [2009] EWCA Civ 753; [2010] ETMR 7, passim, dismissing appeal from Geoffrey Hobbs QC, sitting as a judge in the Community Trade Mark Court.

[200]　Case C-159/09 *Lidl SNC v Vierzon Distribution SA* [2011] 2 CMLR 10; [2011] ETMR 6; Case C-487/07 *L'Oréal SA v Bellure NV* [2009] ECR I-5185.

[201]　Which requires objectivity and like-for-like in comparative advertising and requires that it does not create confusion among traders or their marks, nor discredit or denigrate the marks, trade names, products, activities, or circumstances of a competitor; comparative advertising will also not be allowed under Art 4 if it takes unfair advantage of the reputation of a trade marks, trade name, other distinguishing marks or of the designations of origin; or presents products as imitations or replicas of those bearing a protected trade mark or name.

[202]　[2011] EWHC 250 (Ch) at paras 227–232.

the consumer's advantage, by allowing competitors to highlight objectively the merits of comparable products while, at the same time, prohibiting practices which may distort competition, be detrimental to competitors and have an adverse effect on consumer choice';[203]

(b) 'the conditions listed in Article 4 must be interpreted in the sense most favourable to permitting advertisements which objectively compare the characteristics of goods or services, while ensuring at the same time that comparative advertising is not used anti-competitively and unfairly or in a manner which affects the interests of consumers';[204]

(c) 'the lawfulness of comparative advertising is to be assessed solely by reference to the criteria laid down in the European legislature';[205]

(d) 'Article 4 lists cumulative conditions which the use of a competitor's trade mark in comparative advertising must satisfy in order to be permitted';[206]

(e) 'it is for the national court to ascertain in the circumstances of each case, and bearing in mind the consumers to which the advertising is addressed, whether the latter may be misleading. That court must take into account the perception of the average consumer of the products or services being advertised who is reasonably well informed and reasonably observant and circumspect'.[207]

Domain name registries and dispute resolution bodies

3.40 The case of *British Telecommunications plc v One in a Million Ltd*[208] demonstrated the risk that third parties might register the marks or names of well-known traders as internet domain names, with a view to blocking registration by the owners, threatening to sell them to others and possibly achieving considerable profit by selling them to the companies concerned. The dispute settlement mechanisms for domain names therefore provide protection against inappropriate registration and consequent deception of consumers. A very successful domain name dispute settlement service is that operated by the World Intellectual Property Organization;[209] it publishes analyses of decisions which show the chief classes of dispute.

---

203 [228], citing *Lidl* at para 20; *L'Oréal* at para 68.
204 [229], citing *Lidl* at para 21; *L'Oréal* at para 69; see also Case C-44/01 *Pippig Augenoptik GmbH & Co KG v Hartlauer Handelsgesellschaft mbH* [2003] ECR I-3095, ECJ.
205 [230], citing *Lidl* at para 22;
206 [231], citing *L'Oréal* at paras 54, 63, 65, 67, 70, 72, and 80; also *L'Oréal* [2010] EWCA Civ 535, [2010] RPC 23 at para 44.
207 [232], citing *Lidl* at paras 46–47.
208 [1999] 1 WLR 903 [1998] 4 All ER 476; [1999] ETMR 61 [1999] FSR 1 (CA).
209 See information and links at www.wipo.int/amc/en/domains/.

Plant variety right offices

3.41 New plant varieties may be registered under the Plant Varieties Act 1997 to provide their owners with a period of commercial exclusivity.[210] Section 18 of the Act empowers the relevant Minister to make provision for the selection and registration of varietal names and reg 15 of the Plant Breeders' Rights Regulations 1998/1027 achieves this by requiring the controller of plant varieties to maintain a register of names and record plant variety right applications and grants.[211] An application for protection may be delayed and ultimately refused if an appropriate name is not submitted and approved. Names may be considered unsuitable intrinsically, for example if it causes difficulties of recognition or reproduction or is deceptive as to the characteristics of the variety, or relative to other names and rights, for example if it is too close to an earlier variety name or infringes some other right. Proposed names are published in the *Gazette*[212] and open for objection by third parties for 3 months. Section 19 of the 1997 Act provides that a registered name must be used in the commercialisation of the variety, but the name may be changed, subject to approval of the new name and payment of a fee. Section 20 confers a cause of action against improper use of a registered varietal name.[213] There is no ban on registering a plant variety name as a trade mark,[214] but a variety name should be recognisable as such if used in conjunction with a trade mark.

3.42 Plant variety rights are not harmonised within the EU, but Council Regulation (EC) No 2100/94 of 27 July 1994 creates a system of unitary Community Plant Variety Rights administered by the Community Plant Variety Office in Angers, France.[215] Regulation 2100/94 requires the use of 'variety denominations' in a manner similar to that in the UK; both the UK and the EU are members of UPOV, the International Union for the Protection of New Varieties of Plants.[216]

---

[210] The 'Guide to Plant Breeders' Rights Handbook' (2010) is available at www.fera.defra.gov.uk/plants/plantVarieties/plantbreedersRights/documents/pbrHandbookSept10.pdf. It includes extracts from Explanatory Notes on Variety Denominations Under the UPOV Convention' (UPOV/INF/12/2) of 22 October 2009 (Union pour la Protection des Oeuvres Vegetales), see www.upov.int.

[211] Records may be inspected on application to the Plant Variety Rights Office, Food and Environment Research Agency, Whitehouse Lane, Huntingdon Road, Cambridge CB3 0LF.

[212] Available online back to 2008 at www.fera.defra.gov.uk/plants/publications/gazette.cfm.

[213] See B Sherman 'Taxonomic property' [2008] CLJ 560 on systems of plant nomenclature in general and on plant variety names from p 518.

[214] See, eg www.ipo.gov.uk/types/patent/p-applying/p-before/p-otherprotect/p-plantbreeders.htm: 'You may also be able to register the name of a new variety of plant or seed as a trade mark'. It is may be difficult to overcome an objection that a variety name is generic.

[215] Details available at www.cpvo.europa.eu/main/en/.

[216] See www.upov.int/index_en.html.

Chapter 4

LIMITS TO TRADE MARK PROTECTION

INTRODUCTION

4.1   Registration and passing-off rights do not give a proprietor a monopoly over a mark in all circumstances. First, limits may be inherent in the mark or the rights themselves, or expressly imposed by the legislation.[1] These are described here as 'intrinsic limits'. Secondly, the sovereignty of Parliament, of the European Union (EU) and the jurisdiction of the courts are territorially limited; national rights may not even extend throughout the jurisdiction. Community trade mark rights are unitary, in the sense of extending across the whole of the EU, but scope of protection and available remedies may vary from one member state to another, according to the extent of local reputation, the existence of earlier prior rights, and so forth.[2] Lastly, the enjoyment and exercise of trade mark rights are subject to general rules of law and in particular those rules designed to ensure freedom of trade. This last category of limit is described here as 'extrinsic'.

INTRINSIC LIMITS

'In the course of trade'

Passing off

4.2   Trade mark rights, not surprisingly, are generally confined to the commercial arena. This is certainly true of passing off.[3] A claimant's use of a mark is unprotected if there is no business activity to which goodwill can attach. Thus, a local political party[4] failed to gain protection for their name by suing in passing off. By contrast, the Countryside Alliance were successful in

---

[1]   For marks on the UK and international registers, the Trade Marks Act 1994 ('the 1994 Act') and Trade Marks Harmonisation Directive (codified) 2008/95/EC ('the Directive'), for marks on the Community register, Council Regulation (EC) 207/2009 (codified) on the Community Trade Mark ('the Regulation').

[2]   S Schnell 'The Community trade mark: unitary EU right – EU-wide injunction?' [2011] EIPR 210, citing the opinion of Advocate-General Sharpston in *PAGO International GmbH v Tirolmilch Registrierte Genossenschaft mbH* (C-301/07) [2009] ECR I-9429 (ECJ (2nd Chamber); *DHL Express France SAS v Chronopost SA* (C-235/09) [2011] ETMR 33 (ECJ Grand Chamber) at [46].

[3]   In *Advocaat*, Lord Diplock referred to 'the trader by whom the action is brought' and Lord Fraser referred to the business of the claimant, [1980] RPC 31.

[4]   *Kean v McGivan* [1982] FSR 119 (SDP).

their claim for an injunction in *Burge v Haycock*,[5] having shown that they enjoyed a substantial public reputation and goodwill which might be undermined by the defendant's activities. Well-established professional and charitable organisations like the British Legion,[6] the British Medical Association[7] and the British Diabetic Association[8] have also succeeded in passing-off claims, indicating that 'trade' may be given a generous interpretation.[9] Equally, the defendant's activities need to be commercial for a passing-off action to lie: Lord Diplock in *Advocaat*[10] makes particular reference to misrepresentations by a trader in the course of trade.

Registered trade marks and proprietors

4.3 Similar considerations apply to registered trade marks. Under s 10 of the 1994 Act,[11] an infringing act must be carried out 'in the course of trade', which includes 'any business or profession'.[12] Curiously, the 1994 Act is less explicit when it comes to the activities of registered proprietors – must they be engaged in commercial activity to enjoy protection of their marks? Certainly the very phrase 'trade mark' suggests this. Section 1 refers to the trade marks distinguishing between 'undertakings', a phrase which also suggests economic activity. The Trade Marks Harmonisation Directive ('the Directive') was created[13] in the interests of free movement of goods and undistorted competition within the internal market of the European Union, so EU competition cases may assist in construing this term. In the context of competition law, 'undertaking' has been interpreted as including 'any entity engaged in an economic activity, regardless of its legal status and the way in which it is financed'.[14] 'Economic activity' was said in *FENIN* characteristically to involve offering goods and services on a given market, and not purchasing.[15] However, even if the act of buying does not of itself constitute the 'economic activity' of an 'undertaking', someone offering their services as a buyer to

---

[5]   [2002] RPC 28.
[6]   *British Legion v British Legion Club (Street) Ltd* (1931) 48 RPC 555.
[7]   *BMA v Marsh* (1931) 48 RPC 565.
[8]   [1995] 4 All ER 812, [1996] FSR 1 Ch D.
[9]   For a suggestion that churches might be able to sue in passing off, see S Stokes 'Church names and their protection under English law' [2001] Ent LR 25. The Court of Appeal in *Burge* referred to an Australian church case.
[10] In *Advocaat*, Lord Diplock referred to 'the trader by whom the action is brought' and Lord Fraser referred to the business of the claimant, [1980] RPC 31.
[11] See **7.27–7.28**.
[12] Section 103(1).
[13] First Council Directive (EEC) 89/104, first recital, now codified into Directive 2008/95/EC. See also Regulation (EC) 40/94 ('the Regulation'), first recital, now codified into Regulation (EC) 207/2009.
[14] *Höfner v Macrotron GmbH* (C-41/90): [1991] ECR I-1979; [1993] 4 CMLR 306; applied, inter alia, in *Federación Nacional de Empresas de Instrumentación Científica, Médica, Técnica y Dental (FENIN) v Commission* (T-319/99) [2003] ECR III-357 CFI.
[15] *Federación Nacional de Empresas de Instrumentación Científica, Médica, Técnica y Dental (FENIN) v Commission* (T-319/99) [2003] ECR III-357 CFI, at para 36, citing *Commission v Italy* [1998] ECR I-3851.

others would so qualify.[16] As discussed in *Bettercare v DGFT*,[17] an entity may be an 'undertaking' for some activities and not others. Thus, it may be able to register trade marks for some activities but not others. Further, since the concept of 'undertaking' is based upon economic activity rather than legal personality, different conclusions as to what is an undertaking might be reached for trade mark law purposes and for competition purposes. The crux of the assessment for trade mark being the mode of quality control as contemplated in *Scandecor*.[18] In *Poucet & Pistre*,[19] the European Court of Justice (ECJ, now Court of Justice of the European Union) held that a non-profit making social security scheme which pursued purely social objectives was not an 'undertaking' and therefore not subject to competition law. Would such a scheme be denied trade mark protection? Charitable associations may register their names. Modern government agencies recognise the importance of distinctive and memorable names and logos. The public interest might be served by allowing them to register these signs as trade marks, the better to protect against imitation.[20] But there is at least one problem – a trade mark proprietor must be an entity capable of owning property. This would preclude many government departments from registering. A similar difficulty can also arise in the context of charities and trusts, which the UK Trade Marks Registry contemplates as trade mark applicants.[21] Partnerships pose a slightly different problem – although 'LLPs' under the Limited Liability Partnerships Act 2000 Act are incorporated entities with distinct legal status, generally partnerships do not have legal status distinct from their members. Thus, the partners themselves will be proprietors of a mark (which may for convenience be registered in the partnership name). This can cause problems when membership of the partnership changes.[22] Returning to the 1994 Act, s 32(3) specifies that an applicant for registration[23] must state its use or intention to use the mark for the goods or services concerned, although use in the course of trade is not specified. Failure to make 'genuine' use of a registered mark is a ground for revocation (s 46).[24] Applying these principles to a specific example, there is little scope for the Registry to repeat its refusal under the Trade Marks Act 1938 ('the 1938 Act') to register 'Hospital World'[25] for a

---

16   Class 35 of the Nice classification includes procurement services for others (purchasing goods and services for other businesses).

17   *Bettercare Group Ltd v The Director General of Fair Trading (3)* [2003] ECC 40 CCAT.

18   *Scandecor Development AB v Scandecor Marketing AB (Reference to ECJ)* C-195/01 [2001] OJ C200/53; see also [2001] UKHL 21 at [52].

19   Joined cases C-159/91 and C-160/91 [1993] ECR I-637.

20   The UK Registry contemplates registering names of organisations such as 'The National Association of Tourist Information Offices' on a first-come, first-served basis: 'There is nothing in the Act which requires the registrar, on public policy grounds, to keep names such as "National Guild of Carpenters" free to use in future' Trade Marks Registry *Manual of trade marks practice* (also known as the 'Work Manual'), ch 3, heading 'Organisations (names of)'. A similar approach might work in relation to government agencies.

21   Work Manual, ch 1, section 5 'The applicant'.

22   G Harris 'The Sugababes: the trademark rights associated with band names' [2010] Ent LR 165; Work Manual, ch 1, section 5 'The applicant'.

23   See **5.1** (criteria for registration).

24   See **9.12–9.14** (grounds for revocation, no genuine use).

25   [1967] RPC 595.

magazine because the publication in question was funded by advertisements and distributed free to readers. Selling advertising space and supplying reading matter are clearly activities of an undertaking on the criteria outlined above.

Similarity of marks and products

4.4   Even where claimant and defendant are both traders, an action in passing off or for infringement of a registered trade mark generally requires a degree of similarity between the parties' badges of trade and between their goods or services. Unless these elements are present, the likelihood of damage is remote.[26] If the mark is a 'household name', however, damage may be established in passing off and an injunction will lie even where products are dissimilar.[27] If a registered mark has a reputation, use of an identical or similar mark even on dissimilar goods will be actionable if likely detriment or unfair advantage flows from its use.[28]

Signs in common currency

4.5   Where a sign is wholly descriptive or one which traders at large have a legitimate right to use, the courts are slow to find passing off.[29] Even if one trader enjoys goodwill in such a mark, small differences will suffice to prevent misrepresentation by a rival trader.[30] A wholly descriptive mark is debarred from registration by s 3(1)(b) and (c) of the 1994 Act, unless distinctive character has been acquired by use.[31] Again, the scope of protection of such a registered mark will be narrow – thus 'Aquatite' would not be an infringement of 'Aquascutum' for watertight garments.[32] There are defences for descriptive use[33] and the public may be taken to understand that descriptive matter will be available to other traders.[34]

Non-trade mark use

4.6   If the defendant does not use a sign as a trade mark, it is unlikely that a claimant in a passing-off action will succeed in establishing a misrepresentation.[35] What about signs registered under the 1994 Act?

---

[26] See, e g *Stringfellow v McCain* [1984] RPC 501 (passing off); see further **3.18–3.20** (damages in passing off); **5.38–5.44** (comparison of marks and comparison of products).

[27] As in *Lego v Lego M Lemelstrich* [1983] FSR 155 (passing off); Trade Marks Act 1994, s 10(3) (marks with a reputation).

[28] Trade Marks Act 1994, s 10(3) and s 5(3) may enable the proprietor to oppose another's registration in these circumstances.

[29] As in '*Oven chips*', *McCain v Country Fair* [1981] RPC 69; *BBC v Talksport* [2001] FSR 6. See also **3.10** (descriptive badges of trade), **3.21–3.23** (defences to passing off).

[30] *Office Cleaning Services Ltd v Westminster Window and General Cleaners* (1946) 62 RPC 39.

[31] See **2.35–2.38** (descriptive marks).

[32] As in *Aquascutum v Cohen & Wilks* (1909) 26 RPC 651.

[33] Section 11(2) of the 1994 Act, the Directive, Art 6(1), the Regulation, Art 12.

[34] *Reed Executive v Reed Business Information* [2004] ROC 767; *West v Fuller Smith* [2003] FSR 44 (ESB for Extra Special Bitter).

[35] See, e g *Hodgkinson & Corby v Wards Mobility Services* [1995] FSR 169, discussed in A Firth 'Cushions and confusion' [1994] 11 EIPR 494.

Article 5(5) of the Directive expressly states that the infringement provisions do not affect a member state's rules relating use otherwise than for distinguishing[36] goods and services, provided that such other prohibited use of the sign is without due cause and takes unfair advantage of, or is detrimental to, the distinctive character or repute of the mark.[37] Comparing the text of Art 5 of the Directive with s 10 of the 1994 Act suggests that no new prohibition on non-trade mark use of a registered mark has been introduced.[38] This is reinforced by s 9, which confers exclusive rights in the 'trade mark' rather than in the 'sign'. However, in *Arsenal v Reed*, the ECJ held that there could be infringement by an unlicensed trader's use of the football club's insignia on good for which they were registered if the trade mark proprietor's interest in the marks was affected, notwithstanding the defendant's contention that the marks were being used as badges of allegiance rather than badges of trade.[39]

Use of own name, address, etc

4.7 A variant of the above occurs when the mark, in which a claimant claims rights, constitutes the defendant's own name or address. This may provide a complete defence[40] or lead to a qualified injunction in both the passing-off[41] and registered trade mark regimes.[42] The UK courts have applied this to company names; a reference to the ECJ on the point in *Scandecor*[43] was withdrawn when the dispute settled. However, the 'own name' defence does not apply to new company names.[44]

TERRITORIAL LIMITS

4.8 Passing off may be territorially limited in two respects. First, the claimant's goodwill may be limited to part of the country only. In *Evans v Eradicure*,[45] the defendant's and claimant's businesses under similar names expanded until they overlapped. It was held that, in the area of overlap, they could restrain third parties but not each other from carrying on business under a similar mark. Within the UK, England & Wales, Northern Ireland and

---

[36] The ECJ in *Arsenal v Reed* (C-206/01) [2002] ECR I-7945 re-emphasised the role of the Directive in protecting the distinguishing function of marks; see also [2003] RPC 696 CA.

[37] Article 5(5).

[38] This may be contrasted with the situation in The Netherlands, where non-trade mark use may be enjoined. See, e g the *Philips* case cited by M Kniff in 'Selected Benelux cases' *Trademark World*, July/August 1994, p 14 and further discussion of this issue at **7.9–7.20**.

[39] *Arsenal v Reed* (C-206/01) [2002] ECR I-7945 and see [2003] RPC 696 CA.

[40] As in *Day v Brownrigg* (1878) 10 Ch D 294 (adoption of house name).

[41] *Parker-Knoll v Knoll International* [1962] RPC 265 (injunction against use on goods); *Boswell-Wilkie Circus v Brian Boswell Circus* [1986] FSR 479 (qualified injunction); cf *Gucci v Gucci* [1991] FSR 89 (unqualified injunction).

[42] Section 11(2)(a) of the 1994 Act.

[43] [2001] 2 CMLR 30.

[44] *Asprey v Garrard v WRA (Guns) Ltd* [2001] FSR 31; [2002] FSR 487 (CA).

[45] [1972] RPC 808; [1972] FSR 137.

Scotland are distinct jurisdictions.[46] Although Scotland is a mixed system, with civil and common law juridical heritage, as compared with the other, common law, jurisdictions, the same passing-off principles apply,[47] and goodwill in one may found an action for passing off in another.[48] Secondly, if the claimant does not carry on business in the UK, he may find it difficult to establish an actionable goodwill.[49] However, s 56 of the 1994 Act enables a foreign[50] claimant whose mark is well known in the UK to restrain confusing use even without a registration or passing-off rights in the UK. As far as registered trade marks are concerned, the legislative powers of Parliament are territorially limited. This factor underlies the decision in *Burrough v Speymalt,*[51] where allegedly infringing activities took place in Italy. The UK registration was not infringed by activities in Italy; the Italian trade mark rights were owned by a different party.

4.9   It may be noted that in the Scotch whisky cases,[52] injunctions were granted to restrain the defendants' conduct within the UK on the basis that it would lead to passing off in another jurisdiction, where it was also actionable. These cases may be distinguished from those cited above in that the acts alleged against the defendants took place in England. The courts in passing-off cases have always been astute to restrain passing off at source, even where confusion occurs further down the line.[53] Conversely, misrepresentations issued abroad but intended to take effect within the jurisdiction and liable to damage goodwill may found a passing-off action.[54]

Jurisdiction and applicable law under EU rules

4.10   Infringements occurring in other EU, EEA or European Free Trade Association (EFTA) member states may be actionable in the UK under the 'Brussels' Regulation 44/2001 on civil jurisdiction and judgments[55] and the

---

[46]   The Civil Jurisdiction and Judgments Act 1982 governs private international law issues that stem from this.

[47]   C Ng 'A common law of passing-off? English and Scottish perspectives' [2009] Edin LR 134.

[48]   *Flaxcell v Freedman* [1981] SLT (Notes) 131; see, generally, 'Passing off' in C Colston and J Galloway *Modern Intellectual Property Law* (Routledge, 3rd edn, 2010) ch 14.

[49]   See Chapter 3 (locus of goodwill).

[50]   Section 56 does not avail a UK claimant; since it is designed to satisfy the UK's international obligations (see s 55). Z Ballantyne 'Legal loophole: UK companies may not be able to rely on their well known marks under the Paris Convention' [2002] EIPR 415, commenting on *Imperial Tobacco Ltd v Berry Bros & Rudd* Chancery Division (Patents Court), 31 October 2001.

[51]   *Burrough (James) v Speymalt Whisky Distributors* [1991] RPC 130; where the right to sue in Scotland and to sue for the equivalent wrong in Italy were enjoyed by different parties. The decision refers to the 'double actionability rule' which was abolished by the Private International Law (Miscellaneous Provisions) Act 1995 but it is submitted that the decision would be the same today.

[52]   *John Walker v Ost* [1970] RPC 489; [1970] FSR 63; *White Horse v Gregson* [1984] RPC 61.

[53]   See **4.2**, n 1.

[54]   *Mecklermedia Corp v DC Congress GmbH* [1998] Ch 40; [1997] 3 WLR 479; [1998] 1 All ER 148 [1997] FSR 627 Ch D (refusal to strike out passing-off claim).

[55]   Largely superseding the Brussels Convention of 1968, save for certain territories of EU countries that were excluded from the regulation pursuant to Art 299EC (such as the Channel Islands, Isle of Man), now governed by Art 355TFEU (see J Ziller 'Outermost Regions,

Lugano Convention ('the Conventions').[56] Article 16(4) of the Conventions and Art 22(4) of Regulation 44/2001 confer on the UK courts exclusive jurisdiction as to the registration or validity of UK registered marks. Although pure issues of title usually fall outside this provision, in trade mark cases, title and validity are often interlinked.[57] Jurisdiction in infringement follows the general tort criteria of defendant's domicile,[58] the place of commission of the tort and (at least where damage is an integral element of the tort)[59] or the place where damage is sustained.[60] In contractual disputes, the general jurisdiction based on domicile is supplemented by special jurisdiction of the courts of the place of performance of the obligation in question. This has led to difficulties of interpretation.[61] Regulation 44/2001 deals with the jurisdiction of the courts to hear disputes in civil and commercial matters and also recognition of such judgments as between member states and their enforcement. The other ingredient – the law to be applied – is governed by Regulation (EC) No 864/2007 on the law applicable to non-contractual obligations (Rome II)[62]

Overseas Countries and Territories and Others after the Entry into Force of the Lisbon Treaty', in D Kochenov (ed), *EU Law of the Overseas* (Aspen, 2011), ch 2. Denmark's difficulties with the Reg 44/2001 were overcome by agreement, adopted as Council Decision 2006/325/EC. Further information and a consolidated version of the Regulation, as amended, are available at: http://europa.eu/legislation_summaries/justice_freedom_security/judicial_cooperation_in_civil_matters/l33054_en.htm.

[56] Convention of 27 September 1968; implemented in the UK by means of the Civil Jurisdiction and Judgments Act 1982 (in force from 1 January 1987). Still relevant where dispute has a Danish dimension. Lugano Convention for EFTA. Regulation 44/2001 on jurisdiction and the recognition and enforcement of judgments in civil and commercial matters [2001] OJ L12, in force 1 March 2002.

[57] Eg because an assignment has rendered a mark deceptive or because the wrong person has applied to register: *K SABATIER TM* [1993] RPC 97; s 60 of the 1994 Act. For recent copyright cases relating to title, see P Torremans 'The sense or nonsense of subject-matter jurisdiction over foreign copyright' [2011] EIPR 349. In *Lucasfilm v Ainsworth* [2011] UKSC the Supreme Court held that English courts with *in personam* jurisdiction over a defendant had jurisdiction over claims of copyright infringement in the US. Although the judgment does not apply to rights arising through registration, it may evidence a trend to greater assumption of jurisdiction: J Pila 'The "Star Wars" copyright claim: an ambivalent view of the Empire' [2012] LQR 15.

[58] Article 2 of Reg 44/2001; *Pearce v Ove Arup Partnership Ltd and Others* [2000] Ch 403, [2000] 3 WLR 332 CA, a copyright case.

[59] To allow proceedings wherever damage is felt, e g because a bank account is maintained in a particular jurisdiction, would defeat the purpose of the Convention. In *Sheville v Presse Alliance* [1995] All ER (EC) 289 (defamation) jurisdiction was founded on damage to reputation caused by local circulation of the defamatory statement. Note that the territorial scope of a court's 'special' jurisdicition under Art 5(3) is more limited that its general jurisdiction under Art 2 (domicile).

[60] Article 5(3) refers to the place where the harmful event occurred; this has been used to sustain an action in the jurisdiction where pollution damage occurred, as opposed to the place where the causative discharge of pollutants took place: *Handelskwerij G J Bier v Mines des Potasse d'Alsace* [1976] ECR 1735.

[61] *Falco Privatstiftung v Weller-Lindhorst* [2009] ECR I-3327; see J-J Forner, M Torres 'Jurisdiction in international contracts: new article 5.1 Brussels I and the ECJ' [2011] ICCLR 42; J-J Kuipers 'Determining jurisdiction in international licence agreements: *Falco Privatstiftung v Weller-Lindhorst* (C-533/07)' [2010] EIPR 659.

[62] Regulation (EC) No 864/2007 of the European Parliament and of the Council of 11 July 2007,

and Regulation (EC) No 593/2008 on the law applicable to contractual obligations (Rome I).[63] Rome I will apply to trade mark licensing, Rome II to infringement.

EXTRINSIC LIMITS

4.11   The territorial nature of trade mark and passing-off rights makes them apt to hamper trade. Although an established mark will not usually prevent a competitor from introducing a competing product into the market, the latter will have to gain customer acceptance in the face of the earlier brand. It is not surprising, therefore, that the exploitation of trade mark rights may be subject to the doctrine of restraint of trade, to national competition law and to the provisions of the Treaty on the Functioning of the European Union (TFEU).[64]

Competition law

4.12   Under Arts 101 and 102 of the TFEU, a company may face sanctions if its practices have an actual or potential effect on competition in interstate trade, or if it abuses a dominant position within the internal market, again with effect on trade between member states. Where a restrictive agreement nonetheless has beneficial effects, it may be exempted under Art 101(3). Since Council Regulation (EC) 1/2003 on the implementation of competition rules[65] came into effect,[66] national courts, national competition authorities as well as the European Commission and the ECJ may apply Arts 101 and 102 in full. The European Commission promulgates 'block exemptions' for classes of agreement under Art 101(3), such as that for vertical distribution agreements or technology transfer, which may contain ancillary trade mark provisions. The UK's Competition Act 1998 contains provisions similar to Arts 101 and 102 which apply in the absence of an interstate dimension.

Restraint of trade at common law

4.13   The common law doctrine of restraint of trade will apply to trade mark transactions as to any other.[67] An agreement or term in restraint of trade will be deemed void unless it is reasonably necessary to protect a legitimate interest

---

which came into application on 11 January 2009 including damage occurring from 20 August 2007 onwards. It allows for choice of jurisdiction, subject to Art 8 which specifically governs claims relating to intellectual property rights.

[63]   Regulation (EC) No 593/2008 of the European Parliament and of the Council of 17 June 2008. It applies to contracts concluded from 17 December 2009 onwards. It does not contain any provisions specific to intellectual property rights.

[64]   See **13.17–13.22** (free movement and competition rules in the EU).

[65]   [2003] OJ L/1.

[66]   On 1 May 2004.

[67]   Note that Art 3 of Reg 1/2003 may limit the effect of restraint of trade where it achieves the same objectives as Art 101 of the TFEU: *Days Medical Aids Limited v Pihsiang Machinery Co Ltd* [2004] 1 All ER (Comm) 991; MC Lucey 'Unforeseen consequences of Article 3 of EU Regulation 1/2003' [2006] ECLR 558.

– reasonable as between the parties and in the public interest.[68] Given that trade mark restrictions would not normally fetter trade in the goods or services as such and given the public's particular interest in the indicative power of trade marks, it is not surprising that decisions in this area are uncommon. Indeed, in *Levi Strauss v Kimbyr*,[69] the High Court of New Zealand rejected the argument that a trade mark was a form of monopoly:[70]

> ' . . . the protection of genuine well-established trade marks such as Levi's pocket tab device from free riding competition is in the public interest and pro-competitive rather than the reverse ...'

Restraint of trade has been argued in several cases involving agreements to compromise litigation. Unless the rights are clearly invalid the court will not go into detailed investigation of validity.[71] In *WWF* it was held[72] that a restraint in a settlement agreement would only be considered as a potential restraint of trade if it went beyond any reasonably arguable scope of protection of the intellectual property right in question. In that case it is still open to the person seeking to enforce the restraint to justify it on usual principles.

Consent to marketing and 'exhaustion' of rights

4.14 As a matter of UK law, the territorial nature of trade marks and other intellectual property rights in principle makes it possible for the proprietor to control the movement of products between territories.[73] For example, s 10(4)(c) of the 1994 Act[74] specifies that importing or exporting goods or services under the protected sign may be prohibited by the trade mark owner. Where goods or services have been lawfully marketed in the EU, this would hamper the free movement of goods and services that is required[75] by Art 34 of the Treaty on the Functioning of the European Union (formerly Art 28 of the EC Treaty). This possible effect of trade marks is denied by s 12(2) of the 1994 Act[76] unless the trade mark proprietor has legitimate reason to oppose further circulation of goods, for example, that they have deteriorated. Section 12(2) applies where goods have been put on the internal market by the trade mark proprietor or with his consent. The so-called 'exhaustion' principle – the trade mark proprietor uses up or 'exhausts' his rights when he releases the goods onto the market where they must be free to circulate – does not apply where goods are

---

[68] *Nordenfeldt v Maxim Nordenfeldt* [1894] AC 535 (HL).

[69] [1994] FSR 335, Williams J.

[70] Ibid at p 368.

[71] *WWF-Worldwide Fund for Nature v World Wrestling Federation Entertainment Inc* [2002] FSR 32, Ch D, citing *BAT v Commission* [1985] ECR 363 and *Apple Corp v Apple Computers* [1991] 3 CMLR 49.

[72] At para 28.

[73] Whether this remains true as between states making up the European single market is considered in more detail in Chapter 13.

[74] Directive, Art 5(3)(c); Regulation, Art 9(2)(c).

[75] Subject to the exceptions of Art 30.

[76] Directive, Art 7, Regulation, Art 13.

imported from a country outside the EEA[77] and consent is lacking.[78] Thus in *Quiksilver v Charles Robertson*,[79] the trade mark owner had licensed a Turkish manufacturer to apply the mark to goods destined for Asian and former Soviet markets. Although the defendant had bought them from a Spanish intermediary and (erroneously) believed them to have been previously marketed in the EEA, judgment for trade mark infringement was entered.

International exhaustion not recognised in the UK

4.15 The doctrine of international exhaustion, in which enjoyment of rights in one state renders equivalent rights unenforceable in other states, was emphatically rejected by the Privy Council in *National Phonograph v Menck*[80] in favour of a consent-based approach. But the UK courts have traditionally been quick to infer consent to export or import, unless the proprietor has exercised all powers at his disposal to prevent it. Thus, in *Betts v Willmott*,[81] a patentee was held impliedly to consent to a movement of goods which was within its powers to prevent. This extreme approach was disapproved in *Zino Davidoff*,[82] although the ECJ was obliged to confirm that consent is a matter for national law. The concept of implied consent does not seem to have developed in quite the same way in the rest of Europe, possibly because privity of contract and the corporate veil[83] do not have the same potency[84] as in the UK. However, the issue of consent is crucial to 'exhaustion' in the jurisprudence of the European Court.

Human Rights and Trade Marks

4.16 The Human Rights Act 1998 (HRA 1998) explicitly implemented the European Convention on Human Rights (ECHR) into domestic law. It has assumed an important role in enabling the courts to balance privacy interests (in actions for breach of confidence, reflecting Art 8 of the ECHR)[85] and

---

[77]　*Silhouette v Hartlauer* (C-355/96) [1999] Ch 77.

[78]　*Zino Davidoff v A&G Imports* (C-414/99) [2002] RPC 20 ECJ; P Torremans and I Stamatoudi 'International Exhaustion in the EU in the Light of Zino Davidoff: Contract and Trade Mark Law' [2000] 2 IIC 123.

[79]　[2005] FSR 8.

[80]　*National Phonograph Co of Australia Ltd v Menck* [1911] AC 336; (1911) 28 RPC 229.

[81]　(1871) LR 6 Ch App 239; cf *SA des Manufactures de Glaces v Tilghman's Patent Sand Blast Co* (1884) LR 25 Ch D 1, CA.

[82]　Joined cases C414 to 416/99 *Zino Davidoff* and *Levi Strauss* [2001] ECR I-8691, [2002] RPC 20.

[83]　The legal dividing line between a company, as a distinct legal entity, and its shareholders or members. 'Piercing the corporate veil' – crossing the dividing line – is rarely achieved, unless the company is a sham.

[84]　However, the UK Registry and courts have not always been overly strict in this regard. See, e g *Revlon v Cripps & Lee* [1980] FSR 85.

[85]　Eg *Campbell v Mirror Group Newspapers Ltd* [2004] UKHL 22; [2004] 2 AC 457; [2004] 2 WLR 1232; [2004] 2 All ER 995; [2004] EMLR 15; [2004] HRLR 24; [2004] UKHRR 648.

copyright[86] (a property right recognised under the protocol to Art 1 of the ECHR) with freedom of expression (Art 10 of the ECHR).[87] These balances can assume critical importance in the decision to grant or refuse an interim injunction (in Scotland, interdict) which will result in restraint of speech.[88] However, the messages conveyed by trade marks form part of commercial speech, which typically has been given less weight in ECHR cases than political or cultural speech.[89] Thus, human rights issues arise comparatively infrequently in trade mark cases, at least in the UK.[90] In *Miss World Ltd v Channel 4 Television Corp*,[91] the claimants sought an injunction to restrain the use of 'Miss World' as part of the title 'Mr Miss World' for the defendants' transvestite and trans-sexual beauty parade, imminently to be televised. After considering the interplay of the claimant's goodwill (a property right) and freedom of commercial expression under Art 10 of the ECHR and s 12 of the HRA 1998, the court granted an injunction to restrain the use of 'Mr Miss World', stating:[92]

'Absent a sign which is really telling a political story, making a political point or identifying some matter of public importance, I find the idea that use of a trade mark can of itself generally engage Art.10 of the Convention difficult.'

---

[86]   Eg *Ashdown v Telegraph Group* Ltd [2001] EWCA Civ 1142; [2002] Ch 149; [2001] 3 WLR 1368; [2001] 4 All ER 666; [2002] ECC 19; [2002] ECDR 32; [2001] EMLR 44; [2001] HRLR 57; [2001] UKHRR 1242; [2002] RPC 5.

[87]   See, generally, PLC Torremans (ed) *Intellectual Property and Human Rights* (Wolters Kluwer, 2008) and especially Part III 'Trade Marks, Related Rights and Human Rights', comprising: J Griffiths 'Is There a Right to an Immoral Trade Mark?' (ch 12); A Rahmatian 'Trade marks and Human Rights' (ch 13); C Ng 'Some Cultural Narrative Themes and Variations in the Common Law' (ch 14); and D Ganjee 'Geographical Indications and Human Rights' (ch 15).

[88]   *Cream Holdings v Banerjee* [2005] 1 AC 253.

[89]   But see CR Munro 'The value of commercial speech' [2003] CLJ 134.

[90]   For cases elsewhere, see R Burrell and D Gangjee 'Trade marks and freedom of expression – a call for caution' [2010] IIC 544.

[91]   [2007] EWHC 982 (Pat); [2007] ETMR 66; [2007] FSR 30.

[92]   At [47].

Chapter 5

REGISTRATION

THE CRITERIA

5.1 This chapter considers the substantive and procedural[1] criteria for registration of a mark in the UK under the Trade Marks Act 1994 ('the 1994 Act') and its source, the Trade Marks Harmonisation Directive now codified as 2008/95/EC ('the Directive'), The same substantive criteria apply to registration of marks on the Community Register at the Office for Harmonisation in the Internal Market (OHIM) under the Community Trade Mark Regulation, now codified as Regulation (EC) 207/2009 ('the Regulation'). However, different procedural arrangements apply at OHIM and these are described in Chapter 14. Tables of equivalent provisions of the 1994 Act, the Directive and the Regulation are given at **2.1** above and **5.38** below. Parallel provisions are given a uniform interpretation.[2] Very often the UK courts and Registry will refer directly to the provisions of the Directive. Marks may also be protected in the UK or EU by way of an international application under the Madrid Protocol (Chapter 16). Although these marks are recorded on the International Register, the national or regional criteria for protection and scope of rights apply, as well as procedures for opposition and cancellation.[3]

To obtain registration, the following must be present:

(a) a registrable mark; this in turn presupposes a sign,[4] which:

   (i)   can function as a trade mark;[5]
   (ii) is capable of distinguishing the proprietor's goods or services from others';[6]

---

[1] The website of the UK Intellectual Property (IP) Office has a wealth of information, including links to the texts of legislation, its Manual of Trade Mark Practice ('Work Manual') practice notices, forms, guidance notes on the forms, information on fees, search facilities, information on decided cases of the Registry and Appointed Person (see **5.67**) and so forth: www.ipo.gov.uk/pro-types/pro-tm.htm.

[2] See further, *Zino Davidoff SA v A & G Imports Ltd* (Joined Cases C-414 to 416/99) [2002] Ch 109, 144, paras 41 and 42; *Adam Opel AG v Autec AG (Deutscher Verband der Spielwaren-Industrie eV intervening)* (Case C-48/05) [2007] ECR I-1017; *Hasbro v Nahrmittel* at [195].

[3] The 1994 Act and the Trade Mark Rules 2008 are modified for the purposes of these international registrations by the Trade Marks (International Registration) Order 2008, SI 2008/2206, which came into force on 1 October 2008.

[4] See Trade Marks Act 1994, s 1(1); **2.1–2.8**.

[5] See Chapter 1; cf *Smith Kline & French Laboratories Ltd's Cimetidine TM* [1991] RPC 17.

[6] See **2.31–2.43**.

(iii)   can be represented graphically;[7] and

(iv)   is not prohibited from registration on absolute grounds,[8] nor on relative grounds;[9]

(b)   an applicant with an address for service in the UK;[10]

(c)   who uses the mark or has a bona fide intention to do so,[11] in relation to,

(d)   stated goods and services,[12] in a specified class or classes, for which,

(e)   a request for registration is made to the Registrar,[13]

(f)   together with payment of fees.[14]

A representation[15] of the mark must be attached to the relevant box on form TM3, which is sent or delivered to the IP Office.[16] The Registry publishes very helpful guidance 'How to Apply' which is available[17] from the website, as is the

---

[7]   See **2.25–2.30**.

[8]   Trade Marks Act 1994, s 3; see **2.31–2.43** (non-distinctive, descriptive, deceptive and generic marks); **2.14–2.19** (certain shapes); **2.44** (contrary to public policy and morality, prohibited by law); **2.43** (specially protected emblems); **9.10** (bad faith).

[9]   Trade Marks Act 1994, s 5; see **2.41–2.43** (general), **5.40–5.46** (relative grounds, comparison of marks and products).

[10]   Trade Marks Act 1994, s 32(2)(b) and Trade Mark Rules 2008, r 11. Failure to provide an address for service may result in the application being treated as withdrawn: r 12(4), although the Registrar will first of all give notice for the defect to be put right: r 12(1), if there is sufficient information to contact the applicant. According to *Moviestar Trade Mark* [2005] RPC 26 (App Person) a document sent to the address for service it is not deemed to have been received.

[11]   Section 32(3). If the stated intention is not bona fide, the application may be treated as made in bad faith, and may be refused, opposed or cancelled. See s 3(6), *Ferrero SpA's Trade Marks* [2004] RPC 29; *Laboratoires Goemar SA v La Mer Technology Inc* [2005] EWCA Civ 978 cf *REEF TM* [2002] RPC 19 Ch D and Chapter 9. In *Tesco Stores Ltd's Trade Mark Applications* [2005] RPC 17 it was assumed that the intended use should be for distinguishing goods or services. In *Internetportal und Marketing GmbH v Schlicht* (C-569/08) [2010] ETMR 48, trade mark registrations in the format &R&E&I&F&E&N& made for the purposes of advantage in securing internet domain names, with no intention to use as trade marks, were deemed to evidence bad faith under the domain name legislation. See, also Work Manual, ch 2.

[12]   Section 32(2)(c).

[13]   Section 32(1) and (2)(a). The request is made on form TM3 or its electronic version form e-TM3.

[14]   Rule 4. Fees may accompany the application or be deducted from a deposit account with the Registry. Fees are set by statutory instrument, currently the Trade Marks (Fees) Rules 2008, SI 2008/1958, as amended by SI 2009/2089. Applicants may take advantage of the 'Right Start' examination service, whereby the applicant pays half the filing fee and then the balance only after receiving the examination report if it is favourable. Electronic filing generally for the standard service entitles the applicant to £30 off the standard £200 fee. See UKIPO website under trade marks 'How to apply' at www.ipo.gov.uk/types/tm/t-applying/t-apply.htm.

[15]   Section 32(2)(d); although the box is small (8cm x 8cm), it appears that the Registry will accept representations of up to A4 size: form TM3, guidance note to section 2. See, further, **2.25–2.27** (register) and Work Manual, ch 1, paras 4.3–4.5.

[16]   Rule 5(1). The application may be filed using the electronic filing system on the IP Office web.

[17]   www.ipo.gov.uk/types/tm/t-applying/t-apply.htm.

Registry's own *Manual of Trade Mark Practice* ('Work Manual'), ch 1 'New Applications'.[18] An applicant does not have to show a proprietary interest.[19] However, the Registry may need to inquire whether the applicant is capable of owning property in its own name (an individual or company but not an unincorporated association). Probably in many cases the Registry does not question the nature and status of an applicant; it cannot be assumed that an entity listed as proprietor necessarily has legal capacity or the standing to own property. This problem is likely to increase where applications are made without engaging a trade mark attorney. However, the 1994 Act and the Rules do not require standing to appy, any person may do so provided they can declare the requisite intention to use. In a case of urgency, application may be made electronically, on form e-TM3, for expedited examination, whereby the Registrar will give notice within 10 days whether or not the requirements for registration are met.[20]

Classification of goods and services

5.2 For trade registration purposes, goods and services are classified according to the Nice system;[21] classes 1–34 comprise every imaginable variety of goods, whilst classes 35–45 are for services.[22] The classes are particularly useful for search purposes. Allocation of goods or services to a particular class is a matter ultimately for the Registrar.[23] It usually has no significance as far as infringement or other rights are concerned, although where similar products are listed in different classes, the class may be relevant, even if the specification is not limited by reference to class.[24] Under the 1994 Act, a single application is possible for registration of a mark in a number of classes,[25] subject to payment of fees for each additional class. Chapter 2 of the Work Manual[26] is devoted to classification.

---

[18] www.ipo.gov.uk/tmmanual-chap1-newapp.pdf.

[19] *AL BASSAM Trade Mark* [1994] RPC 315 Ch D; *AL BASSAM Trade Mark* [1995] RPC 511 CA. Special rules apply to the identification of partnerships: Work Manual, ch 1, section 5 'The applicant'.

[20] Rule 5(2)-(6).

[21] Rule 7; this was agreed at Nice in June 1957, revised in 1967 and 1977 and amended in 1979. As at June 2011, 83 states had signed the Nice Agreement, but the classification is used by trade mark registries in many other states. It is in its 9th edition, of which version 2.4 was available as from September 2010. The version in force at the date of application to register is used. At the date of commencement of the 1994 Act, some venerable registrations were classified according to an earlier scheme; the Registrar was empowered by s 65 of the 1994 Act to reclassify these. However, reclassified registrations will be interpreted in the light of the earlier practice: *Avnet Incorporated v Isoact Ltd* [1998] FSR 16.

[22] Which may be consulted on the website of the World Intellectual Property Organization using the link at www.wipo.int/classifications/nivilo/.

[23] Section 34(2).

[24] *Altecnic Ltd's Application* [2002] RPC 34. *Daimler AG v Sany Group Co Ltd* [2009] EWHC 1003 (Ch); [2009] ETMR 58 comments on different practice of OHIM and UK as regards class headings.

[25] Rule 8. Additional classes may be added using form TM3A while a mark is in the application stage.

[26] Chapter 2 can be consulted online at www.ipo.gov.uk/tmmanual-chap2-classi.pdf.

5.3   Rule 8(2)[27] of the Trade Mark Rules 2008 requires that every application to register a UK trade mark shall specify the classes to which it relates; and the goods or services which are appropriate to the class, describing them so as to indicate clearly their nature and to allow them to be classified. In *Minerva TM*[28] Jacob J had described the problems caused to registries and to competitors when an applicants 'specification' of goods or services is too broad or obscure. If these requirements are not met, the Registrar can give the applicant at least one month's notice to put the application right, failing which it is deemed to have been abandoned.[29] Where an application has listed goods or services in the wrong class, they may be moved, the application being amended to include the appropriate class where necessary.[30] There is a general prohibition on broadening specifications post-filing.[31] Form TM3A can only be used whilst the original application is pending. However, the applicant can file a fresh application to cover 'missing' classes of good or service.

Specially protected emblems

5.4   Where the mark consists of or contains an emblem specially protected by s 4 of the 1994 Act, for example, Royal Arms or the Olympic symbol, the appropriate consent to registration must also be filed.[32]

Defective applications

5.5   If the application is defective, the Registrar will notify the applicant and give at least 14 days for the matter to be put right. The effect of failure to do so depends upon the defect in question.[33] Failure to supply the basic information specified in s 32(2) (request for registration, name and address, statement of goods and services and representation of the mark) means that the application is deemed never to have been made.[34] If the default relates to address for service, the application is deemed withdrawn.[35] Where the default is in the statement of use or of intention to use, identification of products or payment of application or class fees, the application is treated as abandoned. The difference is significant in that the abandoned mark will appear on a computer search and deter other applicants, whereas a void application will not.

---

[27]   As amended by the Trade Marks (Amendment) Rules 2004.

[28]   [2000] FSR 734 Ch D; see D Wilkinson 'Broad Trade Mark Specifications' [2002] EIPR 227; Work Manual, ch 2, para 3.5 'Need for clarity in specifications' citing *Postkantoor* (C-363/99).

[29]   Rule 9.

[30]   Rule 9, form TM3A.

[31]   Section 39(2). See Work Manual, ch 2, at para 3.11.

[32]   Rule 10. Sections 57 and 59 also prohibit the registration of the emblems of Convention countries and international organisations unless authorisation is given or unnecessary. Work Manual, ch 3, has much useful detail on this kind of symbol under the heading 'Protected Words and Other Signs', as updated by Practice Amendment Notice PAN1/10 – Examination practice in relation to Protected Symbols, available at www.ipo.gov.uk/pro-types/pro-tm/t-law/t-pan/t-pan-110.htm in the light of *American Clothing Associates SA v OHIM* [2010] ETMR 3.

[33]   Trade Mark Rules 2008, r 13.

[34]   Rule 13(3)(a).

[35]   Rule 12(4).

Filing date

5.6   If and when all the requirements are satisfied, the application will be given a filing date[36] – the date upon which the application became complete. If the mark proceeds to registration, it will be deemed to have been registered as of the filing date,[37] so that infringement rights will be retrospective.

THE PROCESS

5.7   Applications and examination are in English. The Registrar may require translation of any document or part document which is not in English.[38] This presumably also applies where the mark itself appears to be in a foreign language or script. The Registry will then have regard to the meaning of the mark when assessing its registrability.[39] The Registry may also use the internet to investigate foreign descriptive use, especially in fast moving fields, although the Registry traditionally uses dictionaries and other reliable publications.[40]

5.8   Assuming that all the paperwork is formally in order, it remains for the Registry to examine[41] whether the application satisfies the substantive requirements of the 1994 Act. In *Eurolamb*[42] it was held that this process does not involve a presumption of registrability:[43] s 37 is neutral. Although this implies that there is no presumption against registrability either, examination is important to ensure that registered marks do not embarrass honest traders. As expressed in *Cycling is ... TM*:[44]

> 'There is no legal justification for placing traders in jeopardy of proceedings for infringement by registering signs which "are not capable of fulfilling the essential function of a trade mark and so cannot enjoy the protection conferred by registration" (see paragraphs 35 and 36 above). It is also worth noting that a well-founded belief in the unregistrability of a sign which has made its way onto the register appears to provide no defence to liability for unauthorised use of the

---

[36]   Section 33(1).

[37]   Section 40(3).

[38]   Rule 82.

[39]   Work Manual, ch 3 sets out detailed practice on the examination of applications.

[40]   See Work Manual, ch 3, heading 'Internet (Use during examination)'. In *Ruiz-Picasso and Others v OHIM – DaimlerChrysler (PICARO)* Case T-185/02 [2004] ECR II-1739 at [28]–[29] the ECJ indicated that judicial notice of facts might be taken, including information from generally accessible sources.

[41]   Section 37.

[42]   [1997] RPC 279.

[43]   In 'Babydry' – *Procter & Gamble v OHIM* (C383/99 P) [2002] Ch 82 (ECJ) – the ECJ appeared to make such a presumption in relation to a Community trade mark application. However, the principle of availability in the public interest, previously demonstrated in *Windsurfing Chiemsee* – Joined cases C-108/97 and 109/97 [1999] ECR I-2779 – appears to have eclipsed the presumption of registrability in later ECJ decisions, such as *Postkantoor* C-363/99 *KPN Nederland NV v Benelux-Merkenbureau* [2004] ETMR 57, *Libertel* C-104/01 and *Linde, Winward, Rado/DPMA* C-53/01, C-54/01, C-55/01. See, Turner-Kerr 'Trade Mark Tangles: Recent twists and turns in EC trade mark law' [2004] EL Rev 345.

[44]   [2002] RPC 37 (G Hobbs QC, Appointed Person) at para 42.

registered trade mark in criminal proceedings under section 92 of the 1994 Act: *R v Keane* [2001] F.S.R. 7, CA. The whole point of examining applications for registration under Article 3/section 3 is to screen them for compliance with the statutory requirements for protection. I remain of the view that it is not Article 6(1)/section 11(2) or any other saving provision, but the requirement for signs to be free of objection under Article 3/section 3 which should be seen as the first line of protection for the legitimate interests of other traders.'

At present the UK examination process involves assessing the mark on 'absolute grounds' under s 3 and searching for conflicting earlier marks.[45] Since the coming into force of the Trade Marks (Relative Grounds) Order 2007[46] the Registry no longer examines on 'relative grounds'[47] for conflict with prior rights under s 5. Results of searches are notified to the applicant and, where it appears that relative grounds may exist, any 'relevant proprietor' of an earlier mark.[48] The latter may subsequently file opposition.[49] Once the Registry is satisfied that the mark should be accepted for registration, it publishes the mark and takes into account any observations from third parties. If an objector files formal opposition proceedings, these will be determined. If the mark survives these steps in relation to all or some[50] of the goods or services for which registration is sought, it will be entered on the register. The ways in which the application may proceed are mapped out in Figure 5.1 below.

5.9   What appear to be obstacles to the applicant are safeguards for the public[51] and for honest traders. However, the UK Trade Mark Registry does not do its work in isolation. Rights over a mark in the UK may be secured by way of a Community trade mark registration.[52] This influences UK Registry practice in two ways, first, through the formal equivalence of the substantive provisions of the Regulation and Directive. More subtle is the futility of maintaining and financing rigorous examination in the UK if trade mark proprietors can obtain wider rights more easily via a Community trade mark

---

[45]   The definition of 'earlier trade mark', noted below at **5.31–5.37**, means that these conflicting marks may be on the UK register, the Community register or the International register. Because similar goods and services can appear in different Nice classes, the Registry not only searches for identical or similar marks in the class or classes to which the application relates, but also does a 'cross-search' into other classes. See 'Search list' at http://www.ipo.gov.uk/t-class-cross-list.htm n August 2009 the Registry ceased its former practice of searching the registers of coats of arms for the purposes of s 4(4) and r 10: Work Manual, Ch 3, heading 'Armorial bearings, heraldic devices and coats of arms'.

[46]   SI 2007/1976, in force from 1 October 2007 in relation to applications published on or after that date: Art 5. Art 4 provides for search and notification, Art 3 having removed the effect of s 37(2) of the Act. Art 2 ensures that the Registrar refuses marks on relative grounds only in opposition proceedings.

[47]   Ie relative to any conflicting earlier marks.

[48]   Rule 14. Proprietors of UK trade marks may opt out of notification; proprietors of Community marks may opt in for a 3-year period, using form TM6.

[49]   See **5.63ff.**

[50]   See Practice Notice 2/2006 (trade marks): Partial Refusals.

[51]   J Davis 'To Protect Or Serve? European Trade Mark Law and the Decline of the Public Interest' [2003] EIPR 180.

[52]   See Chapter 14. Rights may also be secured by an international designation under the Madrid Protocol, see Chapter 16, but the Protocol allows for rejection and opposition.

Figure 5.1: Process of registration

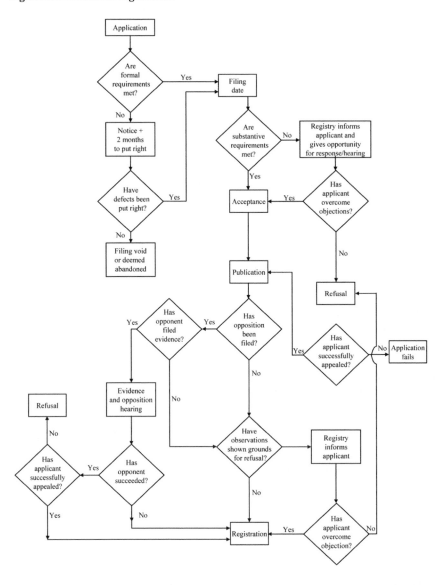

registration. Relative examination was abolished[53] in 2007, the opposition system having been overhauled in 2004.[54] At present the Office for Harmonisation in the Internal Market (OHIM) conducts a search[55] but does

---

53   Section 8 of the 1994 Act contained enabling powers to abolish relative examination, leaving it to proprietors of earlier rights to resist conflicting applications by way of opposition proceedings. This was achieved by the the Trade Marks (Relative Grounds) Order 2007, SI 2007/1976, n 46 above.

54   By the Trade Marks (Amendment) Rules 2004, SI 2004/947, now repealed and replaced by the Trade Mark Rules 2008, SI 2008/1797.

55   For proposals to abandon this and the compromise reached, see Commission 'Report on the

not examine Community trade mark applications 'ex-officio' on relative grounds. User organisations are said to be in favour of retention of the system of search and opposition prior to registration.[56] Some but not all EU member states search their own registers pursuant to a Community trade mark application.

THE OBSTACLES

5.10 In the course of examination, the Registry may raise or adjudicate objections to registrability at various stages. These may be inherent in the mark itself, as applied to the product in question (absolute grounds for non-registration), or based on extrinsic factors, in particular conflict with earlier marks (relative grounds). Relative grounds are considered at **5.38** onwards. In the case of absolute grounds, the Registrar may argue that the alleged sign is descriptive, geographical, misleading or otherwise fails to satisfy the 1994 Act.[57] When the Registry raises an objection, it will notify the applicant in writing and give an opportunity for the applicant to respond. This can be done informally, by correspondence. The applicant may also request an oral hearing, by telephone (the default) or face to face. An appointment with a hearing officer is not held in public[58] and can be quite informal.[59] Hearings may be conducted at the Patent Office in Newport, Wales, or by video-conference link. Hearing accommodation has also been retained in London.[60] The applicant or their agent should consider whether any of the following ways of overcoming obstacles will be needed and prepare accordingly. The Registrar has the power to call for evidence or documents and may do so at the hearing.[61] If the Registrar suspects bad faith,[62] he may call for evidence at an early stage. 'Inter partes' procedures – observations and oppositions – will be considered at **5.63**. We shall next consider what steps an applicant may take to overcome obstacles arising from the Registry's examination – 'ex parte' matters.

---

operation of the system of searches resulting from Article 39 of the Community Trade Mark Regulation' COM(2002) 754 final, available at http://oami.europa.eu/pdf/mark/ec1.pdf.

[56] Max Planck Institute for Intellectual Property and Competition Law Munich 'Study on the Overall Functioning of the European Trade Mark System' February 2001, para 2.34. The study is available at http://ec.europa.eu/internal_market/indprop/docs/tm/20110308_allensbach-study_en.pdf. For arrangements in member states, see para 1.42 ff.

[57] See **2.14–2.18, 2.31–2.44**.

[58] As opposed to an inter partes hearing: r 66.

[59] See Practice Amendment Circular PAC 1/01 'The Conduct of Ex Parte Hearings' at www.ipo.gov.uk/t-pan-101.htm.

[60] See Practice Amendment Notice PAN 02/09 – 'Procedure Governing the Appointment of Ex Parte Hearings', available at www.ipo.gov.uk/pro-types/pro-tm/t-law/t-pan/t-pan-209.htm.

[61] Rule 62.

[62] An absolute ground of refusal: s 3(6); see **9.10**.

OVERCOMING THE OBSTACLES

Argument

5.11 It may be possible to argue that the Registry is mistaken as to fact or law. The law will always be a matter for argument, but unless the Registrar is able to take 'judicial notice' of some factor overlooked, in practice evidence will be needed as to fact.

Evidence of use

5.12 A number of the objections under the absolute grounds[63] of s 3 can be dispelled by evidence of distinctiveness in fact, acquired by use before the application date: proviso to s 3(1).[64] Such evidence may also be used to overcome an objection on the grounds of deceptiveness, if the mark has been used extensively without actually causing deception. The questions arise when, where, to whom, in relation to what, and how distinctiveness may be proved. As to 'when', the proviso to s 3(1) of the 1994 Act states that it must have become distinctive *before* the date of the application to register. Chapter 3 of the Work Manual provides guidance on the evidential requirements.[65] It applies the criteria set forth by the ECJ in *Windsurfing Chiemsee*.[66] Evidence should demonstrate that use has been to distinguish goods and services.[67] The Work Manual recommends that turnover figures be given for a period of about 5 years before the date of application if possible. Evidence of distinctiveness at a point after the date of application may sometimes be relevant on non-deceptiveness or distinctiveness. It may also be possible to argue that distinctiveness acquired after the date of application is evidence of capability to distinguish at the date of application.

5.13 As to 'where', first of all, the mark must have acquired distinctiveness across the UK;[68] local distinctiveness will not suffice. A mark used only outside the UK is unlikely to be registered under the proviso to s 3(1).[69] It is submitted that evidence of distinctiveness in use outside the UK may be relevant to boost local evidence. If it can be shown that a mark has in fact become distinctive outside the UK, this may be persuasive[70] as to capability of distinguishing in this country, but much will depend on linguistic and commercial factors. For this reason, it is unlikely that evidence of foreign use would be persuasive on the issue of deceptiveness.

---

[63] See Chapter 2.
[64] See **2.31**, **2.33** and **2.35**.
[65] Heading 'Evidence of distinctiveness acquired through use'.
[66] C-108 and 109/97, see below.
[67] *Societe des produits Nestle SA v Mars UK Ltd*, Case C-353/03.
[68] *Bovemij Verzekeringen NV v Benelux Merkenbureau*, Case C-108/05; ch 3 of the Work Manual, heading 'Evidence of distinctiveness acquired through use' at point 9 recognises that their relevant public, e g Welsh speakers, may be concentrated in one area, and that failure to show distinctiveness for a small part of the UK will not be fatal to the application.
[69] Chapter 3, of the Work Manual at heading 'Evidence of distinctiveness acquired through use' point 9 states 'if the only use of the mark is outside the UK, the mark cannot be accepted'.
[70] *Henkel KGaA v Deutsches Patent und Markenamt* (C-218/01) [2005] ETMR 45.

5.14   The European Court of Justice (ECJ) addressed the issue of 'to whom' the mark must be distinctive in *Windsurfing Chiemsee*,[71] pointing out that evidence would be relevant as to:

> ' . . . the proportion of the relevant class of persons who, because of the mark, identify goods as originating from a particular undertaking;'

The 'relevant class' of persons depends upon the product's market. For general consumer goods or foodstuffs, it may be the public at large.[72] For others, it may be a very narrow subset.[73] Generally, it will be the average consumer[74] of the goods in question,[75] who is 'reasonably well informed, reasonably observant and circumspect'.

5.15   The best evidence will relate to use of the mark as applied for, in relation to the goods or services in question. However, evidence of use of a similar mark or of use in relation to similar goods or services may be indicative of the distinguishing power of the mark in suit. As pointed out by the Court of Appeal in *Du Pont TM*[76] the relevance of use of the trade mark on other goods depends on the ability to make a sound extrapolation from one type of goods to the other.

5.16   As to 'how', does the evidence have to prove distinctiveness, or will the Registry be prepared to infer distinctiveness from evidence of use? Use is comparatively easy to prove – volume of sales under the mark, advertising, and so forth can be put in evidence.[77] The evidence needs not always be of use of the same sign in isolation. In *'Have a break'*[78] the ECJ held that use of that slogan in conjunction with a trade mark – 'Have a break – have a Kit-Kat' – could lead to the slogan becoming distinctive.[79] But evidence of use is not necessarily conclusive of distinctiveness: the 1994 Act refers to the mark 'having acquired a distinctive character as a result of the use made of it'. Even long use of a sign common to the trade will not necessarily establish

---

[71]   Joined cases C-108/97 and 109/97 [1999] ECR I-2779.

[72]   Eg *Quorn Hunt's Application, Opposition of Marlow Foods Ltd* [2005] ETMR 11 TMR.

[73]   In *Road Tech Computer Systems v Unison Software* [1996] FSR 805, only two of the defendants' 50,000 leaflets had reached the claimant's customers, suggesting very specialised customer bases.

[74]   J Davis 'Locating the Average Consumer: His Judicial Origins, Intellectual Influences and Current Role in European Trade Mark Law' [2005] IPQ 183.

[75]   *Bach and Bach Flower Remedies Trade Marks* [2000] RPC 513 (CA), applying *Windsurfing Chiemsee v Huber* [1999] ECR I-2779, [1999] ETMR 585, ECJ and *Lloyd Schuhfabrik Meyer v Klijsen Handel BV* [1999] ETMR 690, [2000] FSR 77, ECJ.

[76]   [2004] FSR 15 (CA), para 37.

[77]   In *Windsurfing*, the ECJ referred to the market share held by the mark; how intensive, how geographically widespread and long-standing use of the mark has been and the amount invested by the undertaking in promoting the mark as relevant indicators of use.

[78]   *Société des Produits Nestlé SA v Mars UK Ltd* (C-353/03) [2005] 3 CMLR 12, [2005] ETMR 96.

[79]   Contrary to the original finding of the UK Registry and the decision of the referring court at *Nestlé SA's Trade Mark Application (Have a break)* [2004] FSR 2, [2003] ETMR 101 (CA).

distinctiveness.[80] And even evidence of recognition may not be wholly conclusive, especially if the product is unique.[81]

5.17 If evidence of distinctiveness is required, how may it be obtained? The UK courts have been hostile to market survey evidence in infringement actions, even where the survey has been properly conducted.[82] The courts have developed a practice of scrutinising the scope or methodology of any proposed consumer surveys at case management conference.[83] In the '*Raffles*' case[84] Whitford J gave guidance on what constituted the elements of a good survey:

(a)   representative sample;[85]

(b)   statistically significant size;

(c)   fair conduct;

(d)   disclosure of all surveys and responses;[86]

(e)   no leading questions;[87]

(f)   recording of exact answers;

(g)   disclosure of instructions to interviewers; and

(h)   disclosure of coding instructions where computer analysis is used.

The UK Trade Marks Registry suggest including fictitious marks in the survey to act as a 'control'.[88]

---

[80]   *Imperial Group v Philip Morris* [1984] RPC 293.

[81]   *Dualit* [1999] RPC 890.

[82]   See, further, Chapter 9. For an account of survey evidence in infringement cases, see G Lea 'Masters of all they Survey? Some Thoughts upon Official Attitudes to Market Survey Evidence in U.K. Trade Mark Practice' [1999] IPQ 191.

[83]   See,eg, e*sure Insurance v Direct Line Insurance* [2008] RPC 34 per Arden LJ, because 'consumer surveys are costly to produce. They can, moreover, sometimes be based on the wrong questions and thus produce irrelevant or unhelpful responses or for some other reason, as in this case, be of no evidential value'. At 82 she commented that the Registry should also exclude unnecessary expert evidence on confusion.

[84]   *Imperial Group v Philip Morris* [1984] RPC 294.

[85]   Of the relevant public, see Work Manual, ch 3, heading 'Evidence from the trade or from a survey', point 5.

[86]   Which should not disclose the applicant's identity in a questionnaire or covering letter: Work Manual, ch 3, heading 'Evidence from the trade or from a survey', point 5.

[87]   On the design of survey questions to measure whether distinctiveness has been attained, see V Palladino 'Surveying Secondary Meaning' (1994) 84 TMR 1.55.

[88]   Work Manual, ch 3, heading 'Evidence from the trade or from a survey', point 7.

5.18 Although resistant to survey evidence, the UK courts may not be sympathetic to gathering hordes of 'typical consumers' as witnesses either, as Morritt LJ observed in *Bach*:[89]

> 'I do not think the court is assisted by repetitious evidence from individuals put forward by the parties, whether expressly or not, as archetypal average consumers or end-users for, by definition, no one individual is such a consumer or end user and the issue cannot be resolved by counting heads. We were told that the judges before whom cases of this sort are heard have increasingly imposed restrictions on the quantity of such evidence they are prepared to admit. In my view that practice is to be encouraged.'

5.19 The court has pointed out[90] that evidence as to manner of sale or supply, and the circumstances in which confusion may arise, are helpful. Surveys may elicit this kind of information quite effectively, as may evidence from traders. The Registry has traditionally been more receptive of survey evidence, provided of course that the survey is properly carried out.[91] Survey evidence has been much used by Trade Mark Registries in continental Europe.[92] However, 'number-crunching' exercises may be futile. As was pointed out in *Audi v OHIM*[93] there is no set proportion, because the test of distinctiveness cannot be satisfied solely by reference to general, abstract data.

5.20 In providing evidence of use, an applicant needs to consider whether any information is confidential. In principle, all documents filed will be open to public inspection once the relevant stage of the procedure has been completed.[94] The rules permit an applicant to request and the Registrar to rule that a document or part of a document is confidential.[95] Because of the presumption of public access, this power will be used sparingly.[96] It is preferable to prepare evidence in such a way that confidential detail need not be disclosed.

Other evidence

5.21 Other evidence relates to the way in which services or goods are marketed, used, ordered[97] or approved, the character of a geographical location and the likelihood of honest traders there being embarrassed by registration of a geographical mark, and so forth.

---

[89]   Obiter [2000] RPC 513.
[90]   *Dalgety Spillers Foods v Food Brokers* [1994] FSR 504; cf *United Biscuits v Burtons Biscuits (Jaffa Cakes)* [1992] FSR 14.
[91]   See Work Manual, ch 3, heading 'Evidence from the trade or from a survey'.
[92]   See, eg A Kur 'Well-known marks, highly renowned marks and marks having a (high) reputation – what's it all about?' (1992) 23 IIC 218.
[93]   [2004] ETMR 59 CFI.
[94]   Section 67 and rr 56–59.
[95]   Rule 59.
[96]   Work Manual, ch 3, heading 'Confidentiality', point 2 'Handling of requests for confidentiality'.
[97]   Eg doctors are notorious for their bad handwriting on prescriptions.

Invoking an earlier registration

5.22   Where the same or a similar mark is already registered in the name of the applicant, he may wish to rely upon it in support of a later application. This tactic may backfire; the Registry has been known to comment darkly that the earlier registration might be invalid.[98] Usually, the earlier registration is irrelevant.[99] However, if distinctiveness of the earlier mark has been established, this may be relied upon in the later application to register the whole or part of the sign.[100] If a new mark is an equally distinctive variant of an earlier registration, it can help. Thus, a registration of 'Opx' might suggest the distinctiveness of 'Opk' but not 'Opt'. In fact, it is possible to register up to six variants on a basic theme as a series of marks, all in the same application or registration.[101] For example, a mark may be accompanied by model numbers; all being registrable as a series. Thus, 'Cyclops 10', 'Cyclops 20', 'Cyclops 30'. Series registration seems to be peculiar to the UK, Ireland and some Commonwealth jurisdictions. It gives the national route to registration an attractive edge over the competing Community trade mark[102] and international (Madrid)[103] options.

5.23   The Registry recognises that a trader may wish to extend the range of services or goods supplied under the mark. In *Esso*[104] the application for registration of the Esso[105] roundel for tyres was allowed in the light of existing registrations for lubricants and fuels. Tyres were fairly closely allied to the pre-existing fields of activity. However, registration was refused for parts and fittings for land and water vehicles. Since registration now gives protection for goods and services other than those for which the mark is registered,[106] only limited generalisations will be allowed, such as 'footwear' rather than 'shoes'.

5.24   Where the objection is based on deceptiveness or public morality rather than distinctiveness, an earlier registration of the same mark will undoubtedly assist, especially if reinforced by evidence of lack of confusion or offence.

5.25   Under the Trade Marks Act 1938 ('the 1938 Act') a different established mark could be used to support an application. This was because amendment of a mark was possible during prosecution of the application. If a mark was likely

---

[98]   Eg *Avon* [1985] RPC 43 at p 48 where an earlier registration had been obtained after creation of the County of Avon. And see *Agencja Wydawnicza Technopol sp. z o.o. v Office for Harmonisation in the Internal Market (Trade Marks and Designs) (OHIM)* Case C-51/10 P where others' previous number registrations did not assist the applicant for '1000'.

[99]   *British Sugar v Robertson* [1996] RPC 281.

[100]   Work Manual, ch 3, heading 'Evidence of distinctiveness acquired through use'.

[101]   Section 41(1)(c) and r 28; form TM12. The Trade Marks and Trade Marks and Patents (Fees) (Amendment) Rules 2009, SI 2009/2089 limited the number in a series to six.

[102]   See Chapter 14 (Community trade mark).

[103]   See Chapter 16 (international registrations).

[104]   [1972] RPC 283.

[105]   The problem with the mark was, of course, the phonetic equivalent of 'Esso' to the two letters 'SO'. For success with a similar mark from the same stable, see *Exxate* [1986] RPC 567 (equivalent to X8).

[106]   See **5.30ff** (conflicting marks) and Chapter 7 (infringement).

to be rejected due to lack of distinctiveness, it could sometimes be helped on to the register by adding an established sister or house mark. Thus, if Volkswagen were having difficulty in registering a model name, such as 'Golf' or 'Polo', it could amend the mark to 'Volkswagen Golf' or 'Volkswagen Polo'. This practice was sometimes known as 'adding an equity'. The tactic is not possible for 1994 Act applications, however, since the scope for amending marks is now very restricted.[107] To change the mark significantly, for instance, to express a descriptive work in a distinctive style, it is necessary to re-file. Registration of a composite mark does not always help its elements to get on the register at a later stage. For example, in *Cos TM*, the prior registration of 'Cos D'Estournel' did not overcome geographical objection to registration of 'Cos'.[108] Nor will prior registration of an element necessarily assist a later application to register a composite mark. For example, if 'Shake' is registered for hair products, the registry may still refuse 'Rinse & shake'.

Amending the specification of goods or services

5.26   An applicant can amend the specification of goods or services available under s 39(1) to restrict the goods or services covered by the application.[109] An objection may relate only to some of the goods or services concerned, which can be deleted. Since registration now confers infringement rights beyond the products for which the mark is actually registered, the usefulness of this practice is limited.[110] From the applicant's point of view, the usefulness of this tactic depends upon the range of products remaining.

Division or merger of the application

5.27   Division of the application is less drastic than removing or excluding goods or services altogether. Instead, an application may be split[111] so that it may proceed swiftly to registration for the trouble-free goods or services, and the troublesome part of the application may be dealt with separately. The opposite, merger[112] of applications (or indeed registrations), is also possible.[113] Where objections or disputes are anticipated, it may be wise to file separate applications on the same date. If and when the problems are overcome, merger can be sought. Once marks are registered, they can be merged even if their

---

[107]   Section 39(2) permits amendment only when it does not substantially affect the mark's identity, and then only in respect of corrections to name, address or obvious errors of wording or other obvious mistakes. The representation of a mark may be amended under s 39(3). For practice on amendment, see rr 24 and 25 which provide for publication of the amendment and receipt of objections.

[108]   Eg in *Cos TM* [1993] RPC 67, the prior registration of 'Cos D'Estournel' did not overcome geographical objection to registration of 'Cos'; but see *'Have a break'* [2005] ETMR 96.

[109]   See, eg *Pan World Brands Ltd v Tripp Ltd (Extreme Trade Mark)* [2008] RPC 2.

[110]   See, eg *Quorn Hunt's Application, Opposition of Marlow Foods Ltd* [2005] ETMR 11 TMR.

[111]   Section 41(1)(a); r 26.

[112]   Section 41(1)(b); r 27.

[113]   Care must be exerted where the UK registration is used as the basis for an overseas registration, eg not all overseas registries will accept a merged 'mother' registration.

filing dates are different. The merged registration bears the date of registration of the latest component, and is subject to any disclaimer, limitation or licence affecting the component registrations.

Disclaimers and conditions

5.28 Former Registry practice was to impose conditions or a disclaimer on the registration of a doubtful mark. An example was the blank space condition, whereby registration was conditional upon the use only of non-trade mark matter in any blank space. Breach of condition was a ground for cancellation or variation of the registration. The 1994 Act makes no provision for conditions; upon commencement, all conditions ceased to have effect.[114] Disclaimers have often been used where a composite mark was made up of non-distinctive elements. The classic example was *Diamond T*,[115] where the device of a 'T' in a diamond was registered but the applicant had to disclaim exclusive rights under the registration in the diamond or 'T' individually. Voluntary disclaimers are still possible,[116] although it seems unlikely that an applicant would voluntarily disclaim exclusive rights in part of a mark without pressure from the Registry or an opponent, or a prior agreement with a third party to do so. Rights are restricted in accordance with the disclaimer.[117] It was argued in *Phones 4u*[118] that s 13 is a non-permissible derogation from the Directive.[119] The court held, obiter, that this was unlikely, as it would result in identical infringement provisions having different meanings in the Directive and the Regulation. A mark can be made subject to disclaimer after registration, for example, in settlement of a dispute.

Limitations

5.29 A registration may be limited, territorially or otherwise,[120] if requested by the applicant. The registration could be limited to goods for export only. Service marks are more amenable than trade marks for goods to limitation to a particular locality. *Croom's TM*[121] and *Postkantoor*[122] demonstrate that the mark cannot be limited by excluding goods of certain characteristics, such as 'haute couture' clothing. Again, a limitation may be entered after registration.

---

[114] Schedule 3, para 3 of the 1994 Act.
[115] [1921] 2 Ch 583; 38 RPC 373.
[116] Section 13(1)(a); r 2431.
[117] Section 13(1).
[118] *Phones 4u Ltd v Phone4u.co.uk Internet Ltd* [2006] EWCA Civ 244; [2007] RPC 5 at [73]–[74]. It was suggested that a disclaimer could be regarded as 'unconditional binding acceptance by the proprietor that, notwithstanding the rights conferred by the infringement provisions, he cannot assert rights in breach of the condition or outside the limitation', citing *Nestlé SA's Trade Mark Application* [2005] RPC 5 at [33].
[119] The directive does not have a provision on disclaimers, unlike Art 38 of the Regulation.
[120] Section 13(1)(b); r 31.
[121] [2005] RPC 2 (App Person).
[122] C-363/99 *Koninklijke KPN Nederland NV v Benelux-Merkenbureau* [2004] ETMR 57.

CONFLICT WITH EARLIER MARKS

5.30 This involves:

(a) a time dimension, to determine which marks are earlier or have 'priority' over the application;

(b) rules as to which prior marks or other rights are taken into account;

(c) rules for comparison of marks and products to determine whether the conflict will prevent registration; and

(d) strategies for overcoming such conflict.

'Earlier trade mark' and the right of priority

5.31 The timing question is subject to the right of priority established by Art 4 of the Paris Convention on the protection of industrial property.[123] This gives a period of 6 months during which an international trade mark filing programme can be pursued country by country. Once a valid application has been filed in the applicant's 'home' country, it is given a 'priority date'. When applications are filed in other members of the Paris Union,[124] provided they are filed within the 6 months' 'priority interval', they will be assessed for conflict with earlier rights as at the priority date and not at the date when filing was actually effected. Section 35 of the 1994 Act gives effect to this system in the UK by allowing an applicant to claim priority from the earliest application made in a Paris Convention country,[125] provided the priority date does not predate the UK application by more than 6 months.[126] The significance of a priority claim is that the mark is vulnerable only to applications or registrations made before the 'priority date'. Nor is the application affected by any use of the mark in the UK between the two dates. Thus, a priority claim is advantageous to an applicant where the use is by a third party but it means that use by the proprietor during the interim period cannot affect registrability. This may be disadvantageous where the applicant needs evidence of use to support the application.[127] If it is sought to rely on a Convention priority, particulars must be given on the application form. If requested, additional documents must be filed; these do not need to be provided as a matter of course.[128] Provided the UK application is for the same or a narrower specification of goods or services

---

[123] See Chapter 15 (Paris Convention).

[124] Of countries which have acceded to the Paris Convention. See www.wipo.int/treaties/en/ip/paris/index.html for further information about the Paris Convention and a list of members of the Paris Union, which is updated regularly to take account of new accessions.

[125] Priority for the Channel Islands, colonies and other territories is dealt with in s 36.

[126] In accordance with Paris Convention, Art 4. If the first application has failed without being used for priority, a second application date from the same country may be used: s 35(4).

[127] See **5.15–5.20**.

[128] Sections 35 and 36; r 6; Work Manual, ch 3, heading 'Priority claims – International Convention (I.C.) priority claims', point 1.

as the earlier Convention application, the whole will enjoy the earlier priority date. It is also possible to have one or more partial priority claims within a single application.[129]

Kinds of 'earlier trade mark'

5.32 The 'earlier trade marks' which can block a later application are defined in s 6. First, there are UK registrations and applications with an earlier filing[130] or priority[131] date, similar Community trade mark registrations or applications[132] and UK registrations or applications resulting from a Madrid Protocol filing.[133] Secondly, there are Community trade marks which have a valid claim to 'seniority', from an earlier UK mark or international filing designating the UK. Under Arts 34 and 35 of the Regulation, if the proprietor of a national registration applies for and registers a Community trade mark, he can let the national registration lapse but retain equivalent rights in the state of registration.[134] Lastly, 'earlier trade mark' includes a mark which is entitled to protection as a well-known trade mark under Art 6*bis* of the Paris Convention[135] or under Art 16 of the WTO TRIPs (Trade-Related Aspects of Intellectual Property Rights) Agreement. Protection must be afforded to such marks even where they are not registered. In practice, it is likely that many of the marks which would qualify for this category are already registered in the UK.

5.33 The mark with the earlier priority date will form the basis for opposition to that with the later priority date.[136] However, if the conflicting marks happen to have the same priority date, there may be cross-opposition. If neither mark is opposed, both will proceed to registration in the normal manner.[137]

5.34 The effect of an earlier registration endures for a year after its expiry, unless it can be shown to have been out of use for at least the preceding 2 years.[138] The effect of an application is subject to its maturing into a

---

[129] Paris Convention, Art 4F refers specifically to multiple priorities in the case of patent applications; this special mention is required because of the requirement of unity of invention. It is submitted that Paris envisages multiple priorities generally. Work Manual, ch 3, heading 'Priority claims – International Convention (I.C.) priority claims', point 2 refers.

[130] See **5.6** (filing date).

[131] See **5.31** (priority date); Work Manual, ch 3, heading 'Priority claims – International Convention (I.C.) priority claims'.

[132] See Chapter 14 (Community trade mark). Note that the Community may be designated in an international application under the Madrid system (Chapter 16).

[133] Chapter 16 (Madrid).

[134] The number of such claims remain modest: Max Planck Institute for Intellectual Property and Competition Law Munich 'Study on the Overall Functioning of the European Trade Mark System' February 2001, para 4.80.

[135] See, further, **7.32–7.34** (ss 56 and 57 of the 1994 Act) and **12.29–12.36** (well-known trade marks).

[136] Section 6(2).

[137] Work Manual, ch 3, heading 'Priority claims' at point 4 'Marks with the same priority/filing date'.

[138] Section 6(3).

registration (s 6(2)). What if the earlier mark is registered but not used? Section 100 states that if any question of use of a registered mark arises in civil proceedings, it is for the proprietor to show what use has been made of the mark. Section 6A[139] puts use in issue in opposition proceedings; where opposition is based upon an earlier mark the opponent is required to file a statement of use, unless it can be shown to be well known.[140]

Examples of potential conflict

5.35 On 31 January 2011, Albert applies to register 'Grit' for men's toiletries. A search reveals the following, all applications or registrations in the name of third parties:

(a)   a UK registration filed on 31 October 2009 of 'Grid' for aftershave;

(b)   Cecilia filed in France to register 'Gritt' for soap. On 28 September 2010 she applied to the International Bureau under the Madrid Protocol, designating the UK;

(c)   a UK application dated 1 March 2010 to register 'Gryt' for toiletries; fees were not paid and the application is deemed abandoned;

(d)   a Community trade mark application filed on 1 February 2011 claiming priority from a Convention filing in Australia on 30 October 2010, 'Gritty' for talcum powder.

All except 'Gryt' are earlier marks within the meaning of s 6; subject to registration, in the case of the applications.

5.36 Where an earlier mark is not registered, a proprietor of goodwill with 'passing-off rights' may prevent the later registration under s 5(4)(a). In *Saxon TM*[141] Laddie J stated that in respect of s 5(4)(a):

'... the question to be asked is whether any normal use by the proprietors or either of them of the mark as registered for any of the goods or services in respect of which it is registered would be liable to be prevented by passing off proceedings brought by any other person.'

---

[139]   Added to the 1994 Act by the Trade Marks (Proof of Use, etc) Regulations 2004, SI 2004/946, in force from 5 May 2004.

[140]   Section 6A as further emended by the Trade Marks (Earlier Trade Marks) Regulations 2008, SI 2008/1067, which also applied the use requirement to Community and international registrations.

[141]   *Saxon Trade Mark* [2003] FSR 39, sub nom *Byford v Oliver* [2003] EMLR 20 Ch D. For a discussion of the partnership aspects of this case, see P Woolf 'Musicians and Their Assets' [2003] Ent LR 90. Note that goodwill may persist even if trade mark registrations are revoked for non-use: *Group Lotus Plc v 1 Malaysia Racing Team SDN BHD* [2011] EWHC 1366 (Ch).

Other 'rules of law' which might be invoked to prevent registration of a later mark include malicious falsehood,[142] the Consumer Protection from Unfair Trading Regulations 2008[143] and the Business Protection from Misleading Marketing Regulations 2008.[144] It is interesting to speculate whether a registration which is proceeding because of consent by the earlier proprietor[145] might nonetheless be blocked on this ground. Earlier rights of copyright, design right or registered designs are catered for in s 5(4)(b).[146] In *Nellie the Elephant*[147] the applicant for invalidity was able to show that their copyright in the song of that name pre-dated the application to register the trade mark, but the challenge to the mark failed because use of the title could not be restrained as an infringement of copyright.

5.37 Section 5 prohibits registration over earlier rights in various circumstances. Section 5(4), considered in the last paragraph, deals with the relative grounds of refusal where the right is not an 'earlier trade mark'. Section 5(4) has its counterparts in passing off, infringement of copyright and so forth. Sections 5(1)–(3) govern the conflict between a trade mark application and earlier trade marks. They have their counterpart in the infringement sections of the 1994 Act, s 10(1)–(3) and their equivalents in the Directive and Regulation. These provisions and the cases decided under them set out the ground rules for comparison of marks and products.

COMPARISON OF MARKS, GOODS AND SERVICES

The 1994 Act, Directive and Regulation

5.38 The 1994 Act, the Directive and the Regulation all share a very attractive feature. The rules for comparing marks and products for the purpose of assessing relative grounds for refusal of registration are identical with the rules for assessing infringement of a registered mark. The equivalent provisions of the three legislative instruments are shown in Table 5.1. A more detailed 'concordance' is given at the end of Arnold J's judgment in *Hasbro Inc v 123 Nahrmittel GmbH*.[148]

---

[142] See **3.24–3.36**.
[143] SI 2008/1277, reg 5 of which prohibits misleading actions in relation to consumers.
[144] SI 2008/1276, reg 3 of which prohibits misleading advertising to traders.
[145] See **5.59**.
[146] Copyright in a pictorial mark was invoked in *Karo Step* [1977] RPC 255 and *Griggs v Evans* [2004] FSR 31, [2005] EWCA Civ 11. For an Australian perspective, see D Lyons 'Copyright in Trade Marks' [1994] 1 EIPR 21.
[147] *Animated Music Ltd's Trade Mark; Request for a Declaration of Invalidity by Dash Music Co Ltd* [2004] ECDR 27 TMR.
[148] [2011] EWHC 199 (Ch); [2011] ETMR 25; [2011] FSR 21.

Table 5.1: Equivalent provisions giving rules of comparison

Legislation	Relative grounds	Infringement
1994 Act	s 5	s 10(1)–(3)
Directive	Art 4	Art 5
Regulation	Art 8	Art 9(1)

5.39   This means that infringement cases, especially where references are made under Art 5 of the Directive or Art 9 of the Regulation to the ECJ, are highly relevant to registration and to cancellation of registered marks. The converse also holds true, especially since the ECJ and the Court of First Instance hear appeals from the OHIM. There is a rich and interchangeable case-law.[149] We shall gather indicative cases together in the following paragraphs. We shall refer primarily to the sections of the 1994 Act, but increasingly the courts and UK Registry refer directly to the articles and recitals of the Directive. Community trade marks are examined and infringed under the Regulation.

COMPARISON OF MARKS AND PRODUCTS UNDER THE 1994 ACT

5.40   The legislation has a hierarchical scheme which is outlined in Table 5.2. First, one considers whether there is identity of signs and of the relevant goods or services as between the mark in suit and the earlier mark or alleged infringement. In this case, s 5(1) or 10(1) applies. If there is incomplete identity, one then considers whether, because of the combination of identity and/or similarity, there exists a likelihood of confusion of the relevant public. If not, there may still be refusal or infringement if the mark has a reputation and certain effects are shown to be likely. In trying to compare signs and products in this way, the courts and registries have generated useful case-law on comparing signs and products.

Table 5.2: Comparisons of relative grounds for refusal (s 5) and infringement (s 10) – relevant subsections of the 1994 Act

Marks/signs	Identical	Similar	Dissimilar	With a reputation
Goods, services				
identical	s 5(1), 10(1)*	s 5(2), 10(2)**	–	s 5(3), 10(3)***

---

[149]   *ARTHUR ET FELICIE LTJ Diffusion SA v Sadas Vertbaudet SA* (C-291/00) [2002] ETMR 40; [2003] FSR 1 shows that equivalent provisions are to be interpreted uniformly.

Marks/signs	Identical	Similar	Dissimi-lar	With a reputation
similar	s 5(2), 10(2)**	s 5(2), 10(2)**	–	s 5(3), 10(3)***
dissimilar	s 5(3), 10(3)***	s 5(3), 10(3)***	–	s 5(3), 10(3)***

* Where signs and products are identical, protection is said to be 'absolute', although a test of effect on the functions of the mark has crept into European jurisprudence.[150]

** Likelihood of confusion to be shown.

*** Additional elements to be shown: reputation of mark, use involves detriment/unfair advantage, lack of due cause.

How to compare marks/signs

5.41 The ECJ gave important guidance on this in *Sabel v Puma*.[151] It was given for the purposes of assessing confusion, because their 'leaping cat' devices were not identical.[152] However, it is submitted that the rule is of general application. The comparison of signs involves a 'global appreciation', comparing them visually, aurally and conceptually from the viewpoint of the average consumer of the type of goods or services in question.[153] That average consumer was said normally to perceive a mark as a whole and not to analyse its various details. The average consumer is deemed to be reasonably well informed, reasonably observant and circumspect but in the marketplace, consumers confronted with one sign would imperfectly recall the other.[154]

---

[150] Originating with *Arsenal Football Club plc v Reed* (C-206/01) [2002] ECR I-10273; [2003] ETMR 19 at [51], found also in *Adam Opel AG v Autec AG* (C-48/05) [2007] ECR I-1017; [2007] ETMR 33 at [18]–[22] and *Céline Sàrl v Céline SA* (C-17/06) [2007] ECR I-7041; [2007] ETMR 80 at [16]. In *L'Oréal SA v eBay International AG* [2009] EWHC 1094 (Ch); [2009] ETMR 53; [2009] RPC 21 at [300]–[306] Arnold J, analysing the cases, expressed the view that this requirement adds nothing to the other tests for infringement under Art 5(1)(a). See, also, Bonita Trimmer 'An increasingly uneasy relationship – the English courts and the European Court of Justice in trade mark disputes' [2008] EIPR 87.

[151] *Sabel BV v Puma AG, Rudolf Dassler Sport* (C-251/95) [1997] ECR I-6191; [1998] 1 CMLR 445; [1998] ETMR 1; [1998] RPC 199.

[152] Applicant Sabel's showed a cheetah whilst opponent Dassler's showed a puma.

[153] The consumer's level of attention is likely to vary according to the category of goods or services in question: Case C-342/97 *Lloyd Schuhfabrik Meyer* [1999] ECR I-3819 at para 26. In considering composite marks, the overall impression on the consumer must be considered: *Medion AG v Thomson Multimedia Sales Germany & Austria GmbH* (C-120/04) [2005] ECR I-8551.

[154] *Lloyd Schuhfabrik Meyer v Klijsen Handel BV* [1999] ECR I-3819; [1999] ETMR 690; [2000] FSR 77, ECJ.

5.42 This did not represent a departure from earlier UK case-law. In *Pianotist*,[155] the following approach to the comparison of word marks was recommended:

> 'You must take the two words. You must judge them, both by their look and by their sound. You must consider the goods to which they are to be applied. You must consider the nature and kind of customer who would be likely to buy those goods. In fact, you must consider all the surrounding circumstances; and you must further consider what is likely to happen if each of those trade marks is used in a normal way as a trade mark for the goods of the respective owners of the marks.'

Although marks are invariably compared side by side by the Registry or court, in reality customers' recollection may be imperfect. Thus, the concept or idea of a mark was recognised as an important factor.[156] Marks should be considered as a whole, although elements common to the trade would be given less weight than other, more distinctive features.[157] The first syllables of words tend to be more prominent than later syllables.

How to compare goods and services

5.43 As far as the comparison of goods or services under s 10 was concerned, Jacob J elaborated an earlier UK case-law[158] in *British Sugar v Robertson*[159] with the following list of relevant factors:

(a) the respective uses of the respective goods or services;

(b) the respective users of the respective goods or services;

(c) the physical nature of the goods or acts of service;

(d) the respective trade channels through which the goods or services reach the market;[160]

(e) in the case of self-serve consumer items, where in practice they are respectively found or likely to be found in supermarkets and in particular whether they are, or are likely to be, found on the same or different shelves; and

(f) the extent to which the respective goods or services are competitive. This inquiry may take into account how those in trade classify goods, for instance, whether market research companies, who of course act for industry, put the goods or services in the same or different sectors.

---

[155] (1906) 23 RPC 774.

[156] Eg the idea of a cat in *Taw v Notek* (1951) 68 RPC 271.

[157] '*Kleenoff*' – *Bale & Church v Sutton* (1934) 51 RPC 129.

[158] *Jellinek's case (Panda)* (1946) 63 RPC 59.

[159] *British Sugar plc v James Robertson & Sons Ltd* [1996] RPC 281.

[160] See, also, *El Corte Inglés v OHIM* (T-443/05) [2007] ECR II-2579; [2007] ETMR 81.

These factors were cited without disapproval in *Canon Kabushiki Kaisha v Metro Goldwyn Mayer Inc.*[161] In that case the French Government had argued that factors to be taken into account should include the nature of the goods or services, their intended destination and clientele, their normal use and the usual manner of their distribution. The ECJ summed up these approaches as including, inter alia, the nature of the goods or services, their end users and their method of use and whether they are in competition with each other or are complementary.[162] For retail services the UK Registry also consider whether it is normal for the kinds of goods to be brought together and whether there is an 'own brand'.[163]

Are these comparisons independent?

5.44 Jacob J in *British Sugar* thought so.[164] However, the ECJ in *Canon Kabushiki Kaisha v Metro Goldwyn Mayer Inc*[165] held that similarity of marks and similarity of products may interact[166] and the fame of the mark could affect the probability of confusion under ss 5(2) and 10(2).[167] In *Ferrero spA v OHIM*[168] the Court of Justice of the European Union (CJEU – formerly the European Court of Justice or ECJ) ruled that the 'reputation of the earlier mark and the similarity between the goods respectively covered by the marks at issue—even if those factors may be taken into consideration in order to assess likelihood of confusion—d[id] not affect the assessment of the similarity of the signs',[169] although in the global assessment of similarity of signs, a low degree of similarity between the marks might be offset by the strong distinctive character of the earlier mark and similarity of products.[170] Likewise, the fact that there was a 'family' of marks was relevant only when one came to assess

---

[161] (C-39/97) [1998] All ER (EC) 934; [1998] ECR I-5507; [1999] 1 CMLR 77; [1999] ETMR 1; [1999] FSR 332; [1999] RPC 117.

[162] See n 161 at para 23. See, also Work Manual, ch 3, heading 'Notification (Section 5: Relative Grounds)', paras 2 and 3.

[163] Work Manual, ch 3, heading 'Retail, wholesale and shopping centre services'.

[164] *British Sugar plc v James Robertson & Sons Ltd* [1996] RPC 281.

[165] (C-39/97) [1998] All ER (EC) 934; [1998] ECR I-5507; [1999] 1 CMLR 77; [1999] ETMR 1; [1999] FSR 332; [1999] RPC 117.

[166] Interaction was contemplated in a somewhat rambling series of preambles to the Directive: 'Whereas the protection applies also in the case of similarity between the mark and the sign and the goods or services; whereas it is indispensable to give an interpretation of the concept of similarity in relation to the likelihood of confusion; whereas the likelihood of confusion, the appreciation of which depends on numerous elements and, in particular, on the recognition of the trade mark in the market, of the association which can be made with the used or registered sign, of the degree of similarity between the trade mark and the sign and between the goods or services identified, constitutes the specific condition for such protection.'

[167] See **5.47–5.50**. The notion of interdependency in the confusion enquiry – a low degree of similarity between products being offset by a high degree of similarity between the marks and vice versa – was said in *Annco Inc v OHIM* (T-385/09) [2011] ETMR 37 to be expressly referred to in recital 8 of the Regulation.

[168] Case (C-552/09) P [2011] ETMR 30, upholding a decision that 'TiMi KINDERJOGHURT' was not similar to KINDER.

[169] At [68].

[170] Canon, n 165 at para 19; *Lloyd Schuhfabrik Meyer v Klijsen Handel BV* [1999] ETMR 690 at para 21.

confusion. The preferable view seems to be that comparisons of signs and of products are conducted separately, but their interdependence and other factors may be considered in gauging the likelihood of confusion.

Identical marks and identical products

5.45 Section 5(1) prohibits the registration over an identical earlier mark for identical goods or services. This prohibition is 'absolute' in the sense that no confusion need be shown, likewise for infringement under s 10(1). In these provisions, does 'identical' mean identical in every respect[171] – visually, aurally and conceptually? In *Arthur et Felicié*[172] the ECJ ruled that 'identical' has to be strictly construed and in a global appreciation. Thus, 'Scarlet Rain' would not be identical to 'Scarlett Reign', nor 'Swallow Hole' by 'Swallow Whole'. Although phonetically identical, the spelling and ideas of these respective marks are different. The application of these criteria can be seen in *Premier Brands UK Ltd v Typhoon Europe Ltd*:[173] visually 'Typhoon' was distinguished somewhat from 'Typhoo' by the final 'n'; aurally the marks were virtually identical, given the English tendency to slur words. Conceptually, however they were distinct, 'Typhoon' being a dictionary word and 'Typhoo' being invented. A very 'global' approach was taken in *Viagra/Viagrene*,[174] the court noting that the defendants adopted not only a closely similar name for its beverage to that of the claimant's impotency pill, but their product echoed the colour and shape of the pills and claimed aphrodisiac effects.

5.46 Given that identity of all three aspects is required, how identical is identical? Again the perception of the average consumer is important. He would be unlikely to spot the difference between 'Origin' and 'Origins' side by side, let alone apart.[175] What account should be taken of any additional matter used by the defendant in conjunction with the mark as registered? Traditionally, UK trade mark law had disregarded additions, at least where they did not swamp the identity of the mark in suit.[176] A similar approach was taken under the 1994 Act in *British Sugar*[177] and *Decon Laboratories v Fred Baker Scientific*.[178] In due course that question of identity came to the attention of the ECJ in *Arthur et Felicié*.[179] Although 'identical' had to be

---

[171] Parliament wished to avoid lawyers 'stumbling' over this point: *Hansard* (House of Lords), vol 552, no 46, col 731 (24 February 1994).

[172] *LTJ Diffusion SA v Sadas Vertbaudet SA* (C-291/00) [2003] ECR I-2799; [2003] ETMR 83; [2003] FSR 34.

[173] [2000] ETMR 1071; [2000] FSR 767. See, also *Hasbro v 123Nahrmittel* [2011] ETMR 25; [2011] FSR 21 (visual difference meant PLAY-DOH and PLAY-DOUGH not identical).

[174] *Pfizer Ltd v Eurofood Link (UK) Ltd* [2001] FSR 3; [2000] ETMR 896.

[175] In *Origins Natural Resources Inc v Origin Clothing Ltd* [1995] FSR 280 the application for summary judgment was in fact granted under s 10(2).

[176] So, eg, 'Ivory' was not too close to 'Ivy': *Goodwin v Ivory Soap* (1901) 18 RPC 389.

[177] *British Sugar plc v James Robertson & Sons Ltd* [1996] RPC 281.

[178] [2001] ETMR 46; [2001] RPC 17: all the defendants' marks were 'Decon' plus suffix. The suffixes referred to the nature and quality of the goods and could not distinguish them from the proprietor's.

[179] *LTJ Diffusion SA v Sadas Vertbaudet SA* (C-291/00) [2003] ECR I-2799; [2003] ETMR 83; [2003] FSR 34.

strictly construed, in view of imperfect recollection insignificant differences between the sign and the trade mark might go unnoticed by an average consumer and so would not affect identity.[180]

Identical or similar marks – identical or similar products

5.47 Sections 5(2) and 10(2) provide that where the mark and sign and/or the respective goods or services of the plaintiff and defendant are not identical but merely similar, infringement is based on the likelihood of confusion on the part of the public, which 'includes the likelihood of association'. Confusion means that the public will think that there is some sort of trade connection between the suppliers of the goods or services in question.[181] As mentioned above, comparison of marks may interact with comparison of products to produce a likelihood of confusion. The distinctiveness or strength of the mark will also be relevant. Figure 5.2 shows the way in which similarity of marks and products may interact for the purposes of s 10(2).

Figure 5.2: Comparison of marks interacts with comparison of products

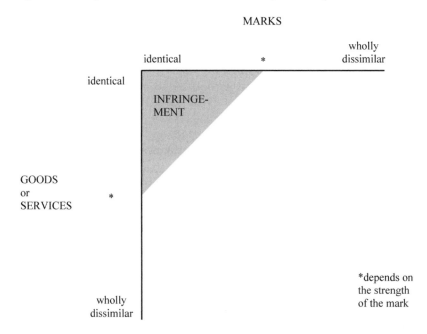

5.48 As mentioned above, the likelihood of confusion must be gauged as to the relevant public – those who are likely to buy or use the goods or services in question are the proper group for which to estimate whether confusion is likely.[182] He is to be regarded as reasonably well informed and reasonably

---

[180] At para 53.
[181] *Canon Kabushiki Kaisha v Metro Goldwyn Mayer Inc* (C-39/97) [1998] All ER (EC) 934 at para 52.
[182] See **5.43**.

observant and circumspect.[183] More metaphysical has been the question of 'likelihood of association': is it merely a factor in establishing confusion, or does it take the arena of conflict beyond mere confusion? Association being a Benelux concept, it is not surprising that resolution came on a reference to the ECJ from that regional trade mark system in *Marca Mode v Adidas*.[184] If association was an alternative to confusion, then for a highly distinctive mark[185] – such that the defendant's use of a similar sign would almost inevitably bring the claimant's to mind – classical confusion need not be shown. The ECJ rejected this approach. The UK Registry's approach to European jurisprudence on the issue of confusion was approved by Arnold J in *Och-Ziff Management Europe Ltd v OCH Capital LLP*[186] and applied in the context of infringement by Floyd J in *Hasbro v 123 Nahrmittel*.[187] In summary:

- confusion assessed globally, taking account of all relevant factors;

- through the eyes of the average consumer (reasonably well informed, circumspect and observant; rarely has chance to make direct comparisons but must rely upon the imperfect recollection; his/her attention varies according to the category of product; normally perceives a mark as a whole);

- visual, aural and conceptual similarities of marks normally assessed by reference to overall impressions; only when all other components of complex mark are negligible is it permissible to make comparison solely on basis of dominant elements;

- nevertheless, overall impression conveyed to relevant public by a composite trade mark may, in certain circumstances, be dominated by one more of its components;

- an element corresponding to an earlier mark may retain an independent distinctive role in a composite mark, without necessarily constituting a dominant element;

- lesser degree of similarity between marks may be offset by greater degree of similarity between goods, and vice versa;

- greater likelihood of confusion where earlier trade mark has a highly distinctive character, either per se or through use;

---

[183] See, also, C-210/96, *Gut Springenheide GmbH v Oberkreisdirektor des Kreises Steinfurt–AMT fur Lebensmitteluberwachung* [1998] ECR I-46577.

[184] *Marca Mode CV v Adidas AG & Adidas Benelux* (C-425/98) [2000] All ER (EC) 694; [2000] ECR I-4861 [2000] 2 CMLR 1061; [2000] ETMR 723 2000.

[185] Intrinsically or with acquired reputation.

[186] [2010] EWHC 2599 (Ch); [2011] ETMR 1 at [72]–[74].

[187] [2011] EWHC 199 (Ch); [2011] ETMR 25 at [195].

- mere association, in the strict sense that later mark brings earlier mark to mind, is not sufficient;

- reputation of a mark does not give grounds for presuming a likelihood of confusion simply because of a likelihood of association; and

- if association between marks causes public wrongly to believe that the goods or services come from the same or economically linked undertakings, there is a likelihood of confusion.

5.49 Two final questions on s 5(2) or 10(2) – first, can confusion work both ways? 'Reverse confusion', where the public think that the claimant's products are connected with the defendant rather than vice versa, is actionable passing off.[188] It is submitted that the ECJ's comments on confusion in *Canon*[189] are apt to describe reverse as well as classic confusion:

> 'The risk that the public might believe that the goods/services in question come from the same undertaking or, as the case may be, from economically-linked undertakings, constitutes a likelihood of confusion.'

Secondly, is there a requirement of effect on the functions of the trade mark, as has been held for s 5(1) and 10(1)? Not surprisingly, this has been held to be the case.[190] In fact it seems inevitable that the presence of confusion will affect the core, distinguishing, function of the trade mark.

Marks with a reputation – identical, similar or dissimilar products

5.50 This is the sphere of ss 5(3) and 10(3). Section 5(3) states that:

> '(3)   A trade mark which is identical with or similar to an earlier trade mark, shall not be registered if, or to the extent that, the earlier trade mark has a reputation in the United Kingdom (or, in the case of a Community trade mark, in the European Community) and the use of the later mark without due cause would take unfair advantage of, or be detrimental to, the distinctive character or the repute of the earlier trade mark.'

Article 10(3) is couched in similar terms for infringement. Evidence of confusion is not required, although it is submitted that a mark can only be 'similar' to the registered trade mark if it calls it to mind in some way. This has been confirmed by the European Court in terms of a 'link' in the mind of relevant public.[191] Additional elements have to be established for the sections to

---

[188] *Provident Financial plc v Halifax Building Society* [1994] FSR 81; *Bristol Conservatories* [1989] RPC 455.

[189] *Canon Kabushiki Kaisha v Metro Goldwyn Mayer Inc* (C-39/97) [1998] All ER (EC) 934.

[190] *O2 Holdings Ltd v Hutchison 3G UK Ltd* (C-533/06) [2008] ECR I-4231; [2008] 3 CMLR 14; [2008] ETMR 55; [2008] RPC 33.

[191] *Adidas-Salomon AG v Fitnessworld Trading Ltd* (C-408/01) [2004] Ch 120; *Intel Corp Inc v CPM United Kingdom Ltd* (C-252/07) [2008] ECR I-8823; [2009] ETMR 13; *L'Oréal SA v*

take effect: reputation, lack of due cause and unfair advantage or detriment to the mark. These have been described as 'cross-pollination' provisions.[192]

5.51   These provisions were amended in 2004 by reg 7(2)(b) of the Trade Marks (Proof of Use, etc) Regulations 2004.[193] Prior to that, and in accordance with optional Art 5(2) of the Directive, these provisions only applied when the goods or services were dissimilar. This resulted in what was described as a 'logical lapse' – infringement and blocking rights could be stronger against dissimilar products than against similar under ss 5(2) or 10(2).[194] Norman argued that this problem had been solved by the cases on the interdependence of comparisons. However, another problem remained; in the absence of confusion, where use related to identical or similar goods, a mark with a reputation could not be protected from damage, especially generic use. In *Davidoff v Gofkid*[195] and *Adidas-Saloman v Fitnessworld Trading*,[196] the ECJ developed a fascinating line of authority – that Art 5(2) of the Directive should not be interpreted literally, but rather so as to give effect to the intention of the Community legislator in protecting trade marks within the Community. Since all member states had implemented Art 5(2), this could be done without undermining harmonisation. *Davidoff* indicated that member states could and *Adidas* that they should extend the protection of Art 5(2) to identical and similar products. However, as Norman points out, this left apparent disharmony between the Directive and the Regulation, which has been eliminated in the codification of these instruments.

5.52   The UK Registry does not examine applications under s 5(3); it has always been left to proprietors of any earlier marks with the requisite reputation to make out the grounds in opposition proceedings. So it will be up to the owners of such marks to keep a watch on the register and to oppose later applications where appropriate. The date at which conflict is assessed is the filing date, or the priority date, if different.[197]

5.53   The meaning of 'reputation' was considered in *General Motors v Yplon*.[198] Its territorial extent can be limited to a substantial part of the territory of a member state. As far as degree of recognition is concerned,

---

Bellure NV (C-487/07) [2000] ECR I-5185; [2009] ETMR 55); *Antartica Srl v OHIM* (C-320/07 P) [2009] ECR I-28; See, also, *Virgin Enterprises Ltd v Casey* [2011] EWHC 1036 (Ch); [2011] ETMR 35 at [26].

[192]   *Electrocoin Automatics v Coinworld* [2005] ETMR 31; [2005] FSR 7.

[193]   SI 2004/946.

[194]   H Norman '*Davidoff v Gofkid*: Dealing with the Logical Lapse or Creating European Disharmony' [2003] IPQ 342, citing WR Cornish *Intellectual Property: Patents, Copyright, Trade Marks and Allied Rights* (4th edn, 1999) at para 17.102.

[195]   (C-292/00) [2003] 1 CMLR 35 ECJ.

[196]   [2004] 1 CMLR 14.

[197]   See **5.31** (priority).

[198]   Case C-375/97 [1999] ECR I-5421 in relation to the Directive and similarly for the Regulation in *PAGO International GmbH v Tirolmilch Registrierte Genossenschaft mbH* (C-301/07) [2009] ECR I-9429; [2010] ETMR 5.

'reputation' connotes that the mark must be known by a significant part of the public interested in the products or services which it covers.

5.54 'Without due cause' was interpreted by Neuberger J in *Premier Brands v Typhoon Europe*.[199] These words, 'somewhat opaque in their effect', govern both use of the mark and the unfair advantage or detriment. They are directed to the defendant's need to use rather than to his honesty or good faith. Following the Benelux decision in *Lucas Bols*,[200] Neuberger held that there would be due cause if the defendant were:

'... under such a compulsion to use this very mark that he cannot honestly be asked to refrain from doing so regardless of the damage the owner of the mark would suffer from such use, or that the user is entitled to the use of the mark in his own right and does not have to yield this right to that of the owner of the mark.'

Thus taking a stance similar to the Benelux Court of Justice in *Claeryn*.[201] As for burden of proof, according to *Premier Brands* and *Intel*[202] it is not for the claimant/opponent to show lack of due cause, but for the defendant/applicant to show cause. It is difficult to imagine due causes which are not provided as express defences to infringement, outlined in Chapter 8.

5.55 'Unfair advantage' has been described as 'intended to encompass instances where there is clear exploitation and free-riding on the coattails of a famous mark or an attempt to trade upon its reputation'.[203] In *L'Oréal v Bellure*,[204] the ECJ characterised the purpose of such conduct – to profit from a transfer of the image of that mark to its own goods, without paying any financial compensation and without being required to make efforts of its own in that regard. Furthermore:

'As regards the concept of "tak[ing] unfair advantage of ... the distinctive character or the repute of the trade mark", also referred to as "parasitism" or "free-riding", that concept relates not to the detriment caused to the mark but to the advantage taken by the third party as a result of the use of the identical or similar sign. It covers, in particular, cases where, by reason of a transfer of the image of the mark or of the characteristics which it projects to the goods identified by the identical or similar sign, there is clear exploitation on the coat-tails of the mark with a reputation.'

---

[199] [2000] FSR 767; considered by the *Singapore Court of Appeal in Novelty Pte Lts v Amanresorts Ltd* [2009] SGCA 13; [2009] FSR 120.

[200] [1976] IIC 420 at 425 'Claeryn'/'Klarein'.

[201] See A Kamperman Sanders 'Some frequently asked questions about the Trade Marks Act 1994' [1995] 2 EIPR 67.

[202] *Intel Corp Inc v CPM United Kingdom Ltd* (C-252/07) [2008] ECR I-8823; [2009] ETMR 13; [2009] RPC 15; ECJ.

[203] *Monopole SpA v OHIM* (T67/04), CFI, 25 May 2005, citing the opinion of Jacobs A-G in *Adidas; L'Oréal SA v Bellure NV* (Case C-487/07) [2010] All ER (EC) 28; [2009] ECR I-5185; [2010] RPC 1; [2009] ETMR 987 at [41].

[204] (Case C-487/07) [2010] All ER (EC) 28; [2009] ECR I-5185; [2010] RPC 1; [2009] ETMR 987 at [41]. For judicial regret at this characterisation, see Jacob LJ in *L'Oréal SA v Bellure NV (No 2)* [2010] EWCA Civ 535; [2010] RPC 687; [2010] ETMR 824, CA.

The claimant or opponent must establish at least a serious likelihood of a future risk, not merely a hypothetical risk, of unfair advantage (or detriment).[205] This requires evidence of an actual or likely change in the economic behaviour of the average consumer of the goods or services for which the earlier mark was registered consequent on the use of the later mark. 'Unfair advantage' might be made out where a defendant unfairly takes advantage of a plaintiff's advertising campaign by using the mark.[206] In *Adidas*[207] the ECJ postulated an example following Schechter[208] – Rolls Royce would be entitled to prevent a manufacturer of whisky from exploiting the reputation of the Rolls Royce mark in order to promote his brand. The court opined that there was no significant difference between taking unfair advantage of the repute and of the distinctive character of the mark.

5.56   The next two alternatives, detriment to the distinctive character or to the repute of the mark, closely resemble two of the forms of dilution[209] by blurring and by tarnishment recognised in the USA[210] and elsewhere. Langvardt has pointed out[211] that lessening of distinctiveness is most likely where the defendant uses the mark in a trade mark sense.[212] Prejudice to reputation usually operates by the trade mark becoming associated in customer's minds with the defendant's deleterious use.[213] These parallels were explored by the ECJ in *Adidas*.[214] Again, it is necessary to establish at least a serious likelihood of such damage occurring.[215]

5.57   Three classic examples of US dilution cases may be used to illustrate dilution. The first is *Godiva/Dogiva*,[216] in which use of 'Dogiva' on dog treats was enjoined as eroding the distinctiveness of the mark 'Godiva' for chocolates. This may be likened to the fear in Intel that use of INTEL-PLAY would undermine the distinctiveness of the INTEL mark. References have been made

---

[205]   *Intel Corp Inc v CPM United Kingdom Ltd* Case C-252/07 [2009] ETMR 13, point 6 of ruling. At point 5 the court opined that the evidence cited in the reference (huge reputation of unique mark plus bringing to mind) would not of itself support a finding of unfair advantage.

[206]   For further examples of 'free-riding' from German case-law and economic and legal arguments against the practice, see M Lehmann 'Unfair use of and damage to the reputation of well-known marks, names and indications of source in Germany. Some aspects of law and economics' (1986) 17 IIC 746.

[207]   *Adidas-Salomon AG v Fitnessworld Trading Ltd* (C408/01) [2003] ETMR 91.

[208]   F Schechter, 'The rational basis of trademark protection' [1927] Harv LR 813, also cited in *Interflora Inc v Marks & Spencer Plc* (C-323/09) [2012] ETMR 1; [2012] FSR 3.

[209]   See S Maniatis 'Dilution in Europe' in H Hansen (ed) *International Intellectual Property Law and Policy* (2002) ch 43.

[210]   From Frank I Schechter 'The rational basis of trademark protection' [1927] *Harvard Law Review* at 813ff.

[211]   82 TMR 671 at 697.

[212]   Eg *Godiva/Dogiva Grey v Campbell Soup Co* 231 USPQ 562 (C D Cal 1986). See I Simon 'Nominative use and honest practices in industrial and commercial matters – a very European history' [2007] IPQ 117.

[213]   As in *Dallas Cowboys Cheerleaders v Pussycat Cinema* 604 F 2d 200, 203 USPQ 161 (2nd Cir, 1979).

[214]   *Adidas-Salomon AG v Fitnessworld Trading Ltd* (C408/01) [2003] ETMR 91.

[215]   *Intel Corp Inc v CPM United Kingdom Ltd* Case C-252/07 [2009] ETMR 13.

[216]   *Grey v Campbell Soup Co* 231 USPQ 562 (CD Cal, 1986).

to the CJEU as to whether the use of keyword INTERFLORA in advertising by a rival supplier of flowers would diminish the distinctiveness of the mark.[217] In *Dallas Cowboys Cheerleaders*,[218] the plaintiffs' uniforms were used as costumes for the participants in a rude film. This was enjoined as detrimental to the plaintiffs' reputation in the appearance of their costumes. In a number of cases involving luxury goods,[219] the ECJ has held that selling outside their top-market distribution networks could damage the reputation of a mark. By contrast, in *Monopole SpA v OHIM*, the Court of First Instance held that the mark 'Spa' would not be tarnished by activities carried on under the 'Spa-Finders' mark.[220] Lastly, in *Lexis/Lexus*,[221] it was alleged that use of 'Lexus' on Toyota motor cars would dilute the distinctiveness of 'Lexis' for legal information services. This was held improbable, given the specialist nature of the market for 'Lexis'. One can see similar considerations at play in Intel.

5.58 UK cases on ss 5(3) and 10(3) include the *Viagra* case, *Pfizer v Eurofoods*,[222] *Sheimer* where an application to register VISA for condoms was rejected after opposition from the credit card company[223] and *MERC*,[224] where the use of the motor mark was not restrained in relation to clothes. In *MERC*[225] Pumfrey J recommended:

'… just to follow the section … remembering Jacobs A.G.'s warning that it is concerned with actual effects, not risks or likelihoods. The enquiry is as follows.

(1)   Does the proprietor's mark have a reputation? If so,

(2)   is the defendant's sign sufficiently similar to it that the public are either deceived into the belief that the goods are associated with the proprietor so that the use of the sign takes unfair advantage of the mark, or alternatively causes detriment in their minds to either (a) the repute or (b) the distinctive character of the mark, or

(3)   even if they are not confused, does the use of the sign nonetheless have this effect, and

(4)   is the use complained of nonetheless with due cause. Detriment can take the form either of making the mark less attractive (tarnishing, to use Neuberger J's word) or less distinctive (blurring). On this analysis, VISA is of course a case of tarnishing.'

---

[217]   *Interflora Inc v Marks & Spencer plc* [2010] EWHC 925 (Ch), notwithstanding the ECJ's ruling in *Google France Sarl v Louis Vuitton Malletier SA & ors* (conjoined cases C-236/08 to 238/08) [2011] Bus LR 1; [2011] All ER (EC) 411; [2010] ETMR 30; [2010] RPC 19.

[218]   604 F 2d 200, 203 USPQ 161 (2nd Cir, 1979).

[219]   *SA v Christian Dior Couture SA* (C-59/08) [2009] ETMR 40 and citations; in the instant case whether the resale of de luxe corsetry by licensees to discount stores was detrimental to 'luxury' aura and therefore infringement a matter for the national court to decide.

[220]   (T-67/04).

[221]   *Mead Data Central v Toyota Sales USA Inc* 875 F 2d 1026 (2nd Cir, 1989).

[222]   *Pfizer Ltd v Eurofood Link (UK) Ltd* [2001] FSR 3; [2000] ETMR 896.

[223]   *CA Sheimer (M) SDN BHD's Trade Mark Application* [2000] RPC 484; cf *'Ever-Ready' Oasis Stores Ltd's TM Application* [1999] ETMR 531; [1998] RPC 631.

[224]   *DaimlerChrysler AG v Javid Alavi* [2001] RPC 42; [2001] ETMR 98; Baloch 'Confused about Dilution' [2001] EIPR 427.

[225]   At para 88.

In *Intel-play*[226] it was held that dilution by blurring would occur if the defendant's 'Intel-play' were used on unsophisticated goods, given that Intel was distinctive of 'high-quality, hi-tech products with a national and international reputation'.

OVERCOMING THE OBSTACLES – RELATIVE GROUNDS

5.59 Taking the last point first, where an earlier mark causes a relative objection,[227] a number of options are open. The most powerful option is to obtain the consent of the earlier mark's proprietor,[228] because the Registrar has no discretion to deny the application if consent is given.[229] However, obtaining the consent may prove a challenge and open a 'Pandora's box' of problems if the earlier proprietor takes objection. Alternatively, the later applicant could seek assignment,[230] surrender,[231] revocation[232] or invalidation[233] of the earlier trade mark. If these strategies are unavailable, the conflict might be resolved by amending the application or the earlier mark to narrow the specification of goods or services of the application.[234] This can be done by 'positively limiting' the specification or by adding an exclusionary phrase 'not including (specific goods)'.[235] The application could[236] also be withdrawn. Withdrawal is usually preferable to refusal; third parties may interpret a Registry refusal as indicating weakness in the applicant's position and cite the decision at some inconvenient moment. If the applicant has used the mark honestly in the UK for a number of years, it may be open to apply for registration as an honest concurrent user under s 8.[237]

Honest concurrent user

5.60 This is now of relevance in opposition proceedings on relative grounds[238] which may be overcome where the applicant has made honest concurrent use of a mark.[239] This provision was introduced to compensate in part for the rigour

---

[226] *Intel Corp Inc v Sihra* [2004] ETMR 44 Ch D.

[227] Which can now only arise under opposition from the proprietor of an earlier mark.

[228] Trade Marks Act 1994, s 5(5). See 'What is a Coexistence agreement?' at www.ipo.gov.uk/pro-types/pro-tm/pro-t-dispute/pro-t-coexist.htm.

[229] An attempt to retain the discretion formerly enjoyed by the Registrar over this aspect of practice was soundly rejected by Parliament: House of Lords Public Bill Committee, col 16 (13 January 1994). However, it was valuable in protecting the public from dangerous confusion. See, eg *Univer TM* [1993] RPC 239.

[230] See Chapter 11 (assignment).

[231] In whole or in part under s 45 (surrender).

[232] In whole or in part under s 46, see **9.12–9.17** (revocation).

[233] In whole or in part under s 47, see **9.6–9.11** (invalidity).

[234] Under s 39(1); see **5.26**.

[235] Work Manual, ch 3, heading 'Disclaimers and limitations (wording of)'. See **5.29** (limitation).

[236] Under s 39(1).

[237] See **5.60–5.62**.

[238] See Work Manual, ch 3, heading 'Honest concurrent use'; *Roadrunner Trade Mark* [1996] FSR 805.

[239] Section 7; practice under s 7 follows that under s 12(2) of the 1938 Act. Note the section limb

of relative examination by the UK Registry when the 1994 Act was passed.[240] In member states of the Community where no relative examination is carried out, a mark may be registered notwithstanding prior conflicting registrations. If the earlier proprietor acquiesces for 5 years in the use of the later registered mark, the earlier proprietor loses the right to challenge the later registration or to oppose further use of the later mark, unless he can show it was applied for in bad faith.[241] Although examination on relative grounds was abolished by the Trade Marks (Relative Grounds) Order 2007[242] the continuing availability of opposition proceedings in the UK favours retention of honest concurrent use. In *Efax Ltd v Protus IP Solutions Inc*[243] an unsuccessful attack was made on the vires of the honest concurrent use provisions. Note that honest concurrent user of itself does not provide a defence to trade mark infringement,[244] unless and until the concurrent mark is registered. Once that is achieved, the proprietor can avail himself of the defence under s 11.[245]

5.61 The criteria for registration of an honest concurrent user were considered in *Pirie's* application.[246] Relevant factors are:

(a)   the length of use (usually 2–3 years at least);[247]

(b)   the volume of use and area of trade;

(c)   the honesty of the concurrent user (knowledge of the earlier registration being pertinent but not conclusive);[248]

(d)   the presence or absence of actual confusion;[249]

---

of s 12(2), which gave a discretion to allow concurrent registration in 'special circumstances' other than honest concurrent use, was repealed by the 1994 Act. See, also, *Budejovicky Budvar v Anheuser-Busch* (C-482/09) [2011] ECR I-0000, which appears to recognize a concept akin to honest concurrent use in European trade mark law.

[240]   *Hansard* (House of Lords) vol 553, no 55, col 72 (14 March 1994).

[241]   Section 45. The Court of Appeal referred questions on acquiescence to the European Court in *Budejovicky Budvar Narodni Podnik v Anheuser-Busch Inc* [2009] EWCA Civ 1022; [2010] RPC 7; a case where two registrations were effected on the same day under the honest concurrent use provisions. The Advocate-General's opnion was published in February 2011: (C-482/09) Unreported.

[242]   SI 2007/1976, in force from 1 October 2007 in relation to applications published on or after that date: Art 5. Art 4 provides for search and notification, Art 3 having removed the effect of s 37(2) of the Act. Art 2 ensures that the Registrar refuses marks on relative grounds only in opposition proceedings.

[243]   [2007] RPC 26.

[244]   *Origins Natural Resources Inc v Origin Clothing Ltd* [1995] FSR 280 Ch D, cf suggestion in *Nucleus Trade Mark* [1998] RPC 233 TMR.

[245]   See **8.13**.

[246]   (1933) 50 RPC 147.

[247]   Just under 3 years in *Buler* [1975] RPC 225. In the case of a mark with high exposure, the period may be less. Of course if the use is not established, the claim will fail: *Nutritive Trade Mark* [1998] RPC 621 TMR.

[248]   *Bali TM* [1978] FSR 193.

[249]   Not necessarily fatal to the later applicant: *Buler* [1975] RPC 275.

(e)   the degree of likely confusion; and

(f)   whether that is tolerable to the public.

Although this list provides useful guidance, in *Budweiser*[250] the Court of Appeal pointed out the dangers in seeking to apply them as decisive factors in every case, quoting with approval a passage from *Kerly*:[251]

> 'The discretion of the tribunal is unfettered and concurrent registration may be allowed even when the probability of confusion is considerable. Every case has to be determined on its own particular merits and circumstances.'

5.62   As regards the combined effects of common law and statute under ss 5(4) and 7 of the 1994 Act, Geoffrey Hobbs QC, sitting as the Appointed Person in *Croom's TM*[252] stated:

> 'the rights of the rival claimants fall to be resolved on the basis that within the area of conflict:
>
> (a)   the senior user prevails over the junior user;
> (b)   the junior user cannot deny the senior user's rights;
> (c)   the senior user can challenge the junior user unless and until is it inequitable for him to do so.'

OPPOSITIONS AND OBSERVATIONS

5.63   Once the Registry has decided to accept an application, it is published in the *Trade Marks Journal*.[253] Interested parties then have 2 months[254] in which to file opposition to registration or to make informal observations to the Registrar.[255] It is at this stage that objections based on earlier marks registered for dissimilar goods or services, well-known marks and honest concurrent user may arise. Anyone may oppose registration.[256] Opposition is filed on form TM7, together with a statement of the grounds on which the opposition is based[257] and a statement of use of marks relied upon (if these have been registered for 5 years or more and are therefore vulnerable to revocation).[258]

---

[250] *Budweiser Trade Marks* [2000] RPC 906 CA.

[251] *Kerly's Law of Trade Marks* (12th edn, 1986) para 10–18.

[252] *Croom's Trade Mark Application* [2005] RPC 23.

[253] Section 38(1); r 16. The rules on opposition were overhauled in 2004 by the Trade Mark (Amendment) Rules 2004, changes now incorporated into the Trade Mark Rules 2008.

[254] Rule 17(2), extendible to 3 months by filing e-form TM7a: r 17(3) and (4). A would-be opponent who misses the deadline will have to seek a declaration of invalidity of the mark once registered: see Chapter 9. See Tribunal Practice Note (TPN) 4/2010 (trade marks): Opposition Proceedings: Calculation of the opposition period.

[255] Section 38(2) and (3); r 1.

[256] For opposition practice in the Registry, see 'How to oppose an application' and links at www.ipo.gov.uk/pro-types/pro-tm/pro-t-object/pro-t-oppose-apply.htm.

[257] Rule 17(5).

[258] Rule 17(5) and see Chapter 9.

The opposition documents are then forwarded by the Registry to the applicant, the date of this being the 'notification date'. The applicant then has 2 months[259] in which to file a counterstatement.[260] Failure to do so will result in the trade mark application being deemed abandoned, unless arrangements have been made for a 'cooling-off period' of up to 9 months from the notification date.[261] Provided the parties agree to extend the time for filing, this can be achieved[262] by either party filing form TM9c. The opponent may end the cooling-off period by filing form TM9t. This has the effect of terminating the cooling-off period one month after filing of form TM9t or 3 months after the notification date, whichever is the later.[263] If the applicant wishes to terminate the cooling-off period, he simply files form TM8. A further period of up to 9 months may be secured by either party filing form TM9e during the cooling-off period.[264] Once counterstatement form TM8 has been filed, it is sent to the opponent.[265]

Preliminary indication

5.64 The Registry then considers the notice of opposition and counterstatement. Where opposition is based upon s 5(1) or (2), the Registrar will send[266] either:

(a) a preliminary view as to whether or not the mark should be registered for the goods or services in question; or

(b) an indication that he feels the case inappropriate for such a view.[267]

If the view is favourable to the applicant, the opponent has one month in which to file form TM53, indicating that he wishes to proceed with the opposition. Failure to do so will result in the opposition being deemed withdrawn.[268] If the Registry view is that the mark should not be registered for any of the goods or services, then the application will be deemed withdrawn unless the applicant files form TM53.[269] In the intermediate position, where the Registry consider the mark should be registered for some but not all of the products, the applicant and the opponent have one month respectively to amend the

---

[259] Rule 18.
[260] Rule 18, form TM8. See TPN 4/2009 (trade marks): Trade mark opposition and invalidation proceedings – defences.
[261] Rule 18(2).
[262] Rule 18(5)(a).
[263] Rule 18(4) and (6).
[264] Rule 18(5).
[265] Rule 18(7).
[266] 19(1)-(2), this date being the 'indication date': r 19(3). See, generally TPN 2/2009 (trade marks): Opposition proceedings Preliminary Indications Rule 19 Trade Marks Rules 2008.
[267] Rule 19(2). See TPN 3/2007 (trade marks): Preliminary Indications in trade mark opposition proceedings: circumstances when they will not be used.
[268] Rule 19(4).
[269] Rule 19(5).

specification or to file form TM53,[270] which should in each case be copied to the other parties.[271] Note that the preliminary indication will not affect other grounds of opposition, for example, under s 5(4). The Registrar need not give reasons for the preliminary indication, nor is it subject to appeal.[272]

'Pleadings', evidence and intervention

5.65 The notices of opposition and counterstatement should define the issues between the parties, as do pleadings in court litigation.[273] Then there may be a round of evidence, with evidence in support of opposition, counterstatement and, if necessary, reply.[274] The Registrar has considerable discretion to set time limits in opposition proceedings[275] and give directions as to evidence, hearings and the like.[276] Failure to file evidence appropriate to the nature of the opposition will result in its being deemed withdrawn.[277] Opposition hearings, being inter partes, are open to the public.[278] The Registrar, in the shape of a hearing officer,[279] may hear oral evidence and call for such documents, information or evidence as he thinks fit, being invested with all the powers of an official referee of the Supreme Court.[280] The hearing officer will normally reserve his decision; parties will be sent notice of the outcome, with reasons.[281] The Registry has power to award reasonable costs and to require security for costs.[282] An interested party in the shape of the licensee of a registered mark, or the authorised used of a certification or collective mark, may intervene in opposition proceedings.[283]

Observations

5.66 It is also possible during the opposition period for an objector to make informal written observations to the Registrar,[284] who sends a copy to the

---

[270] Rule 19(4) and (5).

[271] Rule 19(6).

[272] Rule 19(7).

[273] *Club Europe Trade Mark* [2000] RPC 329 Ch D. See, also TPN 1/2004 (trade marks): Provision of skeleton arguments in Trade Mark proceedings.

[274] Rule 20. See, also TPN 1/2010 (trade marks): Pleadings in opposition and invalidation proceedings relying on s 5(4)(b) of the Trade Marks Act 1994 in relation to copyright, design right and registered designs.

[275] Rule 20(4). See TPN 2/2010 (trade marks): Time periods for the submission of evidence and submissions in inter partes trade mark proceedings.

[276] Rules 62–64. See, also 'Requesting a hearing' at www.ipo.gov.uk/pro-types/pro-tm/pro-t-dispute/pro-t-hearing-request.htm and TPN 3/2008 (trade marks): Time periods for the submission of evidence in inter partes proceedings.

[277] Rule 20(3).

[278] Rule 66.

[279] Who may call for a case management conference or pre-hearing review: r 62.

[280] Rules 62–65; s 69. The power to call for evidence is quite general.

[281] Rule 69; where reasons are not given, parties may request them on form TM5.

[282] Section 68; rr 67 and 68. See TPN 6/2008 (trade marks): Costs in proceedings before the Comptroller.

[283] Rule 21, form TM27. See 'Intervention' at www.ipo.gov.uk/pro-types/pro-tm/pro-t-object/pro-t-oppose-intervention.htm.

[284] Section 38(3); r 22.

applicant. The observer does not become a party to proceedings on the application. Although there are no formal requirements, it is unlikely that the Registrar will give much weight to unsubstantiated allegations in deciding what effect, if any, the observations have.

APPEALS AND STAYS

5.67 Appeals from a refusal to register, an adverse decision in opposition proceedings or other decision[285] of the Registrar may be made to the court[286] or to a person appointed by the Lord Chancellor under s 77.[287] The latter has a discretion to refer the appeal to the court where requested or if an important point of law is involved,[288] but otherwise will hear and determine the appeal. The Appointed Person's judgment is final.[289] This arrangement is popular with users. The Appointed Person is drawn from a highly qualified panel of trade mark lawyers[290] and is seen as cheaper than an appeal to the court, especially as there is no further right of appeal. A procedure for decision on the papers was introduced in 2004, which can be used if all parties indicate they do not require an oral hearing.[291]

5.68 At this point, it should be noted that a stay of Registry proceedings may be sought where there is litigation in court relating to the issue in question.[292]

DURATION AND RENEWALS

5.69 A registration can be renewed indefinitely,[293] although the registration may become vulnerable to attack. Under the 1994 Act, the first period of registration[294] is 10 years, as is the period between renewals. Renewal[295] can be effected up to 6 months before the due date, and for 6 months after, on payment

---

[285] Not as to classification: rr 54, 55 although there is a procedure for the applicant to oppose the Registrar's proposals; arrangements to notify search results (r 14); preliminary indications (r 19); refusal to allow inspection of documents (r 58); see also r 70 as regards final and interim decisions.

[286] See **7.1.**

[287] Section 78; r 71 governs appeals to the Appointed Person, which are filed at the Registry using form TM55. The period for appeal is 28 days. See TPN 2/2008 (trade marks): Appeals to the Appointed Person in Inter Partes proceedings.

[288] Section 76(3); r 72.

[289] Section 76(4).

[290] The hearings diary at www.ipo.gov.uk/types/tm/t-other/t-object/t-challenge/t-hearing/t-hearing-diary/t-diary-appeal.htm gives a flavour of who is hearing what.

[291] Rule 73(3).

[292] The Registrar has power to stay generally under r 62(1)(f). See TPN 1/2009: Requests for stays or suspensions in inter partes proceedings. In *Sears v Sears Roebuck* [1993] RPC 385, it was held that the court has powers to restrain Registry proceedings by interlocutory injunction, even where the Registrar had refused a stay.

[293] Section 42(2).

[294] Section 42(1).

[295] Section 43; rr 34–36, form TM11.

of an additional fee.[296] Where the renewal fee is not paid within these time-limits, the Registrar removes the mark from the register. Where the circumstances of failure to renew warrant sympathy, the proprietor has a further 6 months from removal to seek restoration to the register.[297]

SPECIAL CATEGORY MARKS

5.70 The procedures for registering collective and certification marks[298] largely follow those for ordinary trade marks, except that regulations to govern the use of the mark must be filed within 9 months of the application to register and approved by the Registrar.[299] The regulations can be amended only upon application to the Registrar, who will advertise the amendments for opposition.[300] Certification and collective marks are considered further in Chapter 12.

---

[296] Section 43; r 36.
[297] Section 43(5); r 37.
[298] Sections 49 and 50; Sch 1 & 2; rr 29–33. See Work Manual, ch 4 'Certification and Collective Trade Marks', which may be consulted online at www.ipo.gov.uk/tmmanual-chap4-certcoll. pdf.
[299] Sections 49 and 50; Sch 1, paras 5–8; Sch 2, paras 6–9; r 29, form TM35.
[300] Schedule 3, para 10; Sch 2, para 11; r 32.

Chapter 6

USING THE MARK

INTRODUCTION

6.1 In Chapter 1 we noted that the significance of the use of a trade mark varies according to the national or regional legal system within which such use takes place: in some countries, such as Germany or France, legally enforceable rights in a mark accrue primarily as a result of registration[1] whereas in others, such as the USA, they accrue primarily[2] as a result of use.

6.2 Since the entry into force of the Trade Marks Act 1994 ('the 1994 Act'), the UK has occupied an intermediate position, ie the registration of a trade mark has acquired greater significance[3] but passing-off (use) rights remain significant.[4] In short, use of a mark is still paramount in determining a range of issues relating to the acquisition, perfection, maintenance and violation of trade mark rights registered or unregistered.

6.3 A good example of the continuing potency of the concept of 'use of a mark' under the 1994 Act is that pre-existing rights in an *unregistered* mark (ie those rights protected through the tort of passing off)[5] can still form the basis for refusal of registration for a trade mark application,[6] the invalidation of a registration[7] or even a later registration in the face of a registered trade mark under the rules of 'honest concurrent use'.[8]

6.4 In the case of UK, though not Community, trade mark applications, the applicant must declare that it uses or has a bona fide intention to use the mark in relation to the goods or services for which registration is sought.[9] However,

---

[1] Although misuse of marks may also be characterised as unfair competition. See, eg A Ohly 'The freedom of imitation and its limits – a European perspective' [2010] IIC 506.

[2] In the USA, although Federal applications to register may be based on intention to use, a sworn 'allegation of use' – evidencing actual use in interstate or foreign commerce and accompanied by a specimen exhibiting use in commerce for each class of goods or services – must be filed before registration can issue. See www.uspto.gov/web/offices/tac/doc/basic/addreq.htm.

[3] Or, at least, appeared to do so, as the range of registrable signs expanded.

[4] M Ni Shuilleabhain 'Common-law protection of trade marks – the continuing relevance of passing off' (2003) 34 IIC 722.

[5] See Chapter 3.

[6] See Chapter 5.

[7] See Chapter 9.

[8] See Chapter 5; *Budejovicky Budvar Narodni Podnik v Anheuser-Busch Inc* (C-482/09) [2012] ETMR 2.

[9] Including use by licensees; Form TM3, item 13, see Chapter 5.

the first point at which the significance of use particularly arises is where an objection is raised by the Registry that the subject mark of an application lacks distinctive character or is descriptive under one or more of s 3(1)(b)–(d) of the 1994 Act; the latter can be overcome provided the Registrar can be satisfied that the mark has acquired distinctiveness in fact through use prior to the date of application.[10]

6.5   If a trade mark application succeeds, the resulting registered mark may be used by its proprietor in four principal ways.[11] First, it can be used directly by the proprietor to distinguish its own goods or services from those of others. Secondly, there exists the possibility of licensing the mark for use by third parties.[12] Thirdly, it can be used to prevent use of the mark by unauthorised third parties.[13] Lastly, it can be transferred outright by assignment to a third party.[14] This chapter concentrates on proper use by the proprietor and/or licensees.

THE SIGNIFICANCE OF USE

6.6   Although the provisions of the 1994 Act as a whole make it clear that proper use of a mark is significant, it is surprising that the relevant provisions are scattered about, for example:

(a)   actual use or a bona fide intention to use on the goods or services in question is a prerequisite for registration: s 32(3);[15]

(b)   failure to make genuine use of the mark is one possible ground for removal of the mark from the register: s 46(1)(a) and (b);[16]

(c)   misuse by the proprietor or failure to restrain misuse by others may render the mark liable to revocation, either because it has lost its distinctiveness or because it has become deceptive: s 46(1)(c) and (d);[17]

---

[10]   See the proviso to s 3; it must be emphasised, though, that proof of distinctiveness acquired through use is more than simply showing that use has occurred and assuming distinctiveness follows – the public must be shown to recognise the 'trade mark' as such (this was firmly established by *British Sugar plc v James Robertson & Sons* [1996] RPC 281 and can be seen in decisions of the Court of Justice such as *Windsurfing Chiemsee* (C-108&109/97) [1999] ETMR 585 or *Bovemij Verzekeringen NV v Benelux-Merkenbureau (EUROPOLIS)* (Case C-108/05) [2007] ETMR 29: 'it must be assessed whether the relevant class of persons, or at least a significant proportion thereof, identifies the product or service in question as originating from a particular undertaking because of the trade mark').

[11]   The first and third ways are also possible with unregistered marks. The others are more problematic.

[12]   See Chapter 10.

[13]   See Chapter 7.

[14]   See Chapter 11.

[15]   See Chapter 5.

[16]   See Chapter 9.

[17]   See Chapter 9.

(d) where in civil proceedings a question arises as to the use to which a registered mark has been put, it is for the proprietor to show what use has been made of it: s 100;

(e) where opposition is based upon an earlier trade mark, the opponent must show use made of that earlier mark: s 6A;[18]

(f) similarly, an applicant for invalidity based on conflict with his earlier mark must show use of that earlier mark: s 47(2A)–(2E);[19]

(g) an assignment or licence of a trade mark may be limited to in a particular manner or a particular locality: ss 24(2) and 28(1).

6.7 Additionally, although a trade mark registration may be declared invalid under s 47 if the mark was registered in breach of the requirements of s 3(1)(b)–(d), the registration is protected if it can be demonstrated that the mark has acquired distinctiveness through use in relation to the goods or services for which it was registered.[20]

MANNER OF USE

6.8 Use of a mark should be of the mark as registered, although use in a form which differs only in elements which do not affect its distinctiveness may suffice to prevent revocation on the ground of non-use.[21] This has been applied restrictively; for example, in *Elle*[22] change of case and omission of the symbol for the female gender was held to affect distinctiveness. In *United Biscuits*,[23] device marks showing penguins in different poses were all revoked although other poses had been used. In *Specsavers*,[24] use of a logo with words in was not considered use of the wordless logo – the addition of words was held to affect distinctive character. Although it is true that other decisions have been less strict,[25] if the mark is being used in a new or redesigned form, it is considered safest to make an application to register that later form rather than rely on a registration vulnerable to revocation for non-use.

---

[18] Inserted as of 5 May 2004 by reg 4 of the Trade Marks (Proof of Use, etc) Regulations 2004, SI 2004/946; this is done by filing a 'statement of use': Trade Mark Rules 2008, r 17(5) which must be done if the mark has been registered for more than 5 years (the time after which it becomes liable to revocation).

[19] Inserted as of 5 May 2004 by reg 6 of the Trade Marks (Proof of Use, etc) Regulations 2004, SI 2004/946; this is done by filing a 'statement of use': Trade Mark Rules 2008, r 41(2)(d).

[20] Proviso to s 47(1).

[21] Section 46(2).

[22] *Elle Trade Mark* [1997] FSR 529.

[23] *United Biscuits (UK) Ltd v Asda Stores Ltd* [1997] RPC 513.

[24] *Specsavers International Healthcare Ltd v Asda Stores Ltd (No 2)* [2010] EWHC 2035 (Ch); [2011] FSR 1 App 3 at paras 8–10.

[25] *Anheuser Busch Inc v Budejovicky Budvar Narodni Podnik (Application for Revocation)* [2004] 1 WLR 2577; [2005] FSR 10 (CA) – change of font; *Second Skin Trade Mark* [2001] RPC 30 – use in the form '2nd Skin' saved from total revocation. See also the 'tab' case of *Levi Strauss v Shah* [1985] RPC 371.

6.9   The mark should be used on all the goods or services for which it is registered; if this is not done, the 1994 Act allows the registration in question to be part-cancelled in respect of those goods or services upon or in relation to which the mark has not be used.[26] As eloquently stated in *La Mer*, unused marks '... simply clog up the register and constitute a pointless hazard or obstacle for later traders who are trying actually to trade with the same or similar marks. They are abandoned vessels in the shipping lanes of trade'.[27] The requirement for full use leaves applicants for trade mark registrations with a difficult decision on the width of specification(s) of goods/services on their application forms; in practice, this is a drafting issue which is best resolved by considering what goods/services the mark is already being applied to (if any) and what goods/services the applicant is most likely to apply the mark to within a period of 5 years after completion of registration procedures.[28] If an international filing campaign is to be based upon the UK application,[29] it may be advisable to err on the side of a broader specification.

6.10   Use of a mark should be fully documented throughout its life; this may assist with issues arising during application procedures (eg proving distinctiveness acquired through use in examination or opposition procedures) and once a mark is registered, the 1994 Act specifically provides that where a question arises in civil proceedings as to the use of the mark, the burden of showing what (if any) use has been made lies on the proprietor.[30] Use documentation should show or, at the very least, provide cross-references to the nature of the goods/services in respect of which the mark has been used, the geographical area of use of the mark, sales figures for goods and services sold under the mark, turnover figures, advertising figures, advertisement samples,[31] packaging samples, brochures, samples of the goods (if appropriate) and any other product promotion records. Dates of use are also important; in *BUD*, the Court of Justice held the Court of First Instance to have erred in its view that use by an opponent did not necessarily have to occur before the date of the application for registration of the later mark.[32]

---

[26]   Section 46(5). See Galileo *International Technology, LLC v European Union (formerly European Community)* [2011] EWHC 35 (Ch); [2011] ETMR 22 and, generally, Chapter 9. At para 2, Floyd J stated that he was unable to detect any difference between the approach to revocation of national trade marks, as governed by the Directive, and Community trade marks.

[27]   *Laboratoire De La Mer Trade Marks* [2002] FSR 51 at para 19, cited by C Howell 'No marks for internal promotion – use it or lose it at Covent Garden Market' [2006] Comms L 47 discussing *NEW COVENT GARDEN MARKET Trade Mark* (BL O-015-06) 17 January 2006 (TMR), available at www.ipo.gov.uk/types/tm/t-os/t-find/t-challenge-decision-results/o01506.pdf.

[28]   This being the earliest possible starting date for revocation actions per s 46(1) and (3).

[29]   See Chapters 15 and 16.

[30]   Section 100.

[31]   Preferably showing where and when the advertisement was placed. Practice Amendment Notice PAN 6/07 'Evidence of acquired distinctiveness through use', available at www.ipo.gov.uk/pro-types/pro-tm/t-law/t-pan/t-pan-607.htm provides helpful guidance.

[32]   *Anheuser-Busch Inc v Budějovický Budvar* (Case C-96/09 P) [2011] ETMR 31. In relation to well-known marks, see R Kelbrick '"Gaps" in time: when must a mark be well known?' [2006] IIC 920.

6.11 By whom is use properly made? Logic would dictate that the answer should be the present proprietor of the mark and any licensees and, indeed, Art 10(3) of the Trade Marks Harmonisation Directive ('the Directive') provides that use of the trade mark with the consent or authority of the proprietor shall be deemed to constitute use by the proprietor. The 1994 Act, by contrast, approaches this question piecemeal. Section 9(1) refers twice to the lack of proprietor's consent in defining infringement. Section 28(3) ensures that where the context so requires, the phrase 'consent of the proprietor' will include a predecessor in title. Section 28(4) allows a licensee to permit sub-licensing. Section 32(3) refers not only to the applicant's declaration that he is making actual use of the mark or has a bona fide intention to use a mark but also such use 'with his consent' (ie under licence). Finally, s 46 refers to use by the proprietor or with his consent. However, nowhere in all the above is there a statement in terms as general as those of Art 10(3) and, because of the continued protection for unregistered rights under UK law, it must always be remembered that proprietorship of a trade mark registration does not guarantee the right to use the mark in question.

6.12 The 1994 Act also lacks a comprehensive definition of the activities comprising use. Again, pointers are found in a variety of sections as follows:

(a)　section 103(2) states that use of a trade mark includes use otherwise than by way of graphic representation (this refers to the medium of use which, beside normal physical graphic representation, can include audio-visual or electronic media such as the internet);

(b)　section 10(4) shows that, for the purposes of s 10 (infringement), a person uses a sign if, in particular, he:

　　(i)　affixes it to goods or packaging;
　　(ii)　offers or exposes goods for sale, puts them on the market, stocks them for such purposes, or supplies services under the sign;
　　(iii)　imports or exports goods under the sign; or
　　(iv)　uses the sign on business papers or in advertising;

(c)　section 46(2) states that use in the UK includes affixing the trade mark to goods or to the packaging of goods in the UK solely for export purposes.[33]

6.13 As regards goods, it is clear that the mark need not be attached physically, although that is desirable. Subject to what is said below about genuine use, goods or services do not have to be on the market at the exact time the mark is used on papers or in advertising as it would seem the 1994 Act has

---

[33]　Use on goods solely for export was held genuine use in *Geoffrey Inc's Trade Mark Application (No 12244)* [2004] RPC 30. However, use solely for export will not of itself provide good evidence of acquired distinctiveness in the UK – see Practice Amendment Notice PAN 6/07 'Evidence of acquired distinctiveness through use', available at www.ipo.gov.uk/pro-types/pro-tm/t-law/t-pan/t-pan-607.htm.

preserved the effect of the decision in *Hermes,*[34] where use of the mark during preparations for re-launch of a product was held sufficient to avert removal from the register. In the *Minimax* case,[35] the trade mark proprietors had ceased selling fire extinguishers under the mark, but sold spares and refills and serviced and repaired the fire extinguishers, using the mark in relation to these goods and services. It was held that use in relation to goods no longer marketed could nonetheless be 'genuine use' within the meaning of Art 12 of the Directive.[36] However, the commercial interest in the goods should not be too indirect.[37] Use of a mark as a shop name may be use 'in relation to' goods, though not if such use is limited to identifying a company or its business.[38]

6.14 In order to avoid challenge for non-use, it is stipulated that use of the mark must be genuine, a similar requirement to that of 'genuine commercial use' under the Trade Marks Act 1938 ('the 1938 Act'). The courts and the Registry are astute in detecting sham use. Thus, in *Nerit,*[39] a decision under the 1938 Act, token use of that 'ghost mark' was not permitted to be used to protect the unregistrable mark 'Merit'.[40] Genuine use is more than 'token, minimal or notional for the sole purpose of preserving the rights conferred by the mark'.[41] Under the 1994 Act, in *La Mer,*[42] genuine use was defined as any use going to preservation of an outlet for goods and services bearing the mark as opposed to merely preserving the mark itself. Thus, use of 'WELLNESS' on drinks given to purchasers of clothing but not generally marketed was not 'genuine use' in this sense.[43] However, a non-profit organisation may make genuine use of a mark when advertising events, soliciting donations and the like.[44] The use must be external to the undertaking concerned.[45] The *Invermont* decision[46] also makes clear that where reasons are being put forward to excuse non-use, these have to be cogent and well supported by documentary evidence.

---

[34] [1982] RPC 425.

[35] *Ansul v Ajax* (C-40/01) [2005] Ch 97; [2004] 3 WLR 1048; [2003] ECR I-2439; [2003] ETMR 85; [2003] RPC 40.

[36] Revocation, on which s 46 is based.

[37] C Howell 'No marks for internal promotion – use it or lose it at Covent Garden Market' [2006] Comms L 47, commenting on *NEW COVENT GARDEN MARKET Trade Mark* (unreported) 17 January 2006 (TMR).

[38] *Céline Sàrl v Céline SA* (C-17/06) [2007] ECR I-7041.

[39] *Imperial Group v Philip Morris* [1982] FSR 72.

[40] The ECJ confirmed in *Minimax* that such use would not be considered genuine.

[41] *La Mer Technology Inc v Office for Harmonisation in the Internal Market (Trade Marks and Designs)* (T-418/03) [2008] ETMR 9 at para 90.

[42] *Laboratoires Goëmar v La Mer Technology Inc* [2005] EWCA Civ 978; *Ansul BV v Ajax Brandbeveiliging BV* (C-40/01) [2003] ECR I-2439 at para 37.

[43] *Silberquelle GmbH v Maselli-Strickmode GmbH* (C-495/07) [2009] ECR I-137; [2009] ETMR 28.

[44] *Verein Radetzky-Orden v Bundesvereinigung Kameradschaft 'Feldmarschall Radetzky'* (C-442/07) [2009] ETMR 14.

[45] C Howell 'No marks for internal promotion – use it or lose it at Covent Garden Market' [2006] Comms L 47, commenting on *NEW COVENT GARDEN MARKET Trade Mark* (unreported) 17 January 2006 (TMR).

[46] INVERMONT Trade Mark [1997] RPC 125; insofar as Invermont indicated that the Registrar had a discretion not to revoke when grounds for revocation were established, it was probably wrongly decided – see *ZIPPO Trade Mark* [1999] RPC 173 at 184.

6.15 Does use have to be use as a trade mark? In the context of infringement, the concept of 'use in a trade mark sense' has been problematic.[47] However, the definitions of 'genuine use' outlined above indicate that it is important that use be made for the core purposes of creating or preserving outlets for goods and services, or put another way, for entering or maintaining a distinctive presence in a market. In '*Tesco we sell for less*'[48] the appointed person was prepared to look for 'trade mark use' for the purposes of s 32(3),[49] although she decided that the slogan could be used for the purpose of distinguishing goods or services. In relation to slogans, this approach has been vindicated by the Court of Justice in cases such as '*Vorsprung durch Technik*'.[50] Conversely, in *Montero Padilla v OHIM*[51] a composer's heir opposing another's registration of his name was unable to show that the name had been used as an indicator of commercial origin, rather than as indicating the contents of CDs or by way of tribute. The opposition failed. Some uses, such as generic use described below, are obviously unsuitable but other less obvious dangers arise; for example, use of a mark as part of a company name may not necessarily constitute relevant use of that mark.[52]

6.16 In the view of the authors, the 1994 Act deals badly with the issue of use of a mark; in part, this stems back to the adaptation of UK trade mark law to the Directive which draws more heavily on the principles of laws from European countries with registration/deposit trade mark systems. Problems have arisen as to the proper construction of the 1994 Act in this context and will undoubtedly continue to arise.[53] However, several further practical problems can be clearly identified and are discussed below.

PROBLEMS OF USE

6.17 Particular pitfalls to avoid or restrain are:

(a) Generic use by the proprietor, where the mark is used as a product description. This may bar registration or lead to revocation.[54] If the recommendations at **6.18** onwards are followed, a proprietor's use should avoid this trap. Unfortunately, marketing departments often diverge from good trade mark practice in their enthusiasm to ensure acceptance for

---

[47] Contrast, e g *Trebor Bassett Ltd v The Football Association* [1997] FSR 211 with *Arsenal Football Club plc v Matthew Reed* [2002] ECR I-10273, [2003] 1 CMLR 345, ECJ. See H Norman 'Time to blow the whistle on trade mark use?' [2004] IPQ 1.

[48] *Re Tesco Stores Ltd's Trade Mark Applications* [2005] RPC 17.

[49] Statement of use or intention to use on application.

[50] *Audi AG v OHIM* (C-398/08P) [2010] FSR 24.

[51] T-255/08 [2010] ETMR 55.

[52] *ORIENT EXPRESS Trade Mark* [1996] RPC 25. Cf infringement cases, such as *Smithkline Beecham Ltd v GSKline Ltd* [2011] EWHC 169 (Ch).

[53] See S Maniatis 'Aspects of trade mark use and misuse' ch 11 in N Dawson and A Firth *Trade Marks Retrospective* (2000) vol 7 *Perspectives on Intellectual Property*; J Phillips and I Simon (eds) *Trade Mark Use* (2005).

[54] Such challenge to validity of 'PLAY-DOH' failed in *Hasbro Inc v 123 Nahrmittel GmbH* [2011] EWHC 199 (Ch); [2011] ETMR 25; [2011] FSR 21.

products. A trade mark is the supreme marketing tool and their aims are commendable; the challenge, however, is to ensure that such use of the mark does not undermine its legal status.

(b)   Generic use by others is even more problematic. It must be remembered that not all uses by third parties are infringing and that infringement proceedings do not automatically control generic use;[55] it is even possible that a rival may deliberately try to scupper a mark by such use.[56] Furthermore, the 1994 Act specifically permits certain uses including use for the purpose of identifying goods or services as emanating from the proprietor or a licensee.[57] However, if a person relying on the 'permitted use for reference' provision were to misuse the mark by making generic use of it, such use may well be left unprotected as prejudicial to the distinctive character of the mark.[58]

(c)   Generic use in dictionaries should be discouraged. It is interesting to note that Art 10 of the Community Trade Mark Regulation ('the Regulation') provides Community trade mark proprietors with a right to demand that the publishers of dictionaries or similar publications correct references which give the impression that a mark constitutes the generic name for certain goods or services. The Directive and the 1994 Act do not have any corresponding provision but proprietors should make the same arguments for correction wherever possible, setting out the risks to their property and markets in clear terms. Most publishers, whether in print or electronic media, are likely to be conscientious in this regard, particularly since nearly all are trade mark proprietors themselves.

Misuse as in (b) and (c) above prior to application can prove fatal to any chance of registering the mark. Once on the register, however, the mark will only be removed if it is used generically in the trade and in consequence of the proprietor's acts or inactivity.[59] These principles can be seen in action in *Spambuster*,[60] where it was held that 'Spambuster' had become a common name[61] in the trade for systems to tackle unwanted e-mail but that 'Spam' was not a common name in the trade for tinned meat.

(d)   In addition, deceptive use should be guarded against. The main danger here is that of uncontrolled licensing, which may lead to deceptiveness as

---

[55]   *JERYL LYNN Trade Mark* [2000] ETMR 75; [1999] FSR 491, Laddie J.
[56]   See use of the word 'caplets' in *Johnson & Johnson Australia Pty Ltd v Sterling Pharmaceuticals Pty Ltd* (1991) 21 IPR 1 (Fed Ct of Aus). A colleague of the writers has graphically described this form of use as 'reckless endangerment'.
[57]   Section 10(6).
[58]   Proviso to s 10(6).
[59]   Section 46(1)(c).
[60]   *Hormel Foods Corp v Antilles Landscape Investments NV* [2005] ETMR 54; [2005] RPC 28.
[61]   Richard Arnold QC, sitting as a deputy High Court judge, did not consider an applicant for revocation had to show it was the (only) common name in the trade. As for what trading circles were relevant, he followed (C-371/02) *Björnekulla Frukindustrier AB v Procordia Food AB* [2004] ETMR 69 in considering all stages of the chain of commerce.

to origin and/or quality.[62] Deceptive use by a third party is usually easier to restrain than generic use because, by contrast, it will usually involve infringement.

EDUCATING CUSTOMERS AND CONSUMERS

6.18   In the view of the authors, educating customers and consumers may best be achieved by vigilance and example. Customers and competitors who recognise that a sign is a trade mark, jealously guarded, are likely to respect the mark and use it properly. Proprietors should school their employees, agents, distributors, stockists and advertisers in the basic rules for trade mark use.

6.19   First, where a mark is a word mark which has been registered without restrictions on colour, size, placement or typeface, it should be distinguished from surrounding material or indicia by differential use of such features. If a mark is a word mark which has been registered in such a way that use of all or part in capitals can constitute proper use then do so as this helps to emphasise the mark still further. However, use of the mark 'as registered' is always paramount and, particularly in the case of device marks, there should never be any additions, deletions or alterations which would affect the distinctive character of the mark; this principle extends to maintaining the spelling of word marks and use of specified colour types[63] for marks containing or comprising colours.

6.20   Secondly, a mark should always be used as an adjective and not as a noun or verb: for example:

- Take 'Aspirin' painkillers

- Buy our 'Linoleum' floor coverings

- Wash your hair with 'Tesserae' shampoo

would all be good use whereas the following would be objectionable:

- Take an aspirin

- Treat yourself to new linoleum

- Tesserae your hair.

Following these rules can prove difficult where a trade mark comprises or contains a company name; in this instance, use of the company name and trade

---

[62]   Cf s 46(1)(d).
[63]   Eg by reference to a recognised colour standard.

mark use should be explained by notice in product literature and, within the boundaries of the respective company and trade mark registration rules, distinguished as much as possible.

6.21 Thirdly, as an extension to the above, it must be emphasised that registered marks should not be used in a pluralised, hyphenated or possessive form since this only encourages third parties to treat them as generic names.

6.22 Fourthly, notice should be given as to the status and, possibly, the ownership of the mark whether on literature, labels or packaging. Where a mark is registered, this should be stated in the notice and the ® symbol should be deployed to boost the notice given. It is increasingly common to see the ™ symbol being used to indicate unregistered marks and similar notice being given; this helps to protect rights at common law. Although it is not compulsory to apply information about ownership of the mark, this is helpful and, particularly where the mark is used under licence, some explanation of ownership and use of the mark is a wise precaution against claims that the mark is being used deceptively.

Chapter 7

PURSUING INFRINGEMENTS

INTRODUCTION, FORUM, SPACE AND TIME

7.1   Actions for infringement of a UK registered trade mark are brought under s 14 of the Trade Marks Act 1994 ('the 1994 Act'). Section 75 of the 1994 Act originally defined the relevant courts as the High Court in England and Wales, the High Court in Northern Ireland and the Court of Session in Scotland. However, trade mark matters, including proceedings for infringement of Community trade marks, can now also be heard in the Patents County Court[1] and other county courts where there is a Chancery district registry.[2] Indeed, before this development, it was held that trade mark infringement simpliciter was a tort and therefore actionable in ordinary county courts.[3] The Community Trade Mark (Designation of Community Trade Mark Courts)

---

[1]   Which now has full jurisdiction in passing off and trade mark cases for England and Wales, except appeals from the Registrar: *National Guild of Removers & Storers Ltd v Christopher Silveria* [2010] EWPCC 015; [2011] FSR 9 at [7]–[11]. On transfers between the PCC and the High Court, see *Alk-Abello Ltd v Meridian Medical Technologies* [2011] FSR 13 PCC; *Caljan Rite-Hite Ltd v Sovex Ltd* [2011] EWHC 669 (Ch); [2011] FSR 23.

[2]   See English Civil Procedure Rule 63.13 on allocation: '63.13 Claims relating to matters arising out of the 1994 Act and other intellectual property rights set out in Practice Direction 63 must be started in–
(a) the Chancery Division;
(b) a patents county court;
(c) save as set out in Practice Direction 63, a county court where there is also a Chancery District Registry.'
Practice Direction 63, Section II deals with infringement of registered trade marks and indicates which rights other than patents and registered designs follow the same allocation rule, including:
'(10) hallmarks;
(12) passing off;
(13) protected designations of origin, protected geographical indications and traditional speciality guarantees;
(14) registered trade marks; and
(15) Community trade marks.'
There are Chancery district registries at Birmingham, Bristol, Caernarfon, Cardiff, Leeds, Liverpool, Manchester, Mold, Newcastle-upon-Tyne and Preston. However, the county courts at Caernarfon, Mold and Preston do not have jurisdiction in relation to registered trade marks and Community trade marks.
The complete Civil Procedure Rules for England and Wales with associated Practice Directions are available at www.justice.gov.uk/guidance/courts-and-tribunals/courts/procedure-rules/civil/index.htm. A useful table by Musker summarising jurisdiction may be found in a note by T Gold 'Trade Marks in the Patents County Court' (2005) 35 CIPA J 483.

[3]   *Minerstone Ltd v Be Modern Ltd* [2002] FSR 53 CC (Central London).

Regulations 2005[4] designated the same courts in England and Wales together with the High Court of Northern Ireland and the Scottish Court of Session as Community Trade Mark Courts of First Instance and specified the relevant appeal courts. A Community trade mark seised of an infringement action under Art 97(1)–(4) of the Community Trade Mark Regulation[5] has jurisdiction over infringements in any EU member state. In which case it can grant an injunction in relation to the whole EU.[6] The same remedies are available for infringement of a Community trade mark as of a national mark.[7] Where trade mark rights in the UK are secured by an international registration under the Madrid Protocol[8] these are litigated in the same way as rights obtained by national registration. Courts in other EU member states may have jurisdiction over infringing activity in the UK by virtue of the 'Brussels' Regulation (EC) 44/2001 on civil jurisdiction and judgments[9] or the Community Trade Mark Regulation, Art 97.[10]

7.2   The registration of a person as proprietor of a trade mark is prima facie evidence of the validity of the original UK registration and of any subsequent assignment or other transmission of it.[11] The presumption of validity may be challenged by a defendant who can adduce evidence of invalidity; this in turn

---

4   SI 2005/440, reg 3, replacing reg 9 of the Community Trade Mark Regulations 1996. The Trade Marks (International Registrations Designating the European Community, etc) Regulations 2004, SI 2004/2332, had designated the First Instance courts but not appeal courts. Article 91 of the Community Trade Mark Regulation (EC) 40/94, now consolidated into Regulation (EC) No 207/2009, requires member states to designate Community trade mark courts, while Art 92 gives them exclusive jurisdiction over infringement actions, actions for declaration of non-infringement, counterclaims for revocation or for declaration of invalidity.

5   Regulation (EC) 207/2009 on the Community Trade Mark (hereafter 'Regulation') Under Art 97(1)–(4) of Reg (EC) 207/2009, a consolidating regulation, and Art 93(1)–4) of its predecessor, Reg 40/94, jurisdiction derives from the domicile or establishment of the defendant, or of the plaintiff. Where jurisdiction is based on the location of infringement under Art 97(5), it extends only to that member state.

6   Regulation (EC) 207/2009 on the Community Trade Mark, Art 98(1), formerly Reg 40/94, Art 94(1) as interpreted in *DHL Express France SAS v Chronopost SA* Case C-235/09 [2011] ETMR 33. Sebastian Schnell 'The Community trade mark: Unitary EU right – EU-wide injunction?' [2011] EIPR 210.

7   The Community Trade Mark Regulations 2006, SI 2006/1027, reg 5. However, the Commission's study on the application of Directive 2004/48/EC on the enforcement of intellectual property rights suggests that the courts' powers to grant cross-border relief under provisions such as Art 103(2) of Community Trade Regulation 207/2009 are rarely used: see p 18 of COM(2010) 779, accompanying document to SEC(2010) 1589 final (both 22 December 2010, tendered to the European Parliament and Council 10 January 2011).

8   See, further, Chapter 14 and The Trade Marks (International Registration) Order 2008, SI 2008/2206, art 3(2). The 2008 Order was further amended by SIs 2009/2464 and 2010/32.

9   See **7.3**.

10   See, eg, *G-Star International BV v PepsiCo Inc* [2009] ETMR 18. Arrondissementsrechtbank (Den Haag) G-Star owned CTM 'Raw' for clothes, etc but not soft drinks. D had introduced a soft drink under a mark including 'RAW' onto the UK market. After a couple of complaints it wrote indicating that it would refrain from marketing in other EU member states. G-Star sought an interim injunction to restrain infringement in NL, BeNeLux, EU. Refused – case on the merits appeared weak and insufficient urgency – cross-border injunction with substantive effect in the UK would be too drastic given G-Star's 9 months' inaction in the UK and the 'comfort letter'.

11   Trade Marks Act 1994, s 72. A certified copy of entry on the UK register may be obtained

may be deflected by a proprietor with evidence, for example, of distinctiveness acquired through use.[12] Infringement is actionable by 'the proprietor of the trade mark', but this expression includes a licensee in appropriate circumstances.[13]

7.3 As will be apparent from the above, although the 1994 Act applies throughout the UK and s 9(1) refers to infringement[14] by use of the mark 'in the United Kingdom', the UK actually comprises three separate jurisdictions: England and Wales, Scotland and Northern Ireland. The Civil Jurisdiction and Judgments Act 1982 ('the 1982 Act') governs choice between these possible fora. The 1982 Act implemented the Brussels (EC) and Lugano (EFTA) Conventions on civil jurisdiction and judgments into UK law.[15] The Brussels Convention has been superseded for EU countries other than Denmark by the 'Brussels' Regulation (EC) 44/2001.[16] If jurisdiction is based upon the defendant's place of domicile/residence, the court may hear complaints and grant remedies regarding trade mark infringement throughout the UK, or throughout the EU if a Community trade mark is held. If jurisdiction is based upon the place of occurrence of the harmful event, the court has only local jurisdiction. Jurisdiction may also be based upon a need for provisional measures, joinder, consent and (for Community trade marks) on the state of domicile or establishment of the plaintiff (Regulation, Art 93). The jurisdiction rules do not appear to have caused difficulty within the UK; they are likely to come into greater prominence with increasing use of the Community trade mark system. Within the UK, applicable trade mark law is the same throughout – the 1994 Act or the Regulation. In a cross-border dispute involving another EU member state, it may be necessary to invoke 'Rome I' or 'Rome II' regulations on applicable law,[17] although given the extent of harmonisation, this is unlikely to cause difficulty in pure trade mark cases. It should be noted that the Regulation also deals with questions of applicable law (Art 97), concurrent rights and res judicata (Art 105).[18]

---

using form TM31R, see www.ipo.gov.uk/pro-types/pro-tm/pro-t-formsfees.htm. For Community trade marks, Art 99 of the Regulation stipulates the presumption of validity; for certificates, see http://oami.europa.eu/pdf/forms/inspection_en.pdf; an electronic certified copy of the Community registration certificate can be obtained through the 'CTM ONLINE' database at http://oami.europa.eu/ows/rw/pages/QPLUS/databases/searchCTM.en.do.

[12] *Electrocoin v Coinworld* [2005] FSR 7, applying *British Sugar v Robertson* [1996] RPC 281.

[13] See Chapter 10.

[14] Based upon Art 5 of Directive (EEC) 89/104.

[15] For detailed treatment, see Fawcett and Torremans *Intellectual Property and Private International Law* (Oxford University Press, 2nd edn, 2011).

[16] 22 December 2000, [2001] OJ L21/1. The UK has opted into negotiations for the reform of the Brussels Regulation, which are likely to deal with the position of non-EU defendants, the enforcement of judgments where the enforcing state has qualms as to the judgment and the position relating to arbitration.

[17] Regulation (EC) No 593/2008 on the law applicable to contractual obligations (Rome I, for contracts concluded after 17 December 2009); Regulation (EC) No 864/2007 on the law applicable to non-contractual obligations (Rome II, in force from 11 January 2009).

[18] Considered in *Prudential Assurance Co Ltd v Prudential Insurance Co of America* [2003] 1 WLR 2295; [2003] ETMR 69; [2004] FSR 25; discussed by R Mallinson 'Trade marks in the EU: one right, one law, one decision – or not?' [2007] EIPR 432.

7.4   Infringement of certification (quality) marks and collective (association) marks follows that for 'ordinary' trade marks.[19] Certification and collective marks are considered in Chapter 12, along with the rights conferred under Art 6*bis* of the Paris Convention (well-known marks) and the Olympic association right which protects signs connected with the Olympic Games.

7.5   Section 14(2) of the 1994 Act provides that relief is available as for infringement of any other property right. As with other statutory intellectual property rights, infringement is actionable without proof of damage.[20] Some specific remedies are also provided by the statute: erasure, destruction and delivery up. Section 89 of the 1994 Act and Regulation (EC) 1383/2003 provide for border measures to stem imports of infringing material. Remedies are discussed further below at **7.62–7.71**.

7.6   Regarding the temporal dimension of infringement, first we may note that the 1994 Act applies in actions where the alleged acts of infringement took place after commencement on 31 October 1994.[21] Earlier actions would now be statute-barred. For England and Wales the Limitation Act 1980 set a period of 6 years for claims in tort while the limitation period for delict in Scotland is 5 years. Community trade marks have been in effect since 1 April 1996. The Regulation does not stipulate a limitation period for infringement claims. This is a matter for the complementary application of national law: Art 14 of the Regulation. A mark can only be litigated once registered (1994 Act, s 9(3)(a)). However, s 40(3) provides that once the mark has been registered, its date of registration is deemed to be the date of filing of the application. Consequently, the plaintiff may claim damages retrospectively for infringements occurring in the period between application and registration (s 9(3)). No criminal offence can be committed prior to publication of the registration (s 9(3)(b)). Where evidence is adduced of public perception of a mark, the relevant moment is the outset of infringement.[22]

ALTERNATIVE METHODS OF TRADE MARK DISPUTES AND PRE-ACTION CONDUCT

7.7   It is possible for parties in a trade mark dispute to agree that the matter be resolved by arbitration.[23] The Chartered Institute of Arbitrators has taken an interest in intellectual property[24] and the World Intellectual Property Organisation (WIPO) has an arbitration and mediation centre for private

---

[19]   Trade Marks Act 1994, ss 50 and 49 respectively.
[20]   Save, perhaps, under s 10(3), see below.
[21]   Cf earlier acts of infringement governed by Trade Marks Act 1994, Sch 3, para 4(1).
[22]   *Levi Strauss & Co v Casucci SpA* Case C-145/05 (2006).
[23]   For the relative merits of arbitration, mediation and litigation, see M Alexander 'Settlement in Intellectual Property Disputes' *Trademark World*, December/January 1992/93, p 26; The World Intellectual Property Organisation's Arbitration and Mediation Centre publishes a bibliography at www.wipo.int/amc/en/center/bibliography/general.html.
[24]   See www.ciarb.org.

intellectual property disputes.[25] The UK Intellectual Property Office offers a mediation service, and its website has links to other mediation providers and to the company names adjudicator.[26] The civil courts try to encourage parties to use mediation and may penalise even a successful party as to recovery of their costs if they acted unreasonably in refusing to agree to alternative dispute resolution.[27] In relation to cross-border disputes, Directive 2008/52/EC on certain aspects of mediation in civil and commercial matters[28] empowers the courts in EU member states to invite parties to mediate where appropriate,[29] subject to confidentiality,[30] and requires that settlement agreements be enforceable.[31] It also encourages the development of mediator training and voluntary codes of conduct in member states[32] and requires that limitation or prescription periods do not prejudice attempts to mediate.[33]

7.8   There is no prescribed 'Pre-action protocol' to be followed before commencing trade mark litigation, although the Skrein Committee worked on a draft protocol for intellectual property and formulated a Code of Practice[34] for prospective intellectual property litigants. The general rules of pre-action conduct[35] in theory apply to trade mark disputes. However, in the case of registered marks, the position is complicated by the 'threats' action, whereby certain classes of person aggrieved by threats of infringement proceedings may sue.[36]

THE EXCLUSIVE RIGHTS OF THE PROPRIETOR

7.9   Legislation on the exclusive rights of a trade mark proprietor in the UK can be found in several places:

(a)   Art 5 of the Trade Marks Harmonisation Directive 2008/95/EC ('the Directive');[37]

---

25   See www.wipo.int/amc/en/index.html.
26   See www.ipo.gov.uk/types/tm/t-manage/t-enforce/t-dispute/t-mediation.htm.
27   In which case the burden falls on the unsuccessful party who wishes to avoid paying the successful party's costs: *Halsey v Milton Keynes NHS Trust* [2004] 1 WLR 3002; 4 All ER 920, CA. In *Rolf v De Guerin* [2011] EWCA Civ 78, no order was made as to costs.
28   Of 21 May 2008, [2008] OJ L136/3; implemented in England and Wales by the Cross-Border Mediation (EU Directive) Regulations 2011, SI 2011/1133 and the Civil Procedure (Amendment) Rules 2011, SI 2011/88, in Northern Ireland by the Cross-Border Mediation Regulations (Northern Ireland) 2011, SI 2011/157 and in Scotland by the Cross-Border Mediation (Scotland) Regulations 2011, SI 2011/234. At the time of going to press government is consulting on extending these provisions to domestic disputes.
29   Art 5; UK courts already encourage mediation.
30   Art 7.
31   Art 6.
32   Art 4; UK law was seen as already compliant with this.
33   Art 8.
34   See, R Ashmead 'IP-specific pre-action protocols and threats' [2004] CIPA J 6.
35   See   www.justice.gov.uk/guidance/courts-and-tribunals/courts/procedure-rules/civil/contents/practice_directions/pd_pre-action_conduct.htm.
36   See Chapter 8.
37   A codified version replacing Directive 89/104 as amended: [2008] OJ L 299/25. A study by the

(b)   ss 9 and 10 of the 1994 Act, which implement the mandatory and discretionary provisions of Art 5 and must therefore be interpreted in conformity with Art 5;[38]

(c)   Art 9 of the Regulation,[39] which essentially repeats the provisions of Art 5;

(d)   Art 14 of the Regulation, which provides for complementary application of national law relating to infringement of Community trade marks;

(e)   s 52 of the 1994 Act, which empowers the Secretary of State to make provision by Regulations for Community trade marks, and the Community Trade Mark Regulations[40] promulgated under those powers;

(f)   s 54 of the 1994 Act, which empowers the Secretary of State to make provision for giving effect in the UK to the Madrid Protocol for the International registration of marks, and the Trade Marks (International Registration) Order 1996;[41]

(g)   s 56 of the 1994 Act, which enables the foreign proprietor of a mark which is well known within the UK[42] to restrain its unauthorised use, whether or not the mark is registered or the claimant has a UK business or goodwill.

7.10   Paraphrasing the effect of the provisions for registered marks, a claimant must show:

(a)   that the mark is registered;[43]

Max Planck Institute for Intellectual Property and Competition Law on the operation of European Trade mark system, including both the Community Trade Mark system and harmonisation national systems was presented to the European Commission in February 2011: see http://ec.europa.eu/internal_market/indprop/tm/index_en.htm. In relation to infringement, its main recommendations are that optional provisions of the Directive be made mandatory: Part VII, section 5.1, para 5.

[38]   H Norman 'Time to Blow the Whistle on Trade Mark Use' [2004] IPQ 1 has argued that the drafting of s 9 is narrower than that of Art 5.

[39]   Community Trade Mark Regulation (EC) 207/2009, replacing Reg 40/94.

[40]   The Community Trade Mark Regulations 2006, SI 2006/1027, replacing the Community Trade Mark Regulations 1996, SI 1996/1908.

[41]   SI 1996/714, especially reg 4(1): '4.(1) The proprietor of a protected international trade mark (UK) has, subject to the provisions of this Order, the same rights and remedies as are given by or under sections 9 to 12 and 14 to 20 to the proprietor of a registered trade mark, subject to the limits on effect and to the provisions relating to exhaustion which are applicable to a registered trade mark by virtue of section 11 and section 12 respectively.'
The 1996 Regulations were amended by SI 2006/763 and SI 2006/1080, but not in this regard.

[42]   Within the meaning of Art 6*bis* of the Paris Convention for the Protection of Industrial Property; Art 16 of the WTO TRIPs agreement; WIPO Joint Recommendation concerning Provision on the Protection of Well-Known Marks (1995). See Chapters 12 and 15 and *Hotel Cipriani Srl v Cipriani (Grosvenor Street) Ltd* [2009] EWHC 3032 (Ch); [2009] RPC 9 at [235]–[242].

[43]   See **7.6** (time); no UK registration is required for s 56. See **12.7**, **12.29**ff and **7.9**, **7.49**ff.

(b)   that the claimant has standing to sue, as proprietor or licensee;[44]

(c)   that the defendant has used the registered mark (or a resembling sign):[45]

(i)   in the UK under the 1994 Act[46] or in the EU under the Regulation;[47]

(ii)   in the course of trade;[48]

(iii)   in relation to goods or services in a manner prohibited by the legislation;[49]

(iv)   in one of the activities specified by the legislation;[50]

(v)   without the proprietor's consent.[51]

The interpretative jurisprudence of the Court of Justice of the European Communities on Art 5(1)(a) of the Directive (identical marks and products)[52] suggests an additional factor must be present:

(d)   such that the defendant's use of the sign 'must affect or be liable to affect the functions of the trade mark, in particular its essential function of guaranteeing to consumers the origin of the goods or services'.

The additional factor – effect on trade mark functions

7.11   This additional factor may assist a trade mark proprietor whose mark is being used as a company name, trade name or shop name,[53] or as a badge of allegiance,[54] or as an advertising keyword online (if it is not clear whose goods are being offered)[55] but it complicates the straightforward application of the rules where signs and products are identical, when the Directive suggests that

---

[44]   See **7.2**, **10.18–10.21**, and **12.16** (certification marks), **12.24** (collective marks).

[45]   Trade Marks Act 1994, s 9 and 10. The rules for comparison of marks are identical with those for relative examination of applications to register and are considered in detail in Chapter 5.

[46]   Trade Marks Act 1994, s 9, see **7.1** and **7.3**.

[47]   The infringement provisions of the Regulation do not specify this, but Art 1(2), which deals with the unitary character of the Community Trade Mark, refers to prohibiting its use throughout the Community.

[48]   Trade Marks Act 1994, s 10(1)–(3). See **7.14ff**.

[49]   Trade Marks Act 1994, s 10(1)–(3). See **7.16–7.22** and **5.38–5.58**.

[50]   Trade Marks Act 1994, s 10(4), (5). See **7.42–7.45**.

[51]   Trade Marks Act 1994, s 9(1). Note that, in the context of comparative advertising, s 10(6) ensures that honest use to identify the proprietor's goods or services does not require consent – see **7.53–7.56**.

[52]   Summarised by Arnold J in *L'Oréal SA v eBay International AG* [2009] EWHC 1094 (Ch); [2009] ETMR 53; [2009] RPC 21 at [283]–[288]. This has made inroads into the 'absolute' nature of protection in 'double-identity' cases. The Max-Planck 'Study on the Overall Functioning of the European Trade Mark System' observed at para 2.178: 'There was general agreement among participants that the current jurisprudence of the ECJ in respect of those issues [exclusive rights] is neither consistent nor satisfactory. However, no consensus was reached as to the manner in which more transparency and consistency can be achieved': http://ec.europa.eu/internal_market/indprop/docs/tm/20110308_allensbach-study_en.pdf.

[53]   *Céline Sàrl v Céline SA* Case C-17/06 [2007] ECR I-7041; [2007] ETMR 80; ECJ (Grand Chamber).

[54]   *Arsenal Football Club Plc v Reed* Case C-206/01 [2002] ECR I-10273; [2003] ETMR 19.

[55]   *L'Oréal SA, Lancôme parfums et beauté & Cie, Laboratoire Garnier & Cie, L'Oréal (UK) Limited v eBay International AG, eBay Europe SÀRL and eBay (UK) Limited* Case C-324/09, 12 July 2011 at [93]–[97]; such 'adverse effect' appears tantamount to confusion.

protection is 'absolute'.[56] In *RxWorks v Hunter*, it was said to serve 'a similar purpose to the requirement in earlier English law that use be "trade mark use"', reflecting the fact that a 'registered trade mark is a marketing instrument, not a platform for an absolute monopoly in the use of the term in question'.[57] Arnold J commented in *L'Oréal v eBay* that it was unclear what the additional factor added to the enquiry:[58]

> 'I consider that the current state of the ECJ's jurisprudence is unclear with regard to at least three other inter-related questions. First, it is unclear precisely what the sixth condition [our (d) above] adds to the fifth condition. Secondly, if the sixth condition does add something, it is unclear whether damage to functions other than the origin function can be relied upon to support a claim under Art 5(1)(a), and if so in what circumstances. Thirdly, if damage to functions other than the origin function can be relied on, it is unclear what the relation is between Art 5(1)(a) and Art 5(2) in double identity (identical sign and identical goods) cases.'

7.12   Assuming that all necessary factors are present, the defendant may escape liability by setting up a defence, especially one of the statutory defences in ss 11 and 12 of the 1994 Act, the Directive, Arts 6 and 7, and the Regulation, Arts 12 and 13. These are discussed in Chapter 8. In the rest of this chapter, we shall consider further the effects of ss 9 and 10 of the 1994 Act, and their European counterparts, together with the remedies that a trade mark claimant may seek.

7.13   Note that there is no requirement to prove the defendant's motive or intent in civil proceedings. Consequently, innocence is no defence to a claim of infringement and damages may be claimed against an innocent infringer.[59]

USE OF THE MARK/SIGN: IN THE UK; IN THE COURSE OF TRADE; IN RELATION TO GOODS OR SERVICES

7.14   Section 9 of the 1994 Act begins:

---

[56] Recital 11. The Max Planck Study at p 97, para 2.164 points out that in *Silhouette International Schmied GmbH & Co KG v Hartlauer Handelsgesellschaft mbH* C-355/96 [1998] ECR I-4799; [1998] ETMR 286; [1998] FSR 474, there was no mention of any qualification to a proprietor's rights under Art 5(1)(a). Nor was there in *Gillette Co v LA-Laboratories Ltd Oy* (C-228/03_ [2005] All ER (EC) 940; [2005] ECR I-2337; [2005] 2 CMLR 62; [2005] ETMR 67; [2005] FSR 37.

[57] *RxWorks Ltd v Hunter (t/a Connect Computers)* [2007] EWHC 3061 (Ch); [2008] RPC 13 at [50] per Daniel Alexander QC, sitting as a Deputy High Court Judge.

[58] *L'Oréal SA v eBay International AG* [2009] EWHC 1094 (Ch); [2009] ETMR 53; [2009] RPC 21 at [300]–[306]. For the European Courts' ruling on questions referred by Arnold J, see *L'Oréal SA, Lancôme parfums et beauté & Cie, Laboratoire Garnier & Cie, L'Oréal (UK) Limited v eBay International AG, eBay Europe SÀRL and eBay (UK) Limited* Case C-324/09, 12 July 2011.

[59] *Gillette UK Ltd v Edenwest Ltd* [1994] RPC 279 Ch D; see H Johnson 'Marketing of counterfeit products – innocence is no defence' (1994) 15(4) JML&P 101; R Kelbrick 'Damages against the Innocent Infringer' [1996] EIPR 204.

'(1) the proprietor of a registered trade mark has exclusive rights *in the trade mark* which are infringed by use of the trade mark in the United Kingdom without his consent.

The acts amounting to infringement, if done without the consent of the proprietor, are specified in section 10.'

Sections 10(1)–(3) of the 1994 Act each specify that infringement involves use 'in the course of trade' and set forth the rules for different combinations of identical and similar signs.

7.15 Article 5(1) of the Directive and Art 9(1) of the Regulation both state that the registered/Community trade mark:

'... shall confer on the proprietor exclusive rights therein. The proprietor shall be entitled to prevent all third parties not having his consent from *using in the course of trade* ...'

again, going on elaborate types of infringing activity.

USE OF MARKS PROHIBITED BY S 10 – COMPARISON OF MARKS AND PRODUCTS UNDER THE 1994 ACT

7.16 The tests which the courts and Registry use to compare marks, goods and services are described in detail at **5.38–5.58**. The substantive rules of comparison are identical for refusal of registration on relative grounds and for infringement. However, it should be borne in mind that 'the former requires consideration of notional fair use of the mark applied for, while the latter requires consideration of the use that has actually been made of the sign in context'.[60]

7.17 These tests for comparison in infringement are spelled out in s 10(1), (2) and (3), which enact Arts 5(1) and (2) of the Directive. The equivalent provisions for Community trade marks are found in Art 9(1) and (2) of the Regulation. Their effect is summarised in Table 7.1.

---

[60] *Datacard Corporation v Eagle Technologies Ltd* [2011] EWHC 244 (Pat) [2011] RPC 17 per Arnold J at [75], citing *O2 Holdings Ltd v Hutchison 3G UK Ltd* (C-533/06) [2008] ECR I-4231.

Table 7.1: Comparisons for infringement and relevant subsections of the 1994 Act

Marks	Identical	Similar	Dissimilar	With a reputation
Goods/services				
Identical	10(1)	10(2)*	–	10(3)**
Similar	10(2)*	10(2)*	–	10(3)**
Similar or dissimilar	10(3)**	10(3)**	–	10(3)**

*   Likelihood of confusion to be shown.

**   Additional elements to be shown: reputation of mark, use involves detriment/unfair advantage, lack of due cause.

A COMPOSITE ENQUIRY

7.18   In *Euromarket Designs Inc v Peters and Crate & Barrel Ltd*,[61] Jacob J held that:

> 'The phrase ["using in the course of trade ... in relation to goods or services" from Art 5 of the Directive] is a composite. The right question, I think, is to ask whether a reasonable trader would regard the use concerned as "in the course of trade in relation to goods" within the Member State concerned.'

At the risk of decompiling the enquiry, this section focuses first on location of use, secondly whether use is 'in the course of trade', thirdly the issue of 'trade mark use', and fourthly use 'in relation to goods and services'.

Territorial issues

7.19   Location of use rarely causes problems in the offline world. Section 10(3) and its equivalents require reputation;[62] the difficult passing-off question of whether a trader can show goodwill in the jurisdiction does not arise if the mark is registered, though of course a registration may be vulnerable to revocation for non-use.[63] However, where a foreign website is accessible from within the jurisdiction, interesting questions may arise as to whether there is infringement of local trade marks. Maniatis has argued that 'the nature of a

---

[61]   [2001] FSR 20.

[62]   'The degree of knowledge required must be considered to be reached when the Community trade mark is known by a significant part of the public concerned by the products or services covered by the mark': *PAGO International GmbH* (C-301/07) [2010] ETMR 5 44 (Community Trade Mark); see also *General Motors Corp v Yplon SA* (C-375/97) [1999] ECR I-5421 (Directive).

[63]   Chapter 3; Chapter 9.

commercial or non-commercial use of a trade mark remains the same irrespective of the medium'.[64] Even where the use is clearly a commercial one, however, there may not be infringement by use on websites. In *Euromarket Designs Inc v Peters and Crate & Barrel Ltd*,[65] the defendant advertised its 'Crate and Barrel' shop in Dublin through UK magazine advertising and its Irish website. Jacob J refused summary judgment to the claimant, a US store chain which owned UK and Community trade mark registrations of 'Crate and Barrel'. Jacob J analysed the situation as follows:

> '... if a trader from state X is trying to sell goods or services into state Y, most people would regard that as having a sufficient link with state Y to be "in the course of trade" there. But if the trader is merely carrying on business in X, and an advertisement of his slips over the border into Y, no businessman would regard that fact as meaning that he was trading in Y. This would especially be so if the advertisement were for a local business such as a shop or a local service rather than for goods.'[66]

The defendant's magazine advertisement and website[67] were seen as invitations to visit the Irish shop, rather than trade within the UK.

7.20 A similar distinction was made by the Court of Justice of the European Union (CJEU, formerly ECJ) in *L'Oréal v eBay*.[68] In that case, offers for sale emanating from outside the EU were carried on the defendant's internet auction site at 'www.ebay.co.uk'. The Court held that the 'mere fact that a website is accessible from the territory covered by the trade mark' would not be sufficient to infringe.[69] However, the exclusive rights of the trade mark proprietor would apply 'as soon as it is clear that the offer for sale of a trade-marked product located in a third State is targeted at consumers in the territory covered by the trade mark'. In the absence of evidence to the contrary, the web address 'www.ebay.co.uk' suggested that the advertisements were targeted at UK customers. Another relevant indicator would be inclusion in the advertisement of the geographic areas to which the seller is willing to dispatch the product, or the currency for payment.[70]

---

[64] S Maniatis 'Trade Mark Law and Domain Names: Back to Basics' [2002] EIPR 397; S Maniatis 'New Bottles, but No Wine' in Barendt and Firth (eds) *Yearbook of Copyright and Media Law* (2000). Cases such as *Musical Fidelity Ltd v Vickers* [2003] FSR 50; [2002] EWCA Civ 1989 CA, bear out this assertion.

[65] [2001] FSR 20.

[66] At [19].

[67] The web address was 'www.crateandbarrel.ie', previously 'www.crateandbarrelie.com', where 'ie' denotes the Republic of Ireland.

[68] Case C-324/09 [2011] ECR 0000, 12 July 2011 at [58]–[67].

[69] Referring by analogy to C-585/08 and C-144/09 *Pammer and Hotel Alpenhof* [2010] ECR I-0000.

[70] The use of a dollar sign caused suspicion, although it turned out to be a consequence of the web designer's use of a standard template. See, also *Future Publishing Ltd v Edge Interactive Media Inc, Edge Games Inc and Dr Timothy Langdell* [2011] EWHC 1489 (Ch); [2011] ETMR 50.

7.21 Disputes over domain names – user-friendly web addresses – often involve trade mark issues.[71] Bodies such as WIPO provide dispute resolution services which tend to handle a greater volume of cases than the ordinary courts and WIPO publish consensus views on a number of domain name issues.[72]

7.22 Do both the use of the sign and the trade have to be in the UK? In *Beautimatic International v Mitchell International Pharmaceuticals*[73] there was application of the registered mark 'Lexus' to cosmetics packaging in the UK, mostly intended to be used to package and distribute goods outside of the UK. This was held not to be infringement under s 10(1), save in cases where the packaging and marks were applied to the goods in the UK before export.

'Use in the course of trade'

7.23 From the foregoing, it is clear that wholly non-commercial uses of trade marks will not infringe. In *L'Oréal v eBay*,[74] the Court of Justice, after recalling that the exclusive rights of a trade mark proprietor 'may, as a rule, be relied on only as against economic operators', went on to note that the volume, frequency and other characteristics of sales by individuals on the eBay internet auction site could take the conduct beyond private activity and into 'the course of trade'. The distinction between private and commercial activity was also highlighted in *Arsenal v Reed*.[75]

7.24 A situation on the fringes of commercial activity is comment by a commercial magazine or on a website. Cases cited by a number of writers[76] include *Philips*, where the electrical company's logo was altered to include a swastika and used to illustrate a magazine article about Philips' activities during the Second World War. Examples of political commentary are *Esso v Greenpeace*[77] and similar cases[78] in France. Greenpeace's uses of Esso's marks were held not to infringe the oil company's registrations. Despite the availability

---

71   See K Komaitis 'The Current State of Domain Name Registration: Domain Names as Second-Class Citizens in a Mark-Dominated World' (Routledge, 2010).
72   See *WIPO Overview of WIPO Panel Views on Selected UDRP Questions* (2nd edn), available at www.wipo.int/amc/en/domains/search/overview/index.html.
73   [1999] ETMR 912 Ch D.
74   Case C-324/09 [2011] ECR 0000, 12 July 2011 at [54]–[56], citing Case C-245/02 *Anheuser-Busch* [2004] ECR I-10989, para 62 and (C-487/07) *L'Oréal v Bellure* [2009] ECR I-5185, para 57.
75   *Arsenal Football Club v Reed* C-206/1 [2003] ETMR 19, ECJ. See, also *Céline Sàrl v Céline SA* (C-17/06) [2007] ECR I-7041; [2007] ETMR 80; *UDV North America* [2010] ETMR 25; *L'Oréal v eBay* [2009] EWHC 1094 [2009] RPC 21 at [285].
76   See, in particular, M Kniff 'Selected Benelux cases' *Trademark World*, July/August 1994, p 14; A Kamperman Sanders 'Trade mark dilution – the parting of the ways?' *Managing Intellectual Property*, March 1992, p 42.
77   *Esso Société Anonyme Française SA v Association Greenpeace France and Societe Internet FR* [2003] ETMR 35 Trib Gde Inst (Paris); [2003] ETMR 66 C d'A (Paris); [2004] ETMR 90 Trib Gde Inst (Paris). Critical commentary on the oil company's activities included reference to the altered mark E$$O. Use of Esso's name as a 'metatag' drew internet users to the Greenpeace site.

of T-shirts and requests for 'donations', Greenpeace was not regarded as engaging in economic activity. Use of the marks referred to the company and the environmental effects of its activities rather than to any goods or services for which the mark was registered.[79] Use of trade marks for comment rather than commercial communication will not infringe.[80]

'Trade mark use'

7.25 What if the protected sign is used on commercial products but not explicitly as an indicator of origin? A mark could be used decoratively on the goods for which it is registered ('Kodak' or 'Arsenal' on T-shirts)[81] or to give colour to narrative in a 'blockbuster' novel ('the morning after, Joanna realised that her job at the local branch of the "Halifax"[82] would never feel the same. The lunch at "Maxim's",[83] the journey home through the Channel Tunnel')? In the former case the public may or may not imagine the T-shirt to be connected with the trade mark proprietor[84] and any case will probably turn on this fact. Geoffrey Hobbs QC, sitting as a deputy High Court judge in *Electrocoin v Coinworld*,[85] held that the rights conferred by a trade mark registration were 'not engaged' and therefore not infringed by use of a sign other than to distinguish goods and services. In his opinion in *Adidas-Salomon AG and Adidas Benelux BV v Fitnessworld Trading Ltd*, Jacobs A-G asserted that decorative use would not infringe if members of the public would not perceive the sign as a distinguishing mark.[86] Conversely, in the same case the European Court of Justice (ECJ) ruled[87] that if the decorative use of a mark with a reputation caused the public to 'establish a link between the sign and the mark', there could be infringement. This was reinforced by the ECJ in *Arsenal v Reed*, where it was held that use of the football club's badges of allegiance on avowedly unlicensed merchandise was capable of affecting the function of the marks and therefore of infringing.[88] In the literary scenario above, there is unlikely to be any misapprehension as to the significance of the mark or any ill effect to the functions of the marks. At the time of going to press, this issue was

---

[78]   *Esso, Areva, Danone* (2004) 35 IIC 3 at 342–345 and note 76 above; R Burrell, D Gangjee 'Trade marks and freedom of expression – a call for caution' (2010) IIC 2010.

[79]   In the UK, reference to the proprietor's products is protected under s 10(6) of the 1994 Act – see **7.53–7.56**.

[80]   The need for use to be 'the alleged infringer's own commercial communication' was highlighted by the Max Planck 'Study on the overall functioning of the European Trade Mark system' at p 97, citing C-236/08–238/08 *Google France* at para 56.

[81]   *Kodiak TM* [1990] FSR 49; *'Coast to Coast' Unidoor v Marks & Spencer* [1988] RPC 275; *Arsenal Football Club v Reed* [2003] ETMR 19, ECJ.

[82]   For curious trade mark infringement proceedings under the 1938 Act, see *Provident Financial plc v Halifax Building Society* [1994] FSR 81.

[83]   Subject of the passing off action in *Maxim's v Dye* [1977] 1 WLR 1155; [1975] FSR 364.

[84]   Contrast the doubts expressed in the *Kodiak* and *Coast to Coast* cases with judicial recognition of merchandising in *Mirage Studios v Counter-Feat Clothing* [1991] FSR 145.

[85]   *Electrocoin Automatics Ltd v Coinworld Ltd* [2005] ETMR 31; [2005] FSR 7 (the appearance of sequences of 0s and Xs as winning sequences on gaming machines).

[86]   (C-408/01) [2003] ETMR 91.

[87]   (C-408/01) [2003] ECR I-2537, [2004] 1 CMLR 14, [2004] ETMR 10, [2004] FSR 21.

[88]   *Arsenal Football Club v Reed* C-206/1 [2003] ETMR 19, ECJ.

the subject of rapidly developing jurisprudence from the Court of Justice of the European Union, outlined in the following paragraphs. The Max Planck Study remarked:[89]

> 'It appears appropriate to maintain the requirement established by case law that use must be made for the purpose of (identifying and) distinguishing the commercial origin of goods or services. This requirement is also called for in order to delimit the standard infringement cases from other cases, currently addressed in Article 5 (5) TMD, but now proposed also for the CTMR.'

7.26 A discretionary provision allowing member states to adopt or retain prohibition on 'non-trade mark' use was included in the Directive. This provision is Art 5(5) of the Directive, which states:

> 'Paragraphs 1 to 4 shall not affect provisions in any Member State relating to the protection against the use of a sign other than for the purposes of distinguishing goods or services, where use of that sign without due cause takes unfair advantage of, or is detrimental to, the distinctive character or repute of the trade mark.'

In *Adidas-Salomon v Fitnessworld Trading Ltd*,[90] Jacobs A-G described Art 5(5) as 'clearly directed at provisions of national law in areas other than trade mark regulation – for example, unfair competition and comparative advertising'. In *Robelco*,[91] Art 5(5) was considered to allow a member state to confer protection against the use of an identical or similar sign as a company name. It is perhaps surprising that the existence of Art 5(5) has not had a more profound effect on the interpretation of the trade mark infringement provisions of the Directive.[92] Its existence adds force to the argument that the other provisions of s 10 and Art 5 are limited to 'trade mark' use. However, as outlined below, debate on 'non-trade mark use' has centred upon other provisions, mainly upon the 'double identity' situation under s 10(1), Art 5(1)(a) of the Directive and Art 9(1)(a) of the Regulation, where the legislation does not expressly require confusion or detriment.

7.27 Returning to these provisions, although s 9, Art 5 of the Directive and Art 9 of the Regulation refer to exclusive rights in the *trade mark*, s 10 and the detailed provisions of Arts 5 and 9 speak of infringement by use of a *sign*. Inevitably, this led to debate as to whether the *sign* must be used as a *trade mark* in order to infringe. What does one mean by 'use as a trade mark'? Certainly use to indicate commercial origin would qualify. What about use to indicate a

---

[89] 'Study on the Overall Functioning of the European Trade Mark System' at para 2.208; available at http://ec.europa.eu/internal_market/indprop/docs/tm/20110308_allensbach-study_en.pdf.

[90] (C-408/01) [2003] ETMR 91.

[91] *Robelco NV v Robeco Groep NV* C-23/01 [2002] ECR I-10913, [2003] ETMR 52. Contrast *Céline Sàrl v Céline SA* (C-17/06) [2007] ECR I-7041; [2007] ETMR 80; ECJ (Grand Chamber), nn 53, 75, where it was accepted that such use might infringe Art 5(1).

[92] Art 5(5) was considered in *Bayerische Motorenwerke AG (BMW) v Deenik* (C-63/97) [1999] ECR I-905. The court's interpreting Art 5(1) and (2) in isolation from Art 5(5) means that interpretation of the Directive and Regulation remain uniform.

quality of goods or services?[93] And what about use as an advertising tool? The underlying question seems to be whether the use in question undermines any of these legitimate functions of the trade mark in the hands of its proprietor.[94] Logically, there are three possibilities:

(a)   infringement is present only in the case of 'trade mark use', which must be established by the claimant; or

(b)   a prima facie case of infringement can be defeated if the defendant can show that the sign was not used as a trade mark (or the use has not affected the functions of the mark); or

(c)   use of the registered sign (or a resembling sign) on relevant goods or services will infringe regardless of the nature of the use,

in each case unless one of the specific defences can be established.

7.28   There is overlap, because the defences of s 11(2)(b), Art 6(1) of the Directive and Art 12 of the Regulation provide that various descriptive uses do *not* infringe provided they are in accordance with honest practices in industrial or commercial matters. Reading these defences in conjunction with the above suggests that (c) could be the correct interpretation but hints of all three can be found in the case-law and (b) is probably the correct approach.[95]

7.29   In *Mothercare v Penguin Books*,[96] it was held under the 1938 Act that use of the registered mark as part of the book title *Mothercare/Other Care*, which aptly described the book's contents, did not infringe, because the use was not trade mark use.[97] In *British Sugar v Robertson*,[98] Jacob J considered the 1994 Act a complete departure from earlier legislation and took the view that there was no need to show trade mark use to establish infringement under the 1994 Act. On this authority, (a) cannot be sustained. In *Philips Electronics v Remington Consumer Products*,[99] the Court of Appeal observed that use of a registered sign other than as a trade mark could infringe, suggesting option (c). In *Gillette Co v LA-Laboratories Ltd Oy* (C-228/03),[100] a case on interpretation of the defence in Art 6(1)(c) of the Directive, the ECJ recited Art 5(1)(a) of the

---

93   Which, for luxury goods could include not just only their material characteristics, but also the allure and prestigious image which confer an aura of luxury upon them: *Copad SA v Christian Dior Couture SA* (C-59/08) [2009] ECR I-3421; [2009] ETMR 40; [2009] FSR 22, citing *Parfums Christian Dior SA v Evora BV* (C-337/95) [1997] ECR I-6013.

94   *L'Oréal SA v Bellure NV* Case C-487/07 [2009] ECR I-5185 at [58], [65]; *Datacard Corporation v Eagle Technologies Ltd* [2011] EWHC 244 (Pat); [2011] RPC 17 at [258].

95   See *Datacard Corporation v Eagle Technologies Ltd* [2011] EWHC 244 (Pat); [2011] RPC 17 at [254]–[272].

96   [1988] RPC 113 at 119, CA.

97   For a case where a book series title was held capable of acting as a trade mark, see *Games Workshop v Transworld* [1993] FSR 705.

98   [1996] RPC 281. For a critique of this decision, see H Norman 'Time to Blow the Whistle on Trade Mark Use' [2004] IPQ 1.

99   [1999] RPC 809, CA.

100   [2005] ECR I-2337; [2005] 2 CMLR 62; [2005] ETMR 67; [2005] FSR 37.

Directive without qualification or reference to trade mark function, thus suggesting (c) but did go on to stress the importance of consumers' ability to distinguish products in a competitive free market.[101] In *Bayerische Motorenwerke AG (BMW) v Deenik*[102] the defendant (not a BMW dealer) had used phrases such as 'Repairs and maintenance of BMWs', 'BMW specialist' or 'Specialised in BMWs' to indicate the subject matter of his second-hand sales and motor services. The ECJ held that Mr Deenik 'used' the BMW mark in relation to cars within the meaning of Art 5(1)(a), so that the legitimacy of this use was then considered under Art 6 and (particularly) Art 7. However, the ECJ also stated at para 38 that:

> '... the scope of application of Article 5(1) and (2) of the Directive, on the one hand, and Article 5(5), on the other, depends on whether the trade mark is used for the purpose of distinguishing the goods or services in question as originating from a particular undertaking, that is to say, *as a trade mark as such*, or whether it is used for other purposes.'

7.30   In *Arsenal Football Club v Reed*,[103] Laddie J referred questions to the ECJ along the lines of (b):

> '1. Where a trade mark is validly registered and
>
> (a)   a third party uses in the course of trade a sign identical with that trade mark in relation to goods which are identical with those for whom the trade mark is registered: and
> (b)   the third party has no defence to infringement by virtue of Art 6(1) of Council directive 90/104;
>
> does the third party have a defence to infringement on the ground that the use complained of does not indicate trade origin (i.e. a connection in the course of trade between the goods and the trade mark proprietor)?
>
> 2. If so, is the fact that the use in question would be perceived as a badge of support, loyalty or affiliation to the trade mark proprietor a sufficient connection?'

Arsenal had sued a street trader selling 'unofficial' merchandise bearing Arsenal trade marks – the items had no connection with the club other than their attraction to fans as badges of affiliation. The defendant's sales had been

---

[101] At [25]: 'It should be noted as a preliminary point that trade mark rights are an essential element in the system of undistorted competition which the EC Treaty seeks to establish and maintain. Under such a system, an undertaking must be in a position to keep its customers by virtue of the quality of its products and services, something which is possible only if there are distinctive marks which enable customers to identify them (see, in particular, (C-10/89) *Hag* [1990] ECR I-3711, [13]; (C-517/99) *Merz & Krell* [2001] ECR I-6959, [21], and (C-206/01) *Arsenal Football Club* [2002] ECR I-10273, [47]).'
[102] (C-63/97) [1999] ECR I-905; [1999] 1 CMLR 1099; [1999] ETMR 339.
[103] [2003] ETMR 19, ECJ.

going on for a long time and Laddie J had held that the evidence did not support a claim of passing off by misrepresentation.[104]

7.31 In the meantime, the ECJ decided in *Hölterhoff v Freiesleben*[105] that:

> 'Article 5(1) of First Council Directive 89/104/EEC of 21 December 1988 to approximate the laws of the Member States relating to trade marks is to be interpreted as meaning that the proprietor of a trade mark cannot rely on his exclusive right where a third party, in the course of commercial negotiations, reveals the origin of goods which he has produced himself and uses the sign in question solely to denote the particular characteristics of the goods he is offering for sale so that there can be no question of the trade mark used being perceived as a sign indicative of the undertaking of origin.'

In *Hölterhoff*, there had been use of the claimant's registered marks 'Spirit Sun' and 'Context Cut' to describe the cuts of precious stone which were sold by the proprietor under the marks. 'Spirit Sun' was used for a round cut with facets radiating from the centre whilst 'Context Cut' was used for a square cut with a tapering diagonal cross. The German court had found as fact that the defendant was not using the signs to indicate commercial origin. Indeed, as Norman points out, the use was made by the purchaser rather than the seller.[106] The European Court's decision in *Hölterhoff* suggests that the correct option is either (b) or (a) above. However, it is submitted such generic use by a third party would inevitably undermine the power of the signs to distinguish the proprietor's goods.

7.32 In *Arsenal*, the ECJ considered the functions of a trade mark, stressing its role as a unique indicator of origin but also considering the wider implications of the 'differentiation' function, and using phraseology which hints at the advertising function. The exclusive right under Art 5(1) was given to the proprietor to protect his interest in maintaining the trade mark's functions. The court went on to make detailed observations on the facts of the case, remarking that the defendant's use was in the course of trade, was not merely descriptive, created an impression of a commercial link which was not dispelled by the notice on his stall[107] and could be misleading post-sales. In the circumstances, the court concluded that the use of the signs was liable to jeopardise the guarantee of origin which constituted the essential function of the registered marks and accordingly could be prevented under Art 5(1). Laddie J took the view that, in deviating from the national court's findings of fact, the European Court had exceeded its powers on a reference under Art 234 of the EC Treaty (now Art 267 TFEU). Reverting to his own findings of fact, Laddie J found for Mr Reed. On appeal, the Court of Appeal appeared to reconcile the ECJ's view of the facts (which was 'not binding' upon the national court) with that of Laddie J and held Mr Reed's use to be infringing. Perhaps it

---

[104] [2001] RPC 46.
[105] [2002] FSR 52 ECJ.
[106] See H Norman 'Time to Blow the Whistle on Trade Mark Use' [2004] IPQ 1.
[107] By which Mr Reed made clear that his merchandise was not 'official' Arsenal merchandise.

was not surprising that, in *Philips v Remington*,[108] Rimer J expressed the view that further reference might need to be made to the ECJ on these issues.

7.33 In a number of subsequent references to the Court of Justice, the need for infringing use to affect trade mark functions has been reaffirmed, pointing to (a) or (b) rather than (c). In *Adam Opel v Autec*,[109] the claimants had registered their 'Blitz' logo for real and for replica cars. The defendants asserted that use of the logo on unlicensed 'Cartronic' toy cars did not infringe as it was not 'use as a trade mark', especially in the light of the defendants' use of their own marks on the toys and the public's familiarity with toy cars made by undertaking other than the motor manufacturers. In a judgment which was perhaps unfortunate for the clarity of European trade mark law,[110] the ECJ held that the defendant had 'used' the mark registered for toy cars (though not that for cars[111]) within the meaning of Art 5(1)(a). Such use was not covered by the defence of Art 6(1)(b), but could be saved from infringement because the exercise of a trade mark proprietor's rights 'must be reserved to cases in which a third party's use of the sign affects or is liable to affect the functions of the trade mark, in particular its essential function of guaranteeing to consumers the origin of the goods'.[112] Conversely if use affected or was liable to affect the functions of the trade mark as a trade mark registered for toys, or the mark registered for cars within the meaning of Art 5(2) (s 10(3) of the 1994 Act and Art 9(1)(c) of the Regulation), it would infringe.

7.34 In the light of *Arsenal* and subsequent decisions,[113] it appears that (b) of **7.27** is the best reflection of the current state of the law in 'double identity' cases: the commercial use of a sign in relation to goods or services for which it is registered will prima facie infringe; a defendant using a mark descriptively and in accordance with honest practices or in some other way that does not undermine the functions of the mark[114] may make out a defence – by arguing thus and/or by invoking a specific defence under s 11(2)(b), Art 6(1) of the

---

[108] *Koninklijke Philips Electronics NV v Remington Consumer Products Ltd* [2005] FSR 17. In *Bolton Pharmaceutical Company 100 Ltd v Swinghope Ltd* [2005] EWHC 1600 (Ch) Ch D, Lawrence Collins J navigated skilfully between *Holterhoff* and *Arsenal*; cf *Electrocoin*, nn 12, 85.

[109] (C-48/05) [2007] ECR I-1017; [2007] ETMR 33 ECJ.

[110] Arnold J at in *L'Oréal SA v eBay International AG* [2009] EWHC 1094 (Ch); [2009] ETMR 53; [2009] RPC 21 at [295].

[111] At [26]–[29], distinguishing *BMW v Deenik* (C-63/97) [1999] ECR I-905.

[112] At [21], citing *Arsenal* at [51] and *Anheuser-Busch Inc v Budějovický Budvar národní podnik* (C-245/02) [2004] ECR I-10989 at [59].

[113] Those cited in *L'Oréal SA v Bellure NV* (C-487/07) [2009] ECR I-5185 at [58]; *L'Oréal SA v eBay International AG* [2009] EWHC 1094 (Ch); [2009] ETMR 53; [2009] RPC 21 at [300]–[306]; *Google France Sàrl v Louis Vuitton Malletier SA* C-236/08, European Court of Justice (Grand Chamber), 23 March 2010 [2010] ETMR 30; [2010] RPC 19; *L'Oréal SA, Lancôme parfums et beauté & Cie, Laboratoire Garnier & Cie, L'Oréal (UK) Limited v eBay International AG, eBay Europe SÀRL and eBay (UK) Limited* (C 324/09), 12 July 2011 CJEU; *Die BergSpechte Outdoor Reisen und Alpinschule Edi Koblmuller GmbH v Guni* C-278/08 [2010] ETMR 33; *Datacard Corporation v Eagle Technologies Ltd* [2011] EWHC 244 (Pat) [2011] RPC 17.

[114] In *Google France Sàrl v Louis Vuitton Malletier SA* C-236/08, European Court of Justice

Directive and Art 12 of the Regulation or the misleading advertising directive.[115] Although the phraseology of the Court of Justice[116] may suggest the burden is on the proprietor to show effect on trade mark functions, Arnold J has pointed out in *Datacard*[117] that confusion is presumed in the case of identical marks and products, in accordance with Art 16 of the WTO TRIPs agreement. As regard the origin function, the difference between s 10(1), Art 5(1)(a) of the Directive and Art 9(1)(a) of the Regulation and s 10(2), Art 5(1)(b) of the Directive and Art 9(1)(b) of the Regulation[118] appears to lie in the presumption, versus proof, of confusion. The question is whether:

> '... use of the sign considered in context [does or] does not enable average consumers, or enables them only with difficulty, to ascertain whether the goods or services referred to under the sign originate from the proprietor of the *trade mark* or an undertaking economically connected to it, or from a third party.'[119]

This test has been described by Ohly as introducing a 'novel duty of transparency, which seems to be borrowed from unfair competition law'.[120] Arnold J also regards it as a new test and not arising from *Céline*[121] as asserted by the Court of Justice.[122]

7.35 In relation to infringement under s 10(2), Art 5(1)(b) of the Directive and Art 9(1)(b) of the Regulation, Arnold J confirmed in *Och-Ziff*[123] that 'initial interest confusion' was actionable under these provisions. This form of confusion, also called 'bait and switch', occurs when 'the defendant deliberately

---

(Grand Chamber), 23 March 2010 [2010] ETMR 30; [2010] RPC 19 at [98] it was held that sale of a keyword identical with a mark to another advertiser did not affect the advertising function of the proprietor's mark.

[115] See below at **7.54**.

[116] *Google France Sàrl v Louis Vuitton Malletier SA* (C-236/08), European Court of Justice (Grand Chamber), 23 March 2010 [2010] ETMR 30; [2010] RPC 19 at [76] 'the proprietor of the mark cannot oppose the use of a sign ... if that use is not liable to cause detriment to any of the functions of that mark' citing *Arsenal* [2003] ETMR 19 at [54], and *L'Oréal* [2009] ETMR 55 at [60]; *Die BergSpechte Outdoor Reisen und Alpinschule Edi Koblmuller GmbH v Guni* (C-278/08) [2010] ETMR 33.

[117] *Datacard Corporation v Eagle Technologies Ltd* [2011] EWHC 244 (Pat); [2011] RPC 17 at [266]; D Ribbons 'Trade marks: What's the difference between Article 5(1)(a) and 5(1)(b)? Not a lot ...' [2011] JIPLP 435.

[118] Considered in *BergSpechte: Die BergSpechte Outdoor Reisen under Alpinschule Edi Koblmuüller GmbH v Guni* (C-278/08) [2010] ECR I-0000.

[119] *Google France SÀRL v Louis Vuitton Malletier SA* (C-236/08) to C-238/08 [2010] ECR I-0000, [2010] RPC 19 at [84]; *Datacard Corporation v Eagle Technologies Ltd* [2011] EWHC 244 (Pat) [2011] RPC 17 at [263]; *Die BergSpechte Outdoor Reisen under Alpinschule Edi Koblmuüller GmbH v Guni* Case C-278/08 [2010] ECR I-0000 at [39]; *Portakabin Ltd v Primakabin BV* (C-558/08) [2010] ETMR 52 at [34].

[120] A Ohly 'Keyword advertising or why the ECJ's functional approach to trade mark infringement does not function' [2010] IIC 879.

[121] *Céline SÀRL v Céline SA* (C-17/06) [2007] ECR I-7041; [2007] ETMR 80.

[122] *Datacard Corporation v Eagle Technologies Ltd* [2011] EWHC 244 (Pat); [2011] RPC 17.

[123] *Och-Ziff Management Europe Ltd and another v Och Capital LLP and others* [2010] EWHC 2599 (Ch); [2011] ETMR 1; [2011] FSR 11 at [101]. See, also, *Whirlpool Corp v Kenwood Ltd* [2008] EWHC 1930 (Ch); [2009] RPC 19; [2009] ETMR 63; [2009] EWCA Civ 753; [2010] RPC 51; [2010] ETMR 109, CA.

uses the claimant's trade mark as a bait to attract the consumer's attention, and then exploits the opportunity thus created to switch the consumer's purchasing intention to his own product or service'.[124]

7.36 As for effect on the advertising function, and the trade mark proprietors rights under s 10(3), Art 5(2) of the Directive and Art 9(1)(c) of the Regulation in keyword cases, in *Interflora Inc v Marks & Spencer Plc*[125] the CJEU held that the use of a mark as a search engine keyword, enabled competitors to offer alternatives,[126] would not, on the facts of the case, deny the proprietor of the trade mark 'the opportunity of using its mark effectively to inform and win over consumers'[127] and hence affect advertising function. This was rather curious, given that the CJEU opined that the origin and investment functions might be affected.[128]

7.37 Provided the onus is on the defendant in s 10(1), Art 5(1)(a) and Art 9(1)(a) cases, the Court of Justice's formulations could be helpful, being more capable of nuance than the concept of 'trade mark use'.[129] Some forms of 'non-trade mark use' may be very undermining, for example, to proprietors whose marks are being used 'generically', by competitors[130] or in dictionaries.[131] Might these be caught by an argument that the functions of the mark are adversely affected? Possibly the first, but there is still the requirement that use be 'in relation to goods or services' which would likely defeat the second.

7.38 Finally, it seems that 'use in the course of trade' must involve use in a commercial communication, although the sign may not be visible to customers.[132] In *Google France*,[133] Google used keywords to marshall internet searches and its 'Adwords' service allowed advertisers to purchase keywords, including complainants' trade marks, to achieve higher ranking in the search listings by giving greater weight to users' clicks. It was argued that this infringed the trade mark owners rights. it was held that:

---

[124] *Och-Ziff* at [82].
[125] (C-323/09) [2012] FSR 3; [2010] EWHC 925 (Ch). See, also, S Ott and M Schubert '"It's the Ad text, stupid": cryptic answers won't establish legal certainty for online advertisers' [2011] JIPLP 25, cited in *Datacard*.
[126] At para 58, citing *Google France* [2010] RPC 19 at para 69.
[127] At para 59, citing *Google France* at paras 96 and 97.
[128] At paras 49–53 and 60–66. See also C Morcom 'Trade marks and the internet: Where are we now?' [2012] EIPR 40.
[129] Although Arnold J seems to regard it as 'trade mark use' – plus: *Datacard Corporation v Eagle Technologies Ltd* [2011] EWHC 244 (Pat); [2011] RPC 17 at para 262.
[130] As in 'caplets': *Johnson & Johnson Australia v Sterling Pharmaceuticals* (1991) 21 IPR 1, or indeed *Hölterhoff*.
[131] Art 10 of the Community Trade Mark Regulation provides a remedy for this.
[132] On visibility, see also *Kabushiki Kaisha Sony Entertainment v Nuplayer Ltd* [2006] FSR 9, ChD; *O2 Holdings Ltd v Hutchison 3G Ltd* [2007] RPC 16, CA; *RxWorks Ltd v Dr Paul Hunter* [2007] EWHC 3061 (Ch); [2008] RPC 13.
[133] *Google France Sàrl v Louis Vuitton Malletier SA* C-236/08, European Court of Justice (Grand Chamber), 23 March 2010; [2010] ETMR 30; [2010] RPC 19.

(1) use by advertisers of trade mark proprietors' signs as 'keywords' to attract searching consumers to the websites on which products were offered would constitute use;[134] but

(2) Google's selling the use of those marks as keywords, storing the keywords and arranging for the display of ads on the basis of those keywords, did not constitute use within the meaning of Art 5, because it did not constitute a commercial communication by Google using the mark.[135]

Use in relation to goods or services

7.39   In *Arsenal*, Ruiz-Jarabo Colomer A-G gave an example of non-trade use – the depiction by the artist Andy Warhol of a Campbell's soup can. It seems clear that Mr Warhol does not trade in soup or in cans but he has attained great commercial success as an artist. Does this mean that use 'in the course of trade' must involve trade in the goods or services on which the mark is used? The ECJ's decision as to Google's liability in *Google France*[136] suggests that this may be the case. A number of pre-1994 Act cases provide further illustrations. It should be noted that under the previous UK legislation there was a 'rule of specialism' – only use in relation to goods or services for which the mark was registered could infringe.[137] Nowadays, use in relation to goods or services is assessed under the comparison rules of s 10(1)–(3) and infringement may occur where there is use on similar or even dissimilar products. Arnold J has expressed the view that the 'fifth condition' (point (d) in **7.10**) – use of a sign 'in relation to' goods or services – means 'use "for the purpose of distinguishing" the goods or services in question, that is to say, as a trade mark as such'.[138]

7.40   Whether or not this is eliding different parts of the enquiry, one needs to ascertain in relation to which goods or services the defendant is using a sign in the course of trade – whose trade and whose goods or services? Usually the

---

[134]   At [51]–[52]. In relation to advertisers' use, there was use of identical signs in relation to identical or similar goods, without consent, in the course of trade, because an advertisement was displayed as a result, which would affect one of the essential functions of the mark (origin or quality) and which would infringe unless it were made clear to the public who was supplying the goods or services. So, presenting goods as alternatives would be permissible (like comparative advertising, although the court did not consider whether a form of comparative advertising was involved) but not if confusion or 'riding on coat-tails' was involved.

[135]   At [55]–[56], however, there might be other forms of liability, see [57]. See, also, '*MR SPICY*': *Wilson v Yahoo! UK Ltd* [2008] EWHC 361 (Ch); [2008] ETMR 33); J Cornthwaite 'AdWords or bad words? A UK perspective on keywords and trade mark infringement' [2009] EIPR 347.

[136]   *Google France Sàrl v Louis Vuitton Malletier SA* C-236/08, European Court of Justice (Grand Chamber), 23 March 2010; [2010] ETMR 30; [2010] RPC 19.

[137]   For an example of the contortions this caused, see *Pickwick International v Multiple Sound Producers* [1972] RPC 786; [1972] FSR 427: music cassettes within the specification 'apparatus for wireless telegraphy; parts and fittings therefor'; *Unilever v Johnson Wax* [1989] FSR 145: whether 'Toilet Duck' lavatory cleaner was a 'common soap or detergent'.

[138]   *Datacard Corporation v Eagle Technologies Ltd* [2011] EWHC 244 (Pat); [2011] RPC 17 at [250], citing *Bayerische Motorenwerke AG v Deenik* (C-63/97) [1999] ECR I-905 at [38], *Anheuser-Busch Inc v Budejovicky Budvar np* (C-245/02) [2004] ECR I-10989 at [64] and *Céline SÀRL v Céline SA* (C-17/06) [2007] ECR I-7041 at [20]; and cf Art 5(5) and *Robelco NV v Robeco Groep NV* (C-23/01) [2002] ECR I-10913 at [28]–[34].

goods or services are those in which the defendant is trading, but infringement may also involve reference to the trademark proprietor's goods or services,[139] or even a third party on whose behalf the defendant is acting.[140]

7.41 To illustrate these issues, example cases under earlier legislation where there was a mismatch between the commercial message, the trade and the marked goods and are outlined below. In a previous edition we submitted that 'the correct approach is not to take too technical a view of "in the course of trade" but rather to consider whether there is commercial use which undermines the proprietors' interest in the functioning of their marks. This is in accordance with the broad protection of trade mark functions advocated by the ECJ'. Subsequent decisions of the Court of Justice have stressed the effect on trade mark functions and give pointers for these situations. It is argued that many of these scenarios would be decided in the same way under the current law.

(a) *Nitedals v Lehmann*:[141] a cow mark was registered for matches. A cow mark was used in advertisements for Cow brand milk, carried on match boxes. Thus, the cow was used in the advertiser's commercial communication, which in turn was physically attached to the goods traded – the matches. Held: infringement. In *RxWorks*, Daniel Alexander QC observed that where the sign is physically on (or embedded in) goods, the condition 'in relation to goods' is 'implicitly satisfied. It is only where the sign is not affixed to the goods that one needs to ask what "link" there is between the sign and the goods'.[142] So, prima facie infringement unless it could be shown that average consumers for matches would ascertain without difficulty that the goods did not originate from the proprietor of the COW mark.[143]

(b) *Ind Coope v Paine*:[144] 'John Bull' was registered for beer. It was used on beer kits in relation to the beer that would be made from the kits. The trade was in beer kits. Held: infringement. In the light of *BMW v Deenik*, this could well be considered use in relation to beer; alternatively it could now be argued that there is infringement under s 10(3) or perhaps even s 10(2).

---

[139] As in *Deenik* and subsequent cases such as *O2 Holdings Ltd v Hutchison 3G UK Ltd* [2008] ECR I-04231, [2008] RPC 33; *L'Oréal SA v Bellure NV* C-487/07 [2000] ECR I-5185; [2009] ETMR 55; and *Portakabin Ltd v Primakabin BV* (C-558/08) [2010] ETMR 52. In UK law this is implicit in s 10(6) of the 1994 Act, which allows for such use in appropriate circumstances. For critique of Opel in this regard see Arnold J in *L'Oréal v eBay* [2009] EWHC 1094; [2009] RPC 21 at [291]–[299].

[140] *UDV North America* C-62/08 [2010] ETMR 25 at [43]–[51]; *Google France* at [60]; *L'Oréal v eBay* at [91].

[141] (1908) 25 RPC 793.

[142] *RxWorks Ltd v Hunter (t/a Connect Computers)* [2007] EWHC 3061 (Ch); [2008] RPC 13 at [42], referring to *Céline Sàrl v Céline SA* (C-17/06#0 [2007] ECR I-7041; [2007] ETMR 80 at [22]–[23].

[143] *Datacard* and cases cited.

[144] [1983] RPC 326.

(c) *Spillers*:[145] 'Hovis' was registered for flour. It was used on baking tins to impress the words on loaves. The trade was in loaves. Held: no use in relation to flour, but observed that wording such as 'made from Hovis flour' would be use in relation to flour (though doubted whether this would infringe). If true, the latter use would now be protected by a specific defence under s 11(2)(b), Art 6(1)(b) of the Directive and Art 12(b) of the Regulation, but unlicensed use on tins and, therefore, bread might lead customers to believe that the trade mark proprietors were responsible for the baking of the loaves as well as the supply of flour, so confusion could be shown under the test in s 10(2), Art 5(1)(b) of the Directive and Art 9(1)(b) of the Regulation.[146]

(d) *Du Pont*:[147] 'Du Pont' on garment swing tickets was not use 'in relation to' garments. It indicated the fibre of which the garments were made but did not indicate a trade connection between the applicant for registration and the garments. As a matter of perception of the average consumer, this would probably be decided the same way under the 1994 Act.

(e) *Alicia*:[148] 'Coke' was registered for cola. A 'Coke' bottle appeared in an indecent film sequence. The defendant's trade was in films. Held: infringement. This would likely succeed today under s 10(3) assuming the use of the bottle were regarded as the film-makers' 'commercial communication'.

(f) *Trebor Bassett v Football Association*:[149] Trebor Bassett traded in sweets. They encouraged children to buy their sweets by packing them with 'football cards' bearing photographs of players wearing their official 'strip'. Held: no use of the symbols 'in relation to' the cards. The decision as regards the model cars in *Adam Opel v Autec* suggests that a similar conclusion could be reached under the 1994 Act or Community Trade Mark Regulation.

---

[145] (1954) 71 RPC 234.

[146] *BergSpechte: Die BergSpechte Outdoor Reisen under Alpinschule Edi Koblmüüller GmbH v Guni* Case (C-278/08) [2010] ECR I-0000

[147] *DU PONT Trade Mark* [2004] FSR 15, CA.

[148] [1977] Ned Jur 59, [1976] BIE 214, cited by D W Feer Verkade in 'Unfair use of and damage to the reputation of well-known trademarks, trade names and indications of source – a combination from the Benelux' (1986) 17 IIC 768. In this author's view a number of the cases Feer Verkade classifies as 'non-designatory use' involve use in relation to relevant goods and use in the course of a trade, albeit a different trade.

[149] [1997] FSR 211. Not surprisingly, the Football Association have since relied upon copyright. See, e g *Football Association Premier League Ltd v Panini UK Ltd* [2004] 1 WLR 1147 CA.

ACTIVITIES SPECIFIED AS INFRINGING – PRIMARY INFRINGEMENT

7.42 Section 10(4) of the 1994 Act, Art 5(3) of the Directive and Art 9(2) of the Regulation spell out activities by which infringement may be committed:[150]

(a) affixing the sign to goods or the packaging thereof;

(b) offering or exposing the goods for sale, putting them on the market or stocking[151] them for those purposes under that sign, or offering or supplying services under the sign;

(c) importing or exporting the goods under that sign;[152] or

(d) using the sign on business papers or in advertising.

Although the phraseology of s 10(4) suggests visual use, s 10(2) confirms that non-graphic use counts. By implication, oral use, such as use on the radio, or even use discernible by the senses of touch or smell, could infringe. Where a device mark represents a shape or form, use of the form may infringe, as suggested by the old case of *Carless, Capel & Leonard v Pilmore Bedford.*[153]

7.43 The list in s 10(4), Art 5(3) of the Directive and Art 9(2) of the Regulation is non-exhaustive – the Directive and Regulation use the phrase '*inter alia*' whilst s 10(4) says 'in particular'. In the future, courts will need to consider whether other kinds of use fall within the scope of these provisions, uses which might not have been technically foreseeable when the legislation was promulgated. What, for example, if the use is invisible to the consumer? In *Reed Executive plc v Reed Business Information Ltd,*[154] the defendants used 'metatags' – words used by internet search engines that might lead someone searching for the claimants to the defendants' website. The Court of Appeal, deciding the case on the basis that the marks were non-identical, held that there would be no confusion and hence no infringement under s 10(2). However, Jacob LJ went on to say (obiter):

> 'It may be that an invisible use of this sort is not use at all for the purposes of this trade mark legislation.'

---

[150] 'Article 5(3) of Directive 89/104 provides a non-exhaustive list of the types of use which may be prevented.' *Google France* at [63].

[151] See *Bolton Pharmaceutical Company 100 Ltd v Swinghope Ltd* [2005] EWHC 1600 (Ch) Ch D.

[152] *Pfizer* [2007] EWHC 3137 (Ch).

[153] (1928) 45 RPC 205. The plaintiff's mark, registered for petroleum oil, included a lighthouse device. The defendants sold petrol from lighthouse-shaped pumps. It was held that the defendants did not infringe because the pumps did not, in fact, indicate the origin of the petrol to purchasers. It was recognised, however, that there could in principle be infringement by use of a form represented in a mark.

[154] [2004] ETMR 56; [2004] EWCA Civ 159, CA.

Nonetheless, it appears from *RxWorks*[155] and *Google France*[156] that invisible use by advertisers could infringe, although the perception of consumers and the effect on trade mark functions might be difficult to ascertain.[157]

7.44 From time to time doubts have been expressed as to whether a company uses its name as a trade mark in relation to its products if the latter are labelled with another mark.[158] These doubts were implicit in parliamentary debates on retail service marks.[159] An old case which has often been quoted in this regard was *Autodrome*,[160] where the sale of used motor cars from premises called 'the Autodrome' was held not to be use of a registered mark for cars. However, it is clear from the judgment that, had proper evidence been forthcoming as to the use of 'Autodrome' on invoices,[161] the case would have been decided differently. In *Euromarket Designs Inc v Peters and Crate & Barrel Ltd*,[162] Jacob J commented (obiter) that use on shop signs or shop packaging such as carrier bags might not be use 'in relation to' the goods within. It is submitted that the wording of s 10(4)(a) of the 1994 Act, which refers to offering or exposing goods for sale (etc) under the sign, is apt to include use on a shop sign or as a business name. As stated in the headnote to a Portuguese case:

'The fact that company names and trade marks have different juridical qualities does not prohibit the use of the former from being subject to the law that governs the latter.'[163]

This has been reinforced by the Court of Justice's view in *Céline* that trade mark rights can be engaged by use as a company name.[164] This is just as well as a significant proportion of cases decided by the company names adjudicator involve names incorporating protected marks.[165]

---

[155] *RxWorks Ltd v Hunter (tla Connect Computers)* [2007] EWHC 3061 (Ch); [2008] RPC 13.
[156] *Google France Sàrl v Louis Vuitton Malletier SA* (C-236/08) European Court of Justice (Grand Chamber), 23 March 2010; [2010] ETMR 30; [2010] RPC 19.
[157] See C Morcom 'Trade marks and the internet: Where are we now?' [2012] EIPR 40.
[158] Marks & Spencer escaped liability for infringement of another's trade mark on this basis in *Coast to coast, Unidoor Ltd v Marks and Spencer plc* [1988] RPC 275 Ch D (a case decided under earlier trade mark law but still cited by commentators, e g H Norman 'Time to Blow the Whistle on Trade Mark Use' [2004] IPQ 1).
[159] See **1.25–1.27**.
[160] [1969] RPC 564; [1969] FSR 320.
[161] In *CHEETAH TM* [1993] FSR 263 the court held that use of a mark on invoices and delivery notes was trade mark use under the 1938 Act.
[162] [2001] FSR 20. See, also, *Future Publishing Ltd v Edge Interactive Media Inc, Edge Games Inc and Dr Timothy Langdell* [2011] EWHC 1489 (Ch); [2011] ETMR 50.
[163] *Geoffrey Inc v Nails R Us – Instituto de Beleza e Saúde, Lda* [2005] ETMR 13 Rel (Lisboa).
[164] *Céline Sàrl v Céline SA* (C-17/06) [2007] ECR I-7041; [2007] ETMR 80.
[165] Link available at www.ipo.gov.uk/cna.htm.

ACTIVITIES SPECIFIED AS INFRINGING – CONTRIBUTORY INFRINGEMENT

7.45 Section 10(5) is a curious provision of UK law which makes someone party to infringing use by others.[166] It applies where, without the consent of the proprietor,[167] the person knowingly or recklessly applies the registered mark to material intended to be used:

(a)   for labelling or packaging goods;[168]

(b)   as a business paper; or

(c)   for advertising goods or services.

It is reminiscent of the tort of causing and enabling passing off, as exemplified by the Scotch Whisky cases.[169] However, the printing of the labels, stationery or advertising material is not rendered directly infringing – rather, the printer is made a party to infringing use of the material by others and therefore incurs only *potential* liability. Unlike the passing-off cases, the downstream infringement has therefore to occur in the UK for liability to attach: *Beautimatic International v Mitchell International Pharmaceuticals*.[170] When enacted, this section no doubt caused great concern to the printing and packaging industry, which might be liable for acts over which it has no control. However, the person concerned will only be treated as party to infringing use if he knows or has reason to believe that the application of the mark was not duly authorised by the proprietor or a licensee. The best defence under this section is therefore vigilance in inquiry; if a customer warrants that use of any mark is duly authorised, at best the printer will be able to rely on it as a defence, at worst claim an indemnity. Professor John Adams has posited the case of a printer who makes labels at the request of the proprietor and then supplies some of these to an infringer. Arguably, the latter has been carried out without the consent of the proprietor[171] and thus may be caught by s 10(5). This is supported by the decision in *Primark Stores Ltd v Lollypop Clothing Ltd*,[172] a case on alleged 'over-runs' of jeans, and by analogy with the 'limited purpose' concept in breach of confidence.[173]

---

[166]   In *R v Johnstone* [2003] UKHL 28; [2003] 1 WLR 1736 it was said (obiter) to extend liability to accomplices.

[167]   Section 9(1).

[168]   In *Paterson Zochonis v Merfarken Packaging* [1983] FSR 273, a packaging manufacturer was held not liable for copyright infringements.

[169]   See **4.9**.

[170]   [1999] ETMR 912 Ch D.

[171]   See **7.14**, **7.38**.

[172]   [2001] FSR 37; [2001] ETMR 30 Ch D, per John Martin QC, sitting as a deputy High Court judge: 'In order that the jeans should become Primark's goods, it is not enough that they should have been manufactured to Primark's specification: they must have been adopted by Primark as its goods. Without such adoption, Primark cannot be taken to be saying either that it is the source of the goods or that it accepts responsibility for their quality. In fact, the supplier is the source of the goods; and if anybody has undertaken responsibility to the public

SUMMARY JUDGMENT IN TRADE MARK INFRINGEMENT CASES

7.46   Section 10(1) ensures that use in the course of trade of an identical mark on identical goods or services will infringe the registration. Subject to the question of effect on trade mark function,[174] there is no need for the claimant to prove confusion, damage or intention. This case is eminently suitable for summary judgment under the Civil Procedure Rules 1998 (CPR), Part 24.[175] Under this procedure, once a claim has been served and acknowledged and before a defence is filed,[176] the claimant may apply for judgment on the whole or part of their claim,[177] against one or more defendants.[178] It must be established that the defendant has no real prospect of successfully defending the claim or issue. This may be shown by a short statement or more copious evidence but the court will not engage in a 'mini-trial'. In awarding summary judgment in *Puma AG Rudolf Dassler Sport v Sports Soccer Ltd*,[179] Etherton J discussed this:

> 'It is well established that, on a CPR Part 24 hearing, the judge is not to conduct a mini-trial. That plainly does not mean, however, that in an action which turns on a fact-dependent issue, such as the copying of goods, it is never possible to obtain summary judgment. Save in exceptional circumstances, it is not appropriate for the judge, on a summary judgment application, to choose between opposing

---

for their quality it is the supplier, not Primark. It is irrelevant that, had the jeans been supplied by the supplier to Primark rather than to the defendant, they might have been accepted by Primark and so become Primark's goods.'

[173]   *Coco v Clark* [1969] RPC 41, per Megarry: 'as to the scope of an obligation of confidentiality, where one exists. Sometimes the obligation imposes no restriction on use of the use [sic] of the information, as long as the confidee does not reveal it to third parties. In other circumstances, the confidee may not be entitled to use it except for some limited purpose'. Cf *Seager v Copydex Ltd* [1967] RPC 349 at 368: 'To avoid taking unfair advantage of information does not necessarily mean that the confidee must not use it except for the confider's limited purpose. Whether one adopts the "reasonable man" test suggested by Megarry J or some other, there can be no breach of the equitable obligation unless the court concludes that a confidence reposed has been abused, that unconscientious use has been made of the information.'

[174]   See **7.11**. This requirement must have a chilling effect on applications for summary judgment.

[175]   Civil Procedure Rules 1998, SI 1998/3132, as amended, Part 24 'Summary Judgment', available at   www.justice.gov.uk/guidance/courts-and-tribunals/courts/procedure-rules/civil/contents/parts/part24.htm. See, also, practice direction available at www.justice.gov.uk/guidance/courts-and-tribunals/courts/procedure-rules/civil/contents/practice_directions/pd_part24.htm.

[176]   There is nothing to stop a defendant filing a defence and counterclaim ('Part 20 claim') after an application for summary judgment has been made. A defendant resisting an application for summary judgment will rely upon the contentions in the defence. The court may equally consider an application for summary judgment on a counterclaim. In *Decon Laboratories Ltd v Fred Baker Scientific Ltd* [2001] RPC 17 Ch D, the counterclaim for partial revocation of the registration was successful, but did not prevent judgment being entered for the claimant on infringement.

[177]   If there is summary judgment on infringement but a counterclaim for invalidity goes to trial, as occurred in *AAH Pharmaceuticals Ltd v Vantagemax plc* [2003] ETMR 18, it may be advisable for a defendant to seek stay of the judgment pending trial.

[178]   The application for summary judgment may succeed against one defendant but not another, as in *Beautimatic International Ltd v Mitchell International Pharmaceuticals Ltd* [2000] FSR 267.

[179]   [2003] EWHC 2705 (Ch) Ch D at para 72; see, also, *Daimler AG v Sany Group Co Ltd* [2009] EWHC 1003 (Ch); [2009] ETMR 58.

statements of evidence by, for example, assessing credibility and cogency on a balance of probabilities. In the present case, however, my conclusions do not depend upon resolving conflicting statements of evidence.'

Even a difficult question of law or interpretation[180] may be considered on summary judgment applications, provided that the issue is determinative of the parties' rights.[181] There are several possible outcomes: the court may grant the application, allowing final judgment to be entered for the claimant, or dismiss the application, leaving it open to the defendant to file a defence.[182] In a doubtful case the court may exercise its case management powers in such a way as to make the defence conditional,[183] usually upon payment into court.[184]

7.47 Just as a claimant may seek summary judgment, so may a defendant ask for a claim or issue to be decided in its favour, to be struck out[185] on the grounds that the claimant has no real prospect of success. Whether claimant or defendant (or both) applies for summary judgment, the court must further be satisfied that there is no other compelling reason,[186] such as public policy, why the case or issue should only be disposed of after full trial.

7.48 Summary judgment has also been granted in cases of infringement under s 10(2) and even in passing off.[187] In *Asprey & Garrard Ltd v WRA (Guns) Ltd*,[188] counsel conceded before the Court of Appeal that in the light of a reference[189] to the ECJ as to the meaning of 'identical' in s 10(1), summary

---

[180] Eg of a licence, as in *Pink Floyd v EMI* [2010] EWHC 533 (Ch) (appeal dismissed [2010] EWCA Civ 1429).

[181] Eg *IPC Magazines Ltd v MGN Ltd* [1998] FSR 431 Ch D. This case was decided under earlier Rules of Court, but still good law, it is submitted.

[182] As in *Road Tech Computer Systems v UNISON Software* [1996] FSR 805 Ch D. In these circumstances the defendant may ask for costs occasioned by the unsuccessful application. See, also, *Doncaster Pharmaceuticals Group Ltd v Bolton Pharmaceutical Co 100 Ltd* [2006] EWCA Civ 661; [2006] ETMR 65; [2007] FSR 3. Parallel imports case involved too many factual issues for summary judgment.

[183] CPR PD 24, para 5 states that in an application under CPR Part 24, the court may give judgment on the claim, strike out or dismiss the claim, dismiss the application, or make a conditional order which requires a party to pay a sum of money into court or take a specified step in relation to his claim or defence. In the event of non-compliance with the condition, that party's claim will be dismissed or pleading struck out. Leave to defend conditional upon payment in of royalties under disputed licence was awarded in *Trademark Licensing Co Ltd v Leofelis SA* [2010] EWHC 969.

[184] In *Anglo-Eastern Trust Ltd v Roohallah Kermanshahchi* [2002] CP Rep 36 (CA), the Court of Appeal criticised the time-honoured practice whereby neither the claimant nor defendant would refer to this upon the application, stating that conditional leave to defend should not be granted unless the defendant had prior notice that such an order might be sought. Such notice could be given informally, by letter.

[185] CPR Part 24, r 24.2; CPR Part 3, r 3.4.

[186] CPR Part 24, r 24.2(b).

[187] Eg *British Telecommunications plc v One in a Million Ltd* [1999] 1 WLR 903; [1999] ETMR 61; [1999] FSR 1; cf *Daimler AG v Sany Group Co Ltd* [2009] EWHC 1003 (Ch); [2009] ETMR 58.

[188] [2002] ETMR 47 (CA). For criticism of the decision see, eg Thorne and Bennett 'Domain Names – Internet Warehousing: Has protection of well-known names on the Internet gone too far?' [1998] EIPR 468.

[189] *LTJ Diffusion v SA Sadas Vertbaudet (Arthur et Felicié)* (C-291/00) [2003] ETMR 83, ECJ.

judgment under s 10(1) was not appropriate. However, the Court of Appeal considered summary judgment for *Asprey & Garrard* to be appropriate under s 10(2) and in passing off. In *Smithkline Beecham Ltd v GSKline Ltd* judgment was granted to subsidiaries of a well-known pharmaceutical company in respect of trade mark infringement and passing off claims where, in the absence of any explanation, the inference was that the defendant's company name had been chosen with the deliberate aim of referring to the claimants' group of companies.[190]

WELL-KNOWN MARKS

7.49 Section 56 provides a cause of action for the proprietor of a well-known mark within the meaning of Art 6*bis* of the Paris Convention or Art 16.3 of the WTO TRIPs agreement.[191] The mark has to be well known in the UK as the mark of a person who is a national of, domiciled in, or who has a real and effective commercial presence in, a WTO or Paris Convention country. That person can sue to restrain unauthorised use in the UK, on identical or similar goods or services,[192] of the same or an essentially identical or similar mark. The likelihood of confusion must be established. This special cause of action does not require business or goodwill in the UK.[193] It is subject to the defences of acquiescence and of bona fide continuing use.[194]

7.50 Section 56 raises the questions of whether the mark has to be registered in its country of origin, and how well-known status may be established. In some countries, there is an administrative mechanism for declaring marks to be well known. No such proposals are contained in the 1994 Act. Furthermore, a UK national or resident cannot rely upon s 56, though this might involve discrimination by nationality, contrary to the TFEU. According to s 55(1)(b), 'Convention country' means a country other than the UK. However, someone established in the UK would probably enjoy rights to sue in passing off.

7.51 Article 16.3 of the TRIPs Agreement provides that:

'Article 6*bis* of the Paris Convention (1967) shall apply, mutatis mutandis, to goods or services which are not similar to those in respect of which a trademark is *registered*, provided that use of that trademark in relation to those goods or services would indicate a connection between those goods or services and the owner of the registered trademark and provided that the interests of the owner of the *registered* trademark are likely to be damaged by such use.'

---

[190] [2011] EWHC 169 (Ch).

[191] Well-known marks under the Paris Convention are considered in more detail in Chapter 12 and under TRIPs at **15.19**. See, also, M Blakeney 'Well-Known Marks' [1994] EIPR 481.

[192] Art 6*bis* refers only to goods but its application is extended by virtue of Art 16 TRIPs and the Community trade mark system does not distinguish between goods and services. See, also, *Hotel Cipriani Srl v Cipriani (Grosvenor Street) Ltd* [2009] EWHC 3032 (Ch); [2009] RPC 9.

[193] Section 56(1).

[194] Section 56(2) and (3).

The phraseology is odd since Art 6*bis* actually requires well-known marks to be protected in countries where they are not registered. Assuming that TRIPs, Art 16.3 only requires registered marks to be protected in this way, then s 10(3) of the 1994 Act complies.

USE WITHOUT THE PROPRIETOR'S CONSENT

7.52 Usually this is a matter for recital in pleadings. Dispute as to the existence of consent may arise in a straightforward way, as in *Beiersdorf v Ramlort*,[195] where a defendant avoided summary judgment by producing documents of consent, which the claimant alleged were forged. The court was unable to resolve this crucial dispute as to fact on a summary hearing. In *Pfizer*, Norris J remarked:

> '... when one is considering the concept of consent in this context one is looking for an unequivocal demonstration that the proprietor of the mark has renounced his rights in connection with the intended dealing.'[196]

The question of consent arises in a more subtle way where the mark is used on or in relation to goods or services connected with the proprietor. On the one hand, a seller or reseller may need to use the mark to advertise the availability of goods.[197] On the other hand, the proprietor may have reason to oppose further circulation of the goods or use of the mark. This is considered further in the following paragraphs.

USE IN RELATION TO THE PROPRIETOR'S GOODS OR SERVICES INCLUDING COMPARATIVE ADVERTISING

7.53 Here, s 10(6) of the 1994 Act comes into play. This 'home-grown provision'[198] was introduced, ostensibly under Art 5(5),[199] to enable a proprietor to restrain use of its mark in comparative advertising.[200] Section 10(6) exempts from infringement the use of a mark to identify goods or services as those of the proprietor or a licensee, if that be the case. The last proviso is not expressed, but must be implicit. Section 10(6) is subject to an express proviso which disapplies it where the use is:

---

[195] [2005] ETMR 15.

[196] [2007] EWHC 3137 (Ch) at [9], citing *Roche v Kent Pharmaceuticals* [2006] EWCA Civ 1775 at para 25.

[197] *Parfums Christian Dior v Evora* C337/95 [1997] ECR I-6013.

[198] *Pag Ltd v Hawke-Woods Ltd* [2002] ETMR 70; [2002] FSR 46 Ch D.

[199] S Fletcher, P Fussing, A Indraccolo 'Comparisons And Conclusions: Welcome Clarification From the European Court of Justice on the Interpretation of the Comparative Advertising Directive' [2003] EIPR 570.

[200] *Barclays Bank v RBS Advanta* [1996] RPC 307; *Vodaphone Group plc v Orange Personal Communications* [1997] FSR 34.

(a)   not in accordance with honest practices in industrial or commercial matters;[201]

(b)   without due cause; and

(c)   takes unfair advantage of, or is detrimental to, the distinctive character or repute of the trade mark.[202]

The last two factors also appear in ss 5(3) and 10(3) of the 1994 Act. In *Audi-Med Trade Mark*[203] and *Oasis Stores Ltd's Trade Mark Application*,[204] Registry hearing officer Allan James interpreted s 5(3) in line with Laddie J's interpretation of s 10(6) in *Barclays Bank v RBS Advanta*:[205]

> '"Not in accordance with honest practices" is a venerable phrase which made its appearance in Art 10bis(2) of the Paris Convention, defining an act of unfair competition.[206] It appears to be a subjective test, difficult of elucidation.[207] The complexity of the subsection, and in particular the combination of negatives, make it difficult to be sure on whom the burden of proof lies. It is submitted that a wise plaintiff who wishes to allege infringement by use on her own goods or services will proffer evidence on all three factors in the proviso. As to honest practices, one might suppose it would be helpful to rely upon industry guidelines, such as the Advertising Standards Authority's codes of practice. However, this approach has been rejected.'[208]

7.54 Section 10(6) is most likely to be invoked in comparative advertising cases; the practice of comparative advertising uses the proprietor's mark to identify the proprietor's products for the purposes of comparison with the advertisers.[209] In the words of the Misleading Advertising Directive 2006/114/EC 'Comparative advertising' means any advertising which explicitly or by implication identifies a competitor or goods or services offered by a

---

[201]   See also *Gillette Co v LA-Laboratories Ltd Oy* C-228/03 [2005] ETMR 67 at [42]–[45]; I Simon 'Nominative use and honest practices in industrial and commercial matters – a very European history' [2007] IPQ 117.

[202]   *Anheuser-Busch Inc v Budejovicky Budvar Narodni Podnik* C-245/02 [2005] ETMR 27 confirms this under EU law.

[203]   [1998] RPC 863 TMR (opposition by motor manufacturer Audi).

[204]   [1998] RPC 631 TMR (opposition by battery manufacturer Ever-Ready to registration of the sign for condoms).

[205]   [1996] RPC 307.

[206]   See *Cable & Wireless plc v British Telecommunications plc* [1998] FSR 383 at 391, where Jacob J described it as 'a pretty woolly phrase'.

[207]   House of Lords Public Bill Committee, cols 38–44 (18 January 1994). On 24 February 1994, *Hansard*, vol 552, no 46, col 738, Lord Strathclyde said 'as a matter of principle we should leave industry and commerce to determine those matters themselves'.

[208]   See *Barclays Bank v RBS Advanta* [1996] RPC 307 at 316; *British Airways Plc v Ryanair Ltd* [2001] FSR 32, para 30 at point (6).

[209]   For useful examples of types of comparative advertising, see P Carey 'Comparative Advertising: European Harmonisation' [2000] Ent LR 21.

competitor.[210] If this actually leads to confusion, it is actionable in passing off. Section 10(6) was drafted in the light of proposed amendments to EC Directive (EEC) 84/450 on misleading advertising to permit the necessary use of marks in comparative advertising, subject to safeguards. In due course, Council Directive (EC) 97/55 concerning misleading and comparative advertising amended Directive (EEC) 84/450 to add a new Art 3a which expressly permitted comparative advertising under ten cumulative[211] conditions. The UK government took the view that s 10(6) complied with the misleading advertising Directive, as amended, and contented itself with amending the Control of Misleading Advertising Regulations 1988[212] to reflect Art 3a.[213] These provisions were said in *Lidl v Vierzon* 'to achieve a balance between the different interests which may be affected by allowing comparative advertising'.

7.55 The provisions have been consolidated into Art 4 of Directive 2006/114/EC:

'Comparative advertising shall, as far as the comparison is concerned, be permitted when the following conditions are met:

(a)   it is not misleading within the meaning of Articles 2(b), 3 and 8(1) of this Directive or Articles 6 and 7 of Directive 2005/29/EC of the European Parliament and of the Council of 11 May 2005 concerning unfair business-to-consumer commercial practices in the internal market ("Unfair Commercial Practices Directive");

(b)   it compares goods or services meeting the same needs or intended for the same purpose;[214]

(c)   it objectively compares one or more material, relevant, verifiable and representative features of those goods and services, which may include price;

(d)   it does not discredit or denigrate[215] the trade marks, trade names, other distinguishing marks, goods, services, activities or circumstances of a competitor;

(e)   for products with designation of origin, it relates in each case to products with the same designation;

---

[210]   Directive 2006/114/EC of the European Parliament and of the Council of 12 December 2006 concerning misleading and comparative advertising (codified version) [2006] OJ L 376/21, Art 2(c).

[211]   *L'Oréal v Bellure NV* (C-487/07) [2000] ECR I-5185; [2009] ETMR 55 at [67].

[212]   SI 1988/915.

[213]   Reg 4a. See H Carty 'Registered Trade Marks and Permissible Comparative Advertising' [2002] EIPR 294.

[214]   This supposes a sufficient degree of interchangeability for consumers: *Lidl Belgium GmbH & Co KG v Etablissementen Franz Colruyt NV* C-356/04 [2006] ECR I-8501; [2007] 1 CMLR 9; [2007] CEC 3; [2007] ETMR 28 at [26]; *De Landtsheer Emmanuel SA v Comite Interprofessionnel du Vin de Champagne* C-381/05 [2007] ECR I-3115; [2007] 2 CMLR 43; [2007] ETMR 69 at [44]; *Lidl SNC v Vierzon Distribution SA* C-159/09 [2011] 2 CMLR 10; [2011] ETMR 6 at [28].

[215]   The court took a robust view of the defendants' activity in *British Airways plc v Ryanair Ltd* [2001] FSR 32; [2001] ETMR 24 Ch D ('BA****RDS').

(f)   it does not take unfair advantage of the reputation of a trade mark, trade name or other distinguishing marks of a competitor or of the designation of origin of competing products;[216]

(g)   it does not present goods or services as imitations or replicas of goods or services bearing a protected trade mark or trade name;

(h)   it does not create confusion among traders, between the advertiser and a competitor or between the advertiser's trade marks, trade names, other distinguishing marks, goods or services and those of a competitor.'[217]

7.56 Section 10(6) has proved extremely attractive to those engaging in comparative advertising. The principles of its application were summarised in a series of points[218] which were reiterated in subsequent decisions:[219]

'(1) The primary objective of section 10(6) of the 1996 Act is to permit comparative advertising (see Advanta at pages 312–313 and 315, and Vodafone at pages 4–5 of the transcript of the judgment);

(2) As long as the use of a competitor's mark is honest,[220] there is nothing wrong in telling the public of the relative merits of competing goods or services and using registered trade marks to identify them (see Advanta page 315, Vodafone at page 4);

(3) The onus is on the registered proprietor to show that the factors indicated in the proviso to section 10(6) exist (see Advanta at page 315, Vodafone at page 4);

(4) There will be no trade mark infringement unless the use of the registered mark is not in accordance with honest practices (see Advanta at page 315);

(5) The test is objective: would a reasonable reader be likely to say, upon being given the full facts, that the advertisement is not honest? (See Advanta at page 315, Vodafone at page 4);

---

[216] In *L'Oréal v Bellure NV* C-487/07 [2000] ECR I-5185; [2009] ETMR 55 at [41] 'unfair advantage' was characterised in the following terms: 'As regards the concept of "taking unfair advantage of the distinctive character or the repute of the trade mark", also referred to as "parasitism" or "free-riding", that concept relates not to the detriment caused to the mark but to the advantage taken by the third party as a result of the use of the identical or similar sign. It covers, in particular, cases where, by reason of a transfer of the image of the mark or of the characteristics which it projects to the goods identified by the identical or similar sign, there is clear exploitation on the coat-tails of the mark with a reputation.'

[217] *O2 Holdings Ltd and O2 (UK) Ltd v Hutchison 3G Ltd* (C-533/06) [2008] ECR I-04231, [2008] RPC 33 at [65].

[218] Per Jacob J in *Cable & Wireless plc v British Telecommunications plc* [1998] FSR 383, adding to those listed by Michael Crystal QC (sitting as a deputy High Court judge) in *BT v AT & T Communications*, summarising earlier dicta from *Barclays v RBS Advanta and Vodafone*, see **7.53**.

[219] Including *British Airways plc v Ryanair Ltd* [2001] ETMR 24 and *O2 Ltd v Hutchinson 3G UK Ltd* [2005] ETMR 61 (the latter a case on Community trade mark infringement and Art 12(b) of the Regulation). But see *O2 Holdings Ltd and O2 (UK) Ltd v Hutchison 3G Ltd* C-533/06 [2008] ECR I-04231; [2008] RPC 33.

[220] Cf *Kingspan Group Plc v Rockwool Ltd* [2011] EWHC 250 (Ch).

(6) Statutory or industry agreed codes of conduct are not a helpful guide as to whether an advertisement is honest for the purposes of section 10(6). Honesty has to be gauged against what is reasonably to be expected by the relevant public of advertisements for the goods or services in issue (see Advanta at page 316);

(7) It should be borne in mind that the general public are used to the ways of advertisers and expects hyperbole (see Advanta at page 315; cf. Vodafone at pages 3–4);

(8) The 1994 Act does not impose on the courts an obligation to try and enforce through the back door of trade mark legislation a more puritanical standard than the general public would expect from advertising copy (see Advanta at page 315, Vodafone at page 4);

(9) An advertisement which is significantly misleading is not honest for the purposes of section 10(6) (see Advanta at page 316, Vodafone at page 4–5).

I venture with diffidence to make a number of additional observations.

(10) The advertisement must be considered as a whole (cf Advanta at pages 316–318);

(11) As a purpose of the 1994 Act is positively to permit comparative advertising, the court should not hold words used in the advertisement to be seriously misleading for interlocutory purposes unless on a fair reading of them in their context and against the background of the advertisement as a whole they can really be said to justify that description;

(12) A minute textual examination is not something upon which the reasonable reader of an advertisement would embark;

(13) The court should therefore not encourage a microscopic approach to the construction of a comparative advertisement on a motion for interlocutory relief.'

From this it can be seen that the UK courts in the past have taken a rather robust approach and have tended to permit comparative advertising despite complaints from trade mark proprietors. This is confirmed by the reluctance with which Jacob LJ applied the European Court of Justice's ruling in the 'smell-alike' case, *L'Oréal v Bellure*.[221]

7.57   The statement for entry in the minutes of the EC Council meeting at which the Community Trade Mark Regulation was adopted says of Art 9 of the Community Trade Mark Regulation, which is in identical terms to Art 5(3)(d) of the Directive and s 10(4)(d) of the 1994 Act:

'The Council and the Commission consider that the reference to advertising in paragraph 2(d) does not cover the use of a Community trade mark in comparative advertising.'

---

[221]   *L'Oréal SA v Bellure NV* [2010] EWCA Civ 535; [2010] ETMR 47; [2010] RPC 23; *L'Oréal v Bellure NV* C-487/07 [2000] ECR I-5185; [2009] ETMR 55.

However, given the protection of trade marks envisaged in Art 4 of the misleading advertising Directive and the policy arguments rehearsed by the ECJ in *Toshiba Europe v Katun Germany GmbH*[222] and *Pippig Augenoptik v Hartlauer*[223] it is submitted that this statement is erroneous; trade mark rights may be exercised to enjoin comparative advertising which does not satisfy the criteria of Art 4.

7.58 Section 10(6) may have been designed primarily for comparative advertising cases, but it has been used in other situations. As pointed out in *Scandecor*:[224]

> 'A wholesaler or retailer who buys and re-sells goods on which the manufacturer has placed his trade mark does not need a licence to use the manufacturer's mark. The wholesaler or retailer needs no such licence, for the simple reason that he is merely selling the manufacturer's goods to which the manufacturer has already attached the manufacturer's mark. Re-selling goods bearing the manufacturer's mark is not an infringement of that mark: see section 10(6) of the 1994 Act.'

However, if the goods have been altered in some way, they may cease to fall within s 10(6). In *PAG v Hawk-Woods*,[225] the defendants opened up power cell cases manufactured and sold by the claimant, replaced the cells and returned the batteries to the customer. Pumfrey J rejected a defence under s 10(6), holding that the goods returned to customers under the mark were substantially new; they were not 'those of the proprietor'. Goods marketed abroad by the proprietor or with his consent and imported by a third party, so-called 'parallel imports'[226] have their own specific provisions in s 12. A robust approach similar to that displayed in comparative advertising cases was shown in *Wolters Kluwer (UK) Ltd v Reed Elsevier (UK) Ltd.*[227]

7.59 Other savings from infringement are considered in Chapter 8.

OTHER CAUSES OF ACTION

7.60 Actions for infringement of a registered trade mark may be combined with other causes of action such as passing off[228] or malicious falsehood.[229] It is likely that this practice will continue,[230] especially while uncertainties remain as to the scope and extent of infringement rights and the interplay of the trade marks and misleading advertising directives.

---

[222] (C112/99) [2002] FSR 39.

[223] (C-44/01) [2004] ETMR 5.

[224] *Scandecor Developments AB v Scandecor Marketing AB* [2001] 2 CMLR 30; [2002] FSR 7; [2001] ETMR 74 HL.

[225] [2002] ETMR 70; [2002] FSR 46 Ch D.

[226] See Chapter 4 and 8.

[227] [2005] EWHC 2053 (Ch); [2006] FSR 28.

[228] See **3.5ff**.

[229] See **3.24–3.26**.

[230] G Crown 'Malicious Falsehood: Into the 21st Century' [1997] Ent LR 6; *DSG Retail Ltd v Comet Group plc* [2002] FSR 58.

7.61 Three other special actions for injunctions may be mentioned briefly here. Sections 57, 58 and 60 implement Arts 6*ter*[231] and 6*septies*[232] of the Paris Convention. Sections 57 and 58 enable the competent authority to restrain unauthorised use of flags and other emblems of states and international organisations. In *American Clothing*, a case on registration, the ECJ commented on the 'essential functions which may be attributed to a State emblem. These include that of identifying a State and that of representing its sovereignty and unity'.[233] Section 60 enables the 'true' proprietor of a mark which has been wrongly registered in the name of an agent to restrain the agent's use and to call for transfer or invalidation[234] of the mark.

REMEDIES AND SEIZURE PROVISIONS

7.62 European Directive (EC) 2004/48 on the enforcement of intellectual property rights was promulgated to harmonise good practice throughout the EU.[235] The implementation date was 29 April 2006.[236] The UK government carried out a consultation exercise on implementation.[237] Comparatively minor changes to UK law were thought necessary to comply with the Directive, as can be seen from the implementing Intellectual Property (Enforcement, etc) Regulations 2006.[238] This not only implemented Directive 2004/48, but took into account the WTO TRIPs agreement, which had been declared a Community Treaty by SI 1995/265. Amendments to the Trade Marks Act 1994[239] were particularly brief, but the opportunity was taken to bring the remedial sections of the Registered Designs Act 1949 into line with other intellectual property rights. The amendments were mainly questions of clarification[240] – to order the dissemination of a judgment of the court at the infringer's expense; (Scotland, reg 5[241]) ordering information on origin and distribution networks of goods or services which infringe intellectual property; (Scotland, reg 4)[242] introducing a new head of damages for intellectual property infringement to cover the 'moral prejudice' provision in

---

[231] See *Concept Anlagen und Gerate nach GMP fur Produktion und Labor GmbH v OHIM* T-127/02 [2004] ETMR 81, where a circle of stars regarded as 'an imitation from a heraldic point of view of the European emblem' was refused registration as a Community trade mark.

[232] L Gimeno 'Spain: Trade Marks – Distributor Applying For Rights in Mark Used by Manufacturer – Bad Faith' [2002] EIPR N94.

[233] *American Clothing Associates SA v OHIM* [2010] ETMR 3.

[234] *K SABATIER TM* [1993] RPC 97.

[235] Published in corrected form at [2004] OJ L195/16. See E Bonadio 'Remedies and sanctions for the infringement of intellectual property rights under EC law' [2008] EIPR 320.

[236] Art 20.

[237] See www.ipo.gov.uk/consult-2005-enforce.htm.

[238] SI 2006/1028, in force on 29 April 2006.

[239] Sch 2.

[240] The consultation also considered whether it was necessary to make specific provision to order security for damages against an alleged infringer whilst permitting the infringement to continue and to order that delivery up is at the expense of the infringer.

[241] Implemented in England and Wales by SI 2005/3515 amending the Civil Procedure Rules.

[242] The *Norwich Pharmacal* order was already available in the UK's common law jurisdictions: *Norwich Pharmacal v Customs and Excise Commissioners* [1974] AC 133.

Art 13(a)(reg 3). The European Commission has conducted a review of the Enforcement Directive[243] and made a number of recommendations, few of which affect the UK.[244] However, recognition that remedies are challenging in the digital environment may lead to proposals in this regard. There is also concern that damages awards are too low in many member states and a recommendation that further thought be given to remedying unjust enrichment gained through infringement; the rather oddly drafted Art 3 provided that this might be taken into account in assessing damages.[245]

7.63 Section 14(2) of the 1994 Act makes all the usual remedies available to the court in infringement actions. These include damages; infringement cases are normally fought on specimen instances of infringement. The enumeration of all like acts of infringement and the estimation of damages[246] are usually postponed to a subsequent inquiry as to damages.[247] An account of the defendant's profits from infringement may be claimed as an alternative to damages.[248] Although an inquiry into damages is usually granted as a matter of course to a successful claimant, the courts have occasionally refused claims for damages if satisfied that damages are negligible. An example of this is the curious case of *Emaco v Dyson Appliances*,[249] where there were claims and counterclaims in respect of comparative advertising between competitors.

---

[243] Commission Staff Working Document SEC(2010) 1589 final, available at http://eur-lex.europa. eu/LexUriServ/LexUriServ.do?uri=SEC:2010:1589:FIN:EN:PDF; Report to European Parliament, etc, COM(2010) 779 final, available at http://eur-lex.europa.eu/LexUriServ/LexUriServ. do?uri=COM:2010:0779:FIN:EN:PDF.

[244] Indeed, there is acknowledgement that several of the Directive's provisions were based on UK law, especially the *Anton Piller* order, see SEC(2010) 1589 final, n 10, and the *Norwich Pharmacal* order, see SEC(2010) 1589 final, n 20.

[245] Implemented verbatim into reg 3(2):
'(2) When awarding such damages— all appropriate aspects shall be taken into account, including in particular— the negative economic consequences, including any lost profits, which the claimant has suffered, and any unfair profits made by the defendant; and elements other than economic factors, including the moral prejudice caused to the claimant by the infringement.'

[246] On the basis of profits lost by the plaintiff; or a notional royalty: *Dormeuil v Feraglow* [1990] RPC 449; *Gary Fearns (t/a Autopaint International) v Anglo-Dutch Paint & Chemical Co Ltd* [2010] EWHC 1708 (Ch).

[247] *National Guild of Removers and Storers Ltd v Jones (t/a ATR removals); National Guild of Removers and Storers Ltd v Mabberley (t/a Abbeymove and Clear & Store)* [2011] EWPCC 004; *National Guild of Removers & Storers Ltd v Silveria (t/a C S Movers)* [2010] EWPCC 15.

[248] *Redrow Homes v Betts* [1998] 1 AC 197, a copyright case. Limited disclosure may be ordered to enable a successful claimant to make an informed election between an inquiry as to damages and an account for profits: *Island Records Ltd v Tring International Plc* [1996] 1 WLR 1256. An account may be ordered even in the absence of more than nominal damage: in *Hollister Inc v Medik Ostomy Supplies Ltd* [2011] EWPCC 40, HHJ Birss QC considered UK and EU law and ordered that the defendant account to the claimant for half of its profits gained by parallel importing in breach of a requirement to notify the claimant. This was seen as appropriately deterrent and proportionate.

[249] [1999] ETMR 903 Ch D.

Sections 30(6) and 31(6) of the 1994 Act provide a mechanism whereby a trade mark proprietor can claim damages on behalf of licensees; it does not appear to have been used to date.[250]

INJUNCTIONS

7.64 Injunctions are specifically mentioned: orders that the defendant refrain from infringing being particularly important to a proprietor who wishes to protect a mark. These include final injunctions, granted after judgment, and the interlocutory injunctions, designed to protect the applicant pending trial. Both kinds of injunction are discretionary, but a final injunction will normally be awarded where infringement has been established,[251] but will not be awarded where the wrongdoer does not threaten or intend to repeat acts of infringement.[252] The principles on which an interim restraining order (interlocutory injunction)[253] are granted were set forth by the House of Lords in *American Cyanamid v Ethicon*.[254] Despite the impatience of some judges with these principles, especially where there is a strong case,[255] *Cyanamid* principles continue to be applied.[256] In one or two cases where defendants have put up defences based on the human right to free expression, interlocutory injunctions have been refused.[257] However, as commercial speech, the use of trade marks is a lesser priority in trade mark cases than political speech:

> 'Absent a sign which is really telling a political story, making a political point or identifying some matter of public importance, I find the idea that use of a trade mark can of itself generally engage Art 10 of the Convention difficult.'[258]

---

[250] A Firth 'Damages/Monetary remedies for trade mark infringement' (2008) Anuario Facultad de Derecho – Universidad de Alcala I 73.

[251] *Navitaire Inc v EasyJet Airline Co Ltd (No 2)* [2006] RPC 4; [2005] EWHC 0282 (Ch) Ch D.

[252] Eg *Emaco v Dyson Appliances* [1999] ETMR 903 Ch D; *Numatic International v Qualtex* [2010] EWHC 1797 (Pat); [2010] RPC 26.

[253] Interim interdict in Scotland. *Allied Domecq Spirits & Wine Ltd v Murray McDavid Ltd* [1997] FSR 864 OH provides a useful illustration of the Scots approach and terminology.

[254] [1975] AC 396: the applicant must show that he has an arguable case, that damages would be an inadequate remedy pending trial, he must offer a cross-undertaking in damages which is adequate to protect the defendant. The court will also take into account the status quo, the effect of an injunction on third parties and, as a last resort, the relative strength of the parties' cases.

[255] *Series 5 Software Ltd v Clarke* [1996] 1 All ER 853 (Ch D); A Keay 'Whither American Cyanamid?: Interim Injunctions in the 21st Century' [2004] CJQ 133.

[256] Eg *Kangol Ltd v Sports World International Ltd* [2004] EWHC 3105 (Ch) Ch D, a case involving licensed trade marks.

[257] *Boehringer Ingelheim Ltd and others v VetPlus Ltd* [2007] EWCA Civ 583; [2007] ETMR 67; [2007] HRLR 33; [2007] FSR 29 CA, applying *Cream Holdings Ltd v Banerjee* [2005] 1 AC 253 and distinguishing *American Cyanamid*.

[258] *Miss World Ltd v Channel 4 Television Corp* [2007] EWHC 982 (Pat); [2007] ETMR 66; [2007] FSR 30 at [47]. After considering the interplay of the claimant's goodwill (a property right under the Protocol to Art 1 of the European Convention on Human Rights or ECHR) and freedom of expression under Art 10 ECHR, and s 12 of the Human Rights Act 1998, the court granted an injunction to restrain the use of 'Mr Miss World' as a title for the defendants beauty parade for transvestites and trans-sexuals.

If a trade mark has been incorporated into the defendant's company name,[259] a change of name may be called for. The court will normally grant an injunction with a temporary stay to give the company time to effect this.[260] Other interlocutory orders such as freezing orders (formerly *Mareva* injunctions)[261] and search and seize (formerly *Anton Piller*) orders[262] and disclosure orders (formerly *Norwich Pharmacal*)[263]are also available under s 7 of the Civil Procedure Act 1997. For further details of remedies and procedures, the reader is referred to specialist works.[264]

ADMINISTRATIVE ENFORCEMENT

7.65 Injunctions against traders may also be sought by the Office of Fair Trading (OFT) in consumer protection matters, including cases of unfair commercial practices. Part 8 of the Enterprise Act 2002[265] confers these powers and also gives the OFT a coordinating role amongst consumer protection agencies, which also include Trading Standards Services.[266] An injunction is usually sought as a last resort, if education, guidance and persuasion are ineffective. The OFT's list of closed proceedings indicates that a great many involve internet activities.[267]

7.66 The Company Names Tribunal closes the gap between the companies registration procedure and trade marks by providing a mechanism whereby the registered names of companies and limited liability partnerships[268] may be

---

[259] J Watts, P Walsh 'Company Names' [1996] EIPR 336; there is now a company names tribunal, which provides a cheaper alternative to court litigation where appropriate, see www.ipo.gov.uk/cna.htm.

[260] In the event of failure to comply, the court cannot overrule Companies Act requirements: *Halifax v Halifax Repossessions* [2004] FSR 45.

[261] To preserve assets to meet judgment; see Practice Direction at [1994] RPC 617.

[262] To preserve evidence; see CPR Part 25 (general provisions) and Part 63 (Intellectual Property); *The Gadget Shop Ltd v The Bug.com Ltd* [2001] FSR 26. For the principles on which costs of such an application are awarded, see *Mattel Inc v RSW Group plc* [2005] FSR 5.

[263] *Pfizer* [2007] EWHC 3137 (Ch).

[264] Such as *Kerly's Law of Trademarks and Tradenames* (15th edn, 2011, Sweet & Maxwell) ch 20; D Bean *Injunctions* (2003). Useful and concise guidance can be found in J Lambert 'IP Litigation after Woolf' [1999] EIPR 427 and 'IP Litigation after Woolf Revisited' [2003] EIPR 406.

[265] Which implemented Directive 98/27/EC on injunctions for the protection of consumers' interests [1998] OJ L166/51 as regards breaches of Community rules. See OFT 512 'Enforcement of consumer protection legislation: Guidance on Part 8 of the Enterprise Act', available at www.oft.gov.uk/shared_oft/business_leaflets/enterprise_act/oft512.pdf.

[266] Provided by local government authorities throughout the UK. These are also recognised along with the OFT and other organisations in the European Commission's Communication concerning Art 4(3) of Directive 98/27/EC of the European Parliament and of the Council on injunctions for the protection of consumers' interests, concerning the entities qualified to bring an action under Article 2 of this Directive [2006] OJ C-39/2.

[267] See www.oft.gov.uk/OFTwork/consumer-enforcement/#named4.

[268] The Limited Liability Partnerships (Application of Companies Act 2006) Regulations 2009, SI 2009/1804, regs 2 and 12.

challenged by aggrieved parties under s 69 of the Companies Act 2006.[269] The applicant must enjoy goodwill or reputation in the name.[270] If the disputed company name is identical with the complainant's mark or name, or so similar that use of the company name in the UK would be likely to mislead by suggesting a connection with the applicant, an application to the company names adjudicator[271] will succeed unless the respondent[272] can make out one of five defences under s 69(4).[273] Even if such a defence is made out, the applicant has an opportunity to show that the name was registered for the purpose of extracting money from the applicant or preventing him from registering the name.[274] The decision is published[275] and if the application is upheld, an order will be issued to change the company name by a specified date, in default of which the adjudicator will assign a new name.[276] The tribunal's database of decisions shows that a significant number of applications are undefended.[277]

DECLARATIONS

7.67 Declarations may also be sought, including declarations of non-infringement, for example by compliance with the Misleading Advertising Directive.[278]

STATUTORY REMEDIES

7.68 Section 15 provides a statutory remedy of erasure, removal or obliteration of marks or, if those are impracticable, for the destruction of

---

[269] P Johnson 'I object! The new company names adjudicator in the United Kingdom' [2008] JIPLP 695.

[270] Section 69(1)(a) and 69(7).

[271] Section 69(3) and 70. For forms and procedures, see www.ipo.gov.uk/cna/cna-factsheet.htm, the Practice Direction available at www.ipo.gov.uk/cna/cna-practicenotice.htm and the Company Names Adjudicator Rules 2008, SI 2008/1738. Appeal lies to the court from the decisions of the adjudicators: s 74.

[272] The primary respondent is the company: members and directors may also be joined: s 69(4).

[273] '(a) that the name was registered before the commencement of the activities on which the applicant relies to show goodwill; or
(b) that the company—(i) is operating under the name, or (ii) is proposing to do so and has incurred substantial start-up costs in preparation, or (iii) was formerly operating under the name and is now dormant; or
(c) that the name was registered in the ordinary course of a company formation business and the company is available for sale to the applicant on the standard terms of that business; or
(d) that the name was adopted in good faith; or
(e) that the interests of the applicant are not adversely affected to any significant extent.'

[274] Section 69(5).

[275] Section 72.

[276] Section 73. Section 77 governs the manner in which company names can be changed.

[277] See www.ipo.gov.uk/cna/cna-decisions.htm. See, also, *MB Inspection Ltd v Hi-Rope Ltd* [2010] RPC 18.

[278] *Kingspan Group Plc v Rockwool Ltd* [2011] EWHC 250 (Ch) (Ch D); J Smith, N Ruesink-Brown 'High Court grants declarations of fact on whether comparative advertising satisfied the Misleading and Comparative Advertising Directive' [2011] EIPR 528; Alex Batteson 'The positive rise of the negative declaration' [2008] JIPLP 633.

goods or materials. The defendant may be ordered to carry out these procedures, or to deliver them up to someone else for the purpose. Section 15 makes no explicit reference to general powers of the court to order thus, particularly in support of an injunction;[279] presumably inherent powers are not affected.

7.69 There are also specific orders for delivery up and disposal, conferred by ss 16, 19 and 20 on county courts in Northern Ireland[280] and sheriff courts in Scotland, without prejudice to the powers of the Northern Ireland High Court and the Scots Court of Session.[281] As with the equivalent provisions of the Copyright, Design and Patents Act 1988, it is not clear whether these are meant as free-standing remedies; this must be the case, since county or sheriff courts do not otherwise have express jurisdiction over civil infringements.[282] The relationship between ss 16 and 19 was considered in *Miller Brewing Company v The Mersey Docks and Harbour Company*,[283] a case concerning the seizure of beer and a subsequent application for delivery up under s 19. It was argued on behalf of some defendants that an application under s 19 could only be made if goods had been delivered up under s 16. The court agreed that this was the literal interpretation of s 19, but gave s 19 a 'strained meaning, albeit one that it could bear' to avoid a construction which would involve two separate applications.

7.70 There is a limitation period of 6 years on statutory delivery up, by virtue of s 18. It is submitted that this is inappropriate for trade marks, where use of a mark rather than the marking of goods constitutes the real mischief. The general powers of the courts are not limited if a mark used 6 years after products are marked.

BORDER MEASURES

7.71 A trade mark proprietor may give notice to Customs under s 89 of the impending arrival of infringing goods from outside the European Economic Area (EEA) or from inside the EEA if the goods have not yet been entered for free circulation. These may then be treated as prohibited goods. This procedure is now mainly of importance for parallel imports from outside the EEA and for overruns. In most cases the import of infringing material will be subject to the border measure procedures of Regulation (EC) 1383/2003, given effect in the UK by the Goods Infringing Intellectual Property Rights (Customs)

---

[279] Contrast s 16(4) and s 99(4) of the Copyright, Designs and Patents Act 1988.

[280] But not, it appears, in England and Wales. However, certain county courts now have general trade mark powers, see **7.1**.

[281] *Minerstone Ltd v Be Modern Ltd* [2002] FSR 53. HHJ Fysh seems to have taken the view that the High Court of England and Wales did have jurisdiction under ss 16 and 19 as one of the courts given general trade mark jurisdiction by the 1994 Act, but those courts have inherent jurisdiction.

[282] In *Minerstone Ltd v Be Modern Ltd* [2002] FSR 53 CC (Central London) HHJ Fysh held that the general tort jurisdiction of the county courts covered trade mark infringement.

[283] [2004] FSR 5 [2003] EWHC 1606 (Ch) Ch D.

Regulations 2004.[284] This legislation allows for detention by Customs of suspected infringing goods both pursuant to a notice filed in advance by the proprietor of the trade mark or other right[285] and of Customs' own motion if they come across the goods in the course of their duties.[286] Even goods which are temporarily within the jurisdiction pending re-export have been held subject to border procedures.[287] However, the ability to detain goods in transit appears to depend upon proof that the goods are destined to enter the EU single market.[288] A reference to the Court of Justice of the European Union on this point was made by the Court of Appeal in *Nokia*, this was heard as Joined Cases C-446/09 (*Philips v Lucheng Meijing*) and C-495/09 (*Nokia v HMRC*).[289] The Court of Justice confirmed that the mere presence under a 'suspensive' (transit) procedure could not render them counterfeit and therefore liable to detent. However, if on the evidence the goods appeared destined for a member state, or the destination had not been declared, they could be detained. Proposals for reform have suggested that this rule remain for genuinely transiting goods but that an exception be created to prevent misuse of the transit procedures to cloak illicit activity.[290] There are strict time-limits laid down by the 2004 Regulation. UK Customs, now merged with the Inland Revenue to form HMRC, has published a useful document on border measures, Customs Notice 34 'Intellectual Property Rights' of July 2004.[291]

CRIMINAL PROVISIONS

7.72 Criminal sanctions[292] are applied to certain forms of trade mark infringement in relation to goods but not services. The offences relate only to use of a mark on or in relation to the goods for which the mark is registered, unless the trade mark has a reputation in the UK.[293] In that case, the offences

---

[284] SI 2004/1473.

[285] Regulation (EC) 1383/2003 covers a comprehensive range of rights.

[286] For further details, see A Firth and J Phillips 'Border measures at the national level – United Kingdom' in Vrins and Schneider (eds) *Enforcement of Intellectual Property Rights through Border Measures: Law and Practice in the EU* (2006) ch 28.

[287] *Waterford Wedgwood plc v David Nagli Ltd* [1998] FSR 92; but see *Class International v Colgate-Palmolive* C-405/03 ECJ, 18 October 2005.

[288] *Class International BV v Colgate-Palmolive Co* C-405/03 [2005] ECR I-8735 (ECJ); Christopher Heath 'Customs seizures, transit and trade ch 28 in honour of Dieter Stauder's 70th birthday' [2010] IIC 881.

[289] 1 December 2011 [2011] ECR 000 available at http://curia.europa.eu/juris/liste.jsf?language=en&num=C-446/09.

[290] T Jaeger, H Grosse Ruse-Khan, J Drexl, RM Hilty 'Statement of the Max Planck Institute for Intellectual Property, Competition and Tax Law on the review of EU legislation on customs enforcement of intellectual property rights' [2010] IIC 674.

[291] Notice 34 may be consulted on HM Revenue & Customs' website at: http://customs.hmrc.gov.uk/channelsPortalWebApp/channelsPortalWebApp.portal?_nfpb=true&_pageLabel=pageExcise_ShowContent&propertyType=document&columns=1&id=HMCE_CL_000244 (25 July 2011).

[292] Sections 92–96. For discussion, see P Rawlinson 'The UK Trade Marks Act 1994: It's criminal' [1995] 1 EIPR 54; M Lindsey, M Chacksfield 'Exhaustion of Rights And Wrongs: Section 92 of the Trade Marks Act 1994; Recent Developments and Comments' [2003] EIPR 388.

[293] Section 92(4).

can be made out if the use takes unfair advantage of, or is detrimental to, the distinctive character or repute of the goods.[294] Note that in the latter case, the section does not state such use be without due cause.[295] In this case, the reputation of and effect on the mark have to be shown whether the goods are similar or dissimilar to those for which the mark is registered. It appears unlikely that the prosecution could make out an offence beyond reasonable doubt where dissimilar goods were concerned. If the defendant is convicted, possible consequences include a fine, an order to perform unpaid community service,[296] a term of imprisonment[297] and a confiscation order under the Proceeds of Crime Act 2006.[298] The UK Intellectual Property Office's website has useful pages on intellectual property crime,[299] including a crime report, a 'Supply Chain Toolkit' designed to alert businesses to the problems of counterfeit goods entering the supply chain and possible actions to reduce the risks,

7.73 Section 92 does not specify that use has to be trade mark use. However, in *R v Johnstone*,[300] the House of Lords held that the offence could not be committed in the absence of an indication of trade origin. Given the emphasis of the Court of Justice of the EU on damage to trade mark functions, this remains a tenable approach. However, in *CPS v Morgan*,[301] the Court of Appeal also considered the injurious effects of counterfeiting on the economy and consumers as well as trade marks proprietors and concluded that an offence could be present, even though the designer watches in question were advertised on the internet as 'replica'. The s 92[302] offences have the following elements:

(a) positive or negative commercial purpose ('with a view to gain for himself or with intent to cause loss to another'). This is the closest s 92 gets to

---

[294] For discussion of these criteria, see Chapter 5.

[295] Contrast s 10(3). However, there is a defence that the accused believed on reasonable grounds that the use was not infringing; this would presumably cover any possible justification for the use. Furthermore, the decision of the House of Lords in *R v Johnstone* [2003] UKHL 28; [2003] 1 WLR 1736; [2003] FSR 42; [2004] ETMR 2 shows there can be no criminal infringement absent civil infringement.

[296] 175 hours community service upheld in *R v Pettit* [2009] EWCA Crim 2573.

[297] In *R v Brayford* [2010] EWCA Crim 2329; [2011] 1 Cr App R (S) 107 a sentence of 2 years' imprisonment was upheld where the appellant appeared to have organised the supply from China of unlicensed washing powder and imitation 'Persil' packaging.

[298] *Birmingham City Council v Ram* [2007] EWCA Crim 3084; [2008] Lloyd's Rep FC 183 (judge not wrong to find that Mr Ram's main business was legitimate and to limit the confiscation order to the value of counterfeit goods in question). In *R v Aslam* [2008] EWCA Crim 3250, the amount of a confiscation order in respect of counterfeit items was reduced from £1,003,104.74 to £200,000, with a period of imprisonment in the event of default of payment set at 30 months. In *R v Davies* [2003] EWCA Crim 3110; [2004] 2 Cr App R (S) 12 a confiscation order of £1m was upheld.

[299] See www.ipo.gov.uk/pro-policy/pro-crime/pro-crime-group.htm and links.

[300] [2003] UKHL 28; [2003] 1 WLR 1736; [2003] FSR 42; [2004] ETMR 2, HL.

[301] [2006] EWCA Crim 1742. The case concerned possession of non-genuine 'Rolex', 'Tag Hauer' and 'Cartier' watches.

[302] Section 92(1), (2), (3).

mens rea.[303] In *R v Zaman*[304] 'with a view to' s 92(1)(c) was said to mean that the accused had gain or loss in contemplation as something that might realistically occur, not necessarily that he wanted or intended it to happen;

(b)   lack of consent from the trade mark proprietor;

(c)   infringing acts, including:

   (i)   application of sign to goods, packaging or materials: s 92(1)(a),
   (ii)   application to and use of business papers, labels, advertising: s 92(2),
   (iii) commercial dealing or possession of marked goods or materials: s 92(1)(b), (2)(b),
   (iv)   making or commercially possessing tools (articles) for the above: s 92(3), (1)(c), (2)(c);

(d)   all in relation to an identical mark or one likely to be mistaken for the registered mark.[305]

7.74   There is no element of intent to infringe[306] but a defence that the accused believed on reasonable grounds that use of the mark did not infringe (s 92(5)). This 'reverse burden of proof' was considered in *Roger Sliney v Havering London Borough Council*,[307] where the judge and the Court of Appeal considered that, though potentially contrary to Art 6(2) of the European Convention on Human Rights, it was not incompatible given the 'compelling reasons, having regard not only to the interests of the accused but also to the public interest, why the imposition of legal burden on the accused, as set out in s 92 (5) of the Trade Marks Act 1994, is necessary, justified and proportionate'. A similar ruling was made, obiter, in *R v Johnstone*.[308] In *West Sussex CC v Kahraman*,[309] the Divisional Court observed that 'a market trader ... who purchases goods with well-known designer names on them at very low prices, from a person of unknown identity (even if not positively "disreputable") and with no positive evidence of trade reputation cannot begin to discharge the burden of proof imposed upon him by Section 92(5)'. In *Essex Trading*

---

[303]   In *R v Keane* [2001] FSR 7 Mance LJ considered that attempting to read mens rea into the offences would render the defence of s 92(5) superfluous.

[304]   [2003] FSR 13.

[305]   In *R v Boulter* [2008] EWCA Crim 2375; [2009] ETMR 6, the defence argument that poor counterfeits would not cause confusion failed.

[306]   It was held possible for an innocent infringer to offend in *Torbay Council v Singh (Satnam)* [2000] FSR 158, Div Ct, distinguished and doubted in *R v Rhodes* [2003] FSR 147, CA. Subsequent cases outlined below suggest that the s 92(5) defence is NOT a 'good faith' defence.

[307]   *R v S* [2003] 1 Cr App R 602; [2002] EWCA Crim 2558, CA.

[308]   See, also, the guidance on reverse burdens in *Attorney General's Reference (No 1 of 2004), Re* [2004] EWCA Crim 1025; [2004] 1 WLR 2111.

[309]   [2006] EWHC 1703 (Admin) at [14] per McCombe J, with whom Latham LJ and Dobbs J agreed. See, also, *Stockton-on-Tees BC v Frost* [2010] EWHC 1304 (Admin). Conversely, where apparently genuine goods had been bought from an long-term supplier at full price, the defence should be put to the jury: *R v Malik* [2011] EWCA Crim 1107.

Standards v Singh,[310] the Divisional Court emphasised that the defence involves two elements, honest belief and objectively reasonable grounds for belief. In *R v McCrudden*,[311] the Court of Appeal rejected the contention that a defence could be based on not knowing what a trade marks was:

'... in this class of case requires proof of a positive case to the effect that the defendant knew there was a trade mark in place but reasonably believed that his use of it was no infringement.'

7.75 Curiously, the 'contributory' forms of offence seem wider than their civil equivalents under s 10(4). Section 92 was intended to overcome difficulties with enforcement of the Trade Descriptions Acts and in particular the decision in *Price*,[312] where it was held that a disclaimer 'brand copies' could negate the falsity of a marking.

7.76 The Court of Appeal in *Sliney*[313] spelled out elements of proof for the prosecution:

'By s 92 (1) the following are required to be proved by the prosecuting authorities:

- First, that the accused has acted with a view to gain for himself or another (or with intent to cause loss to another) – that is the only mental element set out in s 92 (1): indeed, it hardly is to be equated with mens rea in the way that phrase is usually understood.
- Second, that the accused has acted without the consent of the proprietor.
- Third, that the accused has done, by reference to a registered trade mark, one (or more) of the things set out in sub-sections (a) (b) or (c) in subsection (1).
- The provisions of subsections (2) and (3) correspond to that approach. If those matters are all proved, then the offence is proved: although no offence is committed unless the matters contained in sub-section (4) are satisfied.
- Finally, s 92 (5) provides, by way of exclusion, a statutory defence.

Nowhere in the section is there indicated any requirement of dishonesty or bad faith on the part of the accused as an element of the offence.'

7.77 As may be inferred from many of the case names referred to above, s 93 imposes a duty[314] on local weights and measures authorities (trading standards officers)[315] in England and Wales[316] to enforce s 92 and gives them like powers

---

[310] [2009] EWHC 520 (Admin)
[311] [2005] EWCA Crim 466 at [13].
[312] *R v Kent CC ex parte Price* [1993] 9 EIPR D-224; (1994) 158 JPN 78. See also *R v Veys* [1993] FSR 366.
[313] *R v S* [2003] 1 Cr App R 35; [2002] EWCA Crim 2558, CA, paras 28 and 29.
[314] An amendment to similar effect of the Copyright Designs and Patents Act 1988 is contained in the Criminal Justice and Public Order Act 1994, s 165.
[315] Much useful information may be obtained at www.lacots.com/pages/trade/lacors.asp.
[316] Not Scotland: s 93(5). The Department of Economic Development has the duty in Northern Ireland (s 93(3)) and powers to extend time for summary proceedings are conferred in Scotland (s 96).

to those they enjoy under the Trade Descriptions Act 1968[317] to make test purchases, enter premises, and so forth. Section 90 enables regulations to be made and s 91 enables Customs to disclose information for prosecutions under s 92 or the Trade Descriptions Act 1968. The 1994 Act was amended by the Copyright, etc and Trade Marks (Offences and Enforcement) Act 2002[318] to insert a new s 92A providing for search warrants and seizure. The 2002 Act removed some discrepancies in the criminal enforcement of trade marks and copyright[319] and made provision for search warrants, forfeiture, etc.

7.78 All offences are triable either way, with a maximum level of fine and/or 6 months' imprisonment on summary conviction or a maximum of 10 years' imprisonment and/or a fine on indictment.

7.79 Forfeiture may be ordered under ss 97 and 98 (Scotland). Under s 97,[320] once proceedings have started, or otherwise by complaint, showing that an offence has been committed, the court has powers to order forfeiture or destruction or obliteration before return. This was introduced to obviate problems which arise when undoubtedly counterfeit goods had been seized but were not subject of a conviction, or where the owner of the infringing goods for obvious reasons makes himself scarce. The criminal courts also have general powers to order forfeiture and compensation in respect of convictions, including offences under s 92, or any offence involving dishonesty or deception.

7.80 There are other offences, of falsification of the register[321] and of falsely representing a trade mark as registered.[322] The latter cannot be made out where the mark is indeed registered somewhere in the EU: see *Pall v Dahlhausen*.[323]

7.81 Section 101 expressly imposes liability upon partners and upon company officers for their firms' and companies' crimes.

7.82 In addition to the offences in the 1994 Act, until May 2008, the Trades Descriptions Acts 1968 and 1972 provided penalties for using false trade descriptions. In many cases these offences did not involve trade marks at all,

---

[317] Now largely repealed and replaced by the Consumer Protection from Unfair Trading Regulations 2008, SI 2008/1277, but not in this regard.

[318] Copyright, Etc and Trade Marks (Offences and Enforcement) Act 2002, s 6.

[319] On copyright, see R Fry 'Copyright Infringement and Collective Enforcement' [2002] EIPR 516.

[320] Because it might be open to a trade mark proprietor to seek forfeiture under s 19 or 97, in *Unic Centre Sàrl v Harrow Crown Court and the London Borough of Brent and Harrow Trading Standards Service* [2000] ETMR 595 QBD the court considered s 97 and an appeal therefrom to be civil proceedings to which the Brussels Convention and the Civil Jurisdiction and Judgments Act 1982 applied. It is submitted that there are important differences between ss 97 and 19, not least the fact that any person into whose hands have come the goods, packaging, etc in the investigation of an offence may apply under s 97. Section 19, which refers back to s 16, is the civil remedy available to the trade mark owner.

[321] Section 94.

[322] Section 95.

[323] *Pall Corp v PJ Dahlhausen & Co* (C-238/89) [1990] ECR I-4827; applied in *Second Sight Ltd v Novell UK Ltd and Novell Inc* [1995] RPC 423 Ch D.

but matters such as falsification of car mileages. However, where resources permitted, Trading Standard Officers exercised their powers under these Acts against misuse of trade marks.[324] The substantive provisions of the Trades Descriptions Act 1968 have been repealed and replaced by the Consumer Protection from Unfair Trading Regulations 2008,[325] which implemented Directive 2005/29/EC concerning unfair business-to-consumer commercial practices. The Regulations set up a series of prohibitions on various forms of unfair practice[326] and then created a set of related criminal offences.[327] The most important from a trade mark point of view are the prohibition in reg 5 on misleading actions which lead consumers to make transactional decisions, and the related offence in reg 9. Regulation 5(3)(a) stipulates that the requirement for a misleading action are satisfied if the action 'concerns any marketing of a product (including comparative advertising) which creates confusion with any products, trade marks, trade names or other distinguishing marks of a competitor'. Regulation 9 provides that such commercial conduct is an offence. The offences are triable either way, with a maximum of 2 years' imprisonment for a conviction on indictment, less than under s 92 of the 1994 Act. These specific provisions have not been tested at the time of going to press, but in *Office of Fair Trading v Purely Creative Ltd*,[328] the court was prepared to grant an order[329] to restrain misleading information relating to prizes and considered the concept of the 'average consumer'.

7.83 The European Commission proposed[330] a Directive and Framework Decision to strengthen the criminal enforcement of intellectual property. This was stated to be justified by growing international counterfeiting and piracy, with links to organised crime and by Art 17(2) of the Charter of Fundamental Rights. The maximum penalties proposed were lower than those described above but the range of offences was wider than current UK law. This came to nought.[331] The European Commission in 2009 issued Communication 'Enhancing the enforcement of intellectual property rights in the internal market'[332] and has set up the 'European Observatory on Counterfeiting and Piracy';[333] there is a strong emphasis on practical and non-legislative measures, but the EU and the UK have participated in negotiation of a proposed international 'Anti-Counterfeiting Trade Agreement' (ACTA) which contains

---

[324] See A Worsdell and A Clark *Anti-counterfeiting* (1998).

[325] SI 2008/1277.

[326] Regs 3–7.

[327] Regs 8–12.

[328] [2011] EWHC 106 (Ch).

[329] Under s 215(5) of the Enterprise Act 2002, or accept undertakings in lieu.

[330] See Modified Proposal for a Directive of the European Parliament and the Council on Criminal Measures aimed at Ensuring the Enforcement of Intellectual Property Rights, 26 April 2006, COM(2006) 168 final.

[331] Having engendered widespread criticism, including RM Hilty, A Kur, A Peukert 'Statement of the Max Planck Institute for Intellectual Property, Competition and Tax Law on the Proposal for a Directive of the European Parliament and the Council on Criminal Measures Aimed at Ensuring the Enforcement of Intellectual Property Rights' [2006] IIC 970.

[332] COM(2009) 467 final, available at http://ec.europa.eu/internal_market/iprenforcement/docs/ip-09-1313/communication_en.pdf.

[333] See http://ec.europa.eu/internal_market/iprenforcement/observatory/index_en.htm.

criminal provisions.[334] This was signed by the EU, UK and 21 other EU member states on 26 January 2012.[335] As well as ratification by the member states, the European Parliament will need to consent to its ratification by the EU.[336]

---

[334] C Geiger 'Of ACTA, "pirates" and organized criminality – how "criminal" should the enforcement of intellectual property be?' [2010] IIC 629.

[335] See www.ipo.gov.uk/pro-crime-acta.htm.

[336] See http://ec.europa.eu/trade/creating-opportunities/trade-topics/intellectual-property/anti-counterfeiting.

Chapter 8

DEFENDING INFRINGEMENT PROCEEDINGS

PRIOR CONSIDERATIONS – THREATS

8.1   Prospective defendants in infringement proceedings should consider whether the action is worth defending at all. If the mark is of no great importance to them, it might be worth offering the trade mark proprietor all that he might achieve at trial: a prospective defendant can undertake to stop using the mark, to sticker catalogues, to return goods to suppliers or at least not part with them until the mark has been removed, and offer information as to the source of infringing articles. This may be the best course for a retailer or service provider in a small way of business. If this is done, the defendant is unlikely to incur costs in any proceedings, especially if the infringement was unwitting.[1]

8.2   The fact that this is so means that there is a temptation for trade mark proprietors to make extravagant threats of litigation against retailers. Indeed, this may be a way to trace infringing goods to their source.[2] Traders are unlikely to 'shop' their suppliers unless threatened with something worse. But over-zealous pursuit may cause damage to suppliers.

8.3   Such use of unjustified threats was seen as a problem, in particular for small businesses.[3] Parliament accordingly enacted s 21 of the Trade Marks

---

[1]   And even more so if proceedings were started without notice, e g *American Tobacco v Guest* (1892) 9 RPC 218.

[2]   Or at least the cheapest way – the court has power to order pre-trial disclosure against a person who gets mixed up in the wrongdoing of others, under the jurisdiction identified in *Norwich Pharmacal Co v Customs and Excise Commissioners* [1974] AC 133. Pre-action disclosure applications against likely parties are governed by the Civil Procedure Rules 1998 (CPR), SI 1998/3132, r 31.16, whilst orders for disclosure against a non-party are made under CPR, r 31.17. Art 8 'Right of information' of Directive (EC) 2004/48 on the enforcement of intellectual property rights [2004] OJ L195/16 required member states to empower their courts in proper cases to order disclosure of (a) the names and addresses of the producers, manufacturers, distributors, suppliers and other previous holders of the goods or services, as well as the intended wholesalers and retailers; (b) information on the quantities produced, manufactured, delivered, received or ordered, as well as the price obtained for the goods or services in question. The Intellectual Property (Enforcement, etc) Regulations 2006, SI 2006/1028 implemented this for Scotland; for the other jurisdictions, *Norwich Pharmacal*-type orders were already available.

[3]   House of Lords Public Bill Committee, col 68 (19 January 1994). For an excellent account, see Lim HG 'The "threats" section in the UK Trade Marks Act 1994: can a person still wound without striking?' [1995] 3 EIPR 138. 'The policy represented by the first statutory threats

Act 1994 ('the 1994 Act'), which provides a remedy for groundless threats of proceedings for infringement of a registered trade mark, including a Community trade mark.[4] This goes wider than direct recipients of threats, who may also have standing to sue for a declaration of non-infringement.[5] Under s 21, anyone 'aggrieved' by the threat, be it the recipient or their supplier or some other person affected by the threat, can apply to the court. The aggrieved person needs to show that 'the threats have or are likely to cause him damage which is not minimal' but this 'does not mean that the claimant must prove loss of identifiable contracts. It is sufficient to show that his commercial interests are or are likely to be adversely affected in a real as opposed to a fanciful or minimal way'.[6] The person aggrieved may seek a declaration that the threat is unjustifiable, an injunction[7] to restrain repetition and damages for any loss sustained. The burden of justifying the threat lies on the person making it; if that burden is not discharged, the plaintiff in threats proceedings is entitled to succeed.[8] Even if justification can be made, it falls away if the registration is invalid or liable to be revoked in a material respect.[9]

8.4   Mere notification that the mark is registered is not a threat.[10] A suggested amendment to the Trade Marks Bill expressly to allow the proprietor to ask for the name of the supplier was not taken up.[11] A similar amendment[12] has been made to the threats provisions in the Patents Act 1977, but as at the time of writing the 1994 Act had not been amended.[13] When Directive (EC)

---

provision (section 32 of the Patents, Designs and Trade Marks Act 1883) was clearly to stop patentees who were (in Pope's words about Addison) "willing to wound but afraid to strike" from holding the sword of Damocles above another's head': *L'Oréal UK Ltd v Johnson & Johnson* [2000] FSR 686; [2000] ETMR 691 Ch D at para 12, per Lightman J.

[4]   Community Trade Mark Regulations 2006, SI 2006/1027, as amended by SI 2008/1959 (replacing SI 1996/1908) reg 6.

[5]   A claim for a declaration of non-infringement as alternative to a claim under s 21 was allowed to stand in *L'Oréal (UK) Ltd v Johnson & Johnson* [2000] FSR 686; [2000] ETMR 691 Ch D; the court holding that the court's inherent jurisdiction to make a declaration co-exists with powers under s 21. Declarations of non-infringement are envisaged by the Community Trade Mark Regulation (EC) 40/94, Art 92.

[6]   *Samuel Smith Old Brewery (Tadcaster) v Lee (t/a Cropton Brewery)* [2011] EWHC 1879 (Ch) at 155, Arnold J citing Laddie J in *Brain v Ingledew Brown Bennision & Garrett (No 3)* [1997] FSR 511 at 516–520.

[7]   If the court concludes that an unjustifiable threat has been made, a declaration and an injunction will usually follow: *Prince plc v Prince Sports Group Inc* [1998] FSR 21.

[8]   As occurred in *Trebor Bassett Ltd v The Football Association* [1997] FSR 211 Ch D.

[9]   Section 21(3).

[10]   Section 21(4).

[11]   House of Lords Public Bill Committee, cols 66–67 (19 January 1994).

[12]   Patents Act 2004 (2004 c 16), s 12, amending s 70 of the Patent Act 1977.

'(5) For the purposes of this section a person does not threaten another person with proceedings for infringement of a patent if he merely—

(a) provides factual information about the patent,

(b) makes enquiries of the other person for the sole purpose of discovering whether, or by whom, the patent has been infringed as mentioned in subsection (4)(a) above, or

(c) makes an assertion about the patent for the purpose of any enquiries so made.'

These amendments are discussed by N Minogue and V Salmon 'You and Whose Army? Problems with Threats Provisions and the Patents Act 2004' [2005] EIPR 294.

[13]   A Murdie 'A threat ahead?' 149(4) Sol J 100 (2005).

2004/48 on the enforcement of intellectual property rights[14] was implemented, the right to seek supplier information[15] in Scotland was reinforced.[16]

8.5   The courts look at how the threat will be perceived: even a veiled threat is actionable under s 21.[17] In *L'Oréal*, a letter reserving the right to bring proceedings in the future, when infringement proceedings were in train in another jurisdiction, was held to be a threat under the 1994 Act, even though the threat was 'veiled and muffled by protestations of a continuing state of indecision'. Could the proprietor allege passing off, threaten proceedings for passing off and then add notice of the trade mark registration as permitted by s 21(4)? The latter is likely to be regarded as a threat, as in the copyright and design case of *Jaybeam v Abru*.[18] In *Best Buy Co Inc v Worldwide Sales Corporation España SL*,[19] the Court of Appeal held that, read as a whole, a letter before action was an admissible threat and not protected by the 'without prejudice' rule as a genuine attempt to settle the dispute. Rather, the paragraphs offering negotiation 'underlined the defendant's belief in its case and its determination to pursue it'.[20] By contrast, in *Samuel Smith Old Brewery (Tadcaster) v Lee (t/a Crompton Brewery)*, Arnold J held that a letter which sought to reach a friendly compromise without involving the defendant's customer was not a threat of infringement proceedings.[21]

8.6   Section 21 is a very powerful mechanism. Where used by the recipient of the threats, he can take the initiative in litigation but the proprietor still has to establish infringement, to escape liability for the threat. The result is to encourage trade mark proprietors to sue first and attempt to resolve the dispute later. The tension between this 'sue first' approach and the 'talk first' approach generally encouraged by the English CPR was discussed in *Reckitt Benkiser UK v Home Pairfum*.[22]

8.7   The threats action is not available where the threats relate to the application of the mark to goods, the import or export of marked goods or the provision of services under the mark.[23] In this respect, it resembles the remedies

---

[14]   Published in corrected form at [2004] OJ L195/16.

[15]   Under Art 8.

[16]   See above at n 2.

[17]   In *Bowden Controls v Acco Cable Controls* [1990] RPC 427 at 432 Aldous J said, apropos of threats of patent infringement proceedings: 'The test is whether the communication would be understood by the ordinary recipient in the position of the claimant as constituting a threat of proceedings for infringement'. Cited in *L'Oréal*; see also *Brain v Ingledew Brown Bennison & Garrett* [1996] FSR 341.

[18]   [1976] RPC 308.

[19]   [2011] EWCA Civ 618; [2011] FSR 30.

[20]   At para 41.

[21]   [2011] EWHC 1879 (Ch).

[22]   [2004] FSR 37.

[23]   Section 21(1) of the 1994 Act. Again, a reasonable recipient's likely perception of an alleged threat is important; in *Best Buy Co Inc v Worldwide Sales Corporation España SL* [2011] EWCA Civ 618; [2011] FSR 30 at paras 32–34 the exception for 'provision of services under the mark' was construed narrowly; it did not extend to threats relating to use of the mark use of the mark 'in advertising and in the media'.

for unjustified threats of patent[24] and design[25] infringement. In the patent case of *Cavity Trays Ltd v RMC Panel Products Ltd,*[26] the court held that this kind of exception refers to the activity rather than to the actor, so that threats to a manufacturer relating to their sale of goods were actionable. This distinction still applies to threats of trade mark infringement, although s 70 of the Patent Act 1977 has been amended to reverse the effect of *Cavity Trays.*[27] There is an important distinction between trade marks, on the one hand, and patents and designs, on the other. The mischief with which trade mark infringement proceedings are concerned is the use of the mark rather than characteristics of products themselves. Provided that retailers can obliterate marks, sticker catalogues, and so forth, the goods are not 'sterilised' in their hands.[28]

8.8 The effect of invalidity on the threats proceedings[29] is probably designed to discourage covetously broad registrations being sought and abused.

CHALLENGING THE CLAIM

8.9 Attack may be the best form of defence. Before or during proceedings, the defendant should consider whether there are grounds to attack the registration,[30] ab initio for invalidity or by way of revocation for non-use, deceptiveness or because the mark has become generic in the trade. If the claim is by a licensee, it may be possible to challenge their standing to sue.[31] In a case which will turn on confusion, the defendant can log calls and correspondence for any complaints, and seek the views of representatives and customers.

INTERLOCUTORY TACTICS

8.10 A defendant faced with an application for an interlocutory injunction or other relief has a number of options. He may seek to undermine the plaintiff's substantive case or raise effective defences. However, the criteria for an interlocutory injunction (or 'interim restraining order') require only an arguable case or 'serious issue to be tried' under the *American Cyanamid* criteria, and injury for which damages would be inadequate.[32] However, it was observed in *Cowshed Products Ltd v Island Origins Ltd*[33] that it is difficult to

---

[24] Patents Act 1977, s 70 prior to its amendment by the Patents Act 2004.

[25] Registered Designs Act 1949, s 26 (note the Act as amended appears as Sch 4 to the Copyright Designs and Patents Act 1988).

[26] [1996] RPC 361, CA.

[27] By the Patent Act 2004, s 12, substituting a new s 70(4).

[28] Obliteration was discussed in *I N Newman Ltd v Adlem* [2005] EWCA Civ 741.

[29] Section 21(3) of the 1994 Act. Again, the position has been ameliorated for good faith patent owners by the Patents Act 2004, s 12, but not for trade marks.

[30] Invalidity may be raised by way of defence, but a defendant who challenges validity will probably also counterclaim for a declaration of invalidity and/or for revocation. These are considered further in Chapter 9.

[31] See **10.18–10.23**.

[32] See **7.64**.

[33] [2010] EWHC 3357 (Ch); [2011] ETMR 42.

apply *American Cyanamid* to trade mark cases, since the likelihood of injury follows substantive issues, such as confusion. The defendant may also avert an interlocutory injunction by persuading the court that damages would be perfectly adequate to compensate the plaintiff pending trial. Tactics here include establishing that the defendant's products are not inferior, offering to log any shift of sales towards the defendant's goods or services (and conceding that damages would be available if so),[34] showing that the defendant is good for damages, or offering to make payments into an account in the name of the defendant's solicitors (or both).[35] If these tactics are ineffective, it may be preferable to give undertakings not to use the mark pending trial.

JUSTIFYING USE – SUBSTANTIVE DEFENCES

8.11 A number of specific defences come under this general heading. They will be useful at trial and in showing an arguable defence to avert summary judgment. Most of them are to be found in parallel provisions of the 1994 Act, Trade Marks Harmonisation Directive (EC) 89/104 ('the Directive') (which prevails if improperly implemented in the 1994 Act) and Community Trade Mark Regulation (EC) 40/94 ('the Regulation'). They are, briefly:

(a) defences under s 10(6) of the 1994 Act: the circumstances of s 10(6) are related to consent of the proprietor and were considered in detail in at **7.53–7.58**;

(b) defences under s 11 of the 1994 Act (Art 6 of the Directive, Art 12 of the Regulation);

(c) 'exhaustion' defences under s 12 of the 1994 Act (Art 7 of the Directive, Art 13 of the Regulation); and

(d) miscellaneous other defences.

Defences under s 11 of the 1994 Act (Art 6 of the Directive, Art 12 of the Regulation)

8.12 Section 11 provides five statutory exceptions to infringement of registered trade marks:

---

[34] This ploy was used to good effect in *Beecham v Sainsbury* [1987] EIPR D-234.
[35] In *Cowshed Products Ltd v Island Origins Ltd* [2010] EWHC 3357 (Ch); [2011] ETMR 42 the defendant offered to undertake, pending trial, not to discount their products and to pay a proportion net profits on sales into an escrow account. Also the court was persuaded against grant of an injunction by the possibility that the defendant might go out of business.

(a)   Overlapping registrations: s 11(1)[36]

8.13   If the defendant has a concurrent registration for the goods or services in question, s 11(1) provides that use within the scope of defendant's registration will not infringe other marks.[37] It reflects the fact that the UK Registry has traditionally been rigorous in examining trade mark applications on relative grounds. Conflicting marks are unlikely to co-exist on the UK register unless there is good reason, such as honest concurrent use or former common ownership, or one party has consented to the other's registration.[38] In this last case, consent to registration might be taken to imply consent to use.[39] The defence under s 11(1) is subject to validity[40] of the registration relied upon, so it is not absolute. However, if there is 5 years' acquiescence by the senior proprietor in the use of the junior registered mark, within the meaning of s 48,[41] the junior mark becomes immune to invalidity over the senior mark (on relative grounds). *Newman v Adlem*[42] reiterated that s 11(1) does not confer an entitlement to use the registered mark if there is otherwise passing off.

8.14   The next three defences (b)–(d) are subject to the proviso that the defendant's 'use is in accordance with honest practices in industrial or commercial matters'.[43] The phrase 'honest practices' was considered by the European Court of Justice (ECJ), now Court of Justice of the European Union (CJEU) in *Gerolsteiner Brunnen v Putsch*[44] to 'constitute in substance the expression of a duty to act fairly in relation to the legitimate interests of the trade mark owner'. In *Anheuser-Busch v Budejovicky Budvar Narodni Podnik*,[45]

---

[36]   This defence has no direct equivalent in the Directive. In *Electrocoin Automatics Ltd v Coinworld Ltd* [2005] FSR; [2005] ETMR 31, Geoffrey Hobbs QC, sitting as a deputy High Court judge, queried (obiter) whether s 11(1) 'goes further than the Community law of trade marks permits or requires'. In *Inter Lotto (UK) Ltd v Camelot Group plc* [2004] RPC 8 Laddie J said that s 11(1) 'may be open to challenge'. The contrast between s 11(1) and the position under Art 106 of the Regulation was noted in *Compass Publishing v Compass Logistics* [2004] RPC 41 Ch D.

[37]   The usefulness of this provision was outlined in *Group Lotus plc v 1Malaysia Racing Team SDN BHD* [2011] EWHC 1366 (Ch), although the marks in question were revoked for non-use. However, the defence is only available to one entitled under the parallel mark: *Nanjing Automobile (Group) Corp v MG Sports & Racing Europe Ltd* [2010] EWHC 270 (Ch) (MG sports car business had been excluded from sale to Chinese company, but not trade marks).

[38]   See *Omega Engineering Inc v Omega SA* [2011] EWCA Civ 645; [2011] ETMR 40, where the court was called upon to interpret a co-existence agreement from the 1980s.

[39]   In practice the consent to registration might be achieved by way of an agreement on the extent of acceptable use.

[40]   Section 11(1) refers explicitly to s 47(6). For invalidity, see Chapter 9.

[41]   See **8.24.**

[42]   *IN Newman Ltd v Richard T Adlem* [2005] EWCA Civ 741 at para 51, citing s 2(2) of the 1994 Act and *Inter Lotto (UK) Ltd v Camelot Group plc* [2003] 4 All ER 575; [2004] RPC 9.

[43]   See **7.53** for the origins of the term.

[44]   (C-100/02) [2004] RPC 39 ECJ at paras 24–26 see, also, *BMW v Deenik* (C-63/97) [1999] ECR I-905 at para 61; Case 228/03 *Gillette Co v LA-Laboratories Ltd Oy* [2005] ECR I-2337 at para 41, (C-17/06) *Céline SARL v Céline SA* [2007] ECR I-7041 at para 33, *Datacard Corporation v Eagle Technologies Ltd* [2011] EWHC 244 (Pat); [2011] RPC 17 at paras 296–299.

[45]   (C-245/02) [2005] ETMR 27 ECJ; see, *Samuel Smith Old Brewery (Tadcaster) v Lee (t/a Cropton Brewery)* [2011] EWHC 1879 (Ch) at para 210.

this in turn was stated to be 'essentially the same condition as that laid down by Article 17 of the TRIPs Agreement'. This requires the court to carry out assessment of all relevant circumstances, especially whether the defendant is competing unfairly with trade mark proprietor.[46] The court in *Gerolsteiner*[47] considered the drafting history of the phrase, which had been substituted for an earlier provision 'provided he does not use them as a trade mark'. Accordingly the ECJ felt that 'use as a trade mark' was not a helpful concept in interpreting Art 6(1)(b). 'Honest practices' appears to connote an objective standard. In *Asprey and Garrard Ltd v WRA (Guns) Ltd*,[48] the Court of Appeal remarked, obiter, that however honest a defendant's subjective intentions were, any use of his own name which amounted to passing off would not be in accordance with honest practice. Thus, in most circumstances the proviso will not be met where there is confusion unless there is a good reason for tolerating it.[49] In *Samuel Smith Old Brewery (Tadcaster) v Lee (t/a Crompton Brewery)*,[50] Arnold J gave a useful, though non-exhaustive, checklist of materials factors for assessing the proviso:

'(i)   whether the defendant knew of the existence of the trade mark, and if not whether it would have been reasonable for it to conduct a search;

(ii)   whether the defendant used the sign complained of in reliance on competent legal advice based on proper instructions;

(iii)   the nature of the use complained of, and in particular the extent to which it is used as a trade mark for the defendant's goods or services;

(iv)   whether the defendant knew that the trade mark owner objected to the use of the sign complained of, or at least should have appreciated that there was a likelihood that the owner would object;

(v)   whether the defendant knew, or should have appreciated, that there was a likelihood of confusion;

(vi)   whether there has been actual confusion, and if so whether the defendant knew this;

(vii) whether the trade mark has a reputation, and if so whether the defendant knew this and whether the defendant knew, or at least should have appreciated, that the reputation of the trade mark would be adversely affected;

(viii) whether the defendant's use of the sign complained of interferes with the owner's ability to exploit the trade mark;

---

[46] *Datacard Corporation v Eagle Technologies Ltd* [2011] EWHC 244 (Pat); [2011] RPC 17 at para 298: 'this makes sense, since the wording of the proviso to Art 12 [of the Regulation] appears to reflect Art 10*bis* Paris'. Use of a mark in comparative advertising will not satisfy the similar proviso to s 10(6) if the conditions of the Misleading Advertising Directive are not complied with: *L'Oréal v Bellure* [2010] EWCA Civ 535; [2010] ETMR 47; [2010] RPC 23; applying *L'Oréal SA v Bellure NV* (C-487/07) [2009] ECR I-5185; [2009] ETMR 55; [2010] RPC 1.

[47] At para 14 of the judgment.

[48] [2002] FSR 31, CA.

[49] *Samuel Smith Old Brewery (Tadcaster) v Lee (t/a Cropton Brewery)* [2011] EWCA Civ 618; [2011] FSR 30 at paras 116–117.

[50] [2011] EWHC 1879 (Ch) at paras 118–119, citing his earlier decisions in Hotel Cipriani, upheld at [2010] EWCA Civ 110; [2010] Bus LR 1465; [2010] RPC 16; *Och-Ziff Management Europe Ltd v Och Capital LLP* [2010] EWHC 2599 (Ch); [2011] FSR 11; and *Datacard Corporation v Eagle Technologies Ltd* [2011] EWHC 244 (Pat); [2011] RPC 17.

(ix)   whether the defendant has a sufficient justification for using the sign complained of; and

(x)   the timing of the complaint from the trade mark owner.'

(b)   Use of own name or address under s 11(2)(a)
(Art 6(1)(a) of the Directive, Art 12(1)(a) of the Regulation)

8.15   In *Reed Executive v Reed Business Information*[51] the Court of Appeal confirmed that s 11(2)(a) covered use by the defendant as a trade mark,[52] but was less certain as to the application of the defence to company names as opposed to individual names.[53] The following statement had been made for inclusion in the minutes of adoption of the Community Trade Mark Regulation:

'The Council and Commission consider that the words "his own name" in subparagraph (a) apply only to natural persons.'

8.16   However, the ECJ in *Anheuser-Busch v Budvar*[54] rejected such a limitation of Art 6(1)(a), holding the quoted statement to be of 'no legal significance'. In the UK, the 'own name' defence under the 1994 Act had been used successfully by companies as well as individuals,[55] continuing a practice long established under the Trade Marks Act 1938[56] (as pointed out by Jacob J in *Euromarket Designs Inc v Peters and Crate & Barrel Ltd*).[57] Jacob J gave positive grounds for this:

'There is good reason in some circumstances to give immunity to company names used in accordance with honest practices. A company may well have built up a business honestly under its name. It is then rather stuck with its name in a similar way as an individual is stuck with his. For a registration to interfere with the use of that name in those circumstances would be a strong thing. It might well involve destruction of goodwill. English law regards goodwill as property. So do most businessmen. It is unlikely that the goodwill in a personal name would be protected but not that of a company, assuming of course that in both cases that the use is in accordance with honest practices.'[58]

---

51   [2004] RPC 40.
52   Citing *Premier Luggage and Bags Ltd v Premier Co (UK) Ltd* [2003] FSR 5, CA and *Gerolsteiner*.
53   At para 116, stating that whether Art 6(1)(a) of the Directive was available to a company was not acte clair and subject to any question of a reference to the ECJ.
54   *Anheuser-Busch Inc v Budejovicky Budvar Narodni Podnik* (C-245/02), [2004] ECR I-10989, [2005] ETMR 27 at paras 78–79.
55   D Nissen and G Pratt 'What's in a name? The own name defence under English and European law' (2004) 172 TW 24.
56   Eg 'The honest use by the person of his own name without any intention to deceive anybody or without any intention to make use of the goodwill which has been acquired by another trader': *Baume v Moore* [1958] RPC 226 at 235.
57   [2001] FSR 20.
58   [2001] FSR 20 at para 31.

In *Hotel Cipriani*,[59] the Court of Appeal confirmed that a company could rely on the 'own name' defence in relation to an established trading name as well as company name. However, in *Group Lotus plc v 1Malaysia Racing Team SDN BHD*,[60] the use of the different name, 'Team Lotus' did not attract the defence.

8.17 Thus, a company name must be used in full,[61] although omitting 'Limited' or 'plc' will not destroy the defence.[62] The courts recognise the ease with which company names can be changed; in the absence of established goodwill the use of a new company's own name may be permitted only in the short term or not at all.[63] In *Och-Ziff*,[64] Arnold J distinguished between a mere formal identification of a company name and 'upfront in-your-face' trade mark use, for which the defence was less likely to be available. In the case of a defendant who is an individual rather than a company, the court will need to take care in framing an injunction: *Asprey and Garrard Ltd v WRA (Guns) Ltd.*[65]

8.18 The ECJ in *Anheuser-Busch* also remarked that the availability of the defence under Art 6(1)(a) was irrelevant to questions of registrability.[66]

(c) Descriptive use under s 11(2)(b) (Art 6(1)(b) of the Directive, Art 12(1)(b) of the Regulation)

8.19 Under s 11(2)(b), a registered mark is not infringed by use as an indication of 'kind, quality, quantity, intended purpose, value, geographical origin, the time of production of goods or of rendering of services, or other characteristics of goods or services'. Again, the use must be in accordance with honest practices. This provision was described in *Electrocoin v Coinworld* as ensuring that the rights conferred by registration operate with due regard for freedom of expression, which is guaranteed by Art 10 of the European Convention on Human Rights.[67] If use of a sign in a purely descriptive way can infringe a registered mark, s 11(2)(b) is vital. Even if the disputed use might be

---

59   [2010] EWCA Civ 110; [2010] Bus LR 1465; [2010] RPC 16.
60   [2011] EWHC 1366 at para 268.
61   *Origins Natural Resources Inc v Origin Clothing Ltd* [1995] FSR 280; *Hart v Relentless Records Ltd* [2003] FSR 36.
62   *NAD Electronics v NAD Computer Systems* [1997] FSR 380.
63   *Asprey and Garrard Ltd v WRA (Guns) Ltd* [2002] FSR 31, CA at para 43, otherwise 'the route to piracy would be obvious'. See, also, *International Business Machines Corp v Web-Sphere Ltd* [2004] EWHC 529; [2004] ETMR 94 (Ch) ('late' change of defendant company name). For the work of the Company Names Adjudicator, see **7.66** and www.ipo.gov.uk/cna.htm.
64   *Och-Ziff Management Europe Ltd v Och Capital LLP* [2010] EWHC 2599 (Ch); [2011] FSR 11 at para 145, citing Jacob LJ in *Reed* [2004] RPC 40.
65   [2002] FSR 31, CA.
66   *Nichols plc v Registrar of Trade Marks* (C-404/02) [2005] All ER (EC) 1; [2005] ETMR 21; [2005] RPC 12; [2005] 1 WLR 1418 at para 32.
67   See *L'Oréal v Bellure* [2010] EWCA Civ 535; [2010] ETMR 47; [2010] RPC 23 par Jacob LJ at paras 10–13. In *BMW v Deenik* [1999] All ER (EC) 235; [1999] 1 CMLR 1099; [1999] ECR I-905; [1999] ETMR 339 at para 62, the ECJ stressed justification for Art 6 of the Directive in terms of single market aims. For a discussion of freedom of expression issues arising from trade marks and copyright, see C Geiger 'Fundamental rights: a safeguard for the coherence of

perceived as an indication of origin, there may be some other reason to permit it, for example, because the defendant's sign is a valuable indication of geographical origin. In *Gerolsteiner*,[68] the proprietors of a German mark 'Gerri' alleged that their mark was infringed by use of 'Kerry' on mineral waters and soft drinks deriving from the Kerry Spring in Ireland, a recognised geographical indication. Even in the presence of confusion, in view of Art 6(1)(b), the proprietors of 'Gerri' could only enjoin the use of 'Kerry' if it were contrary to honest practices. That was for the national court to decide in all the circumstances, including the shape and labelling of the bottles. As indicated above, the ECJ felt that the question whether the use was 'as a trade mark' was unhelpful under Art 6(1)(b), although in *Windsurfing Chiemsee*, the ECJ had stated firmly that Art 6(1)(b) did 'not confer on third parties the right to use the name as a trade mark but merely guarantees their right to use it descriptively'. *Gerolsteiner* also laid to rest a line of argument that s 11(2)(b) only applied where the mark and sign were identical. In *Hölterhoff v Freiesleben*[69] Jacobs A-G refuted a suggestion from the French government that the use had to be necessary. Other cases under this defence include *Electrocoin* (signs used as indication of a winning line on a fruit machine), *Bravado Merchandising Services Ltd v Mainstream Publishing (Edinburgh) Ltd*[70] (use of band name 'Wet Wet Wet' to indicate the subject matter of a book).

(d)   Intended purpose under s 11(2)(c) (Art 6(1)(c) of the Directive, Art 12(1)(c) of the Regulation)

8.20   Use of a trade mark will also be permitted where it is necessary to indicate the purpose of other goods or services. Section 11(2)(c) makes particular reference to accessories or spare parts; however, it is not limited to these examples, as the ECJ remarked of Art 6(1)(c) in *Gillette Co v LA-Laboratories Ltd Oy*.[71] Gillette sold 'Gillette' and 'Sensor' razors with detachable handles and blades. LA sold similar blades and handles under the marks 'Parason Flexor'. However, the packaging stated 'All Parason Flexor and Gillette Sensor handles are compatible with this blade'. The ECJ held that this could potentially fall within the defence. 'Necessary' meant that 'information cannot in practice be communicated to the public by a third party without use being made of the trade mark'. In deciding whether use was necessary, the national court could take account of factors such as the possible existence of technical standards or norms known to the relevant public. There is again the requirement of honesty. In this context, the ECJ observed that:

---

intellectual property law' (2004) 35(3) IIC 268. See, also, *Red Dot Technologies Ltd v Apollo Fire Detectors Ltd* [2007] EWHC 1166 (Ch) at paras 11–13.

[68]   *Gerolsteiner Brunnen v Putsch* (C-100/02) [2004] RPC 39 ECJ; note 35 above. See, also, J Reed 'Water from Kerry Spring and Honest Practices' [2004] EIPR 429.

[69]   (C-2/00) [2002] ECR I-4187; [2002] ETMR 7; [2002] FSR 23.

[70]   [1996] FSR 205.

[71]   (C-228/03) [2005] ECR I-2337; [2005] All ER (D) 305. See also the comment at [2005] EIPR N137. Applied in *Datacard Corporation v Eagle Technologies Ltd* [2011] EWHC 244 (Pat); [2011] RPC 17 at para 299 and *Samuel Smith Old Brewery (Tadcaster) v Lee (t/a Cropton Brewery)* at para 114.

'The use of the trade mark will not be in accordance with honest practices in industrial and commercial matters if, for example:

– it is done in such a manner as to give the impression that there is a commercial connection between the third party and the trade mark owner;
– it affects the value of the trade mark by taking unfair advantage of its distinctive character or repute;
– it entails the discrediting or denigration of that mark;
– or where the third party presents its product as an imitation or replica of the product bearing the trade mark of which it is not the owner.'

8.21 Repairs and servicing also come within this exception. In *Volvo v Heritage*,[72] a former Volvo dealer continued to use the word 'Volvo' in letterheads and signs, together with the words 'specialist' and 'independent'. The court held that this use of the 'Volvo' mark was calculated to cause confusion or the belief that there was still a trading connection, and so was not honest. Thus 'spares for all Rover models' or 'we repair Canon cameras' would be permitted under s 11(2)(c), but probably not 'Rover spares', for other manufacturers' spare parts for 'Rover' cars, or 'Canon repairs' for a repairer outside the Canon network. In *BMW v Deenik*,[73] Mr Deenik ran a garage which sold second-hand BMW cars and offered maintenance and repair services. He was not a BMW dealer. Some of his uses of the BMW marks were held by the Dutch courts improperly to suggest affiliation. However, other advertisements such as 'repairs and maintenance of BMWs', 'BMW specialist' or 'specialised in BMWs' were thought permissible. The ECJ ruled that the trade mark proprietor could not restrain the uses unless the mark was being used to create the impression of a commercial connection such as affiliation or a special relationship with the trade mark proprietor. Cases in passing off[74] have shown that descriptions like 'factory reconditioned Hoovers' may be actionable, because members of the public would imagine reconditioning to have been done by or on behalf of the mark's proprietor, with original spares. Contrast 'We recondition vacuum cleaners – all makes – Hoover, Electrolux, Goblin, etc'.

(e)   The use of local signs under s 11(3) (Art 6(2) of the Directive, Art 12(2) of the Regulation)

8.22 The defendant may be able to show an earlier local right in the mark, for example, the right to sue in passing off.[75] If so, s 11(3) provides a defence in

---

[72] *Aktiebolaget Volvo v Heritage (Leicester) Ltd* [2000] FSR 253 (Ch D). T Martino, A Robinson 'Car Wars: The Volvo Empire Strikes Back' [1999] EIPR 630.

[73] *Bayerische Motorenwerke AG v Deenik* (C-63/97) [1999] All ER (EC) 235; [1999] 1 CMLR 1099; [1999] ECR I-905; [1999] ETMR 339.

[74] Eg *Hoover v Air-Way* (1936) 53 RPC 399 ('reconditioned Hoover'); *Levi Strauss v Wingate* [1993] EIPR D-258; (1993) 26 IPR 215 (Fed Ct of Aus).

[75] The ECJ has said little to date about Art 6(2) but has acknowledged that it refers to non-registered rights recognised by EU member states: *Anheuser-Busch Inc v Budejovicky Budvar Narodni Podnik* (C-245/02) [2005] ETMR 27; *Arsenal Football Club Plc v Reed* (C-206/01) [2002] ECR I-10273; [2002] ETMR 82.

that locality. Note that the text of s 11(3) diverges mysteriously from that of the Directive by substitution of 'locality' for 'territory' at the end of the first sentence.[76]

'Exhaustion' defences under s 12 of the 1994 Act (Art 7 of the Directive, Art 13 of the Regulation)

8.23 The defendant's products may be 'parallel imports' – goods marketed elsewhere by or with the consent of the trade mark proprietor. If such goods emanate from the European Economic Area (EEA), s 12(1) provides a defence. The background to this section and the case-law of the CJEU as applied by the UK courts are discussed in Chapter 13. It appears that the consent has to be voluntary.[77] Section 12(2) disapplies s 12(1) where there are legitimate reasons to oppose further dealings, especially where the condition of goods is changed/impaired. In *Sun Microsystems*,[78] the Court of Appeal held it arguable that the Directive (and hence s 12) did not provide an exhaustive code, so that a free-standing and distinct defence might be available under EU free movement rules. Many of the EU cases involve pharmaceutical products, where low cost of transport combined with differentials between the prices set in member states makes parallel importing a lucrative business.

Other defences

8.24

(a) If the proprietor's rights are restricted[79] by disclaimer or limitation, the defendant may be able to argue that his activities fall within that disclaimer, and thus cannot be enjoined. A defendant should get sight of the registration certificate or entry in the *Trade Mark Journal* as quickly as possible, to ascertain whether the plaintiff's rights may be limited in this way.

(b) *Acquiescence under s 48/Art 9 of the Directive/Art 53 of the Regulation and generally* – Where the defendant has registered and used the mark in suit and the plaintiff has been aware of its use but has acquiesced in that use for a continuous period of 5 years, s 48 applies. In *Sunrider v Vitasoy* it was held that the marks must be actually registered before the 5-year period can start to run so an application to register is insufficient.[80] However, in *Budejovicky Budvar Narodni Podnik v Anheuser-Busch Inc*, the Court of Appeal doubted this and referred questions on the nature of

---

[76] D Lyons 'Vested Rights Unbuttoned: Section 11(3) Trade Marks Act 1994' [1995] EIPR 608.

[77] Cf *Pharmon v Hoechst* [1985] 3 CMLR 775 where a compulsory licence was in effect.

[78] *Sun Microsystems Inc v M-Tech Data Ltd* (or *Oracle America Inc v M-Tech Data Ltd*) [2010] EWCA Civ 997; [2011] 1 CMLR 43; [2010] ETMR 64; [2011] FSR 2.

[79] Section 13.

[80] Despite s 40(3), which deems the application to be the date of registration once the mark is registered: *Sunrider Corp (t/a Sunrider International) v Vitasoy International Holdings Ltd* [2007] EWHC 37 (Ch); [2007] Bus LR 602; [2007] RPC 29.

acquiescence and the start date of the 5-year period to the Court of Justice.[81] The Court of Justice held that the prerequisites for the running of the 5-year period were registration of the later mark, in good faith, use and knowledge by the proprietor of the earlier registration. The Court also observed that there could not be acquiescence where the proprietor of the earlier mark was not in a position to oppose use of the later mark. Section 48 provides a defence to infringement claims and disables the claimant from applying for a declaration of invalidity. Section 48 does not appear to preclude an application for revocation under s 46. However, the CJEU in para 3 of its ruling in *Budejovicky Budvar v Anheuser-Busch* ruled that cancellation of the mark would be unavailable 'where there has been a long period of honest concurrent use of those two trade marks where, in circumstances such as those in the main proceedings, that use neither has nor is liable to have an adverse effect on the essential function of the trade mark which is to guarantee to consumers the origin of the goods or services'. The relationship between s 48 and s 2(2) – which states that the 1994 Act is without prejudice to passing off – was considered in *Inter Lotto (UK) Ltd v Camelot Group plc*.[82] It is submitted that the better view is that s 48 does not extinguish passing-off rights,[83] although equitable defences of acquiescence, estoppel or laches may make it impossible to restrain passing off by injunction where the claimant has failed to exert passing-off rights for an extended period.

(c) The courts prize finality in litigation and discourage relitigation of the same dispute. This principle is enshrined in the concepts of 'res judicata', 'cause of action estoppel'[84] and 'issue estoppel'. Once a claim or legal point has been finally concluded between two parties, the courts will bar attempts to resurrect it. However, the defendant has to raise the point to resist the second claim. This can be seen in action in *Omega Engineering v Omega SA*.[85] Revocation of the disputed mark as of a particular date had been refused in earlier proceedings[86] because the pleadings were unclear. The second action raised points that should have been put forward in the first proceedings. The defendant applied to strike out was successful,[87] not because the points had been decided, but because it was oppressive to have to meet a second set of proceedings when the first should have been

---

[81] *Budejovicky Budvar Narodni Podnik v Anheuser-Busch Inc* [2009] EWCA Civ 1022; [2010] RPC 7 at para 63; (C-482/09) [2012] ETMR 2.

[82] [2004] RPC 9, CA.

[83] M Lim and G Kwek 'Conflict Between Common Law and Statutory Trade Mark Rights: Does Registration Confer Immunity Against a Claim for Passing Off' [2004] EIPR 36 discuss the Court of Appeal's decision in *Inter Lotto (UK) Ltd* and make interesting comparisons with Canada, Australia and Singapore.

[84] *Hormel Foods Corp v Antilles Landscape Investments NV* [2005] EWHC 13; [2005] ETMR 54 (Ch D). See K Stephens 'Trade marks: res judicata' (2005) 34(2) CIPA J 118.

[85] [2005] FSR 12; and see [2011] EWCA Civ 645; [2011] ETMR 40.

[86] *Omega SA v Omega Engineering Inc* [2003] FSR 49.

[87] After an appeal from the High Court Master to the judge.

enough. However, in *Special Effects Ltd v L'Oréal SA,* the Court of Appeal held that there was no estoppel from opposition proceedings in the trade marks Registry.[88]

(d) The Limitation Acts apply to infringement just as to any other torts. The limitation period of 6 years (5 in Scotland) will apply to debar any instances of infringement occurring more than 6 years prior to commencement of proceedings.[89] A 6-year limitation period is also built into the special provisions on delivery up in s 18.

(e) Innocence is not, strictly speaking, a defence in civil proceedings, since no requirement of intention or knowledge is built into the definitions of infringement. It may incline the court to refuse a discretionary remedy such as an account of profits.

(f) Non-infringing use started prior to commencement of the 1994 Act can be continued, by virtue of Sch 3, para 4(2). This applies where the mark was registered prior to commencement, or a new registration was obtained for essentially the same mark, for the same goods and services. It compensates for the broadening of the infringement provisions.[90]

SETTLEMENT

8.25 Compromise of litigation is always desirable. The public policy in favour of settlement of disputes[91] is the basis of many aspects of civil procedure – the award of litigation costs, the 'without prejudice' rule[92] which prevents statements in settlement negotiations being revealed to the court,[93] and so forth. However, those seeking to settle a trade mark infringement action must be particularly careful. Inappropriate partitioning arrangements may offend against Art 101 of the Treaty on the Functioning of the European Union (ex Art 81 of the EC Treaty).[94] Furthermore, a settlement agreement which

---

[88]   [2007] EWCA Civ 1; [2007] Bus LR 759; [2007] ETMR 51; [2007] RPC 15, applying *Buehler AG v Chronos Richardson Ltd* [1998] 2 All ER 960 and distinguishing *Hormel Foods Corp v Antilles Landscape Investments NV* [2005] EWHC 13; [2005] ETMR 54.

[89]   See, further **7.06**. For a patent case in which the defendant's acts were statute-barred before grant of the patent, see *Sevcon v Lucas* [1986] RPC 609.

[90]   See **7.16–7.18, 7.41**.

[91]   See, eg *Naylor v Preston AHA* [1987] 1 WLR 958 at 967.

[92]   *Prudential Assurance Co Ltd v Prudential Insurance Co of America* [2004] ETMR 29 (CA). Said to be the subject of an implied agreement as well as public policy in *Reed Executive plc v Reed Business Information Ltd (No 2)* [2005] FSR 3.

[93]   Save as to costs.

[94]   See Chapter 13; S Singleton 'Intellectual property disputes: settlement agreements and ancillary licences under EC and UK competition law' [1993] 2 EIPR 48; E McKnight 'Trade Mark Agreements and EC Law' [1996] EIPR 271. S Maniatis and D Botis 'Competition and Trade Marks', in *Trade Marks in Europe: A Practical Jurisprudence* (Sweet and Maxwell, 2009).

involves licensing the defendant to continue to use the mark in some way may endanger the mark's validity by rendering it deceptive.[95]

---

[95] See Chapter 9.

Chapter 9

CANCELLATION OF UK REGISTRATIONS

INTRODUCTION

9.1   Under the Trade Marks Act 1994 ('the 1994 Act'), anyone[1] may seek removal of a trade mark from the UK register,[2] in respect of some or all of the goods or services for which it is registered.[3] In contrast, under the Trade Marks Act 1938 ('the 1938 Act'), a person applying for removal of a mark had to be a 'person aggrieved';[4] this status was normally shown by the citation of the mark against an application, or threat of infringement proceedings.[5] At the entry into force of the 1994 Act, concerns were expressed that the liberality of the new provisions would lead to vexatious applications, or to the use of nominees in attacking marks; fortunately, largely due to the costs of mounting such proceedings, neither these nor the related abilities of persons to 'intervene' in proceedings for either revocation or invalidation of registrations[6] appear to have been abused. In *Galileo v EU*, no point was taken on the standing of the EU, represented by the Commission.[7] Of course the applicant must be able to establish grounds for cancellation of the mark.

---

[1]   An attempt to limit the possibility to those with a bona fide interest in removal of the mark from the register was rejected in Parliament: *Hansard*, House of Lords, vol 553, no 55, col 78 (14 March 1994); Directive 2008/95/EC and (its predecessor 89/104/EEC) to approximate the laws of the member states relating to trade marks merely refer in Art 12 to the trade mark being liable to revocation. Recital 6 clarifies that member states should remain free to fix the provisions of procedure concerning registration, revocation and invalidity of registered marks. However, where the grounds of an attack on validity are 'relative grounds' – based on a prior right – the 'proprietor' of that right as defined in s 5(4) of the 1994 Act must bring the application to cancel the mark. See the Trade Marks (Relative Grounds) Order 2007, SI 2007/1976 and below at **9.11**.

[2]   As regards Community trade marks (CTMs), it was held in *Lancôme v OHIM* (C-408/08 P) [2010] ETMR 34 at paras 36–44 that a lawyer had standing to apply in relation to absolute grounds of validity, though in relation to relative grounds the application had to be made by the proprietor of the earlier right. This is because (what is now) Art 56(1) of codified Reg (EC) No 207/2009 on the Community trade mark distinguishes between these cases. It also provides that any person with legal personality may apply to revoke.

[3]   Sections 45(1), 46(5), 47(5) of the 1994 Act.

[4]   Sections 26, 27(4), 32, 33 and Sch 1, para 4 of the 1938 Act.

[5]   For a case in which the applicant for removal of a mark failed to satisfy this requirement, see *OSCAR TM* [1979] RPC 173.

[6]   A process initiated on Form TM27 by virtue of Trade Mark Rules 2008, r 45; it is also possible to intervene in proceedings to rectify the register conducted under s 64.

[7]   *Galileo International Technology, LLC v European Union (formerly European Community)* [2011] EWHC 35 (Ch) [2011] ETMR 22, per Floyd J.

9.2   The proprietor himself may apply to the Registry to surrender the registration,[8] either in whole or in part. In this case, the 1994 Act recognises that licensees or those with other interests in the registration might be affected.[9] Accordingly, the proprietor is required to give the name and address of any person having a registered interest in the mark and to certify that they have received 3 months' notice of the application. The proprietor must further certify either that such persons are not affected by surrender or that they have given consent. Licensees, chargeholders and others having registrable interests should register[10] in order to enjoy this (and other) protection. It appears that the Registry need not look behind the certificate, nor notify the registered interests directly.[11]

9.3   In lieu of surrender, the proprietor may simply fail to renew the registration. This requires no forms or consents; it is free and, in some circumstances, reversible as, subject to payment of the relevant fees, s 43 provides for submission of the request for renewal up to 6 months after expiry[12] and for restoration of marks after that date; however, the latter is only permitted if the Registrar is satisfied that it is just to restore the mark to the register.[13] It should be noted, though, that the effect of failing to renew a registration is not identical to that of surrender; this is because, although showing as 'expired' on the register, the registration will not be removed for 6 months after the renewal date in order to allow for late renewal. Thus, during the 6 months after expiry, a non-renewed registration enjoys a more substantial 'afterlife' than a surrendered one: whilst it is true that, like a surrendered registration, various operations relating to a non-renewed registration (eg recordal of assignment, recordal of licence or merger) cannot be conducted on the register, this is only the case pending any possible late renewal or restoration. Moreover, unlike a surrendered registration, a non-renewed registration can still be cited against later applications (thereby potentially blocking them) pending late renewal and, subject to late renewal or restoration occurring, it can even ground infringement proceedings; this is because even if the registration is renewed late, it is deemed renewed retroactively from the expiry of the previous registration[14] and, subject to any possible gaps in registration arising from a non-contiguous restoration date,[15] this is also true for restored registrations.

---

8   Section 45(1) of the 1994 Act; Trade Marks Rules 2008, r 33.
9   Section 45(2)(b) and r 33(3).
10   See **10.21–10.23, 11.17, 11.19** and **11.27**.
11   Unless they have filed a request for information, or 'caveat', on Form TM31C; Form TM31M is used to request information on international (Madrid) registrations with effect in the UK.
12   Section 43(3) and r 36.
13   Section 43(5) and r 37.
14   Section 43(4).
15   On the face of the wording of r 37(2), a gap between the expiry date and the restoration date is possible.

9.4   Applications by third parties to remove a mark may be divided into two broad categories; both can be made to the Registry or to the court.[16] The first category of application, for a declaration of invalidity, is based on grounds existing at the time of registration. If the application is successful, in relation to some or all of the goods or services, the registration will be deemed never to have been made, subject to 'transactions past and closed'.[17] The Registrar himself may apply to the court for cancellation on the ground of bad faith.[18]

9.5   The second category is the application for revocation. This is based on grounds arising after registration: non-use, deceptiveness or a shift to generic meaning. The revocation may take effect from the date of the application, or from an earlier date at which the grounds for revocation subsisted.[19] In both categories, evidence will be required, in due form,[20] and appropriate fees must be paid.[21]

GROUNDS – INVALIDITY (S 47)

9.6   The grounds of invalidity include all those which could form a basis for refusal under ss 3 to 6. The applicant for a declaration of invalidity may allege that the registered sign does not satisfy s 1, because it is not a sign capable of graphic representation. At first glance, this seems a hopeless objection, because a graphic representation of something must have been entered on the register. However, it may still be open to argue that the representation is embarrassingly inadequate, and fails to show in what sign the proprietor has exclusive rights. Another ground based on s 1 is that of non-distinctiveness. If the mark is shown incapable of being distinctive[22] or devoid of distinctive character,[23] then the registration may be declared invalid. Where a claim of invalidity is based on

---

[16]   To the court if proceedings are pending there: s 47(3)(a) and s 46(4)(a). Note that the Registrar may transfer applications to the court: s 47(3)(b) and s 46(4)(b).

[17]   Section 47(6).

[18]   Section 47(4). Note that the test for bad faith 'contains both a subjective element, what did the applicant know, and an objective element, what would the ordinary person adopting proper standards think': *Harrison's Trade Mark Application (CHINAWHITE)* [2005] FSR 10, CA, applied in *Jules Rimet Cup Ltd v Football Association Ltd* [2007] EWHC 2376 (Ch) at paras 74–76.

[19]   Section 46(6). Note that the earliest date that revocation may occur is 5 years after the completion of the registration process (or date of conferral of protection of a trade mark on the International Register which extends to the UK): *George Lowden v The Lowdon Guitar Company Ltd* [2004] EWHC 2531 (Ch). For calculation of this date, see *Philosophy di Alberta Ferretti Trade Mark* [2003] RPC 15 and *WISI Trade Mark* [2006] RPC 17, explained in Tribunal Practice Notice (TPN) 1/2007 'Applications for revocation on the grounds of non-use: calculation of the date of revocation', available at www.ipo.gov.uk/pro-types/pro-tm/t-law/t-tpn.htm.

[20]   See TPN 2/2010 'Time periods for the submission of evidence and submissions in inter partes trade mark proceedings' and TPN 5/2009 'Correspondence solicited for proceedings', available at www.ipo.gov.uk/pro-types/pro-tm/t-law/t-tpn.htm.

[21]   Trade Marks and Trade Marks and Patents (Fees) (Amendment) Rules 2009, SI 2009/2089.

[22]   Contrary to s 1(1) and 3(1)(a). See **2.32**.

[23]   Contrary to s 3(1)(b); see further **2.34–2.40**; COMBI STEAM TM (*Matsushita Electric Industrial Co Ltd Trade Mark Application*) O-363–09 (AP).

s 3(1)(b) or (c) and (d) (descriptive and generic marks),[24] the proprietor may be able to show that the mark has acquired distinctiveness after registration by virtue of use, on the goods or services for which it is registered.[25] The case-law on passing off shows that a descriptive mark may indeed acquire 'secondary meaning'.[26] Difficulty arises, however, where the proprietor faces no competition. In *Shredded Wheat*,[27] the mark was held to be non-distinctive[28] despite long and extensive use for breakfast cereal. This was partly because the product had been patented, so no other manufacturer could compete directly while the patent was in force, and partly because the proprietors' advertising had highlighted the descriptiveness of the name. By analogy, it may be more difficult to show acquired distinctiveness in a mark which has been protected by registration than in an unregistered mark.[29]

9.7   Other provisions in s 3 will provide grounds for invalidity: that the mark is merely a prohibited shape,[30] is contrary to public order or accepted morals[31] or has always been deceptive at the date of application.[32] In practice, evidence of the way the mark has been used and perceived may be relevant to these issues as well as that of distinctiveness. The applicant for invalidity may further argue that the use of the mark is prohibited by UK or Community law.[33] For example, there may be some infraction of labelling laws.

9.8   Like s 46, s 47 does not appear to cater for removal of a mark on the ground that its use has subsequently become contrary to public order or morality. Presumably the assumption is that standards in these matters usually relax rather than tighten. This is not true of legal rules, especially those designed to protect the health and safety of the consumer. Nor is there the

---

[24]   See, in this context, the genesis and usage of the terms 'Extra Special Bitter' and the acronyms E.S.B./ESB in *David West (t/a Eastenders) v Fuller Smith & Turner Plc* [2003] EWCA (Civ) 48 (Pumfrey J at para 21ff). In *Paul Reber GmbH & Co KG v OHIM* (Case T-304/06) [2008] ETMR 68, the then Court of First Instance upheld cancellation of 'MOZART' as a CTM for confectionery, on the basis that it would be understood as indicating 'Mozartkugel' a name admittedly generic for balls of marzipan and praline coated in chocolate.

[25]   Section 47(1). In *Hasbro Inc v 123 Nahrmittel GmbH* [2011] EWHC 199 (Ch); [2011] ETMR 25; [2011] FSR 21 at para 167 it was held an appropriate short cut to see if distinctive in the present. This distinctiveness should be established for the whole of the UK, or at least the whole of the area where the linguistic problem arises: *Bovemij Verzekeringen NV v Benelux-Merkenbureau* (C-108/05) [2007] ETMR 29.

[26]   The classic example being Camel Hair Belting: *Reddaway v Banham* [1896] AC 199; 13 RPC 218.

[27]   (1938) 55 RPC 125 (Canada) and (1938) 55 RPC 271 (UK) and (1940) 57 RPC 137.

[28]   And therefore invalidly registered.

[29]   See *BP Amoco plc v John Kelly Ltd* [2002] FSR 5 (CA NI).

[30]   See s 3(2); for detailed consideration of this ground under s 47, see *Koninklijke Philips NV v Remington Consumer Products Ltd* [2004] EWHC 2327; [2005] FSR 17 and the discussion of shape marks at **2.15–2.21**.

[31]   Section 3(3); see **2.40**, **2.44**. Note under this ground it is the use of the mark that must be contrary to public policy, not the underlying business: *Sportwetten GmbH Gera v OHIM* [2006] ETMR 15 (the proprietor lacked the necessary gaming licence to offer betting under the mark).

[32]   Section 3(3)(b) and see **2.40**. Deceptiveness subsequent to registration is a ground for revocation under s 46(1)(d), referred to below.

[33]   Section 3(4).

possibility of invalidity proceedings if the mark acquires an overpowering geographical significance because of news coverage of disasters or the reorganisation of local government.[34]

9.9　Where the mark is or incorporates one of the specially protected emblems referred to in ss 3(5) and 4, a declaration of invalidity may be sought.[35]

9.10　The applicant in invalidity proceedings may argue that the mark has been applied for in bad faith.[36] An attack on this ground is likely to fail where based merely on the allegation that there was no bona fide intention to use the mark, especially where there has been use on some of the goods or services within the specification.[37] In this case, the challenger must pursue revocation, rather than invalidity. An allegation of bad faith is often likely to overlap with other grounds for removal, such as failure to use the mark. It may also coincide with relative grounds of refusal – that the mark was unregistrable in the face of an earlier mark, especially a well-known earlier mark.[38]

9.11　Validity may be impugned on the basis of identity or similarity to an earlier trade mark,[39] where registration was prohibited by s 5(1), (2), (3), or where the proprietor of an earlier right in passing off,[40] copyright[41] or design could prevent use and registration.[42] An application must be made by the 'proprietor' of the earlier right, defined as the person who can prevent use of the (later) trade mark. This may include an exclusive licensee under relevant legislation.[43] In relation to validity disputes centred on earlier trade marks, applicants asserting such rights have faced tougher time requirements since 5

---

[34]　'Avon', eg became the name of a county as well as of a river (cf *Avon* [1985] RPC 43). However, a mark which becomes geographically deceptive by virtue of the proprietor's use might be liable to revocation: s 46(1)(d).

[35]　See *American Clothing Associates SA v OHIM* [2010] ETMR 3, a case on refusal of a CTM.

[36]　See *DAAWAT TM* [2003] RPC 11.

[37]　*Second Sight TM* [1995] RPC 423, per Lightman J, obiter, but cited with approval in *Road Tech Computer Systems Ltd v UNISON Software (UK) Ltd* [1996] FSR 805 Ch D. Curiously, in *Chocoladefabriken Lindt & Sprüngli AG v Franz Hauswirth GmbH*, the Commission argued, unsuccessfully, that the bad faith ground be limited to cases of applications made without a genuine intention to use the mark. See Ron Moscona 'Bad faith as grounds for invalidation under the Community Trade Mark Regulation – the ECJ decision in *Chocoladefabriken Lindt & Sprüngli AG v Franz Hauswirth GmbH*' [2010] EIPR 48.

[38]　Even if that mark is no longer in use, if the goodwill has not been abandoned: *Jules Rimet Cup Ltd v Football Association Ltd* [2007] EWHC 2376 (Ch) (WORLD CUP WILLIE).

[39]　See **5.8, 5.10, 5.30–5.37**.

[40]　Section 5(4)(a). See *Dixy Fried Chickens (Euro) Ltd v Dixy Fried Chickens (Stratford) Ltd* [2003] EWHC 2902 (Ch) and *Byford v Oliver* [2003] EWHC 295 (Ch).

[41]　Though note the possible limitation imposed by rules of copyright infringement demanding taking of the whole or a substantial part (eg the general lack of protection for book titles under copyright): *Animated Music Ltd's Trade Mark; Request for a Declaration of Invalidity by Dash Music Co Ltd* [2005] ECDR 27.

[42]　See s 5(4)(b). For helpful details as to how such an applicant may plead their case, see TPN 1/2010, available at www.ipo.gov.uk/pro-types/pro-tm/t-law/t-tpn.htm.

[43]　See Copyright, Designs and Patents Act 1988, ss 101 and 234; Registered Designs Act 1949, s 24F.

May 2004;[44] from that date, the 1994 Act, as amended requires that the earlier marks in question must have completed their registration procedures less than 5 years before the application date,[45] have still been going through the application procedure at that date[46] or satisfy prescribed use conditions.[47] For further details of 'relative' grounds for refusal and techniques for comparison of marks, goods and services, see Chapter 5 (registration) and Chapter 7 (infringement). Note that the Office's findings in invalidity proceedings may be relied upon to found an estoppel,[48] unlike those in opposition proceedings.[49]

Invalidity – defending the registration

9.12 Where confusion is objectively likely across the breadth of the registration, a defence based solely on lack of actual confusion in the marketplace may well fail.[50] Absence of confusion may be due to dearth of use by the proprietor of the earlier mark, or extraneous factors. In both EU and UK law, attempts by the proprietor of the mark under attack to rely on earlier trade marks of its own have failed. If they predate the attacker's mark, the correct course of action is to apply to invalidate that mark.[51] In this case proceedings may be consolidated if both are before the UK Registry.[52]

GROUNDS – REVOCATION (S 46)

9.13 Revocation may be sought instead of or in addition to a declaration of invalidity. The first ground for revocation, and the one likely to be employed most frequently, is non-use. There are two possibilities. First, the applicant[53] may allege that the mark has not been put to genuine[54] use,[55] by the proprietor

---

44 Because of the insertion of s 47(2A)–(2E) by the Trade Marks (Proof of Use, etc) Regulations 2004, SI 2004/946.

45 Section 47(2A)(a).

46 Section 47(2A)(b); this is the better reading of a somewhat obscure passage.

47 Section 47(2A)(c)–(2E); note that the prescribed use conditions are similar to those for revocation for non-use under s 46 and in s 6A (raising of relative grounds in opposition proceedings in case of non-use).

48 *Evans (t/a Firecraft) v Focal Point Fires* [2009] EWHC 2784 (Ch). For this reason, the Registry insists upon a hearing in invalidity applications based on s 5 of the 1994 Act: TPN 6/2009, available at www.ipo.gov.uk/pro-types/pro-tm/t-law/t-tpn.htm.

49 *Special Effects Ltd v L'Oréal SA* [2007] EWCA Civ 1; [2007] ETMR 51; [2007] RPC 15.

50 TPN 4/2009, citing *Compass Publishing v Compass Logistics* [2004] RPC 41; *Rousselon Freres v Horwood Homewares* [2008] EWHC 881 and *The European v The Economist* [1998] FSR 283; available at www.ipo.gov.uk/pro-types/pro-tm/t-law/t-tpn.htm.

51 TPN 4/2009, citing *PepsiCo v OHIM* (T-259/02) [2005] ECR II-1341; *MATRATZEN* (T-6/01) [2002] ECR II-4335; *Ion Associates v Stainton* BL O-211–09.

52 Eg *THE ORIGINAL BUCKS FIZZ TM* O/296/11 (Allan James, 22 August 2011), available at www.ipo.gov.uk/pro-types/pro-tm/pro-t-os/pro-t-find/t-challenge-decision-results.htm.

53 There is no provision for ex officio revocation by the Registry.

54 For a discussion of 'genuine use', see **6.6, 6.14–6.16** and *Laboratoires Goëmar v La Mer Technology Inc* [2005] EWCA Civ 978 (ie genuine use defined as any use going to preservation of an outlet for goods and services bearing the mark as opposed to merely preserving the mark itself). Unused registrations have been described as 'abandoned vessels in the shipping lanes of trade': Howell 'No marks for internal promotion – use it or lose it at Covent Garden Market'

or with his consent, for at least 5 years since it was placed on the register.[56] Alternatively, the revocation may be sought on the ground that the mark has been out of use for an uninterrupted period of 5 years. Once an allegation of non-use has been made in revocation proceedings, it is for the proprietor to show what use has in fact been made. This is the effect of s 100. Unless use is shown on all the goods or services for which the mark is registered, its registration is liable to be revoked in whole or in part.[57] Where use is resumed after 5 or more years' non-use, the mark might still be saved but use in the 3 months prior to the application for revocation is disregarded, unless preparations were made before the proprietor became aware that the application might be made.[58] This is designed to enable the applicant to approach the proprietor with a view to compromise, in the knowledge that commencement of use will not count after warning is given. The costs regime encourages the giving and heeding of notice.[59]

9.14 Section 46(1)(a) and (b) refers to 'proper reasons for non-use'. Although it may be for the applicant to establish that there are no proper reasons for non-use, a wise proprietor will be prepared to justify failure to use. Parliament declined to particularise the proper reasons which might subsist;[60] construction of s 46(1) and the provisions of the Trade Marks Harmonisation Directive (EEC) 89/104 ('the Directive') on which it was based (and equivalent provisions of the Community Trade Mark Regulation) is therefore left to the courts. In decisions under the equivalent provisions of the 1938 Act, reasons for non-use had to be fairly extreme to save a mark: 'special circumstances in the trade' such as wartime prohibitions.[61] Historically, there was also some recognition

---

[2006] Comms L 47 citing *NEW COVENT GARDEN MARKET TM* O/026/06 (Trade Mark Registry or TMR) and *Laboratoires Goëmar SA v La Mer Technology Inc* [2005] EWCA Civ 978.

[55] This key concept is discussed in Chapter 6, eg the requirement for use of the mark in a form which does not differ materially from the form in which it was registered; in relation to s 46(2), see *Bud and Budweiser Budbräu Trade Marks* [2002] RPC 38. See, also, J Phillips and I Simon (eds) *Trade Mark Use* (2005). For extent of use, see *Ansul* [2003] ETMR 85; *Anheuser-Busch Inc v OHIM* (T-191/07) [2009] ECR II-691; [2009] ETMR 50 has been said to use the same approach to genuine use of a CTM: *Galileo International Technology, LLC v European Union (formerly European Community)* [2011] EWHC 35 (Ch); [2011] ETMR 22, per Floyd J. Use must be in the course of trade in the products in question: free promotional use relating to other products does not avail: *Silberquelle GmbH v Maselli-Strickmode GmbH* (C-495/07) [2009] ETMR 28.

[56] Section 46(1)(a) refers to 5 years following the date of completion of the registration procedure; the latter was also held to be the relevant starting point under the 1938 Act: *BON MATIN TM* [1989] RPC 537, Ch D; affirming [1988] RPC 553, TMR. For calculation of this date, see *Philosophy di Alberta Ferretti Trade Mark* [2003] RPC 15 and *WISI Trade Mark* [2006] RPC 17, explained in TPN 1/2007 'Applications for revocation on the grounds of non-use: calculation of the date of revocation', available at www.ipo.gov.uk/pro-types/pro-tm/t-law/t-tpn.htm.

[57] Section 46(5).

[58] Section 46(3).

[59] TPN 6/2008 (trade marks): costs in proceedings before the Comptroller, available at www.ipo.gov.uk/pro-types/pro-tm/t-law/t-tpn/t-tpn-2008/t-tpn-62008.htm.

[60] House of Lords Public Bill Committee, col 84 (19 January 1994).

[61] *Manus v Fullwood & Bland* (1948) 65 RPC 329; (1949) 66 RPC 71.

that, if the goods or services were very valuable, sales could be sporadic and that, by parity of reasoning, lack of demand could be a legitimate reason for non-use.[62] In its explanatory memorandum to Art 13 of the 1980 draft of the Community Trade Mark Regulation (EC) 40/94 ('the Regulation'), the European Commission likewise suggested that a manufacturer of pharmaceuticals who was prevented from using a mark because of marketing constraint would not be liable to lose the mark for non-use.[63] Today, the main emphasis lies in determining whether there exist 'obstacles to non-use arising independently of the will of the proprietor'[64] and whether these obstacles are 'exceptional' or merely the 'normal difficulties' of commercial life.[65]

9.15	Where a mark is used on some but not all of the goods for which it is registered, partial revocation is possible.[66] Consider a mark registered in Class 18 for umbrellas, parasols and riding whips which is used only on umbrellas. Revocation may be sought in respect of parasols and riding whips. Under the 1938 Act, there was discretion to allow a mark to remain on the register if used for goods and services of the same description.[67] There was no equivalent provision in the 1994 Act. In its memorandum on the creation of an EEC trade mark the European Commission wrote:

> 'If a trade mark is used only for some of the goods for which it is registered, it should be maintainable ... only for those goods. In the case of proceedings for invalidation or cancellation, the remaining goods should be removed from the list of goods. This strict provision does not prejudice the rule that the protection of a trade mark extends to goods which are similar to the used goods. However, if use for similar goods were sufficient to maintain the registration for unused goods, the result would be an extension of the trade mark right beyond what is fair and reasonable.'

Since the entry into force of the 1994 Act, the courts have become progressively stricter in ensuring that the specification of goods/services for which a mark is registered accurately reflect those upon which it is used, partly because of the much wider net of infringement the Act creates when compared to the 1938 Act: in *David West (t/a Eastenders) v Fuller Smith & Turner plc*,[68] Pumfrey J, sitting in the Court of Appeal, adopted the reasoning of Aldous LJ in *Thomson Holidays Ltd v Norwegian Cruise Line Ltd*[69] in searching for a 'fair specification' which should be entered on the register in such cases; by analogy to infringement testing under s 10(2), this should be devised by reference to the

---

[62]	A Spencer 'European harmonisation use and abuse' *Trademark World*, May 1994, p 27, citing s 30 of the WIPO Model Law.

[63]	*Bulletin of the European Communities*, 5/1980, p 61.

[64]	*Philosophy Inc v Ferretti Studio Srl* [2002] EWCA Civ 921; judgment of Peter Gibson LJ at para 25 (drawing on Art 19.1 of the WTO Trade-Related Aspects of Intellectual Property Rights (TRIPs) Agreement).

[65]	Ibid at para 22.

[66]	Section 46(5).

[67]	Section 26(1). In our example, this would probably have saved the mark for parasols but perhaps not for riding whips.

[68]	[2003] EWCA (Civ) 48.

[69]	[2002] EWCA Civ 1828.

intended use of the proprietor's goods, the channels of trade through which they were sold, and the likely purchasers of the goods. In the instant case, registration was cut back in class 32 from 'beer' to 'bitter beer' on the basis that 'Beer drinkers in the main drink either lager or bitter, but not both. There is little overlap of trade marks between those two classes'.[70]

9.16 A mark which has become 'generic' in the trade (used by traders as the common name for a product or service for which it is registered) is vulnerable to revocation under s 46(1)(c). The applicant must show that the mark has become generic by virtue of the proprietor's acts or inactivity. Already we have seen in Chapter 6 that a proprietor who has used his own mark in a generic way, or has stood idly by[71] whilst others do so is likely to lose the registration, but a vigilant if ineffective proprietor may be able to keep the mark on the register. Until recently it appeared that the 1994 Act did not provide fully effective means to prevent generic use by other traders and the Australian '*Caplets*'[72] case shows that this can be a problem as such use may be quite deliberate. However, the danger of 'genericide' has now been recognised in EU trade mark law by the Court of Justice in *Interflora v Marks & Spencer*.[73]

9.17 Where, after registration, a mark merely loses its distinctiveness, as was also the law under the 1938 Act.

9.18 Registration of a mark may be revoked on the ground that use has rendered it misleading to the public, particularly as to the nature, quality or geographical origin of the goods or services concerned. The wording of this section follows that of Art 12 of the Directive. It is submitted that other forms of deceptiveness, especially as to commercial origin, are not excluded.[74]

PROCEDURES

9.19 Surrender of a mark is relatively straightforward, subject to notification of those with a registered interest in the mark, and to provision of the

---

[70] See judgment of Pumfrey J in *David West (t/a Eastenders) v Fuller Smith & Turner plc* [2003] EWCA (Civ) 48 at para 61.

[71] As Lord Trowie of Troon remarked whilst the Trade Marks Bill was in committee stage, proprietors whose marks become generic may (misguidedly) be 'quite pleased': House of Lords Public Bill Committee, col 83 (19 January 1994).

[72] *Johnson & Johnson v Sterling Pharmaceuticals* (1991) 21 IPR 1.

[73] Case C-323/09, 22 September 2011 at para 94: 'Advertising on the basis of such a keyword is detrimental to the distinctive character of a trade mark with a reputation (dilution) if, for example, it contributes to turning that trade mark into a generic term.' See also, for useful comparisons of European and US approaches to dilution and related issues, I Simon 'Dilutive trade mark applications: trading on reputations or just playing games?' [2004] EIPR 67. Article 10 of the Community Trade Mark Regulation 207/2009 has a mechanism for correcting dictionary references that suggest a Communuity trade mark is a generic term.

[74] See H Norman 'Trade mark licences in the United Kingdom' [1994] 4 EIPR 154. It is interesting to speculate whether the splitting assignment in *IHT Internationale Heiztechnik v Ideal Standard* [1995] FSR 59 might render the marks vulnerable to attack on this ground.

necessary names, addresses and certificates.[75] Form TM22 is used for total surrender, while Form TM23 is prescribed for partial surrender, in respect of only some of the goods and services.[76]

9.20   Applications for revocation and for declarations of invalidity are rather more elaborate. Revocation for non-use is now governed by r 38 of the Trade Mark Rules 2008.[77] Rule 38(1) prescribes application for revocation on ground of non-use using a Form 26(N); this was revised in light of *Omega SA v Omega Engineering Inc* [2003] EWHC 1334.[78] Rule 38(2) provides for transmission of the application to revoke for non-use to the registered proprietor,[79] who may then file a counterstatement on Form TM8(N), including a clear statement of any proper reasons for non-use.[80] If the proprietor fails to file a counterstatement as prescribed the registration for the mark being revoked, unless the Registrar directs otherwise.[81] If filed, Form TM8(N) will be forwarded to the applicant for revocation, along with any evidence.[82] Timetabling and formalities of submission of evidence via pre-hearing 'evidence rounds' is now tightly controlled;[83] where the proprietor fails to file evidence in due time, the Registrar may treat the application as unopposed, and revoke the registration.[84] Applications and subsequent Registry procedures for revocation on grounds other than non-use and invalidation are similarly structured.[85] Once any one of the three applications is made, the hearings procedures are broadly similar to those for opposition proceedings.[86] However, as invalidity proceedings, unlike opposition proceedings, may give rise to estoppels, extra care has to be taken as regards the evidence and an application will not be decided without a hearing.[87] Appeals may be made to the court or

---

[75]   Described at **9.2**.

[76]   Rule 33(1).

[77]   Note, the valuable guidance given under TPN 1/2005 (Revocation (non-use) procedures); TPN 1/2007 (calculation of the date of revocation); TPN 4/2009 (defences) and TPN 1/2020 (pleadings under s 5(4)(b)).

[78]   In this case, Jacob J (as he then was) held that if applicants for revocation were to seek a revocation date earlier than the date of application, they had to specifically allege the grounds existing at that earlier date and also specify the date of revocation. The then-existing Form 26(N) neither had space for (nor otherwise encouraged) providing such information and was criticised accordingly.

[79]   Rule 38(2). See para 1.4 of TPN 1/2005 on procedure for 'sending'.

[80]   Rule 38(3); Form TM8(N). If evidence is lacking the Registrar shall provide a further period of at least 2 months for that: r 38(4).

[81]   Rule 38(6). A possible reason might be where a third party intervener becomes involved.

[82]   Rule 38(5).

[83]   See TPN 2/2011 'Case management of inter partes proceedings: efficient, fair and less costly resolution of disputes before the Trade Marks Tribunal' and TPN 2/2010 (trade marks): 'Time periods for the submission of evidence and submissions in inter partes trade mark proceedings'. Rule 38(8) gives discretion to the Registrar to give leave to file evidence subject to conditions.

[84]   Rule 38(7).

[85]   See Form 26(O) and 26(I) plus rr 39–40, 43 and 41–43 respectively.

[86]   See **5.63–5.65**.

[87]   See TPN 3/2011 (trade marks) 'Requirement to attend hearings in relation to applications for invalidation on relative grounds'.

to the appointed person,[88] again as for oppositions. Costs awarded to the successful party against the unsuccessful party are usually scale-based and modest. However, more generous costs may be awarded where the expense of proceedings has been greatly exacerbated by the conduct of a party.[89]

DATE AS AT WHICH THE REGISTRATION IS TO BE CANCELLED OR AMENDED

9.21   Where an application is made to surrender[90] a registration, in whole or in part, the proprietor should date and submit Form TM22 (surrender) or Form TM23 (partial surrender) as at the date on which surrender is sought. Subject to the interests of others, surrender will take effect as from that date.[91] Successful application to invalidate[92] a registered mark takes effect ab initio, but subject to 'transactions past and closed'.[93] An application to revoke[94] can take effect, if successful, from the date of application or an earlier date on which the grounds for revocation existed.[95] There is no provision to restore any marks affected by such procedures, but, in theory at least, the former proprietor may make a subsequent application to re-register the mark afresh if it is 'recaptured' from a generic usage or it otherwise becomes registrable once more.

---

[88]   Rules 70–73.
[89]   In *Death before Dishonour* O/307/11, costs were ordered on an indemnity basis.
[90]   See **9.2–9.3** and **9.19**.
[91]   The authors are grateful to the Trade Marks Registry for help on this point.
[92]   See **9.6–9.12** and **9.20**. ·
[93]   Proviso to s 47(6).
[94]   See **9.13–9.18, 9.20**.
[95]   Section 46(6).

Chapter 10

LICENSING OTHERS TO USE THE MARK

INTRODUCTION

10.1 A trade mark licence is, in essence, a permission by the trade mark proprietor to do something which would otherwise be an infringement. Although simple in concept, trade mark licensing has proven to be a difficult issue in the evolution of UK trade mark law.[1]

10.2 Prior to the Trade Marks Act 1938 ('the 1938 Act'), the prevailing view was that a trade mark was supposed to show a single source of goods; thus licensing was seen as a derogation from the basic function of a trade mark in that it would destroy distinctiveness and, more significantly, mislead the public.[2] The loss of distinctiveness or risk of deception could lead to the mark in question being expunged from the register.

10.3 In the end, the demands of commercial life partially prevailed: initially, the 1938 Act instituted the system of 'registered users' whereby, if a licensing agreement was made and recorded on the Register, use of the mark by the licensee was deemed to be use by the proprietor,[3] thereby automatically nullifying arguments over deception as to source. Eventually, the courts came to accept that licensing was not inherently deceptive to the public and that, accordingly, even an unregistered licence agreement would not automatically damage a trade mark registration.[4]

10.4 However, there remained a problem: in order to prevent trade mark registrations being treated as mere commodities, s 28(6) of the 1938 Act directed that the Registrar should not register any registered user agreement which would 'tend to facilitate trafficking'. The difficulty was that in relation to most licence agreements, those practices which the courts dismissed as trafficking amounted to the whole commercial point of the exercise; this was an issue which came to a head in the '*Holly Hobbie*' character merchandising case.[5]

---

[1] The history of trade mark licensing in the UK was charted by Lord Nicholls in *Scandecor Developments v Scandecor Marketing* [2001] UKHL 21; [2001] ETMR 74; [2002] FSR 122, HL, from para 16. See, also, N Wilkof and D Burkitt *Trade Mark Licensing* (Sweet & Maxwell, 2nd edn, 2005).

[2] *Bowden Wire v Bowden Brake* (1914) 31 RPC 385.

[3] Section 28(2) of the 1938 Act.

[4] *Bostitch Trade Mark* [1963] RPC 183.

[5] [1984] 1 WLR 189; [1984] FSR 199.

10.5 In passing the Trade Marks Act 1994 ('the 1994 Act'), both the government and Parliament took the view that trade mark licensing should be fully deregulated;[6] taking their cue from the position in the Trade Marks Harmonisation Directive ('the Directive') that trade marks may be licensed[7] and that use of a mark with the consent of the proprietor[8] should be deemed to constitute use by the proprietor.[9] The previous UK system of registered users was scrapped and a fully facilitative framework for licensing was inserted at ss 28–31.[10] The view that the 1994 Act represented a complete departure from earlier, more restrictive, regimes under the Trade Marks Act 1905 and the 1938 Act gained support from the opinions of the House of Lords in *Scandecor*.[11] The position of licensing under the Directive and 1994 Act is consonant with the approach in Regulation (EC) No 207/2009 ('the Regulation') on the Community trade mark (CTM) and its predecessor Regulation 40/94, which make clear that CTM rights are proprietary and capable of licensing.[12]

10.6 However, even under the current system, proprietors must still 'police' use of their marks by licensees: as we have already seen in Chapter 6, improper use of a mark can lead to revocation of the relevant registration and, in the case of licensing, the following considerations are always present:

(a) the risk of the mark becoming generic in the trade because of the inactivity of the proprietor (ie a failure to control a licensee's misuse of the mark) per s 46(1)(c); and

(b) the risk of misleading the public arising from use made with the proprietor's consent (ie under licence) per s 46(1)(d).

10.7 In addition, a trade mark licensor may still incur liability for defective products under the Consumer Protection Act 1987[13] and use of a trade mark in such a way as to deceive the public may also amount to a prohibited unfair commercial practice under the Consumer Protection from Unfair Trading Regulations 2008.[14] Given these commercial risks,[15] it is essential that a licensor

---

[6] See White Paper 'Reform of Trade Marks Law' Cm 1203 (1990) para 4.36; *Hansard*, House of Lords, vol 550, no 10, col 752 (6 December 1993).

[7] Article 8 of Directive 89/104/EEC to approximate the laws of the member states relating to trade marks, and of its successor, Directive 2008/95/EC.

[8] Or use of a collective or certification mark with the appropriate authorisation.

[9] Article 10(3) of Directive 89/104/EEC; Art 10(2) of Directive 2008/95/EC. This provision is integrated into the 1994 Act in negative form by way of limitation upon revocation at s 46.

[10] See NJ Wilkof 'Same old tricks or something new? A view of licensing and quality control' [1996] 5 EIPR 261.

[11] *Scandecor Developments v Scandecor Marketing* [2001] UKHL 21; [2001] ETMR 74; [2002] FSR 122, HL, at para 40. See NJ Wilkof and D Burkitt *Trade Mark Licensing* (Sweet & Maxwell, 2nd edn, 2005) paras 1–27; Chapter 6.

[12] Recital 11, Arts 22, 23 of Reg 207/2009; Recital 10, Arts 22 and 23 of Reg 40/94.

[13] Sections 2(2)(b) and 3(2). See, further, D Good and C Easter 'Product safety and product liability: the implications for licensing' [1993] 1 EIPR 10; P Giliker 'Consumer law; Torts Strict liability for defective products: the ongoing debate' [2003] Bus LR 87.

[14] SI 2008/1277, especially regs 3 and 5; Sch 1; a successor offence to that of false trade description under the Trade Descriptions Acts 1968–72. See **3.1**, **3.32** and **7.55**, **7.65**.

should have proper oversight and a degree of control over a licensee's activities; the mechanism for achieving this is the proper use of contract terms.

10.8 In practice, therefore, although there is no requirement that a trade mark licence should be granted within a contractually binding framework, many are. Furthermore, because of the need to control a licensee, any sensible licence agreement will go far beyond the basic act of giving permission:[16] quality control, duration, payment of royalties and many other matters have to be considered. The existence of a contractual backing for a licensing agreement means that the licensor has both contractual and trade mark rights to fall back on to deal with an erring licensee; in the case of the latter, English law makes clear that use outside the scope of a licence agreement is infringement,[17] a position echoed in Art 8(2) of the Directive and Art 22(2) of the Regulation.

LICENSING AND 'COMMON LAW' MARKS

10.9 The effect of licensing unregistered marks and other similar subject matter protected by passing off is unclear.[18] On the one hand, it is clear that, as between the licensee and licensor, a licence relating to an unregistered mark will work in much the same way as one relating to a registered mark:[19] on the other, it is difficult to argue that goodwill will inure to the benefit of the licensee such that it will acquire rights to take legal action against infringing third parties.[20]

10.10 These difficulties have been nowhere more evident than in relation to character merchandising[21] and business format franchising;[22] taking the former first, initially the courts were sceptical that a licence of an unregistered mark

---

[15] See DM Downing 'The risks of trade mark licensing' (2002) 122 MIP 59 for a discussion informed by unfortunate US experiences.

[16] See A Nette and H Strattmann 'Trademark licensing: an overview of the associated risks' (1999) 99 TW 22.

[17] See, e g *Crittall Windows v Stormseal* [1991] RPC 265, a case involving use of the mark in a form and style not sanctioned by the licence agreement. In *Copad SA v Christian Dior Couture SA* (C-59/08) [2009] ETMR 40, the ECJ held that it was for the national court to decide if resale of de luxe corsetry by licensees to discount stores was detrimental to 'luxury' aura and therefore infringement.

[18] For a detailed analysis of the problem, see NJ Wilkof and D Burkitt *Trade Mark Licensing* (Sweet & Maxwell, 2nd edn, 2005) p 45ff.

[19] This is because there will usually be contractual provisions governing the relationship and any action by the licensee outside the scope of the licence could be both passing off and a breach of contract; this argument was raised, albeit unsuccessfully on the facts, in the domain name case of *Pitman Training Ltd v Nominet UK Ltd* [1997] EWHC Ch 367; [1997] FSR 797.

[20] This being a significant feature of most licences of registered trade marks: see **10.18–10.20**.

[21] See, generally, H Stallard (ed) *Bagehot on Sponsorship, Merchandising and Endorsement* (1998); G Scanlan 'Personality, Endorsement and Everything: The Modern Law of Passing Off and the Myth of the Personality Right' [2003] EIPR 563, discussing *Irvine v Talksport Ltd* [2002] EWHC 367; [2002] 1 WLR 2355 (Ch D); *Irvine v Talksport Ltd (Damages)* [2003] EWCA Civ 423; [2003] 2 All ER 881 (CA).

[22] See, generally, M Mendelsohn *The Guide to Franchising* (Cengage Learning EMEA, 7th edn, 2004); J Adams, J Hickey and K Pritchard Jones: 'Franchising' (Tottel, 5th rev edn, 2005).

could stand at all and, in the *Kojak Lollipops* case,[23] Walton J memorably described the licence in question as 'a thing writ in water'.[24] A trio of other cases involving *ABBA*,[25] the *Beatles*[26] and the *Wombles*[27] seemed to confirm this but the later and much-celebrated *Ninja Turtles*[28] decision suggested that goodwill could inure to the benefit of a person other than a manufacturer or marketer.

10.11 At first, the *Ninja Turtles* decision was hailed for ensuring that licences of unregistered trade marks were valid and enforceable against third parties. However, closer analysis of the case[29] revealed that it was the licensor and its licensing agents that took action rather than end licensees and that, more significantly, the licence was coupled to a copyright licence; it was primarily the latter that gave the licensing agents the standing to sue.[30]

10.12 Since *Ninja Turtles*, the courts appear to have returned to their former position. In *NASA*,[31] it was held that a third party had parasitically built up goodwill in an unregistered mark even in the face of a licence agreement; this, in effect, meant that the neither the licensor nor its licensee had any standing to sue the third party for passing off.

10.13 More recently, the Court of Appeal has cast a further shadow by stating, albeit in the context of trade mark registrability, that it did not accept that the public would assume a licensee to be the source of origin for merchandise;[32] if this view were to be transposed into the context of unregistered marks, it would be tantamount to saying that a licensee could not acquire goodwill and, therefore, would be effectively barred from suing for passing off.

10.14 Turning to franchisors, the same problems arise as, in licensing their business formats, they will frequently be providing the licensee with the right to use not only registered trade marks but also unregistered marks and other 'trade badges'.[33] Accordingly, although the powerful arguments raised by Lane[34] that unregistered marks are capable of being licensed could be prayed in

---

[23] *Tavener Routledge v Trexapalm Ltd* [1975] FSR 479, [1977] RPC 275, 119 SJ 792, Ch D.

[24] Judgment at 486.

[25] *Lyngstad v Annabas* [1977] FSR 62.

[26] *Harrison & Starkey v Polydor* [1977] FSR 1.

[27] *Wombles v Womble Skips* [1977] RPC 99.

[28] *Mirage Studios v Counter-Feat Clothing* [1991] FSR 145.

[29] See B Cordery and J Watts 'Character merchandising – all shook up?' [1997] 4 Ent LR 145.

[30] This coupling effect may also explain *GE Electric Co's Trade Mark* [1969] RPC 418, a decision in which Graham J apparently upheld a licence of unregistered marks as valid (in that case, the licence also covered patent rights).

[31] *Nice And Safe Attitude v Flook* [1997] FSR 14; see also *Julian Higgins' Trade Mark Application* [2000] RPC 321 Ch D.

[32] *ELVIS PRESLEY Trade Marks* [1999] RPC 567.

[33] Eg customised shop interiors, fixtures and fittings.

[34] *The Status of Licensing Common Law Marks* (1991); S Lane 'Goodwill Hunting: Assignments and Licences in Gross after *Scandecor*' [1999] IPQ 264.

aid by a licensee as litigant, the best protection is still that offered by registered trade marks[35] or through other intellectual property rights.[36]

THE LICENCE AGREEMENT AND THE LICENSEE

10.15 Licence agreements fall into three broad categories.[37] First, the proprietor may authorise a manufacturer to apply the mark on the proprietor's behalf.[38] In this case, the proprietor is effectively subcontracting the use, the benefit of which will inure to him in any event. Secondly, the trade mark owner may license use of the marks on goods or services in which he has a direct commercial interest. Many business format franchises fall into this category[39] and, in this instance, the proprietor will have an even greater incentive than usual to exercise control over the quality of such goods or services.[40] Lastly, the proprietor may regard the trade mark merely as an asset from which a return may be made by licensing. Into this category come most aspects of character merchandising.[41]

10.16 One additional point to remember in this context is that not all forms of permission devolve from a licence agreement: for example, use in relation to the proprietor's own goods does not infringe in normal circumstances.[42] Whether this is use 'by or with the consent of the proprietor' is a nice point; presumably, consent will be implied into the circumstances of the trade.

10.17 Turning next to the licensee, the need for the trade mark owner to police the mark means that considerable care must be taken in selecting the licensee. A good licensee will be solvent, reliable, have good distribution arrangements, advertising policy and other business methods. Indeed, it is not uncommon for contractual terms to specify or demand such things: for example, a licence agreement may automatically terminate if the licensee becomes insolvent.

---

[35] Assuming, of course, that the subject matter in question is capable of being registered.

[36] Eg copyright, registered designs, design right.

[37] Note, however, that specialist agreements exist, e g so-called 'co-existence agreements' which delineate boundaries of registration and use between two legitimate holders of overlapping trade mark rights: see *MGW Group Inc v Gourmet Cookie Bouquets.com* (2004), noted at (2005) 7(1) WLLR 19.

[38] Such agreements can be at 'arm's length' or, alternatively, within a corporate group.

[39] See J Pratt 'Franchise agreements' (1997) 8(7) PLC 13; M Abell 'Franchising and the internationalisation of UK retail brands' (1997) 101 TW 31, RM Absill and MG Brennan 'International franchising: establishing and maintaining a healthy relationship' (1997) 25(5) IBL 208 and S Rose 'The future of distribution in Europe' (1999) 1 IJFDL 3.

[40] This is because of the need to maintain a sufficiently high level of goodwill and/or reputation so as to ensure a steady supply of both customers and new franchisees.

[41] See IC Baillie 'Trade marks and marketing images' (1997) 26(7) CIPAJ 495 and P Jaffey 'Merchandising and the law of trade marks' [1998] IPQ 240; on specific problems relating to the control of exploitation of human likenesses, see B Isaac 'Merchandising or fundraising? Trade marks and the Diana, Princess of Wales Memorial Fund' [1998] 12 EIPR 441 and H Johnson 'Do we need a publicity right?' (1999) 4(2) Comms L 41.

[42] Section 10(6).

10.18 From the licensee's point of view, one of the most important things is whether the licence is exclusive,[43] sole,[44] or non-exclusive, with the effect of the distinction lying in the level of action that the licensee can take against infringing third parties. Subject to the terms of the licence agreement, an exclusive licensee has all the rights and remedies of an assignee,[45] except title. He can bring infringement proceedings in his own name[46] against anyone except the proprietor[47] except where the licence agreement expressly excludes the right to do so.[48] Where the proprietor has acted in breach of an exclusive licence agreement by authorising a third party to use the mark, the licensee's remedy is in contract against the proprietor.[49] The exclusive licensee must be joined in infringement proceedings brought by the proprietor where they have concurrent rights of action.

10.19 A sole or other non-exclusive licensee may also bring proceedings for infringement unless the agreement provides to the contrary.[50] The licensee must first call upon the proprietor to take proceedings. If the proprietor fails to do so within 2 months, or refuses to do so, the licensee is then free to start litigation; this procedure represents an improvement upon the 1938 Act, under which the licensee had to wait for 2 months even if the proprietor expressly refused to institute proceedings.[51] Ultimately, the proprietor must be joined, although the licensee may seek interim relief prior to joinder.[52] Where the proprietor brings proceedings, the courts have the power to order that pecuniary relief be held on behalf of the licensee.[53]

10.20 Directive (EC) 2004/48 on the enforcement of intellectual property rights[54] by Art 4, entitled 'Persons entitled to apply for the application of the measures, procedures and remedies', recognises the rights of licensees to sue, 'in so far as permitted by and in accordance with the provisions of the applicable law'. An English court hearing claims for trade mark infringement in other EU member states under the Brussels Regulation (see **7.1** and **7.3**) may have to apply the law of another member state, which may differ as to standing of

---

[43] Authorising the licensee to use the mark to the exclusion of all others, including the proprietor: s 29(1).

[44] So that the use of the mark is limited to the licensee and the proprietor. This designation is not recognised in the 1994 Act but it is in common use for this particular type of non-exclusive licence.

[45] Section 31.

[46] The proprietor should be joined as co-plaintiff or nominal defendant per s 31(4) and (5), although interim relief may be sought prior to joinder. The court apportions pecuniary relief: s 31(6).

[47] Section 31(1).

[48] This is the better interpretation of the combined effect of s 30(1) and (7).

[49] Since the third party may defend infringement proceedings by referring to the proprietor's consent: s 31(3). See *Northern & Shell v Condé Nast* [1995] RPC 117.

[50] Section 30(2). To the same effect under registered user provisions of the 1938 Act, see *Levi Strauss v The French Connection* [1982] FSR 443.

[51] Section 28(3) of the 1938 Act.

[52] Section 30(4).

[53] Section 30(6).

[54] [2004] OJ L195/16 (corrected version).

licensees to sue. One must bear in mind also that a CTM may be licensed separately for different territories within the EU.[55] Subject to the licensing contract, Art 22(3) of the Regulation allows an exclusive CTM licensee to initiate infringement proceedings while Art 22(4) allows a non-exclusive licensee to intervene to claim compensation. It appears that, by virtue of Art 16, CTM licences will all be governed by the trade mark law of a single member state.

10.21 In order for the licensee to enjoy rights of action, a UK licence must be recorded under the provisions relating to registrable transactions.[56] If the licence is not recorded within 6 months from grant, the licensee's remedies are limited in that damages or account of profits cannot be had for the period from grant to eventual recordal.[57] Furthermore, failure to record means that the licence is ineffective as against a person acquiring a conflicting interest in or under the registered trade mark in ignorance of the same.[58]

10.22 A licensee will also be interested to see whether or not sub-licensing is permitted under the licence agreement. In the past, sub-licensing was regarded with a great deal of suspicion as it diminished the ability of the licensor to control the actual 'end use' of the mark and, even today, it is not uncommon to see express provisions barring it. However, interestingly, the 1938 Act did not ban sub-licensing; it merely stated that registered users were not automatically granted 'assignable or transmissible rights' by virtue of their status.[59] In practice, therefore, the ability of a licensee to sub-licence under the 1938 Act was dictated solely by the provisions of the licence agreement itself.[60]

10.23 The 1994 Act expressly recognises the possibility of sub-licensing, provided that the licence agreement in question allows it;[61] this, in effect, codifies the position reached under the 1938 Act. In addition, however, references in the 1994 Act to 'licence' or 'licensee' are extended to cover sub-licences and sub-licensees;[62] this opens up the possibility of sub-licensees acquiring rights to sue for infringement under s 30. Sub-licences should be registered in the same way as licences (although Form TM50 does not appear to provide for it and should be reworded as necessary when applying).

---

[55] Regulation (EC) 40/94, Art 22. In *Jean Christian Perfumes Ltd v Thakrar* [2011] EWHC 1383 (Ch); [2011] FSR. 34 it was held that even an oral licensee of a CTM could sue with the consent of the proprietor.

[56] See s 25(2)(b) and (3)(b). Rule 40(b) sets out the required particulars whilst r 41(1)(b)–(c) requires use of Form TM50 for recordal of grant of a licence and Form TM51 for amendment or termination.

[57] Section 25(4)(a). Note, however, that if the court can be convinced that it was not practicable for such an application to be made before the 6-month limit and that an application was made as soon as practicable thereafter, it may waive the limitation of remedies: s 25(4)(b).

[58] Section 25(3)(a).

[59] Section 28(12). For Australian jurisprudence on the assignability of licences, see *Pacific Brands Sport & Leisure Pty Ltd v Underworks Pty Ltd* [2006] FCAFC 40 (Fed Ct (Aus) (Full Ct)), noted at [2007] IIC 114.

[60] *Accurist Watches v King* [1992] FSR 80.

[61] Section 28(4).

[62] Section 28(4).

GENERAL AND LIMITED LICENCES

10.24 The licence may be general or limited to some of the goods or services for which it is registered.[63] Preferably the licence should be specific on this point[64] and, in any event, great care should be taken to define the scope of use under such agreements to avoid any possibility that there is 'crossover' of users such as would deceive the public and render the mark liable to revocation.[65]

10.25 Territorial limitations may also apply, as specifically provided for by s 28(1)(b). Both the territorial and product limitation provisions in s 28 derive from Art 8(1) of the Directive but it is important to ensure that any limitations imposed do not fall foul of overriding competition laws,[66] EC free movement of goods rules[67] and, more specifically, provisions relating to exhaustion of rights.[68]

10.26 The licence may be limited to use of the mark in a particular manner:[69] for example, where a mark is registered without reference to colour or typescript, the licence may nevertheless insist upon use in a particular colour or font. It may also be wise for the proprietor to specify the size and placement of any representations of the mark and to restrict the use of other marks in conjunction with that licensed. It may not be in the best interests of a licensee to use another mark in direct combination with the licensed mark; the marks may become difficult to use independently.

10.27 So far, 'manner of use' has been interpreted in terms of the mode of display of the mark. It may or may not extend to the field of use, for example, where the proprietor supplies one sector, say the veterinary sector, while the licensee supplies another, say the retail pharmacy sector. This really amounts to market sharing. Neither the Directive nor the 1994 Act refers to limitations by customer type. In principle, a licence could thus be limited but, again, care should be taken when defining any such limitation to avoid any risk of deceiving the public or infringing competition law (see **10.31**).

QUALITY CONTROL

10.28 Control by the proprietor of the quality of goods or services supplied under the mark is an important mechanism for maintaining a nexus between

---

[63] Section 28(1)(a).

[64] Not least because such limitations have to be recorded anyway: r 40(b)(iii).

[65] Section 46(1)(d).

[66] See, generally, N Parr 'Avoiding antitrust pitfalls in drafting and enforcing IP agreements in the EU' [1997] 2 EIPR 37.

[67] Articles 28–30 (ex Arts 30, 34 and 36) of the EC Treaty.

[68] Article 7 of the Directive and s 12 of the 1994 Act: for an example of acceptable territorial limitation, see *Microsoft v Computer Future Distribution* [1998] FSR 597.

[69] Section 28(1)(b). See, also, N Wilkof 'Don't forget the "trade mark" in a trade mark licence agreement' (2005) 7(3) WLLR 14 on the need for proper definitions of the trade mark(s) to be included.

the proprietor and those products. Traditionally, quality control supported both the 'origin' functions of the mark and its 'quality' function.[70] Although the House of Lords indicated in *Scandecor*[71] that failure of a licensor to control quality by the granting of a so-called 'bare licence' was not automatically fatal to the validity of a mark, and that the public could now properly regard an exclusive licensee as a unique source, that rather convoluted decision did not rule on non-exclusive licensing; subsequently, a reference to the European Court of Justice (ECJ) was halted by settlement of the action.[72] Additionally, quality control is directed towards maintaining the goodwill and reputation connected to a trade mark.[73] Failure to control quality may diminish the mark's value, render it deceptive or both.[74] Loss of reputation is not just commercially significant; it could also affect the proprietor's ability to sue for infringement under s 10(3) to restrain use on dissimilar services or goods.[75] The importance of quality control is a factor which lies behind the licence agreement providing for termination in the event of change of corporate control of a licensee.[76]

10.29 Quality control[77] may be carried out by the proprietor,[78] by a third party equipped to do so[79] or, subject to suitably stringent 'self policing' controls embedded within the licence agreement, by the licensee.[80] The necessary quality threshold may be set by reference to a recognised industry or technical standard for goods or services, or by setting out specific quality criteria within the licence agreement itself.[81] Where this is not possible, it may be necessary to place restrictions on the licensee's suppliers.[82]

OTHER TERMS

10.30 In addition to defining the scope of use and laying down quality controls, a licence agreement should adequately identify the marks,

---

[70] See Chapter 1.
[71] *Scandecor Developments v Scandecor Marketing* [2001] UKHL 21; [2001] ETMR 74; [2002] FSR 122, HL.
[72] See NJ Wilkof and D Burkitt *Trade Mark Licensing* (2nd edn, 2005) paras 6–57 to 6–70.
[73] For a critical evaluation, see J Phillips 'Quality control and the Napoleon principle' (2001) 109 MIP 42.
[74] For a discussion, see H Norman 'Trade mark licences in the United Kingdom: time for *Bostitch* to be re-evaluated?' [1994] 4 EIPR 155.
[75] See **7.39**, **5.50ff**.
[76] See, e g *Philip Morris Products Inc v Rothmans International Enterprises Ltd* [2001] All ER (D) 48 CA.
[77] For a discussion as to the optimum level of quality control, see W Borchard and A Lewis 'The US experience with quality control in trade mark licensing' (1994) 11 CIPR 3.
[78] Who will need provisions in the agreement for the taking of samples for analysis; but note that this, on its own, will not suffice unless it leads to regular contact with the licensee: *JOB Trade Mark* [1993] FSR 118.
[79] Eg a laboratory or testing station.
[80] See, e g *MOLYSLIP Trade Mark* [1978] RPC 211.
[81] See S Burshstein 'Licensing fundamentals: quality standards' (2001) 3(4) WLLR 34.
[82] Provided that competition law permits it. Note that where a standard is impossible to set or enforce in practice, restrictions on suppliers may be valid notwithstanding competition laws: *Pronuptia v Schillgalis* [1986] ECR 353; [1986] 1 CMLR 414 at para 21.

registrations, and names and addresses of the parties. A licensee can record its interest on the register without the co-operation of the licensor, but it is preferable for the licensor to agree to join in taking whatever steps are necessary to effect registration.[83] The licence should also provide terms for dealing with the following important matters:[84]

(a)   spot inspection of goods or services provided;

(b)   the auditing of royalty accounts by the licensor;

(c)   the maintenance of the mark[85] by the licensor;

(d)   licensor/licensee confidentiality;

(e)   warranties[86] and indemnities;[87]

(f)   termination;[88]

(g)   'force majeure' (ie external events which would disrupt licensed activities);

(h)   arbitration; and

(i)   jurisdiction (ie governing law, relevant courts).

THE IMPACT OF COMPETITION LAWS

10.31   Both UK and EC competition laws apply. With the remodelling of UK competition law under the Competition Act 1998 to reflect the provisions of Arts 81 and 82 of the EC Treaty,[89] the principles to be applied should mirror

---

[83]   Or at least to agree to sign Form TM50: see r 41(1) and (2). The issue of allocation of recordal expenses will also have to be dealt with.

[84]   For a detailed treatment on licence agreement drafting, see N Byrne and A McBratney *Licensing Technology* (Jordans, 3rd edn, 2005).

[85]   In particular, the renewal of a registration or registrations.

[86]   Eg that the licensor has rights sufficient to allow the grant of the licence in question.

[87]   Eg that the licensee is indemnified against infringement claims made by third parties.

[88]   This is important for a licensor as well as a licensee because of the risks of breach of contract: *Glolite Ltd v Jasper Conran Ltd* (unreported) (1998) *The Times,* January 28. Termination provisions should cover termination on notice, breaches giving rise to automatic termination, post-termination covenants, and disposal of goods or supplies held at the point of termination: see M Abell 'Trade mark licensing in the UK: when the plug is pulled' (1999) 99 TW 19; *Hay & Robertson Plc v Kangol Ltd* [2004] EWCA Civ 63; [2005] FSR 13 (interpretation of termination provisions); *Vivat Holdings Ltd v Indus Clothing Ltd* [2006] EWHC 2157 (TCC) (injunction granted to prevent damage caused by activities on the defendant's part in breach of the run-off provisions after termination of licence agreement); *Leofelis SA v Lonsdale Sports Ltd* [2008] EWCA Civ 640; [2008] ETMR 63 (attempt to terminate but keep agreement in force without prejudice to termination was legally impossible without consent of the other party).

[89]   Ex Arts 85 and 86.

those laid out in Chapter 13.[90] Council Regulation (EC) 1/2003[91] transferred the focus of enforcement of EU competition law from the European Commission to a situation where national competition authorities and courts may apply not only Arts 81(1) and 82, but also Art 81(3).

10.32 Those licences that constitute agreements with effect on interstate trade are subject to Art 81[92] of the EC Treaty whilst, s 2 of the Competition Act 1998 governs licences constituting agreements with effect on trade within the UK. Under the present EC system,[93] there is no block exemption which specifically deals with trade mark licences, although trade mark licences which are ancillary to vertical distribution agreements[94] or technology transfer agreements[95] may be exempted under those heads. These laws apply equally to licences reached in compromise of litigation,[96] often described as 'trade mark delimitation' agreements.[97]

10.33 If trade is significant[98] in the European market as defined,[99] a territorial licence which restricts the rights of licensee to make passive or unsolicited sales outside of the territory may fall foul of competition law, particularly under Art 81 of the EC Treaty. Enforcement may be contrary to Art 28.[100]

10.34 Field of use restrictions are usually regarded by the European Commission as disguised market partitioning arrangements;[101] they, and customer sharing restrictions, should be approached with particular caution.[102]

---

[90] Section 60 of the Competition Act 1998 requires that questions arising should be determined by reference to principles established in EC law as far as is practicable.

[91] [2003] OJ L1/1, in force 1 May 2004. See J Ratliff 'Major Events and Policy Issues in EC Competition Law, 2003–2004: Part 1' [2005] ICCLR 47.

[92] Ex Art 85.

[93] N Parr 'Avoiding Antitrust Pitfalls in Drafting and Enforcing Intellectual Property Agreements in the European Union' [1997] EIPR 43 deals with competition aspects of trade mark licensing, as do NJ Wilkof and D Burkitt *Trade Mark Licensing* (2nd edn, 2005) ch 13.

[94] Commission Regulation (EC) 2790/1999 of December 22, 1999, on the application of Art 81(3) of the EC Treaty to categories of vertical agreements and concerted practices [1999] OJ L336/21; Commission Guidelines on Vertical Restraints [2000] OJ C291/1.

[95] Commission Regulation (EC) 772/2004 on the application of Art 81(3) of the Treaty to categories of technology transfer agreements [2004] OJ L123/11; Commission Guidelines on the Application of Art 81 to Technology Transfer Agreements [2004] OJ C141/2; P Treacy and T Heide 'The New EC Technology Transfer Block Exemption' [2004] EIPR 421. See, also, *Moosehead/Whitbread* [1991] 4 CMLR 391; *Campari-Milano SpA Agreements, Re* [1978] 2 CMLR 397, [1978] FSR 528, CEC, [1978] OJ L70/69.

[96] Eg *Sirdar/Phildar* OJ 1975 L125/27; 1975 1 CMLR D93.

[97] For a survey of cases on delimitation agreements under Art 81 (ex Art 85) of the EC Treaty, see E McKnight 'Trade Mark Agreements and EC Law' [1996] EIPR 271.

[98] See 'Notice on Agreements of Minor Importance which do not fall under Art 81(1) [ex. Art. 85(1)] of the Treaty establishing the European Community' [2001] OJ C368/13.

[99] See 'Commission Notice on the Definition of Relevant Market for the Purposes of Community Competition Law' [1997] OJ C372/5.

[100] Ex Art 30.

[101] See, e g *Bay-o-Nox* [1990] 4 CMLR 429. See also AF Gagliardi 'Territorial restraints in pure trade mark licence agreements: an unsettled issue' [1997] 12 EIPR 723.

[102] For a very useful note, see *ITMA Information*, No 5/94, June 1994, p 1.

TAXATION ISSUES

10.35　In considering the applicability of taxation to intellectual property transactions,[103] there are five UK taxes to consider: income tax, capital gains tax (CGT),[104] corporation tax, value added tax (VAT) and stamp duty. Taking the first three, we can observe that the first two are applicable to individuals whilst the third applies to companies. Being assets used in the course of trade, trade marks and trade mark licences will be held for the purposes of trade. The taxation of trade mark transactions follows corporation tax rules where companies are involved (see **10.39ff**).

10.36　Income tax for non-corporate persons covers receipts from income whilst CGT covers capital gains arising from disposal of an asset. Although apparently simple, the distinction between capital and income can be difficult but, in the present context, one can say that consideration from a trade mark assignment would be treated as a capital receipt whereas royalties under a licence would be treated as income. A relevant difficulty here is that royalties paid under an exclusive trade mark licence may be treated as capital if the effect of the licence is to deprive the licensor of the ability to exploit the mark in the same way as if it had been disposed of outright.[105] Conversely, in *Gunn v Commissioners for Her Majesty's Revenue and Customs*,[106] an inventor who had caused patent and trade mark registrations to be made in the name of a UK company was held to have licensed rather than assigned rights to the company. Royalties payable from business in the US were held to arise from the individual's trade in the UK as an inventor. He was liable to income tax on licence fees as and when they arose.

10.37　Trading income received by individuals and partnerships is governed by the Income Tax (Trading and Other Income) Act 2005 (ITA 2005).[107] This Act rewrote much of the 'source' legislation – the Income and Corporation Taxes Act 1988 (ICTA 1988) – as part of a 'Tax Law Rewrite Project'. In most cases ITA 2005 was intended to produce the same effect as ICTA 1988, to 'clarify existing provisions, make them consistent or bring the law into line with well established practice'.[108] There are helpful Explanatory Notes to the ITA 2005 prepared by the Revenue authority.[109] ITA 2005 repealed the various 'cases' of ICTA 1988, Sch D referred to in previous editions of this book and simplified the rules on allowable deductions.

---

[103]　For an excellent review of principles and laws prior to 2002, see JB Hickey 'Taxation of Technology and Intellectual Property' [1997] IPQ 319.

[104]　The capital gains taxation of registered trade marks is discussed in HMRC Manual at CG68220 'Intellectual Property Rights: registered trade marks', available at www.hmrc.gov.uk/manuals/cgmanual/cg68220.htm; unregistered marks are said at CG68210 to form an intrinsic part of the goodwill of a business; taxation of goodwill being discussed at CG68300.

[105]　Eg in relation to a territory, a range of goods or services, or both.

[106]　[2010] UKFTT 419 (TC), appeal dismissed [2011] UKUT 59 (TCC).

[107]　ITA 2005, s 5. Section 5 charges profits of a trade to income tax.

[108]　ITA 2005, Explanatory Notes, para 7.

[109]　Readers should be aware that ITA 2005 and its Explanatory Notes refer to a number of detailed provisions on intellectual property, though not of immediate relevance to trade marks, which have been repealed by the Finance Act 2006, s. 25 or the Income Tax Act 2007, s. 3.

Where licensing activity *is* the trade in question (formerly Sch D, Case I) the general principles of ITA 2005 apply: Part 2 – trading income.[110] In other cases, s 579(1) makes royalties and other income from intellectual property to income tax.[111] Intellectual property is defined to include (a) any trade mark, (b) similar rights under the law of any part of the United Kingdom and (c) any rights under the law of any territory outside the United Kingdom which correspond or are similar to (trade marks).[112]

Section 579 applies whether the mark is a foreign registered mark[113] or UK registered mark if the licence is exclusive.[114] If the licence is non-exclusive, the income is likely to be regarded as general trading income.[115] Income tax may be payable even if royalties are routed through a company.[116]

10.38 Once the status of taxable income is established, the general principle is that certain deductions are allowed and the tax payable is calculated on the net amount. Thus, in the case of royalties under s 579 of ITA 2005, expenditure on the registration and renewal of marks[117] can be deducted as of right in the calculation of profits. Capital expenditure may be the subject of allowances under the Capital Allowances Act 2001.

10.39 Originally, corporation tax was calculated exactly in the same way as income tax for corporate income receipts[118] save that, in place of the capital receipts taxation element of CGT, there was taxation of 'chargeable gains'.[119] However, with effect from 1 April 2002, the corporation tax treatment of a company's gains and losses in respect of intangible fixed assets, including intellectual property, was significantly modified by Schs 29–30 of the Finance Act 2002; the new approach to be taken was much closer to accounting practice[120] than the previous regime. (The taxation of companies is now governed by the Corporation Tax Act 2009.)[121] This divergence meant that the tax treatment of a trade mark transaction depended critically on whether the

---

[110] Explanatory Notes, para 817.
[111] Categories of income formerly classified under ICTA 1988 as annual payments from a UK source (Sch D Case III), overseas income from intellectual property (Sch D Case V) and casual profits of an income nature from the exploitation of intellectual property outside the course of a trade (Sch D Case VI): see Explanatory Notes, paras 817 and 818.
[112] Section 579(2).
[113] Formerly Sch D, Case V ('receipts in respect of income arising from possessions out of the United Kingdom').
[114] Schedule D, Case III ('receipts from investments') or Sch D, Case VI ('receipts from miscellaneous sources not falling within any other Case of Schedule D') will apply depending on whether the royalty is a 'pure income profit'.
[115] Formerly Sch D, Case I ('receipts in respect of a trade'), now Part 2 of the 2005 Act.
[116] *Gunn v Commissioners for Her Majesty's Revenue and Customs* [2010] UKFTT 419 (TC), appeal dismissed [2011] UKUT 59 (TCC).
[117] ITA 2005, s 90. Note that s 90(2) excludes professions and vocations from this provision.
[118] ICTA 1988, s 9.
[119] Taxation of Chargeable Gains Act 1992, s 8.
[120] D Hole 'Finance Act Notes: References to Accounting Practice and Periods of Account – Section 103' [2002] BTR 326.
[121] Where profits are chargeable to UK corporation tax, income taxation and capital gains taxation are excluded: Corporation Tax Act 2009, ss 2 and 3.

parties were individuals or partnerships on the one hand, or companies on the other. The situation became even more complex when there was a mixture. However, ITA 2005 brought income taxation of trade mark transactions closer to general accounting practice.

10.40 Where companies are concerned, trade marks and trade mark licences fall within the definition of 'intangible assets' under s 906(2) of the Corporation Tax Act 2009.[122] Gains in respect of intangible assets are generally chargeable to corporation tax as income.[123] Credits from such assets are treated as income from the trade in question and debits as expenditure.[124] There are special provisions on royalties as between related companies.[125] Note also that, in the examples above, the general assumption has been that both the licensor and licensee are UK based: the tax treatment where one or other of the parties is based abroad is a complex field in its own right.[126]

10.41 VAT is chargeable on the supply of certain goods or services made by a person who is or is required to be registered for VAT[127] under the relevant criteria.[128] The grant of a trade mark licence is a taxable 'supply of services' for VAT purposes and is made if the supplier 'belongs' in the UK.[129] Subject to complex rules on 'international supply',[130] a licensor who is a taxable person and belongs in the UK must charge VAT at 17.5% on royalties received from a UK-based licensee, regardless of whether the payments are for use at home or abroad.

10.42 Finally, stamp duty, discussed in more detail in Chapter 11, is a tax which is paid in respect of certain written documents; if it is not paid, the document in question cannot be adduced in evidence in civil proceedings[131] and any official who registers it commits a criminal offence.[132] Stamp duty on documents effecting transfers of intellectual property and goodwill was abolished by s 129 of the Finance Act 2000. Ostensibly, this change eliminated a significant problem: the Stamp Office had previously treated exclusive trade mark licences of indefinite duration as if they were assignments of trade marks (thereby usually catching them as 'conveyance or transfers on sale') and, accordingly, required that they should be stamped.[133] However, for documents effecting transactions before 28 March 2000, the former rules remain in effect;

---

[122] See *Halsbury's Laws* Vol 15, para 1496A.1.
[123] Corporation Tax Act 2009, s 906(1).
[124] Corporation Tax Act 2009, s 747(1)–(3); Halsbury's Laws Vol 15, para 1496A.5.
[125] Corporation Tax Act 2009, s 851; Halsbury's Laws Vol 15 para 1496A.16.
[126] J Irvine and L Bartels 'Finding and using tax havens' (1998) 80 MIP 11.
[127] This is the so-called 'taxable person'.
[128] Eg the size of business turnover.
[129] Value Added Tax Act 1994, s 9.
[130] Where trade mark licensing forms part of a larger transaction, it may be possible to identify a 'single source of supply' to simplify matters.
[131] Stamp Act 1891, s 14(4). For a useful reminder of the difficulties that this can cause, see *Coflexip Stena Offshore Ltd's Patent* [1997] RPC 179.
[132] Stamp Act 1891, s 17. This would apply to the Registrar of Trade Marks.
[133] See C Ghosh and S Lewis 'UK stamp duty on assignment and licences of trade marks' [1999] EIPR 592.

this has created serious problems (ie mounting stamp duty penalties) for 'old' unrecorded documents which govern transactions for which recordal is now being sought and, potentially, any new documents which effect 'old' transactions retrospectively.

Chapter 11

ASSIGNMENT OF MARKS

MARKS AND GOODWILL

11.1   As noted in Chapter 3, after the enactment of trade marks legislation in 1875, the action for passing-off has been used to protect property in goodwill. No property right in a trade mark per se is now recognised at common law.[1] In order validly to transfer a mark at common law, goodwill must be transferred.[2] In fact, assignment of goodwill is deemed to include assignment of any marks used in the course of the business[3] or part of the business in question.[4] An attempt to assign a mark 'in gross' results in deemed abandonment of the mark by the vendor;[5] the purchaser may gain immunity from suit by the vendor, but no right to sue third parties.[6]

11.2   Registration, however, confers a property right in the mark itself.[7] This was also the case under previous statutes,[8] although in *GE TM*[9] Lord Diplock expressed the view that the 1875 Act did not create property rights in marks because they were previously recognised at common law. The Trade Marks Act 1938 ('the 1938 Act') had a curious provision requiring the applicant for registration to claim to be 'the proprietor' of the mark.[10] The meaning of this was particularly obscure in the case of an unused mark. Section 17(1) was

---

[1]   For contrary views on historical causes, see C Wadlow, *Passing Off* (3rd edn, 2004) pp 16–36 and Lupton 'Trade Marks as Property' (1991) 2 IPJ 29–34 (Aus). In *AL BASSAM Trade Mark* [1995] RPC 511, the Court of Appeal regarded the 1938 Act as 'superimposed' on earlier common law rights.

[2]   '[T]he right to the used mark as an indication of the origin of the goods could not be assigned separately from the goodwill of the business in which it had been used for that would have been to assign the right to commit a fraud on the public', *AL BASSAM Trade Mark* [1995] RPC 511 (CA).

[3]   *Kerly's Law of Trade Marks and Trade Names* (15th edn, 2011) para 13–062.

[4]   *Kerly's Law of Trade Marks and Trade Names* (14th edn, 2005) para 13–065, citing *Sunbeam* (1916) 33 RPC 389. For a critical analysis of the *Sunbeam* case, see S Lane, *The Status of Licensing Common Law Marks* (1991) pp 18–19 and 22–3.

[5]   See *Star Industrial v Yap Kwee Kor* [1976] FSR 256 on loss of passing off rights by abandonment.

[6]   *Pinto v Badman* (1891) 8 RPC 181.

[7]   Trade Marks Act 1994, ss 2(1) and 22. Maniatis 'Trade Mark Rights – a Justification Based on Property' [2002] IPQ 123 explores theoretical bases for this.

[8]   See s 22(1) of the 1938 Act: registered trade marks assignable and transmissible with or without goodwill; Trade Marks Act 1905, s 22: trade mark assignable and transmissible, but only with goodwill; see also *Pinto v Badman* (1891) 8 RPC 181.

[9]   [1973] RPC 297; cited in *AL BASSAM Trade Mark* [1995] RPC 511 (CA).

[10]   Section 17(1).

considered in *AL BASSAM Trade Mark*,[11] where Morritt LJ observed, 'in the case of an unused mark the person with the best right to use it was the designer or inventor'.[12]

11.3   Not surprisingly, the 1938 Act contained no provision for the assignment of an application to register. This was alleviated somewhat by the effect of s 29(1)(a), which enabled an application to be made with the intention of assigning it to a company not yet incorporated. However, the Trade Marks Act 1994 ('the 1994 Act') goes further in stating that the sections as to assignment and so forth apply, with necessary modifications, to applications to register. Thus, it appears that applications are an evanescent form of property, vanishing if the application fails to mature into a registration, but hardening into personal property if and when it does. This has logic, because once a mark is registered, rights date back to the application date, deemed to be the date of registration.[13] Where evidence of use by the assignor is likely to be important in securing registration, the assignee of an application should seek to acquire goodwill, so that he may rely upon the use.

11.4   Section 22 of the 1994 Act states that a registered mark is personal property or, in Scotland, incorporeal moveable property. From an English viewpoint one may note that s 22 does not state whether or not a mark is to be considered as a chose in action. This is in contrast to a patent, which is stated not to be a chose in action.[14] The editors of the *UK Trade Marks Handbook* express the view that little turns on whether a trade mark is a chose in possession or a chose in action.[15] The trade mark does have one important characteristic of a chose in action: any assignment must be in writing,[16] signed by the proprietor.[17]

ASSIGNMENT WITH BUSINESS GOODWILL

11.5   Section 24(6) makes clear that the 1994 Act does not affect the assignment or transmission of unregistered marks along with the goodwill of a business. As noted above, assignment of goodwill will transfer marks in the absence of contrary intention.[18] Provided that the assignment is in writing, this may be effective to transfer registered marks, although it is always desirable to

---

[11]   [1995] RPC 511 CA; [1994] RPC 315 Ch D.

[12]   At 521; Aldous J at first instance regarded s 17(1) as a procedural provision, requiring merely a bona fide intention to use. Cf *Vitamin Ltd's Application* [1956] RPC 1; [1956] 1 WLR 1. If a designer is contracted to produce artwork for a stylised trade mark it is advisable to have any copyright in the artwork assigned to the would-be trade mark owner.

[13]   Section 40(3).

[14]   Patents Act 1977, s 30(1). For characteristics of choses in action, see J Fitzgerald and A Firth 'Equitable Assignments in Relation to Intellectual Property' [1999] IPQ 228.

[15]   Paragraph 116-001.

[16]   See Law of Property Act 1925, s 136.

[17]   Section 24(3) of the 1994 Act; an assent must likewise be in writing.

[18]   *Kerly's Law of Trade Marks and Trade Names* (15th edn, 2011) 13–064, citing *Roger's TM* (1895) 12 RPC 149. For a discussion of the decision in *Roger*, see S Lane, *The Status of Licensing Common Law Marks* (1991) pp 32–3.

identify these clearly by reference to registration numbers. Where the assignment is expressed not to include marks, it is unlikely that an assignor retains any common law right to protect them. In the case of registered marks which are retained, the assignor of goodwill will enjoy continued proprietorship unless the marks become vulnerable by reason of deceptiveness or non-use.

11.6 Where part only of the goodwill is transferred, it is a delicate question as to whether the business can be severed in an appropriate way.[19] Thus, in *Sinclair Ltd's TM*,[20] an attempt was made to transfer the mark together with that portion of goodwill as attached to the mark. The assignor's interest in the business was otherwise unchanged. The assignment was held to be void. However, assignment without goodwill has since been made possible by statute, as outlined below.

11.7 A merger or other transmission by operation of law will often cause an automatic transfer of ownership of a trade mark. Such transmissions should be recorded as 'assignments', not least in order to secure the right to claim damages in an infringement action.[21]

ASSIGNMENT WITHOUT BUSINESS GOODWILL

11.8 The 1938 Act broke with common law tradition by permitting the assignment of registered marks without goodwill. The interest of the public in avoiding confusion or deception was protected by conferring on the Registrar the power to direct advertisements; unless and until such directions were sought[22] and complied with, the assignment was ineffective. If advertisements were duly made, the assignment was effective to transfer not only the registered marks but any unregistered marks used in the same business as the registered marks and transferred with those registered. This was achieved by virtue of s 22(3) of the 1938 Act; that section was of general application but it is difficult to envisage a transfer of goodwill which was effective to transfer registered but not unregistered marks.

11.9 The White Paper, *Reform of Trade Marks Law*,[23] observed that the advertisement requirements of s 22(7) were 'of little practical effect as a safeguard to the public' and proposed their removal.[24] This has been done; s 24(1) of the 1994 Act states that a trade mark is transmissible, by assignment, testamentary disposition or operation of law, in connection with the goodwill

---

[19] It is not possible to assign trade marks registered as a series separately from each other: s 41(2).

[20] (1932) 49 RPC 123.

[21] See **11.14** and *MyFotoshop Ltd v Fotostop Group Ltd* [2006] EWHC 2729 (Ch).

[22] Within the 6 months' time-limit afforded to the assignee: s 22(7).

[23] Cm 1203 (1990) para 4.46.

[24] For arguments that trade mark provisions designed to protect the consumer should generally be repealed, see Pendleton 'Excising Consumer Protection – the Key to Reforming Trade Mark Law' (1992) 3 AIPJ 110 (Aus). Cf Davis 'To Protect or Serve? European Trade Mark Law and the Decline of the Public Interest' [2003] EIPR 180.

of a business or independently. The assignment may effect a transfer of the mark for all or only some of the goods or services for which it is registered[25] or for a particular manner or territory of use.[26] There are no requirements for advertising an assignment without goodwill, nor is there any prohibition upon an assignment which would lead to the likelihood of deception or confusion.[27] The lack of restriction on transfer does not ensure, however, that an assignee will always enjoy the fruits of the assignment. There may be defects to title which undermine the transaction, while the assignment may render the mark deceptive and liable to revocation.[28]

11.10 Furthermore, there is no longer any provision for the automatic assignment of unregistered marks along with registered marks when the assignment is without goodwill.[29]

FORMALITIES AND PITFALLS

11.11 The essential elements for an assignment of a registered mark may be summarised[30] as:

(a)   an identified mark;

(b)   registered and transferred for identified goods or services;[31]

(c)   as of a specified date;

(d)   the number of the registration;

(e)   identification of the assignor;

(f)   some form of warranty of title;[32]

(g)   name and address of the assignee;

(h)   identification of the territory for which the mark is to be assigned;[33]

---

[25]   Section 24(2)(a).

[26]   Section 24(2)(b).

[27]   Contrast s 22(4) of the 1938 Act, which prohibited assignments resulting in a deceptive split of ownership for the same products or descriptions of product.

[28]   The decision in *JOB* [1993] FSR 118 illustrates the dangers of careless transactions.

[29]   Cf s 22(3) of the 1938 Act which applied to transactions prior to commencement but not thereafter: Sch 3, para 8(1).

[30]   See, in particular, rule 48 of which Rules, Trade Mark Rules 2008, SI 2008/1797.

[31]   It is possible to 'part assign' in relation to a selection of goods or services covered by the registration; in doing this, the assignor must ensure that there is no risk of deception such as would give rise to grounds for revocation under s 46.

[32]   See **11.12**.

[33]   For a case where arguments on territory were canvassed, see *Fyffes v Chiquita* [1993] FSR 83. It is also important to consider the effect of free movement and competition rules under Arts 28,

(i)   consideration (unless under seal);

(j)   details of any goodwill transferred;

(k)   stamp duty, if payable (rarely so today; see **11.26**).

11.12   Warranties of title are a difficult matter as the assignor will wish to give none whilst the assignee will seek cast iron guarantees. Accordingly, the warranties actually given are largely a matter for negotiation between the parties and the resulting provision will be contractually binding. In the UK, it is not uncommon to see the phrases 'full title guarantee' and 'limited title guarantee' appearing in assignments; the first derives from the Law of Property (Miscellaneous Provisions) Act 1994[34] and, when used, the majority view[35] is that they have the effect of implying certain covenants as to title which affect intellectual property ownership.[36] However, because the LPA 1925 applies only to England and Wales, it is probably better to formulate specific warranties taking effect by virtue of contract law alone.[37] In addition, it would also be wise for an assignee to seek a specific warranty against adverse changes of title stemming from wrongful attribution of ownership of a mark to an agent or representative.[38]

11.13   Execution of an assignment document by the assignor is sufficient; an assignee need not countersign. However, assignment of a Community trade mark (CTM) requires the signature of all parties to the contract.[39] This is curious given that a CTM is dealt with as an object of property as if it were a national trade mark.[40] Thought should be given, therefore, when assigning a CTM simultaneously with a UK registration whether separate assignment documents would be more appropriate.

29, 30 and 81 (ex Arts 30, 34, 36, and 85) of the EC Treaty when determining territory: see *IHT Internationale v Ideal-Standard* [1994] ECR I-2789; [1995] FSR 59.

[34]   Formerly, it was common to see the phrase 'beneficial ownership' per s 76 of the Law of Property Act 1925 (LPA 1925); this latter implied covenants including full power to convey, quiet enjoyment, freedom from encumbrance of title and agreement to execute documents. The 'beneficial ownership' provision at LPA 1925, s 76 was repealed by the Law of Property (Miscellaneous Provisions) Act 1994; transitional provisions set out at ss 10–13 of the latter deal with contracts to transfer made before 1 July 1995 but where actual execution occurred afterwards.

[35]   For interesting arguments that, although referring to 'property', the LPA 1925 should not be construed as covering intellectual property, see Henry 'Mortgages of Intellectual Property in the United Kingdom' [1992] 5 EIPR 158.

[36]   Common to both is the assignor's right to dispose and the obligation to do all that can be reasonably done to give title at its own cost. Full title guarantee also provides that the assignor assigns free from all charges and encumbrances and all other rights exercisable by third parties, other than charges, which the assignor does not and could not be reasonably expected to know about (s 3(1)). Limited title guarantee merely provides that the assignor has not charged or encumbered the property or allowed the same to happen and, furthermore, that the assignor is not aware of anybody else having done so (s 3(3)). Note the loss of implied 'quiet enjoyment'.

[37]   Particularly where the assignment relates additionally to foreign marks.

[38]   See s 60 of the 1994 Act.

[39]   Article 17(3) of Council Regulation 207/2009 of 26 February 2009 ('the CTMR').

[40]   Article 16(1). See **14.70**.

11.14 It is useful to assign a trade mark registration together with the right to bring infringement proceedings for infringements which commenced prior to the assignment and also with any other benefit the registration brings in addition to benefits defined by statute.[41] Examples include contractual arrangements with third parties which stem from the registration such as consents, co-existence agreements and undertakings as well as contentious actions based on the registration such as invalidation and oppositions.

11.15 What if the assignor's title is defective? Where the assignor is registered as proprietor, there may be equitable interests in the mark, which are not registrable.[42] The assignee will take subject to any registered assignment, licence, security interest, assent or court order. He will not take subject to any such interest for which an application to register has not been made, unless he has knowledge of it.[43]

11.16 Where the assignor can show good title notwithstanding that it has not been registered, it seems that this is sufficient to show that a valid chain of transactions leads to the assignee. A problem which frequently occurs when a UK trade mark is assigned along with foreign registrations is that the document which assigns the trade marks is not in a format which is acceptable to a foreign trade mark office for the purpose of recordal. The issue rarely arises at UK recordal since the Registrar does not require to see an assignment document in order to effect a recordal. A common mistake is to draft a 'confirmatory assignment'; this is not acceptable because not only has the property already passed from the assignor to the assignee, but the assignee no longer has the power to assign.[44] The solution is to ensure in the first place that the proposed assignment document format is acceptable in each foreign jurisdiction or, if necessary, to assign the trade mark back as a precursor to assigning it afresh.

11.17 Once a mark has been assigned, the assignee or any other person claiming to be affected by the transaction may apply to register it.[45] Registration is desirable for a number of reasons: it protects the assignee against inconsistent transactions after the application to register[46] and the assignee is able to prove title in infringement proceedings by putting in evidence a certificate of registration.[47] Where the assignee fails to register within 6

---

[41] *Trendtex v Credit Suisse* [1982] AC 679 shows that assignment of the right to sue for past infringements in these circumstance would be regarded as ancillary to the trade mark assignment and not contrary to rules on champerty.

[42] Section 26(1).

[43] Section 25(3)(a) actually says that an unregistered transaction is ineffective against a person taking a conflicting interest in ignorance of it, which suggests absence of actual knowledge.

[44] *Coflexip Stena Offshore Ltd's Application* [1997] RPC 179.

[45] Section 25(1), on Form TM16: r 49(1)(d) Trade Mark Rules 2008.

[46] Section 25(3), which is curiously worded. It suggests that an unregistered transaction is ineffective as against a person acquiring a conflicting interest. Presumably this is not so until the latter is registered; otherwise unregistered transactions would enjoy reverse priority.

[47] Infringement proceedings may be commenced under a UK registration before a change of title has been recorded but not under a CTM. Article 17(6) CTMR.

months, damages and accounts of profits are unavailable until registration is effected.[48] Recordal of an assignment part way through an infringement action could, therefore, prevent a plaintiff receiving a sizeable financial recompense for the infringement. Preferably, the assignor should sign the application to register the transaction; otherwise it must be accompanied by adequate documentary evidence.[49] The Registrar also needs to be satisfied that any instrument that was subject to stamp duty was duly stamped.[50]

11.18 A trade mark registration may be assigned in whole or in part[51] but particular care should be taken not to lay the foundations for a scenario where separate ownership of the same mark for closely allied goods or services might mislead the public.[52] So long as the effect of the assignment is not to obscure the original function of the now separate trade marks (or to divide the market contrary to European law) it will not be vulnerable.[53]

SPECIFIC CASES AND TRANSACTIONS

Transmission by testamentary disposition

11.19 Property rights in the mark will devolve upon the testator's personal representatives. The latter's assent must be made in writing and signed by or on behalf of the personal representative.[54] For the reasons indicated above, the assent should be registered.[55]

Transmission by operation of law

11.20 This is likely to arise in one of three circumstances: intestacy, insolvency or partnership. In the first two cases, the former proprietor is unable to co-operate in the registration of the transaction. An order of the court may form part of the chain of transmission. Registration of the order of a court or other authority competent to effect transfer is applied for on Form TM24.[56] Form TM16 (assignments) is also used for transactions not allotted a separate form.

---

[48] Section 25(4) – unless the court is satisfied that it was not practicable to apply to register before.

[49] Rule 49(2)(a).

[50] Trade Marks Rules 2000, r 41(3); stamp duty is no longer levied on intellectual property transactions but failure to stamp at the relevant time may affect chain of title (see **10.42** and **11.30**).

[51] Section 24(2).

[52] Grounds for revocation of a registration under s 46(1)(d).

[53] See *Scandecor Development AB v Scandecor Marketing AB* [2001] UKHL 21, [2001] 2 CMLR 30, [2001] ETMR 74, [2002] FSR7, and also Case C-259/04 *Elizabeth Florence Emanuel v Continental Shelf 128 Ltd* [2006] ETMR 56. See Chapter 13.

[54] Section 24(3).

[55] By filing Form TM24: r 49(1)(e).

[56] Rule 49(1)(e).

11.21 Intellectual property generally may pass by operation of partnership law.[57] However, the enjoyment of a trade mark by a partnership will normally involve use on goods or services emanating from the partnership. That case is suitable for joint proprietorship (**11.21-11.22**). One partner may not undermine the other's enjoyment of shared goodwill by 'elbowing them out',[58] but exiting partners may abandon their interest in shared goodwill.[59]

Jointly owned trade marks

11.22 The 1938 Act permitted the registration of marks in joint names, but only when the relationship between the proprietors was such that they each used the mark on behalf of them all or the mark indicated a connection with all of them.[60] Annand and Norman[61] point out that this ensured joint tenancy in the marks. This was desirable when the joint owners were actually trading under the mark, but was not necessarily suitable for other forms of exploitation, such as the grant of an exclusive licence to a third party.

11.23 Section 23 of the 1994 Act refers to the grant of a mark to two or more persons 'jointly', but goes on to say that each is entitled to an 'equal undivided share'. This smacks of a tenancy in common,[62] which may be more suitable where marks are held as assets or by way of security, but less suitable where the proprietors use the marks. Section 25(3) and (4) limits the powers of the co-proprietors to deal with the mark as they please; each is entitled to use the mark for his own benefit without accounting to the others for its use, but a licence, assignment or charge[63] requires the consent of co-proprietors. This arrangement is similar to that for patents.[64]

Collective marks[65]

11.24 There is no special regime for the transfer of collective marks. However, the rules governing the use of the mark must specify the persons authorised to use the mark;[66] any change will necessitate amendment of the regulations and acceptance of the amended regulations by the Registrar.[67]

---

[57] *Murray v King* [1986] FSR 116 (copyright: Fed Ct of Australia).

[58] *Sir Robert McAlpine Ltd v Alfred McAlpine plc* [2004] RPC 36 Ch D.

[59] Eg *Saxon Trade Mark* [2003] FSR 39, sub nom *Byford v Oliver* [2003] EMLR 416 Ch D.

[60] Not necessarily the same connection for each joint owner: *Val Marks* (1923) 40 RPC 103 (manufacturer and distributor).

[61] R Annand and H Norman, *Blackstone's Guide to the Trade Marks Act 1994* (1994) ch 11.

[62] See, eg Annand and Norman *Blackstone's Guide to the Trade Marks Act 1994* (1994) ch 11, where an unattractive scenario is outlined.

[63] But not transmission by operation of law, at least in the case of insolvency: *Hansard*, House of Lords, vol 552, no 46, col 745 (24 February 1994).

[64] Patents Act 1977, s 36.

[65] See, further, Chapter 12.

[66] Schedule 1, para 5(2).

[67] Schedule 1, para 10.

Certification marks[68]

11.25 The proprietor must not trade in the goods or services of the kind certified.[69] It is not surprising, therefore, that the Registrar's consent is required for any assignment or other transmission.[70]

Assignment of the right of priority

11.26 The right of priority is the right to claim the priority date of a first filing within the preceding 6 months in another Paris Convention country.[71] This may be assigned, with or without the application on which it is based.[72] Thus, applicant A in France may assign to B the right to use the French filing date as priority date for a UK application.

Security interests over trade marks

11.27 A trade mark may be subject to a fixed or floating charge[73] or may be assigned by way of security.[74] In the latter case, it will usually be appropriate for the assignee to grant a licence back. In any event, all registrable elements of the transaction should be registered, for the reasons outlined above.[75]

TAXATION ISSUES

11.28 For individuals and partnerships as assignors, the consideration payable is normally classifiable as capital rather than income and, as such, income tax will not apply. In consequence, however, capital gains tax (CGT) is an important consideration; the outright disposal of a trade mark[76] will usually give rise to a charge to tax on the capital gain arising if one of three conditions is met: the owner is UK resident, the owner ordinarily UK resident or if the mark is used in a UK trade carried out through a UK branch or agency.[77] From a corporation tax perspective, again we note that, since 1 April 2002, Schs 29–30 of the Finance Act 2002 have applied to trade mark transactions entered into by companies.[78]

---

[68] See, further, Chapter 12.
[69] Schedule 2, para 4.
[70] Schedule 2, para 12.
[71] See, generally, **5.31**, **14.34**, **15.11–15.12**.
[72] Section 33(6).
[73] Section 24(5); for an example of a fixed charge over assets including trade marks, see *Re Rayford Homes Ltd (in admin rec)* [2011] EWHC 1948.
[74] Section 24(4).
[75] See **11.16**.
[76] Including an assignment without goodwill.
[77] There are additional rules which affect (a) non-residents receiving sums in the UK in relation to foreign registered marks and (b) persons receiving sums taxable under both UK and foreign law.
[78] See **10.40**.

11.29   Value added Tax (VAT) rules apply to assignment transactions in the same way that they affect licensing.[79]

11.30   Although, as discussed in **10.42**, stamp duty on trade mark transactions was abolished with effect from 28 March 2000, for earlier transactions (including 'old assignments') it is still relevant whether a document is duly stamped. Looking at old assignments, first one must see what head of charge applied and whether any exemptions or reliefs are payable: for example, if the assignment was not for consideration then 50p fixed duty was payable,[80] and intra-group transfers benefited from group relief. However, the vast majority of old assignments for value will be classified as 'conveyance or transfer on sale' and the following rates of duty applied:[81]

Consideration	Rate of duty
Up to £60,000	Nil duty
£60,000–£249,999	£1.00 per £100
£250,000–£499,999	£2.50 per £100
£500,000 upwards	£3.50 per £100

For assignments in the first three bands, even if the actual consideration paid was stated in the relevant agreement, certificates of value should be incorporated or endorsed on the assignment document stating that the transaction in question did not exceed the stated band level.[82]

11.31   Where a document has been stamped outside the prescribed time-limits, double duty, a £10 fine and interest of 5% per year could be applied as a fine. One interesting point related to old assignments of UK marks executed outside the UK; although these were immediately chargeable to tax, payment could be deferred for 30 days until after they were first brought into the UK. However, this was not carte blanche to avoid stamp duty and it was controlled by the overriding need to record an assignment. The result of r 41(3) is that, where a chargeable instrument such as an old assignment is involved, a party seeking

---

[79]   See **10.41**.

[80]   A certificate claiming exemption under the Stamp Duty (Exempt Instruments) Regulations 1987, SI 1987/516 also had to be incorporated or endorsed on the assignment document.

[81]   These rates were set in the 1999 Budget; under the Finance Act 1998, the top two bands were charged at £2 and £3 per £100 respectively. Note that there were important stamp duty exemptions which affect instruments dealing with Community trade marks and international trade mark (UK) rights: see s 61 of the 1994 Act.

[82]   In addition, the certificate was only valid if the transaction did not form part of a larger series, the aggregate value of which did not exceed the stated band value, and the certificate expressly stated this to be so.

registration of an assignment must either provide a copy of the stamped document or make the declaration on Form TM16 that the document has been 'duly stamped'.[83]

TRANSITIONAL PROVISIONS

11.32 Transitional provisions are spelled out in Sch 3, para 8 to the 1994 Act. The new law applies to transactions effected after commencement, and to applications made after commencement to register prior transactions. Applications made prior to commencement but not yet determined by the Registrar are also dealt with under the new law. Surprisingly, as of 2004, applications under the 1938 Act were still being litigated.[84]

---

[83] See Hiddlestone 'Stamp Duty and the Recordal of Assignments at the UK Trade Marks Registry' (1995) 82 TW 31.
[84] Eg *DU PONT Trade Mark* [2004] FSR 293, CA.

Chapter 12

SPECIAL CATEGORY MARKS

INTRODUCTION

12.1 Although the proprietor of a mark has exclusive control over the use of a mark, there are a number of ways in which more than one person can legitimately use a mark.[1] The proprietor may grant licences,[2] or several persons may be registered as co-proprietors of a registered mark.[3] This chapter principally deals with two more systems for multiple use, the certification mark[4] and the collective mark,[5] but it also briefly touches on other special category marks and legally protected symbols.

12.2 A collective mark signifies that the goods or services are connected with a member of the association which owns the mark. The latter may or may not trade in the goods or services in question. Thus, the collective mark indicates origin, although the association may include quality standards as a condition of membership.[6] Registration of collective marks was introduced by the Trade Marks Act 1994 ('the 1994 Act'). Collective purchasing organisations[7] and other groups of small enterprises may find them particularly useful. A certification mark, by contrast, indicates that the services or goods are certified as to some quality by the association which owns the mark. In this case, the proprietor must not trade in the certified goods/services; it would be inappropriate for one trader to certify the products of a competitor.[8]

---

[1] As outlined in Chapter 10.

[2] See A Firth 'Collectivity, Control and Joint Adventure – observations on marks in multiple use' in N Dawson and A Firth (eds) *Trade Marks Retrospective* (Sweet & Maxwell, 2000).

[3] See **11.22–11.23**.

[4] See J Belson 'Certification Marks, Guarantees and Trust' [2002] EIPR 340.

[5] The now largely subsumed categories of 'association marks' (related to collective) and 'guarantee marks' (related to certification) are not covered separately here although it is interesting that there are still perceived sufficient differences within the EU for guarantee marks to be separately referenced within Directive 2008/95 to approximate the laws of the member states relating to trade marks (Trade Marks Harmonisation Directive): see, e g Arts 1 and 14.

[6] Subject, of course, to the rules of competition law: see White Paper 'Reform of Trade Mark Laws' (1990) Cm 1203, para 5.02.

[7] For brief details of such an organisation, see *Spar (UK) Ltd v Audits of Great Britain Ltd* [1986] 5 EIPR D-74.

[8] Some jurisdictions outside the UK, such as Australia, allow the proprietor to use the mark on goods/services it provides whereas others, such as New Zealand, act like the UK in specifically barring the certification authority from so acting. The underlying principle at stake in barring such use – prevention of conflict of interest – should not be discarded lightly.

Certification marks for goods have been registrable in the UK since 1905;[9] the 1994 Act extended them to services. Both collective and certification marks are permitted by Art 15 of the Trade Marks Harmonisation Directive ('the Directive'). The Council Regulation (EC) on the Community Trade Mark (EC) 207/2009[10] ('the Regulation') provides for the registration of Community collective marks, but not certification marks. However, Dawson[11] has observed that the distinction between collective and certification marks is not absolute.[12] Use of a collective mark may involve formal certification of goods or services or may carry informal connotations of quality in just the same way as an ordinary trade mark.[13] Indeed, it appears that the Trade Marks Act 1905, as liberally construed, may have permitted registration of what we now call collective marks. In *Re an Application by Union Inter-Syndicate des Marques Collectives*,[14] reference was made to the exercise of:

'... a sufficient supervision and control over the affixing of marks upon goods by ... the careful selection and control of members of the association or other persons who are permitted to affix the mark.'

12.3 A key difference to note is that, unlike ordinary trade marks, both certification and collective marks may directly move to designate geographical origin.[15] Indeed, for some jurisdictions like the US, this is the principal method of providing requisite protection for geographical designations of products such as Florida Oranges: however, in other jurisdictions like the EU and its member states, sui generis protection of certain special geographical designations[16] such as indications of source[17] and appellations of origin[18] has

---

9   For a useful historical survey covering the UK and a number of other EC countries, see J Joseph 'Certification Marks, Collective Marks or Guarantee Marks' [1979] 6 EIPR 111.

10 Articles 66–74. See *Muñoz Arraiza v OHMI-Consejo Regulador de la Denominación de Origen Calificada Rioja* [2010] EUECJ T-138/09.

11 N Dawson *Certification Trade Marks: Law and Practice* (Intellectual Property Publishing, 1988) at p 84, citing *Creusois v Seguy* [1982] 10 EIPR D-213 (France).

12 Indeed, it is possible to emulate at least some of the functionality of collective or certification marks through multiple licensing under a suitable licensing scheme of a 'standard' mark: see, albeit as a cautionary tale of what not to do, *Rousselon Freres et Cie v Horwood Homewares Ltd* [2008] EWHC 881.

13 See Chapter 1. A collective mark tends to be cheaper and quicker to register than a certification mark, with fewer restrictions on its use.

14 *'UNIS'* [1922] 2 Ch 653; (1922) 39 RPC 97, discussed by N Dawson *Certification Trade Marks: Law and Practice* (1988) at pp 17–20.

15 Schedule 1, para 3(1); for an overview of this and other pertinent differences, see AF Ribeiro de Almeida 'Key Differences Between Trade Marks and Geographical Indications' [2008] EIPR 406.

16 Referred to collectively by the World Intellectual Property Organisation (WIPO) and the World Trade Organisation (WTO) as 'geographical indications'; this usage should be distinguished from the term 'Protected Geographical Indication' (PGI) which has a more specific meaning in EC law: see, e g Art 2 of Regulation (EC) 510/2006. To compare usages, definitions and approaches further, see D Rogitis 'EU Geographical Indications v US Trademarks: TKO Against the International Harmonisation of Geographical Indications?' [2010] IPQ 403.

17 An indication mark is applied to goods to show the territory of production.

18 An appellation mark is applied to goods possessing certain defined qualities which essentially derive from the geographical area of production, e g 'Cognac'.

developed. As such, geographical designations are now protected by a complex and uneven patchwork of national, regional and international laws;[19] at present, the most significant of the latter for the UK[20] are a set of EC Regulations under which the national authorities of the member states are obliged to provide protection for an assortment of designations relating to wines,[21] spirits[22] and agricultural foodstuffs and products.[23] Leaving aside geographical matters, it should also be noted that certification marks may often extend into other areas quite remote from a trade mark's traditional function as a 'badge of origin'; these range from compliance with technical standards[24] through to a possible solution to the problem of regulating the use of the creations and symbols of indigenous peoples.[25]

12.4 This chapter mainly deals with *registered* collective and certification marks. However, it should be remembered that where these are not registered, or protected by other laws or regulations, the users may build up a collective goodwill in their shared mark such as to found an action in passing off to restrain improper use. This was the case in *Taittinger*,[26] in *Advocaat*,[27] in

---

[19] See the Madrid Agreement for the Protection of Indications of Source 1891, the Lisbon Agreement for the Protection of Appellations of Origin and their International Registration 1958 (discussed in Chapter 15). See, more recently, Arts 22 and 23 of TRIPs: HR Ortiz 'Geographical indications in TRIPs' (1997) 102 TW 34; N Dawson 'Locating Geographical Indications: Perspectives from English Law' (2000) 90 Trademark Reporter 590.

[20] A signatory to the Madrid Agreement 1891 but not the Lisbon Agreement 1958. WIPO is still working towards revision of the international treaty framework to provide more effective protection and to encourage greater participation and the WTO is seeking to deal with such issues within the corresponding TRIPS framework but both are being hampered because of differences in existing approaches as between major players: see Geiger et al 'Towards a Flexible International Framework for the Protection of Geographical Indications' [2010] WIPOJ 147 and T Kongolo 'Any New Developments With Regard to GI Issues Debated Under WTO?' [2011] EIPR 83.

[21] Regulation (EC) 1493/1999; in *Taittinger v Allbev* [1993] FSR 641, the Court of Appeal held that use of the term 'Elderflower Champagne' contravened the preceding Regulation (EEC) 823/1999 and held that it would be enforced by injunction; for an interesting decision relating to use of a foreign language in this context, see *Schneider v Land Rheinland-Pfalz* [2008] EUECJ C-285/06.

[22] Regulation (EC) 110/2008.

[23] Regulation (EC) 510/2006. For examples of difficulties that can arise, see *CTFG v Kaserei* [1999] ETMR 454 ('Gorgonzola'), *Denmark v EC Commission* [1999] ETMR 478 ('Feta'), *CPP v Asda* [2004] ETMR 23 ('Parma Ham') and *Severi v Regione Emilia-Romagna* [2009] ETMR 64; J Reed 'ECJ Protects Simple Geographical Indications for Their Bud-Dy' [2005] EIPR 25; W Van Caenegem 'Registered GIs: Intellectual Property, Agricultural Policy and International Trade' [2004] EIPR 170. See also Regulation (EC) 509/2006 covering 'Traditional Specialities Guaranteed', eg Traditionally Farmed Gloucestershire Old Spots Pork (TSG) in *Axle Associates Ltd v Gloucestershire Old Spots Pig Breeders' Club* [2010] ETMR 12.

[24] Certification marks sometimes being referred to as 'standardisation' marks.

[25] See, eg O Morgan 'Protecting Indigenous Signs and Trade Marks – The New Zealand Experiment' [2004] IPQ 58; J Gibson 'Intellectual Property Systems, Traditional Knowledge and the Legal Authority of Community' [2004] EIPR 280; C-C Yang 'A Critical Perspective on Taiwan's Aboriginal Traditional Knowledge Creation Protection Ordinance' [2010] EntLR 229.

[26] See *Taittinger v Allbev* [1993] FSR 641 (CA) and **12.3**; see also, 'Parma Ham' in *CPP v Asda* [1999] ETMR 319.

[27] *Erven Warnink v Townend* [1980] RPC 31.

Chocosuisse,[28] in *Long Point*[29] and other cases discussed in Chapter 3. Passing off may also be actionable at the suit of authorised users of a certification mark.[30]

12.5   Collective marks are referred to in Art 7*bis* of the Paris Convention for the Protection of Industrial Property,[31] which states:

> 'The Countries of the Union undertake to accept for filing and to protect collective marks belonging to associations the existence of which is not contrary to the law of the country of origin, even if such associations do not possess an industrial or commercial establishment.'

12.6   Another kind of sign finds itself in multiple use – the symbols associated with the Olympic Games. There is an international treaty about these signs – the Nairobi Treaty on the Protection of the Olympic Symbol (1981), discussed in Chapter 15. However, this chapter has a brief note on the protection of Olympic symbols in the UK as the UK is not a party to the Nairobi Treaty as at the time of writing.

12.7   The last 'special' category of mark, the 'well-known' mark, is a creature of the Paris Convention. By Art 6*bis*, Paris Union members undertake to protect well-known marks against unauthorised use and registration by another person. Where a foreign trade mark owner with reputation but no (or minimal) trade in this country is concerned, the action in passing off may not assist.[32] The 1994 Act explicitly discharges the UK's obligation to protect the well-known marks of other countries.[33]

CERTIFICATION MARKS

12.8   The certification trade mark system has been used to register marks such as the Woolmark, 'Lurpak' and other 'Lur' marks for Danish butter and dairy products, 'Stilton' for blue cheese made in the Melton Mowbray region of England[34] and the British Standards Institute's kite marks for all manner of goods and services.[35] The marks are administered by the proprietor associations. Sometimes the mark itself suggests the qualities of the product

---

[28]   *Chocosuisse Union des Fabricants Suisses de Chocolat v Cadbury Ltd* [1999] RPC 826; [1999] ETMR 1020, CA.

[29]   *Artistic Upholstery Ltd v Art Forma (Furniture) Ltd* [2000] FSR 311 Ch D.

[30]   N Dawson *Certification Trade Marks: Law and Practice* (1988) at pp 77–78, discussing *Argyllshire Weavers v A Macaulay (Tweeds) Ltd* [1964] RPC 477.

[31]   Of 1883, with revisions in 1900, 1911, 1925, 1934, 1958 and 1967.

[32]   See the '*Budweiser*' case (*Anheuser-Busch v Budjovicky Budvar* [1984] FSR 413) and other 'foreign plaintiff' cases discussed in Chapter 3.

[33]   Section 56 of the 1994 Act. Note that domestic traders cannot rely upon s 56 because of the definition of 'Convention country' in s 55.

[34]   Although the cheese had not actually been manufactured in Stilton: [1967] RPC 173.

[35]   For an interesting global view of the interaction of standards setting and certification marks, see R Rozas and H Johnston 'Impact of Certification Marks on Innovation and the Global Marketplace' [1997] EIPR 599.

which are certified, but usually these are found in the regulations governing use of the mark,[36] in the regulations or statutory order establishing the proprietor, or in the relevant British or European standard. Historically, the Registry often required that the phrase 'certification mark' be used upon the goods to indicate the kind of mark involved.[37] Similar requirements are set out in the 1994 Act;[38] exceptionally, amendment of the mark during the application procedure may be made to meet these.[39] The Registry is especially conscious that an application to register a certification mark must be carefully scrutinised:[40]

> '... it is subject to an element of control in the public interest, in that a government agency (the Trade Marks Registry) has a say in its acceptance for registration through the regulations controlling use, and in the circumstances in which it may be assigned.'

It appears that some applicants have sought to avoid this rigour of examination by applying to register an ordinary trade mark for 'certification services'. Although it is legitimate to apply in relation to such certification services, in cases where it is clear that a certification mark is what is, in effect, being sought, the Registry will give the applicant the opportunity to amend the application to bring it under s 50, or to clarify that the mark will be used as an ordinary trade mark.[41]

12.9 The qualities which are certified are objectively verifiable, rather than subjective standards like 'good design'.[42] An organisation seeking to promote subjective qualities of products could resort to a prize or award system[43] or to business format franchising. Section 50 of the 1994 Act sets out the qualities which a certification mark may indicate; most certification marks signify more than one of these;[44] the examples given in Table 12.1 below are by way of illustration only.

---

36   *Hansard*, House of Lords, vol 552, no 46, col 730 (24 February 1994).

37   See Trade Marks Act 1938, Sch 1, para 1(3).

38   Schedule 2, para 5.

39   Cf s 39; see **5.25** for the tight limitations imposed.

40   *UK Trade Marks Registry Work Manual*, ch 4.

41   UK Registry Practice Amendment Notice PAN 12/02 'Certification Services being Claimed in Trade Mark Applications'. See also Practice Amendment Circular PAC 2/01 'Section 3 and Section 5 Practice in Relation to Applications Made to Register a Mark as Both a Trade Mark and a Collective Mark, or as Both a Trade Mark and Certification Mark'.

42   N Dawson *Certification Trade Marks: Law and Practice* (1988) at p 103, citing the 'Molony Committee on Consumer Protection', Cmnd 1781 (1962) para 373.

43   For the tribulations of '*Oscar*', see [1979] RPC 173.

44   See N Dawson *Certification Trade Marks: Law and Practice* (1988) at pp 50–54. See also an intriguing reference to the 'Harris Tweed' orb mark by way of possible defence in trade mark and passing off proceedings: *Westwood v Knight* [2010] EWPCC 16.

Table 12.1: Qualities and certification marks

Quality certified (s 50)	Example mark
Origin	'Lurpak'
Material	Woolmark
Mode of manufacture of goods	'Harris Tweed' orb mark
Mode of performance of services	British Standard mark for firms
Quality (specific qualities)	'Commanderia' wines
Accuracy	National Physical Laboratory (NPL)
Other characteristics	British Standard safety mark

12.10 Unless otherwise specified, the general criteria of the 1994 Act apply to certification marks.[45] Special conditions which appertain are set out in Sch 2. The mark must be capable of graphical representation and of distinguishing the certified goods and services from those not certified.[46] Absolute and relative grounds for refusal appear to follow those for trade marks in general, save that geographical indications are expressly permitted, with a saving for bona fide use by others.[47] Concern was expressed in Parliament that the other exclusions of s 3(1)(c)[48] would prevent the registration of certification marks. An assurance was given that this would not be the case.[49]

12.11 The applicant/proprietor must not carry on a business involving the supply of goods or services of the kind certified.[50] The applicant applies in the normal way, giving name and address, details of the goods and services[51] and a representation of the mark applied for. Within 9 months of filing for registration of a certification mark, the applicant must file a copy of the regulations governing use of the mark.[52] These must show who is entitled to use it. There should be appropriate restrictions in terms of the quality of the product but, subject to this:[53]

> 'There must be no discrimination in authorising use of the mark. Any persons trading in the United Kingdom in goods or services with the required characteristics – whether as manufacturers or, if the certification scheme extends

---

[45] Section 1(2).

[46] Schedule 2, para 2.

[47] Schedule 2, para 3; see *Proceedings Brought by Bureau National Interprofessionnel du Cognac* (C-4/10) and *Gust Ranin Oy* (C-27/10) (conjoined cases) and cases cited therein on conflict between geographical indications protected under EU rules and trade marks.

[48] Kind, quality, quantity, intended purpose, value or time of production of goods or of rendering of services or other characteristics.

[49] *Hansard*, House of Lords, vol 552, no 46, col 730 (24 February 1994).

[50] Schedule 2, para 4.

[51] As with ordinary trade marks a multi-class application may be filed. In practice, however, the regulations governing the use of the mark are likely to differ significantly from product to product.

[52] Schedule 2, para 6(1); Trade Marks Rules 2008, SI 2008/1797, r 29; the relevant form is Form TM35. Failure to file regulations results is deemed withdrawal of the application: Sch 2, para 7(2). This is referred to as the two-stage registration process: *UK Trade Marks Registry Work Manual*, ch 4.

[53] *Trade Marks Registry Work Manual*, ch 4, para 3.3.1.

to them, as other traders – shall be eligible for authorisation to use it, provided that they can and will comply with the regulations, which must not include provisions restricting use to any particular group drawn from among traders qualified in all other respects to use the mark.

It is not a statutory requirement that a certification mark shall be open for use by any person who is competent to produce goods of the required standard but in practice this "open door" policy is invariably pursued. The undertaking that the applicant gives that use of the mark will be permitted to anyone who complies with the regulations and produces goods which have the certified characteristic is intended to prevent a scheme of certification becoming a restrictive trade practice . . .'

Some certification marks are intended for use only by members of the association owning the mark.[54] Given the above strictures, however, membership of such association should be accessible without discrimination or artificial entry barriers such as high membership fees. Some certification marks are merely licensed to third parties and some may be used by members or non-members. In this case, as the Registry points out:

'It is permissible to charge different fees to members and non-members of the applicant association, provided that it is obvious that the fee differential has not been introduced with the intention of discouraging non-members from seeking permission to use the mark. It may be worthwhile for a non-member to pay the higher fee for using the mark when he does not have to pay membership fees. The fees schedule should make this clear.'[55]

The regulations should spell out the characteristics to be certified, and how the certifying body is to test those characteristics and supervise the use of the mark.[56] The applicant will need to satisfy the Registry that it is competent[57] and prepared to do so, fairly.

12.12 The regulations must stipulate the fees (if any) to be paid in connection with the operation of the mark. There is no statutory requirement for the operation to be non-profit making, although this was often required in the past.[58] A mechanism for the resolution of disputes must be established.[59] Finally, the regulations must comply with public policy and accepted principles of morality.[60] Chapter 4, para 3.3.9 of the *Trade Marks Registry Work Manual*

---

[54] The 'Board of Trade', latterly the Consumer Affairs Division of the Department of Trade and Industry (White Paper 'Reform of Trade Mark Law' (1990) Cm 1203, para 5.01), has in the past shown itself strict in ensuring that certification is open to all qualified persons: N Dawson *Certification Trade Marks: Law and Practice* (1988) at p 32.

[55] *Trade Marks Registry Work Manual*, ch 4, para 3.3.4.

[56] Schedule 2, para 6(2).

[57] Schedule 2, para 7(1)(b).

[58] N Dawson *Certification Trade Marks: Law and Practice* (1988) at p 33, para 12.10, n 4; see now *Trade Marks Registry Work Manual*, ch 4, para 3.3.4 (fees must be reasonable).

[59] Schedule 2, para 6(2).

[60] Schedule 2, para 7(1)(a)(ii).

gives helpful advice on the drafting of regulations. These must make clear that amendments require the Registrar's consent.

12.13 Once a certification mark passes formalities and its regulations have been accepted, it is published in the normal way, together with the regulations, and open for observations and opposition.[61] If it survives the opposition process, it is registered in the normal register. The regulations are open to public inspection.[62]

12.14 The mark may be assigned or transmitted only with the consent of the Registrar.[63] Amendment of the regulations also requires approval.[64]

12.15 Infringement of a certification mark is governed by the general provisions. As noted above, the 1994 Act is silent as to whether only trade mark use infringes.[65] It was stated in Parliament that it was 'implicit'.[66] It is submitted that use which suggests any kind of trade mark function – as indicating origin, quality or certification – should be capable of 'implicitly' infringing a certification mark.

12.16 Authorised users are equated for most purposes to licensees under 'ordinary' trade marks.[67] However, an authorised user has no right of action for infringement. Such right was proposed in an early version of the Trade Marks Bill, but removed by amendment.[68] Only the registered proprietor can sue.[69] In proceedings brought by the proprietor the court may take into account any loss or likely loss to authorised users, and can order the plaintiffs to hold the proceeds of pecuniary remedies on behalf of authorised users.[70]

12.17 Revocation of a certification mark may be sought on all the grounds specified in s 46[71] and additionally on the following grounds:[72]

(a)   the proprietor is trading in the goods or services concerned;

---

[61]   The *UNIS* case, at **12.2**, involved opposition. Opposition or observations may also be based on the content of the regulations: Sch 2, para 9.

[62]   Schedule 2, para 10.

[63]   Although transmission by operation of law would appear to be automatic: see *Hansard*, House of Lords, vol 552, no 46, col 745 (24 February 1994), on the related issue of jointly owned marks in the case of insolvency.

[64]   Schedule 2, para 11. The application to amend is filed on Form TM36.

[65]   See **7.11, 7.25–7.37**.

[66]   *Hansard*, House of Lords, vol 552, no 46, col 733 (24 February 1994), referring to the recital of the Directive.

[67]   Schedule 2, para 13 specifically applies ss 10(5), 19(2) and 89. The last appears to enable an authorised user to request Customs stoppage of infringing goods, which is odd, since the user at present has no right to sue for infringement. See **7.71, 10.18–10.21**.

[68]   *Hansard*, House of Lords, vol 553, no 55, cols 88–89 (14 March 1994), reversing col 748 (24 February 1994).

[69]   If the proprietor will not sue, the user may have a remedy in passing off, see **12.5**.

[70]   Schedule 2, para 14.

[71]   See **9.5, 9.13–9.18**.

[72]   Schedule 2, para 15.

(b)   the proprietor has used the certification mark in such a way that the public is liable to be misled as to its nature;[73]

(c)   the regulations have not been observed or enforced;[74]

(d)   an inappropriate amendment of the regulations has been made;

(e)   the proprietor is no longer competent to certify.

12.18   A declaration of invalidity may be sought on the grounds set forth in s 47[75] and also on the grounds[76] that:

(a)   the proprietor traded in the products;

(b)   the public is liable to be misled as to the nature of the mark;

(c)   the regulations do not conform to the requirements.

12.19   Previously, one interesting question raised by Dawson[77] was whether a civil action would lie for breach of statutory duty where the Trade Descriptions Act 1968 was contravened by misuse of a certification mark; this was by analogy to decision in *Rickless v United Artists*,[78] in which it was held that a performer's personal representatives could sue for breach of the Performers' Protection Acts (criminal statutes). However, given that the vast bulk of the Trade Descriptions 1968 Act has now been repealed as part of the implementation of EU Unfair Commercial Practices Directive by the Unfair Trading Regulations 2008 (the 'CPRs'), the question appears to be presently settled in the negative, at least to the extent of such repeal; only enforcement bodies may currently take action under the CPRs and, pending necessary amendment to allow them (under discussion at the time of writing), private actions will not lie.

COLLECTIVE MARKS

12.20   Collective marks are defined, in s 49, as marks distinguishing the goods or services of members of the association which is the proprietor from those of other undertakings. The first question this raises is whether collective marks may be registered in the name of an association of non-traders. It will be recalled that Art 7*bis* of the Paris Convention requires them to be protected

---

[73]   Ie not a certification mark.

[74]   For an application to revoke a certification mark on this basis, see '*Sea Island Cotton*' *Certification Trade Marks* [1989] RPC 87; N Dawson 'The West Indian Sea Island Cotton Association's Certification Trade Mark: Application to Expunge' [1989] EIPR 375.

[75]   See **9.6–9.11**.

[76]   Schedule 2, para 16.

[77]   N Dawson *Certification Trade Marks: Law and Practice* (1988) at pp 63–64.

[78]   [1988] QB 40; [1987] FSR 362.

even if the association does not possess an industrial or commercial establishment.[79] Gilson[80] says of the collective mark in the US:

> 'It is also widely used by fraternal organisations, service clubs, automobile clubs and the like to indicate membership, where the members do not engage in any kind of commercial activity under the mark.'

It is submitted that a generous construction of s 49 is called for; this would be consistent with the wide interpretation of 'undertaking' in EC law.[81]

12.21 An association seeking to register a collective mark is not prohibited from trading, however. As with certification marks, geographical indications are permitted, subject to bona fide use by others.[82] It is submitted that the other prohibitions in s 3 should be applied to collective marks in the same way as to ordinary trade marks.[83] As mentioned previously, the mark should not mislead as to its nature and can be amended during prosecution to ensure this.[84]

12.22 The mode of application for registration is similar to that for certification marks. Regulations governing use of the mark must be filed[85] specifying the persons authorised to use the mark and the conditions of membership of the association. This is rather oddly worded, since the collective mark is designed for use by members of the association. Perhaps different categories of membership are envisaged for different categories of user. If that is so, it may be difficult to ensure that the public is properly educated or informed as to the nature of the mark. Schedule 1, para 5(2) refers to 'any sanctions against misuse'. It is to be hoped that the Registry will insist, in practice, upon sanctions for misuse.[86]

12.23 The regulations must be approved by the Registrar, who shall allow the applicant the opportunity to make representations or amendments.[87] Assuming that everything is in order, the collective mark and regulations are published and opponents may formally oppose and file observations as before.[88] Unless refused as a result of opposition or observations, the mark will proceed to

---

[79] See **12.5**.

[80] J Gilson *Trade Mark Protection and Practice* (Matthew Bender, 1997) para 1.02[2] (US).

[81] See, Case C-41/90 *Hofner & Elser v Macrotron* [1991] ECR I-1979 at para 21; C Graham *EU and UK Comeptition Law* (Pearson Longman, 2010) at p 66 (maintaining consistency with competition law is an increasingly significant issue in relation to collective marks: see *Duales System Deutschland v Commission* [2007] EUECJ T-289/01 ('Grüne Punkt')).

[82] Schedule 1, para 3.

[83] Contrast certification marks, **12.8**.

[84] Schedule 1, para 5(1).

[85] Schedule 1, para 5(2); Trades Marks Rules 2008, r 29; Form TM35. For an actual set of regulations, see J Boff 'Regulations for Marks' (1996) 25(11) CIPAJ 905.

[86] Although in the context of conflicting marks, Parliament observed that the Registrar was no longer to have a consumer protection role: *Hansard*, House of Lords, vol 550, no 10, col 752 (6 December 1993).

[87] Schedule 1, para 7. In practice, the Registry appears to scrutinise regulations for collective marks somewhat less minutely than those for certification marks.

[88] See *CFA Institute v Chartered Insurance Institute* [2007] ETMR 76 and **12.13**, **5.63–5.65**.

registration and the regulations will be open to inspection.[89] Fees for use are not specifically mentioned. The regulations should, presumably, provide a fee structure for membership of the association. Any amendment to the regulations is subject to acceptance by the Registrar.[90]

12.24 The practice for collective marks follows the general pattern established for certification marks, although in practice the Registry appear to scrutinise applications for collective marks less rigorously. Given this rather more laissez-faire approach, in keeping with the deregulatory ethos of the 1994 Act, proprietors and users of collective marks need to pay especial attention to compliance with competition law.[91]

OLYMPIC SYMBOLS

12.25 The Nairobi Treaty on the Protection of the Olympic Symbol (1981) requires contracting parties to refuse the registration of symbols associated with the Olympic Games, and to prohibit their use, except with the authorisation of the International Olympic Committee. There are derogations for prior rights and during periods when the Olympic Committee of the country concerned does not have an agreement with the International Olympic Committee. The UK, like many other EU countries, is not a signatory to the Nairobi Treaty,[92] but has enacted the Olympic Symbol etc (Protection) Act 1995 ('the 1995 Act')[93] and the London Olympic Games and Paralympic Games Act 2006 ('the 2006 Act'). During a prior unsuccessful bid to hold the Olympic Games in Manchester, the UK Government gave a commitment to regulate the use of Olympic symbols in the UK; the International Olympic Committee accepted the UK Government's view that rights should best be held by the British Olympic Association, which had already registered as trade marks certain signs combining Olympic symbols.[94] The 'Olympics Association Rights' created by the 1995 Act were more extensive than trade marks – they were not limited to particular goods or services and did not have to be used to remain valid. The rights did not depend upon registration, so were unlimited in time and did not need to be renewed. Nor was there any requirement that the symbols be used. The 'proprietor' was appointed by the Secretary of State by statutory instrument.[95] Subsequently, the 2006 Act amended the 1995 Act including expanding the range of covered signs, designators and symbols to the Paralympic Games; it also created a new London Olympic Association Right (LOAR) to prevent unauthorised persons doing anything likely to create an association between the London Olympics and goods and services or a person

---

[89] Schedule 1, para 9.
[90] Schedule 1, para 10, who has a discretion to publish the changes for opposition.
[91] On which, see Chapters 4 and 13.
[92] As at December 2010, there were 48 contracting parties.
[93] 1995 c 32. The Act came into force on 20 September 1995.
[94] *Hansard*, House of Commons, vol 253, col 1379 (3 February 1995).
[95] The Olympics Association Right (Appointment of Proprietor) Order 1995, SI 1995/2473 appointed the British Olympic Association (a company limited by guarantee).

providing goods or services, such right vested in the London Organising Committee of the Olympic Games Limited (LOCOG).

12.26   Under the 1995 Act, the relevant signs are the familiar Olympic symbol consisting of five interlocking rings, the word Olympic and variants and the motto 'Citius, altius, fortius'.[96] The 'proprietor' is given an exclusive right over the symbols but may not dispose of the right or create any interest in or over the right (s 2). So the right is not fully proprietary, despite the availability of property-like remedies for infringement.[97] The right is infringed by the unauthorised use in the course of trade of one of the protected signs, or a sign so similar as to create an association in the public mind (s 3(1)). Prohibited use includes incorporation in a flag or banner as well as the more usual trade mark-type activities – affixing to goods or packaging, offering or exposing for sale, import, export or the supply of services under the sign and use on business papers or in advertising (s 3(2)). Having conferred very broad rights, the 1995 Act then goes on to create elaborate exceptions to infringement,[98] for example for use in books or programmes about the Olympics, provided such use is honest. There are also savings for continuing of prior use or the exercise of prior rights. Section 16 establishes the right to sue for groundless threats of infringement proceedings, providing some protection against overweening exercise of the rights. Section 8 creates criminal offences and is largely modelled upon the provisions of s 92 of the 1994 Act. Acquisition of competing rights by way of registered designs or design right is restricted by ss 13 and 14.

12.27   The 1995 and 2006 Acts appear to have generated little significant case-law in the UK, although this may well change during the countdown to the London Olympics in 2012.[99] At the EU level, the Office for Harmonisation in the Internal Market has refused a number of Community trade marks application after opposition from the International Olympic Committee.[100] In *Groupement d'Achat des Centres Leclerc (SCA Galec) v Comité National Olympique et Sportif Francais (CNOSF)*,[101] the French Supreme Court held that the national Olympic committee had standing to challenge Leclerc's use of 'Olymprix' but that the lower court had misapplied statutory provisions on

---

[96]   Section 18.

[97]   Section 6. Further remedies were made available by secondary legislation, the Olympics Association Right (Infringement Proceedings) Regulations 1995, SI 1995/3325. There are also Regulations in support of the LOAR: see now the Olympics, Paralympics and London Olympics Association Rights (Infringement Proceedings) Regulations 2010, SI 2010/2477. Note also that ambush marketing and other 'on the spot' ploys will be additionally controlled by temporary local street trading regulations.

[98]   Section 4.

[99]   Though perhaps one early sign of things to come is a domain name dispute involving 'ticket' domain names: *LOCOG v Tiley* [2010] DRS 8302 (16 April 2010). On trade mark problems thrown up by previous games, see C Pina and A Gil-Roble 'Sponsorship of Sports Events and Ambush Marketing' [2005] EIPR 93.

[100]   Cf *Belmont Olympic SA's Application; Opposition of the Comité International Olympique* [2000] ETMR 919 OHIM (Opposition Div).

[101]   *Groupement d'Achat des Centres Leclerc (SCA Galec) v Comité National Olympique et Sportif Francais (Cnosf), SA Proximité, Cie Uap and Cie AGF* [2001] ETMR 33 (Cour de Cass, Comm Div, Fr).

famous trade marks, which did not expressly prohibit the evocation or the use of a similar form of sign. The case was remanded for further hearing on the merits.

WELL-KNOWN MARKS

12.28 Another type of protection available in the UK without registration is conferred on foreign marks in accordance with Art 6*bis* of the Paris Convention. Art 6*bis* provides:

'(1) The countries of the Union undertake, ex officio if their legislation so permits, or at the request of an interested party, to refuse or to cancel the registration, and to prohibit the use, of a trade mark which constitutes a reproduction, an imitation, or a translation, liable to create confusion, of a mark considered by the competent authority of the country of registration or use to be well known in that country as being already the mark of a person entitled to the benefits of this Convention[102] and used for identical or similar goods. These provisions shall also apply when the essential part of the mark constitutes a reproduction of any such well-known mark or an imitation liable to create confusion therewith.

(2) A period of at least five years from the date of registration shall be allowed for requesting the cancellation of such a mark. The countries of the Union may provide for a period within which the prohibition of use must be requested.

(3) No time limit shall be fixed for requesting the cancellation of the prohibition of the use of marks registered or used in bad faith.'

12.29 The UK, as a signatory to the Paris Convention, is obliged to provide such protection to nationals of, and those domiciled or established in, other Convention countries.[103] Prior to enactment of the 1994 Act, such protection was afforded informally, by exercise of the Registrar's discretion[104] and by virtue of the action in passing off.

12.30 The 1994 Act defines a well-known mark in s 56 as the mark which is well known in the UK as being the mark of a person national, domiciled or established in a Convention country other than the UK,[105] whether or not that person carries on business, or has goodwill, in the UK. That person may sue for an injunction to restrain use of the mark[106] on identical or similar goods or

---

[102] Ie nationals of Union countries or those who are domiciled or have real and effective industrial or commercial establishments in the territories of one of the Paris Union Countries: Arts 2 and 3. Further countries which provide protection for UK trade marks may be declared 'Convention countries' by statutory instrument under s 36 for the purposes of priority claims under s 35 but these powers do not seem to extend to the definition of 'Convention country' for the purposes of ss 55 and 56.

[103] Article 2(1). And WTO countries: see s 56, **12.32–12.33, 15.16–15.27**.

[104] Eg in calling for evidence of use or intention to use, advertising a mark before acceptance under the proviso to s 18(1) of the 1938 Act, or refusing to register on judicial grounds: *Rawhide TM* [1962] RPC 133.

[105] Section 55(1)(b).

[106] Or a similar mark: s 56(2).

services where the use is likely to cause confusion. The claimant does not have to show lack of consent, although it is submitted that a defence of estoppel would lie where consent has been given.[107] There is explicit application of the defence of 5 years' acquiescence in s 48; to make out that defence, however, the defendant has to have registered the mark in question.

12.31 Section 56 thus goes beyond Art 6*bis* in protecting well-known marks for goods and for services. Thus, if 'Coca-Cola' is a well-known mark for soft drinks, its use can be enjoined on restaurant services. In this respect, the UK already complies with Art 16.2 of the GATT Agreement on Trade-Related Aspects of Intellectual Property Rights (TRIPs).[108] Article 16.3 requires application of Art 6*bis* to goods or services which are not similar to those for which the mark is registered,[109] provided use would indicate a connection and be deleterious to the owner of the registered mark; this is considered further below.

12.32 The registration of a well-known mark by someone else is prevented by including the well-known mark within the definition of 'earlier trade mark' in s 6.[110] In effect, this will give the 'proprietor' of the well-known mark a ground for opposition.[111] The provisions of s 5(3)[112] are more generous than those of Art 6*bis* or TRIPs.

12.33 A limited class of well-known marks was afforded some protection under s 27 of the 1938 Act. Where an invented word mark had become so well known in respect of the words for which it was registered and used that its use on other goods was likely to be taken as indicating a connection in the course of trade with the proprietor, he could register for those other goods, notwithstanding that there was no use made or proposed. Such defensive registration served to block subsequent attempts to register and could be used to restrain infringements in the usual manner. Defensive registration was sparingly granted, however,[113] and the system was therefore little used in the UK and other countries with related legislation.[114] It is gradually being abandoned elsewhere. The system did, however, have the merit of comparative certainty for owners of defensive marks and for their competitors. Wheeldon[115] has pointed out that defensive trade mark legislation was interpreted more

---

[107] For the equitable defences of estoppel, acquiescence and laches, see *Habib Bank Ltd v Habib Bank AG* [1981] 1 WLR 1265; [1982] RPC 1.

[108] Text available at www.wto.org/english/docs_e/legal_e/27-trips.pdf; see **15.16–15.27**.

[109] Presumably in the country where protection is sought.

[110] See **5.31–5.37**.

[111] Under the former examination system, there was no specific attempt to examine marks for conflict against well-known marks which were not registered in the UK for the same or similar products, these being left for opposition as a s 5(3) matter.

[112] See **5.50–5.58**.

[113] See, e g *Ferodo Ltd's Application* (1945) 62 RPC 111.

[114] M Tierney *Irish Trade Marks Law and Practice* (Gill & MacMillan, 1987) at p 106 reported no defensive marks on the Irish Register.

[115] R Wheeldon 'The Community Trademark and the Concept of Dilution: Was the Case for Defensive Trademarks Adequately Considered?' (November 1994) *Trademark World* at p 12.

generously in South Africa, and regrets that it was not seriously considered to prevent dilution under the Community Trade Mark Regulation. There is no provision for defensive registration under the 1994 Act. Existing defensive registrations were immune from revocation on the ground of non-use for a period of 5 years from commencement.[116] This transitional period has now long since expired, so any remaining defensive registrations are vulnerable to revocation on the grounds of non-use.[117]

12.34 The most difficult question lies with the definition of 'well known'. It is not defined in the 1994 Act. Clearly, the world's 'top 20' marks are likely to be regarded as well known.[118] Although it has proven difficult in the past to establish international agreement on what constitutes 'well known', WIPO has adopted a 'Joint Recommendation' setting out an assessment framework;[119] it is envisaged that this may, in due course, be directly incorporated into the international trade mark treaty framework. The Joint Recommendation was considered in *Le Mans TM*,[120] which also referred to the following criteria suggested by Mostert[121] and cited by the Advocate-General in *General Motors Corp v Yplon*:[122]

'(i)   the degree of recognition of the mark;
(ii)   the extent to which the mark is used and the duration of the use;
(iii) the extent and duration of advertising and publicity accorded to the mark;
(iv)   the extent to which the mark is recognised, used, advertised, registered and enforced geographically or, if applicable, other relevant factors that may determine the mark's geographical reach locally, regionally and worldwide;
(v)   the degree of inherent or acquired distinctiveness of the mark;
(vi)   the degree of exclusivity of the mark and the nature and extent of use of the same or a similar mark by third parties;
(vii) the nature of the goods or services and the channels of trade for the goods or services which bear the mark;
(viii) the degree to which the reputation of the mark symbolises quality goods;
(ix)   the extent of the commercial value attributed to the mark.'

Ultimately, it is a matter for national decision-making;[123] markets, awareness, language and legal attitudes are so diverse that international harmonisation in

---

[116] Schedule 3, proviso to para 17(2).

[117] See, eg *Premier Brands UK Ltd v Typhoon Europe Ltd* [2000] FSR 767; [2000] ETMR 1071 Ch D.

[118] See R Abnett 'AIPPI: Famous Trademarks Require a New Legal Weapon' (December 1990/January 1991) *Trademark World* at p 23. In Case R-91/2002–3 *McDonald's International Property Co Ltd v Aydemir* (OHIM Third Board of Appeal, 5 March 2003) the McDonald's 'Golden Arches' was accepted to be well known.

[119] The full text may be consulted on the internet at www.wipo.int/about-ip/en/development_iplaw/pub833.htm.

[120] R Arnold, Appointed Person, 8 November 2004, available as Decision O-012–05 on the UK Patent Office website at www.patent.gov.uk/tm/legal/decisions/2005/o01205.pdf. He held Le Mans to be well known for the services of organising and managing motor racing events, both among consumers of, and traders in, such services and among the public at large.

[121] F Mostert *Famous and Well-Known Marks* (LexisNexis UK, 1997) at pp 8–17.

[122] (C-375/97) [1999] ECR I-5421; [1999] ETMR 122.

[123] See country reports to question 100 (1990) *AIPPI Annual Report* (Barcelona, 1990).

relation to specific marks would seem impossible. In countries like Japan, the trade mark administration declares marks to be well known. A glance at the listings in any issue of the journal *AIPPI Japan* will suggest that awareness of marks is high and/or the threshold for 'well-known' status is low. In countries like Germany, the Registrar and courts use consumer awareness surveys to determine degrees of reputation.[124] In a UK decision, *Paco/Paco Life in Colour TMs*,[125] the Registry Hearing Officer observed that:

'(a) a trade mark could only be well known in respect of the goods or services in respect of which it has been used, and (b) accordingly PACO RABANNE was not a well-known trade mark for clothing even though it had a reputation in relation to perfume.'

This 'common-sense' approach was cited with approval in *Le Mans* and was subsequently adopted in the landmark case of *Hotel Cipriani Srl & Ors v Cipriani (Grosvenor Street) Ltd & Ors* to deal with issues affecting the use of the Cipriani mark for hotel and restaurant services.[126]

12.35 The relationship between well-known marks and 'marks with a reputation' was considered by Jacobs A-G in his opinion in *General Motors Corp v Yplon*.[127] As to well-known marks he stated:

'33 The protection of well-known marks under the Paris Convention and TRIPs is accordingly an exceptional type of protection afforded even to unregistered marks. It would not be surprising therefore if the requirement of being well-known imposed a relatively high standard for a mark to benefit from such exceptional protection. There is no such consideration in the case of marks with a reputation. Indeed as I shall suggest later, there is no need to impose such a high standard to satisfy the requirement of marks with a reputation in Article 5(2) of the Directive.'

The European Court of Justice spent little time on these matters, merely echoing the Advocate-General's remarks about marks with a reputation with the finding that:[128]

---

[124] See, eg A Kur 'Well-known Marks, Highly Renowned Marks and Marks Having a (High) Reputation – What's it all About?' (1992) 23 IIC 218 and citations therein; M Lehmann 'Unfair Use of and Damage to the Reputation of Well-Known Marks, Names and Indications of Source in Germany. Some Aspects of Law and Economics' (1986) 17 IIC 746.

[125] [2000] RPC 451.

[126] *Le Mans* O-012–05, see n 124 above and *Hotel Cipriani* [2008] EWHC 3032 respectively. In the latter case, Arnold J was applying his own earlier reasoning as Appointed Person in *Le Mans*; this was upheld on appeal (cf *Hotel Cipriani Srl & Ors v Cipriani (Grosvenor Street) Ltd & Ors* [2010] EWCA Civ 110).

[127] (C-375/97) [1999] ECR I-5421; [1999] ETMR 122.

[128] [1999] ECR I-5421; [1999] ETMR 950; [2000] RPC 572. As to corresponding issues of the proper treatment of 'marks having a reputation', see *Intel Corporation Inc v CPM United Kingdom Ltd* [2007] EWCA Civ 431 and *Intel Corporation Inc v CPM United Kingdom Ltd* [2008] EUECJ C-252/07 ('INTELMARK').

'Article 5(2) of the Directive is to be interpreted as meaning that, in order to enjoy protection extending to non-similar products or services, a registered trade mark must be known by a significant part of the public concerned by the products or services which it covers.'

Chapter 13

TRADE MARKS AND EUROPEAN UNION LAW

INTRODUCTION

13.1 Trade mark law, like other areas of intellectual property law,[1] has been influenced profoundly by the European Union (EU). A programme of intellectual property measures designed to hasten the single market in the wake of the Single European Act[2] was based on the premise that disparities in national laws impeded the free movement of goods and services.[3] Free movement is one of the cornerstones of the EC Treaty, now revised and renamed the Treaty on the Functioning of the European Union (TFEU) by the Lisbon Treaty.[4] The free movement principle[5] has been held to affect the exercise of trade mark rights,[6] along with competition laws governing restrictive practices[7] and abuses of dominant position.[8]

13.2 In 1980 proposals for a Trade Mark Harmonisation Directive were published[9] and considered subsequently by the Economic and Social Committee and the European Parliament.[10] After further deliberation the

---

[1] For other areas see AEL Brown 'Post Harmonisation Europe – United, Divided or Unimportant?' [2001] IPQ 275; G Tritton *Intellectual Property in Europe* (3rd edn, 2008). Useful tables showing the progress of EU legislation are published monthly in EIPR. The Europa website maintains lists of intellectual property laws and other materials with legal effect which can be accessed from http://ec.europa.eu/internal_market/top_layer/index_52_en. htm by following the links to 'copyright' or 'industrial property'.

[2] For an index and links to treaties see http://europa.eu/abc/treaties/index_en.htm. For commentary, see, eg, J Steiner, L Woods *EU Law* (OUP, 10th edn, 2009); or P Craig, G de Búrca *EU Law* (OUP, 5th edn, 2011).

[3] See Second Recital to the Trade Marks Harmonisation Directive 2008/95/EC and to the Community Trade Mark Regulation (EC) 207/2009.

[4] In 2008, the UK Foreign and Commonwealth Office helpfully published 'A Comparative Table of the Current EC and EU Treaties as Amended by the Treaty Of Lisbon' Cm7311, available at www.official-documents.gov.uk/document/cm73/7311/7311.asp.

[5] And is covered by Arts 34-36 (formerly Arts 28–30 of the EC Treaty, Arts 30–36 of the EEC Treaty) for goods and Art 56 (formerly Art 49 of the EC Treaty, Art 59 of the EEC Treaty) for services.

[6] See P Koutrakos 'In Search of a Common Vocabulary in Free Movement of Goods: The Example of Repackaging Pharmaceuticals' [2003] EL Rev 53; C Stothers *Parallel Trade in Europe: Intellectual Property, Competition and Regulatory Law* (2007).

[7] Article 101 of the TFEU – formerly Art 81 of the EC Treaty, Art 85 of the EEC Treaty.

[8] Article 102 of the TFEU – formerly Art 82 of the EC Treaty, Art86 of the EEC Treaty.

[9] Proposal from the Commission [1980] OJ C351/1; revised proposal at [1985] OJ C351/4.

[10] European Parliament [1983] OJ C307/66 and [1988] OJ C309, 5 December 1988; Economic and Social Committee [1981] OJ (C-310/22).

proposals came to fruition as the First Council Directive ('the Directive').[11] The purpose of the Directive was to 'approximate', that is to say, harmonise the national trade mark laws of the EU member states. Article 16(1) of the Directive required the member states to introduce legislation with the object of fulfilling its specific requirements. A codified version incorporating minor amendments was promulgated in 2008.[12] Many of the Directive's provisions, and hence the equivalent provisions of the Trade Marks Act 1994, have been subject to interpretation by the Court of Justice of the European Union (CJEU, or ECJ) and the Court's rulings have been noted in earlier chapters.

13.3 The Directive was followed in 1994 by the creation of the unitary Community Trade Mark (CTM) system under Community Trade Marks Regulation (EC) 40/94 ('the Regulation') (considered in more detail in Chapter 14). Again, this has been reissued in a codified from as Reg (EC) 207/2009.[13] Despite suggestions that (harmonised) national trade mark laws and systems are now unnecessary,[14] registration statistics suggest that national and Community systems will co-exist for the foreseeable future, not least because linguistic differences between member states render some marks unsuitable for Community-wide use.[15] Linguistic differences may also cause apparent non-uniformity in the application of the harmonised national laws to specific marks in different member states. The European Commission has commissioned a study of the functioning of the European trade mark system,[16] including the relationship between Community and national systems, and in May 2011 indicated its intention to introduce legislation to modernise the system.[17] This will be considered further below; here it may be noted that the Max Planck study states that 'coexistence between the supranational CTM system and the national trade mark systems is one of the basic principles of

---

[11] Trade Marks Harmonisation Directive (EEC) 89/104, promulgated on 21 December 1988. For the significance of preparatory materials for the interpretation of EC legislation, see S Schonberg and K Frick 'Finishing, Refining, Polishing: On the Use of Travaux Preparatoires as an Aid to the Interpretation of Community Legislation' [2003] EL Rev 149.

[12] Directive 2008/95/EC of the European Parliament and of the Council of 22 October 2008 to approximate the laws of the Member States relating to trade marks (Codified version) [2008] OJ L299/25 ('the Directive').

[13] Council Regulation (EC) No 207/2009 of 26 February 2009 on the Community Trade Mark (codified version) [2009] OJ L78/1 ('the Regulation').

[14] H Laddie 'National IP Rights: A Moribund Anachronism in Federal Europe' [2001] EIPR 402. 'But if it be true that it makes sense to have, in substance, the same I.P. diet, what is the justification for splitting it into national helpings?'

[15] Note also that, in the USA, state-level registration or deposit systems for marks still exist alongside the federal system, eg Art 24 of the General Business Law (NY), ch 6–2, General Laws of Rhode Island 1956, etc. Furthermore, some enterprises simply have neither the requirement nor the desire for any protection beyond a national registration.

[16] 'Study on the Overall Functioning of the European Trade Mark System', presented by the Max Planck Institute for Intellectual Property and Competition Law, 8 March 2011, available, with annexes, from http://ec.europa.eu/internal_market/indprop/tm/index_en.htm ('Max Planck Study' hereafter).

[17] Commission Communication of 24 May 2011 COM(2011) 287 final 'A Single Market for Intellectual Property Rights: Boosting creativity and innovation to provide economic growth, high quality jobs and first class products and services in Europe', para 3.2: 'Modernisation of the trade mark system in Europe'.

European trade mark law'.[18] The continued existence of national offices is seen as important for Small and Medium-Sized Enterprises (SMEs); evidence submitted to the study suggests that larger enterprises, especially foreign and multinational ones are abandoning national or BeNeLux offices in favour of the CTM system.[19]

13.4 In addition to the member states, the EU itself is party to the WTO Trade-Related Aspects of Intellectual Property Rights (TRIPs) Agreement.[20] Thus, TRIPs can influence interpretation of Community law and the ECJ/CJEU has jurisdiction to interpret it.[21] However, in proceedings before the CJEU, TRIPs has not been not given direct horizontal effect as between litigants.[22] Other aspects of European law, such as the Convention on Human Rights,[23] and the Charter of Fundamental Rights[24] may also influence the acquisition, enjoyment and enforcement of trade mark rights in the EU.

IMPLEMENTATION OF THE DIRECTIVE AND ENFORCEMENT OF TRADE MARK RIGHTS IN OTHER EU MEMBER STATES

13.5 The Directive governs the definition and registrability of marks, the grounds for refusal of registration, for revocation and invalidity. It also touches upon licensing and sets out exhaustive criteria for infringement. However, the Directive does not purport to affect registry or court procedures, or national rules as to ownership.[25] Likewise, it leaves member states free to recognise rights acquired by use, save where they interact with registered marks and to protect marks by national rules as to unfair competition, civil liability and consumer protection.

---

[18] Ibid Max Planck Study, Part VII – Conclusions, para 43.

[19] Max Planck Study, Part II 'Fact finding' para 1.22.

[20] See www.wto.org/English/docs_e/legal_e/27-trips_01_e.htm and Chapter 15.

[21] *Parfums Christian Dior v Tuk* (joined cases C-300/98 and C-392/98) [2000] ECR I-11307, [2001] ETMR 26, [2001] ECDR 12. The CJEU may also consider whether an envisaged international agreement is compatible with the EU treaties: Art 218 of the TFEU (formerly Art 300 of the EC Treaty).

[22] Case C-53/96 *Hermes* [1998] ECR I-3603; Case C89/99 *Schieving-Nijstad VOF v Groeneveld* [2001] ECR I-5851, [2001] 3 CMLR 44, [2002] ETMR 4, [2002] FSR 22 (provisional measures). See also *Azrak-Hamway* [1997] RPC 134, where the UK IPO declined to give direct effect to TRIPs; T Cottier and KN Schefer 'The relationship between World Trade Organisation law, national and regional law' [1998] JIEL 83.

[23] T Pinto 'The influence of the European Convention on Human Rights on intellectual property rights' [2002] EIPR 209; P Torremans *Intellectual Property and Human Rights* (Wolters Kluwer, 2008).

[24] Charter of Fundamental Rights of the European Union, Art 17(2) states that intellectual property shall be protected. Protocol to the Lisbon Treaty contains a derogation from the Charter for the UK and Poland.

[25] Article 6 of the Directive. Article 245 of the TEFU (formerly Art 295 of the EC Treaty) provides that the Treaty is without prejudice to national systems of property ownership.

13.6   Member states were required to implement the Directive by 31 December 1992. Although many states failed to meet the deadline,[26] each of the pre-Enlargement member states did eventually introduce trade mark legislation which took the Directive into account, although the Max Planck study suggests that 'differences in understanding and practical implementation' have led to divergence.[27] Member states acceding by way of the Enlargement of the EU in May 2004[28] were required to accept and conform to the 'acquis' of pre-existing Community law.[29] The Max Planck report concludes that the optional provisions, which were incorporated into the Trade Marks Act UK, should be made mandatory for all member states.[30] It further recommended the introduction of new provisions to bring national law into line with the Community Trade Mark Regulation in relation to certain proprietary aspects, such as licensing, transfer, rights in rem, levy of execution, insolvency proceedings and the protection of collective marks.[31]

13.7   Thus, in theory, one may expect convergence, assisted in areas of difficulty by decisions of the CJEU.[32] The Court can become seised of trade mark issues by way of reference under Art 267 of the TFEU[33] from national courts and in review of decisions under the Regulation. As noted in Chapter 5, the substantive provisions of the Regulation and Directive are often identical, so a ruling of the CJEU on interpretation of the Directive also serves to clarify the law under the Regulation, and vice versa. A significant stage towards

---

[26]   In the event of failure to implement a directive, the European Commission may bring proceedings against the member state in default before the CJEU. The legitimacy of implementation may also be raised by parties to litigation, as in *Oakley Inc v Animal Ltd and Ors, The Secretary of State for Trade and Industry* [2005] EWCA Civ 1191 CA (Civ Div) (a reference to the ECJ from the High Court – (C-267/05) – was withdrawn and deleted from the ECJ's register of pending cases as of 7 February 2006).

[27]   Max Planck Study, Part III 'Legal analysis', para 1.19 and Part V p 213ff.

[28]   The Accession Treaty for the Czech Republic, Estonia, Cyprus, Latvia, Lithuania, Hungary, Malta, Poland, Slovenia and Slovakia was signed at Athens, 16 April 2003; that for Bulgaria and Romania on 25 April 2005 and for Croatia on 9 December 2011 (subject to referendum and ratifications, Croatia is expected to join the EU on 1 July 2013).

[29]   The OHIM website has useful information on Enlargement and links to key documents: http://ec.europa.eu/enlargement/index_en.htm. See, also, A Folliard-Monguiral, D Rogers 'The Community Trade Mark and Designs System and the Enlargement of the European Union' [2004] EIPR 48. These authors deal in some detail with transitional provisions. The effect of Enlargement on the Community trade mark system is considered in Chapter 14.

[30]   Max Planck Study Part VII 'Conclusions' at para 5.

[31]   At para 8.

[32]   For this reason, Parliament was inclined to follow the wording of the Directive. House of Lords Public Bill Committee, col 11 (13 January 1994).

[33]   Formerly Art 234 of the EC Treaty. In principle the court rules on the interpretation of the Treaty and legislation thereunder, while national courts apply the ruling to the facts. For comment on the blurring of this distinction see C Worth and K Warburton 'ECJ v National Courts: The Division of Powers after Clinique' [1994] 6 EIPR 247. See, also, H Norman 'Perfume, Whisky and Leaping Cats of Prey. A UK Perspective on Three Recent Trade Mark Cases before the European Court of Justice' [1998] EIPR 306 for comment on the 'open-ended nature of the [ECJ]'s pronouncements'. This makes it possible for national courts to apply the guidance in accordance with national notions of, for example, consent to marketing. However, in some cases, the UK courts have applied the rulings reluctantly. See, eg, *Arsenal v Reed* [2003] EWCA Civ 696; *L'Oréal v Bellure* [2010] EWCA Civ 535.

approximation of the trade mark laws of the member states has, therefore, been concluded. The Max Planck study has commented on the vital role of the Court in this process.[34]

13.8 During the process of implementing the Directive, several member states also took the opportunity to amend their civil procedure as it related to trade mark infringement. Thus, new investigative measures to obtain information prior to action and interlocutory injunctions were introduced in Spain.[35] France opened up infringement actions to exclusive licensees and clarified the law relating to temporary injunctions in trade mark cases.[36] Oppositions were introduced in France, and in Germany were postponed until after registration.[37] Italy's reform of civil procedure relating to the preliminary stages of trade mark infringement proceedings was considered to improve matters for trade mark proprietors.[38]

13.9 However, all member states had to reconsider their civil procedure as it relates to enforcement of trade marks and other forms of intellectual property right in the light of the IP Enforcement Directive (EC) 2004/48,[39] by the implementation date of 29 April 2006.[40] At the time of writing the European Commission is engaged in a review of the Enforcement Directive, an exercise somewhat vitiated by failure of many member states to meet the implementation deadline.[41] A directive on aspects of mediation in civil and commercial matters was passed in 2008.[42]

13.10 In the sphere of criminal enforcement of trade marks, further strengthening has also been suggested: in July 2005 the European Commission proposed a Directive and framework Decision[43] to strengthen criminal

---

[34]   At 5.1(1)(a)(2).

[35]   N Jenkins 'Pre-action Proof of Facts and Preliminary Measures under the New Spanish Industrial and Intellectual Property Acts' [1993] 9 EIPR 347. Spain amended its trade mark law in 1988.

[36]   C Le Stanc 'The enforcement of trade mark rights in France' [1994] 8 EIPR 352. France's new trade mark law came into effect in 1992.

[37]   M Fammler 'The new German Act on marks: EC harmonisation and reform' [1995] 1 EIPR 22.

[38]   M Franzosi and G de Sanctis 'Intellectual and industrial property litigation in Italy: a change for the better' [1994] 9 EIPR 392.

[39]   Directive (EC) 2004/48 Of the European Parliament and of the Council of 29 April 2004 on the enforcement of intellectual property rights [2004] OJ L195/16. Note that unfair competition was excluded from the ambit of this instrument.

[40]   Article 20. Implementation in the UK was achieved by the Intellectual Property (Enforcement, etc) Regulations 2006, SI 2006/1028, in force from 29 April 2006.

[41]   Thus giving less experience from tardy member states. See http://ec.europa.eu/internal_market/iprenforcement/directives_en.htm and especially the Commission's report COM(2010) 779 final and SEC(2010) 1589 final.

[42]   Directive 2008/52/EC of 21 May 2008 on certain aspects of mediation in civil and commercial matters.

[43]   Proposal for a European Parliament and Council Directive on criminal measures aimed at ensuring the enforcement of intellectual property rights and Proposal for a Council Framework Decision to strengthen the criminal law framework to combat intellectual property offences, Brussels, 12 July 2005, COM(2005) 276 final.

measures for protection of intellectual property. At the same time, the Summit of the G8 group of countries at Gleneagles[44] also agreed an action to reduce counterfeiting and piracy.[45] The proposed criminal enforcement directive ran into objections from the European Parliament and procedural difficulties connected with the 'pillars' of the EC, which assigned intellectual property and criminal matters to different areas of competence (since dismantled, with transitional provisions, by the Lisbon Treaty). An amended proposal in 2006 likewise did not mature into legislation.[46] The Commission's Communication in 2009 referred to the establishment of an 'Observatory' on counterfeiting and piracy, the need to improve administrative co-operation across Europe and the encouragement of voluntary arrangements between stakeholders.[47] The Commission has observed that the civil enforcement direction is 'the cornerstone of the EU's contribution to the fight against counterfeiting and piracy',[48] but also remarked that it 'continues to believe that Member States need to put in place effective criminal law measures'.[49] The EU has expressed support for the plurilateral Anti-Counterfeiting Trade Agreement (ACTA), Art 23 of which requires criminal measures to be available at least for 'wilful trademark counterfeiting or copyright or related rights piracy on a commercial scale'.[50]

13.11 Although trade mark registration procedures are not affected by the Trade Marks Harmonisation Directive, a parallel development may ultimately lead to a worldwide harmonisation. A diplomatic conference of the World Intellectual Property Organisation (WIPO) concluded a Trademark Law Treaty to this end.[51] Furthermore, the Max Planck study noted that variations in procedure exist as between different national offices. It proposed increased

---

[44] 6–7 July 2005. For a convenient table of existing criminal measures in the UK, see the UK Intellectual Property Office's 'Guide to Offences' at www.ipo.gov.uk/ipenforce/ipenforce-resources/ipenforce-offenceguide.htm.

[45] Reducing IPR Piracy and Counterfeiting through Effective Enforcement; noted at www.ipo.gov.uk/policy-notices-g8.htm.

[46] COM(2006) 168 of 26 April 2006.

[47] 'Enhancing the enforcement of intellectual property rights in the internal market' COM(2009) 467 final.

[48] Commission Communication COM(2008) 465/3 at 5.1; see, also Commission Communication COM (2011) 287 'A Single Market for Intellectual Property Rights – Boosting creativity and innovation to provide economic growth, high quality jobs and first class products and services in Europe' at para 3.5; available at http://ec.europa.eu/internal_market/copyright/docs/ipr_strategy/COM_2011_287_en.pdf.

[49] COM (2008) 465/3 at para 5.1.

[50] As regards support, see http://ec.europa.eu/trade/creating-opportunities/trade-topics/intellectual-property/anti-counterfeiting. For the final text of ACTA, see http://trade.ec.europa.eu/doclib/docs/2011/may/tradoc_147937.pdf. Eight states signed ACTA on 1 October 2011 – United States, Australia, Canada, Korea, Japan, New Zealand, Morocco, and Singapore, but not the EU. On 26 January 2012, the EU and 22 member states signed the treaty; at the time of writing the European Parliament was due to consider the issue in June 2012 before ratification could take place: see www.bbc.co.uk/news/technology-16757142. An idea of the scale of criminal activity in the field of intellectual property in the UK can be gained from the IP Crime Group's annual report for 2010/11, available at www.ipo.gov.uk/ipcreport10.pdf.

[51] WIPO Trademark Law Treaty, adopted at Geneva on 27 October 1994 and Regulations there

co-operation between the Office of Harmonisation in the Internal Market (OHIM) and the national trade mark registries and transfer from OHIM to national registries of a proportion for renewal fees to support their work.

THE LAW MAKING INSTITUTIONS

13.12 At this point, a brief outline of the European Union's law making framework may be helpful.

(a) *The European Commission* is the administrative body which initiates law proposals. It has been chiefly responsible, insofar as intellectual property matters are concerned, for enforcing European competition law. Now, as discussed below, much of this has been devolved to national courts and national competition authorities under Regulation (EC) 1/2003.[52]

(b) *The Council of Ministers* makes law either in the form of Regulations which bind all member states automatically without further implementing measures, or Directives which become binding once national legislation has been passed to implement them. The Council is composed of the relevant ministers from member states, depending upon the legislation proposed, and is assisted by a permanent committee of Heads of Mission and Deputy Heads of Mission (ie member state civil servants acting in a quasi-ambassadorial role) named CoRePer from the French '*Comité des Représentants Permanents*'. CoRePer has numerous sub-committees and working parties of civil servants scrutinising proposed legislation.

(c) *The European Parliament* is a body of directly elected MEPs whose powers have increased from scrutinising and making recommendations on Commission proposals to a more active legislative role;[53] the extent of its legislative power depends upon the legislative procedure concerned.

(d) *The legislative procedure* depends upon which provision of the Treaty empowers the European legislator. The EC Treaty provided for the 'co-operation procedure'[54] under Art 252, which applied to economic and monetary union; and the 'co-decision procedure'[55] under Art 251, which

---

under. See www.wipo.int/treaties/en/ip/tlt. The Treaty has entered into force; the UK acceded on 1 August 1996 and as of December 2011 there were 49 contracting parties. See, further, Chapter 15.

[52] Council Regulation (EC) No 1/2003 of 16 December 2002 on the implementation of the rules on competition laid down in Arts 81 and 82 of the Treaty [2003] OJ L1/1. For the text of Reg 1/2003, implementing Reg (EC) No 773/2004 and related documents, including the 2009 report on the functioning of Reg 1/2003, see http://ec.europa.eu/competition/antitrust/legislation/regulations.html.

[53] Under the 'consultation procedure' used for taxation and similar matters, the European Parliament's views must be considered by the Council but not necessarily followed.

[54] See helpful diagram in TC Vinje 'Harmonising Intellectual Property Laws in the European Union: Past, Present and Future' [1995] EIPR 361.

[55] See diagram in TC Vinje 'Harmonising Intellectual Property Laws in the European Union: Past, Present and Future' [1995] EIPR 361.

gave the European Parliament power to legislate jointly with the Council. This came to be used for internal market legislation and hence trade mark matters. Article 294 of the Lisbon Treaty retains the co-decision procedure (more or less unchanged), applies it to more instances and renames it the 'ordinary legislative procedure'.[56] Procedures involving consultation and assent by the European Parliament are now described as 'special legislative procedures'. Furthermore, the Lisbon Treaty extended the ambit of Qualified Majority Voting with a new system in place from 1 November 2014. Article 118 of the TFEU now provides the legal basis for EU-wide intellectual property rights.

(e)   *The Court:* the Court has two tiers, the lower court being known as the General Court (formerly Court of First Instance or CFI)[57] and the higher court the Court of Justice (CJEU, formerly 'ECJ').[58] The CJEU is the longer-standing and national courts may refer questions of EU law to it for preliminary rulings under Art 267 of the TEFU (formerly Art 234 of the EC Treaty, Art 177 of the EEC Treaty).[59] An Advocate General considers any question referred and provides a written opinion, which is considered in turn by the CJEU prior to making an official ruling. National courts will be bound by the ruling, provided that the CJEU keeps within the limits of its powers.[60] The CFI was created in 1989 to assist the court with the work of hearing appeals from decisions of Community institutions and staff cases. Community trade mark decisions are subject to internal appeals to the OHIM boards of appeal and thence to the General Court and finally to the CJEU.

HARMONISATION IN THEORY AND IN PRACTICE

13.13   The theoretical basis for harmonisation of trade mark laws has now been laid. What still remains, however, is for harmonisation in practice to be reached.[61] It should also be noted that whilst much of the Directive was compulsory in nature, there were optional provisions, for example, as to refusal of an application made in bad faith, whether evidence of acquired

---

[56]   On which, see http://europa.eu/about-eu/basic-information/decision-making/index_en.htm. If the Council and Parliament cannot agree, a 'conciliation' procedure is used: www.europarl. europa.eu/code/about/default_en.htm.

[57]   See link at http://europa.eu/about-eu/institutions-bodies/court-justice/index_en.htm.

[58]   See http://europa.eu/about-eu/institutions-bodies/court-justice/index_en.htm.

[59]   The criteria for referring issues were discussed in *O2 Holdings v Hutchison 3G* [2005] ETMR 62, Ch D.

[60]   *Arsenal v Reed* [2003] EWCA Civ 96; [2003] ETMR 36.

[61]   Eg the UK and Swedish courts found differently when asked to rule on the alleged infringement of the Philips three-headed shaver mark: *Philips Electronics NV v Remington Consumer Products Ltd* [1999] RPC 809, [1999] ETMR 816, CA; *Ide Line AG v Philips Electronics NV* [1997] ETMR 377. Would a Spanish court have held 'Harvard' and 'Jarvard' not to be confusingly similar as the UK Registry held, in view of their being almost phonetically identical in Spanish? [1998] ETMR 178.

distinctiveness after the date of application is admissible[62] and whether to protect a trade mark against use of a sign other than for the purposes of distinguishing goods or services.[63] The Max Planck study has recommended that these be made compulsory. Equally, national registries have remained free to decide whether to examine applications against earlier registrations and applications or whether to put the onus on the owners of earlier registrations or applications to oppose or file invalidity actions. Again, gaining access to information on practice at the local level remains difficult in view of different traditions in publishing decisions and, of course, since national decisions are published in the language of the local court.[64] In order to counteract the problem, OHIM has for a number of years organised biannual symposia for European judges,[65] which contribute to judicial co-operation and understanding. The Max Planck study contains useful information on the practices of the national offices, including the average time to registration, which varies from 2 months to 4–5 years.[66]

13.14 How national trade mark offices in Europe responded to the Directive varied widely. Most modified their examination procedures insofar as they relate to absolute grounds[67] and it is the authors' perception[68] that standards were raised in the Benelux, France, Italy and Portugal, but lowered in Denmark, Germany, Spain and the UK. There is a reluctance by some offices to be persuaded by office decisions taken elsewhere in the Community.[69] Finland, Portugal, Sweden and the UK traditionally refused to accept that surnames were inherently registrable whereas other member states did not adopt such a hard-line approach; however, there has been convergence in this area, prompted by the ECJ.[70] Although the UK Registry has abandoned

---

[62] A number of member states accept use after the application date. OHIM takes it into consideration.

[63] Where use of that sign without due cause takes unfair advantage of, or is detrimental to, the distinctive character or the repute of the trade mark; *Robelco v Robeco* (C-23/01).

[64] Decisions of the CJEU are of course available in all official languages of the EU and local cases considered to be of general interest appear in European Trade Mark Reports (ETMR) in English. OHIM has a database of decisions of the CTM Courts of First Instance designated in the member state, see
http://oami.europa.eu/ows/rw/pages/CTM/caseLaw/judgementsCTMCourtsList.en.do.

[65] For details see http://oami.europa.eu/ows/rw/pages/QPLUS/networks/EJS.en.do.

[66] Part II, para 1.31.

[67] Benelux introduced examination in January 1996.

[68] Most have modified their examination procedures insofar as they relate to absolute grounds and have had to take due note of decisions made in other jurisdictions even if they have chosen not to be influenced by them. The UK has revised progressively most of the 'Examination & Practice' chapter of its historic *Work Manual*.

[69] In the UK they are regarded as persuasive but not binding. See *Trade Marks Registry Work Manual*, ch 6, part 5, citing *Henkel v Deustches Patent und Markenamt* (C-218/01).

[70] Practice on this has been amended in the light of the ECJ's decision in Case C-404/02 *Nichols v Registrar of Trade Marks* [2005] All ER (EC) 1, [2005] ETMR 21, [2005] RPC 12, [2005] 1 WLR 1418. See *Trade Marks Registry Work Manual*, ch 6, part 20.

examination on relative grounds in favour of provision of a search (a practice shared by Denmark), 12 national offices do examine ex-officio on relative grounds.[71]

13.15 It is increasingly to the CJEU which one must turn for interpretation of the harmonised framework of European law. Initially, cases which involved trade marks alone were rarely heard at the ECJ, which concerned itself primarily with issues which impacted on national trade mark rights on account of the provisions in the Treaty relating to the free movement of goods.[72] Now, because of the CJEU's dual role in deciding references on the interpretation of the Directive and appeals from OHIM under the Regulation, it has developed a rich trade mark jurisprudence, which is considered throughout this book under the substantive issues concerned. Brief details of some of the main issues decided to date are given in the next section.

SOME ISSUES IN THE DIRECTIVE AND REGULATION ON WHICH THE ECJ/CJEU HAS COMMENTED

13.16

(a)   The relevant public, in whose eyes marks are assessed, consists of average consumers, reasonably well-informed, observant and circumspect: *Linde/Winward/Rado/DPMA;*[73] *Libertel;*[74] *Postkantoor.*[75]

(b)   Non-traditional signs such as colours and non-visual marks may be registered if, and only if, they can adequately be recorded on the register and they serve to distinguish the applicant's goods from others: *Libertel; Shield;*[76] *Sieckmann;*[77] *Blue & Yellow.*[78]

(c)   In order to be registered validly, shapes must not be objectionable under Art 3(1)(e)/Art 7(1)(e) and must be distinctive: *Philips v Remington; Linde.*

(d)   Slogans may be registered if they perform the distinguishing function, otherwise not: *Have A break;*[79] cf *Das Princip Der Bequemlichkeit.*[80]

---

[71]   Bulgaria, Cyprus, Czech Republic, Estonia, Finland, Greece, Ireland, Malta, Poland, Portugal, Slovakia and Sweden: Max Planck study, Part II, paras 1.42–1.43.

[72]   These issues are considered at **13.17–13.25**.

[73]   Joined cases C53, 54, 55/01; [2003] ECR I-3161.

[74]   *Libertel Groep BV v Benelux-Merkenbureau* (C-104/01) [2003] ETMR 63 (colour orange).

[75]   'Postkantoor' *Koninklijke KPN Nederland NV v Benelux-Merkenbureau* (C-363/99) [2004] ETMR 57.

[76]   *Shield Mark BV v Kist* (C-283/01) [2004] ETMR 33 (sound mark).

[77]   *Sieckmann v Deutsches Patent-und-Markenamt* (C-273/00) [2003] ETMR 37 (olfactory mark).

[78]   *Hiedelberger Bauchemie GmbH's TM Application* (C-49/02) [2004] ETMR 99 (combination of colours).

[79]   (C-353/03) *Société des Produits Nestlé SA v Mars UK Ltd* [2005] 3 CMLR 12, [2005] ETMR 96.

[80]   *Erpo Mobelwerk GmbH v OHIM* (T-138/00) *Das Prinzip der Bequemlichkeit TM* [2002] ETMR 39, [2005] EIPR N30.

(e)   The general standard of distinctiveness is not unduly high but there is no presumption in favour of registration; rather there is a balance with the principle that non-distinctive signs should be free for others to use: *Windsurfing Chiemsee v Boots;*[81] *Doublemint;*[82] *Bravo;*[83] *SAT1;*[84] *New Born Baby.*[85]

(f)   Geographical names are registrable so long as they do not refer to the nature or quality of the goods for which application has been made and if the place has no reputation in the particular goods or services: *Windsurfing Chiemsee.*[86]

(g)   Marks should not be registered if deceptive for the products in question, or significantly offensive or objectionable on public policy grounds: *Postkantoor;*[87] *Fuhrer;*[88] possibly the official euro symbol.[89]

(h)   Marks may be registered for retail services, in which case it is not necessary to specify the services in detail but rather the goods to which those services relate: *Praktiker.*[90]

(i)   For relative grounds of refusal and for assessing infringement, marks should be compared by way of a 'global appreciation' of visual, aural and conceptual aspects of the marks: *Sabel v Puma;*[91] *Lloyd Schuhfabrik.*[92] Additions render marks non-identical if they go to distinctive character: *Arthur et Felicié.*[93]

---

[81]   *Windsurfing Chiemsee v Boots* (C-108/97) [2000] Ch 523; [2000] 2 WLR 205; [1999] ECR I-2779; [1999] ETMR 585.

[82]   (C-191/01 P) *OHIM v Wrigley* [2004] ETMR 9.

[83]   *Merz & Krell v Deutsches Patent-und-Markenamt* (C-517/99) [2002] All ER (EC) 441; [2001] ECR I-6959; [2002] ETMR 21.

[84]   *SatellitenFernsehen GmbH v OHIM* (T-323/00) [2003] ETMR 49.

[85]   *Zapf Creation v OHIM (T-140/00) New Born Baby TM* [2002] ETMR 10.

[86]   C-108/97 and 109/97 [2000] Ch 523; [2000] 2 WLR 205; [1999] ECR I-2779; [1999] ETMR 585. The ECJ also give guidance on how to show that a geographical mark had acquired a distinctive character by virtue of its use. It is interesting to speculate in the light of this decision whether there will be future attempts to bring invalidity proceedings against early acceptances of geographic names by OHIM, e g Registration No 207886 for 'Wimbledon'.

[87]   *Koninlijke KPN Nederland NV v Benelux-Merkenbureau* (C-363/99) [2004] ETMR 57.

[88]   J Phillips and I Simon 'No Marks for Hitler: A Radical Reappraisal of Trade Mark Use and Political Sensitivity' [2004] EIPR 327; CPL van Woensel 'At your Local Store: Legal Means Against Commercial Exploitation of Intolerable Portrayals' [2005] EIPR 37.

[89]   In *Travelex Global and Financial Services Ltd (Formerly Thomas Cook Group Ltd), Interpayment Services Ltd v Commission of the European Communities* [2003] ETMR 90 CFI (5th Chamber) (T-195/00), the claimants sued claiming that in adopting the euro symbol, the Community had adopted a symbol too close to its registered device mark. The action was dismissed by the CFI.

[90]   C-418/02, ECJ, 3 September 2005.

[91]   *Sabèl BV v Puma AG, Rudolph Dassler Sport* (C251–95) [1998] ETMR 1, [1998] RPC 1991.

[92]   *Lloyd Schuhfabrik Meyer & Co GmbH v Klijsen Handel BC* (C-342/97) [1997] ETMR 690.

[93]   *LTJ Diffusion SA v Sadas Vertbaudet SA* (C-291/00) [2003] ETMR 83.

(j)   Where two trade marks are conceptually similar, mere association is not enough to show that there is a likelihood of confusion: in determining whether there is a likelihood of confusion account must be taken of the perception of marks in the mind of the average consumer who does not make a detailed analysis thereon: *Sabel v Puma*.[94] This reasoning was followed in the comparison of 'Lloyd' and 'Loint's' for footwear[95] in which the ECJ advocated making a global assessment and taking all relevant factors into account; making a finding on the basis of aural similarity alone was not sufficient.

(k)   The strength of a mark may make confusion likely over a wider range of products. For example, it is appropriate to take into account inherent distinctive character together with evidence of reputation when assessing whether goods or services are similar and a likelihood of confusion exists: *Canon/Cannon*.[96]

     This was a departure from the UK's hitherto objective analytical approach[97] and has forced the UK to accept that marks which have acquired a reputation will attract enhanced protection.

     The effect of the decisions in *Sabel* and *Canon* has to introduce greater uncertainty into the issue of whether marks are confusingly similar; a new test depending partly on the degree of inherent distinctiveness of the earlier mark and any acquired reputation has been born.

(l)   A trade mark should be protected against unfair advantage or damaging use for similar and dissimilar products alike: *Davidoff v Gofkid*;[98] *Adidas-Salomon v Fitnessworld*.[99]

(m)   An unauthorised party may use another's trade mark in advertising where services provided in connection with the genuine goods are being provided only so long as the reputation of the trade mark is not damaged thereby and no false impression of a trade connection between the unauthorised party and the trade mark owner is given: *BMW v Deenik*.[100]

---

[94] [1998] RPC 1991. It should be noted that the ECJ has not by means of *Sabel and Puma* set out what 'likelihood of confusion' means; it has simply stated what appears to be the obvious, namely that all the circumstances surrounding the case must be taken into account, echoing *Pianotist Co's Application* [1906] 23 RPC 774.

[95] *Lloyd Schuhfabrik*, n 92 above.

[96] *Canon Kabushiki Kaisha v Metro-Goldwyn-Meyer Inc* (C-39/97) [1998] ETMR 366, [1999] RPC 117.

[97] Eg *Treat; British Sugar plc v James Robertson & Sons Ltd* [1997] ETMR 118, [1996] RPC 281.

[98] C-292/00 [2003] ECR I-389, [2002] ETMR 99, [2003] FSR 4.

[99] [2004] FSR 21; [2004] Ch 120; [2004] 2 WLR 1095. Sections 5(3) and 10(3) of the Trade Marks Act 1994 have been amended accordingly.

[100] (C-63/97) [1999] ETMR 339. However, is any unauthorised use of a trade mark inherently capable of damaging its reputation?

(n) Meaning of 'reputation' (Art 5(2)). A mark must be known to a significant proportion of the relevant sector of the public in order to have a reputation.[101]

(o) Internet advertising using the trade mark as keyword renders the advertiser liable if it would be difficult or impossible for the average internet user to ascertain the origin of the goods.[102]

(p) Where the operator of an electronic marketplace participates actively in advertisers' use of trade marks and reasonably well-informed and observant internet users cannot ascertain the commercial origin of the goods, the operator may be liable for infringement as well as the advertiser: *L'Oréal v eBay International.*[103]

(q) The Court's rulings where the mark is used to refer to the trade mark proprietor's goods have created confusion and complexity: *Adam Opel v Autec*;[104] *O2 v Hutchinson.*[105]

(r) These cases and others where the court has used a 'functional' approach to double identity infringement have made such protection less 'absolute': *Arsenal v Reed.*[106]

FREE MOVEMENT AND COMPETITION RULES

13.17 Trade marks do not prevent the marketing or movement of goods or services as such, but the existence of a strong brand may constitute a significant barrier to a newcomer wishing to compete.[107] Trade mark registrations can be renewed indefinitely, so any effect on competition can be long-lasting. It is not surprising therefore, that the ECJ and Commission's earliest judgments were somewhat hostile[108] to the territorially divisive nature of national marks and

---

[101] *General Motors v Yplon* (C-375/97) [1999] ECR I-5421.

[102] *Die BergSpechte Outdoor Reisen und Alpinschule Edi Koblmuller GmbH v Guni* (C-278/08) [2010] ETMR 33.

[103] *L'Oréal SA v eBay International AG* (C-324/09) [2011] ETMR 52; [2011] RPC 27.

[104] *Adam Opel AG v Autec AG* (C-48/05); [2007] ECR I-1017.

[105] *O2 Holdings Ltd v Hutchison 3G UK Ltd* (C-533/06) [2008] ECR I-4231; [2008] 3 CMLR 14 ECJ (1st Chamber). The Max Planck study has recommended clarification of Art 5(1) of the Directive and Art 9(1) of the Regulation: Part VII – Conclusions, para 62 and also that infringment include the ingredient that use is to distinguish goods or services: para 61.

[106] *Arsenal Football Club plc v Reed* (C-206/01) [2003] Ch 454.

[107] It is also thought that so-called 'cluttering' of the Register, whereby unused marks prevent others from registering can have an anti-competitive effect. The cure for this probably lies mainly in procedures for cancellation, but the Max Planck study has recommended abolishing the system whereby marks in up to 3 classes can be registered for a single fee, replacing it wityh a system of fees for each additional class? See para 67, 83–85, rejecting for the moment the possibility of requiring a declaration of use for renewals: para 84.

[108] See J Flynn 'Intellectual Property and Anti-Trust: EC Attitudes' [1992] EIPR 49. For subsequent swings of attitude, see J Phillips 'Pariah, Piranha or Partner? The New View of Intellectual Property in Europe' [1998] IPQ 107.

the exercise of the rights attached to them.[109] However, marks are today recognised as playing an important positive role in a competitive market, in facilitating identification and choice by consumers.[110] The Community trade mark was intended to achieve this without some of the disadvantages of national marks yet the Regulation was a long time coming. Moreover, national trade mark systems will still be required for those marks which are unable to get on to the Community register because of conflict with marks in other states, for marks which are linguistically or otherwise unsuitable as Community marks, and for the benefit of localised trading interests.[111]

13.18 National trade mark rights can, in principle, be used to prevent the movement of goods and services across borders. An injunction prohibiting sales of trade marked goods can be a 'measure' equivalent to a quantitative restriction on imports within the meaning of Art 34 of the Treaty.[112] Trade marks can be used to tie others to restrictive agreements contrary to Art 101 or to practise discrimination (contrary to Art 102 if the trade mark proprietor enjoys a dominant position). The ECJ has had to reconcile the effect of trade mark laws with these principles of the single market. The next sections of this chapter review a number of decisions relevant to trade marks; for a more comprehensive view of EC law in this area the reader is referred to specialist works.[113]

13.19 It is on Art 34[114] which the ECJ has had to rely in its attempt to resolve the dilemma, on the one hand of recognising that national trade mark rights have to be respected and preserved, and, on the other, that there should be a free movement of goods around the EU.[115] The ECJ arrived at the concept of there being a difference between the existence and the exercise of intellectual property rights.[116] It applied the doctrine of 'exhaustion' of trade mark (and

---

[109] Though note Memorandum on the creation of an EEC trade mark *Bulletin of the European Communities*, Supplement 8/96, paras 11–14.

[110] Max Planck study, paras 1.23–1.39. See also V Liakatou, S Maniatis 'Red soles, gas bottles and ethereal market places: competition, context and trade mark law' [2012] EIPR 1, commenting on *Viking Gas A/S v Kosan Gas A/S (formerly BP Gas A/S)* (C-46/10) [2011] ETMR 58 (ECJ (1st Chamber)) and *L'Oréal SA v eBay International AG* (C-324/09) [2011] ETMR 52; [2011] RPC 27.

[111] See **13.13**.

[112] See, e g *Fratelli Graffione v Ditta Fransa* [1997] 1 CMLR 925 ECJ ('Cotonelle'), para 14.

[113] Such as P Roth *Bellamy and Child: European Community Law of Competition* (6th edn, 2007); V Korah *An Introductory Guide to EC Competition Law and Practice* (9th rev edn, 2007); DT Keeling *Intellectual Property Rights in EU Law: Free Movement and Competition Law* (2004); G Tritton *Intellectual Property in Europe* (4th edn, 2011); R Whish *Competition Law* (6th edn, 2008); P Joseph and J Watts 'The Impact of Competition Law on Trade Marks' (2005) 321 ITMA Rev 10.

[114] Formerly Art 28 of the EC Treaty, Art 30 of the EEC Treaty.

[115] There is also a principle of free movement of services which has received less judicial attention; the Treaty language is much less specific than that for goods. See M Andenas (ed) *Services and Free Movement* (2005). However, in *Football Association Premier League Ltd and Others v QC Leisure and Others* (C-403/08) and *Karen Murphy v Media Protection Services Ltd* (C-429/08) (4 October 2011) the CJEU gave an apparently expansive reading of Art 56 of the TFEU.

[116] *Deutsche Grammophon Gmbh v Metro-SB-Grossmarkte GmbH & Co KG* (C-78/70) [1971] ECR 487; this distinction is also used in competition cases (see **13.26ff**).

other intellectual property) rights,[117] whereby the owner of a trade mark shall not be entitled to object to its further use in relation to goods which have been put on the market in the EU by him or with his consent unless there are compelling reasons, such as where the goods or their packaging have undergone detrimental change. This is the extent to which Art 36, which allows for protection of industrial and commercial property, has been permitted to override Art 34 in trade mark cases.[118] Much of the case-law has focused on the issues of consent to marketing and on reasons why goods released onto the EU internal market might be controlled subsequently by a trade mark owner.

13.20 Via a line of cases the ECJ set out that in deciding whether a trade mark proprietor's action is deemed to be contrary to the principle of free movement of goods, regard must also be had to the 'specific subject matter' of a trade mark or its 'essential function', namely 'to guarantee to the owner that he has the exclusive right to use that trade mark for the purpose of putting a product on the market for the first time and therefore to protect him against competitors wishing to take advantage of the status and reputation of the trade mark by selling products bearing it illegally'.[119] The effect of prior case-law on free movement was enshrined in the Directive (Art 7), Regulation (Art 13) and the Trade Marks Act 1994 (s 12): first, a registered trade mark 'shall not entitle the proprietor to prohibit its use in relation to goods which have been put on the market in the Community under that trade mark by the proprietor or with his consent'; this consent may be express or implied.[120] Secondly, this is disapplied in situations where 'there exist legitimate reasons for the proprietor to oppose further commercialization of the goods, especially where the condition of the goods is changed or impaired after they have been put on the market'. More recent ECJ cases involve the interpretation of these provisions in the light of the Treaties, the single market objective and the role of trade marks. Many decisions involve pharmaceuticals,[121] where price differentials between different member states make 'parallel importing' profitable, or luxury goods,

---

[117] N Gross 'Trade Mark Exhaustion: The UK Perspective' [2001] EIPR 224; N Gross 'Trade Mark Exhaustion: The Final Chapter' [2002] EIPR 93.

[118] There may also be conflict between Art 34 and other principles, such as the protection of the environment. See, e g *Der Grune Punkt, EC Commission v Germany* (C-463/01), noted at (2005) EU Focus 157/8 13; *Der Grune Punkt-Duales System Deutschland v Commission* (No 1 – Art 82) T-151/01 [2007] 5 CMLR 4 and (No 2 – Art 81) T-289/01 [2007] 5 CMLR 5.

[119] C-16/74 *Centrafarm BV v Winthrop BV* [1974] ECR 1183; C-192/73 *Hag I (Van Zuylen Frères v Hag AG)* [1974] ECR 731; C-102/77 *Hoffman La Roche & Co AG v Centrafarm Vertriebsgesellschaft Pharmazeutische Erzeugnisse mbH* [1978] ECR 1139; C-3/78 *Centrafarm BV v American Home Products Corporation* [1978] ECR 1823; C-10/89 *Hag II (SA CNL – Sucal v Hag GF AG)* [1990] ECR I-3711; and *Ideal Standard v Ideal-Standard GmbH* [1995] ECR I-2789 [1995] FSR 59.

[120] Zino Davidoff; implied consent can be dispelled by appropriate marking: *Coty Prestige Lancaster Group GmbH v Simex Trading AG* (C-127/09) [2010] ETMR 41; [2010] FSR 875.

[121] L Harrold and N Gross 'Fighting for Pharmaceutical Profits' [2002] EIPR 497.

where again profits are high.[122] These provisions extend not only to the EU, but to the slightly wider European Economic Area (EEA).[123]

13.21   These provisions preclude a trade mark owner from exercising his rights so as to prevent imports from other member states where:

(a)   the imported goods have been placed on the market in the EEA by the trade mark proprietor, a related company[124] or licensee: *Deutsche Grammophon v Metro-Grossmarkte*.[125] Note that the burden of proving this will usually fall on the defendant, with certain exceptions;[126]

(b)   the proprietor has adopted different marks in different member states deliberately to partition the market and the importer substitutes the local mark: *Centrafarm v American Home Products*;[127] *Upjohn v Paranova*;[128]

(c)   the importer repacks the proprietor's products without affecting the quality of the goods or any marks on the product/inner packaging and makes its activities clear to the proprietor and consumers: *Hoffmann-La Roche v Centrafarm*;[129] *Pfizer v Eurimpharm*;[130]

(d)   the importer is obliged[131] to repackage in order to market the product in the country of importation, where the original condition is unaffected, where the importer has stated clearly on the packaging who is the proprietor and repackager, where notice has been given to the proprietor: *Bristol Myers Squibb v Paranova A/S*;[132] *Merck v Paranova*;[133] *Boehringer Ingheim v Swingward*;[134] *Orifarm A/S v Merck Sharp & Dohme*;[135]

---

[122]   However, in *Copad SA v Christian Dior Couture SA* (C-59/08) [2009] ECR I-3421 it was recognised that the luxury aura of goods might be impaired if they were sold outside a selective distribution system.

[123]   This area was created in 1994 by agreement with the European Free Trade Area (EFTA), so that EFTA countries could participate in the internal market without joining the EU: see [1994] OJ L1/3; http://eeas.europa.eu/eea. Switzerland was excepted, so the EEA now consists of EU countries plus Iceland, Liechtenstein and Norway. There is a series of bilateral agreements with Switzerland which allows access between Swiss and EU markets. These now-numerous agreements may be rationalised but at the time of writing could be consulted on the EU's treaty database at http://ec.europa.eu/world/agreements/SimpleSearch.do.

[124]   *Centrafarm v Winthrop* [1974] ECR 1183: [1974] 2 CMLR 480; [1975] FSR 161; it does not matter if goods were manufactured outside the EEA if they have been marketed in the EEA with the trade mark proprietor's consent.

[125]   See above, n 116.

[126]   Eg if there is a real risk of market partitioning: *Van Doren v Lifestyle Sports* (C-244/00) [2003] ECR I-3051; P Turner-Kerr 'Trade Mark Tangles' [2004] EL Rev 345.

[127]   [1978] ECR 1823, [1979] 1 CMLR 326.

[128]   Opinion of Advocate General C-379/97.

[129]   [1978] ECR 1139, [1978] 3 CMLR 217, [1978] FSR 598.

[130]   [1981] ECR 2913, [1982] 1 CMLR 406, [1982] FSR 269.

[131]   For regulatory reasons or possibly to overcome market resistance to other methods of re-labelling, such as 'stickering'.

[132]   [1997] ECR 1-3457.

[133]   [2002] ECR I-3703.

[134]   [2002] ECR I-3759; N Gross 'EU: Trade Marks – Parallel Imports – Repackaging –

(e)   it is necessary to re-brand goods in order to be able to market them in the importing country, if a refusal to allow re-branding would otherwise partition the market: *Upjohn SA v Paranova A/S;*

(f)   note that, where the mark is registered in one member state, the law of another member state which provides penalties for falsely stating that a mark is registered will be of no effect, even if the mark is not registered in the state of import: *Pall v Dallhausen.*[136]

13.22 In the following classes of case, the proprietor may exercise its exclusive rights where:

(a)   the goods in question have not actually been put on the EU market in the sense of being available to consumers: *Peak Holding,*[137] even though similar goods have been marketed in the EU: *Sebago v GB-Unic,*[138] goods are sold on the internet and sourced from outside the EU: *Sony v Nuplayer;*[139] goods have been sold as testers and marked 'not for sale': *Coty v Simex;*[140]

(b)   the goods are repackaged in a way which affects their quality: *Hoffmann-La Roche v Centrafarm;*[141]

(c)   the goods are repackaged in a way which deceives consumers: *Boehringer Sohn v Paranova;*[142]

(d)   different marks were chosen in different states for objectively justifiable reasons *Centrafarm;*[143] *Upjohn v Paranova;*[144]

(d)   the goods were put on the market by someone entirely unconnected with the trade mark proprietor: *Terrapin v Terranova;*[145]

Requirement of Necessity – Requirement of Notice'; N Gross and L Harrold *'Boehringer Ingelheim v Swingward*: Repackaging Revisited' [2003] EIPR 582. Note that a further reference has been made to the ECJ on burden of proof: C-348/04 (as yet undecided).

[135] C-400/09 [2011] ETMR 59 – the actual repackager need not be identified on the packs as long as the person responsible for repackaging is.

[136] C-238/89 [1990] ECR I-4827.

[137] *Peak Holding v Axolin-Elinor* (C-16/03) [2005] All ER (EC) 723, [2005] 1 CMLR 45, [2005] Ch 261, [2005] ETMR 28, [2005] 2 WLR 650 ECJ. The goods in question had been imported and distributed but not sold to the public.

[138] [1999] ECR I-4103.

[139] [2005] EWHC 1522 Ch D.

[140] *Coty Prestige Lancaster Group GmbH v Simex Trading AG* (C-127/09) [2010] ETMR 41; [2010] FSR 875.

[141] See n 129 above.

[142] *CH Boehringer Sohn v Paranova A/S* [2008] ETMR 6.

[143] See n 129 above.

[144] C-379/97, *Pharmacia & Upjohn v Paranova* [1999] ECR I-6927.

[145] [1976] ECR 1039; [1976] 2 CMLR 482.

(e)   ownership of the mark was previously split by expropriation: *CNL-Sucal v Hag*;[146]

(f)   ownership of the mark was previously split due to financial difficulties: *Ideal Standard*;[147]

(g)   use of the trade mark by another party was likely to interfere with the guarantee of origin which the trade mark must carry with it; namely that the original condition of the marked product had not been impaired or altered without the agreement of the trade mark owner and that the reputation of the trade mark had been damaged: *Bristol Myers Squibb v Paranova A/S*;[148] *Fritz Loendersloot v George Ballantine*;[149]

(h)   damage to the reputation of high-quality goods could occur by reason of repackaging or advertising of a lower quality or standard than that put out by the trade mark proprietor: *Parfums Christian Dior v Evora*.[150]

INTERNATIONAL EXHAUSTION

13.23 Although the UK historically did not recognise a doctrine of *international* exhaustion of intellectual property rights,[151] a number of other EU and EFTA countries did. The case-law of the ECJ that was incorporated into Art 7 of the Directive[152] had been applied to prevent proprietors of national trade mark rights relying on them to impede the free movement of goods *within* the EU.[153] The ECJ had held that Art 34 (ex Art 28 of the EC

---

[146]   [1990] 3 CMLR 571; [1991] FSR 99.

[147]   [1995] FSR 59; G Tritton 'Articles 30 to 36 and intellectual property; is the jurisprudence of the ECJ now of an Ideal Standard?' [1994] 10 EIPR 422. If this decision were seen as representing a relaxation in the attitude of the ECJ to the exercise of intellectual property, it might diminish the attractiveness of the Community trade mark. However, Community trade mark filings have shown no sign of abating: see Chapter 14.

[148]   [1997] ECR I-3457, [1998] 1 CMLR 1–15.

[149]   C-349/95 [1997] ECR I-6227. This case concerned parallel trade in alcohol; previously case-law on repackaging and re-labelling had focused on pharmaceutical products.

[150]   C-337/95 [1998] ETMR 26; [1998] 1 CMLR 737 ECJ. This was a step beyond *Hoffmann-La Roche v Centrafarm*, and seemed to indicate that the Court of Justice now accepts that there is damageable property in a mark itself irrespective of alterations to product packaging having a potentially damaging affect. This was an important development.

[151]   *National Phonograph Co of Australia v Walter T Menck* [1911] AC 3376.

[152]   And s 12(2) of the Trade Marks Act 1994. A faithful transposition, according to KA Sorensen 'Reconciling secondary legislation with the Treaty rights of free movement' [2011] ELRev 339, but not one that ousts the general application of Arts 34–36: *Sun Microsystems Inc v M-Tech Data Ltd* [2010] EWCA Civ 997; [2011] 1 CMLR 43; [2010] ETMR 64; [2011] FSR 2.

[153]   See Chapter 8; cases include *Centrapharm v Winthrop* [1974] ECR 1147; [1974] CMLR 480; *Loendersloot (t/a F Loendersloot Internationale Expeditie) v George Ballantine & Son Ltd* (C-349/95) [1997] ECR I-6227; [1998] 1 CMLR 1015; *Sebago & Ancienne Maison Dubois v GB Unic* [1999] 2 CMLR 1317; *Van Doren + Q GmbH v Lifestyle Sports* (C-244/00) [2003] ECR I-3051 (ECJ); *Peak Holding AB v Axolin-Elinor AB* (C-16/03) [2004] ECR I-11313 (ECJ); *Boehringer Ingelheim KG v Swingward Ltd* (C-348/04) [2007] 2 CMLR 52; [2007] ETMR 71;

Treaty) did not apply to goods entering the EU from without its borders[154] and so parallel imports from other parts of the world could be intercepted, if national law so permitted. (Note that it was immaterial whether a product was manufactured outside the EU if it had already been put on the market lawfully within the EU with the consent of the trade mark proprietor; the import of such goods manufactured outside the EC was subject to exhaustion throughout the EU.)[155] It was argued that the Directive did not affect national laws on international, as opposed to internal, exhaustion of rights. This, however, would create inequalities in the market – the status of goods imported from outside the EEA would depend on which state the goods had initially been imported through.

13.24 By its decision in *Silhouette*[156] the ECJ decided that the concept of worldwide exhaustion of rights was incompatible with existing Community law; to have some national rules providing for exhaustion of trade mark rights in goods put on the market outside the EU whilst others did not, would be contrary to the spirit of the internal market. In other words, a uniform interpretation of Art 7 would be applied so that trade mark rights held in the EU can only be exhausted when a product's first marketing occurs within the EU rather than outside it. The Court of Justice has since ruled against 'international exhaustion' in the case of other intellectual property rights.[157] The TRIPs agreement permits WTO members to choose whether to operate a rule of international exhaustion; it has been argued that such a rule is consistent with the aims of the WTO.[158] However, the EFTA court abandoned the principle comparatively recently.[159]

13.25 In cases post-*Silhouette* involving imports from third countries, the presence or absence of consent has proved a crucial factor. Although there is scope for variation in national concepts of consent, these are subject to limits, as demonstrated by the ECJ's decision in *Davidoff*.[160] The ECJ ruled that an intention to renounce trade mark rights must be 'unequivocally demonstrated'.[161] This decision highlights the importance of trade marks to the

---

CH Boehringer Sohn v Paranova A/S [2008] ETMR 6; *Copad SA v Christian Dior Couture SA* (C-59/08) [2009] ECR I-3421; *Orifarm A/S v Merck Sharp & Dohme Corp (formerly Merck & Co Inc)* (C-400/09) [2011] ETMR 59.

[154] *EMI Records Ltd v CBS United Kingdom Ltd* (C-51/75) [1976] ECR 811.

[155] *Phytheron International SA v Jean Bouordon SA* (C-352/95) [1997] ECR I-1729.

[156] *Silhouette v Hartlauer* (C-355/96) [1998] ETMR 539 [1998] FSR 729.

[157] Copyright/neighboouring rights – *Laserdisken ApS v Kulturministeriet* (C-479/04) [2007] 1 CMLR 6; plant variety rights – *Greenstar-Kanzi Europe NV v Hustin & Goossens* (C-140/10) 20 October 2011. Peukert has argued that this is based on presumption in favour of strong protection: 'Intellectual property as an end in itself?' [2011] EIPR 67.

[158] E Bonadio 'Parallel imports in a global market: should a generalised international exhaustion be the next step?' [2011] EIPR 153.

[159] *L'Oréal Norge AS v Per Aarskog AS* [2008] ETMR 60.

[160] *Zino Davidoff SA v A & G Imports Ltd and Levi Strauss & Co and Others v Tesco Stores Ltd and Others, joined cases* C-414/99 to C-416/99 [2002] All ER (EC) 55, [2002] 1 CMLR 1, [2002] Ch 109, [2001] ECR I-8691, [2002] ETMR 9, [2002] RPC 20, [2002] 2 WLR 321, ECJ, 20 November 2001.

[161] At para 45, [2001] ECR I-8695. Such intent was found in *Makro Zelfbedieningsgroothandel CV*

proper working of the internal market and the seriousness of denying the exclusive rights of proprietors. The importance to a trade mark proprietor of being able to control the first sale of trade-marked goods into the EU was re-emphasised by the Court of Justice in *L'Oréal v e-Bay*.[162] This being said, it can be difficult for traders downstream from the importer to distinguish between licensed or non-licensed imports, or indeed, counterfeit products.[163]

ARTICLE 101 – AGREEMENTS AND TRANSACTIONS WHOSE EFFECTS RESTRICT, PREVENT OR DISTORT COMPETITION WITHIN THE COMMON MARKET

13.26　Early decisions were based upon Art 85 of the EEC Treaty (now Art 101 of the TFEU), which prohibits agreements which may affect interstate trade[164] and which have an object or effect deleterious to competition. In *Consten v Grundig*,[165] a trade mark assignment coupled with an exclusive distribution agreement had the effect of partitioning the market between the parties. It was held contrary to (then) Art 85.[166] The court made a distinction between the existence of national rights, which were preserved by the EC Treaty, and their exercise, which was subject to control by EC law.[167] Although this doctrine has since been criticised as illogical[168] and obsolete,[169] the distinction initially proved very potent in enabling the court to rule on the effect of national rights. The UK's competition legislation was reformed along EU lines by the Competition Act 1998; it follows that much of the case-law discussed below is relevant to UK and EU competition law alike. Although the agreement need not be legally binding, it must be reciprocal. Thus in *P Bundesverband der Arzneimittel-Importeure eV (BAI) v Bayer and Commission*[170] it was held that the Commission had not discharged its burden of proof to show that distributors had agreed to Bayer's limiting supply of pharmaceutical products (to discourage exports). However, acquiescence (if

　　　v Diesel SpA (C-324/08) [2009] ECR I-10019, where 'DIESEL' goods made by a sub-licensee could not be restrained by the trade mark proprietor.
[162]　*L'Oréal SA v eBay International AG* (C-324/09) [2011] ETMR 52; [2011] RPC 27.
[163]　See *Torbay Council v Singh (Satnam)* [2000] FSR 158, Div Ct, albeit distinguished and doubted in *R v Rhodes* [2003] FSR 147, CA and overruled in *R v Johnstone (Robert Alexander)* [2003] UKHL 28; [2003] 1 WLR 1736.
[164]　For which now see 2004 Commission Notice 'Guidelines on the effect on trade concept contained in Articles 81 and 82 of the Treaty' [2004] OJ C-101/07.
[165]　[1996] ECR 299.
[166]　See also the trade marks licensing case of *Campari-Milano SpA Agreements, Re* [1978] 2 CMLR 397, [1978] FSR 528, CEC.
[167]　A distinction made in *Deutsche Grammophon v Metro-Grossmarkte* [1971] ECR 487; [1971] CMLR 631.
[168]　CG Miller 'Magill: Time to abandon the "Specific Subject-matter" concept' [1994] 10 EIPR 415.
[169]　G Tritton 'Articles 30 to 36 and intellectual property: is the jurisprudence of ECJ now of an Ideal Standard?' [1994] 10 EIPR.
[170]　Cases C-2/01 and C-3/01 [2004] ECR I-23.

proven) could amount to agreement. A unilateral refusal to supply for this purpose might amount to abuse of dominant position.[171]

13.27 Excessively restrictive repackaging bans[172] and field-of-use restrictions[173] have been found to fall foul of Art 101. It has even been suggested that an agreement to bring trade mark infringement proceedings might in certain circumstances infringe Art 101.[174] Trade mark delimitation agreements which seek to reduce confusion between conflicting marks have also been subjected to scrutiny under Art 101. In *Re the Agreement of Sirdar Ltd*[175] an opposition was settled on the basis that one company would use the marks 'Phildar' and 'Le Fil D'Art' in France, and the other would use 'Sirdar'. It was held that this would prevent cross supplies – supplies of products into the others' territories – and that this agreement should not be exempt from Art 101. Where cross supplies are feasible and confusion prevented by distinguishing means, the agreement will not infringe.[176] Nor will restrictions on the quality of products sold under a trade mark (eg obligations to manufacture to a strict recipe) within the EU or on the right to sell competing products under a different trade mark fall foul of Art 101, so long as the restrictions are nothing more than that.[177] An agreement not to challenge the validity of a trade mark could infringe Art 101, but not an agreement not to challenge ownership as between licensor and licensee.[178] In certain circumstances an agreement whose effect is to restrict activities of an entity *outside* the EU vis-à-vis its relationship with an entity inside the EU can offend Art 101.[179] If, as a matter of the relevant contract law, an objectionable clause may be deleted without affecting the validity of the rest of an agreement, Art 101(2) will only extend to the objectionable term,[180] and not make the whole contract void.

13.28 Formerly, a trade mark owner could apply to the European Commission for exemption of his agreement if he was in doubt about its legality under Art 101.[181] This procedure has now been abolished[182] and jurisdiction under Art 101(3) extended to national courts and competition

---

[171] *Sot Lelos kai Sia EE v GlaxoSmithKline AEVE Farmakeftikon Proionton (formerly Glaxowellcome AEVE)* (C-468/06) [2009] ECR I-3421.

[172] *Bayer Dental* [1992] 4 CMLR 61.

[173] *Bay-O-nox* [1990] 4 CMLR 429.

[174] See S Preece '*Glaxo and Others v Dowelhurst and Swingward* : Litigation and the Scope of Article 81' [2000] ECLR 330.

[175] [1995] 1 CMLR 395.

[176] *Persil* [1978] 1 CMLR 395.

[177] *Campari-Milano SpA Agreements* (Decision 78/253/EEC) [1978] 2 CMLR 397. *Moosehead Breweries Ltd and Whitbread & Co plc's Agreement* [1991] 4 CMLR 391.

[178] *Moosehead* [1991] 4 CMLR 391; [1990] OJ L100/32.

[179] Eg the effective splitting of the use of 'Wilkinson Sword' in *Warner-Lambert Co v Gillette Co* (Cases IV/33.400 and IV/33.486). Decision 93/252/EEC [1993] 5 CMLR 559.

[180] *Chemidus Wavin* [1978] 3 CMLR 514.

[181] By requesting 'negative clearance' and/or exemption under Art 81(3).

[182] In very limited circumstances, where 'Community public interest' is in issue, the Commission may rule: Art 10 of Regulation (EC) 1/2003. Informal guidance may also be sought from the Commission on 'novel or unresolved questions'.

authorities under the so-called 'Modernisation' Regulation (EC) 1/2003.[183] The emphasis is now on self-assessment, with the assistance of Guidelines.[184] The agreement may be exempt in any case if it falls within the 'de minimis' rule which permits agreements considered to be of minor effect when the products concerned reflect a small percentage of the relevant market in the EU in the goods;[185] however, care should be exercised to ensure that no 'hard core' restrictive clauses (relating, e g to market sharing or price fixing) appear in the agreement. For guidance on what is the relevant market the Commission has published a Notice.[186]

13.29 A defendant in trade mark infringement proceedings may plead Art 101 by way of a 'Euro-defence' – that a breach of Art 101 disentitles the claimant to assert their trade mark rights. This argument depends on there being a nexus between the alleged breach of Art 101 and the infringement; if such a nexus is not proven, the defence will fail.[187]

13.30 Several forms of intellectual property licensing are exempted under Art 101(3) by way of the Technology Transfer Block Exemption.[188] Trade mark provisions which are ancillary to such an agreement may be exempt. Likewise the 'Verticals' Block Exemption Regulation[189] and guidelines[190] allow for

---

[183] [2003] OJ L1/1, in force from 1 May 2004 (the date of Enlargement of the Community). See, also, the Commission's procedural Regulation (EC) 773/2004 [2004] OJ L123/18. The UK Office of Fair Trading website has useful pages and a Guideline devoted to competition law under Regulation (EC) 1/2003: see www.oft.gov.uk/OFTwork/publications/publication-categories/guidance/competition-act/oft442.

[184] Commission Guidelines on the application of Art 81(3) of the Treaty, [2004] OJ C-101/97. See J Ratliff 'Major Events and Policy Issues in EC Competition Law, 2003–2004: Part 1' [2005] ICCLR 47; J Kallaugher and A Weitbrecht 'Developments under Articles 81 and 82 EC – The Year 2004 in Review' [2005] ECLR 188.

[185] Commission Notice on agreements of minor importance which do not appreciably restrict competition under Article 81(1) of the Treaty establishing the European Community [2001] OJ C-368/13. In the case of agreements between actual or potential competitors, the agreement will be regarded as de minimis and not having an appreciable effect on competition if the aggregate market share held by the parties does not exceed 10%. In the case of agreements between non-competitors, the market share held by each of the parties is relevant and the threshold is 15% – para 7. The notice also indicates that agreements between SMEs will not have sufficient effect on trade between member states to be caught by Art 101.

[186] Commission Notice on the definition of the relevant market for the purposes of Community competition law [1997] OJ C-372/5. For a summary, see http://europa.eu/legislation_summaries/competition/firms/l26073_en.htm.

[187] *Sportswear v Ghattaura* [2005] EWHC 2087 (Ch) Ch D; appeal allowed on facts but principle confirmed at [2006] EWCA Civ 380; [2007] FSR 2.

[188] Commission Regulation (EC) 772/2004 [2004] OJ L123/11. Guidelines on the application of Art 81 of the EC Treaty to technology transfer agreements were published at [2004] OJ C-101/02. There is a heavy reliance here on market share thresholds; for a criticism of this approach, see Vrins 'Intellectual Property Licensing and Competition Law: Some News from the Front – The Role of Market Power and Double Jeopardy in the EC Commission's New Deal' [2001] EIPR 576.

[189] Commission Regulation 330/2010 of 20 April 2010 on the application of Article 101(3) of the Treaty on the Functioning of the European Union to categories of vertical agreements and concerted practices [2010] OJ L102/1.

[190] Commission Notice 'Guidelines on Vertical Restraints' [2010] OJ C-130/1.

exemption of trade mark licences, but only if ancillary to a distribution arrangement, the licence is downward, directly related to the downstream transaction, and not the 'primary object of the agreement'.[191] Thus the 'verticals' block exemption does not spare 'the pure licence of a trade mark or sign for the purposes of merchandising' from Art 101.[192]

13.31 The Office of Fair Trading (OFT) published draft guidelines on the application of competition law to intellectual property, but these were never promulgated in final form, the OFT preferring for EU guidelines to be followed.[193] This is in conformity with the principle that the Competition Act 1998 should have the same effect in the UK as do Arts 101 and 102 across the EU, but means that guidance is less than complete for trade mark transactions.

ASSIGNMENTS

13.32 A trade mark assignment will be declared void for falling foul of Art 101(1)(c) when its effect is perceived to create market sharing, thereby distorting competition in the EU.[194] Otherwise, case-law has developed to the point where assignments are recognised as not being inherently anti-competitive.

13.33 The ECJ first considered the question of an identical trade mark being assigned to unrelated parties in different member states in its *Sirena v Eda* judgment.[195] Its finding that this was contrary to Art 101 was, however, heavily criticised. A similarly questionable judgment followed in *Hag I*, finding that the integrity of the Common Market could not be split by a mark which had once enjoyed 'common origin'.[196] However, in *EMI*[197] the ECJ overturned its *Sirena* judgment finding that, for Art 101 to apply, the effects of the assignment should exceed those flowing from the mere exercise of national trade mark rights.

13.34 *Sirena*, *EMI* and *Hag I* were considered when the ECJ's primary thinking on trade marks was that they should serve to indicate origin of goods and that, irrespective of the fact that the marks' history had determined their fate (e g expropriation in the case of *Hag*, where there had once been a common origin), that fact needed to be emphasised in order to preserve the integrity of the Common Market. In *Hag II*, the overriding concern was to recognise that a

---

[191] Article 2(3); guideline 31.
[192] Guideline 32.
[193] P Joseph and J Watts 'The Impact of Competition Law on Trade Marks' (2005) 321 ITMA Rev 10.
[194] *IHT Internationale Heiztechnik GmbH v Ideal-Standard GmbH* (C-9/93) [1994] ECR I-2789, [1995] FSR 59.
[195] *Sirena Srl v Eda Srl (*40/70) [1971] ECR 69, [1971] CMLR 260, [1971] CMR 8101, ECJ.
[196] *Hag I.* In this case the ECJ relied on Art 30.
[197] *EMI Records Ltd v CBS UK Ltd* [1976] ECR 811.

trade mark needed to guarantee the quality of goods and that a trade mark owner needed to be able to control that quality.

13.35 In *Ideal Standard*, the ECJ went further, holding that 'national trade mark rights are not only territorial but independent of each other', suggesting that territoriality reigns supreme and is over and above the concept of a Common Market so long as the intention behind an assignment is not to circumvent the principle of free movement of goods.

ARTICLE 102 – ABUSE OF DOMINANT POSITION

13.36 It is not ownership of an intellectual property right such as a trade mark (particularly a very well-known one such as a brand leader) per se which gives rise to an abuse of Art 102, but a rights holder who enjoys a dominant position in the market for a product in a substantial part of the Community must take care to avoid abuse of that position. Market definitions tend to be drawn narrowly.[198] Forms of abuse which may infringe include the limitation of production or markets, discriminatory practices, the imposition of unwanted obligations and refusals to supply or grant access to an essential facility.[199] Although a mere refusal to grant a licence may not infringe,[200] it may do so if accompanied by other forms of abuse[201] or possibly if it prevents the creation of a separate market,[202] or use of a de facto standard.[203] Oppressive use of opposition procedure was held contrary to Art 102 in *BAT v Commission*.[204] The marks were 'Toltecs' and 'Dorcet'.

13.37 Registration of a competitor's trade mark by a company in a dominant position where it is known that the competitor is using the mark might be an

---

[198] Eg *Eurofix and Bauco v Hilti* [1989] 4 CMLR 677; appeal dismissed [1994] 4 CMLR 614, ECJ; see S Topping 'Finally Nailed Down – The Hilti Appeal to the ECJ' [1994] EIPR 543.

[199] *Der Grune Punkt-Duales System Deutschland v Commission* (No 1 – Art 82) T-151/01 [2007] 5 CMLR 4 and (No 2 – Art 81) T-289/01 [2007] 5 CMLR 5. It was held that although the Commission had been right to suggest that charging a licensee for the use of recycling facilities that a proportion of its product did not enter, there was a non-zero benefit to using the 'green dot' mark, which indicated availability of recycling through the licensor's facility. For the business model, see www.tradeangles.fsbusiness.co.uk/articles/green_dot.htm. On essential facilities generally, see *Oscar Bronner v Media Print* [1998] ECR I 7791; [1999] 4 CMLR 112 (access to dominant rival's home delivery service not essential for smaller competitor).

[200] Eg *Volvo v Veng* [1989] 4 CMLR 122, a principle reiterated in the Advocate General's opinion in Magill 'Commission v Radio Telefis Eireann and Others' [1991] 4 CMLR 586; see C Miller, n 168.

[201] Eg *Hilti*, n 198.

[202] Magill, 669, 745.

[203] *IMS Health v NDC Health* (C-418/01) [2004] ECR I-5039 ECJ; E Derclaye 'The IMS Health Decision and the Reconciliation of Copyright and Competition Law' [2004] EL Rev 687; Net Le 'What does "capable of eliminating all competition" mean' [2005] ECLR 6. On the problems of standards and competition law more generally, see G Lea 'Ever decreasing circles? The crisis in standards setting in the wake of *US v Microsoft* ' (2000) YC&ML 166 (cited decision affirmed in part at 253 f 3d 34 (DC Cir, 2001)).

[204] [1985] 2 CMLR 470.

abuse.[205] An agreement by a company not to use its trade mark for a period of 20 years in the face of a larger competitor was held to stifle competition.[206] Acquisition of a substantial shareholding, in a key competitor and subsequent restrictions on the assignee's freedom to advertise goods bearing the mark 'Wilkinson Sword' beyond the EC infringed what was then Art 82.[207]

THE UK COMPETITION ACT 1998

13.38 As mentioned above, the intentions of the UK Competition Act 1998 ('the 1998 Act') are to import the effects of Arts 101 and 102 closely into UK law to act as a deterrent to agreements of an anti-competitive nature and abuses of dominant position. The Office of Fair Trading regulates the 1998 Act's provisions,[208] with the assistance of the Competition Commission[209] and a specialist appeal route to the Competition Appeal Tribunal.[210] The 1998 Act came into effect on 1 March 2000.

ANTI-COUNTERFEITING MEASURES

13.39 The progressive reduction in customs tariffs and barriers and the principles of free movement mean that goods may circulate freely inside the single market. The corollary is that counterfeit products are unlikely to meet with obstacles to movement as brand owners are less able to control the appearance and distribution of their goods. This problem was recognised in *Bristol-Myers Squibb*[211] in which it was considered necessary for a repackager to notify the brand owner of his activities and supply samples so that the brand owner might be better placed to distinguish between parallel imports and counterfeit goods. Although a defendant who relies on free movement may be required to show lawful manufacture and sale in the Internal Market,[212] positive measures to restrain counterfeiting are necessary.[213] Council

---

[205] *OSRAM/AIRAM* (11th Report on Competition Policy) 1981, European Commission, point 97; [1982] 3 CMLR 614.

[206] *Chiquita v Fyffes* (Commission Press release of 4 June 1992).

[207] *Warner-Lambert Co* (see n 179).

[208] Detailed guidance, including OFT 401 'Agreements and concerted practices' (2004); OFT 402 'Abuse of a dominant position' (2004); OFT403 'Market definition' (2004) and OFT1263 'A guide to the OFT's investigation procedures in competition cases' (2011) are available from the website at www.oft.gov.uk.

[209] Which conducts detailed investigations; it is currently separate from the OFT and maintains its own website at www.competition-commission.org.uk.

[210] See www.catribunal.org.uk. The Tribunal also hears actions for damages following on from findings of infringement, under s 47A of the Entrerprise Act 2002.

[211] [1997] ECR I-3457.

[212] *Renault v Thevenoux* [1988] CMLR 686.

[213] Concern over counterfeiting is widespread and long-running: see DP Harvey 'Efforts under GATT, WIPO and other multinational organisations against trade mark counterfeiting' [1993] 12 EIPR 446 and A Clark 'Trade marks and the Relabelling of Goods in the Single Market'; 'Anti-counterfeiting Implications of the *Loendersloot v Ballantine*' [1998] 9 EIPR 328; INTA resolutions of 2005, available at www.inta.org/Advocacy/Pages/MeasurestoCombatTrademarkCounterfeiting.aspx.

Regulation (EC) 1383/2003[214] lays down measures including customs retention upon request or ex officio, to prohibit the release for free circulation of counterfeit and pirated goods.[215] This was implemented in the UK by the Goods Infringing Intellectual Property Rights (Customs) Regulations 2004.[216]

13.40 Goods transiting through the EU without being entered for free circulation present a problem of enforcement. The ECJ has held that a trade mark proprietor cannot under the external transit procedure or the customs warehousing procedure contest the entry into the EU of goods bearing his mark which were originally his, notwithstanding that he had not put them on the market in the EU. However, he could prevent their being offered for sale in the Community.[217] In *Montex v Diesel*, the CJEU interpreted Reg 1383/2003 in combination with Art 5(1) and 5(3) of the Directive to hold that goods could be detained in transit only if circumstances would 'necessarily entail their being put on the market in that Member State of transit'.[218] *Philips and Nokia* confirmed that such goods could not be detained unless they were destined for a European customer, had been advertised to consumers in the European Union, or 'where it is apparent from documents or correspondence concerning the goods that their diversion to European Union consumers is envisaged'.[219]

13.41 These decisions are consonant with the definition of 'counterfeit' in Reg 1383/2003 and the CJEU's 'functional' interpretation of infringement under Art 5(1)(a) of the Directive, which requires the alleged infringement to impinge on the functions of the mark, even where there is identity of marks and goods. The Max Planck study recommended that Reg 1383/2003 be clarified so as to enable counterfeit goods to be caught in transit if their use would infringe in the country of transit and the country of destination[220] but it is thought unlikely that this will be achieved.

13.42 Proposals for criminal enforcement of intellectual property also stem from concern over counterfeiting, see **7.71–7.73** and **13.10**.

---

[214] Council Regulation (EC) 1383/2003 of 22 July 2003 concerning customs action against goods suspected of infringing certain intellectual property rights and the measures to be taken against goods found to have infringed such rights [2003] OJ L196/7 and HM Revenue & Customs website www.hmrc.gov.uk.

[215] See, further, Chapter 7; K Daele 'A New Step in the Fight Against Counterfeit and Pirated Goods at the Borders of the European Union' [2004] EIPR 214; Vrins and Schneider (eds) *Enforcement of Intellectual Property Rights through Border Measures: Law and Practice in the EU* (2006), with updates at www.bordermeasures.com.

[216] SI 2004/1473. See HM Revenue & Customs website for further details: www.hmrc.gov.uk.

[217] *Class International BV v Colgate-Palmolive Company and others* (C-405/03), [2006] Ch 154; [2006] 2 WLR 507; [2005] ECR I-8735; [2006] 1 CMLR 14.

[218] *Montex Holdings Ltd v Diesel SpA* (C-281/05) [2006] ECR I-10881; [2007] ETMR 13.

[219] *Koninklijke Philips Electronics NV v Lucheng Meijing Industrial Company Ltd, & others* and *Nokia Corporation v HMRC*, 1 December 2011, Joined Cases C-446/09 and C-495/09.

[220] Part VII – Conclusions, para 63.

Chapter 14

THE COMMUNITY TRADE MARK

BACKGROUND AND IMPLEMENTATION

14.1 The idea of a single, unitary Community trade mark system was conceived in the 1960s. Preliminary proposals were prepared in 1964[1] and published in 1973,[2] though ensuing legislation was a long time coming. In 1980, proposals for a Community Trade Mark Regulation were published.[3] However, not until the principle of harmonisation was accepted and implemented could the creature in the shape of the present Community trade mark be born.

14.2 On 20 December 1993, the European Council issued Council Regulation (EC) 40/94 ('the Regulation') on the Community trade mark (CTM) which came into force on 15 March 1994. It established a unitary system for registration of marks throughout the European Community and signalled the Commission's objective of preventing trade mark owners partitioning the European market by adopting different trade marks for different countries and, thereby, thwarting the concept of a single market as originally envisaged by the Treaty of Rome.[4] It was replaced by Council Regulation 207/2009 of 26 February 2009 ('the CTMR') which came into force on 13 April 2009 and is supported by Commission Regulation 2868/95 of 13 December 1995 (Implementing Regulation, 'the Rules'), which has been amended from time to time.[5]

14.3 The CTMR is independent of the Trade Marks Harmonisation Directive ('the Directive') and is binding on all EU member states.[6] The Commission

---

[1] By a Trade Mark Working Group convened in 1961. More recently, the Max Planck Institute for Intellectual Property and Competition Law Munich were commissioned to produce a 'Study on the Overall Functioning of the European Trade Mark System', delivered in early 2011 and available at http://ec.europa.eu/internal_market/indprop/docs/tm/20110308_allensbach-study_en.pdf ('Max Planck Study'). Some of its conclusions and recommendations will be noted in this chapter. Adoption of its recommendations to extend harmonisation of national trade mark rights and to bring them even more into line with the Community Trade Mark Regulation – Part VII, paras 5 and 8 – would reduce the differences between Community and national trade mark systems.

[2] By HMSO in unofficial translation. See Memorandum on the creation of an EEC Trade Mark 1976, *Bulletin of the European Communities*, Supplement 8/76, paras 3–6.

[3] In the *Bulletin of the European Communities*, Supplement 5/80.

[4] As in *Centrafarm BV v American Home Products Corporation* Case 3/78 [1978] ECR 1823.

[5] For the Regulation and a codified/annotated version of the Rules, see the Office for Harmonisation in the Internal Market (Trade Marks & Designs) (OHIM) website at http://oami.europa.eu/ows/rw/pages/CTM/legalReferences/regulations.en.do.

[6] Under Art 249 (formerly Art 189) of the EC Treaty, legislation in the form of a regulation

pursued the double objective of harmonising national laws and creating a CTM registration system to a single goal: the convergence of trade mark law throughout Europe under the jurisdictional control of the European Court of Justice (ECJ) which is the ultimate arbiter in Europe of legal dispute whether approached by a national court or a Community Trade Mark Court.[7] As the recitals to the Regulation makes clear, an orderly expansion of the European single market was envisaged. We shall examine how the CTM system dealt with enlargement of the Community at **14.83**.

CO-EXISTENCE, CONVERSION AND SENIORITY – INTRODUCTION

14.4   The CTM system has three distinctive features by which it relates to the registration systems of member states: co-existence, conversion and seniority. These are considered in more detail below. Briefly, *co-existence* of a CTM with national or regional registrations[8] is permitted; this requires specific provisions to ensure that proceedings for infringement of a CTM do not conflict unduly with proceedings relating to equivalent national marks, which may or may not be in common ownership. Secondly, there may be localised prior rights which for some reason have not prevented registration of the Community mark; these may be exercised (subject to acquiescence). On the other hand, if a localised prior right or other ground of objection results in failure of a CTM application, then *conversion* comes into play: the CTM application can be converted into a bundle of national applications for unaffected parts of the Community and keep the same priority date. Lastly, *seniority* is a mechanism whereby earlier national registrations[9] can be tacked onto a later Community application or registration, to be renewed and enforced along with the CTM.

IMPLEMENTATION IN THE UK

14.5   In the UK it was s 52 of the Trade Marks Act 1994 ('the 1994 Act') which empowered the Secretary of State to implement measures so that the Regulation (EC) 40/94 might become operative. In particular, she or he may make provision with respect to:

(a)   applying for CTM registration via the UK Patent Office (now UK Intellectual Property Office or IPO);[10]

---

requires no additional national legislation to implement it since it is directly applicable throughout the member states and, therefore, has uniform effect.

[7]   See, for designation at member state level, **14.64–14.66**.
[8]   Belgium, the Netherlands and Luxembourg ('Benelux') have a regional trade mark system.
[9]   Of the same mark for the same products and in the same ownership.
[10]   Section 52(2)(a). See **14.33–14.42**.

(b) the procedures for determining the invalidity or liability to revocation of the registration of a trade mark from which a CTM claims seniority;[11]

(c) conversion of a CTM;[12]

(d) designation of UK courts to have jurisdiction over CTM matters.[13]

All measures have since been implemented.

14.6 It is to be noted that the effect of the Regulation is to subsist as an alternative system for the registration of trade marks across the member states rather than as a replacement for national law and procedures.

UNITARY NATURE

14.7 The CTM was designed to be an indivisible entity, having equal effect throughout the whole Community.[14] It can be registered,[15] assigned, surrendered or revoked only for the whole Community.[16] This, one of its key attractions, is also a fundamental weakness; registration must be available in all member states in order for the right to be granted, which means effectively that no opposition based on a prior right must succeed, and the owner of a CTM must accept that he cannot in future divide it territorially between assignees.[17] Since its coming into being, it has been accepted universally that use in one member state is sufficient to maintain the unitary right.[18] However, doubt has been cast on this position by the Benelux Office for Intellectual Property

---

[11] Section 52(2)(b). See **14.35–14.39**.

[12] Section 52(2)(c). See **14.51–14.53**.

[13] Section 52(2)(d). See **14.64**.

[14] At January 2012 the Community consisted of Austria, Belgium, Bulgaria, Cyprus (Greek part), Czech Republic, Denmark, Estonia, Finland, France, Germany, Greece, Hungary, Ireland, Italy, Latvia, Lithuania, Luxembourg, Malta, Netherlands, Poland, Portugal, Romania, Slovenia, Slovakia, Spain, Sweden and the UK. Croatia is due to join on 1 July 2013.

[15] At OHIM, in Alicante. OAMI, an alternative frequently seen, is the Spanish acronym for OHIM.

[16] This posed problems when assimilating new EU members into the CTM system. At the second meeting of the OAMI Trade Mark Group on 26 April 1999 (as reported in the INTA Bulletin, 15 May 1999, vol 54, no 10) the President of OHIM stated the Office's priorities in the event of Enlargement as:
(1) Maintenance of the unitary character of the CTM.
(2) Extension of the principles of the CTM to new states whilst respecting their national laws.
(3) The date of accession should be the criterion for implementation of the CTMR.
(4) The present language regime should stay.
See also Pretnar 'Is the Future Enlargement of the European Union an Immediate Issue for the Community Trade Mark System?' [1997] EIPR 185 and reply by Tatham at [1997] EIPR 267.

[17] The acknowledgement of the ECJ in *Ideal Standard* [1995] ECR 1–2789; [1995] FSR 59 that the right to exercise national trade mark rights is by nature territorial means that trade mark owners whose businesses are by nature geographically fragmentary may not regard the CTM as an attractive option.

[18] As set out in the Joint Statements established by the European Commission and European Council in relation to the CTM Regulation and discussed in the Max Planck study, n 1 above.

(BOIP), in the *Onel* case, who decided recently that use in one member state only is insufficient.[19] Although the Hungarian Trade Marks Office has already followed the decision in one case,[20] the decision is otherwise criticised heavily, including by OHIM.[21] Notwithstanding this, it is interesting to speculate as the Community expands its membership whether the ECJ will in the future find it necessary to look to assessing genuine use more by market share in the whole Community than by activity in one jurisdiction.

ACHIEVEMENTS TO DATE

14.8 There is no doubt that the CTM system has been popular and that OHIM in the first years of operation received substantially more applications than was originally anticipated. OHIM's business plan envisaged 15,000 applications in its first year but received 40,000.[22] Its 100,000th application was received in January 1999. Since 1998, the number of applications has grown year on year, save for in 2008 when the figure dropped by just 0.5% over the previous year. In 2011, 105,000 applications were filed (the highest annual figure since the introduction of this system) and by the end of that year 1,030,307 applications had been received in total since 1994 of which 792,000 had been accepted and registered. Naturally, OHIM was overwhelmed by the early popularity of the CTM. One casualty of the volume of applications to process was the suspension of examination of seniority claims.[23]

14.9 In view of the need for a CTM to be available for registration in all member states, it was commonly believed at the outset that the majority of applications would face oppositions. In reality, however, about 24% of applications published in Bulletins 1/97 to 84/98 were opposed.[24] The overall figure fell to just under 20% in the period 2005–09; the majority of oppositions

---

The Study concludes that 'genuine use' should be assessed without regard to political boundaries, so that use in more than one member state should not necessarily be required: Part VII, paras 27–33.

[19] Decision No 2004448 of 15 January 2010, *Leno Merken BV v Hagelbruis Bekeer bv* [2010] ETMR 21. See www.boip.int/pdf/opposition/BBIE_OMEL-ONELenglish.pdf; on appeal the District Court of the Hague referred several questions to the ECJ: decision of 1 February 2011, case 200.057.983/01).

[20] 1 February 2011, No. M0900377. See E Bolton 'Defining Genuine Requirements of an Expanding European Union' at www.wipo.int/edocs/mdocs/modocs/en/wipo_ipr_ge_11_topic3.pdf.

[21] Pending a possible appeal of this decision, OHIM – applying the principle of the unitary character of the CTM – continues to consider that boundaries of Member States should not play a part in assessing genuine use within the EU single market. See Bolton, ibid, at para 8.

[22] See the OHIM website at http://oami.europa.eu/ows/rw/resource/documents/OHIM/statistics/ssc009-statistics_of_community_trade_marks_2011.pdf for statistics.

[23] Communication No 1/97 of the President of the Office of 17 June 1997, OJ No 9/97, p 751. The examination of seniority claims was resumed in May 2000. See **14.35–14.39** for the current situation.

[24] OAMI Trade Mark Group Meeting of 26 April 1999 reported in ECTA OHIM Link Report No 29 of 28 June 1999. This figure was still high compared with the percentage of applications opposed in the UK.

continuing to be settled rather than proceeding to a judgment.[25] Fewer applications than expected were opposed in the early years of the system, it is assumed, because a large percentage of those applications were of a consolidating nature and simply replicated earlier national rights, claiming seniority from them. The CTM system has proved particularly popular with UK applicants but less so with some other EU-based applicants: between 1996 and 2010, US applicants accounted for around 20% of filings, followed by German applicants at 18%; 11% of applications originated from the UK, well ahead of Spain, Italy and France's 7–8% share each and Japan's 2%. In 2011, Germany headed the table of applicants at 18%, forcing the US into second place with 13% which was presumably a reflection of the weak US economy. The number of applications from China has remained at 1% or less.[26]

14.10 In 2006 the first CTMs became due for renewal. In that year 72% of the registrations eligible for renewal were renewed but the proportion has dropped steadily year on year to 52% in 2011. This might reflect difficult economic times, or given that new filings continue to rise, that trade mark owners are rejuvenating their trade mark portfolios.[27] Comparable renewal figures for UK registrations in the period 2006–09 rose year on year from 69% to 95%.[28]

RELATIONSHIP OF THE CTM SYSTEM WITH UK LAW

14.11 The ideal of the CTM registration system eventually replacing the national route to registration may have been present in the minds of some of those who conceived the idea of a unitary system. However, it seems likely that there will always be a co-existence, not least since some marks will not be available for use and registration throughout the member states,[29] and since replacement is a Eurocentric view; other regions in the world do not necessarily wish to incur the cost and risks associated with obtaining CTM registrations.[30]

---

[25] See http://oami.europa.eu/ows/rw/resource/documents/OHIM/statistics/ssc009-statistics_of_community_trade_marks_2011.pdf.

[26] Ibid.

[27] Ibid.

[28] See www.ipo.gov.uk/about-facts0809.pdf. In 2010 the percentage dropped to 86%: www.ipo.gov.uk/about-facts0910.pdf.

[29] See also Joly 'Can the Community Trade Mark Succeed National Trade Marks in the European Union?' *Trademark World* (1997) 101, pp 25–7; the Max Planck Study (n 1 above) envisages that the two systems will continue to exist in parallel, performing 'important complementary functions': Part VII, para 18.

[30] Eg Australia's key trading partner in Europe is the UK. Hence the UK national system remains the most attractive to Australians; between 1996 and 2008 there were 6,200 CTM applications from Australia, averaging 480 per annum. Applications (including additional classes) to the UK from Australian applicants averaged 1,200 a year between 2006 and 2009 inclusive of UK designations via the Madrid Protocol. See www.ipo.gov.uk/about-facts0809.pdf. Figures for 2010 show that the Madrid system was popular with Australian applicants: see www.ipo.gov.uk/about-facts0910.pdf.

14.12   Articles 110 and 111 of the CTMR recognise that notwithstanding the grant of a CTM, the existence of prior national rights may prevent its use throughout the entire Community. Those rights are defined in Arts 8 and 53(2).

14.13   The importance of ensuring compatibility with existing laws led to Art 32 declaring that a CTM application shall be deemed equivalent to a national filing. This enables a CTM application to be used as the basis for a priority claim. The principle manifests itself elsewhere in the shape of the conversion mechanism providing for national applications to be born out of the spent shell of a failed CTM application,[31] and also in infringement being governed by national law.[32]

14.14   The definition of a trade mark, the criteria for registration, duration, renewals, restoration, restrictions on amendment of applications and marks, the rules of comparison for infringement, defences to infringement, arrangements for surrender and the grounds of revocation or invalidity closely parallel those of the Directive and hence of the 1994 Act. Some features specific to the CTM are:

(a)   prior to amendment of the Regulation in 2004[33] there were significant restrictions as to who could apply for a CTM;

(b)   absolute grounds will block registration even if they pertain only in part of the Community;[34]

(c)   bad faith is not mentioned in the absolute grounds for refusal but appears as an absolute ground of invalidity in Art 52;

(d)   earlier trade marks or applications which can block a later Community application comprise[35] CTMs, marks registered in member states or the Benelux, international registrations having effect in a member state or the Community and well-known marks within the meaning of Art *6bis* of the Paris Convention;

(e)   the proprietor of rights acquired by use can oppose a CTM only if his mark is 'of more than mere local significance';[36]

---

[31]   Article 112.

[32]   Article 14 provides for the complementary application of national law, whilst Art 101 determines which is applicable law in litigation, usually that of the member state where the Community Trade Mark Court in question has its seat. Transactions are governed by the national law of the proprietor's member state of seat, domicile or establishment, or if none, Spain: Art 16.

[33]   See **14.22–14.23**.

[34]   Article 7(2).

[35]   Article 8(2).

[36]   Article 8(4); the owner of the local rights will have a defence to infringement in that area under Art 111 and may be able to oppose use of the CTM if national law permits.

(f) an opponent must have standing and may oppose only on relative grounds,[37] but any person may make observations objecting to registration on absolute grounds;[38]

(g) there is a specific provision to restrain the use of CTMs in dictionaries without indicating their trade mark status;[39]

(h) a proprietor may oppose use of a mark registered in the name of his agent or representative;[40]

(i) use in part of the Community will be sufficient to maintain the mark on the register in the event of a non-use attack;[41]

(j) invalidity can be based on a right of personal portrayal;[42]

(k) there is provision for Community collective marks,[43] but not certification marks;[44]

(l) a CTM or application may be converted into one or more national trade mark applications.[45] This is convenient where an application is refused by virtue of a successful opposition based on an earlier national or Benelux registration;

---

[37] Article 41 spells out the classes of prior right owner who are able to oppose.

[38] Article 40.

[39] Article 10.

[40] Article 11.

[41] Article 15 refers merely to 'genuine use in the Community', but the statement for inclusion in the minutes of adoption of the Regulation reads:
'The Council and the Commission consider that use which is genuine within the meaning of Article 15 in one country constitutes genuine use in the Community.'
However, see **14.7** regarding the *Onel* decision.
OHIM refer to 'genuine and effective use' in a single member state at www.oami.eu.int/en/mark/role/raisons.htm.

[42] Article 53.2(b). The possibilities for preventing use by a right to a name, copyright or industrial property right are also listed in Art 53 as grounds of invalidity, but do not appear under relative grounds for refusal. They do not appear to be available for opposition, but only cancellation, which is to be regretted. However, Art 8 was amended by Regulation (EC) 422/2004 to refer to Community law, so that earlier Community rights, such as Community designs, may found opposition as well as validity.

[43] Articles 66–74. By the end of December 2011, 1,151 such applications had been registered. See http://oami.europa.eu/ows/rw/resource/documents/OHIM/statistics/ssc009-statistics_of_community_trade_marks_2011.pdf.

[44] See **12.8**. 'Community guarantee-marks' were included in earlier drafts, see, eg, Art 86 of the proposal published at *Bulletin of the European Communities*, Supplement 5/1980, p 18. It is clear from a statement prepared for inclusion in the minutes of adoption of the Regulation that collective marks are not intended to include certification marks:
'… the Council and Commission consider that a collective mark which is available for use only by members of an association which owns the mark is liable to mislead within the meaning of Article 66(2) [now Art 68(2)] if it gives the impression that it is available for use by anyone who is able to meet certain objective standards.'

[45] Articles 112–14.

(m) there is no equivalent in the Directive to s 10(6) of the 1994 Act on comparative advertising.[46]

THE COMMUNITY TRADE MARKS OFFICE AND MACHINERY

14.15 Council Regulation (EC) 40/94 created a Community Trade Marks Office ('the Office'),[47] which is located in Alicante, Spain. It is an EC body with legal personality,[48] and subject to legal control by the EC Commission[49] where not under the general jurisdiction of the ECJ.[50] The Office has a President, two Vice-Presidents and an administrative board. Its work is carried out[51] by examiners, opposition divisions, an administration of trade marks and a legal division, cancellation divisions and boards of appeal. These carry out their work under Implementing Regulation (EC) 2868/95, as amended,[52] Fees Regulation (EC) 2869/95[53] and Regulation (EC) 216/96 on the rules of procedure of the Boards of Appeal. The Office has published Guidelines to its proceedings, and a Manual of trade marks practice ('OHIM Manual') which are regularly updated on its website.[54] It has a staff of about 700 and an annual income of over €180m.[55]

14.16 The Office publishes the *Community Trade Marks Bulletin*, which advertises CTM applications for opposition purposes and an Official Journal

---

[46] Partly because the UK's attitude to comparative advertising as being acceptable in principle differed from most other European countries' approaches, but also because the European Comparative Advertising Directive was under consideration. This came into force on 26 May 2008 as the Comparative Advertising Directive 2006/114 and repealed the Misleading Advertising Directive 84/450 and also Directive 97/55. The UK implemented 2006/114 as the Business Protection from Misleading Marketing Regulations 2008 (SI 2008/1276) (see **7.54**). Directive (EC) 97/55 was adopted on 6 October 1997 with an implementation date of April 2000. See Fletcher, Fussing and Indraccolo 'Comparisons and Conclusions: Welcome Clarification From the European Court of Justice on the Interpretation of the Comparative Advertising Directive' [2003] EIPR 570.

[47] Article 2. The Office also administers Community Registered Designs, see D Musker, *Community Design Law – Principles and Practice* (2003).

[48] Article 115.

[49] Article 122; the internal market directorate of the Commission has responsibility for OHIM.

[50] The power of the Court to review decisions of the boards of appeal is spelled out in Art 65.

[51] Articles 130–37.

[52] Commission Regulation (EC) 2868/95 of 13 December 1995 implementing the Regulation, amended by Commission Regulation (EC) 782/2004 and Commission Regulation (EC) 1041/2005. A consolidated version is published on the OHIM website: http://oami.europa.eu/en/mark/aspects/reg/reg4094.htm.

[53] As amended by Regulations (EC) 782/2004, (EC) 1041/2005 and (EC) 1687/2005.

[54] See http://oami.europa.eu/ows/rw/pages/CTM/legalReferences/guidelines/OHIMManual.eu.do. Users of the CTM system should take care to use the OHIM Manual rather than the Guidelines as the most up-to-date point of reference.

[55] See http://oami.europa.eu/ows/rw/pages/OHIM/institutional/institutional.eu.do and Decision No ADM-11-26 of 10 May 2011 concerning the internal structure of the Office at http://oami.europa.eu/ows/rw/pages/CTM/legalReferences/decisionsPresident.en.do.

('OJ OHIM') which contains notices and general information on a variety of issues.[56] Other publications and notices appear from time to time.[57]

Legal representation

14.17 Representation before the Office is not mandatory[58] but, where a legal entity is neither domiciled in nor has a real and effective industrial or commercial establishment in the Community, it must be represented before the Office.[59] For entities either domiciled in or having the requisite business establishment an employee may act.[60]

Languages

14.18 The Office works in five languages:[61] English, French, German, Italian and Spanish. Official publications appear in the five languages but each entry in the Register is made in all the EU official languages.[62] The accession of Bulgaria to the EU in 2008 means that the EU now works in three different alphabets.

14.19 An application for registration may be filed in any of the EU official languages, but the applicant must nominate a second language which must be chosen from amongst the five working languages. Where no third party becomes involved in proceedings all communications with the Office are made in the primary chosen language. However, an opposition may be filed in the second language as may subsequent revocation or invalidity action. There is scope for the parties to proceedings to choose any official Office language, subject to the detailed rules contained in Art 119.[63]

14.20 There are occasions when for tactical reasons an applicant may choose to file in a language other than his own. For example, if a UK applicant wanted to ensure that any opposition was conducted in English (perhaps if opposition from a known source was anticipated) he might choose to file his application in, say, Finnish, Finnish not being one of the five working languages. Such tactical language choosing needs approaching with great caution, however,

---

[56] Article 89. The Bulletin is published daily online. See http://oami.europa.eu/ows/rw/pages/ CTM/CTMBulletin.eu.do. The journal has been available online since January 2007. See http://oami.europa.eu/ows/rw/pages/OHIM/OHIMPublications/officialjournal.en.do.

[57] Eg *OAMI News*.

[58] Article 92

[59] Article 92(2).

[60] Article 92(3).

[61] Article 119.

[62] Article 120.

[63] See *Salomon SA v Hubert Schurr GmbH & Co KG* (Decision No 6/1997 of the Opposition Division of 17 December 1997, ruling on opposition No B 2784); the opponent filed its opposition in French without a translation into either German or English (these being the two languages nominated by the applicant) within the prescribed period. OHIM ruled the opposition inadmissible: [1998] OJ OHIM 653.

since all non-contentious communications with the Office (including the registration certificate) would be conducted in Finnish.

14.21 English has so far proved to be the most popular language of applications and oppositions. About 40% of applications filed between 1996 and 2011 claimed English as their first language and over 50% their second.[64] It is believed that most oppositions continue to be filed in English.

OBTAINING A REGISTRATION

Who is entitled to own a registration?

14.22 Article 5 states that: 'Any natural or legal person, including authorities established under public law, may be the proprietor of a Community trade mark.' This is a welcome liberalisation; prior to amending Regulation (EC) 422/2004 there was an elaborate definition, which caused a number of problems. For example, legal entities emanating from the Channel Islands were not entitled to own a CTM,[65] non-Paris Union and non-WTO applicants had to show that their country accorded reciprocal trade mark protection to nationals of all EC member states.[66]

14.23 It is unclear whether Art 3 actually permits entities without legal personality (eg UK partnerships) to own a registration. Article 3 of the Regulation is headed 'Capacity to act' and states:

> 'For the purpose of implementing this Regulation, companies or firms and other legal bodies shall be regarded as legal persons if, under the terms of the law governing them, they have the capacity in their own name to have rights and obligations of all kinds, to make contracts or accomplish other legal acts and to sue and be sued.'

OHIM announced its intention to accept applications from English partnerships.[67] It has been suggested that registration must be applied for in the names of all members of the partnership.[68] However, OHIM follows the UK model of accepting applications in the partnership name and, in the opinion of the writers, this is the correct method of filing, especially in the light of the decision in *Saxon*.[69]

---

[64] See http://oami.europa.eu/ows/rw/resource/documents/OHIM/statistics/ssc009-statistics_of_community_trade_marks_2011.pdf.

[65] Any application filed by such an entity was suspended at OHIM. Jersey amended its laws to extend the protection of CTMs to its territory: Trade Marks (Jersey) Law 2000; and the Regulation was amended by Regulation (EC) 422/2004 of 19 February 2004 to correct this anomaly. It has been possible since 1 June 2006 to re-register a CTM in Guernsey.

[66] Article 5(1)(d), as amended by Council Regulation (EC) 3288/94, and 5(3).

[67] *OAMI News*, 3–1998, at 2–3, cited by Humphreys 'Territoriality in Community Trade Mark Matters: The British Problem' [2000] EIPR 405.

[68] RE Annand and HE Norman, *Guide to the Community Trade Mark* (1998) p 21.

[69] *Saxon TM* [2003] FSR 39. See, also UK Registry's Practice Amendment Notice PAN 2/04 'Trade Marks Owned by Partnerships' at www.ipo.gov.uk/t-pan-204.htm.

Representation

14.24   Although any person may *apply* to register a CTM at OHIM, natural or legal persons not having domicile, their principal place of business or a real and effective industrial or commercial establishment in the Community must appoint a qualified representative[70] to act in all other matters before OHIM.[71] See Art 92 generally for rules in connection with representation, and Art 93 outlining criteria under which OHIM will enter a person on the official list of professional representatives.[72]

What can be registered as a CTM?

14.25   To secure a registration, the following must be present:

(a)   a registrable mark; this in turn presupposes a sign,[73] which:

    (i)   functions as a trade mark;
    (ii)   is capable of being distinctive;
    (iii) can be represented graphically; and
    (iv)   is not prohibited from registration on either absolute or on relative grounds;[74]

(b)   an applicant with a stated name and address and having an authorised representative;

(c)   stated goods and/or services, in a specified class or classes;

(d)   a request for registration is made;

(e)   together with payment of fees.

A representation of the mark must be submitted at the appropriate point in the application form.

14.26   The meaning of 'sign', the emphasis on distinguishing function and so forth are the same as in the Directive; cases on both have been considered in earlier chapters. Some details are given below of practical aspects at OHIM.

14.27   So long as the terms of the CTMR are met an OHIM examiner's function is to assist applicants to obtain registration.[75] This represents a sea

---

[70]   Article 92(2).
[71]   A legal practitioner, qualified in trade mark law in a member state and having a place of business within the Community, or some other professional recognised by OHIM whose name and qualifications appear in a list maintained by OHIM.
[72]   OHIM Manual at Part A, Section 5; discusses professional representation: http://oami.europa. eu/ows/rw/resource/documents/CTM/legalReferences/partasection5_profrep.pdf.
[73]   Article 4. Cf the 1994 Act, s 1(1).
[74]   See Chapter 5.
[75]   OHIM's original Guidelines Concerning Proceedings (Trade Marks and Design) (of the Office

change from the UK Registry's historic approach which championed its position as 'guardian of the Register' and was perceived thereby as reluctant to register.[76] The UK Registry's position has itself changed in recent years (assisted no doubt by 'competition' from Alicante), but appears to have set its registrability standard above that of OHIM; most UK practitioners can by now cite examples of marks refused registration in the UK but which have been accepted by OHIM.[77] Nevertheless, OHIM examiners are reminded that Art 7 'is a European provision and has to be interpreted on the basis of a common European standard. It would be incorrect to apply different standards of distinctiveness, based on different national traditions, or to apply different, that is more lenient or stricter, standards on the breach of public order or morality, depending on the country concerned.'[78]

'Capable of being represented graphically'

14.28   The need for graphic representation of a mark is chiefly to assist others in being able to determine the extent of the right granted, but also to ensure an accurate description of the mark when either OHIM or third parties wish at a later date to locate confusingly similar marks in a search. For refusal of an application on the basis of lack of graphic representation see *Antoni & Alison's Application*[79] and the *Sieckmann* criteria set out in the *Cinnamon Smell* case.[80] DaimlerChrysler's car seat mechanism application for a tactile mark failed to secure a filing date[81] and the Tarzan Yell sound mark application with graphic representation in the form of a sonogram was rejected.[82]

'Capable of distinguishing'

14.29   For UK practitioners used traditionally to a relatively thorough UK Trade Mark Registry Work Manual, OHIM's initial Examination Guidelines

---

for the Harmonisation in the Internal Market) were issued by Decision of the President of the Office on 28 October 1996 and came into force on 1 November 1996 as published in OJ OHIM 9/96 p 1324. The Guidelines have been augmented continually and the most up-to-date version may be inspected on the OHIM website: http://oami.europa.eu/ows/rw/resource/documents/CTM/legalReferences/partb_examination.pdf.

[76]   On merits of such approach, see Davis ' To Protect or Serve? European Trade Mark Law and the Decline of the Public Interest' [2003] EIPR 180.

[77]   Eg one of the authors', CTM Reg No 191833 as against UK TM App No 2108578 Cat's Head device for pet food.

[78]   OHIM Manual, Examination Part B at para 7.1.3. Though note in OHIM BoA Decision R 20/97-1 'X-tra' trade mark that 'even if the competent authorities in one or more Member States, or a fortiori in non-member countries, had held the mark to be sufficiently distinctive, the same findings would not necessarily have been reached by the Examiner at the Office, who must in each case make his own assessment as to the existence of absolute grounds of refusal'.

[79]   *Antoni & Alison's App* (OHIM BoA) [1998] ETMR 460 in which the mark given was 'the vacuum packing of an article of clothing in an envelope of plastic'.

[80]   Case C-273/00 *Ralf Sieckmann v Deutsches Patent-und Markenamt* [2003] ETMR 37; [2003] RPC 38. The Max Planck Study (n 1 above) somewhat delphically recommends that the requirement for graphical representation be deleted from the CTMR but that the level of security provided by *Sieckmann* be retained: Part VII, para 59.

[81]   Decision R 1174/2006-1 *DaimlerChrysler AG*.

[82]   Decision R 0708/2006-4 *Edgar Rice Burroughs Inc*.

were regarded as sparse. However, as practice has evolved, so OHIM has provided more assistance in the form of its Examination Manual, amended periodically and available online.[83] There is now guidance inter alia on the registrability of marks consisting of one or two words, misspellings, slogans, shapes (including UFOs),[84] colours and a recent thorough exposition on state flags and symbols.[85]

14.30 Although OHIM might be forgiven for not wanting to have appeared too dogmatic in its infancy in laying down apparently strict criteria for registrability (after all, it needed to attract applicants and compete not only with established national filing systems but also the Madrid system), the effect of the 'blank sheet of paper' approach adopted made it very difficult for applicants and representatives to know how high the registrability hurdle had been set. This led to many 'testing of the water' applications. Would the UK Registry have followed OHIM's example and accepted *Swiss Formula* in respect, inter alia, of cosmetic and hygiene preparations for registration?[86] It should be noted, however, that OHIM objections to applications based on absolute grounds have remained at 8–10% since the introduction of the CTM.[87]

Absolute grounds for refusal

14.31 In addition to refusing under Art 7 signs which do not conform to the requirements of Art 4, trade marks which are devoid of distinctive character and trade marks which are considered descriptive, or otherwise have some pertinent meaning for the goods or services in question, as outlined in the preceding paragraphs, OHIM will refuse to register:

(a) trade marks which consist of terms customary to the trade,[88] for example, 'Network' for computers;

(b) signs which consist of the shape which results from the nature of the goods themselves (an egg box or a toothbrush) or the shape of goods which is necessary to obtain a technical result (the shape of an electric plug with no stylisation), or the shape of goods which gives substantial value to the goods;[89]

---

[83] The Manual Concerning Proceedings Before the Office for Harmonization in the Internal Market (Trade Marks and Designs) Part B Examination. See http://oami.europa.eu/ows/rw/pages/CTM/legalReferences/guidelines/OHIMManual.en.do. It was last updated in February 2011.

[84] Unidentified filing date-seeking objects. Ibid at para 7.6.2.

[85] Ibid at para 7.8.3.

[86] See Application No 149914. Probably not: the UK Registry would not be persuaded by one of these authors (admittedly under the Trade Marks Act 1938) that the mark was registrable for cosmetics and other goods in Class 3 even after filing substantial evidence of use.

[87] For a list of refused marks, searchable on various criteria, see OHIM's website at http://oami.europa.eu/ows/rw/resource/documents/OHIM/statistics/ssc009-statistics_of_community_trade_marks_2011.pdf.

[88] Article 7(1)(d).

[89] Article 7(1)(e). In the case of giving 'substantial value', does the shape of the product have 'eye

(c)   trade marks which are contrary to public policy or to accepted principles of morality;[90]

(d)   trade marks which are inherently deceptive, for example, as to nature, quality or geographical origin;[91]

(e)   national emblems, flags, armorial bearings, official signs, hallmarks and other symbols of intergovernmental organisations, unless the applicant has permission;[92]

(f)   badges, emblems and escutcheons other than those covered by Art 6*bis* of the Paris Convention and which are of particular public interest, unless the applicant has permission;[93]

(g)   marks for wines or spirits containing a geographical indication which do not have that origin;[94]

(h)   marks which contain or consist of a designation of origin or a geographical indication registered in accordance with Council Regulation (EC) No 510/2006 protecting agricultural products and foodstuffs.[95]

Evidence of use

14.32   Notwithstanding prima facie unregistrability under Arts 7(1)(b), (c) and (d) if the applicant can demonstrate that the trade mark has acquired

---

appeal' such that the consumer purchases it primarily for that reason? It is interesting that OHIM will accept applications to register the shape of food products and perfume or shampoo bottles, despite the fact that it is often the shape which is attractive to a purchaser, especially children, in the case of food products. See Registrations Nos 234476, 297671 and 473983 for three-dimensional shapes of perfume or cosmetics bottles, together with accepted Application No 635706 of Beaute Prestige International for a bottle in the shape of a female figure. See Registrations Nos 324673 and 364083 for three-dimensional chocolate shapes in the name of Kraft Jacobs Suchard SA, together with accepted Application No 609875 of Kellogg Company for a biscuit shape. See OHIM Manual, Examination Part B at para 7.8.2. See Chapter 2 also.

[90]   Article 7(1)(f). OHIM Manual, Examination Part B at para 7.8.1 states only that offensive, blasphemous or racially derogatory matters are unacceptable; marks 'in poor taste' are not disbarred. It is suggested that European society being predominantly liberal and tolerant will facilitate the registration of trade marks which may be disbarred in other jurisdictions. See Case R 495/2005-G *Kenneth (SCREW YOU trade mark)* [2007] ETMR 7 and Case R111/2002-4 *Dick Lexic Ltd (DICK & FANNY trade mark)*. See also *Basic Trademark SA's TM* [2005] RPC 25 (App Person) (the mark in question being 'Jesus').

[91]   Article 7(1)(g). OHIM Manual, Examination Part B at para 7.8.2. In assessing whether customers are deceived or misled OHIM should 'use the criterion of the presumed expectations of an average consumer who is reasonably well informed and reasonably observant and circumspect'. Opinion of Advocate General Jacobs in C-87/97 (*Cambazola*).

[92]   Article 7(1)(h). See Chapter 15.

[93]   Article 7(1)(i).

[94]   Article 7(1)(j).

[95]   Article 7(1)(k).

distinctiveness by virtue of its use, registration will be permitted.[96] OHIM provides only very general comments on the type of evidence which should be submitted, but presentation must be in a format which is acceptable to the relevant national authority (eg statutory declaration or witness statement in the UK)[97] and evidence from independent sources carries particular weight. Further, unlike in the UK, evidence can be filed at the appeal stage,[98] and may be taken into account if pertaining to the period after the application's filing.[99]

THE APPLICATION PROCESS

14.33 Classification of goods and services is made according to the Nice System. The 9th edition came into force on 1 January 2007 and was adopted by OHIM on that day. OHIM developed a listing of goods and services called 'Euronice', which has blossomed into an online resource called EUROCLASS.[100] Where applicants use descriptions of goods or services from the database, they will be accepted by OHIM. Multi-class applications are permitted; the application fee (currently €1050 (€900 if the application is filed electronically[101]) is in respect of an application claiming up to three classes. Each additional class attracts a fee of €150. An optional extra fee of €120 is payable in order to receive the results of national searches. All but 10 jurisdictions have now opted out of the possibility of providing these.[102] OHIM too provides a search report listing earlier CTMs of potential relevance to the application. OHIM permits wide specifications of goods and/or services even where it is clear that the applicant is unlikely to trade in all the claimed goods or provide all the claimed services[103] and considers that the class heading covers

---

[96] Article 7(3). The mark must be distinctive throughout the member state(s) to which the objection applies. Trade marks which consist of or contain English words are at a disadvantage when compared with words of other languages given the knowledge of English throughout the Community. This was illustrated in CFl Case T-435/07 *New Look Ltd v OHIM (NEW LOOK trade mark)* [2008] ECR II-296. There is also a particular difficulty for single colour or three-dimensional trade marks for which evidence may need to be gathered from all member states, or at least from representative regions of the entire Community. This difficulty may worsen as the Community expands. See Case T-28/08 *Mars, Inc v OHIM (BOUNTY trade mark)* [2009] ECR II-106. The Max Planck Study (n 1) recommended the adoption of a less compartmentalised approach: Part VII, para 81.

[97] OHIM Manual, Examination Part B at paras 8.12.1 and 8.12.2. See OHIM circular letter of 15 March 1999 to International Non-Governmental Organisations (eg as reproduced in *CIPA Journal*, May 1999) and OHIM's Practice Note 'Evidence of Use' of 1 March 1999 which appears on its website.

[98] *Baby-Dry* (Case T163/98 of 8 July 1999 on appeal from Case R35/1998–1 of 31 July 1998).

[99] See Case T-365/06 *Compagnie des bateaux mouches v OHIM (BATEAUX MOUCHES trade mark)* [2008] ECR II-00310.

[100] See http://oami.europa.eu/ec2.

[101] Fees and arrangements for their payment were revised as from 1 May 2009. See Commission Regulation (EC) 355/2009 amending previous fee Regulations, available on the OHIM website at http://oami.europa.eu/ows/rw/pages/CTM/feesPayment/listfees.en.do.

[102] Austria, Czech Republic, Denmark, Finland, Greece, Hungary, Lithuania, Poland, Romania and Slovak Republic.

[103] Article 26(1)(c). Filing class headings is permitted; if 'all goods in Class X' are filed OHIM converts this to the class heading. See OHIM Manual, Examination Part B at para 3.3.

all the goods and services which fall under that class.[104] This is unlike UK Registry practice which under the 1994 Act will raise a s 3(6) objection on the basis of alleged lack of bona fides regarding intent to use. Other member states' national offices (e g France and Germany) will allow broad specifications without question.

Claiming of Paris Convention priority

14.34 Articles 29–32 set out the criteria under which priority may be claimed from the earliest application made in a Paris Convention country.[105] An applicant must within 3 months from claiming priority provide details of the application from which priority is claimed to enable OHIM to view it online from the official Trade Marks Registry website. Where this is not available, OHIM will ask for a copy of the application.[106] Priority can also be claimed within 2 months of filing the CTM application.[107]

Claiming seniority

14.35 When the CTM appeared, seniority was a concept new to trade mark law. It is designed to allow the recorded trade mark proprietor to consolidate his European trade mark rights under one unitary CTM. This is further manifestation of the goal of a single territorial market served by a single trade mark rather than a bundle of national rights. The effect of claiming seniority of a national right against a CTM is to backdate it to the original filing date of the national right. In other words, if the proprietor of the existing national right claimed as a seniority allows it to lapse, he shall be deemed to continue to have the same rights as he would have had if the earlier trade mark had continued to be registered.[108]

---

[104] OHIM Manual, Examination Part B at para 3.5. See Chapter 5 at **5.3**. This may contribute to undesirable cluttering of the register, but the Max Planck Study recommended that all offices should accept generic terms, including Nice class headings, unless there are members of the class which do not properly correspond: Part VII, paras 66–67.

[105] See Chapter 5 for comment on the UK position. Practice at OHIM is explained in the OHIM Manual, Examination Part B at Section 4. The 'Allensbach' survey underlying the Max Planck Study (n 1) showed strong support for more rigorous examination of priority claims by OHIM, but the Study recommended no change: Part VII, paras 68–89.

[106] A certified copy is not needed. See Decision No EX-05-5 of 1 June 2005 of the President concerning the evidence to be provided when claiming priority or seniority at http://oami.europa.eu/en/office/aspects/pdf/EX-05%20ATMDD.pdf.

[107] Rule 6(2) of the Implementing Regulation.

[108] Regulation (EC) 40/94, Arts 34 and 35. See Debrett Lyons 'Community Trade Marks Office: Trade marks – seniority and security of claims: Pts 1 and 2' [1996] EIPR D311 and D339; ECTA Special Newsletter No 30, May 1996, 'Seniority'. The Max Planck Study (n 1) considered that the possibility of claiming the right at any time as well as non-identity of national and CTM registrations might explain low use of seniority claims; the Study recommended dropping the requirement to relinquish the corresponding national rights: Part VII, paras 35–38.

14.36 Seniority may be claimed either when applying to register a CTM (or within 2 months thereof)[109] or at any point after registration. OHIM requires factual information about the earlier trade mark such as its registered date, number and specification of goods, when the claim to seniority is made and proceeds as for priority claims see **14.34** insofar as documentary proof is concerned.[110] Partial seniority can be claimed, for example, when the specification of the registered mark and the new CTM application do not match completely.[111] Details of the relevant registration must be provided to OHIM within 3 months (extendible) of the date of the claim.[112] Seniority may be claimed only from a registered mark and registered status must have been achieved when the claim is made.[113] Seniority may not be claimed from a CTM.

14.37 In view of the important provision that a national right which forms the basis of a seniority claim can be relinquished, OHIM is careful to check for so-called 'triple identity', namely same proprietor,[114] same mark[115] and same goods, or services.

14.38 Upon conversion of a CTM (see **14.50** and **14.52**), a national right which is born out of the failed CTM will in its own country benefit from the seniority claim,[116] though it is questionable whether conversion would be requested by an applicant for a CTM in a country where he had an earlier identical right already registered.

14.39 Whether a consensus is reached by trade mark proprietors that it is always safe to relinquish national rights and rely on their continuation via the seniority mechanism under a CTM remains to be seen. The full impact of removal from a national register of a registered right is not yet clear; for example, the owner of a former national right in a member state which examines on relative grounds will be dependent on the Registry locating the relevant CTM right with a seniority claim attached should the Registry be faced with a third party application for a confusingly similar mark. In the

---

[109] Rule 8(2) IR; OHIM Manual, Examination Part B at Section 5.

[110] Rule 1(1)(h) IR; ibid, Section 5 at para 5.3.

[111] See Communication No 1/97 of the President of OHIM of 17 June 1997, OJ OHIM 9/97, pp 751–757; OHIM Manual, Examination Part B, Section 5 at para 5.7.

[112] Ibid, Section 5 at para 5.1.

[113] Articles 34(1) and 35(1) and ibid, Section 5 at paras 5.1 and 5.4.

[114] The Austrian and Greek registrations of the 'Viceroy' trade mark were recorded in the name of Brown & Williamson Tobacco Corporation (Export) Ltd and used as bases of seniority claims by Batmark Inc in its CTM application since it had required the rights but had not yet had the proprietorship change effected in Austria and Greece. OHIM accepted, on appeal, that it is actual ownership rather than recorded proprietorship which should be taken into account in a seniority claim. *Batmark Inc's Application* (OHIM BoA) [1998] ETMR 448. However, subsidiaries or associated companies are not considered the same proprietor. See Communication of the President No 2/00 of 25 February 2000: http://oami.europa.eu/en/office/aspects/communications/02-00.htm.

[115] 'Thinkpad' (one word) trade mark was deemed to be the same as 'Think Pad' (two words) in BoA Decision R10/1998–2. However, change of a single letter will destroy identity. Capitalisation or typefaces are not taken into account.

[116] Article 112.

meantime, a CTM application with a relevant seniority claim is a signal to would-be opponents to check the relative positions of the parties prior to opposing.

Making the application: official procedures

14.40   Application for a CTM may be made direct to OHIM (preferably online using e-filing[117] or by fax) or through a national Registry, which will forward it to the Office.[118] OHIM issues a filing acknowledgement (immediately if filed using e-filing), which allocates a provisional filing date and an application number subject to the appropriate fees having been paid. On e-filing, an application number is accorded immediately. So long as the minimum requirements for filing have been met the provisional date becomes the effective filing date.[119]

14.41   OHIM examines the application from a formalities perspective[120] and permits 'deficiencies' or default on payment to be remedied within 2 months (extendable).

14.42   As soon as the application has been accorded a filing date OHIM transmits a copy of it to the national offices which have declared an intention to conduct their own prior right searches against the application.[121] The national offices must send the results of their searches to OHIM within 3 months of receipt of notice of an application.[122] OHIM conducts its own search amongst prior CTMs for the information of the applicant[123] and also notifies the earlier owners of the new application. The quality of the national searches varies from country to country and is particularly lacking in that no goods, services or device mark representations are revealed and the tendency is towards much superfluous, irrelevant and uninformative material.

Publication, opposition and observations

14.43   After transmission of the search results to the applicant,[124] OHIM publishes the application for opposition purposes once it is satisfied that no absolute grounds for refusal exist. OHIM does not during examination raise

---

[117]   Fax number +34 965 131 344. A direct application may also be sent by regular mail, sent via a private delivery service, or handed in personally at OHIM. See OHIM's website for assistance. OHIM encourages e-filing by lowering the filing fee by €150. 80% of applications were filed electronically in 2011. See http://oami.europa.eu/ows/rw/resource/documents/OHIM/statistics/ssc009_statistics_of_community_trade_marks_2011.pdf.

[118]   Article 25. The UK Office levies a charge (currently £15) for handling a CTM filing. See www.ipo.gov.uk/applyctm.pdf. The Max Planck Study (n 1) recommended that this option be retained: Part VII, para 26.

[119]   Article 27; OHIM Manual, Examination Part B, Section 2 at paras 2.1–2.3.

[120]   Article 36.

[121]   Article 38(2).

[122]   Article 38(3).

[123]   Article 38(1).

[124]   Article 38(6).

objections to registration on the basis of earlier rights ('relative grounds') and so it is left to the owners of earlier rights to oppose, if appropriate.

14.44 Within a non-extendable period of 3 months from publication the proprietor of an earlier mark as defined variously in Art 8 may oppose.[125] Alternatively, any party (including those without earlier rights on which to base an opposition) may file observations and explain why OHIM should refuse the application on absolute grounds.[126] An 'observer' does not become party to proceedings, but his observations are sent to the applicant for comment.[127]

14.45 An opposition fee[128] is payable and the opposition must be in writing. OHIM supplies a pro forma opposition form. Opposition may be filed online.[129] The grounds of opposition must be specified.[130] The opposition must be filed in one of the two languages nominated originally by the applicant, which must be one of the five OHIM languages.[131]

14.46 Once the opposition has been found admissible both parties to it are notified of this and informed that the opposition proceedings will commence 2 months after the notification.[132] The opponent is advised about the nature of the information he should submit to OHIM about the earlier rights he claims and a 2-month 'cooling off' period is set.[133] This is extendable up to a total of 24 months if the parties to the opposition make a joint request.[134] This is in order to facilitate friendly settlement, for example, by an applicant amending his specification of goods/services. The requirement for the opponent to substantiate his opposition in evidence is postponed until after the cooling off period expires. Should friendly settlement have not been achieved, the opponent is required to file evidence within 2 months (extendable). OHIM copies the applicant's observations (arguments) to the opponent and invites

---

[125] Article 41. See OHIM Manual, Opposition Part C.
[126] Article 40(1).
[127] Article 40(2).
[128] Currently €350.
[129] See http://oami.europa.eu/ows/rw/pages/QPLUS/forms/electronic/fileOpposition.en.do.
[130] Article 41(3). See Decision No 1/1997 published in OJ OHIM 6/98, p 710 on opposition by Ciba Speciality Chemicals Holdings Inc which was dismissed through failure to specify grounds.
[131] See **14.18–14.21**. Under r 17(1) the opponent can file in any of the 20 languages of the Community so long as a translation is filed within one month of the opposition deadline.
[132] Rule 18(1). Oppositions are considered admissible if all absolute and relative requirements are complied with for at least one of the earlier rights. See Communication No 05/07 of the President of the Office of 12 September 2007 on change of practice in opposition proceedings available at http://oami.europa.eu/en/office/aspects/pdf/co5-07en.pdf.
[133] Rule 19.
[134] Rule 18(1). It cannot be suspended, but it can be terminated (irrevocably) early by one of the parties. See Communication No 01/06 of the President of the Office of 2 February 2006 on extensions of the cooling off period: available at http://oami.europa.eu/en/office/aspects/pdf/co1-06en.pdf.

him to respond[135] within an extendable 2-month period. The applicant is given a further opportunity to comment on any subsequent observations made by the opponent.[136]

14.47 The applicant is entitled to ask the opponent to justify his grounds of opposition by filing evidence to demonstrate that the mark on which he relies in opposition has been in genuine use in respect of the relevant goods or services.[137] It is advised to make the request early in proceedings,[138] it must do so before the applicant files observations in reply to the opposition.[139] Failure on the part of the opponent to comply will cause OHIM to reject the opposition.[140]

Examination of the opposition

14.48 Whilst any party to an opposition may request oral proceedings, OHIM seeks to dissuade these.[141] Otherwise, OHIM takes a decision from written submissions by the parties, notifies the parties and publishes its decision.[142] By December 2011, 52,000 decisions had been handed down.[143] The Opposition Division applies the principles set out by the ECJ in *Sàbel*, *Canon* and *Lloyd* (see **5.41**, **5.43**) when determining confusing similarity and tends to issue decisions framed within a set structure, whilst remaining free to interpret the 'global assessment' and 'all relevant factors' of *Lloyd* at will. This may simply be because every case does have to be assessed on its merits; it is perhaps too tempting to look for trends in an attempt to discern patterns emerging as to how OHIM regards confusing similarity.[144]

Costs

14.49 The losing party in the proceedings shall bear the costs of them[145] but a cost award is not compensatory. Article 85(6) provides for OHIM to fix costs when they are limited to official fees and representation costs. In other circumstances, the losing party may be liable for remuneration for legal advice, travel and subsistence and costs incurred by the winning party essential to the

---

[135] Rule 20(4).

[136] Rule 18(1)(2), 20(2).

[137] Article 42(2). This applies only to marks which have been registered for not less than 5 years (and, bearing in mind *BON MATIN TM* [1989] RPC 537, Ch D; affirming [1988] RPC 553, TMR, it would be safer to assume 'entered in the Register' for UK registrations).

[138] Eg, if it is made after the opponent has completed its filing of observations and evidence.

[139] Rule 22(1).

[140] Article 42(2) and r 22(1). See, eg Decisions Nos 370/1999 and 389/1999 in which both the registered proprietors failed to satisfy OHIM as to use having been made.

[141] Article 77(1).

[142] Tatham and Gevers 'The Opposition Procedure in the Community Trade Mark System' [1998] EIPR 22.

[143] See http://oami.europa.eu/ows/rw/resource/documents/OHIM/statistics/ssc009-statistics_of_community_trade_marks_2011.pdf.

[144] For a current list of Opposition decisions see http://oami.europa.eu/ows/rw/pages/CTM/caselaw/decisionsOffice.en.do and follow the link to Opposition decisions.

[145] Article 85.

proceedings subject to the scale determined in the Implementing Regulation[146] In reality the fixed cost award is the norm.

Registration

14.50   Where an application meets the requirements of the Regulation, where no opposition has been filed or any opposition rejected, the trade mark proceeds to registration.[147] The registration will be for a period of 10 years from date of application and renewals are for further 10-year periods.[148] No proof of use is due at renewal.

CONVERSION

14.51   Given that an application for registration must be available for registration in all member states both in terms of inherent registrability and also having regard to earlier national rights, it was important from the outset that a mechanism be devised whereby the 'all or nothing' nature of the right would not deter would-be applicants. Hence the concept of conversion was born.[149] Where an application to register a CTM is refused, withdrawn, deemed to be withdrawn or ceases to have effect, the applicant or proprietor may request that it be converted into one or more national trade mark applications.[150] 'Ceases to have effect' includes surrender,[151] failure to renew,[152] being declared invalid or being revoked[153] and being renounced as a designation in an International Registration.[154] However, conversion is not permitted if the CTM is revoked for non-use[155] or otherwise prevented from being registered in the relevant member state.[156] Partial conversion is permitted.[157]

14.52   The key benefit of conversion is the retention of the original filing date.[158] A request for conversion must be filed within an unextendable 3-month period from receipt of notification by OHIM of an applicant's right to apply

---

[146]   Article 85(1).

[147]   Article 45.

[148]   Articles 46 and 47. The current renewal fee is €1,500 (€1,350 if requested electronically).

[149]   Olivier and Haman 'Analysis of the Westlife Decision and the Concept of Conversion of a Community Trade Mark Right' [2005] Ent LR 187.

[150]   Article 112. OHIM has published Guidelines to conversion at http://oami.europa.eu/ows/rw/resource/documents/CTM/legalReferences/parte_conversion.pdf. See Tatham 'Conversion and Transformation' in *Trademark World* (1995) 78; Tatham and Gevers 'The Opposition Procedure in the Community Trade Mark System' [1998] EIPR 22.

[151]   Article 50 and Rules 44–47.

[152]   Article 47 and Rule 31(4)(a) or (b) CR.

[153]   Articles 55 and 158.

[154]   Rules 25(1), 27 CR.

[155]   Unless in the relevant member state any use made of the CTM is deemed genuine. Article 112(2)(a).

[156]   Eg on absolute or relative grounds.

[157]   Ie for some goods or services. Article 112(1).

[158]   Article 112(3).

for conversion.[159] A conversion fee[160] is payable to OHIM and national offices can elect to levy standard national application fees.[161] Thereafter, save for the filing date having been determined by OHIM, the converted application in its constituent part or parts assumes the mantle of a national application.

14.53 Where the CTM application resulted from designation of the Community under the Madrid system,[162] it may be converted into a bundle of national applications as already outlined, or into a bundle of Madrid designations under Art 154.

APPEALS

14.54 Each decision of an application examiner, or issued by an official in Opposition, Legal or Cancellation Divisions is open to appeal.[163] A Notice of Appeal must be filed in writing within 2 months of the date of notification of the decision and must be accompanied by the appropriate fee. Rules 48–51 set out OHIM's requirements for appealing. A written statement setting out the grounds of appeal must be filed within 4 months of notification of the decision.[164] The appeal is heard by one of OHIM's boards of appeal which may be referred by one of those boards to the Grand Board of Appeal if the subject matter is considered sufficiently important.[165] Referrals are rare, the most high profile thus far having concerned the three-dimensional Lego brick.[166]

14.55 Further appeal is to the Court of Justice (Court of First Instance) under Art 63.

14.56 Following *Baby-Dry*,[167] OHIM will permit evidence on appeal new to the case and not previously put before an examiner. Though note that it remains at the discretion of the Board of Appeal.[168] New evidence will not be admitted by the Court of First Instance.[169]

INFRINGEMENT

14.57 A CTM registration confers on its owner the right to sue for trade mark infringement. The registered proprietor is entitled to prevent all unauthorised

---

[159] Article 112(4).
[160] Currently €200.
[161] The UK Registry levies the full national fee.
[162] See Chapter 16 and the Regulation, 'Title XIII: International registration of marks' added by Regulation (EC) 1992/2003.
[163] Article 58(1).
[164] Article 60. A pro forma 'Notice of Appeal Form' is available on OHIM's website.
[165] Introduced by Regulation 2082/2004.
[166] Case R 856/2004-G *Lego Juris A/S v Mega Brands Inc.*
[167] Case T-163/98 *Procter & Gamble* [1999] ECR II-2383; [1999] ETMR 767.
[168] Case C-29/05-P *Kaul GmbH v Bayer AG (ARCOL/CARPOL trade marks)* [2007] ETMR 37.
[169] Eg Case T-194/03 Il *Ponte Finanziaria SpA v OHIM (BAINBRIDGE/BRIDGE trade marks)* [2006] ECR II-445.

use of the identical or similar marks in relation to goods or services identical or similar to those registered.[170] Use of the identical or a similar mark for dissimilar goods can be prevented where the mark has a reputation in one country and where the unauthorised use takes unfair advantage of or is detrimental to the distinctive character or repute of the CTM.[171] For a fuller examination of what constitutes trade mark infringement see Chapters 5, 7 and 13. Theoretically, infringement of a CTM should be on a par with infringement of a UK national registration, as harmonised by the Directive with the laws of other member states. Note, however, that Art 14(1) counsels that it is the Regulation and the Regulation alone which governs the effect of a CTM, and that there are some differences between the Regulation and the Directive. Where the Regulation does not provide for an eventuality, Art 14 mandates the complementary application of national law relating to infringement. Which national law will depend upon the conflicts rules, outlined below.

14.58 Acquiring a registration does not convey the right to *use* the mark, the subject of the registration. There is no reminder in the Regulation as in s 2(2) of the 1994 Act that earlier rights may prevent a CTM being put into use. However, the Regulation does not prohibit the exercise of prior rights to oppose use of the Community mark, subject to acquiescence under Art 53.[172]

14.59 Acts which amount to infringement include:

(a) affixing the sign to the goods or to the packing thereof;

(b) offering the goods, putting them on the market or stocking them for these purposes under that sign, or offering or supplying services thereunder;

(c) importing or exporting the goods under that sign;

(d) using the sign on business papers or in advertising.[173]

The extent to which goods held by customs ('goods in transit') might infringe has received recent attention. If the intention is not to release the goods for general circulation in the EU, this is not importing and therefore not infringement.[174] Further, it is a fiction to contend that there is 'use in the course of trade' akin to production of goods in a member state which applies to goods

---

[170] Article 9(1).
[171] Article 9(1)(c).
[172] See **14.76**.
[173] Article 9(2).
[174] Case C-405/03 *Class International BV v SmithKline Beecham plc* [2005] ECR I-8735; [2006] ETMR 12.

seized by customs[175] but EU customs authorities may seize non-Community goods bearing a CTM in transit if there are reasonable grounds to believe that the goods are counterfeit.[176]

14.60 The effective date from which a CTM registration can be used against an infringer is the date of publication of the registration, though 'reasonable compensation' may be claimed for acts committed between publication and registration which would subsequently count as infringement.[177] Further, the court may not decide upon the merits of the case until the registration has been published. This suggests that proceedings may be commenced prior to publication. Whether such action is available will depend upon the attitude of the CTM Court of First Instance, under the principle of complementary application of national law. The Community Trade Mark Regulations 1996[178] did not specifically provide rules on commencement of actions for infringement of CTMs.

14.61 A CTM does not entitle the proprietor to prevent the use in the course of trade of:

(a) someone's own name or address;

(b) indications concerning characteristics of the goods/services;

(c) the mark itself where it is necessary to indicate the intended purpose of a product or service; such as an accessory or spare part.[179]

However, such use must be 'in accordance with honest practices in industrial or commercial matters'.

14.62 Dealing in goods which have been put on the market in the Community under the trade mark by the proprietor or with his consent cannot be prevented by means of a CTM unless the condition of the goods has been changed or impaired after having been first marketed.[180] This concept has become part of CTM law as a result of the 'exhaustion of rights' doctrine.[181]

---

[175] Case C-446/09 *Koninklijke Philips Electronics NV v Lucheng Meijng Industrial Company Ltd, Far East Sourcing Ltd, Röhlig Hong Kong Ltd and Röhlig Belgium NV.*

[176] Case C-495/09 *Nokia Corporation v Her Majesty's Commissioners of Revenue and Customs (fake Nokia goods).*

[177] Article 9(3).

[178] SI 1996/1908.

[179] Article 12. See, further, Chapter 8.

[180] Article 13.

[181] See Chapter 13 for further discussion.

14.63 Further limitations placed on the proprietor of a CTM are that:

(a) where the proprietor has acquiesced for a period of 5 successive years in the use of a later CTM he is prevented from attacking the later right.[182] Acquiescence requires awareness on the part of the proprietor of the later mark having been used;

(b) earlier national rights can provide bases on which to attack the use of a CTM so long as the owner of the earlier national right has not acquiesced for a continuous period of 5 years in the use of the CTM.[183]

Enforcing the CTM

14.64 Article 95 requires the member states to nominate particular national courts to function as Community Trade Mark Courts of First and Second Instance.[184] In England and Wales at first instance these are the High Court, the Patents County Court and certain other county courts with Chancery District Registries; in Scotland the Court of Session (Inner House) and in Northern Ireland, the High Court.[185] The Courts of Appeal of England and Wales and Northern Ireland are designated as appeal courts, along with the Court of Session in Scotland (Outer House). Curiously, the House of Lords (now Supreme Court) was not mentioned; this may be because the Regulation provides only for Courts of First and Second Instance. There is no one central Community Trade Mark Court and so the designated national courts, sitting as Community Trade Mark Courts, have exclusive jurisdiction over infringement actions as well as actions for validity and revocation.[186] Despite harmonisation it is to be assumed that plaintiffs will engage in 'forum shopping' to select legal systems and procedures suited to their particular needs. Readers will need to bear in mind the Brussels Regulation on Jurisdiction and the Enforcement of Judgments in Civil and Commercial Matters when considering jurisdictional issues.[187]

Jurisdiction over infringements as between Community Trade Mark Courts

14.65 Article 97(1)–(3) confers Community-wide[188] jurisdiction to the Community Trade Mark Court of the member state where the defendant has

---

[182] Unless it was made in bad faith. Article 54.

[183] Articles 110 and 111.

[184] These are listed on the OHIM website at http://oami.europa.eu./pdf/mark/ctmcourts.pdf.

[185] The Community Trade Mark (Designation of Community Trade Mark Courts) Regulations 2005, SI 2005/440. See **7.1**.

[186] Article 96. But note that cancellation may also be sought at OHIM under Arts 51–57 of the Regulation – see **14.67–14.70**.

[187] Article 94 of the CTM Regulation refers Regulation (EC) 44/2001 on jurisdiction and the recognition and enforcement of judgments in civil and commercial disputes, known as the Brussels Regulation. This replaced the earlier Brussels Convention. The Brussels Regulation was implemented in the UK by the Civil Jurisdiction and Judgments Order 2001, SI 2001/3929.

[188] Article 98(1).

their domicile or establishment, or if the defendant is not domiciled in the EU, then the plaintiff's domicile or establishment, or failing this Spain, the member state where OHIM has its seat. However, other courts may have jurisdiction if the parties so agree, or if the defendant enters an appearance.[189] Article 97(5) also confers jurisdiction on the court of the state in which infringement has been committed or threatened. In this latter case, however, the court's jurisdiction extends only to local infringements.[190]

Applicable law

14.66 Article 101 provides that the Community Trade Mark Courts shall apply the Regulation, supplementing it with its own national law where necessary, including private international law and procedural law. Note, however, that trade mark transactions may be governed by another law, under Art 16.[191]

REVOCATION AND INVALIDITY

14.67 A CTM can be revoked on the grounds of failure to put into use, continuous non-use, genericism, or acquired deceptiveness.[192] If challenged for non-use, the registered proprietor would need to show genuine rather than token use, but use in a single member state has from the inception of the CTM been believed to be sufficient,[193] as would export use from a member state to a territory outside the Community.[194] Use need not be made by the proprietor; third party use to which the proprietor had consented would be acceptable.[195] Guidance has been handed down from the ECJ in *Ansul*[196] and *La Mer*[197] on what constitutes genuine use.[198] Notwithstanding these cases, it is important to remember that each case must be considered on its own merits and that a de

---

[189] Article 97(4).

[190] Article 98(2).

[191] The member state where the proprietor has his seat, domicile or establishment, failing which, Spain. See, further, **14.77**. Promulgation of Directive 2004/48/EC on the enforcement of intellectual property rights had reduced differences in remedies available in different EU member states.

[192] Article 51. The grounds are the same as for revocation of a national trade mark. See Chapter 9. Continuous non-use is by far the most common ground of attack. For registrations cancelled on the grounds of genericism see Case T-365/06 *Bateaux Mouches v OHIM (BATEAUX MOUCHES trade mark)* [2008] ECR II-00000 and Cancellation Division Decision 1020C 835033 *Osotspa Co Ltd v Red Bull GmbH (STIMULATION trade mark)*.

[193] This is one of the main advantages attaching to the CTM, yet flies in the face of the need for availability for registration in all member states at the outset. See **14.6**.

[194] Article 15(1)(b). Case R 1209/2005-1 *Reno Schuhcentrum GmbH v Payless ShoeSource Worldwide Inc (PAYLESS SHOESOURCE trade mark)*.

[195] Article 15(2).

[196] C-40/01 *Ansul BV v Ajax Brandbeveiliging BV.*

[197] C-259/02 [2004] ECR I-1159.

[198] See also OHIM Manual, Part D Section 2 at para 3.1.2.

minimis rule cannot be laid down.[199] Goods given away free of charge under a sign used as a trade mark for other goods does not constitute genuine use.[200]

14.68 Article 50 allows a proprietor not to use his trade mark when he has 'proper reasons' for non-use.[201] Although no definition of 'proper reasons' is given in the Regulation, it is likely that they will amount to circumstances beyond the control of the trade mark owner.[202] Voluntary suspension of trade for whatever reason would seem unable to save the position, but a government restriction on trade in the goods might provide an acceptable reason for delay in introduction of the mark, waiting for the grant of a product licence for a pharmaceutical product or medicine. Similarly, the European ban on use of a tobacco mark for non-tobacco goods[203] might have prevented a registration being used, but may save it from being attacked. OHIM considers that issues such as insolvency, bankruptcy and temporary stoppage of activities are difficulties which constitute the natural part of running a business.[204]

14.69 An application to revoke a CTM may be made direct to OHIM or within a counterclaim to infringement.[205] The fee is currently €700. Rule 37 sets out what OHIM requires an application for revocation or a declaration of invalidity to contain and r 38 sets out the language requirements. On the face of it the onus of proof in a non-use action lies with the challenger. Article 99 requires the Community Trade Mark Courts to regard the mark as valid unless its validity is questioned. It should be noted that there is no equivalent in the Regulation to s 100 of the 1994 Act which makes clear that it is down to the proprietor to show what use has been made of the mark. Given the apparent impossibility of an applicant for revocation being able to show non-use across the entire Community for a continuous 5-year period, the burden of proof in reality shifts quite easily to the registered proprietor once a challenge is made;[206] compare, for example, the requirement of the owner of an earlier mark to show use when called upon to do so in the course of opposition or invalidity proceedings.[207] Partial revocation is permitted where only some of the goods or services for which the mark is registered are affected by the revocation application. Some official discretion is present in the extent to which

---

[199] Case C-416/04 [2006] ECR I-4237 (VITAFRUIT trade mark).

[200] Case C-495/07 *Silberquelle GmbH v Maselli-Strickmode GmbH (WELLNESS trade mark)* [2009] ECR I–*137*.

[201] Article 51(1)(a). See Chapter 9.

[202] Eg the need to follow a regulatory procedure for the renaming of a pharmaceutical product in Decision R155/2006-1 *Laboratorios Ern SA v Sepracor Inc (LEVENIA trade mark)*. See also CFI T-156/01, GIORGI/GIORGIO AIRE.

[203] See *R ex p British American Tobacco (Investments) Ltd) v Secretary of State for Health* (C-491/01) (2003) All ER (EC) 604, and 'Court Upholds New Tobacco Rules' [2003] EU Focus 113; for earlier commentary on the prohibitive principle, see Maniatis and Kamperman Sanders 'A Quixotic Raid against the Tobacco Mill' [1997] EIPR 237.

[204] OHIM Manual, Cancellation Part D at para 3.1.6. See http://oami.europa.eu/ows/rw/resource/documents/CTM/legalReferences/partd_cancellation_subs_provi.pdf.

[205] Articles 51(1) and 99(3).

[206] Cancellation Division Decision 686C 405555/1 *The Welding Institute v Stockhausen GmbH & Co KG (BARRICADE trade mark)*.

[207] Articles 42(2) and (3). See for comparison, **14.67**.

revocation shall take effect where a trade mark is used for some but not all goods for which the mark is registered. For example, use only on 'socks' may not be sufficient to save the broader registered term 'footwear'.[208] It may depend on whether the particular goods for which use can be shown are identifiable as a distinct subcategory within the broader term.[209]

14.70 If an application for revocation is successful the cancellation will be effective as of the date of application for revocation (unless an earlier date is requested)[210] or the date of the counterclaim.

INVALIDITY

14.71 Unless a CTM's validity is questioned, it shall be treated by the courts as valid. A CTM may be declared invalid either on absolute or relative grounds, or a combination of the two.[211] Essentially, the challenger seeks a declaration of invalidity, namely that the mark should never have been registered. The consequence of a successful attack is that the CTM is deemed never to have existed.[212]

14.72 An application can be made either direct to OHIM or on the basis of a counterclaim to infringement proceedings.[213] The fee is currently €700.

Absolute grounds

14.73 A registration will be declared invalid if the proprietor was not entitled to registration under Art 5, if at the time of registration absolute grounds for refusal under Art 7 existed.[214] The shape of the Lego brick[215] was determined by the need to obtain a technical result. OZARK trade mark survived an attempt to invalidate it notwithstanding that it was a place name in the US; the place name was remote and unlikely to be recognised as such by Europeans.[216] Similarly, WIMBLEDON's recognition as the identifier of a tennis championship outweighed its geographical significance.[217] A crown device registration was deemed invalid since it did not have permission from the

---

[208] Use for 'bath salts' and 'bath gels' saved the registration for 'soaps' in Cancellation Division Decision 712C 141366/1 *Out of the Blue KG v Kamsut Inc (KAMA SUTRA trade mark)*.

[209] Case T-126/03 *Reckitt Benckiser (España) SL v OHIM (ALADDIN/ALADIN trade marks)* [2005] ECR II-2861; [2006] ETMR 50 at paras 45 and 46 and applied in Case T-256/04 *Mundipharma v OHIM RESPICUR trade mark* [2007] ECR II-449.

[210] Article 55(1).

[211] An application based on one of these grounds may not be amended to introduce the other. See case R 252/2006-I *Telesis Entwicklungs-und Management GmbH v Telesis Communications France Sarl (TELESIS trade mark)*.

[212] Article 55.

[213] As with revocation actions, rr 37–41 outline procedures.

[214] Article 52(1)(a).

[215] Article 7(1)(e)(i). Case C-48/09 P *Lego Juris A/S v OHIM* [2010] ETMR 63.

[216] Case 135C 966044/1 *Wal-Mart Stores Inc v Ozark London Ltd (OZARK trade mark)*.

[217] Cases 621 207886/1 and 638C 207866/2 *Think Promotions Ltd, David Heller v All England Lawn Tennis Club (Wimbledon) Ltd (WIMBLEDON trade mark)* [2006] ETMR 36.

Danish Royal Family to be registered.[218] Acquiring distinctiveness notwithstanding a fatal flaw at the time of application will, however, save the registration.[219]

14.74 A registration may also be declared invalid where the application was made in bad faith.[220] This may be shown by behaviour falling short of acceptable commercial standards, or dishonesty.[221] The intentions, honest or otherwise, were considered in *East Side Mario's*.[222] Unlike a UK trade mark application which requires the applicant to have a bona fide intention that he should use the mark[223] a CTM does not. Hence a CTM with a broad specification of goods or services will not be invalidated simply because the applicant did not intend to use this mark as widely as claimed.[224] A successful applicant for invalidity will need to show dishonest intent or some other 'similar motive' on the part of the trade mark proprietor to stand a chance of invalidating a registration.[225]

Relative grounds

14.75 A registration will be declared invalid where an earlier trade mark or right existed at the time of registration, such as outlined in Art 8(2), (3) and (4). 'Any other earlier right' may also form a basis for application, including (but not limited to) a right to a name, a right of personal portrayal, a copyright and an industrial property right.[226]

14.76 Since an attack on relative grounds requires the existence of an earlier right it is incumbent on the challenger to act quickly. Acquiescence for a period of 5 successive years in the use of the later CTM will prevent a successful application,[227] as will consent from the proprietor of the earlier right.[228]

---

[218] Case 1190 C-147749 *Carlsberg Breweries AS v Kopparbergs Bryggerie AB (DANSK FADÄL trade mark)*.

[219] Article 52(2). See Decisions 169C 76059/1 and 184C 76059/2 *Manpower Austria Temporapersonal GmbH v Manpower Inc (MANPOWER Trade Mark)*.

[220] Article 52(1)(b).

[221] OHIM Manual, Cancellation Part D, Section 2 at para 4.3. See http://oami.europa.eu/ows/rw/ resource/documents/CTM/legalReferences/partd_cancellation_subs_provi.pdf.

[222] Case 232C 447730/1 *Prime Restaurant Holdings Inc v John Arthur Slater (EAST SIDE MARIO's trade mark)*.

[223] Section 32(3). See Chapter 5.

[224] Case R436/2000-1 *Harte-Hanks Data Technologies, Inc v Trillium Digital Systems, Inc (TRILLIUM trade mark)*.

[225] Case C-529/07 *Chocoladefabriken Lindt & Sprüngli AG v Franz Hauswirth GmbH* [2009] ECR I-4893; [2009] WLR (D) 182. The defendant knew of the plaintiff's successful sales of Easter bunnies wrapped in gold foil and sporting a red ribbon and bell.

[226] Article 53(3).

[227] Article 54.

[228] Article 53(3).

ASSIGNMENT

14.77 For the purposes of property and transactions, a CTM is dealt with as a national trade mark registered in the state where the proprietor has its seat or domicile on the relevant date, or if none, where the proprietor has an establishment, or failing that, Spain.[229] Consequently, a CTM owned by a UK company will be governed by the law of property as it affects a UK national registration.[230] Where a mark is owned jointly the domicile of the first-named proprietor is used first.[231]

14.78 Whilst under the 1994 Act the sections as to assignment and so forth apply equally to registrations as to applications, and so recording an assignment of an application can be made – as it can for a CTM application – it is observed at Chapter 11[232] that UK trade mark applications are an evanescent form of property. Article 24 makes clear that the application for a CTM is an object of property, yet Art 6 equally makes clear equally that rights are obtained by registration. So again, if the CTM application is refused, this 'property' vanishes. An assignment document which transfers a CTM application only should perhaps, therefore, speak of an 'applicant for registration' rather than an 'owner', and should convey the benefit of the application which would fully harden into personal property if and when it proceeded to registration.

14.79 The following issues need to be borne in mind when assigning a CTM:[233]

(a)   *territorial splitting cannot occur*: the unitary nature and effect of a CTM means that it must be assigned as a whole for all member states;[234] but

(b)   *partial assignment is permissible*: a CTM may be transferred in respect of some of the goods or services for which it is registered.[235] It is incumbent on a proprietor to ensure that the effect of a partial transfer is not likely to mislead the public.[236] Although the act of assignment and recordal may not in themselves be problematic (e g deception as to origin) the effect of the split could be to lay the blueprint for future public deception given the disappearance of central control over the destiny of the mark's use.

---

[229]   Where OHIM has its seat: Art 16.

[230]   Property laws of England and Wales, Northern Ireland or Scotland, as appropriate.

[231]   See OHIM Manual, Transfer Part E and http://oami.europa.eu/ows/rw/resource/documents/CTM/legalReferences/parte_transfer.pdf.

[232]   See **11.3**.

[233]   See, again, Chapter 11 for comparison purposes.

[234]   The issue of seniority needs to be kept in mind when assigning CTMs. If a CTM has seniority claims attached, it is recommended that this be mentioned in the assignment document. Equally, should a national registration from which a CTM claims seniority be assigned, the CTM should be assigned too.

[235]   Article 17(1).

[236]   Article 17(4).

OHIM is empowered under Art 17(4) not to record an assignment which it deems is inherently 'likely to mislead';[237]

(c)   *assignment of a CTM may be with or without the goodwill of the business in which it is used*;[238]

(d)   *it must be in writing and signed by all parties to it*;[239]

(e)   *do not delay in recording*: although there is no time-limit by which to record the change in title, early recordal is recommended since failure to do so means that:

   (i)   an assignee cannot rely on its acquisition to sue for infringement until recordal has been made;[240]
   (ii)   the transfer will not have any effect vis-à-vis third parties until its recordal except where they acquired rights in the CTM after the transfer date and where they had prior knowledge of the transfer;
   (iii) neither OHIM nor any third party will be aware of the transfer, meaning that the recorded proprietor will continue to be regarded as proprietor and would receive any official or third party notice affecting the maintenance and renewal of the CTM;

(f)   *procedure for recordal*: r 31 sets out the recordal procedures which OHIM requires, including documentary evidence of transfer.[241] A pro forma Recordal Application Form is available online.[242] The official recordal fee was abolished in 2005;[243]

(g)   *stamp duty:* this is no longer chargeable on documents conveying a CTM, but care should be taken to check the status of pre-2000 transactions.[244]

LICENSING

14.80   Article 22 provides that a CTM may be licensed for some or all of the goods or services for which it is registered, for the whole or part of the

---

[237] See r 31(6) IR.

[238] Article 17(1).

[239] Article 17(3). The recordal applicant may be either the recorded proprietor or the successor in title.

[240] Article 17(6).

[241] Rule 31(5). OHIM will record an assignment on receipt of a photocopy of the original document. The original or a certified copy is not needed. OHIM prefers documents to be signed by all parties to it, though under English law at least a transfer executed only by the assignor would be valid. If the recordal application form is signed by all parties to the transfer no further documentary proof of the transfer is needed by OHIM.

[242] See http://oami.europa.eu/ows/rw/pages/QPLUS/forms/nonelectronic/nonelectronic.en.do.

[243] By Commission Regulation 1041/2005 of 29 June 2005.

[244] Section 61 of the 1994 Act states that stamp duty is not chargeable on an instrument conveying a CTM purely because the mark has legal effect in the UK; but if the document was executed in the UK the normal rules relating to payment applied. See **10.42** and **11.30**.

Community, exclusively or non-exclusively.[245] Marks the subject of CTM applications can be licensed, as well as registrations.[246] OHIM has published a practice manual on the licensing of CTMs.[247]

14.81   The following general principles and issues should be borne in mind when licensing a CTM:[248]

(a)   *EC competition law*: it is necessary to ensure that any territorial restriction does not fall foul of EC competition policy;[249]

(b)   *licensees and infringement proceedings*: subject to the terms of the licence saying otherwise, an exclusive licensee may bring infringement proceedings (presumably in his own name) should the registered proprietor fail to do so within 'an appropriate period'. Non-exclusive licensees require the consent of the proprietor to do so;[250]

(c)   *licences should preferably be in writing*: although the Regulation does not specify this, a written arrangement is more likely to define clearly the relationship between the parties and the ensuing rights of a licensee. OHIM does not require proof of the licence unless the application to record it is made by the licensee. Nor does OHIM make any enquiry as to the validity of the licence. The official fee payable is currently €200;

(d)   *recordal is advisable (but not mandatory)*: any one of the parties may apply to record.[251] There is no time-limit by which to record a licence, though see **14.80** point (e) in connection with recording assignments for corresponding reasons why early recordal should be effected;

(e)   *procedure for recordal*: as with recordal of assignments, r 31 governs the process and information OHIM requires. A pro forma Recordal Application Form is available online.[252] Rule 34(2) deals with partial licences, and r 35 with the cancellation or modification of a recorded entry;

(f)   *need for effective policing of the arrangement by the proprietor*: There should be a high state of vigilance on the part of a CTM proprietor to ensure that the benefit of licensed use accrues to him;[253]

---

[245]   Article 22(1).
[246]   Article 24.
[247]   See   http://oami.europa.eu/ows/rw/resource/documents/CTM/legalReferences/parte_licenses. pdf.
[248]   See Chapter 10 for comparison purposes.
[249]   See Chapter 13.
[250]   Article 22(3).
[251]   Article 22(5).
[252]   See http://oami.europa.eu/ows/rw/pages/QPLUS/forms/nonelectronic/nonelectronic.en.do.
[253]   In order to safeguard the registration from attack under the provisions of Art 51(1)(b) and (c).

(g) *specifically for the licensee*: the impact on a licensee of the CTM's transfer being given as security, licensing or surrender shall have effect only after recordal of the licence.[254]

Other registrable transactions

14.82 A CTM can be given as security and the arrangement can be recorded.[255] Further, a creditor can seize a CTM as property in satisfaction of a debt and record the levy of execution.[256] Article 21, as amended, deals with insolvency – unless the debtor is an insurance or credit institution, the only insolvency proceedings in which a CTM may be involved are those opened in the member state where the debtor has his 'centre of main interests'. Moreover, a bankruptcy notice affecting a CTM shall on request of the competent national authority be recorded against the CTM and published.[257] It would appear that a memorandum outlining the terms of an agreement between two or more parties (eg where an earlier proprietor consents to the registration by a later proprietor of a confusingly similar mark as an alternative to opposition) cannot be recorded.[258]

ENLARGEMENT OF THE COMMUNITY AND THE CTM

14.83 Since the CTM is a unitary right, intended to have a uniform effect throughout the countries of the EU, the system posed a problem when the EU was enlarged in 2004 to embrace 10 new member states.[259] As Folliard-Monguiral and Rogers put it, efforts had to be made 'to reconcile the two objectives of legal certainty for the owners of Community trade marks and designs, and respect for rights in the new Member States which pre-date enlargement'.[260] The CTM system already contained the concepts of prior local rights[261] as a defence to trade mark infringement and acquiescence.[262] However, unlike the UK regime at the time, it did not have a defence of overlapping registration[263] or the concept of honest concurrent user.[264]

---

[254] Articles 23(1) and 50(3).

[255] Article 19(1). For the approach of the European Patent Office to transactions, see Lise Osterberg Dybdahl 'Transfer of Rights and their Registration in the European Patent and Community Patent Registers' (1998) IIC 387.

[256] Article 20.

[257] Article 21.

[258] See r 84(3) for a list of registrable transactions; the President may determine that other items be registered: r 84(4).

[259] Cyprus, Czech Republic, Estonia, Hungary, Latvia, Lithuania, Malta, Poland, Slovakia and Slovenia. The Accession Treaty was signed at Athens in April 2003; Annex II to the Treaty amended Community legislation including the Regulation. Acceding member states were obliged to bring their trade mark legislation into line with the Directive.

[260] Folliard-Monguiral and Rogers 'The Community Trade Mark and Designs System and the Enlargement of the European Union' [2004] EIPR 48.

[261] Articles 110 and 111; see **8.22**.

[262] Article 55(2)of the Regulation; see **8.24** at point (b).

[263] Trade Marks Act 1994, s 11(1); see **8.13**.

14.84　In brief summary, these difficulties were addressed as follows:[265]

(a)　CTMs were extended automatically to the new member states;[266]

(b)　in the face of this, earlier rights in the accession countries which were acquired in good faith enjoy the protection of Arts 12, 110 and 111 of the Regulation;

(c)　CTM applications filed before the accession date, 1 May 2004, were examined under the old rules: thus applications as well as registrations were 'grandfathered', to use the President's terminology;

(d)　to prevent misuse of this in the period immediately before accession, CTM applications filed between 1 November 2003 and 30 April 2004 could be opposed on the basis of earlier rights in the new member states under Art 142a(3) of the Regulation;

(e)　OHIM services were extended into the new languages (right to apply in own official language, availability of classification guides, staffing of the Office, etc).

14.85　Following the success of the strategy to deal with enlargement in 2004 OHIM adopted the same approach at the accession of Bulgaria and Romania in 2007. As at January 2012, Croatia, the Yugoslav Republic of Macedonia and Turkey are negotiating to join the EU. Other potential future candidates include Albania, Bosnia and Herzegovina, Kosovo, Iceland, Montenegro and Serbia.

ADVANTAGES AND DISADVANTAGES OF THE CTM SYSTEM VIS-À-VIS THE NATIONAL FILING ROUTE

14.86　The CTM system is not suitable for recommendation to all business undertakings, particularly small, geographically restricted ones. For those, where the effort and cost of maintaining registered protection across all the member states could outweigh the benefits of the system, a traditional route to registration via the national offices or the Madrid systems (see Chapter 16) may be more appropriate. The key criteria to consider are the extent of geographical protection required and the cost of securing and maintaining a unitary right. The following overview of the strengths and weaknesses of the CTM system will give further pointers.

---

[264]　Note that this is not a defence but a means to concurrent registration and indirectly to the defence of s 11(1). See **5.60–5.62**.

[265]　Communication No 05/03 of the President of the Office of 16 October 2003 concerning the enlargement of the EU in 2004, available at http://oami.europa.eu/en/office/aspects/communications/05-03.htm.

[266]　The right to claim seniority under Arts 34 and 35 was also extended to new states, and the right to convert an unsuccessful application into a bundle of national applications.

Characteristics of the CTM system	*Comparison with national rights*
One application process leading to a unitary right.	Separate applications process following national laws and practice.
Cost effectiveness begins once two countries would have been claimed as individual national rights.	Securing 24 national (and one Benelux) registrations would be significantly more expensive than a single CTM.
Use in one member state only maintains the unitary right (see **14.7**).	Use of each national registration needed to maintain its continued registration.
Existence of a CTM registration may be used to prevent later use and registration of a confusingly similar mark in all or part of the EU.	Existence of a national right has no effect beyond the state's borders (but can be used as a basis on which to oppose a CTM).
One central renewal only required.	Separate renewals required.
Concept of seniority provides for consolidation of national rights into one unitary right.	Need to maintain separate national rights.
Central assignment and licence recordal.	Separate assignment and licence recordal requiring separate procedures.
Availability of conversion process to extend CTM application to a string of national applications.	No provision to extend beyond national right (subject to Madrid system).
Lack of relative grounds examination leaves a perpetual question over a CTM's validity vis-à-vis earlier rights.	Better presumption as to validity in countries which have retained relative grounds examination.
One language (but designating a second).	Need to work in the national language.
Automatic expansion to include future member states.	National registration will remain static, geographically.
The CTM may be designated as a jurisdiction in an International Registration.	Each national jurisdiction may be designated individually.
OHIM notifies the owner of a CTM if a later CTM application is filed which could conflict with the registered CTM.	Only the UK in the Community notifies existing trade mark owners of a later conflicting application.

Disadvantages of the CTM system	Comparison with national rights
Registration process slower than in some countries (eg UK).	Registration process quicker in some countries.
If opposition is encountered, application costs can mount rapidly, particularly where translations are required, and, if successful, the CTM will fail entirely, the losing party being liable for the successful party's costs.	Opposition to a national registration has no repercussions beyond national boundaries.
A CTM can be assigned only as a geographical entity.	National rights can be assigned individually.
Successful revocation or invalidity action leads to loss of unitary right.	Successful revocation or invalidity actions leads to loss of national right only.
Must be available for registration throughout the EU.	Being unavailable for registration in one territory has no bearing on availability elsewhere.
A CTM may be assigned for the entire EU only.	National registrations may be assigned individually.

Chapter 15

TRADE MARK SYSTEMS WORLDWIDE: INTERNATIONAL CO-OPERATION AND HARMONISATION

INTRODUCTION

15.1 Since trade marks and the rights which attach to them are by nature territorial, a person or a business wishing to register, or protect a trade mark is obliged to investigate law and practice in each separate country. Despite incremental efforts at international harmonisation, some of which are outlined below, a huge and bewildering variety of local law and practice is still to be found worldwide: by way of contrast to the UK and EU, Burma has no trade mark legislation per se but relies on an administrative combination of registration with the Office of the Registration of Deeds and triennial publication of Cautionary Notices. Although providing detail for all countries is beyond the scope of this work, it should be noted that encyclopaedic works exist which, in a structured format, illuminate the details for each country.[1] However, even armed with such useful intelligence, the fact remains that, in some countries, either or both of the registration system and enforcement system are in abeyance or are excruciatingly slow.[2]

15.2 Most systems afford trade mark rights either to a party who is 'first to file' (ie applies for registration first) or to the 'first to use'. In the former case trade mark rights may only be acquired by registration. The first person to apply to register a particular mark for certain goods or services becomes the proprietor; only prior registrations or applications are able to block a subsequent application. Examples of this kind of system are to be found in France and in the Benelux countries. The first to use country may require commencement of use before an application is filed or a registration granted. A mark filed in the US, for example, solely on an intention to use basis must be

---

[1] Eg, JR Olsen, SM Maniatis, C Garrigues *Trade Marks, Trade Names and Unfair Competition: World Law and Practice* (Sweet & Maxwell, 1996 and releases).

[2] Eg, Somalia where the Registry stopped functioning due to the civil war. Similarly, in Libya, the Registry received applications but did not prosecute them for well over a decade. In June 2004, owners were formally invited to revive their trade mark claims (P Johns of Stevens Hewlett & Perkins, personal communication). However, all trade mark applications files prior to August 2002 were deemed invalid, with fresh filings and fees required, and the next registration certificate was only actually issued on 25 May 2010 after a gap of nearly 30 years.

put into use before registration will be granted.[3] Moreover, a first to use country may give precedence in the event of conflict to the earlier user, even of an unregistered mark – as under the UK Trade Marks Act 1938 ('the 1938 Act').[4] As we have noted elsewhere, one effect of the UK Trade Marks Act 1994 ('the 1994 Act') was to shift the UK from being squarely within the 'first to use' type of country further towards a 'first to file' type.[5]

15.3 Another distinction is between countries which undertake a thorough examination of applications and those which leave any objections to be raised in cancellation proceedings, often in the courts rather than in the trade marks office. Systems which do not provide substantive examination of applications are sometimes called 'deposit' systems, though applications will in practice always receive a degree of inspection as to form, not least to ensure that the relevant Registry or office receives its fees.

15.4 Most national registration systems will consist of the following elements:

(a) filing of application at the national trade mark office;

(b) official examination as to formalities;

(c) substantive examination as to inherent registrability (distinctiveness); and

(d) issuance of registration certificate or notice of refusal.[6]

A substantial number of other systems contain one or more of the following stages, whose order varies from country to country:

(e) official search as to prior conflicting statutory rights, with or without Registry objections being raised as a result of examination on 'relative grounds';

(f) advertisement for the purposes of third party opposition or observations;

(g) opposition or observations;

(h) declaration confirming commencement of use.

---

3   15 USC 1501: note, however, that the position is somewhat different for applications made under the provisions of international conventions and treaties to which the US has become a party (15 USC 1126).

4   Prior UK Registry examination practice of treating earlier pending applications as citations ensured that priority of filing was maintained. Earlier applicants still enjoy the benefit of notification under post-2007 arrangements.

5   Eg, see Christopher Morcom QC in a letter to *The Times* on 22 November 1994: 'The most fundamental change is shifting the emphasis from common law action for passing off to the protection of marks by registration, which has become considerably easier and more effective. The risk of failing to register marks has undoubtedly increased.'

6   For the problems caused where there is no mechanism for refusal, see Romo de Vivar and Luna 'The Problem of Trade Mark Denials' (2004) MIP 138 Supplement 17–21.

15.5 The current trend seems to be in favour of 'streamlining': as has been discussed elsewhere, partly as a result of the need to improve integration with faster-moving regional and international processing, since 2007, the UK has moved from raising substantive objections based on examination on relative grounds to conducting an advisory search with notifications to potentially affected owners of earlier rights.

15.6 Other features of individual systems include the registration of service marks as well as trade marks for goods, provision for collective marks and/or certification marks, and distinct schemes for trade or business names. The kinds of mark eligible for registration, the classification systems for products and the possibility of multi-class applications also vary, as do renewal frequency, use requirements and procedures for cancellation. Some countries permit licensing, either with or without registration of the licensee, while others do not.

DIFFICULTIES AND SOLUTIONS IN OBTAINING AN INTERNATIONAL PORTFOLIO OF MARKS

15.7 In light of all the above, it will be evident to the reader that the skill and money needed to obtain and maintain an international portfolio of marks is considerable. Local agents usually have to be retained, and translations of documents filed. Enforcement also has its vagaries; rules of comparison of marks and products differ from jurisdiction to jurisdiction as do court procedures and remedies.

15.8 However, several mechanisms exist which reduce the problems of obtaining protection internationally. The first is the regional system under which a single Registry handles applications for the whole region by virtue of a uniform law.[7] A number of regional systems exist, including the Benelux, OAPI,[8] ARIPO,[9] and the Community trade mark (CTM).[10] Secondly, international agreements facilitate direct registration into other systems, by aligning classification or reducing formalities. Thirdly, international 'registration' of marks is possible through the so-called 'Madrid system', discussed further in Chapter 16. Other treaties with relevance to trade marks are outlined below.

---

[7]   See, eg, Blakeney and Willis 'Intellectual property and regional trade arrangements in Europe, Asia and the Western Hemispheres' (1998) 4 Int TLR 73–80.

[8]   French-speaking Africa, consisting of Benin, Burkina Faso, Cameroon, Central African Republic, Chad, Congo, Côte d'Ivoire, Gabon, Guinea, Guinea-Bissau, Equatorial Guinea, Mali, Mauritania, Niger, Senegal and Togo. See www.wipo.int/africa/en/partners_org/partners/oapi_bg.html.

[9]   African Regional Industrial Property Organisation, which was created in December 1979 (Lusaka Agreement). As at January 2012, members are: Botswana, Gambia, Ghana, Kenya, Lesotho, Malawi, Mozambique, Namibia, Sierra Leone, Somalia, Sudan, Swaziland, Tanzania, Uganda, Zambia and Zimbabwe. See also www.wipo.int/africa/en/partners_org/partners/aripo.html.

[10] See Chapter 14.

15.9 At a practical level, although not binding because of the underlying principle of territoriality, obtaining registration in one country can be persuasive to another country's office;[11] in some countries registration is merely a formality on presentation of evidence of registration elsewhere,[12] as with certain UK overseas territories and Commonwealth countries.

15.10 Apart from international arrangements for easing the path to registration of trade marks, other systems for international protection exist, including, as noted in Chapter 12, the Lisbon Agreement for the protection of geographical appellations and the Nairobi Treaty on the protection of Olympic symbols, both of which are outlined below.

15.11 The parent treaty of many of these is the Paris Convention.[13]

THE PARIS CONVENTION FOR THE PROTECTION OF INDUSTRIAL PROPERTY 1883 AND REVISIONS

15.12 The Paris Convention of 1883[14] had 174 member countries by January 2011.[15] The members are known collectively as the Paris Union.[16] By establishing the principle of national treatment[17] the Paris Convention obviates discrimination in its signatory states between domestic and foreign applicants. It is administered by the World Intellectual Property Organisation (WIPO), which became a specialised agency in the United Nations system of organisations in 1974. Its headquarters are in Geneva. Another key feature of the Paris Convention is that priority can be claimed from the earliest

---

[11] Eg, although now somewhat less so because of divergence in examination practices, previously, trade mark registries in Hong Kong and Ireland were frequently favourably influenced to accept a mark for registration where the UK Registry had already done so: experience of P Cornford (co-author of this book).

[12] Eg, in the Channel Islands, filing a certified copy of a UK registration leads to automatic registration in Jersey and/or Guernsey. In Jersey, similar rules now apply to CTMs but, pending implementing legislation, not in Guernsey. The UK Registry holds a list of territories into which UK and EU trade mark rights can be thus 'extended'. See, as at January 2012, www.ipo.gov.uk/pro-policy/policy-information/extendukip.htm.

[13] For text of the treaties and commentary, see A Ilardi and M Blakeney *International Encyclopaedia of Intellectual Property Treaties* (Oxford University Press, 2004).

[14] With effect from 7 July 1884 (revised in 1900, 1911, 1925, 1934, 1958 and 1967, amended in 1979) www.wipo.int/treaties/en/ip/paris/trtdocs_wo020.html.

[15] See 'contracting parties' link at www.wipo.int/treaties/en/index.jsp.

[16] Article 1(1) establishes the Paris Union. Article 19 gives the power to members of the Paris Union to create arrangements or sub-unions. An important example of this is the Madrid Union, see Chapter 16.

[17] Articles 2 and 3, under which nationals of each Union country are given, in each other country, treatment under law no less favourable than nationals of that other country. See further Evans 'The Principle of National Treatment and the International Protection of Industrial Property' [1996] EIPR 149 and Rotstein 'Is There an International Intellectual Property System? Is There an Agreement Between States as to What the Objectives of Intellectual Property Should be?' [2011] EIPR 1.

application made in a Convention country.[18] The other most significant provisions which relate to trade marks are:

(a)   use of a trade mark by the proprietor in a form differing in elements which do not alter the distinctive character of the mark in the form in which it was registered will not invalidate it or diminish the protection granted to it;[19]

(b)   a signatory country shall refuse to register a mark when it constitutes a reproduction of a well-known mark or an imitation liable to create confusion therewith;[20]

(c)   well-known marks must be protected against unlicensed use, regardless of registration in the country in question;[21]

(d)   a signatory country shall refuse to register as trade marks armorial bearings, flags, state emblems, official signs, hallmarks or imitations thereof;[22]

(e)   the principle of independence of foreign filings from the priority filing;[23]

(f)   the protection of business names;[24] and

(g)   the duty of Union members to provide protection against unfair competition.[25]

In the UK, the Convention's provisions were introduced into legislation on a piecemeal basis; the 1994 Act represents a significant consolidation of the same.

15.13   Other Treaties and Conventions affecting trade marks include:

•   the Nice Agreement Concerning the International Classification of Goods and Services for the Purposes of the Registration of Marks 1957 and revisions;

•   the Vienna Agreement Establishing an International Classification of the Figurative Elements of Marks 1973, revised in 1985;

---

18   See Chapter 5.
19   Article 5C(2).
20   Article 6*bis*.
21   Article 6*bis*.
22   Article 6*ter*.
23   Article 6(3).
24   Article 8.
25   Article 10*bis*.

- the World Trade Organisation (WTO) Agreement on Trade-Related Aspects of Intellectual Property Rights (TRIPs) 1994;

- the Trademark Law Treaty (TLT) 1994;

- the Singapore Treaty on the Law of Trademarks 2006 (ST);

- the Madrid Agreement for the Repression of False or Deceptive Indications of Origin 1891;

- the Lisbon Agreement for the Protection of Appellations of Origin and their International Registration 1958 and revisions;

- the Nairobi Treaty on the Protection of the Olympic Symbol 1981;

- the Hague System for the International Registration of Designs (London 1934, Hague 1960, Geneva 1999).

NICE AGREEMENT CONCERNING THE INTERNATIONAL CLASSIFICATION OF GOODS AND SERVICES FOR THE PURPOSES OF THE REGISTRATION OF MARKS 1957 AND REVISIONS

15.14 This treaty, concluded at Nice in 1957, revised in 1967 and 1977, and amended in 1979, established the Nice classification of goods and services; WIPO, many territories and many IGOs now use this system to classify the goods and services in trade mark applications and registrations while others either directly shadow it or, in a few cases, still maintain their own variants (eg Canada). Now in its tenth edition, Nice classification currently consists of 34 classes of goods and 11 classes of service, with explanatory notes and recommendations where appropriate. WIPO publishes an alphabetical list of goods and services showing their class and also class-by-class alphabetical lists.[26] Versions are available in printed form and on CD-ROM. The legal effect of using the classification scheme is a matter for national law[27] and indeed the scheme is used by non-members of the Nice Special Union.[28] The scheme is kept under review by a Committee of Experts[29] and a new edition is published approximately every 5 years. Although the scheme is regularly updated, its basic structure reflects the patterns of trade and industry of its time. Modern patterns of trade may cut across class boundaries to a greater extent than formerly.

---

[26] See www.wipo.int/classifications/nice/en/classifications.html.
[27] Article 2.
[28] As at January 2012, there were 83 contracting parties.
[29] Article 3. Assisted by an 'electronic forum', see www.wipo.int/nef.

VIENNA AGREEMENT ESTABLISHING AN INTERNATIONAL CLASSIFICATION OF THE FIGURATIVE ELEMENTS OF MARKS 1973, REVISED IN 1985

15.15 This treaty creates a sub-union of the Paris Union.[30] There are comparatively few contracting parties – 31 states as at January 2012, including several EU member states but not the UK. However, as with Nice, the classification scheme is widely used by non-members, including the Office for Harmonisation in the Internal Market (OHIM).[31] As with other classification treaties, a Committee of Experts keeps the scheme under review; the sixth edition was released in 2008. It consists of 29 categories[32] ranging from 'celestial bodies, natural phenomena, geographical maps' (category 1) to colours (category 29).

GATT AND THE WTO AGREEMENT ON TRADE-RELATED ASPECTS OF INTELLECTUAL PROPERTY RIGHTS (TRIPS) 1994

15.16 During the course of the Uruguay round of the General Agreement on Tariffs and Trade (GATT) talks, impatience with the dearth of intellectual property rights in many countries and with the lack of national and international mechanisms for enforcement led to the conclusion of the TRIPs[33] Agreement which sets out minimum standards in acquiring[34] trade mark rights, in their enforcement,[35] in customs and criminal procedures and in dispute prevention and settlement.[36] Trade mark provisions of the so-called 'Dunkel draft' which formed the basis of TRIPs were based on European trade mark texts. Consequently, European and UK trade mark laws were already in substantial conformity with the substantive provisions of TRIPs.[37] The Agreement is, however, significant for UK trade mark interests

---

[30] See www.wipo.int/treaties/en/classification/vienna/summary_vienna.html.

[31] See www.wipo.int/treaties/en/classification/vienna/summary_vienna.html. OHIM is the Community Trade Mark Office (see Chapter 14).

[32] See, along with Nice classification, www.wipo.int/classifications/nivilo.

[33] Trade-Related Aspects of Intellectual Property Rights. The Agreement was concluded on 15 December 1993 at Geneva and became Annex 1C of the Marrakesh Agreement Establishing the World Trade Organization (WTO). The UK and the EU joined the WTO at its inception on 1 January 1995. As from 23 July 2008, the WTO has had 153 members, see www.wto.org/english/thewto_e/whatis_e/tif_e/org6_e.htm. There is much literature on TRIPs. See, as a good overview, Arup 'TRIPs: Across the Global Field of Intellectual Property' [2004] EIPR 7.

[34] Part II, Section 2, Arts 15–21.

[35] Part III.

[36] Part V.

[37] Developing nations had a compliance deadline of 1 January 2000; the Doha round of negotiations resulted in relaxation of the timetables for least developed nations, see www.wto.org/english/tratop_e/dda_e/dda_e.htm and **15.26**.

internationally.[38] The EU's role in GATT and TRIPs was clarified by the European Court of Justice (ECJ) in a way which suggested that EU competence in intellectual property matters was shared with member states.[39] This had a significant effect within the Union as time went by, with the Commission taking an ever-increasing role in international IP-related activities and negotiations as compared to the member states' representatives. The Lisbon Treaty conferred exclusive competence on the EU to conclude agreements with third countries on intellectual property matters as part of the Union's common commercial policy, under Arts 207 and 218 of the Treaty on the Functioning of the Economic Union (TFEU). Indeed, even before Lisbon, the EU had concluded a number of bilateral trade agreements with intellectual property content.

15.17 As with the Paris Convention, TRIPs requires national treatment (Art 3). World Trade Organisation (WTO) members must comply with Arts 1–12 and 19 of the Paris Convention (1967 revision) (Art 2(1)). The TRIPs agreement is said not to derogate from obligations under the Paris and other Conventions (Art 2(2)). It adds the principle of most-favoured nation treatment (Art 4) and is explicitly neutral on the exhaustion of rights (Art 6). The objectives clause in Art 7 is slanted at the relation and transfer of technology rather than the market objectives which underlie trade mark protection, but there is reference to social and economic welfare, and the balancing of rights and obligations. Public health and public interest are specifically mentioned, as is the right of states to prevent abuse of intellectual property or undue restraints on trade[40] (Art 8).

15.18 Section 2 of Part II deals specifically with trade marks. Article 15 provides that any sign maybe a trade mark if it is capable of distinguishing the proprietor's goods and services. Colours are explicitly mentioned. WTO member states may limit trade mark registration to signs which are perceptible visually. Intent-to-use applications must be allowed, but actual registration may be conditional upon use. Trade marks must be advertised before or promptly after registration and third party cancellation must be permitted (Art 15).

15.19 Infringement rights are primarily based upon confusion as between identical or similar marks and products (Art 16). However, the protection afforded to well-known marks under Art 6*bis* of the Paris Convention must be available for services as well as goods, and for goods or services which are not similar to those 'in respect of which the trade mark is registered'. The meaning of this is not wholly clear; it is submitted, however, that s 10(3) of the 1994 Act complies with this obligation.[41]

---

[38] See, eg, Xin Zhang 'Direct Effect of the WTO Agreements: National Survey' [2003] Int TLR 35.

[39] Originally confirmed in Opinion 1/94 of 15 November 1994.

[40] Article 40 of TRIPs also contains general provisions allowing states to control anti-competitive licensing.

[41] See Chapter 5.

15.20 Cancellation on the ground of non-use must require at least 3 years' non-use (Art 19) and use by a licensee must count, subject to quality control. Licensing and assignment are left to national law,[42] but compulsory licensing is not permitted and assignment without goodwill must be possible.

15.21 Section 3 of Part II (Arts 22–24) contains quite detailed provisions on the protection of geographical indications. Principally because of differences of approach as between the US and EU, the form of legal protection is left to member states but must include the repression of misleading indications and of uses which amount to unfair competition within the meaning of Art 10*bis* of the Paris Convention (Art 22(2)). Broader protection is envisaged for wines and spirits (Art 23).

15.22 A key feature of TRIPs is the emphasis on the enforcement of intellectual property rights (Part III, Arts 41–61) and the availability of effective final and interim remedies and border measures. Criminal procedures and penalties must be provided at least in cases of 'wilful trademark counterfeiting or copyright piracy on a commercial scale' (Art 61).

15.23 TRIPs also requires that procedures for acquisition and maintenance of rights must be reasonable (Art 62).

15.24 As with other international treaties and conventions, TRIPs is not regarded as having direct effect in the UK,[43] but national law will be interpreted, when possible, in compliance with the UK's obligations under TRIPs.

15.25 At the conclusion of the Uruguay round, the WTO was established as a permanent body in Geneva. Relations between the WTO and WIPO will be a matter of considerable interest in coming years. On 22 December 1995, WIPO and the WTO signed their first co-operation agreement with the aim:[44]

> 'to establish a mutually supportive relationship between them, and with a view to establishing appropriate arrangements for cooperation between them.'

15.26 WIPO also recognised that compliance with TRIPs can be arduous for developing countries[45] and has provided advice on using the derogations or 'flexibilities' that are available as part of what is now its Development Agenda.[46] The WTO has a dispute settlement mechanism for intellectual

---

[42] See Chapter 10.

[43] See *Azrak-Hamway International Inc's Application* [1997] RPC 134 and *Lenzing AG's European Patent* [1997] RPC 245. However, with the increasing role of the EU institutions and EU law in this area, the exclusive effect of domestic law examined in those cases is becoming increasingly irrelevant.

[44] Preamble: see www.wipo.int/treaties/en/agreement/trtdocs_wo030.html.

[45] On the difficulties see, eg Correa 'Implementation of the TRIPs Agreement in Latin America and the Caribbean' [1997] EIPR 435.

[46] See www.wipo.int/ip-development/en.

property disputes between states,[47] something that WIPO has been trying to achieve for some time. However, WIPO does have an active arbitration centre for private intellectual property disputes and, as a major part of its caseload, domain name disputes.[48]

15.27 Since the major burst of multilateral activity in the late 1990s exemplified by TRIPs, there has been an increasing tendency towards creating bilateral international agreements,[49] especially by the US and, to a lesser extent, the EU, to enhance the level of intellectual property protection over and above TRIPs standards.

TRADEMARK LAW TREATY (TLT) 1994 AND SINGAPORE TREATY (ST) 2006

15.28 A diplomatic conference concluded the TLT and accompanying regulations in Geneva on 27 October 1994.[50] Although the purpose behind the TLT negotiations was to attempt to unify substantive trade mark law and to provide a universal definition of terms such as 'distinctive' and 'confusingly similar', the end result is a treaty whose provisions, it is believed, will 'remove the aggravating and apparently unnecessary idiosyncratic procedural requirements of different trade mark offices'.[51]

15.29 The TLT came into force in 1996, when the UK became the fifth contracting party to ratify it. In short, the TLT lays down basic procedural requirements which contracting parties must agree not to exceed. The most important provisions are:

(a)   limits to what an office may demand when an application is filed (no entitlement to require commercial register extract, evidence of commercial activity or a supporting overseas registration);[52]

(b)   a power of attorney may be required;[53]

(c)   multi-class applications shall be allowed;[54]

---

[47]   See www.wto.org/english/tratop_e/dispu_e/dispu_e.htm; Part V of TRIPs, Arts 63–4, refers to dispute settlement and the need for transparency in compliance.

[48]   Originally announced at (1995) 34(2) Industrial Property and Copyright, pp 117–123. Details of the Arbitration and Mediation Center's activities may be found at www.wipo.int/amc/en/index.html.

[49]   Eg, Ribeiro de Almeida 'The TRIPs Agreement, the Bilateral Agreements Concerning Geographical Indications and the Philosophy of the WTO' [2005] EIPR 150; http://ec.europa.eu/trade/creating-opportunities/trade-topics/intellectual-property and links.

[50]   See www.wipo.int/treaties/en/ip/tlt/index.html.

[51]   Kunze 'The Trade Mark Law Treaty' (1995) MIP 46 23–27.

[52]   Article 3.

[53]   Article 4.

[54]   Article 6.

(d)   division of an application and registration shall be allowed;[55]

(e)   no attestation, notarisation, legalisation or other certification of signatures shall be required;[56]

(f)   the Nice Classification of goods and services shall be used;[57]

(g)   no evidence shall be required to substantiate a request to change a trade mark owner's name or address or to record an assignment of a mark (unless there is reason to doubt the request);[58]

(h)   no evidence of use shall be required on renewal.[59]

As at January 2012, 45 states were party to the TLT. Given that the provisions of the treaty required contracting parties to amend their legislation, it took some time coming into operation; indeed, the date for compliance was 28 October 2004, some 10 years after the treaty's adoption in Geneva.

15.30   Although the TLT represented a worthy effort in harmonisation of national approaches to trade mark issues, nevertheless much remained to be done in terms of simplifying and standardising national rules and practice. The TLT also contained significant restrictions on the kinds of marks to which it applied, including a broad restriction to visible signs, such that many 'modern favourites' (eg smell, sound and holograms marks)[60] were not subject to it. Accordingly, even before the TLT compliance date, plans were laid and negotiations commenced for a second treaty which would increase the overall level of harmonisation and deal with modernisation issues (eg use of electronic communication); the result of these was the Singapore Treaty on the Law of Trademarks (ST) 2006 and accompanying Regulations.[61] Today, strictly speaking, the TLT and ST stand as separate instruments, open to separate contracting party entry, but, in practice, TLT entry now is often seen as a first step (optional at that) to ST entry.[62] When compared to the TLT, ST extends its net to all mark types save for collective, certification and guarantee[63] and, in addition to modifying and updating the various provisions found in the TLT as necessary, has the following totally new features:

(a)   a free choice of the means of communication with contracting party trade mark offices including electronic communication;

---

[55]   Article 7.
[56]   Article 8. This was probably the most attractive feature of the TLT for UK trade mark proprietors.
[57]   Article 9.
[58]   Articles 10 and 11.
[59]   Article 13.
[60]   Article 2(1).
[61]   Gold 'Report on the WIPO Diplomatic Conference: the STLT, March 2006' (2006) CIPAJ 35(7) 459–460.
[62]   Indeed, as at January 2015, there were already 25 contracting parties.
[63]   Article 2.

(b)   relief measures in respect of time-limits;

(c)   provisions on the recording of trade mark licences; and

(d)   an Assembly to deal with the implementation and development of the Treaty and its Regulations.[64]

THE MADRID AGREEMENT FOR THE REPRESSION OF FALSE OR DECEPTIVE INDICATIONS OF ORIGIN 1891 AND REVISIONS

15.31   This early treaty dealt with misuse of geographical indications.[65] As at January 2012, there were 35 contracting parties, including the UK and a number of other European countries. Signatories undertake to repress false indications of source by seizing goods upon import or removing them from circulation in the country where the sign has been applied or where the product is being marketed. It relies upon national law, which often has considered indications of source to be generic in its own territory. This treaty was revised in 1911, 1925, 1934, and at Lisbon on 31 October 1958. At the Lisbon diplomatic conference, the 'Lisbon Agreement' (outlined below) was concluded. A further conference in Stockholm in 1967 dealt with the relationship between this Madrid Agreement and the Lisbon Agreement.

LISBON AGREEMENT FOR THE PROTECTION OF APPELLATIONS OF ORIGIN AND THEIR INTERNATIONAL REGISTRATION 1958 AND REVISIONS

15.32   This treaty has comparatively few contracting parties: 27 states in January 2012.[66] Most EU countries, including the UK, are not members.[67] It establishes a special union within the Paris Union – membership is open to any signatory to the Paris Convention. The treaty provides for registration at the International Bureau operated by WIPO in Geneva.[68] Application is made by the competent authority in the country of origin, which requests protection in the name of the relevant person. English, French or Spanish may be used. The Bureau notifies other member states which then have up to a year to declare that they cannot protect the appellation. According to Art 2(1) 'appellation of origin' means 'the geographical name of a country, region, or locality, which serves to designate a product originating therein, the quality and characteristics

---

[64]   See www.wipo.int/treaties/en/ip/singapore/summary_singapore.html.
[65]   For a good historical account, see O'Connor 'The Legal Protection of Geographical Indications' [2004] IPQ 35.
[66]   See www.wipo.int/export/sites/www/treaties/en/documents/pdf/lisbon.pdf.
[67]   The EU members are Bulgaria, Czech Republic, France, Hungary, Italy, Portugal and Slovakia.
[68]   Article 5. On registration of geographical indications generally, see Van Caenegem 'Registered GIs: Intellectual Property, Agricultural Policy and International Trade' [2004] EIPR 170.

of which are due exclusively or essentially to the geographical environment, including natural and human factors'. Registration gives protection against 'any usurpation or imitation, even if the true origin of the product is indicated or if the appellation is used in translated form or accompanied by terms such as "kind", "type", "make", "imitation", or the like'. The protection of appellations of origin within the UK is discussed further in Chapters 3 and 12.

NAIROBI TREATY ON THE PROTECTION OF THE OLYMPIC SYMBOL 1981

15.33 By this treaty, contracting parties agree to protect the Olympic symbol against unauthorised registration or use. The UK is not a signatory, although it protects a wider range of Olympic symbols by the Olympic Symbols Protection Act 1995.[69] The list of signatories as at January 2012 included a number of EU member states where the Treaty was in force: Bulgaria, Cyprus, Estonia Greece, Hungary, Italy, Poland, Romania and Slovenia. The Olympic symbol is defined by description, as consisting of five interlaced rings, which in colour are specified as blue, yellow, black, green and red. It is also protected in black and white. There are exceptions for earlier rights, for use in the media when reporting Olympic news, and so forth.[70] A signatory's obligations are suspended during periods when there is no national agreement with the International Olympic Committee.[71]

THE HAGUE SYSTEM FOR THE INTERNATIONAL REGISTRATION OF DESIGNS (LONDON 1934, HAGUE 1960, GENEVA 1999)

15.34 Finally, originally described as the Hague Agreement for the international deposit of designs, this system of treaties allowing for international design filings[72] was reformed and re-badged by a diplomatic conference in Geneva in 1999, with the hope of enticing countries such as the UK and US to join. These countries are not currently members, but many EU member states are.[73] The system allows for a single international filing of an 'industrial design' with the International Bureau at WIPO; no originating application or registration in the country of origin is required. As the system's earlier name suggests, the International Bureau examines only as to form. An international registration will take effect under the national laws of signatory states unless the designs office of a member state indicates within the

---

[69] See Lynd 'A Herculean Task' (2004) TW 168 34–36 and Chapter 12.
[70] Article 2.
[71] Article 3.
[72] See www.wipo.int/treaties/en/registration/hague. There were also the Monaco Act of 1961 and the Stockholm Act of 1967.
[73] For membership, see www.wipo.int/export/sites/www/treaties/en/documents/pdf/hague.pdf – the Agreement itself had 60 contracting parties as at January 2012.

prescribed period of 6 months that national registration is liable to be refused.[74] As national design laws apply, there is no harmonised definition of 'industrial design' but the phrase embraces both two- and three-dimensional designs; most systems require eye-appeal or aesthetic content. The International Register has its limitations, for example, there is no mechanism for recording licences. Registration of a design confers rights for a limited period.[75] Although the aesthetic appeal of a registrable 3D design would probably confer substantial value to the shape of a product and therefore render it ineligible for registration in the UK or EU,[76] a search of the International Register[77] of designs may indicate the presence of earlier rights over devices and motifs. It should be noted that deferment of publication may occur.[78] The International Register is classified under the Locarno scheme;[79] unfortunately this differs from the Nice classification of goods for trade mark purposes.

TRADITIONAL KNOWLEDGE, CULTURE, BIODIVERSITY AND TRADE MARKS

15.35 There has been debate[80] as to whether Western models of intellectual property protection are suitable for protecting the traditional knowledge[81] and culture of indigenous peoples and in providing a mechanism for the sharing of benefits derived from biodiversity under the Rio Convention.[82] Stakeholders in countries such as Australia[83] and New Zealand have developed systems to protect marks or labels of authenticity as a means of regulating the use of traditional cultural expression. At the international level, concern has already been expressed to WIPO about the registration of indigenous words, names and other marks: building on prior experience with protected symbols (e g state emblems and flags, the Olympic rings) and 'ring-fence' protection of certain indigenous emblems under US and New Zealand law, suggestions have been made that trade mark laws should be revised in order to protect such emblems,

---

[74] See Art 12 (1999 Act), Art 8 (1960 Act) and Common Regulations 1999, rule 18.
[75] A maximum of 25 years in the EU; see Art 12 of Council Regulation (EC) No 6/2002 of 12 December 2001 on Community designs and Art 10 of Directive (EC) 98/71 of the European Parliament and of the Council of 13 October 1998 on the legal protection of designs.
[76] See Chapter 2.
[77] See www.wipo.int/hague/en/services.
[78] Article 11.
[79] Under the Locarno Agreement Establishing an International Classification for Industrial Designs (concluded in 1968). See www.wipo.int/classifications/nivilo/locarno/index.htm?lang= EN.
[80] For earlier WIPO initiatives, see J Gibson 'Intellectual Property Systems, Traditional Knowledge and the Legal Authority of Community' [2004] EIPR 280. For current work, see WIPO's pages on 'Traditional Knowledge, Genetic Resources and Traditional Cultural Expressions/Folklore' at www.wipo.int/tk/en.
[81] Eg, Heath and Weidlich 'Intellectual Property: Suitable for Protecting Traditional Medicine' [2003] IPQ 69.D Zografos *Intellectual Property and Traditional Cultural Expressions* (Edward Elgar, 2010).
[82] The Convention on Biological Diversity, 5 June 1992; see www.cbd.int.
[83] L Wiseman 'The Protection of Indigenous Art and Culture in Australia: The Labels of Authenticity' [2001] EIPR 14; D Zografos, 'New Perspectives for the Protection of Traditional Cultural Expressions in New Zealand' [2005] IIC.

to allow for opposition/cancellation if necessary and to allow for registration of such words, names or other marks as a special form of 'defensive' registration.[84]

---

[84] See, on WIPO developments, Roberts 'Protecting Traditional Knowledge' (2009) CIPAJ 39(1) 26.

Chapter 16

INTERNATIONAL REGISTRATION: THE MADRID AGREEMENT AND PROTOCOL

BACKGROUND

16.1 Producers, traders and others with branding interests are generally in agreement that finding trade marks available for use and registration throughout the world is a worthwhile pursuit as part of a large-scale branding exercise, given that trading patterns are nowadays truly global. In reality, few undertakings need to use and register a trade mark in every single territory, but, on the other hand, unless a business is to remain small or have as an objective trading in its home country only, most will, at some point, look beyond national boundaries for trading purposes.

16.2 Except where regional or international agreements specifically provide to the contrary, trade marks and the rights which attach to them are by nature territorial, which principally means that their use and registration is subject to national law. Consequently, obtaining registrations on a country-by-country basis is an expensive exercise and at the end of the process (which itself is subject to local practice and language) one is potentially left, if at all, with a collection of rights of varying scope and duration. The need to remedy the inconvenience of the country-by-country route to trade mark protection and the financial burden it placed on manufacturers was first recognised at the end of the nineteenth century; accordingly, in 1891 the Madrid Agreement Concerning the International Registration of Marks was concluded ('the Madrid Agreement'[1]). The Agreement has been revised on seven occasions since 1891, the last time in 1979.[2]

16.3 The Agreement instituted a centralised trade mark application system which provides for the obtaining, simultaneously, of registered protection in as many countries party to the Agreement as is desired, by means of a single application designating countries of interest which is processed through the International Bureau of the World Intellectual Property Organisation (WIPO) in Geneva.

---

[1] Note that there is another 'Madrid Agreement' of 1891, for the Repression of False or Deceptive Indications of Source on Goods (discussed briefly at **15.29**); see, on this and on related EU legislation, O'Connor 'The Legal Protection of Geographical Indications' [2004] IPQ 35.

[2] At Stockholm; it had been revised previously in 1900, 1911, 1925, 1934, 1957 and 1967. See, generally, www.wipo.int/treaties/en/registration/madrid.

16.4 It will be understood readily that the creature resulting from an Agreement application is still not a truly 'international' registration, but instead is a bundle of national rights, obtained by means of a simplified and cheaper application procedure, with central recording and renewal.

LIMITATIONS OF THE AGREEMENT

16.5 Moreover, what one might imagine to be an application procedure which should meet with universal acclaim has important drawbacks when it is scrutinised more closely. It was as a result of the perceived disadvantages that many commercially important countries remained outside the Agreement. Weighed against the clear advantages set out above, and administrative benefits which flow therefrom, such as central recordal of assignments, renewals and changes of name and address, are the following disadvantages:

(a)   *'Central attack':* if the base registration is invalidated during the first 5 years, then the international registration falls, resulting in total loss of protection in all designated countries.[3]

(b)   *Too short a period within which an application may be refused by a national office:* designated countries have one year from the date of registration or demand for extension of protection within which to issue a refusal. This timescale is too short for those countries with full examination systems.[4]

(c)   *Language restriction:* the only language originally recognised for applications under the Madrid Agreement was French.[5]

(d)   *Low fee structure:* again, disadvantageous for countries with a full examination system.

16.6 The Agreement has been successful in terms of the number of marks protected under it,[6] though when compared with the number of applications received by OHIM since 1996, its success is relatively modest.[7] Until the early 1990s, membership was always below 30 and it needs to be recognised that the apparent popularity of membership during the 1990s was simply the result of

---

[3]   See **16.31**.

[4]   Article 5(2) of the Agreement.

[5]   However, changes have been made: Rule 6 of the Common Regulations under the Madrid Agreement Concerning the International Registration of Marks and the Protocol Relating to that Agreement (in force 1 September 2009) (hereinafter, the 'Common Regulations') now allows for English, Spanish and French as official application languages plus, for some other communications with WIPO, use of the applicant's 'home' language.

[6]   Under the Agreement and Protocol together (see **16.7**) by the beginning of 1999 over 345,000 registrations were in force. During 2010, some 37,533 new registrations were effected and 21,949 renewed: see www.wipo.int/stats/en/madrid/general_stats.jsp.

[7]   See Chapter 14.

the break up of the Soviet Union, Yugoslavia and Czechoslovakia and the ability of their successor states to join in their own right.[8]

16.7 Spurred by the moves toward creating a Community trade mark in the 1980s, attention was focused on how to overcome the Agreement's limitations and, in 1989, a Protocol[9] relating to the Madrid Agreement ('the Protocol') was signed by 28 countries including the UK.[10] It came into force on 1 April 1996 once nine countries had ratified it[11] and applications were first received on that day.

16.8 The Protocol shares many features of the Agreement,[12] but the following innovations will continue to encourage ratification of the Protocol:

(a) an applicant filing a Protocol application may base his request for registration on an application; an applicant under the Agreement must base his application on a registration;[13]

(b) a contracting party has a period of 18 months as opposed to 12 under the Agreement to issue a refusal.[14] If an opposition is notified within the 18-month period a contracting party has a longer period within which to refuse;

(c) the national office of a contracting party may receive higher fees than under the Agreement;[15]

(d) if the base application fails to mature into a registration or is cancelled at the request of the office of origin (as a result of receiving a 'central attack' application), the Madrid Protocol application may be converted or 'transformed' into one or more national applications,[16] thereby preserving the filing date;

---

[8] As at January 2011, the Agreement had still only attracted 56 states as parties. This number is unlikely to grow significantly as, in practice, the Agreement is increasingly being displaced by the Madrid Protocol (1989) (see **16.7** and Eckhartt 'Is There Still a Need for the 1891 Madrid Agreement' (2007) CW 170 (Supp) 22-4, 26).

[9] The text can be consulted at www.wipo.int/madrid/en/legal_texts/trtdocs_wo016.html. It has been amended twice so far (2006 and 2007).

[10] At its entry into force, not all countries viewed the Protocol as beneficial and the US did not accede until November 2003: see Nedeltscheff 'Turning Theory into Reality: the Expansion of the Madrid Protocol' (2004) 167 (Supp) *Trademark World* 6.

[11] China, Cuba, Denmark, Finland, Germany, Norway, Spain, Sweden and the UK. At least four contracting parties were needed, including one country party to the Agreement and one not.

[12] See Tramposch 'The Dream: has the Protocol Lived up to its Founders' Ambitions?' (2004) 167 (Supp) *Trademark World* 14 and Ghafele 'Trade Mark Owners' Perspectives on the Madrid System: Practical Experiences and Theoretical Underpinnings' (2007) 2(3) JIPLP 160-9.

[13] Protocol, Art 2.1.

[14] Protocol, Art 5(2)(b), (c) and (d).

[15] Protocol, Art 8(7).

[16] See **16.33–16.35**.

(e)   renewals are for 10 years rather than 20;[17]

(f)   English and Spanish were immediately recognised as official languages in addition to French;[18]

(g)   not only can states be contracting parties but also intergovernmental organisations;[19] making use of this provision, the EU[20] became a party on 1 October 2004.

16.9   The Agreement and the Protocol are two separate treaties. However, the Protocol is based firmly on the Agreement despite its new departures from the latter and, consequently, there is much common numbering of Articles,[21] and both systems share 'Common Regulations' for administrative purposes.[22]

16.10   The Protocol was originally implemented in the UK via s 54 of the Trade Marks Act 1994 ('the 1994 Act') and given effect by means of Order on 11 March 1996.[23] It did not generate amongst UK business the interest which might have been expected; only 50 applications were filed by UK applicants in the first year,[24] with some suggestion that this was a result of UK applicants being able to nominate fewer than 20 contracting parties in that initial period (of which only a handful were in western Europe); indeed, even with some 83 contracting parties as at January 2011, a slight braking effect is said to remain in that, where a 'home' contracting party to which an applicant is affiliated is a Madrid Protocol member only, such as the UK, an application using the Protocol mechanism may correspondingly designate contracting parties to the Protocol only.[25] Since the EU, as an Inter Governmental Organisation (IGO), can only be a contracting party to the Protocol, one might reasonably suspect

---

[17]   Protocol, Arts 6(1) and 7(1). Note, however, that renewal payments fall due every 10 years regardless of whether the registration arises via the Agreement or Protocol: in the case of Agreement registrations, they are treated as instalments under Rule 30(4), Common Regulations.

[18]   Rule 6, Common Regulations reflects.

[19]   Protocol, Arts 1 and 14(1)(b).

[20]   In its EC aspect and with OHIM as the relevant Office. See http://oami.europa.eu/ows/rw/pages/CTM/communityTradeMark/extending.en.do.

[21]   Reference in this chapter to 'Art' is made where the Article is common to both the Agreement and the Protocol. Otherwise references are given either as 'Agreement, Art X' or as 'Protocol, Art X'.

[22]   See note 5 above.

[23]   Originally, this was done via the Trade Marks (International Registration) Order 1996, SI 1996/714 (revoked in 2008).

[24]   Paper delivered by Malcolm Todd on general filing trends at Madrid Protocol Seminar, Trade Marks Registry, 28 April 1997. Between August 1998 and August 1999, just 314 applications were filed by UK applicants, a figure which compared unfavourably with the 8,646 applications made by non-UK applicants in the same period in which the UK was designated a territory of interest. The authors are grateful for this information which was provided by Mr Salvatore Di Palma, Deputy Director and Head, Administration Section International Registration Department, WIPO.

[25]   On the basis that there is no link to a contracting party in the Agreement and, therefore, Rule 9(4)(a)(xv) is not satisfied; any designation defective in this respect is advised to the applicant and disregarded thereafter.

this braking effect also to have operated on it but, increasingly for many applicants, use of OHIM as a Protocol 'point of departure' plus reliance on a Community trade mark (CTM) basic application in preference to member state national-level filings has siphoned in many such filings that would otherwise have occurred, including, logically, at least some relating to the UK.[26] In any event, UK participation in the Madrid system has remained at a lower level than was originally anticipated in the 1990s, being, in 2010, still only one place ahead of Australia (with approximately one-third of the population) in the registrations league table: the top five biggest numbers of registrations classed by office of origin were from Germany (4,548), the EU (OHIM) (4,356), the US (3,897), France (3,734) and Switzerland (3,093) respectively (the UK, by contrast, managed just 1,062).[27]

ENTITLEMENT TO APPLY

16.11 The Agreement or Protocol can be used as a filing mechanism by natural or legal persons whose country of origin is or falls within the territory of one of the contracting parties.[28] In the case of the Protocol only, additional rules have had to be devised to cover the question of origin which arises when an intergovernmental organisation rather than a state is involved at the point of filing.[29]

16.12 If the Agreement route is used, the country of origin is where an applicant has a 'real and effective commercial or industrial establishment'.[30] If he does not, the state of domicile may be used, if applicable. If it is not, the country of which the applicant is a national will be considered the country of origin.[31] These strict rules serve to prevent a user 'shopping' for the state where registration is most easily obtained. This is relevant because a national registration in the country of origin must be secured as a basis for the international filing. This makes the arrangement less suitable for countries where examination is strict, because the base registration takes longer to procure and is likely to be narrower in scope.

---

[26] Indeed, the UK accounted for over 16.6% of CTM applications in 2010, the second highest percentage after Germany: see http://oami.europa.eu/ows/rw/resource/documents/OHIM/statistics/ssc009-statistics_of_community_trade_marks_2010.pdf.

[27] Until the entry of the US into the Madrid system in 2003, many UK trade mark attorneys tended to be more reluctant than their continental European counterparts to endorse the Madrid system; against this background, see Muhlberg 'Madrid: Playing the Game' (2001) 141 *Trademark World* 12.

[28] Agreement, Art 1(2) and 2; Protocol, Art 2(1).

[29] See **16.13**.

[30] This wording also occurs in relation to the trade mark provisions in the Paris Convention – it is intended to prevent stockpiling of marks through sham economic links: see Humphreys 'Territoriality in Community Trade Mark Matters: the British Problem' [2000] EIPR 405.

[31] Agreement, Art 1(3).

16.13 For the Protocol applicant, the above strict entitlement rules do not apply; so long as the country of origin chosen is party to the Protocol the applicant may elect to base his filing on either:

(a) an application made in the country of origin in which the applicant is a national or has a real and effective industrial or commercial establishment; or

(b) an application made at the office of a contracting organisation where the applicant is a national of a state party to the organisation or where the applicant is domiciled or has a real and effective industrial or commercial establishment in the territory of the organisation.[32]

An applicant using the Agreement can only use an existing registration in his country of origin on which to base his international filing,[33] whereas under the Protocol the basis can be a registration or an application made in a contracting country where the applicant has a real and effective commercial or industrial establishment.[34]

16.14 The following are members of the Agreement as at January 2011.

Albania (AL)	Algeria (DZ)
Armenia (AM)	Austria (AT)
Azerbaijan (AZ)	Belarus (BY)
Belgium (BE)	Bhutan (BT)
Bosnia and Herzegovina (BA)	Bulgaria (BG)
China (People's Republic) (CN)	Croatia (HR)
Cuba (CU)	Cyprus (CY)
Czech Republic (CZ)	Egypt (EG)
France (FR)	Germany (DE)
Hungary (HU)	Iran (Islamic Republic of) (IR)
Italy (IT)	Kazakhstan (KZ)
Kenya (KE)	Korea (Democratic People's Republic) (KP)
Kyrgyzstan (KG)	Latvia (LV)

---

[32] Protocol, Art 2(1)(i) and (ii).
[33] Agreement, Art 1(2).
[34] Protocol, Art 2(1).

Lesotho (LS)	Liberia (LR)
Liechtenstein (LI)	Luxembourg (LU)
Macedonia (Former Yugoslav Republic) (MK)	Moldova (MD)
Monaco (MC)	Mongolia (MN)
Montenegro (ME)	Morocco (MA)
Mozambique (MZ)	Namibia (NA)
Netherlands (NL)	Poland (PL)
Portugal (PT)	Romania (RO)
Russian Federation (RU)	San Marino (SM)
Serbia (RS)	Sierra Leone (SL)
Slovakia (SK)	Slovenia (SI)
Spain (ES)	Sudan (SD)
Swaziland (SZ)	Switzerland (CH)
Syrian Arab Republic (SY)	Tajikistan (TJ)
Ukraine (UA)	Vietnam (VN)

16.15   The following are members of the Protocol as at January 2011.

Albania (AL)	Antigua and Barbuda (AG)	Armenia (AM)
Australia (AU)	Austria (AT)	Azerbaijan (AZ)
Bahrain (BH)	Belarus (BY)	Belgium (BE)
Bhutan (BT)	Bosnia and Herzegovina (BA)	Botswana (BW)
Bulgaria (BG)	China (People's Republic) (CN)	Croatia (HR)
Cuba (CU)	Cyprus (CY)	Czech Republic (CZ)
Denmark (DK)	Egypt (EG)	Estonia (EE)
European Community (OHIM) (EM)	Finland (FI)	France (FR)

Georgia (GE)	Germany (DE)	Ghana (GH)
Greece (GR)	Hungary (HU)	Iceland (IS)
Iran (IR)	Ireland (IE)	Israel (IL)
Italy (IT)	Japan (JP)	Kazakhstan (KZ)
Kenya (KE)	Korea (Democratic People's Republic) (KP)	Korea (Republic) (KR)
Kyrgyzstan(KG)	Latvia (LV)	Lesotho (LS)
Liberia (LR)	Liechtenstein (LI)	Lithuania (LT)
Luxembourg (LU)	Macedonia (Former Yugoslav Republic) (MK)	Madagascar (MG)
Moldova (MD)	Monaco (MC)	Mongolia (MN)
Montenegro (ME)	Morocco (MA)	Mozambique (MZ)
Namibia (NA)	Netherlands (NL)	Norway (NO)
Oman (OM)	Poland (PL)	Portugal (PT)
Romania (RO)	Russian Federation (RU)	San Marino (SM)
Sao Tome and Principe (ST)	Serbia (RS)	Sierra Leone (SL)
Singapore (SG)	Slovakia (SK)	Slovenia (SI)
Spain (ES)	Sudan (SD)	Swaziland (SW)
Sweden (SE)	Switzerland (CH)	Syrian Arab Republic (SY)
Turkey (TR)	Turkmenistan (TM)	Uzbekistan (UZ)
Ukraine (UA)	United Kingdom (GB)	United States (US)
Vietnam (VN)	Zambia (ZM)	

Application procedure

16.16 An international application is filed in the country of origin which certifies that the details of the application correspond with the details of the basic application or registration as the case may be.[35] The mark, the subject of the Madrid application, must be identical to the earlier mark, relate only to goods and/or services of the earlier right and be in the same ownership. Priority

---

[35] Article 3.

may be claimed either from the application/registration on which the international application is based, or from an earlier filing so long as the claim is made within 6 months[36] of the latter.

16.17 The UK Trade Marks Registry charges a handling fee to receive and process the initial request for an international application.[37] Although international applications governed by the Agreement originally had to be made in French, today, like an application governed by the Protocol, they may be in French, English or Spanish.[38]

16.18 The applicant must designate those contracting parties for which protection is sought.[39] Entitlement to designate is dependent on whether the applicant's office of origin is party to the Agreement only, the Protocol only or to both.

16.19 Article 8 and Rule 10 set out the structure of standard fees, which, in its basic form, is the same both for the Protocol as for the Agreement. The fees payable (in Swiss francs) are set out in the Schedule of Fees to the Common Regulations. The fee structure provides that the total fees payable consists of three components:

(1)   a basic fee[40] payable on every application;

(2)   a supplementary fee[41] for each product class beyond three;

(3)   a complementary fee[42] for each country designation made.

16.20 However, although Art 8 provides that the annual fee returns are to be divided amongst the contracting parties on a pro rata basis, parties contracting to the Protocol may opt for 'individual' fees instead of their proportional share. So far the UK and a number of others have exercised this option,[43] the effect of

---

[36]   Article 4(2). See, further, Chapter 5 (priority) and Chapter 15 (Paris Convention).

[37]   As at the time of writing, £40.

[38]   Rule 6.

[39]   Articles 3*bis* and 3*ter*(1).

[40]   Currently 653 Swiss francs unless the mark is in colour, in which case 903 Swiss francs.

[41]   Currently 100 Swiss francs.

[42]   Currently 100 Swiss francs.

[43]   See the various 'Declarations made by Contracting Parties of the Madrid System under the Agreement, the Protocol and the Common Regulations' at www.wipo.int/madrid/en/notices/index.jsp.

which is to increase dramatically the cost of Protocol applications.[44] In order to assist applicants, a fee calculator is available from the International Bureau's website.[45]

16.21 Once the office of origin is satisfied that the request for international registration is identical in all respects to the earlier right on which it is based, the office transmits the application to the International Bureau.[46] Upon receipt, the International Bureau checks the certified formalities, enters the mark on the International Register, and sends a Certificate of Registration to the applicant. If the Bureau discovers a classification discrepancy or other irregularity, a limited period is set to remedy the deficiency,[47] and to pay any appropriate fee. If and when accepted, the application is published in *Les Marques Internationale* and details of it are forwarded to the designated countries.[48] So long as the International Bureau receives details of an application within 2 months of filing at an office of origin, the registration will bear the date of application in the country of origin. Otherwise, the registration date will be the date on which the Bureau receives the notification of an application having been made.[49]

16.22 Once a mark has been registered, each contracting party must treat the international registration as if it had been filed directly at the trade mark office of that party.[50] For a mark filed under the Agreement, national offices have 12 months to refuse it,[51] failing which the mark automatically becomes protected as of the date of international registration.[52] A refusal in one designated country does not affect protection in others. The receiving office may issue a partial refusal or limit the specification of goods or services.[53] Again, this has no bearing on the position in other countries. The equivalent period for Protocol marks is 18 months, unless opposition is filed, in which case the period can be longer.[54] Insofar as the UK is concerned, WIPO was been notified under Art 5(2)(c) that oppositions may be filed outside the 18-month period; however, this is increasingly unlikely given the accelerated processing of applications under the post-2007 system.

---

[44] When designating Japan or Cuba it also needs to be borne in mind that a significant sum at the end of a successful designation will be payable in the form of those jurisdictions' registration fees. However, notwithstanding this and the individual fees issue generally, registering a mark overseas via Madrid should still be cheaper than using individual national routes. Unless a national office raises an issue that requires an applicant to nominate a local attorney to resolve it, no local address for service is required.

[45] See www.wipo.int/madrid/en/fees.

[46] Article 3(1).

[47] Typically 3 months, depending on the nature of the irregularity: see, in detail, Rules 11–13.

[48] Article 3(4).

[49] Article 3(4).

[50] Article 4(1).

[51] For an example of such refusal on absolute grounds, see *Basic Trademark SA's TM Application* [2005] RPC 25 (Appointed Person).

[52] Agreement, Art 5(5).

[53] See Wilkinson 'Broad Trade Mark Specifications' [2002] EIPR 227.

[54] Protocol, Art 5(1) and (2).

16.23 The UK Registry examines the UK portion of the international registration as if it were a direct national filing, requiring a valid address for service with which to correspond if an official objection is raised.[55] So long as any official objection is overcome, the application is published in the *Trade Marks Journal* along with other national applications,[56] and is subject to a 3-month opposition period as are national applications.[57] Where no opposition is filed, or where opposition is overcome, the mark becomes 'protected as a protected international trade mark (UK)'.[58]

16.24 In terms of when to commence an infringement action in the UK, based on an international registration which designates the UK, the right to do so runs from the date the mark becomes protected in the UK as opposed to entry in the Register (since no Register entry is made as such). It should be noted that the date of protection will vary from country to country, depending, inter alia, on whether a country provides for opposition. Bearing these factors in mind, a competitor conducting a search for protected marks in the UK will need to search the international as well as the UK and Community registers.

16.25 Similarly, the period of 5 years during which there must be genuine use of the mark commences on the date of protection as opposed to any entry in the Register date, the original filing date, or entry in the International Register.[59] Renewal periods are calculated, however, from the date of international registration.[60]

POST-REGISTRATION MATTERS

Territorial extension

16.26 Further countries may be grafted on to the international registration by the process of 'extension'.[61] A request for extension is generally treated in the same way as the original registration in terms of procedures.[62] Extensions may not go beyond the scope of the original registration in terms of goods and/or services. It should be noted further that renewal fees are due on the tenth anniversary from the original filing date and so an applicant requesting a territorial extension in, say, year nine of a renewal period will be paying

---

[55] A Form TM33 must be filed.

[56] Though in a separate section.

[57] By virtue of the Trade Marks (International Registration) Order 2008, SI 2008/2206; as with national procedures, they may result in the international registration being refused for some or all of the goods or services concerned: *Giorgio Armani SpA v Sunrich Clothing Ltd* [2010] EWHC 2939 (Ch); [2011] ETMR 13.

[58] An official letter issues to that effect.

[59] The 'first vulnerability' date varies from country to country. See Folliard-Monguiral and Rogers 'Significant Case Law from 2004 on the Community Trade Mark from the Court of First Instance, the European Court of Justice and OHIM' [2005] EIPR 133.

[60] Article 6; 20 years for an Agreement registration, 10 for a Protocol registration.

[61] Article 3*ter*(2); see Rule 24(1) for entitlement to make subsequent designations.

[62] For an example of refusal of a request for extension to the UK, see *Casa Damiani SpA's App* [2004] ETMR 68 TMR.

renewal fees hard on the heels of the application fee. Conversely, a designation may be renounced, for example in consequence of dispute settlement.

Assignment

16.27   Article 9 provides that an international registration may be assigned in whole or in part so long as the assignee is entitled to hold an international registration.[63] Rule 25(2) sets out the International Bureau's requirements in terms of formalities. If the assignment application is in order the Bureau records it, notifies each office of the designated contracting parties[64] and publishes details of the recordal in the *WIPO Gazette of International Marks.*

16.28   Fortunately, an increasingly historical issue, insofar as any UK portion of an international registration is concerned, if the relevant assignment transaction was executed in the UK prior to 28 March 2000, then the normal rules as to stamp duty applied.[65] Although stamp duty is no longer levied on intellectual property transactions, an assignee or other interested party should check to see whether the rules were complied with.[66]

Other registrable transactions

16.29   The following are recordable changes which are notifiable by the International Bureau to the offices of the contracting parties;[67] most are publishable:

(i)   limitation of the list of goods and/or services in respect of all or some of the designated territories;

(ii)   voluntary cancellation;[68]

(iii)   correction of errors;[69]

(iv)   change of name and/or address;

(v)   enforced cancellation or invalidity action;

(vi)   any other relevant fact (presumably includes a memorandum or charge);[70]

---

[63]   See **16.11–16.13**.
[64]   Rule 27(1).
[65]   Although s 61 of the 1994 Act stated that stamp duty was not chargeable on an instrument conveying an international trade mark purely because the mark had legal effect in the UK, if the document was executed in the UK then the normal rules relating to payment nevertheless applied.
[66]   See Chapter 10 and Chapter 11.
[67]   Article 9 and Rule 25(1)(l).
[68]   Agreement, Art 8*bis*; Protocol, Art 9*bis*.
[69]   Rule 28.
[70]   Agreement, Art 9, Protocol, Art 9*bis*.

(vii) division or merger of the basic registration or application during the first 5 years of its life.[71]

16.30 Applications to record changes are made via the office of origin or, in permitted cases, to the International Bureau and may, in some instances, be subject to a fee.[72]

SPECIAL FEATURES OF THE MADRID SYSTEM

Dependence on the national mark and 'central attack'

16.31 Once the first period of 5 years from the date of the international registration has expired the registration becomes independent of the national mark registered earlier in the country of origin.[73] Until that point is reached, if the basic mark is withdrawn, partially refused, opposed, revoked in whole or in part, or is the subject of invalidity proceedings, the effect of action on the basic mark follows through to all the country designations. Third party action against the basic mark is known as 'central attack'. Its importance should not be overestimated: WIPO stated in 1997 that less than one half of a per cent of international registrations were cancelled as a result of central attack.

16.32 It is the responsibility of the office of origin to notify the International Bureau of action affecting the basic application or registration[74] and of the Bureau in turn to notify the offices of the designated contracting parties.

Transformation

16.33 It will be appreciated that the vulnerability of an international registration to 'central attack' action by a third party against the application or registration on which it is based is theoretically high and the effect potentially devastating. For marks governed by the Agreement the issue cannot be avoided. For marks governed by the Protocol, however, the alleviative concept of 'transformation' has been introduced.[75]

16.34 In the event of a successful attack on a base registration under the terms of the Protocol, so long as the holder of the registration within a period of 3 months from its cancellation applies to register the same mark with any contracting party in the territory in which the international registration had effect, the holder shall be permitted to 'transform' as many of the territorial designations as are required into national registrations. These will then continue to enjoy the same date of protection as was previously enjoyed under the international registration.

---

71 Rule 23.
72 See Schedule of Fees to the Common Regulations.
73 Article 6(3).
74 Article 6(4); Rule 22.
75 Protocol, Art 9.

16.35 It should be noted that the transformation mechanism does not exist to save a Protocol filing based on an *application*; so an applicant for registration is advised to proceed with extreme care if he chooses such a basis. For international registrations based on a UK application, the position is somewhat better than in other countries; not only is the registration process in the UK relatively quick, but the fact that examination takes place at all gives applicants some comfort as to potentially conflicting marks and inherent validity. Once a positive report on an application has been received, or at least a UK clearance search has suggested the mark is a good candidate for registration, it may be safe to proceed with the Madrid application. Inevitably though, waiting until the application has proceeded to grant before using it as a base remains the securest option.

Replacement of national rights

16.36 Where a mark which is the subject of a national registration in the office of a contracting party is also the subject of an international registration and where both registrations are identical in terms of ownership, list of goods and/or services, and where the international registration is later than the national mark, the international registration is deemed to replace the earlier right.[76] Although the benefit of the provision is financial in that cheaper renewal fees result, it is not sensible to relinquish an earlier national right until the period of dependency has passed.[77]

16.37 In the UK the holder of a protected international mark must apply on the Form TM28 to have his national mark replaced.

THE MADRID SYSTEM AND THE COMMUNITY TRADE MARK

Points of contact and comparisons

16.38 It will be understood for those based in the UK and who trade in continental Europe that three routes to protection of their trade marks can now be used:

(a)   national registrations;

(b)   the Community trade mark (CTM) system;

(c)   the Protocol system leading to a bundle of national rights and/or a regional right.[78]

---

[76]   Article 4*bis*.
[77]   See **16.31**.
[78]   Such as the Community trade mark itself.

The routes are not mutually exclusive; it is often highly advisable to use a combination. Factors influencing which route(s) to follow include cost, territories of interest, nature of the mark, speed of application procedure, the mark's importance in relation to others in the proprietor's portfolio and perception of the relative advantages inherent in each system. For an analysis of the pros and cons of CTMs versus national registrations see **14.76**.

Designating the European Community under the Protocol

16.39 Since 1 October 2004, it has been possible to designate the EU as a single territory within a Protocol application;[79] although the latter instrument was designed with the emerging CTM system specifically in mind, a lengthy series of obstacles prevented implementation of the necessary linkage scheme,[80] including such issues as conversion to national applications or extension to contracting parties, which languages were to be those officially recognised, and voting rights for the EU (one of the original sticking points for US accession).[81] The first two technical issues having been satisfactorily resolved, the political issue of the existence or exercise of an EU vote was eventually overcome by a 'gentleman's agreement' whereby the EU would not exercise its vote in the Madrid Union if all the member states had voted unanimously,[82] and, in any event, the total number of votes would not exceed the number of EU member states.

International registration based on a CTM application or registration

16.40 With the definition of 'basic applications' and 'basic registrations' already covering those from contracting parties (rather than just states only as under the Agreement), since the accession of the EU to the Protocol in 2004, it has been possible to use a CTM application or registration as a basis for an international registration.[83] However, in practice, there is some degree of risk in this strategy. Many months will elapse before an OHIM examination report issues and, in 2011, over 15% of published CTM applications were opposed[84]; this is not surprising given that OHIM carries out only a limited search and report using member state data and their own internal databases (results

---

[79] See, now, Title XIII (International Registration of Marks) in Council Regulation (EC) No 207/2009 of 26 February 2009 on the Community trade mark.

[80] See the original Proposal for a Council Regulation modifying Council Regulation (EC) 40/94 of 20 December 1993 on the Community trade mark to give effect to the accession of the European Community to the Protocol relating to the Madrid Agreement concerning the international registration of marks (96/C 300/09) COM (96) 372 final – 96/01988CNS; De Ranitz and Von Muhlendahl 'Alexander von Muhlendahl in Conversation with Remco de Ranitz' [2000] EIPR 528.

[81] See Nooteboom 'The Madrid Agreement and Protocol: Links with the CTM' (1998) ECTA 14.

[82] For the problem and its compromise see REP De Ranitz, A Von Muhlendahl 'Alexander Von Muhlendahl in conversation with Remco De Ranitz' [2000] EIPR 528.

[83] Cf Rule 1(xiii) and (xiv) of the Common Regulations.

[84] Based on figures from OHIM statistics at http://oami.europa.eu/ows/rw/resource/documents/OHIM/statistics/ssc009-statistics_of_community_trade_marks_2011.pdf.

available on fee-bearing request to applicant) and do not examine on 'relative grounds', ie for conflict with earlier marks. However, given that the EU now consists of 27 member states, due to rise to 28 with the accession of Croatia in July 2013, the actual scope for opposition is considerable.

Do the Madrid system and the Community trade mark system compete?

16.41   Prior to the EU's accession to the Protocol in 2004, it was argued by some that the two systems operated in competition to one another; although the proponents of both the Madrid and the CTM systems worked hard from their conception and inception to deny this, competition within Europe was the inevitable consequence so long as they remained separate.[85] Today, following linkage, the situation is much more relaxed and the systems can be simply compared 'on the merits';[86] this is especially so given that, as at January 2012, all of the EU countries (except Malta) have also ratified the Protocol.[87] Ultimately, cost calculations and the range of countries which are of genuine interest to the trade mark proprietor will determine which system or combination is used. With significant fee reductions under the CTM system in 2009, there is a somewhat greater incentive than previously to use the 'CTM plus Protocol' hybrid option.

16.42   The following highlights some of the points of contact between the Madrid and CTM systems and may be used to compare their relevant strengths and weaknesses. It should be stressed that, especially since linkage of the two systems in 2004, neither system is clearly 'better' than the other; ultimately, it is the circumstances surrounding the type of protection required which will determine each route's usefulness.[88]

---

[85]   Indeed, it is interesting to note that in 2004, only 42 international registrations had OHIM as their Office of origin.

[86]   See Weberndorfer 'The Integration of the Office for Harmonization in the Internal Market into the Madrid System: a First Field Report' [2008] EIPR 216.

[87]   Malta is likely to join eventually and has already made provision for doing so; s 48 of its Trademarks Act 2000 (as amended) provides that local implementation of the Protocol can occur via Ministerial Order.

[88]   A comparison is made between the Protocol and the CTM rather than between the Madrid system as a whole and the CTM given that the former provides a better comparison from a UK perspective: see also Vern 'Two Tracks, One Destination: International Registration or Community Trade Mark?' (2004) 172 *Trademark World* 32.

Advantages of the Madrid Protocol	Comparison with the CTM
Central application procedure resulting in a bundle of rights.	Central application procedure resulting in a unitary right.
Can select contracting parties of interest and extend protection at a later date to others.	No choice: all EU member states are included automatically.
Application filed in English at the UK Registry.	Application filed in English at the UK Registry or direct in an official language at the CTM Office.
Central renewal, licence and assignment recordal.	Central renewal, licence and assignment recordal.
Filing costs depend on number of classes and contracting parties designated.	All EU member states included automatically; extra class fees payable above specified limit.
Can be used to circumvent a complex local route (eg China), where local attorneys fees are expensive (eg Spain) or where local procedures are slow (eg Russia).	N/A except that there is an obvious cost saving on not having to pay continental European attorneys' fees.
Marks are protected within 18 months unless an official objection or opposition is successfully maintained.	The registration process remains slow.
Refusal in one territory does not affect other designated territories.	A successful objection in one territory will lead to the collapse of the application.[89]
Separate rights in the bundle can be assigned individually (though needs the consent of the assignee's country of origin if within the first 5 years).	Can be assigned only as a totality, though can be licensed for part of the Community.
Successful revocation or invalidity action (after first 5 'dependence' years) in relation to one contracting party has no effect on the other designations.	Successful revocation or invalidity action removes entire right.
The system is becoming more attractive as more contracting parties ratify.	N/A but note the EU now has 27 member states with other candidate countries at hand.
Single renewal fee and 10-year renewal period.	Single renewal fee and 10-year renewal period.

---

[89] Although a Community trade mark application may be converted into a bundle of national applications in EU member states. See **14.4–14.5**; **14.51–14.53** (conversion).

Disadvantages of the Madrid Protocol	Comparison with the CTM
Underlying application/registration needed.	No base application or registration required.
An international registration based on an application is dependent on the fate of the 'home' application.	N/A
Major potential contracting parties (eg Brazil) still remain outside the system.[90]	N/A
Use is required for each contracting party to maintain the relevant registrations in force.	Use in one country maintains the unitary right.
Assignment to legal entities not entitled to hold international registrations under a contracting party's rules is not permitted.	N/A
Fee structure is complex.	Fee structure is simple.
Necessary to pursue infringements in each contracting party's designated courts.	'CTM Courts' designated nationally have jurisdiction throughout the EC.
Subject to 'central attack' (though tempered with ability to 'transform').	N/A
Need to appoint local attorneys if there is a local Registry/third party objection.	All issues handled by one attorney.
Specification of goods and services will be scrutinised by many trade mark offices.	Specification of goods and services will be scrutinised by only one trade mark office.

---

[90]   At time of writing, a number of significant UK trading partners, such as India, Thailand, Malaysia, South Africa, Canada and much of the Middle East, still remain outside.

Appendix 1

TRADE MARKS ACT 1994

PART I
REGISTERED TRADE MARKS

Introductory

1 Trade Marks

(1) In this Act a 'trade mark' means any sign capable of being represented graphically which is capable of distinguishing goods or services of one undertaking from those of other undertakings.

A trade mark may, in particular, consist of words (including personal names), designs, letters, numerals or the shape of goods or their packaging.

(2) References in this Act to a trade mark include, unless the context otherwise requires, references to a collective mark (see section 49) or certification mark (see section 50).

2 Registered trade marks

(1) A registered trade mark is a property right obtained by the registration of the trade mark under this Act and the proprietor of a registered trade mark has the rights and remedies provided by this Act.

(2) No proceedings lie to prevent or recover damages for the infringement of an unregistered trade mark as such; but nothing in this Act affects the law relating to passing off.

3 Absolute grounds for refusal of registration

(1) The following shall not be registered –

   (a)   signs which do not satisfy the requirements of section 1(1),
   (b)   trade marks which are devoid of any distinctive character,
   (c)   trade marks which consist exclusively of signs or indications which may serve, in trade, to designate the kind, quality, quantity, intended purpose, value, geographical origin, the time of production of goods or of rendering of services, or other characteristics of goods or services,
   (d)   trade marks which consist exclusively of signs or indications which have become customary in the current language or in the bona fide and established practices of the trade:

Provided that, a trade mark shall not be refused registration by virtue of paragraph (b), (c) or (d) above if, before the date of application for registration, it has in fact acquired a distinctive character as a result of the use made of it.

(2) A sign shall not be registered as a trade mark if it consists exclusively of –

    (a)   the shape which results from the nature of the goods themselves,

    (b)   the shape of goods which is necessary to obtain a technical result, or

    (c)   the shape which gives substantial value to the goods.

(3) A trade mark shall not be registered if it is –

    (a)   contrary to public policy or to accepted principles of morality, or

    (b)   of such a nature as to deceive the public (for instance as to the nature, quality or geographical origin of the goods or service).

(4) A trade mark shall not be registered if or to the extent that its use is prohibited in the United Kingdom by any enactment or rule of law or by any provision of Community law.

(5) A trade mark shall not be registered in the cases specified, or referred to, in section 4 (specially protected emblems).

(6) A trade mark shall not be registered if or to the extent that the application is made in bad faith.

4 Specially protected emblems

(1) A trade mark which consists of or contains –

    (a)   the Royal arms, or any of the principal armorial bearings of the Royal arms, or any insignia or device so nearly resembling the Royal arms or any such armorial bearing as to be likely to be mistaken for them or it,

    (b)   a representation of the Royal crown or any of the Royal flags,

    (c)   a representation of Her Majesty or any member of the Royal family, or any colourable imitation thereof, or

    (d)   words, letters or devices likely to lead persons to think that the applicant either has or recently has had Royal patronage or authorisation,

shall not be registered unless it appears to the registrar that consent has been given by or on behalf of Her Majesty or, as the case may be, the relevant member of the Royal family.

(2) A trade mark which consists of or contains a representation of –

    (a)   the national flag of the United Kingdom (commonly known as the Union Jack), or

    (b)   the flag of England, Wales, Scotland, Northern Ireland or the Isle of Man,

shall not be registered if it appears to the registrar that the use of the trade mark would be misleading or grossly offensive.

Provision may be made by rules identifying the flags to which paragraph (b) applies.

(3) A trade mark shall not be registered in the cases specified in –

section 57 (national emblems, &c of Convention countries), or section 58 (emblems, &c of certain international organisations).

(4) Provision may be made by rules prohibiting in such cases as may be prescribed the registration of a trade mark which consists of or contains –

(a) arms to which a person is entitled by virtue of a grant of arms by the Crown, or

(b) insignia so nearly resembling such arms as to be likely to be mistaken for them,

unless it appears to the registrar that consent has been given by or on behalf of that person.

Where such a mark is registered, nothing in this Act shall be construed as authorising its use in any way contrary to the laws of arms.

(5) A trade mark which consists of or contains a controlled representation within the meaning of the Olympic Symbol etc (Protection) Act 1995 shall not be registered unless it appears to the registrar

(a) that the application is made by the person for the time being appointed under section 1(2) of the Olympic Symbol etc (Protection) Act 1995 (power of Secretary of State to appoint a person as the proprietor of the Olympics association right), or

(b) that consent has been given by or on behalf of the person mentioned in paragraph (a) above.

Amendments–Olympic Symbol etc (Protection) Act 1995, s 13(2), (3).

5 Relative grounds for refusal of registration

(1) A trade mark shall not be registered if it is identical with an earlier trade mark and the goods or services for which the trade mark is applied for are identical with the goods or services for which the earlier trade mark is protected.

(2) A trade mark shall not be registered if because –

(a) it is identical with an earlier trade mark and is to be registered for goods or services similar to those for which the earlier trade mark is protected, or

(b) it is similar to an earlier trade mark and is to be registered for goods or services identical with or similar to those for which the earlier trade mark is protected,

there exists a likelihood of confusion on the part of the public, which includes the likelihood of association with the earlier trade mark.

(3) A trade mark which –

(a) is identical with or similar to an earlier trade mark,

(b) *(repealed)*

shall not be registered if, or to the extent that, the earlier trade mark has a reputation in the United Kingdom (or, in the case of a Community trade mark or international trade mark (EC), in the European Community) and the use of the later mark without due cause would take unfair advantage of, or be detrimental to, the distinctive character or the repute of the earlier trade mark.

(4) A trade mark shall not be registered if, or to the extent that, its use in the United Kingdom is liable to be prevented –

> (a)   by virtue of any rule of law (in particular, the law of passing off) protecting an unregistered trade mark or other sign used in the course of trade, or
>
> (b)   by virtue of an earlier right other than those referred to in subsections (1) to (3) or paragraph (a) above, in particular by virtue of the law of copyright, design right or registered designs.

A person thus entitled to prevent the use of a trade mark is referred to in this Act as the proprietor of an 'earlier right' in relation to the trade mark.

(5) Nothing in this section prevents the registration of a trade mark where the proprietor of the earlier trade mark or other earlier right consents to the registration.

Amendments–SI 2004/946; SI 2004/2332.

6 Meaning of 'earlier trade mark'

(1) In this Act an 'earlier trade mark' means –

> (a)   a registered trade mark, international trade mark (UK), Community trade mark or international trade mark (EC) which has a date of application for registration earlier than that of the trade mark in question, taking account (where appropriate) of the priorities claimed in respect of the trade marks,
>
> (b)   a Community trade mark or international trade mark (EC) which has a valid claim to seniority from an earlier registered trade mark or international trade mark (UK),
>
> (ba) a registered trade mark or international trade mark (UK) which –
> > (i)   has been converted from a Community trade mark or international trade mark (EC) which itself had a valid claim to seniority within paragraph (b) from an earlier trade mark, and
> > (ii)   accordingly has the same claim to seniority, or
>
> (c)   a trade mark which, at the date of application for registration of the trade mark in question or (where appropriate) of the priority claimed in respect of the application, was entitled to protection under the Paris Convention or the WTO agreement as a well known trade mark.

(2) References in this Act to an earlier trade mark include a trade mark in respect of which an application for registration has been made and which, if registered, would be an earlier trade mark by virtue of subsection 1(a) or (b), subject to its being so registered.

(3) A trade mark within subsection (1)(a) or (b) whose registration expires shall continue to be taken into account in determining the registrability of a

later mark for a period of one year after the expiry unless the registrar is satisfied that there was no bona fide use of the mark during the two years immediately preceding the expiry.

Amendments–SI 1999/1899; SI 2004/2332.

6A Raising of relative grounds in opposition proceedings in case of non-use

(1) This section applies where –

    (a)   an application for registration of a trade mark has been published,

    (b)   there is an earlier trade mark of a kind falling within section 6(1)(a), (b) or (ba) in relation to which the conditions set out in section 5(1), (2) or (3) obtain, and

    (c)   the registration procedure for the earlier trade mark was completed before the start of the period of five years ending with the date of publication.

(2) In opposition proceedings, the registrar shall not refuse to register the trade mark by reason of the earlier trade mark unless the use conditions are met.

(3) The use conditions are met if –

    (a)   within the period of five years ending with the date of publication of the application the earlier trade mark has been put to genuine use in the United Kingdom by the proprietor or with his consent in relation to the goods or services for which it is registered, or

    (b)   the earlier trade mark has not been so used, but there are proper reasons for non-use.

(4) For these purposes –

    (a)   use of a trade mark includes use in a form differing in elements which do not alter the distinctive character of the mark in the form in which it was registered, and

    (b)   use in the United Kingdom includes affixing the trade mark to goods or to the packaging of goods in the United Kingdom solely for export purposes.

(5) In relation to a Community trade mark or international trade mark (EC), any reference in subsection (3) or (4) to the United Kingdom shall be construed as a reference to the European Community.

(6) Where an earlier trade mark satisfies the use conditions in respect of some only of the goods or services for which it is registered, it shall be treated for the purposes of this section as if it were registered only in respect of those goods or services.

(7) Nothing in this section affects –

    (a)   the refusal of registration on the grounds mentioned in section 3 (absolute grounds for refusal) or section 5(4)(relative grounds of refusal on the basis of an earlier right), or

    (b)   the making of an application for a declaration of invalidity under section 47(2) (application on relative grounds where no consent to registration).

Amendments–SI 2004/946; SI 2008/1067.

7 Raising of relative grounds in case of honest concurrent use

(1) This section applies where on an application for the registration of a trade mark it appears to the registrar –

    (a)   that there is an earlier trade mark in relation to which the conditions set out in section 5(1), (2) or (3) obtain, or

    (b)   that there is an earlier right in relation to which the condition set out in section 5(4) is satisfied,

but the applicant shows to the satisfaction of the registrar that there has been honest concurrent use of the trade mark for which registration is sought.

(2) In that case the registrar shall not refuse the application by reason of the earlier trade mark or other earlier right unless objection on that ground is raised in opposition proceedings by the proprietor of that earlier trade mark or other earlier right.

(3) For the purposes of this section 'honest concurrent use' means such use in the United Kingdom, by the applicant or with his consent, as would formerly have amounted to honest concurrent use for the purposes of section 12(2) of the Trade Marks Act 1938.

(4) Nothing in this section affects –

    (a)   the refusal of registration on the grounds mentioned in section 3 (absolute grounds for refusal), or

    (b)   the making of an application for a declaration of invalidity under section 47(2) (application on relative grounds where no consent to registration).

(5) This section does not apply when there is an order in force under section 8 below.

8 Power to require that relative grounds be raised in opposition proceedings

(1) The Secretary of State may by order provide that in any case a trade mark shall not be refused registration on a ground mentioned in section 5 (relative grounds for refusal) unless objection on that ground is raised in opposition proceedings by the proprietor of the earlier trade mark or other earlier right.

(2) The order may make such consequential provision as appears to the Secretary of State appropriate –

    (a)   with respect to the carrying out by the registrar of searches of earlier trade marks, and

(b) as to the persons by whom an application for a declaration of invalidity may be made on the grounds specified in section 47(2) (relative grounds).

(3) An order making such provision as is mentioned in subsection (2)(a) may direct that so much of section 37 (examination of application) as requires a search to be carried out shall cease to have effect.

(4) An order making such provision as is mentioned in subsection (2)(b) may provide that so much of section 47(3) as provides that any person may make an application for a declaration of invalidity shall have effect subject to the provisions of the order.

(5) An order under this section shall be made by statutory instrument, and no order shall be made unless a draft of it has been laid before and approved by a resolution of each House of Parliament.

No such draft of an order making such provision as is mentioned in subsection (1) shall be laid before Parliament until after the end of the period of ten years beginning with the day on which applications for Community trade marks may first be filed in pursuance of the Community Trade Mark Regulation.

(6) An order under this section may contain such transitional provisions as appear to the Secretary of State to be appropriate.

Effects of registered trade mark

9 Rights conferred by registered trade mark

(1) The proprietor of a registered trade mark has exclusive rights in the trade mark which are infringed by use of the trade mark in the United Kingdom without his consent.

The acts amounting to infringement, if done without the consent of the proprietor, are specified in section 10.

(2) References in this Act to the infringement of a registered trade mark are to any such infringement of the rights of the proprietor.

(3) The rights of the proprietor have effect from the date of registration (which in accordance with section 40(3) is the date of filing of the application for registration):

Provided that –

(a) no infringement proceedings may be begun before the date on which the trade mark is in fact registered; and
(b) no offence under section 92 (unauthorised use of trade mark, &c in relation to goods) is committed by anything done before the date of publication of the registration.

10 Infringement of registered trade mark

(1) A person infringes a registered trade mark if he uses in the course of trade a sign which is identical with the trade mark in relation to goods or services which are identical with those for which it is registered.

(2) A person infringes a registered trade mark if he uses in the course of trade a sign where because –

(a) the sign is identical with the trade mark and is used in relation to goods or services similar to those for which the trade mark is registered, or

(b) the sign is similar to the trade mark and is used in relation to goods or services identical with or similar to those for which the trade mark is registered,

there exists a likelihood of confusion on the part of the public, which includes the likelihood of association with the trade mark.

(3) A person infringes a registered trade mark if he uses in the course of trade, in relation to goods or services, a sign which –

(a) is identical with or similar to the trade mark,

(b) *(repealed)*

where the trade mark has a reputation in the United Kingdom and the use of the sign, being without due cause, takes unfair advantage of, or is detrimental to, the distinctive character or the repute of the trade mark.

(4) For the purposes of this section a person uses a sign if, in particular, he –

(a) affixes it to goods or the packaging thereof;

(b) offers or exposes goods for sale, puts them on the market or stocks them for those purposes under the sign, or offers or supplies services under the sign;

(c) imports or exports goods under the sign; or

(d) uses the sign on business papers or in advertising.

(5) A person who applies a registered trade mark to material intended to be used for labelling or packaging goods, as a business paper, or for advertising goods or services, shall be treated as a party to any use of the material which infringes the registered trade mark if when he applied the mark he knew or had reason to believe that the application of the mark was not duly authorised by the proprietor or a licensee.

(6) Nothing in the preceding provisions of this section shall be construed as preventing the use of a registered trade mark by any person for the purpose of identifying goods or services as those of the proprietor or a licensee.

But any such use otherwise than in accordance with honest practices in industrial or commercial matters shall be treated as infringing the registered trade mark if the use without due cause takes unfair advantage of, or is detrimental to, the distinctive character or repute of the trade mark.

Amendments–SI 2004/946.

11 Limits on effect of registered trade mark

(1) A registered trade mark is not infringed by the use of another registered trade mark in relation to goods or services for which the latter is registered (but see section 47(6) (effect of declaration of invalidity of registration)).

(2) A registered trade mark is not infringed by –

(a) the use by a person of his own name or address,

(b) the use of indications concerning the kind, quality, quantity, intended purpose, value, geographical origin, the time of production of goods or of rendering of services, or other characteristics of goods or services, or

(c) the use of the trade mark where it is necessary to indicate the intended purpose of a product or service (in particular, as accessories or spare parts),

provided the use is in accordance with honest practices in industrial or commercial matters.

(3) A registered trade mark is not infringed by the use in the course of trade in a particular locality of an earlier right which applies only in that locality.

For this purpose an 'earlier right' means an unregistered trade mark or other sign continuously used in relation to goods or services by a person or a predecessor in title of his from a date prior to whichever is the earlier of –

(a) the use of the first-mentioned trade mark in relation to those goods or services by the proprietor or a predecessor in title of his, or

(b) the registration of the first-mentioned trade mark in respect of those goods or services in the name of the proprietor or a predecessor in title of his;

and an earlier right shall be regarded as applying in a locality if, or to the extent that, its use in that locality is protected by virtue of any rule of law (in particular, the law of passing off).

12 Exhaustion of rights conferred by registered trade mark

(1) A registered trade mark is not infringed by the use of the trade mark in relation to goods which have been put on the market in the European Economic Area under that trade mark by the proprietor or with his consent.

(2) Subsection (1) does not apply where there exist legitimate reasons for the proprietor to oppose further dealings in the goods (in particular, where the condition of the goods has been changed or impaired after they have been put on the market).

13 Registration subject to disclaimer or limitation

(1) An applicant for registration of a trade mark, or the proprietor of a registered trade mark, may –

    (a)   disclaim any right to the exclusive use of any specified element of the trade mark, or

    (b)   agree that the rights conferred by the registration shall be subject to a specified territorial or other limitation;

and where the registration of a trade mark is subject to a disclaimer or limitation, the rights conferred by section 9 (rights conferred by registered trade mark) are restricted accordingly.

(2) Provision shall be made by rules as to the publication and entry in the register of a disclaimer or limitation.

Infringement proceedings

14 Action for infringement

(1) An infringement of a registered trade mark is actionable by the proprietor of the trade mark.

(2) In an action for infringement all such relief by way of damages, injunctions, accounts or otherwise is available to him as is available in respect of the infringement of any other property right.

15 Order for erasure, &c of offending sign

(1) Where a person is found to have infringed a registered trade mark, the court may make an order requiring him –

    (a)   to cause the offending sign to be erased, removed or obliterated from any infringing goods, material or articles in his possession, custody or control, or

    (b)   if it is not reasonably practicable for the offending sign to be erased, removed or obliterated, to secure the destruction of the infringing goods, material or articles in question.

(2) If an order under subsection (1) is not complied with, or it appears to the court likely that such an order would not be complied with, the court may order that the infringing goods, material or articles be delivered to such person as the court may direct for erasure, removal or obliteration of the sign, or for destruction, as the case may be.

16 Order for delivery up of infringing goods, material or articles

(1) The proprietor of a registered trade mark may apply to the court for an order for the delivery up to him, or such other person as the court may direct, of any infringing goods, material or articles which a person has in his possession, custody or control in the course of a business.

(2) An application shall not be made after the end of the period specified in section 18 (period after which remedy of delivery up not available); and no order shall be made unless the court also makes, or it appears to the court that there are grounds for making, an order under section 19 (order as to disposal of infringing goods, &c).

(3) A person to whom any infringing goods, material or articles are delivered up in pursuance of an order under this section shall, if an order under section 19 is not made, retain them pending the making of an order, or the decision not to make an order, under that section.

(4) Nothing in this section affects any other power of the court.

17 Meaning of 'infringing goods, material or articles'

(1) In this Act the expressions 'infringing goods', 'infringing material' and 'infringing articles' shall be construed as follows.

(2) Goods are 'infringing goods', in relation to a registered trade mark, if they or their packaging bear a sign identical or similar to that mark and –

 (a) the application of the sign to the goods or their packaging was an infringement of the registered trade mark, or
 (b) the goods are proposed to be imported into the United Kingdom and the application of the sign in the United Kingdom to them or their packaging would be an infringement of the registered trade mark, or
 (c) the sign has otherwise been used in relation to the goods in such a way as to infringe the registered trade mark.

(3) Nothing in subsection (2) shall be construed as affecting the importation of goods which may lawfully be imported into the United Kingdom by virtue of an enforceable Community right.

(4) Material is 'infringing material', in relation to a registered trade mark if it bears a sign identical or similar to that mark and either –

 (a) it is used for labelling or packaging goods, as a business paper, or for advertising goods or services, in such a way as to infringe the registered trade mark, or
 (b) it is intended to be so used and such use would infringe the registered trade mark.

(5) 'Infringing articles', in relation to a registered trade mark, means articles –

 (a) which are specifically designed or adapted for making copies of a sign identical or similar to that mark, and
 (b) which a person has in his possession, custody or control, knowing or having reason to believe that they have been or are to be used to produce infringing goods or material.

18 Period after which remedy of delivery up not available

(1) An application for an order under section 16 (order for delivery up of infringing goods, material or articles) may not be made after the end of the period of six years from –

 (a) in the case of infringing goods, the date on which the trade mark was applied to the goods or their packaging,
 (b) in the case of infringing material, the date on which the trade mark was applied to the material, or

(c)   in the case of infringing articles, the date on which they were made,

except as mentioned in the following provisions.

(2) If during the whole or part of that period the proprietor of the registered trade mark –

(a)   is under a disability, or
(b)   is prevented by fraud or concealment from discovering the facts entitling him to apply for an order,

an application may be made at any time before the end of the period of six years from the date on which he ceased to be under a disability or, as the case may be, could with reasonable diligence have discovered those facts.

(3) In subsection (2) 'disability' –

(a)   in England and Wales, has the same meaning as in the Limitation Act 1980;
(b)   in Scotland, means legal disability within the meaning of the Prescription and Limitation (Scotland) Act 1973;
(c)   in Northern Ireland, has the same meaning as in the Limitation (Northern Ireland) Order 1989.

19 Order as to disposal of infringing goods, material or articles

(1) Where infringing goods, material or articles have been delivered up in pursuance of an order under section 16, an application may be made to the court –

(a)   for an order that they be destroyed or forfeited to such person as the court may think fit, or
(b)   for a decision that no such order should be made.

(2) In considering what order (if any) should be made, the court shall consider whether other remedies available in an action for infringement of the registered trade mark would be adequate to compensate the proprietor and any licensee and protect their interests.

(3) Provision shall be made by rules of court as to the service of notice on persons having an interest in the goods, material or articles, and any such person is entitled –

(a)   to appear in proceedings for an order under this section, whether or not he was served with notice, and
(b)   to appeal against any order made, whether or not he appeared;

and an order shall not take effect until the end of the period within which notice of an appeal may be given or, if before the end of that period notice of appeal is duly given, until the final determination or abandonment of the proceedings on the appeal.

(4) Where there is more than one person interested in the goods, material or articles, the court shall make such order as it thinks just.

(5) If the court decides that no order should be made under this section, the person in whose possession, custody or control the goods, material or articles were before being delivered up is entitled to their return.

(6) References in this section to a person having an interest in goods, material or articles include any person in whose favour an order could be made –

    (a)   under this section (including that section as applied by regulation 4 of the Community Trade Mark Regulations 2006 (SI 2006/1027));

    (b)   under section 24D of the Registered Designs Act 1949;

    (c)   under section 114, 204 or 231 of the Copyright, Designs and Patents Act 1988; or

    (d)   under regulation 1C of the Community Design Regulations 2005 (SI 2005/2339).

Amendments–SI 2006/1028.

20 Jurisdiction of sheriff court or county court in Northern Ireland

Proceedings for an order under section 16 (order for delivery up of infringing goods, material or articles) or section 19 (order as to disposal of infringing goods, &c) may be brought –

    (a)   in the sheriff court in Scotland, or

    (b)   in a county court in Northern Ireland.

This does not affect the jurisdiction of the Court of Session or the High Court in Northern Ireland.

21 Remedy for groundless threats of infringement proceedings

(1) Where a person threatens another with proceedings for infringement of a registered trade mark other than –

    (a)   the application of the mark to goods or their packaging,

    (b)   the importation of goods to which, or to the packaging of which, the mark has been applied, or

    (c)   the supply of services under the mark,

any person aggrieved may bring proceedings for relief under this section.

(2) The relief which may be applied for is any of the following –

    (a)   a declaration that the threats are unjustifiable,

    (b)   an injunction against the continuance of the threats,

    (c)   damages in respect of any loss he has sustained by the threats;

and the plaintiff is entitled to such relief unless the defendant shows that the acts in respect of which proceedings were threatened constitute (or if done would constitute) an infringement of the registered trade mark concerned.

(3) If that is shown by the defendant, the plaintiff is nevertheless entitled to relief if he shows that the registration of the trade mark is invalid or liable to be revoked in a relevant respect.

(4) The mere notification that a trade mark is registered, or that an application for registration has been made, does not constitute a threat of proceedings for the purposes of this section.

Registered trade mark as object of property

22 Nature of registered trade mark

A registered trade mark is personal property (in Scotland, incorporeal moveable property).

23 Co-ownership of registered trade mark

(1) Where a registered trade mark is granted to two or more persons jointly, each of them is entitled, subject to any agreement to the contrary, to an equal undivided share in the registered trade mark.

(2) The following provisions apply where two or more persons are co-proprietors of a registered trade mark, by virtue of subsection (1) or otherwise.

(3) Subject to any agreement to the contrary, each co-proprietor is entitled, by himself or his agents, to do for his own benefit and without the consent of or the need to account to the other or others, any act which would otherwise amount to an infringement of the registered trade mark.

(4) One co-proprietor may not without the consent of the other or others –

    (a)   grant a licence to use the registered trade mark, or
    (b)   assign or charge his share in the registered trade mark (or, in Scotland, cause or permit security to be granted over it).

(5) Infringement proceedings may be brought by any co-proprietor, but he may not, without the leave of the court, proceed with the action unless the other, or each of the others, is either joined as a plaintiff or added as a defendant.

A co-proprietor who is thus added as a defendant shall not be made liable for any costs in the action unless he takes part in the proceedings.

Nothing in this subsection affects the granting of interlocutory relief on the application of a single co-proprietor.

(6) Nothing in this section affects the mutual rights and obligations of trustees or personal representatives, or their rights and obligations as such.

24 Assignment, &c of registered trade mark

(1) A registered trade mark is transmissible by assignment, testamentary disposition or operation of law in the same way as other personal or moveable property.

It is so transmissible either in connection with the goodwill of a business or independently.

(2) An assignment or other transmission of a registered trade mark may be partial, that is, limited so as to apply –

(a) in relation to some but not all of the goods or services for which the trade mark is registered, or

(b) in relation to use of the trade mark in a particular manner or a particular locality.

(3) An assignment of a registered trade mark, or an assent relating to a registered trade mark, is not effective unless it is in writing signed by or on behalf of the assignor or, as the case may be, a personal representative.

Except in Scotland, this requirement may be satisfied in a case where the assignor or personal representative is a body corporate by the affixing of its seal.

(4) The above provisions apply to assignment by way of security as in relation to any other assignment.

(5) A registered trade mark may be the subject of a charge (in Scotland, security) in the same way as other personal or moveable property.

(6) Nothing in this Act shall be construed as affecting the assignment or other transmission of an unregistered trade mark as part of the goodwill of a business.

25 Registration of transactions affecting registered trade mark

(1) On application being made to the registrar by –

(a) a person claiming to be entitled to an interest in or under a registered trade mark by virtue of a registrable transaction, or

(b) any other person claiming to be affected by such a transaction,

the prescribed particulars of the transaction shall be entered in the register.

(2) The following are registrable transactions –

(a) an assignment of a registered trade mark or any right in it;

(b) the grant of a licence under a registered trade mark;

(c) the granting of any security interest (whether fixed or floating) over a registered trade mark or any right in or under it;

(d) the making by personal representatives of an assent in relation to a registered trade mark or any right in or under it;

(e) an order of a court or other competent authority transferring a registered trade mark or any right in or under it.

(3) Until an application has been made for registration of the prescribed particulars of a registrable transaction –

(a) the transaction is ineffective as against a person acquiring a conflicting interest in or under the registered trade mark in ignorance of it, and

(b) a person claiming to be a licensee by virtue of the transaction does not have the protection of section 30 or 31 (rights and remedies of licensee in relation to infringement).

(4) Where a person becomes the proprietor or a licensee of a registered trade mark by virtue of a registrable transaction and the mark is infringed before the prescribed particulars of the transaction are registered, in proceedings for such an infringement, the court shall not award him costs unless –

   (a)   an application for registration of the prescribed particulars of the transaction is made before the end of the period of six months beginning with its date, or
   (b)   the court is satisfied that it was not practicable for such an application to be made before the end of that period and that an application was made as soon as practicable thereafter.

(5) Provision may be made by rules as to –

   (a)   the amendment of registered particulars relating to a licence so as to reflect any alteration of the terms of the licence, and
   (b)   the removal of such particulars from the register –
         (i)   where it appears from the registered particulars that the licence was granted for a fixed period and that period has expired, or
         (ii)   where no such period is indicated and, after such period as may be prescribed, the registrar has notified the parties of his intention to remove the particulars from the register.

(6) Provision may also be made by rules as to the amendment or removal from the register of particulars relating to a security interest on the application of, or with the consent of, the person entitled to the benefit of that interest.

Amendments–SI 2006/1028.

26 Trusts and equities

(1) No notice of any trust (express, implied or constructive) shall be entered in the register; and the registrar shall not be affected by any such notice.

(2) Subject to the provisions of this Act, equities (in Scotland, rights) in respect of a registered trade mark may be enforced in like manner as in respect of other personal or moveable property.

27 Application for registration of trade mark as an object of property

(1) The provisions of sections 22 to 26 (which relate to a registered trade mark as an object of property) apply, with the necessary modifications, in relation to an application for the registration of a trade mark as in relation to a registered trade mark.

(2) In section 23 (co-ownership of registered trade mark) as it applies in relation to an application for registration the reference in subsection (1) to the granting of the registration shall be construed as a reference to the making of the application.

(3) In section 25 (registration of transactions affecting registered trade marks) as it applies in relation to a transaction affecting an application for the registration of a trade mark, the references to the entry of particulars in the

register, and to the making of an application to register particulars, shall be construed as references to the giving of notice to the registrar of those particulars.

Licensing

28 Licensing of registered trade mark

(1) A licence to use a registered trade mark may be general or limited.

A limited licence may, in particular, apply –

- (a) in relation to some but not all of the goods or services for which the trade mark is registered, or
- (b) in relation to use of the trade mark in a particular manner or a particular locality.

(2) A licence is not effective unless it is in writing signed by or on behalf of the grantor.

Except in Scotland, this requirement may be satisfied in a case where the grantor is a body corporate by the affixing of its seal.

(3) Unless the licence provides otherwise, it is binding on a successor in title to the grantor's interest.

References in this Act to doing anything with, or without, the consent of the proprietor of a registered trade mark shall be construed accordingly.

(4) Where the licence so provides, a sub-licence may be granted by the licensee; and references in this Act to a licence or licensee include a sub-licence or sub-licensee.

29 Exclusive licenses

(1) In this Act an 'exclusive licence' means a licence (whether general or limited) authorising the licensee to the exclusion of all other persons, including the person granting the licence, to use a registered trade mark in the manner authorised by the licence.

The expression 'exclusive licensee' shall be construed accordingly.

(2) An exclusive licensee has the same rights against a successor in title who is bound by the licence as he has against the person granting the licence.

30 General provisions as to rights of licensees in case of infringement

(1) This section has effect with respect to the rights of a licensee in relation to infringement of a registered trade mark.

The provisions of this section do not apply where or to the extent that, by virtue of section 31(1) below (exclusive licensee having rights and remedies of assignee), the licensee has a right to bring proceedings in his own name.

(2) A licensee is entitled, unless his licence, or any licence through which his interest is derived, provides otherwise, to call on the proprietor of the registered trade mark to take infringement proceedings in respect of any matter which affects his interests.

(3) If the proprietor –

    (a)   refuses to do so, or

    (b)   fails to do so within two months after being called upon,

the licensee may bring the proceedings in his own name as if he were the proprietor.

(4) Where infringement proceedings are brought by a licensee by virtue of this section, the licensee may not, without the leave of the court, proceed with the action unless the proprietor is either joined as a plaintiff or added as a defendant.

This does not affect the granting of interlocutory relief on an application by a licensee alone.

(5) A proprietor who is added as a defendant as mentioned in subsection (4) shall not be made liable for any costs in the action unless he takes part in the proceedings.

(6) In infringement proceedings brought by the proprietor of a registered trade mark any loss suffered or likely to be suffered by licensees shall be taken into account; and the court may give such directions as it thinks fit as to the extent to which the plaintiff is to hold the proceeds of any pecuniary remedy on behalf of licensees.

(7) The provisions of this section apply in relation to an exclusive licensee if or to the extent that he has, by virtue of section 31(1), the rights and remedies of an assignee as if he were the proprietor of the registered trade mark.

31 Exclusive licensee having rights and remedies of assignee

(1) An exclusive licence may provide that the licensee shall have, to such extent as may be provided by the licence, the same rights and remedies in respect of matters occurring after the grant of the licence as if the licence had been an assignment.

Where or to the extent that such provision is made, the licensee is entitled, subject to the provisions of the licence and to the following provisions of this section, to bring infringement proceedings, against any person other than the proprietor, in his own name.

(2) Any such rights and remedies of an exclusive licensee are concurrent with those of the proprietor of the registered trade mark; and references to the proprietor of a registered trade mark in the provisions of this Act relating to infringement shall be construed accordingly.

(3) In an action brought by an exclusive licensee by virtue of this section a defendant may avail himself of any defence which would have been available to him if the action had been brought by the proprietor of the registered trade mark.

(4) Where proceedings for infringement of a registered trade mark brought by the proprietor or an exclusive licensee relate wholly or partly to an infringement in respect of which they have concurrent rights of action, the proprietor or, as the case may be, the exclusive licensee may not, without the leave of the court, proceed with the action unless the other is either joined as a plaintiff or added as a defendant.

This does not affect the granting of interlocutory relief on an application by a proprietor or exclusive licensee alone.

(5) A person who is added as a defendant as mentioned in subsection (4) shall not be made liable for any costs in the action unless he takes part in the proceedings.

(6) Where an action for infringement of a registered trade mark is brought which relates wholly or partly to an infringement in respect of which the proprietor and an exclusive licensee have or had concurrent rights of action –

    (a)   the court shall in assessing damages take into account –
        (i)   the terms of the licence, and
        (ii)   any pecuniary remedy already awarded or available to either of them in respect of the infringement;
    (b)   no account of profits shall be directed if an award of damages has been made, or an account of profits has been directed, in favour of the other of them in respect of the infringement; and
    (c)   the court shall if an account of profits is directed apportion the profits between them as the court considers just, subject to any agreement between them.

The provisions of this subsection apply whether or not the proprietor and the exclusive licensee are both parties to the action; and if they are not both parties the court may give such directions as it thinks fit as to the extent to which the party to the proceedings is to hold the proceeds of any pecuniary remedy on behalf of the other.

(7) The proprietor of a registered trade mark shall notify any exclusive licensee who has a concurrent right of action before applying for an order under section 16 (order for delivery up); and the court may on the application of the licensee make such order under that section as it thinks fit having regard to the terms of the licence.

(8) The provisions of subsections (4) to (7) above have effect subject to any agreement to the contrary between the exclusive licensee and the proprietor.

Application for registered trade mark

32 Application for registration

(1) An application for registration of a trade mark shall be made to the registrar.

(2) The application shall contain –

    (a)   a request for registration of a trade mark,
    (b)   the name and address of the applicant,
    (c)   a statement of the goods or services in relation to which it is sought to register the trade mark, and
    (d)   a representation of the trade mark.

(3) The application shall state that the trade mark is being used, by the applicant or with his consent, in relation to those goods or services, or that he has a bona fide intention that it should be so used.

(4) The application shall be subject to the payment of the application fee and such class fees as may be appropriate.

33 Date of filing

(1) The date of filing of an application for registration of a trade mark is the date on which documents containing everything required by section 32(2) are furnished to the registrar by the applicant.

If the documents are furnished on different days, the date of filing is the last of those days.

(2) References in this Act to the date of application for registration are to the date of filing of the application.

34 Classification of trade marks

(1) Goods and services shall be classified for the purposes of the registration of trade marks according to a prescribed system of classification.

(2) Any question arising as to the class within which any goods or services fall shall be determined by the registrar, whose decision shall be final.

Priority

35 Claim to priority of Convention application

(1) A person who has duly filed an application for protection of a trade mark in a Convention country (a 'Convention application'), or his successor in title, has a right to priority, for the purposes of registering the same trade mark under this Act for some or all of the same goods or services, for a period of six months from the date of filing of the first such application.

(2) If the application for registration under this Act is made within that six-month period –

(a) the relevant date for the purposes of establishing which rights take precedence shall be the date of filing of the first Convention application, and

(b) the registrability of the trade mark shall not be affected by any use of the mark in the United Kingdom in the period between that date and the date of the application under this Act.

(3) Any filing which in a Convention country is equivalent to a regular national filing, under its domestic legislation or an international agreement, shall be treated as giving rise to the right of priority.

A 'regular national filing' means a filing which is adequate to establish the date on which the application was filed in that country, whatever may be the subsequent fate of the application.

(4) A subsequent application concerning the same subject as the first Convention application, filed in the same Convention country, shall be considered the first Convention application (of which the filing date is the starting date of the period of priority), if at the time of the subsequent application –

(a) the previous application has been withdrawn, abandoned or refused, without having been laid open to public inspection and without leaving any rights outstanding, and

(b) it has not yet served as a basis for claiming a right of priority.

The previous application may not thereafter serve as a basis for claiming a right of priority.

(5) Provision may be made by rules as to the manner of claiming a right to priority on the basis of a Convention application.

(6) A right to priority arising as a result of a Convention application may be assigned or otherwise transmitted, either with the application or independently.

The reference in subsection (1) to the applicant's successor in title shall be construed accordingly.

36 Claim to priority from other relevant overseas application

(1) Her Majesty may by Order in Council make provision for conferring on a person who has duly filed an application for protection of a trade mark in –

(a) any of the Channel Islands or a colony, or

(b) a country or territory in relation to which Her Majesty's Government in the United Kingdom have entered into a treaty, convention, arrangement or engagement for the reciprocal protection of trade marks,

a right to priority, for the purpose of registering the same trade mark under this Act for some or all of the same goods or services, for a specified period from the date of filing of that application.

(2) An Order in Council under this section may make provision corresponding to that made by section 35 in relation to Convention countries or such other provision as appears to Her Majesty to be appropriate.

(3) A statutory instrument containing an Order in Council under this section shall be subject to annulment in pursuance of a resolution of either House of Parliament.

Registration procedure

37 Examination of application

(1) The registrar shall examine whether an application for registration of a trade mark satisfies the requirements of this Act (including any requirements imposed by rules).

(2) (*repealed*)

(3) If it appears to the registrar that the requirements for registration are not met, he shall inform the applicant and give him an opportunity, within such period as the registrar may specify, to make representations or to amend the application.

(4) If the applicant fails to satisfy the registrar that those requirements are met, or to amend the application so as to meet them, or fails to respond before the end of the specified period, the registrar shall refuse to accept the application.

(5) If it appears to the registrar that the requirements for registration are met, he shall accept the application.

Amendments–SI 2007/1976.

38 Publication, opposition proceedings and observations

(1) When an application for registration has been accepted, the registrar shall cause the application to be published in the prescribed manner.

(2) Any person may, within the prescribed time from the date of the publication of the application, give notice to the registrar of opposition to the registration.

The notice shall be given in writing in the prescribed manner, and shall include a statement of the grounds of opposition.

(3) Where an application has been published, any person may, at any time before the registration of the trade mark, make observations in writing to the registrar as to whether the trade mark should be registered; and the registrar shall inform the applicant of any such observations.

A person who makes observations does not thereby become a party to the proceedings on the application.

39 Withdrawal, restriction or amendment of application

(1) The applicant may at any time withdraw his application or restrict the goods or services covered by the application.

If the application has been published, the withdrawal or restriction shall also be published.

(2) In other respects, an application may be amended, at the request of the applicant, only by correcting –

(a)   the name or address of the applicant,
(b)   errors of wording or of copying, or
(c)   obvious mistakes,

and then only where the correction does not substantially affect the identity of the trade mark or extend the goods or services covered by the application.

(3) Provision shall be made by rules for the publication of any amendment which affects the representation of the trade mark, or the goods or services covered by the application, and fofor the making of objections by any person claiming to be affected by it.

40 Registration

(1) Where an application has been accepted and –

(a)   no notice of opposition is given within the period referred to in section 38(2), or
(b)   all opposition proceedings are withdrawn or decided in favour of the applicant,

the registrar shall register the trade mark, unless it appears to him having regard to matters coming to his notice since the application was accepted that the registration requirements (other than those mentioned in section 5(1), (2) or (3)) were not met at that time.

(2) A trade mark shall not be registered unless any fee prescribed for the registration is paid within the prescribed period.

If the fee is not paid within that period, the application shall be deemed to be withdrawn.

(3) A trade mark when registered shall be registered as of the date of filing of the application for registration; and that date shall be deemed for the purposes of this Act to be the date of registration.

(4) On the registration of a trade mark the registrar shall publish the registration in the prescribed manner and issue to the applicant a certificate of registration.

Amendments–SI 2004/946.

41 Registration: supplementary provisions

(1) Provision may be made by rules as to –

(a)   the division of an application for the registration of a trade mark into several applications;

(b)   the merging of separate applications or registrations;

(c)   the registration of a series of trade marks.

(2) A series of trade marks means a number of trade marks which resemble each other as to their material particulars and differ only as to matters of a non-distinctive character not substantially affecting the identity of the trade mark.

(3) Rules under this section may include provision as to –

(a)   the circumstances in which, and conditions subject to which, division, merger or registration of a series is permitted, and

(b)   the purposes for which an application to which the rules apply is to be treated as a single application and those for which it is to be treated as a number of separate applications.

Duration, renewal and alteration of registered trade mark

42 Duration of registration

(1) A trade mark shall be registered for a period of ten years from the date of registration.

(2) Registration may be renewed in accordance with section 43 for further periods of ten years.

43 Renewal of registration

(1) The registration of a trade mark may be renewed at the request of the proprietor, subject to payment of a renewal fee.

(2) Provision shall be made by rules for the registrar to inform the proprietor of a registered trade mark, before the expiry of the registration, of the date of expiry and the manner in which the registration may be renewed.

(3) A request for renewal must be made, and the renewal fee paid, before the expiry of the registration.

Failing this, the request may be made and the fee paid within such further period (of not less than six months) as may be prescribed, in which case an additional renewal fee must also be paid within that period.

(4) Renewal shall take effect from the expiry of the previous registration.

(5) If the registration is not renewed in accordance with the above provisions, the registrar shall remove the trade mark from the register.

Provision may be made by rules for the restoration of the registration of a trade mark which has been removed from the register, subject to such conditions (if any) as may be prescribed.

(6) The renewal or restoration of the registration of a trade mark shall be published in the prescribed manner.

44 Alteration of registered trade mark

(1) A registered trade mark shall not be altered in the register, during the period of registration or on renewal.

(2) Nevertheless, the registrar may, at the request of the proprietor, allow the alteration of a registered trade mark where the mark includes the proprietor's name or address and the alteration is limited to alteration of that name or address and does not substantially affect the identity of the mark.

(3) Provision shall be made by rules for the publication of any such alteration and the making of objections by any person claiming to be affected by it.

Surrender, revocation and invalidity

45 Surrender of registered trade mark

(1) A registered trade mark may be surrendered by the proprietor in respect of some or all of the goods or services for which it is registered.

(2) Provision may be made by rules –

(a) as to the manner and effect of a surrender, and
(b) for protecting the interests of other persons having a right in the registered trade mark.

46 Revocation of registration

(1) The registration of a trade mark may be revoked on any of the following grounds –

(a) that within the period of five years following the date of completion of the registration procedure it has not been put to genuine use in the United Kingdom, by the proprietor or with his consent, in relation to the goods or services for which it is registered, and there are no proper reasons for non-use;
(b) that such use has been suspended for an uninterrupted period of five years, and there are no proper reasons for non-use;
(c) that, in consequence of acts or inactivity of the proprietor, it has become the common name in the trade for a product or service for which it is registered;
(d) that in consequence of the use made of it by the proprietor or with his consent in relation to the goods or services for which it is registered, it is liable to mislead the public, particularly as to the nature, quality or geographical origin of those goods or services.

(2) For the purposes of subsection (1) use of a trade mark includes use in a form differing in elements which do not alter the distinctive character of the mark in the form in which it was registered, and use in the United Kingdom includes affixing the trade mark to goods or to the packaging of goods in the United Kingdom solely for export purposes.

(3) The registration of a trade mark shall not be revoked on the ground mentioned in subsection (1)(a) or (b) if such use as is referred to in that

paragraph is commenced or resumed after the expiry of the five year period and before the application for revocation is made:

Provided that, any such commencement or resumption of use after the expiry of the five year period but within the period of three months before the making of the application shall be disregarded unless preparations for the commencement or resumption began before the proprietor became aware that the application might be made.

(4) An application for revocation may be made by any person, and may be made either to the registrar or to the court, except that –

    (a)   if proceedings concerning the trade mark in question are pending in the court, the application must be made to the court; and

    (b)   if in any other case the application is made to the registrar, he may at any stage of the proceedings refer the application to the court.

(5) Where grounds for revocation exist in respect of only some of the goods or services for which the trade mark is registered, revocation shall relate to those goods or services only.

(6) Where the registration of a trade mark is revoked to any extent, the rights of the proprietor shall be deemed to have ceased to that extent as from –

    (a)   the date of the application for revocation, or

    (b)   if the registrar or court is satisfied that the grounds for revocation existed at an earlier date, that date.

47 Grounds for invalidity of registration

(1) The registration of a trade mark may be declared invalid on he ground that the trade mark was registered in breach of section 3 or any of the provisions referred to in that section (absolute grounds for refusal of registration).

Where the trade mark was registered in breach of subsection (1)(b), (c) or (d) of that section, it shall not be declared invalid if, in consequence of the use which has been made of it, it has after registration acquired a distinctive character in relation to the goods or services for which it is registered.

(2) The registration of a trade mark may be declared invalid on the ground –

    (a)   that there is an earlier trade mark in relation to which the conditions set out in section 5(1), (2) or (3) obtain, or

    (b)   that there is an earlier right in relation to which the condition set out in section 5(4) is satisfied,

unless the proprietor of that earlier trade mark or other earlier right has consented to the registration.

(2A) But the registration of a trade mark may not be declared invalid on the ground that there is an earlier trade mark unless –

    (a)   the registration procedure for the earlier trade mark was completed within the period of five years ending with the date of the application for the declaration,

(b)   the registration procedure for the earlier trade mark was not completed before that date, or

(c)   the use conditions are met.

(2B) The use conditions are met if –

(a)   within the period of five years ending with the date of the application for the declaration the earlier trade mark has been put to genuine use in the United Kingdom by the proprietor or with his consent in relation to the goods or services for which it is registered, or

(b)   it has not been so used, but there are proper reasons for non-use.

(2C) For these purposes –

(a)   use of a trade mark includes use in a form differing in elements which do not alter the distinctive character of the mark in the form in which it was registered, and

(b)   use in the United Kingdom includes affixing the trade mark to goods or to the packaging of goods in the United Kingdom solely for export purposes.

(2D) In relation to a Community trade mark or international trade mark (EC), any reference in subsection (2B) or (2C) to the United Kingdom shall be construed as a reference to the European Community.

(2E) Where an earlier trade mark satisfies the use conditions in respect of some only of the goods or services for which it is registered, it shall be treated for the purposes of this section as if it were registered only in respect of those goods or services.

(2F) Subsection (2A) does not apply where the earlier trade mark is a trade mark within section 6(1)(c).

(3) An application for a declaration of invalidity may be made by any person, and may be made either to the registrar or to the court, except that –

(a)   if proceedings concerning the trade mark in question are pending in the court, the application must be made to the court; and

(b)   if in any other case the application is made to the registrar, he may at any stage of the proceedings refer the application to the court.

(4) In the case of bad faith in the registration of a trade mark, the registrar himself may apply to the court for a declaration of the invalidity of the registration.

(5) Where the grounds of invalidity exist in respect of only some of the goods or services for which the trade mark is registered, the trade mark shall be declared invalid as regards those goods or services only.

(6) Where the registration of a trade mark is declared invalid to any extent, the registration shall to that extent be deemed never to have been made:

Provided that this shall not affect transactions past and closed.

Amendments–SI 2004/946; SI 2008/1067.

48 Effect of acquiescence

(1) Where the proprietor of an earlier trade mark or other earlier right has acquiesced for a continuous period of five years in the use of a registered trade mark in the United Kingdom, being aware of that use, there shall cease to be any entitlement on the basis of that earlier trade mark or other right –

    (a)   to apply for a declaration that the registration of the later trade mark is invalid, or

    (b)   to oppose the use of the later trade mark in relation to the goods or services in relation to which it has been so used,

unless the registration of the later trade mark was applied for in bad faith.

(2) Where subsection (1) applies, the proprietor of the later trade mark is not entitled to oppose the use of the earlier trade mark or, as the case may be, the exploitation of the earlier right, notwithstanding that the earlier trade mark or right may no longer be invoked against his later trade mark.

Collective marks

49 Collective marks

(1) A collective mark is a mark distinguishing the goods or services of members of the association which is the proprietor of the mark from those of other undertakings.

(2) The provisions of this Act apply to collective marks subject to the provisions of Schedule 1.

Certification marks

50 Certification marks

(1) A certification mark is a mark indicating that the goods or services in connection with which it is used are certified by the proprietor of the mark in respect of origin, material, mode of manufacture of goods or performance of services, quality, accuracy or other characteristics.

(2) The provisions of this Act apply to certification marks subject to the provisions of Schedule 2.

PART II
COMMUNITY TRADE MARKS AND INTERNATIONAL MATTERS

Community trade marks

51 Meaning of 'Community trade mark'

In this Act –

    'Community trade mark' has the meaning given by Article 1(1) of the Community Trade

    'the Community Trade Mark Regulation' means Council Regulation (EC) No 40/94 of 20th December 1993 on the Community trade mark.

52 Power to make provision in connection with Community Trade Mark Regulation

(1) The Secretary of State may by regulations make such provision as he considers appropriate in connection with the operation of the Community Trade Mark Regulation.

(2) Provision may, in particular, be made with respect to –

(a) the making of applications for Community trade marks by way of the Patent Office;

(b) the procedures for determining a posteriori the invalidity, or liability to revocation, of the registration of a trade mark from which a Community trade mark claims seniority;

(c) the conversion of a Community trade mark, or an application for a Community trade mark, into an application for registration under this Act;

(d) the designation of courts in the United Kingdom having jurisdiction over proceedings arising out of the Community Trade Mark Regulation.

(3) Without prejudice to the generality of subsection (1), provision may be made by regulations under this section –

(a) applying in relation to a Community trade mark the provisions of –
    (i) section 21 (remedy for groundless threats of infringement proceedings);
    (ii) sections 89 to 91 (importation of infringing goods, material or articles); and
    (iii) sections 92, 93, 95 and 96 (offences); and

(b) making in relation to the list of professional representatives maintained in pursuance of Article 89 of the Community Trade Mark Regulation, and persons on that list, provision corresponding to that made by, or capable of being made under, sections 84 to 88 in relation to the register of trade mark attorneys and registered trade mark attorneys.

(4) Regulations under this section shall be made by statutory instrument which shall be subject to annulment in pursuance of a resolution of either House of Parliament.

Amendments–Legal Services Act 2007, s 208(1), Sch 21, paras 109, 110.

The Madrid Protocol: international registration

53 The Madrid Protocol

In this Act –

'the Madrid Protocol' means the Protocol relating to the Madrid Agreement concerning the International Registration of Marks, adopted at Madrid on 27th June 1989;

'the International Bureau' has the meaning given by Article 2(1) of that Protocol;

'international trade mark (EC)' means a trade mark which is entitled to protection in the European Community under that Protocol; and

'international trade mark (UK)' means a trade mark which is entitled to protection in the United Kingdom under that Protocol.

Amendments–SI 2004/2332.

54 Power to make provision giving effect to Madrid Protocol

(1) The Secretary of State may by order make such provision as he thinks fit for giving effect in the United Kingdom to the provisions of the Madrid Protocol.

(2) Provision may, in particular, be made with respect to –

(a) the making of applications for international registrations by way of the Patent Office as office of origin;

(b) the procedures to be followed where the basic United Kingdom application or registration fails or ceases to be in force;

(c) the procedures to be followed where the Patent Office receives from the International Bureau a request for extension of protection to the United Kingdom;

(d) the effects of a successful request for extension of protection to the United Kingdom;

(e) the transformation of an application for an international registration, or an international registration, into a national application for registration;

(f) the communication of information to the International Bureau;

(g) the payment of fees and amounts prescribed in respect of applications for international registrations, extensions of protection and renewals.

(3) Without prejudice to the generality of subsection (1), provision may be made by regulations under this section applying in relation to an international trade mark (UK) the provisions of –

(a) section 21 (remedy for groundless threats of infringement proceedings);

(b) sections 89 to 91 (importation of infringing goods, material or articles); and

(c) sections 92, 93, 95 and 96 (offences).

(4) An order under this section shall be made by statutory instrument which shall be subject to annulment in pursuance of a resolution of either House of Parliament.

The Paris Convention: supplementary provisions

55 The Paris Convention

(1) In this Act –

(a)   'the Paris Convention' means the Paris Convention for the Protection of Industrial Property of March 20th 1883, as revised or amended from time to time,

(aa) 'the WTO agreement' means the Agreement establishing the World Trade Organisation signed at Marrakesh on 15th April 1994, and

(b)   a 'Convention country' means a country, other than the United Kingdom, which is a party to that Convention or to that Agreement.

(2) The Secretary of State may by order make such amendments of this Act, and rules made under this Act, as appear to him appropriate in consequence of any revision or amendment of the Paris Convention or the WTO agreement after the passing of this Act.

(3) Any such order shall be made by statutory instrument which shall be subject to annulment in pursuance of a resolution of either House of Parliament.

Amendments–SI 1999/1899; SI 2006/1028.

56 Protection of well-known trade marks: Article 6bis

(1) References in this Act to a trade mark which is entitled to protection under the Paris Convention or the WTO agreement as a well known trade mark are to a mark which is well-known in the United Kingdom as being the mark of a person who –

(a)   is a national of a Convention country, or

(b)   is domiciled in, or has a real and effective industrial or commercial establishment in, a Convention country,

whether or not that person carries on business, or has any goodwill, in the United Kingdom.

References to the proprietor of such a mark shall be construed accordingly.

(2) The proprietor of a trade mark which is entitled to protection under the Paris Convention or the WTO agreement as a well known trade mark is entitled to restrain by injunction the use in the United Kingdom of a trade mark which, or the essential part of which, is identical or similar to his mark, in relation to identical or similar goods or services, where the use is likely to cause confusion.

This right is subject to section 48 (effect of acquiescence by proprietor of earlier trade mark).

(3) Nothing in subsection (2) affects the continuation of any bona fide use of a trade mark begun before the commencement of this section.

Amendments–SI 1999/1899.

57 National emblems, &c of Convention countries: Article 6ter

(1) A trade mark which consists of or contains the flag of a Convention country shall not be registered without the authorisation of the competent

authorities of that country, unless it appears to the registrar that use of the flag in the manner proposed is permitted without such authorisation.

(2) A trade mark which consists of or contains the armorial bearings or any other state emblem of a Convention country which is protected under the Paris Convention or the WTO agreement shall not be registered without the authorisation of the competent authorities of that country.

(3) A trade mark which consists of or contains an official sign or hallmark adopted by a Convention country and indicating control and warranty shall not, where the sign or hallmark is protected under the Paris Convention or the WTO agreement, be registered in relation to goods or services of the same, or a similar kind, as those in relation to which it indicates control and warranty, without the authorisation of the competent authorities of the country concerned.

(4) The provisions of this section as to national flags and other state emblems, and official signs or hallmarks, apply equally to anything which from a heraldic point of view imitates any such flag or other emblem, or sign or hallmark.

(5) Nothing in this section prevents the registration of a trade mark on the application of a national of a country who is authorised to make use of a state emblem, or official sign or hallmark, of that country, notwithstanding that it is similar to that of another country.

(6) Where by virtue of this section the authorisation of the competent authorities of a Convention country is or would be required for the registration of a trade mark, those authorities are entitled to restrain by injunction any use of the mark in the United Kingdom without their authorisation.

Amendments–SI 1999/1899.

58 Emblems, &c of certain international organisations: Article 6ter

(1) This section applies to –

    (a)   the armorial bearings, flags or other emblems, and
    (b)   the abbreviations and names,

of international intergovernmental organisations of which one or more Convention countries are members.

(2) A trade mark which consists of or contains any such emblem, abbreviation or name which is protected under the Paris Convention or the WTO agreement shall not be registered without the authorisation of the international organisation concerned, unless it appears to the registrar that the use of the emblem, abbreviation or name in the manner proposed –

    (a)   is not such as to suggest to the public that a connection exists between the organisation and the trade mark, or
    (b)   is not likely to mislead the public as to the existence of a connection between the user and the organisation.

(3) The provisions of this section as to emblems of an international organisation apply equally to anything which from a heraldic point of view imitates any such emblem.

(4) Where by virtue of this section the authorisation of an international organisation is or would be required for the registration of a trade mark, that organisation is entitled to restrain by injunction any use of the mark in the United Kingdom without its authorisation.

(5) Nothing in this section affects the rights of a person whose bona fide use of the trade mark in question began before 4th January 1962 (when the relevant provisions of the Paris Convention entered into force in relation to the United Kingdom).

Amendments–SI 1999/1899.

59 Notification under Article 6ter of the Convention

(1) For the purposes of section 57 state emblems of a Convention country (other than the national flag), and official signs or hallmarks, shall be regarded as protected under the Paris Convention only if, or to the extent that –

(a) the country in question has notified the United Kingdom in accordance with Article 6ter(3) of the Convention that it desires to protect that emblem, sign or hallmark,
(b) the notification remains in force, and
(c) the United Kingdom has not objected to it in accordance with Article 6ter(4) or any such objection has been withdrawn.

(2) For the purposes of section 58 the emblems, abbreviations and names of an international organisation shall be regarded as protected under the Paris Convention only if, or to the extent that –

(a) the organisation in question has notified the United Kingdom in accordance with Article 6ter(3) of the Convention that it desires to protect that emblem, abbreviation or name,
(b) the notification remains in force, and
(c) the United Kingdom gas not objected to it in accordance with Article 6ter(4) or any such objection has been withdrawn.

(3) Notification under Article 6ter(3) of the Paris Convention shall have effect only in relation to applications for registration made more than two months after the receipt of the notification.

(4) The registrar shall keep and make available for public inspection by any person, at all reasonable hours and free of charge, a list of –

(a) the state emblems and official signs or hallmarks, and
(b) the emblems, abbreviations and names of international organisations,

which are for the time being protected under the Paris Convention by virtue of notification under Article 6ter(3).

(5) Any reference in this section to Article 6ter of the Paris Convention shall be construed as including a reference to that Article as applied by the WTO agreement

Amendments–SI 1999/1899.

60 Acts of agent or representative: Article 6septies

(1) The following provisions apply where an application for registration of a trade mark is made by a person who is an agent or representative of a person who is the proprietor of the mark in a Convention country.

(2) If the proprietor opposes the application, registration shall be refused.

(3) If the application (not being so opposed) is granted, the proprietor may –

   (a) apply for a declaration of the invalidity of the registration, or
   (b) apply for the rectification of the register so as to substitute his name as the proprietor of the registered trade mark.

(4) The proprietor may (notwithstanding the rights conferred by this Act in relation to a registered trade mark) by injunction restrain any use of the trade mark in the United Kingdom which is not authorised by him.

(5) Subsections (2), (3) and (4) do not apply if, or to the extent that, the agent or representative justifies his action.

(6) An application under subsection (3)(a) or (b) must be made within three years of the proprietor becoming aware of the registration; and no injunction shall be granted under subsection (4) in respect of a use in which the proprietor has acquiesced for a continuous period of three years or more.

61 (*repealed*)

Amendments–Repealed by Finance Act 2000, s 156, Sch 40, Pt III this repeal applies to instruments executed on or after 28 March 2000 see the Finance Act 2000, s 129(5), Sch 40, Pt III.

PART III
ADMINISTRATIVE AND OTHER SUPPLEMENTARY PROVISIONS

The registrar

62 The registrar

In this Act 'the registrar' means the Comptroller-General of Patents, Designs and Trade Marks.

The register

63 The register

(1) The registrar shall maintain a register of trade marks.

References in this Act to 'the register' are to that register; and references to registration (in particular, in the expression 'registered trade mark') are, unless the context otherwise requires, to registration in that register.

(2) There shall be entered in the register in accordance with this Act –

    (a)   registered trade marks,

    (b)   such particulars as may be prescribed of registrable transactions affecting a registered trade mark, and

    (c)   such other matters relating to registered trade marks as may be prescribed.

(3) The register shall be kept in such manner as may be prescribed, and provision shall in particular be made for –

    (a)   public inspection of the register, and

    (b)   the supply of certified or uncertified copies, or extracts, of entries in the register.

64 Rectification or correction of the register

(1) Any person having a sufficient interest may apply for the rectification of an error or omission in the register:

Provided that an application for rectification may not be made in respect of a matter affecting the validity of the registration of a trade mark.

(2) An application for rectification may be made either to the registrar or to the court, except that –

    (a)   if proceedings concerning the trade mark in question are pending in the court, the application must be made to the court; and

    (b)   if in any other case the application is made to the registrar, he may at any stage of the proceedings refer the application to the court.

(3) Except where the registrar or the court directs otherwise the effect of rectification of the register is that the error or omission in question shall be deemed never to have been made.

(4) The registrar may, on request made in the prescribed manner by the proprietor of a registered trade mark, or a licensee, enter any change in his name or address as recorded in the register.

(5) The registrar may remove from the register matter appearing to him to have ceased to have effect.

65 Adaptation of entries to new classification

(1) Provision may be made by rules empowering the registrar to do such things as he considers necessary to implement any amended or substituted classification of goods or services for the purposes of the registration of trade marks.

(2) Provision may in particular be made for the amendment of existing entries on the register so as to accord with the new classification.

(3) Any such power of amendment shall not be exercised so as to extend the rights conferred by the registration, except where it appears to the registrar that

compliance with this requirement would involve undue complexity and that any extension would not be substantial and would not adversely affect the rights of any person.

(4) he rules may empower the registrar –

    (a)   to require the proprietor of a registered trade mark, within such time as may be prescribed, to file a proposal for amendment of the register, and

    (b)   to cancel or refuse to renew the registration of the trade mark in the event of his failing to do so.

(5) Any such proposal shall be advertised, and may be opposed, in such manner as may be prescribed.

Powers and duties of the registrar

66 Power to require use of forms

(1) The registrar may require the use of such forms as he may direct for any purpose relating to the registration of a trade mark or any other proceeding before him under this Act.

(2) The forms, and any directions of the registrar with respect to their use, shall be published in the prescribed manner.

67 Information about applications and registered trade marks

(1) After publication of an application for registration of a trade mark, the registrar shall on request provide a person with such information and permit him to inspect such documents relating to the application, or to any registered trade mark resulting from it, as may be specified in the request, subject, however, to any prescribed restrictions.

Any request must be made in the prescribed manner and be accompanied by the appropriate fee (if any).

(2) Before publication of an application for registration of a trade mark, documents or information constituting or relating to the application shall not be published by the registrar or communicated by him to any person except –

    (a)   in such cases and to such extent as may be prescribed, or
    (b)   with the consent of the applicant;

but subject as follows.

(3) Where a person has been notified that an application for registration of a trade mark has been made, and that the applicant will if the application is granted bring proceedings against him in respect of acts done after publication of the application, he may make a request under subsection (1) notwithstanding that the application has not been published and that subsection shall apply accordingly.

68 Costs and security for costs

(1) Provision may be made by rules empowering the registrar, in any proceedings before him under this Act –

    (a)   to award any party such costs as he may consider reasonable, and

    (b)   to direct how and by what parties they are to be paid.

(2) Any such order of the registrar may be enforced –

    (a)   in England and Wales or Northern Ireland, in the same way as an order of the High Court;

    (b)   in Scotland, in the same way as a decree for expenses granted by the Court of Session.

(3) Provision may be made by rules empowering the registrar, in such cases as may be prescribed, to require a party to proceedings before him to give security for costs, in relation to those proceedings or to proceedings on appeal, and as to the consequences if security is not given.

69 Evidence before registrar

Provision may be made by rules –

    (a)   as to the giving of evidence in proceedings before the registrar under this Act by affidavit or statutory declaration;

    (b)   conferring on the registrar the powers of an official referee of the Senior Courts or of the Court of Judicature as regards the examination of witnesses on oath and the discovery and production of documents; and

    (c)   applying in relation to the attendance of witnesses in proceedings before the registrar the rules applicable to the attendance of witnesses before such a referee.

Amendments–Constitutional Reform Act 2005, s 59(5), Sch 11, Pt 4, para 31.

70 Exclusion of liability in respect of official acts

(1) The registrar shall not be taken to warrant the validity of the registration of a trade mark under this Act or under any treaty, convention, arrangement or engagement to which the United Kingdom is a party.

(2) The registrar is not subject to any liability by reason of, or in connection with, any examination required or authorised by this Act, or any such treaty, convention, arrangement or engagement, or any report or other proceedings consequent on such examination.

(3) No proceedings lie against an officer of the registrar in respect of any matter for which, by virtue of this section, the registrar is not liable.

71 Registrar's annual report

(1) The Comptroller-General of Patents, Designs and Trade Marks shall in his annual report under section 121 of the Patents Act 1977, include a report on the execution of this Act, including the discharge of his functions under the Madrid Protocol.

(2) The report shall include an account of all money received and paid by him under or by virtue of this Act.

Legal proceedings and appeals

72 Registration to be prima facie evidence of validity

In all legal proceedings relating to a registered trade mark (including proceedings for rectification of the register) the registration of a person as proprietor of a trade mark shall be prima facie evidence of the validity of the original registration and of any subsequent assignment or other transmission of it.

73 Certificate of validity of contested registration

(1) If in proceedings before the court the validity of the registration of a trade mark is contested and it is found by the court that the trade mark is validly registered, the court may give a certificate to that effect.

(2) If the court gives such a certificate and in subsequent proceedings –

    (a)   the validity of the registration is again questioned, and
    (b)   the proprietor obtains a final order or judgment in his favour,

he is entitled to his costs as between solicitor and client unless the court directs otherwise.

This subsection does not extend to the costs of an appeal in any such proceedings.

74 Registrar's appearance in proceedings involving the register

(1) In proceedings before the court involving an application for –

    (a)   the revocation of the registration of a trade mark,
    (b)   a declaration of the invalidity of the registration of a trade mark, or
    (c)   the rectification of the register,

the registrar is entitled to appear and be heard, and shall appear if so directed by the court.

(2) Unless otherwise directed by the court, the registrar may instead of appearing submit to the court a statement in writing signed by him, giving particulars of –

    (a)   any proceedings before him in relation to the matter in issue,
    (b)   the grounds of any decision given by him affecting it,
    (c)   the practice of the Patent Office in like cases, or

(d)   such matters relevant to the issues and within his knowledge as registrar as he thinks fit;

and the statement shall be deemed to form part of the evidence in the proceedings.

(3) Anything which the registrar is or may be authorised or required to do under this section may be done on his behalf by a duly authorised officer.

75 The court

In this Act, unless the context otherwise requires, 'the court' means –

(a)   in England and Wales, the High Court or a county court having jurisdiction by virtue of an order made under section 1 of the Courts and Legal Services Act 1990,

(aa)   in Northern Ireland, the High Court, and

(b)   in Scotland, the Court of Session.

Amendments–SI 2005/587.

76 Appeals from the registrar

(1) An appeal lies from any decision of the registrar under this Act, except as otherwise expressly provided by rules.

For this purpose 'decision' includes any act of the registrar in exercise of a discretion vested in him by or under this Act.

(2) Any such appeal may be brought either to an appointed person or to the court.

(3) Where an appeal is made to an appointed person, he may refer the appeal to the court if –

(a)   it appears to him that a point of general legal importance is involved,

(b)   the registrar requests that it be so referred, or

(c)   such a request is made by any party to the proceedings before the registrar in which the decision appealed against was made.

Before doing so the appointed person shall give the appellant and any other party to the appeal an opportunity to make representations as to whether the appeal should be referred to the court.

(4) Where an appeal is made to an appointed person and he does not refer it to the court, he shall hear and determine the appeal and his decision shall be final.

(5) The provisions of sections 68 and 69 (costs and security for costs; evidence) apply in relation to proceedings before an appointed person as in relation to proceedings before the registrar.

(6) In the application of this section to England and Wales, 'the court' means the High Court.

Amendments–SI 2005/587.

77 Persons appointed to hear and determine appeals

(1) For the purposes of section 76 an 'appointed person' means a person appointed by the Lord Chancellor to hear and decide appeals under this Act.

(2) A person is not eligible for such appointment unless –

(a) he satisfies the judicial-appointment eligibility condition on a 5-year basis;

(b) he is an advocate or solicitor in Scotland of at least 5 years' standing;

(c) he is a member of the Bar of Northern Ireland or solicitor of the Court of Judicature of Northern Ireland of at least 5 years' standing; or

(d) he has held judicial office.

(3) An appointed person shall hold and vacate office in accordance with his terms of appointment, subject to the following provisions –

(a) there shall be paid to him such remuneration (whether by way of salary or fees), and such allowances, as the Secretary of State with the approval of the Treasury may determine;

(b) he may resign his office by notice in writing to the Lord Chancellor;

(c) the Lord Chancellor may by notice in writing remove him from office if –

(i) he has become bankrupt or made an arrangement with his creditors or, in Scotland, his estate has been sequestrated or he has executed a trust deed for his creditors or entered into a composition contract, or

(ii) he is incapacitated by physical or mental illness,

or if he is in the opinion of the Lord Chancellor otherwise unable or unfit to perform his duties as an appointed person.

(4) The Lord Chancellor shall consult the Secretary of State before exercising his powers under this section.

(5) The Lord Chancellor may remove a person from office under subsection (3)(c) only with the concurrence of the appropriate senior judge.

(6) The appropriate senior judge is the Lord Chief Justice of England and Wales, unless –

(a) the person to be removed exercises functions wholly or mainly in Scotland, in which case it is the Lord President of the Court of Session, or

(b) the person to be removed exercises functions wholly or mainly in Northern Ireland, in which case it is the Lord Chief Justice of Northern Ireland.

Amendments–SI 1999/678; Constitutional Reform Act 2005, s 59(5), Sch 11, Pt 3, para 5; Tribunals, Courts and Enforcement Act 2007, s 50, Sch 10, Pt 1, para 25(1), (2).

Rules, fees, hours of business, &c

78 Power of Secretary of State to make rules

(1) The Secretary of State may make rules –

(a)   for the purposes of any provision of this Act authorising the making of rules with respect to any matter, and

(b)   for prescribing anything authorised or required by any provision of this Act to be prescribed,

and generally for regulating practice and procedure under this Act.

(2) Provision may, in particular, be made –

(a)   as to the manner of filing of applications and other documents;

(b)   requiring and regulating the translation of documents and the filing and authentication of any translation;

(c)   as to the service of documents;

(d)   authorising the rectification of irregularities of procedure;

(e)   prescribing time limits for anything required to be done in connection with any proceeding under this Act;

(f)   providing for the extension of any time limit so prescribed, or specified by the registrar, whether or not it has already expired.

(3) Rules under this Act shall be made by statutory instrument which shall be subject to annulment in pursuance of a resolution of either House of Parliament.

79 Fees

(1) There shall be paid in respect of applications and registration and other matters under this Act such fees as may be prescribed.

(2) Provision may be made by rules as to –

(a)   the payment of a single fee in respect of two or more matters, and

(b)   the circumstances (if any) in which a fee may be repaid or remitted.

80 Hours of business and business days

(1) The registrar may give directions specifying the hours of business of the Patent Office for the purpose of the transaction by the public of business under this Act, and the days which are business days for that purpose.

(2) Business done on any day after the specified hours of business, or on a day which is not a business day, shall be deemed to have been done on the next business day; and where the time for doing anything under this Act expires on a day which is not a business day, that time shall be extended to the next business day.

(3) Directions under this section may make different provision for different classes of business and shall be published in the prescribed manner.

81 The trade marks journal

Provision shall be made by rules for the publication by the registrar of a journal containing particulars of any application for the registration of a trade mark (including a representation of the mark) and such other information relating to trade marks as the registrar thinks fit.

Trade mark agents

82 Recognition of agents

Except as otherwise provided by rules and subject to the Legal Services Act 2007, any act required or authorised by this Act to be done by or to a person in connection with the registration of a trade mark, or any procedure relating to a registered trade mark, may be done by or to an agent authorised by that person orally or in writing.

Amendments–Legal Services Act 2007, s 184(1), (2).

83 The register of trade mark attorneys

(1) There is to continue to be a register of persons who act as agent for others for the purpose of applying for or obtaining the registration of trade marks.

(2) In this Act a registered trade mark attorney means an individual whose name is entered on the register kept under this section.

(3) The register is to be kept by the Institute of Trade Mark Attorneys.

(4) The Secretary of State may, by order, amend subsection (3) so as to require the register to be kept by the person specified in the order.

(5) Before making an order under subsection (4), the Secretary of State must consult the Legal Services Board.

(6) An order under this section must be made by statutory instrument.

(7) An order under this section may not be made unless a draft of it has been laid before, and approved by a resolution of, each House of Parliament.

Amendments–Legal Services Act 2007, s 184(1), (3).

83A Regulation of trade mark attorneys

(1) The person who keeps the register under section 83 may make regulations which regulate –

    (a)   the keeping of the register and the registration of persons;
    (b)   the carrying on of trade mark agency work by registered persons.

(2) Those regulations may, amongst other things, make –

    (a)   provision as to the educational and training qualifications, and other requirements, which must be satisfied before an individual may be registered or for an individual to remain registered;

(b)   provision as to the requirements which must be met by a body (corporate or unincorporate) before it may be registered or for it to remain registered, including provision as to the management and control of the body;

(c)   provision as to the educational, training or other requirements to be met by regulated persons;

(d)   provision regulating the practice, conduct and discipline of registered persons or regulated persons;

(e)   provision authorising in such cases as may be specified in the regulations the erasure from the register of the name of any person registered in it, or the suspension of a person's registration;

(f)   provision requiring the payment of such fees as may be specified in or determined in accordance with the regulations;

(g)   provision about the provision to be made by registered persons in respect of complaints made against them;

(h)   provision about the keeping of records and accounts by registered persons or regulated persons;

(i)   provision for reviews of or appeals against decisions made under the regulations;

(j)   provision as to the indemnification of registered persons or regulated persons against losses arising from claims in respect of civil liability incurred by them.

(3) Regulations under this section may make different provision for different purposes.

(4) Regulations under this section which are not regulatory arrangements within the meaning of the Legal Services Act 2007 are to be treated as such arrangements for the purposes of that Act.

(5) Before the appointed day, regulations under this section may be made only with the approval of the Secretary of State.

(6) The powers conferred to make regulations under this section are not to be taken to prejudice –

(a)   any other power which the person who keeps the register may have to make rules or regulations (however they may be described and whether they are made under an enactment or otherwise);

(b)   any rules or regulations made by that person under any such power.

(7) In this section –

'appointed day' means the day appointed for the coming into force of paragraph 1 of Schedule 4 to the Legal Services Act 2007;

'manager', in relation to a body, has the same meaning as in the Legal Services Act 2007 (see section 207);

'registered person' means –

(a)   a registered trade mark attorney, or

(b)   a body (corporate or unincorporate) registered in the register kept under section 83;

'regulated person' means a person who is not a registered person but is a
manager or employee of a body which is a registered person;

'trade mark agency work' means work done in the course of carrying on the
business of acting as agent for others for the purpose of –

(a)   applying for or obtaining the registration of trade marks in the
United Kingdom or elsewhere, or

(b)   conducting proceedings before the Comptroller relating to
applications for or otherwise in connection with the registration
of trade marks.

Amendments–Legal Services Act 2007, s 184(1), (3); SI 2009/3339.

84 Unregistered persons not to be described as registered trade mark agents

(1) An individual who is not a registered trade mark attorney shall not –

(a)   carry on a business (otherwise than in partnership) under any name or
other description which contains the words 'registered trade mark
agent' or registered trade mark attorney; or

(b)   in the course of a business otherwise describe or hold himself out, or
permit himself to be described or held out, as a registered trade mark
agent or a registered trade mark attorney.

(2) A partnership or other unincorporated body shall not –

(a)   carry on a business under any name or other description which
contains the words 'registered trade mark agent' or registered trade
mark attorney; or

(b)   in the course of a business otherwise describe or hold itself out, or
permit itself to be described or held out, as a firm of registered trade
mark agents or registered trade mark attorneys,

unless the partnership or other body is registered in the register kept under
section 83.

(3) A body corporate shall not –

(a)   carry on a business (otherwise than in partnership) under any name or
other description which contains the words 'registered trade mark
agent' or registered trade mark attorney; or

(b)   in the course of a business otherwise describe or hold itself out, or
permit itself to be described or held out, as a registered trade mark
agent or a registered trade mark attorney,

unless the body corporate is registered in the register kept under section 83.

(4) A person who contravenes this section commits an offence and is liable on
summary conviction to a fine not exceeding level 5 on the standard scale; and
proceedings for such an offence may be begun at any time within a year from
the date of the offence.

Amendments–Legal Services Act 2007, s 208(1), Sch 21, paras 109, 111(a)(i).

85 (*repealed*)

Amendments–Repealed by the Legal Services Act 2007, ss 184(1), (5), 210, Sch 23.

86 Use of the term 'trade mark attorney'

(1) No offence is committed under the enactments restricting the use of certain expressions in reference to persons not qualified to act as solicitors by the use of the term 'trade mark attorney' in reference to a registered trade mark attorney.

(2) The enactments referred to in subsection (1) are section 21 of the Solicitors Act 1974, section 31 of the Solicitors (Scotland) Act 1980 and Article 22 of the Solicitors (Northern Ireland) Order 1976.

Amendments–Legal Services Act 2007, s 208(1), Sch 21, paras 109, 112.

87 Privilege for communications with registered trade mark agents

(1) This section applies to –

(a) communications as to any matter relating to the protection of any design or trade mark, or as to any matter involving passing off, and

(b) documents, material or information relating to any matter mentioned in paragraph (a).

(2) Where a trade mark attorney acts for a client in relation to a matter mentioned in subsection (1), any communication, document, material or information to which this section applies is privileged from disclosure in like manner as if the trade mark attorney had at all material times been acting as the client's solicitor.

(3) In subsection (2) 'trade mark attorney' means –

(a) a registered trade mark attorney, or

(b) a partnership entitled to describe itself as a firm of registered trade mark attorneys, or

(c) any other unincorporated body or a body corporate entitled to describe itself as a registered trade mark attorney.

Amendments–Legal Services Act 2007, s 208(1), Sch 21, paras 109, 113(a).

88 Power of registrar to refuse to deal with certain agents

(1) The Secretary of State may make rules authorising the registrar to refuse to recognise as agent in respect of any business under this Act –

(a) a person who has been convicted of an offence under section 84 (unregistered persons describing themselves as registered trade mark agents);

(b) a person whose name has been erased from and not restored to, or who is suspended from, the register of trade mark *agents* [attorneys] on the ground of misconduct;

(c)   a person who is found by the Secretary of State to have been guilty of such conduct as would, in the case of a person registered in the register of trade mark *agents*[attorneys], render the person liable to have the person's name erased from the register on the ground of misconduct;

(d)   a partnership or body corporate of which one of the partners or directors is a person whom the registrar could refuse to recognise under paragraph (a), (b) or (c) above.

(2) The rules may contain such incidental and supplementary provisions as appear to the Secretary of State to be appropriate and may, in particular, prescribe circumstances in which a person is or is not to be taken to have been guilty of misconduct.

Amendments–SI 2009/3348.

Prospective Amendments–Words in italics prospectively repealed and words in square brackets prospectively substituted by Legal Services Act 2007, s 211(2), with effect from a date to be appointed.

Importation of infringing goods, material or articles

89 Infringing goods, material or articles may be treated as prohibited goods

(1) The proprietor of a registered trade mark, or a licensee, may give notice in writing to the Commissioners of Customs and Excise –

(a)   that he is the proprietor or, as the case may be, a licensee of the registered trade mark,

(b)   that, at a time and place specified in the notice, goods which are, in relation to that registered trade mark, infringing goods, material or articles are expected to arrive in the United Kingdom –
(i)   from outside the European Economic Area, or
(ii)   from within that Area but not having been entered for free circulation, and

(c)   that he requests the Commissioners to treat them as prohibited goods.

(2) When a notice is in force under this section the importation of the goods to which the notice relates, otherwise than by a person for his private and domestic use, is prohibited; but a person is not by reason of the prohibition liable to any penalty other than forfeiture of the goods.

(3) This section does not apply to goods placed in, or expected to be placed in, one of the situations referred to in Article 1(1), in respect of which an application may be made under Article 5(1), of Council Regulation (EC) No 1383/2003 concerning customs action against goods suspected of infringing certain intellectual property rights and the measures to be taken against goods found to have infringed such rights.

Amendments–SI 2004/1473.

90 Power of Commissioners of Customs and Excise to make regulations

(1) The Commissioners of Customs and Excise may make regulations prescribing the form in which notice is to be given under section 89 and requiring a person giving notice –

    (a) to furnish the Commissioners with such evidence as may be specified in the regulations, either on giving notice or when the goods are imported, or at both those times, and

    (b) to comply with such other conditions as may be specified in the regulations.

(2) The regulations may, in particular, require a person giving such a notice –

    (a) to pay such fees in respect of the notice as may be specified by the regulations;

    (b) to give such security as may be so specified in respect of any liability or expense which the Commissioners may incur in consequence of the notice by reason of the detention of any goods or anything done to goods detained;

    (c) to indemnify the Commissioners against any such liability or expense, whether security has been given or not.

(3) The regulations may make different provision as respects different classes of case to which they apply and may include such incidental and supplementary provisions as the Commissioners consider expedient.

(4) Regulations under this section shall be made by statutory instrument which shall be subject to annulment in pursuance of a resolution of either House of Parliament.

(5) (*repealed*)

Amendments– Commissioners for Revenue and Customs Act 2005, ss 50(6), 52(2), Sch 4, para 57, Sch 5.

91 Power of Commissioners for Revenue and Customs to disclose information

Where information relating to infringing goods, material or articles has been obtained or is held by the Commissioners for her Majesty's Revenue and Customs for the purposes of, or in connection with, the exercise of functions of Her Majesty's Revenue and Customs in relation to imported goods, the Commissioners may authorise the disclosure of that information for the purpose of facilitating the exercise by any person of any function in connection with the investigation or prosecution of an offence under –

    (a) section 92 below (unauthorised use of trade mark, &c in relation to goods),

    (b) the Trade Descriptions Act 1968,

    (c) the Business Protection from Misleading Marketing Regulations 2008, or

    (d) the Consumer Protection from Unfair Trading Regulations 2008.

Amendments– Commissioners for Revenue and Customs Act 2005, s 50(6), Sch 4, para 58(2); SI 2008/1277.

Offences

92 Unauthorised use of trade mark, &c in relation to goods

(1) A person commits an offence who with a view to gain for himself or another, or with intent to cause loss to another, and without the consent of the proprietor –

    (a)   applies to goods or their packaging a sign identical to, or likely to be mistaken for, a registered trade mark, or

    (b)   sells or lets for hire, offers or exposes for sale or hire or distributes goods which bear, or the packaging of which bears, such a sign, or

    (c)   has in his possession, custody or control in the course of a business any such goods with a view to the doing of anything, by himself or another, which would be an offence under paragraph (b).

(2) A person commits an offence who with a view to gain for himself or another, or with intent to cause loss to another, and without the consent of the proprietor –

    (a)   applies a sign identical to, or likely to be mistaken for, a registered trade mark to material intended to be used –

        (i)   for labelling or packaging goods,

        (ii)   as a business paper in relation to goods, or

        (iii) for advertising goods, or

    (b)   uses in the course of a business material bearing such a sign for labelling or packaging goods, as a business paper in relation to goods, or for advertising goods, or

    (c)   has in his possession, custody or control in the course of a business any such material with a view to the doing of anything, by himself or another, which would be an offence under paragraph (b).

(3) A person commits an offence who with a view to gain for himself or another, or with intent to cause loss to another, and without the consent of the proprietor –

    (a)   makes an article specifically designed or adapted for making copies of a sign identical to, or likely to be mistaken for, a registered trade mark, or

    (b)   has such an article in his possession, custody or control in the course of a business,

knowing or having reason to believe that it has been, or is to be, used to produce goods, or material for labelling or packaging goods, as a business paper in relation to goods, or for advertising goods.

(4) A person does not commit an offence under this section unless –

    (a)   the goods are goods in respect of which the trade mark is registered, or

(b)   the trade mark has a reputation in the United Kingdom and the use of the sign takes or would take unfair advantage of, or is or would be detrimental to, the distinctive character or the repute of the trade mark.

(5) It is a defence for a person charged with an offence under this section to show that he believed on reasonable grounds that the use of the sign in the manner in which it was used, or was to be used, was not an infringement of the registered trade mark.

(6) A person guilty of an offence under this section is liable –

(a)   on summary conviction to imprisonment for a term not exceeding six months or a fine not exceeding the statutory maximum, or both;

(b)   on conviction on indictment to a fine or imprisonment for a term not exceeding ten years, or both.

92A   Search warrants

(1) Where a justice of the peace (in Scotland, a sheriff or justice of the peace) is satisfied by information on oath given by a constable (in Scotland, by evidence on oath) that there are reasonable grounds for believing –

(a)   that an offence under section 92 (unauthorised use of trade mark, etc in relation to goods) has been or is about to be committed in any premises, and

(b)   that evidence that such an offence has been or is about to be committed is in those premises,

he may issue a warrant authorising a constable to enter and search the premises, using such reasonable force as is necessary.

(2) The power conferred by subsection (1) does not, in England and Wales, extend to authorising a search for material of the kinds mentioned in section 9(2) of the Police and Criminal Evidence Act 1984 (c 60) (certain classes of personal or confidential material).

(3) A warrant under subsection (1) –

(a)   may authorise persons to accompany any constable executing the warrant, and

(b)   remains in force for 28 days three months from the date of its issue.

(4) In executing a warrant issued under subsection (1) a constable may seize an article if he reasonably believes that it is evidence that any offence under section 92 has been or is about to be committed.

(5) In this section 'premises' includes land, buildings, fixed or moveable structures, vehicles, vessels, aircraft and hovercraft.

Amendments– Copyright, etc and Trade Marks (Offences and Enforcement) Act 2002, s 6; Serious Organised Crime and Police Act 2005, s 174(1), Sch 16, para 8.

93 Enforcement function of local weights and measures authority

(1) It is the duty of every local weights and measures authority to enforce within their area the provisions of section 92 (unauthorised use of trade mark, &c in relation to goods).

(2) The following provisions of the Trade Descriptions Act 1968 apply in relation to the enforcement of that section as in relation to the enforcement of that Act –

section 27 (power to make test purchases),
section 28 (power to enter premises and inspect and seize goods and documents),
section 29 (obstruction of authorised officers), and
section 33 (compensation for loss, &c of goods seized).

(3) Subsection (1) above does not apply in relation to the enforcement of section 92 in Northern Ireland, but it is the duty of the Department of Economic Development to enforce that section in Northern Ireland.

For that purpose the provisions of the Trade Descriptions Act 1968 specified in subsection (2) apply as if for the references to a local weights and measures authority and any officer of such an authority there were substituted references to that Department and any of its officers.

(4) Any enactment which authorises the disclosure of information for the purpose of facilitating the enforcement of the Trade Descriptions Act 1968 shall apply as if section 92 above were contained in that Act and as if the functions of any person in relation to the enforcement of that section were functions under that Act.

(5) Nothing in this section shall be construed as authorising a local weights and measures authority to bring proceedings in Scotland for an offence.

94 Falsification of register, &c

(1) It is an offence for a person to make, or cause to be made, a false entry in the register of trade marks, knowing or having reason to believe that it is false.

(2) It is an offence for a person –

(a) to make or cause to be made anything falsely purporting to be a copy of an entry in the register, or
(b) to produce or tender or cause to be produced or tendered in evidence any such thing,

knowing or having reason to believe that it is false.

(3) A person guilty of an offence under this section is liable –

(a) on conviction on indictment, to imprisonment for a term not exceeding two years or a fine, or both;
(b) on summary conviction, to imprisonment for a term not exceeding six months or a fine not exceeding the statutory maximum, or both.

95 Falsely representing trade mark as registered

(1) It is an offence for a person –

(a)   falsely to represent that a mark is a registered trade mark, or

(b)   to make a false representation as to the goods or services for which a trade mark is registered

knowing or having reason to believe that the representation is false.

(2) For the purposes of this section, the use in the United Kingdom in relation to a trade mark –

(a)   of the word registered, or

(b)   of any other word or symbol importing a reference (express or implied) to registration,

shall be deemed to be a representation as to registration under this Act unless it is shown that the reference is to registration elsewhere than in the United Kingdom and that the trade mark is in fact so registered for the goods or services in question.

(3) A person guilty of an offence under this section is liable on summary conviction to a fine not exceeding level 3 on the standard scale.

96 Supplementary provisions as to summary proceedings in Scotland

(1) Notwithstanding anything in section 136 of the Criminal Procedure (Scotland) Act 1995, summary proceedings in Scotland for an offence under this Act may be begun at any time within six months after the date on which evidence sufficient in the Lord Advocate's opinion to justify the proceedings came to his knowledge.

For this purpose a certificate of the Lord Advocate as to the date on which such evidence came to his knowledge is conclusive evidence.

(2) For the purposes of subsection (1) and of any other provision of this Act as to the time within which summary proceedings for an offence may be brought, proceedings in Scotland shall be deemed to be begun on the date on which a warrant to apprehend or to cite the accused is granted, if such warrant is executed without undue delay.

Amendments–Criminal Procedure (Consequential Provisions) (Scotland) Act 1995, s 5, Sch 4, para 92(2).

Forfeiture of counterfeit goods, &c

97 Forfeiture: England and Wales or Northern Ireland

(1) In England and Wales or Northern Ireland where there has come into the possession of any person in connection with the investigation or prosecution of a relevant offence –

(a)   goods which, or the packaging of which, bears a sign identical to or likely to be mistaken for a registered trade mark,

(b) material bearing such a sign and intended to be used for labelling or packaging goods, as a business paper in relation to goods, or for advertising goods, or

(c) articles specifically designed or adapted for making copies of such a sign,

that person may apply under this section for an order for the forfeiture of the goods, material or articles.

(2) An application under this section may be made –

(a) where proceedings have been brought in any court for a relevant offence relating to some or all of the goods, material or articles, to that court;

(b) where no application for the forfeiture of the goods, material or articles has been made under paragraph (a), by way of complaint to a magistrates' court.

(3) On an application under this section the court shall make an order for the forfeiture of any goods, material or articles only if it is satisfied that a relevant offence has been committed in relation to the goods, material or articles.

(4) A court may infer for the purposes of this section that such an offence has been committed in relation to any goods, material or articles if it is satisfied that such an offence has been committed in relation to goods, material or articles which are representative of them (whether by reason of being of the same design or part of the same consignment or batch or otherwise).

(5) Any person aggrieved by an order made under this section by a magistrates' court, or by a decision of such a court not to make such an order, may appeal against that order or decision –

(a) in England and Wales, to the Crown Court;

(b) in Northern Ireland, to the county court;

and an order so made may contain such provision as appears to the court to be appropriate for delaying the coming into force of the order pending the making and determination of any appeal (including any application under section 111 of the Magistrates' Courts Act 1980 or Article 146 of the Magistrates' Courts (Northern Ireland) Order 1981 (statement of case)).

(6) Subject to subsection (7), where any goods, material or articles are forfeited under this section they shall be destroyed in accordance with such directions as the court may give.

(7) On making an order under this section the court may, if it considers it appropriate to do so, direct that the goods, material or articles to which the order relates shall (instead of being destroyed) be released, to such person as the court may specify, on condition that that person –

(a) causes the offending sign to be erased, removed or obliterated and

(b) complies with any order to pay costs which has been made against him in the proceedings for the order for forfeiture.

(8) For the purposes of this section a 'relevant offence' means

(a)   an offence under section 92 above (unauthorised use of trade mark, &c in relation to goods),

(b)   an offence under the Trade Descriptions Act 1968,

(c)   an offence under the Business Protection from Misleading Marketing Regulations 2008,

(d)   an offence under the Consumer Protection from Unfair Trading Regulations 2008, or

(e)   any offence involving dishonesty or deception.

Amendments–SI 1994/2550; SI 2008/1277.

98 Forfeiture: Scotland

(1) In Scotland the court may make an order for the forfeiture of any –

(a)   goods which bear, or the packaging of which bears, a sign identical to or likely to be mistaken for a registered trade mark,

(b)   material bearing such a sign and intended to be used for labelling or packaging goods, as a business paper in relation to goods, or for advertising goods, or

(c)   articles specifically designed or adapted for making copies of such a sign.

(2) An order under this section may be made –

(a)   on an application by the procurator-fiscal made in the manner specified in section 134 of the Criminal Procedure (Scotland) Act 1995, or

(b)   where a person is convicted of a relevant offence, in addition to any other penalty which the court may impose.

(3) On an application under subsection (2)(a), the court shall make an order for the forfeiture of any goods, material or articles only if it is satisfied that a relevant offence has been committed in relation to the goods, material or articles.

(4) The court may infer for the purposes of this section that such an offence has been committed in relation to any goods, material or articles if it is satisfied that such an offence has been committed in relation to goods, material or articles which are representative of them (whether by reason of being of the same design or part of the same consignment or batch or otherwise).

(5) The procurator-fiscal making the application under subsection (2)(a) shall serve on any person appearing to him to be the owner of, or otherwise to have an interest in, the goods, material or articles to which the application relates a copy of the application, together with a notice giving him the opportunity to appear at the hearing of the application to show cause why the goods, material or articles should not be forfeited.

(6) Service under subsection (5) shall be carried out, and such service may be proved, in the manner specified for citation of an accused in summary proceedings under the Criminal Procedure (Scotland) Act 1995.

(7) Any person upon whom notice is served under subsection (5) and any other person claiming to be the owner of, or otherwise to have an interest in, goods, material or articles to which an application under this section relates shall be entitled to appear at the hearing of the application to show cause why the goods, material or articles should not be forfeited.

(8) The court shall not make an order following an application under subsection (2)(a) –

(a) if any person on whom notice is served under subsection (5) does not appear, unless service of the notice on that person is proved; or

(b) if no notice under subsection (5) has been served, unless the court is satisfied that in the circumstances it was reasonable not to serve such notice.

(9) Where an order for the forfeiture of any goods, material or articles is made following an application under subsection (2)(a), any person who appeared, or was entitled to appear, to show cause why goods, material or articles should not be forfeited may, within 21 days of the making of the order, appeal to the High Court by Bill of Suspension; and section 182(5)(a) to (e) of the Criminal Procedure (Scotland) Act 1995 shall apply to an appeal under this subsection as it applies to a stated case under Part II of that Act.

(10) An order following an application under subsection (2)(a) shall not take effect –

(a) until the end of the period of 21 days beginning with the day after the day on which the order is made; or

(b) if an appeal is made under subsection (9) above within that period, until the appeal is determined or abandoned.

(11) An order under subsection (2)(b) shall not take effect –

(a) until the end of the period within which an appeal against the order could be brought under the Criminal Procedure (Scotland) Act 1995; or

(b) if an appeal is made within that period, until the appeal is determined or abandoned.

(12) Subject to subsection (13), goods, material or articles forfeited under this section shall be destroyed in accordance with such directions as the court may give.

(13) On making an order under this section the court may if it considers it appropriate to do so, direct that the goods, material or articles to which the order relates shall (instead of being destroyed) be released, to such person as the court may specify, on condition that that person causes the offending sign to be erased, removed or obliterated.

(14) For the purposes of this section –

'relevant offence' means 77

(a)   an offence under section 92 above (unauthorised use of trade mark, &c in relation to goods),

(b)   an offence under the Trade Descriptions Act 1968,

(c)   an offence under the Business Protection from Misleading Marketing Regulations 2008,

(d)   an offence under the Consumer Protection from Unfair Trading Regulations 2008, or

(e)   any offence involving dishonesty or deception,

'the court' means –

(a)   in relation to an order made on an application under subsection (2)(a), the sheriff, and

(b)   in relation to an order made under subsection (2)(b), the court which imposed the penalty.

Amendments–Criminal Procedure (Consequential Provisions) (Scotland) Act 1995, s 5, Sch 4, para 92(3). Sub-s (14); SI 2008/1277.

PART IV
MISCELLANEOUS AND GENERAL PROVISIONS

Miscellaneous

99 Unauthorised use of Royal arms, &c

(1) A person shall not without the authority of Her Majesty use in connection with any business the Royal arms (or arms so closely resembling the Royal arms as to be calculated to deceive) in such manner as to be calculated to lead to the belief that he is duly authorised to use the Royal arms.

(2) A person shall not without the authority of Her Majesty or of a member of the Royal family use in connection with any business any device, emblem or title in such a manner as to be calculated to lead to the belief that he is employed by, or supplies goods or services to, Her Majesty or that member of the Royal family.

(3) A person who contravenes subsection (1) commits an offence and is liable on summary conviction to a fine not exceeding level 2 on the standard scale.

(4) Contravention of subsection (1) or (2) may be restrained by injunction in proceedings brought by –

(a)   any person who is authorised to use the arms, device, emblem or title in question, or

(b)   any person authorised by the Lord Chamberlain to take such proceedings.

(5) Nothing in this section affects any right of the proprietor of a trade mark containing any such arms, device, emblem or title to use that trade mark.

100 Burden of proving use of trade mark

If in any civil proceedings under this Act a question arises as to the use to which a registered trade mark has been put, it is for the proprietor to show what use has been made of it

101 Offences committed by partnerships and bodies corporate

(1) Proceedings for an offence under this Act alleged to have been committed by a partnership shall be brought against the partnership in the name of the firm and not in that of the partners; but without prejudice to any liability of the partners under subsection (4) below.

(2) The following provis.

ions apply for the purposes of such proceedings as in relation to a body corporate –

   (a)   any rules of court relating to the service of documents;
   (b)   in England and Wales or Northern Ireland, Schedule 3 to the Magistrates' Courts Act 1980 or Schedule 4 to the Magistrates' Courts (Northern Ireland) Order 1981 (procedure on charge of offence).

(3) A fine imposed on a partnership on its conviction in such proceedings shall be paid out of the partnership assets.

(4) Where a partnership is guilty of an offence under this Act, every partner, other than a partner who is proved to have been ignorant of or to have attempted to prevent the commission of the offence, is also guilty of the offence and liable to be proceeded against and punished accordingly.

(5) Where an offence under this Act committed by a body corporate is proved to have been committed with the consent or connivance of a director, manager, secretary or other similar officer of the body, or a person purporting to act in any such capacity, he as well as the body corporate is guilty of the offence and liable to be proceeded against and punished accordingly.

Interpretation

102 Adaptation of expressions for Scotland

In the application of this Act to Scotland –

'account of profits' means accounting and payment of profits;
'accounts' means count, reckoning and payment;
'assignment' means assignation;
'costs' means expenses;
'declaration' means declarator;
'defendant' means defender;
'delivery up' means delivery;
'injunction' means interdict;
'interlocutory relief' means interim remedy; and
'plaintiff' means pursuer.

103 Minor definitions

(1) In this Act –

'business' includes a trade or profession;

'director', in relation to a body corporate whose affairs are managed by its members, means any member of the body;

'infringement proceedings', in relation to a registered trade mark, includes proceedings under section 16 (order for delivery up of infringing goods, &c);

'publish' means make available to the public, and references to publication –

    (a)   in relation to an application for registration, are to publication under section 38(1), and

    (b)   in relation to registration, are to publication under section 40(4);

'statutory provisions' includes provisions of subordinate legislation within the meaning of the Interpretation Act 1978;

'trade' includes any business or profession.

(2) References in this Act to use (or any particular description of use) of a trade mark, or of a sign identical with, similar to, or likely to be mistaken for a trade mark, include use (or that description of use) otherwise than by means of a graphic representation.

(3) References in this Act to a Community instrument include references to any instrument amending or replacing that instrument.

104 Index of defined expressions

In this Act the expressions listed below are defined by or otherwise fall to be construed in accordance with the provisions indicated –

account of profits and accounts (in Scotland)	Section 102
appointed person (for purposes of section 76)	Section 77
assignment (in Scotland)	Section 102
business	Section 103(1)
certification mark	Section 50(1)
collective mark	Section 49(1)
commencement (of this Act)	Section 109(2)
Community trade mark	Section 51
Community Trade Mark Regulation	Section 51

Convention country	Section 55(1)(b)
costs (in Scotland)	Section 102
the court	Section 75
date of application	Section 33(2)
date of filing	Section 33(1)
date of registration	Section 40(3)
defendant (in Scotland)	Section 102
delivery up (in Scotland)	Section 102
director	Section 103(1)
earlier right	Section 5(4)
earlier trade mark	Section 6
exclusive licence and licensee	Section 29(1)
infringement (of registered trade mark)	Section 9(1) and 2 and 10
infringement proceedings	Section 103(1)
infringing articles	Section 17
infringing goods	Section 17
infringing material	Section 17
injunction (in Scotland)	Section 102
the International Bureau	Section 102
international trade mark (EC)	Section 53
international trade mark (UK)	Section 53
Madrid Protocol	Section 53
Paris Convention	Section 55(1)(a)
plaintiff (in Scotland)	Section 102
Prescribed	Section 78(1)(b)

protected under the Paris Convention	
–well-known trade marks	Section 56(1)
–state emblems and official signs or hallmarks	Section 57(1)
–emblems, &c of international organisations	Section 58(2)
publish and references to publication	Section 103(1)
register, registered (and related expressions)	Section 63(1)
registered trade mark attorney	Section 83 (2)
registrable transaction	Section 25 (2)
the registrar	Section 62
rules	Section 78
statutory provisions	Section 103 (1)
trade	Section 103 (1)
trade mark	
–generally	Section 1(1)
–includes collective mark or certification mark	Section 1(2)
United Kingdom (references include Isle of Man)	Section 108(2)
use (of trade mark or sign)	Section 103(2)
well-known trade mark (under Paris Convention)	Section 56(1)

Amendments–SI 2004/2332; Legal Services Act 2007, s 208(1), Sch 21, paras 109, 115(a).

Other general provisions

105 Transitional provisions

The provisions of Schedule 3 have effect with respect to transitional matters, including the treatment of marks registered under the Trade Marks Act 1938, and applications for registration and other proceedings pending under that Act, on the commencement of this Act.

106 Consequential amendments and repeals

(1) The enactments specified in Schedule 4 are amended in accordance with that Schedule, the amendments being consequential on the provisions of this Act.

(2) The enactments specified in Schedule 5 are repealed to the extent specified.

107 Territorial waters and the continental shelf

(1) For the purposes of this Act the territorial waters of the United Kingdom shall be treated as part of the United Kingdom.

(2) This Act applies to things done in the United Kingdom sector of the continental shelf on a structure or vessel which is present there for purposes directly connected with the exploration of the sea bed or subsoil or the exploitation of their natural resources as it applies to things done in the United Kingdom.

(3) The United Kingdom sector of the continental shelf means the areas designated by order under section 1(7) of the Continental Shelf Act 1964.

108 Extent

(1) This Act extends to England and Wales, Scotland and Northern Ireland.

(2) This Act also extends to the Isle of Man, subject to such exceptions and modifications as Her Majesty may specify by Order in Council; and subject to any such Order references in this Act to the United Kingdom shall be construed as including the Isle of Man.

109 Commencement

(1) The provisions of this Act come into force on such day as the Secretary of State may appoint by order made by statutory instrument.

Different days may be appointed for different provisions and different purposes.

(2) The references to the commencement of this Act in Schedules 3 and 4 (transitional provisions and consequential amendments) are to the commencement of the main substantive provisions of Parts I and III of this Act and the consequential repeal of the Trade Marks Act 1938.

Provision may be made by order under this section identifying the date of that commencement.

110 Short title

This Act may be cited as the Trade Marks Act 1994.

Schedule 1

Collective Marks

Section 49

1 General

The provisions of this Act apply to collective marks subject to the following provisions.

2 Signs of which a collective mark may consist

In relation to a collective mark the reference in section 1(1) (signs of which a trade mark may consist) to distinguishing goods or services of one undertaking from those of other undertakings shall be construed as a reference to distinguishing goods or services of members of the association which is the proprietor of the mark from those of other undertakings.

3 Indication of geographical origin

(1) Notwithstanding section 3(1)(c), a collective mark may be registered which consists of signs or indications which may serve, in trade, to designate the geographical origin of the goods or services.

(2) However, the proprietor of such a mark is not entitled to prohibit the use of the signs or indications in accordance with honest practices in industrial or commercial matters (in particular, by a person who is entitled to use a geographical name).

4 Mark not to be misleading as to character or significance

(1) A collective mark shall not be registered if the public is liable to be misled as regards the character or significance of the mark, in particular if it is likely to be taken to be something other than a collective mark.

(2) The registrar may accordingly require that a mark in respect of which application is made for registration include some indication that it is a collective mark.

Notwithstanding section 39(2), an application may be amended so as to comply with any such requirement.

5 Regulations governing use of collective mark

(1) An applicant for registration of a collective mark must file with the registrar regulations governing the use of the mark.

(2) The regulations must specify the persons authorised to use the mark, the conditions of membership of the association and, where they exist, the conditions of use of the mark, including any sanctions against misuse.

Further requirements with which the regulations have to comply may be imposed by rules.

6 Approval of regulations by registrar

(1) A collective mark shall not be registered unless the regulations governing the use of the mark –

  (a)   comply with paragraph 5(2) and any further requirements imposed by rules, and
  (b)   are not contrary to public policy or to accepted principles of morality.

(2) Before the end of the prescribed period after the date of the application for registration of a collective mark, the applicant must file the regulations with the registrar and pay the prescribed fee.

If he does not do so, the application shall be deemed to be withdrawn.

7

(1) The registrar shall consider whether the requirements mentioned in paragraph 6(1) are met.

(2) If it appears to the registrar that those requirements are not met, he shall inform the applicant and give him an opportunity, within such period as the registrar may specify, to make representations or to file amended regulations.

(3) If the applicant fails to satisfy the registrar that those requirements are met, or to file regulations amended so as to meet them, or fails to respond before the end of the specified period, the registrar shall refuse the application.

(4) If it appears to the registrar that those requirements, and the other requirements for registration, are met, he shall accept the application and shall proceed in accordance with section 38 (publication, opposition proceedings and observations).

8

The regulations shall be published and notice of opposition may be given, and observations may be made, relating to the matters mentioned in paragraph 6(1).

This is in addition to any other grounds on which the application may be opposed or observations made.

9 Regulations to be open to inspection

The regulations governing the use of a registered collective mark shall be open to public inspection in the same way as the register.

10 Amendment of regulations

(1) An amendment of the regulations governing the use of a registered collective mark is not effective unless and until the amended regulations are filed with the registrar and accepted by him.

(2) Before accepting any amended regulations the registrar may in any case where it appears to him expedient to do so cause them to be published.

(3) If he does so, notice of opposition may be given, and observations may be made, relating to the matters mentioned in paragraph 6(1).

11 Infringement: rights of authorised users

The following provisions apply in relation to an authorised user of a registered collective mark as in relation to a licensee of a trade mark –

(a)   section 10(5) (definition of infringement: unauthorised application of mark to certain material);

(b)   section 19(2) (order as to disposal of infringing goods, material or articles: adequacy of other remedies);

(c)   section 89 (prohibition of importation of infringing goods, material or articles: request to Commissioners of Customs and Excise).

12

(1) The following provisions (which correspond to the provisions of section 30 (general provisions as to rights of licensees in case of infringement)) have effect as regards the rights of an authorised user in relation to infringement of a registered collective mark.

(2) An authorised user is entitled, subject to any agreement to the contrary between him and the proprietor, to call on the proprietor to take infringement proceedings in respect of any matter which affects his interests.

(3) If the proprietor –

(a)   refuses to do so, or

(b)   fails to do so within two months after being called upon,

the authorised user may bring the proceedings in his own name as if he were the proprietor.

(4) Where infringement proceedings are brought by virtue of this paragraph, the authorised user may not, without the leave of the court, proceed with the action unless the proprietor is either joined as a plaintiff or added as a defendant.

This does not affect the granting of interlocutory relief on an application by an authorised user alone.

(5) A proprietor who is added as a defendant as mentioned in sub-paragraph (4) shall not be made liable for any costs in the action unless he takes part in the proceedings.

(6) In infringement proceedings brought by the proprietor of a registered collective mark any loss suffered or likely to be suffered by authorised users shall be taken into account; and the court may give such directions as it thinks fit as to the extent to which the plaintiff is to hold the proceeds of any pecuniary remedy on behalf of such users.

13 Grounds for revocation of registration

Apart from the grounds of revocation provided for in section 46, the registration of a collective mark may be revoked on the ground –

(a) that the manner in which the mark has been used by the proprietor has caused it to become liable to mislead the public in the manner referred to in paragraph 4(1), or

(b) that the proprietor has failed to observe, or to secure the observance of, the regulations governing the use of the mark, or

(c) that an amendment of the regulations has been made so that the regulations –

   (i)   no longer comply with paragraph 5(2) and any further conditions imposed by rules, or

   (ii) are contrary to public policy or to accepted principles of morality.

14 Grounds for invalidity of registration

Apart from the grounds of invalidity provided for in section 47, the registration of a collective mark may be declared invalid on the ground that the mark was registered in breach of the provisions of paragraph 4(1) or 6(1).

Schedule 2
Certification Marks

Section 50

1 General

The provisions of this Act apply to certification marks subject to the following provisions.

2 Signs of which a certification mark may consist

In relation to a certification mark the reference in section 1(1) (signs of which a trade mark may consist) to distinguishing goods or services of one undertaking from those of other undertakings shall be construed as a reference to distinguishing goods or services which are certified from those which are not.

3 Indication of geographical origin

(1) Notwithstanding section 3(1)(c), a certification mark may be registered which consists of signs or indications which may serve, in trade, to designate the geographical origin of the goods or services.

(2) However, the proprietor of such a mark is not entitled to prohibit the use of the signs or indications in accordance with honest practices in industrial or commercial matters (in particular, by a person who is entitled to use a geographical name).

4 Nature of proprietor's business

A certification mark shall not be registered if the proprietor carries on a business involving the supply of goods or services of the kind certified.

5 Mark not to be misleading as to character or significance

(1) A certification mark shall not be registered if the public is liable to be misled as regards the character or significance of the mark, in particular if it is likely to be taken to be something other than a certification mark.

(2) The registrar may accordingly require that a mark in respect of which application is made for registration include some indication that it is a certification mark.

Notwithstanding section 39(2), an application may be amended so as to comply with any such requirement.

6 Regulations governing use of certification mark

(1) An applicant for registration of a certification mark must file with the registrar regulations governing the use of the mark.

(2) The regulations must indicate who is authorised to use the mark, the characteristics to be certified by the mark, how the certifying body is to test those characteristics and to supervise the use of the mark, the fees (if any) to be paid in connection with the operation of the mark and the procedures for resolving disputes.

Further requirements with which the regulations have to comply may be imposed by rules.

7 Approval of regulations, &c

(1) A certification mark shall not be registered unless –

    (a)   the regulations governing the use of the mark –
          (i)   comply with paragraph 6(2) and any further requirements imposed by rules, and
         (ii)   are not contrary to public policy or to accepted principles of morality, and
    (b)   the applicant is competent to certify the goods or services for which the mark is to be registered.

(2) Before the end of the prescribed period after the date of the application for registration of a certification mark, the applicant must file the regulations with the registrar and pay the prescribed fee.

If he does not do so, the application shall be deemed to be withdrawn.

8

(1) The registrar shall consider whether the requirements mentioned in paragraph 7(1) are met.

(2) If it appears to the registrar that those requirements are not met, he shall inform the applicant and give him an opportunity, within such period as the registrar may specify, to make representations or to file amended regulations.

(3) If the applicant fails to satisfy the registrar that those requirements are met, or to file regulations amended so as to meet them, or fails to respond before the end of the specified period, the registrar shall refuse the application.

(4) If it appears to the registrar that those requirements, and the other requirements for registration, are met, he shall accept the application and shall proceed in accordance with section 38 (publication, opposition proceedings and observations).

9

The regulations shall be published and notice of opposition may be given, and observations may be made, relating to the matters mentioned in paragraph 7(1).

This is in addition to any other grounds on which the application may be opposed or observations made.

10 Regulations to be open to inspection

The regulations governing the use of a registered certification mark shall be open to public inspection in the same way as the register.

11 Amendment of regulations

(1) An amendment of the regulations governing the use of a registered certification mark is not effective unless and until the amended regulations are filed with the registrar and accepted by him.

(2) Before accepting any amended regulations the registrar may in any case where it appears to him expedient to do so cause them to be published.

(3) If he does so, notice of opposition may be given, and observations may be made, relating to the matters mentioned in paragraph 7(1).

12 Consent to assignment of registered certification mark

The assignment or other transmission of a registered certification mark is not effective without the consent of the registrar.

13 Infringement: rights of authorised users

The following provisions apply in relation to an authorised user of a registered certification mark as in relation to a licensee of a trade mark –

    (a)   section 10(5) (definition of infringement: unauthorised application of mark to certain material);

(b) section 19(2) (order as to disposal of infringing goods, material or articles: adequacy of other remedies);

(c) section 89 (prohibition of importation of infringing goods, material or articles: request to Commissioners of Customs and Excise).

14

In infringement proceedings brought by the proprietor of a registered certification mark any loss suffered or likely to be suffered by authorised users shall be taken into account; and the court may give such directions as it thinks fit as to the extent to which the plaintiff is to hold the proceeds of any pecuniary remedy on behalf of such users.

15 Grounds for revocation of registration

Apart from the grounds of revocation provided for in section 46, the registration of a certification mark may be revoked on the ground –

(a) that the proprietor has begun to carry on such a business as is mentioned in paragraph 4,

(b) that the manner in which the mark has been used by the proprietor has caused it to become liable to mislead the public in the manner referred to in paragraph 5(1),

(c) that the proprietor has failed to observe, or to secure the observance of, the regulations governing the use of the mark,

(d) that an amendment of the regulations has been made so that the regulations –

(i)   no longer comply with paragraph 6(2) and any further conditions imposed by rules, or

(ii) are contrary to public policy or to accepted principles of morality, or

(e) that the proprietor is no longer competent to certify the goods or services for which the mark is registered.

16 Grounds for invalidity of registration

Apart from the grounds of invalidity provided for in section 47, the registration of a certification mark may be declared invalid on the ground that the mark was registered in breach of the provisions of paragraph 4, 5(1) or 7(1).

Schedule 3
Transitional Provisions

Section 105

1 Introductory

(1) In this Schedule –

'existing registered mark' means a trade mark, certification trade mark or service mark registered under the 1938 Act immediately before the commencement of this Act;

'the 1938 Act' means the Trade Marks Act 1938; and

'the old law' means that Act and any other enactment or rule of law applying to existing registered marks immediately before the commencement of this Act.

(2) For the purposes of this Schedule –

    (a)   an application shall be treated as pending on the commencement of this Act if it was made but not finally determined before commencement, and

    (b)   the date on which it was made shall be taken to be the date of filing under the 1938 Act.

2 Existing registered marks

(1) Existing registered marks (whether registered in Part A or B of the register kept under the 1938 Act) shall be transferred on the commencement of this Act to the register kept under this Act and have effect, subject to the provisions of this Schedule, as if registered under this Act.

(2) Existing registered marks registered as a series under section 21(2) of the 1938 Act shall be similarly registered in the new register.

Provision may be made by rules for putting such entries in the same form as is required for entries under this Act.

(3) In any other case notes indicating that existing registered marks are associated with other marks shall cease to have effect on the commencement of this Act.

3

(1) A condition entered on the former register in relation to an existing registered mark immediately before the commencement of this Act shall cease to have effect on commencement.

Proceedings under section 33 of the 1938 Act (application to expunge or vary registration for breach of condition) which are pending on the commencement of this Act shall be dealt with under the old law and any necessary alteration made to the new register.

(2) A disclaimer or limitation entered on the former register in relation to an existing registered mark immediately before the commencement of this Act shall be transferred to the new register and have effect as if entered on the register in pursuance of section 13 of this Act.

4 Effects of registration: infringement

(1) Sections 9 to 12 of this Act (effects of registration) apply in relation to an existing registered mark as from the commencement of this Act and section 14 of this Act (action for infringement) applies in relation to infringement of an existing registered mark committed after the commencement of this Act, subject to sub-paragraph (2) below.

The old law continues to apply in relation to infringements committed before commencement.

(2) It is not an infringement of –

(a) an existing registered mark, or

(b) a registered trade mark of which the distinctive elements are the same or substantially the same as those of an existing registered mark and which is registered for the same goods or services,

to continue after commencement any use which did not amount to infringement of the existing registered mark under the old law.

5 Infringing goods, material or articles

Section 16 of this Act (order for delivery up of infringing goods, material or articles) applies to infringing goods, material or articles whether made before or after the commencement of this Act.

6 Rights and remedies of licensee or authorised user

(1) Section 30 (general provisions as to rights of licensees in case of infringement) of this Act applies to licences granted before the commencement of this Act, but only in relation to infringements committed after commencement.

(2) Paragraph 14 of Schedule 2 of this Act (court to take into account loss suffered by authorised users, &c) applies only in relation to infringements committed after commencement.

7 Co-ownership of registered mark

The provisions of section 23 of this Act (co-ownership of registered mark) apply as from the commencement of this Act to an existing registered mark of which two or more persons were immediately before commencement registered as joint proprietors.

But so long as the relations between the joint proprietors remain such as are described in section 63 of the 1938 Act (joint ownership) there shall be taken to be an agreement to exclude the operation of subsections (1) and (3) of section 23 of this Act (ownership in undivided shares and right of co-proprietor to make separate use of the mark).

8 Assignment, &c of registered mark

(1) Section 24 of this Act (assignment or other transmission of registered mark) applies to transactions and events occurring after the commencement of this Act in relation to an existing registered mark; and the old law continues to apply in relation to transactions and events occurring before commencement.

(2) Existing entries under section 25 of the 1938 Act (registration of assignments and transmissions) shall be transferred on the commencement of this Act to the register kept under this Act and have effect as if made under section 25 of this Act.

Provision may be made by rules for putting such entries in the same form as is required for entries made under this Act.

(3) An application for registration under section 25 of the 1938 Act which is pending before the registrar on the commencement of this Act shall be treated as an application for registration under section 25 of this Act and shall proceed accordingly.

The registrar may require the applicant to amend his application so as to conform with the requirements of this Act.

(4) An application for registration under section 25 of the 1938 Act which has been determined by the registrar but not finally determined before the commencement of this Act shall be dealt with under the old law; and sub-paragraph (2) above shall apply in relation to any resulting entry in the register.

(5) Where before the commencement of this Act a person has become entitled by assignment or transmission to an existing registered mark but has not registered his title, any application for registration after commencement shall be made under section 25 of this Act.

(6) In cases to which sub-paragraph (3) or (5) applies section 25(3) of the 1938 Act continues to apply (and section 25(3) and (4) of this Act do not apply) as regards the consequences of failing to register.

9 Licensing of registered mark

(1) Sections 28 and 29(2) of this Act (licensing of registered trade mark; rights of exclusive licensee against grantor's successor in title) apply only in relation to licences granted after the commencement of this Act; and the old law continues to apply in relation to licences granted before commencement.

(2) Existing entries under section 28 of the 1938 Act (registered users) shall be transferred on the commencement of this Act to the register kept under this Act and have effect as if made under section 25 of this Act.

Provision may be made by rules for putting such entries in the same form as is required for entries made under this Act.

(3) An application for registration as a registered user which is pending before the registrar on the commencement of this Act shall be treated as an application for registration of a licence under section 25(1) of this Act and shall proceed accordingly.

The registrar may require the applicant to amend his application so as to conform with the requirements of this Act.

(4) An application for registration as a registered user which has been determined by the registrar but not finally determined before the commencement of this Act shall be dealt with under the old law; and sub-paragraph (2) above shall apply in relation to any resulting entry in the register.

(5) Any proceedings pending on the commencement of this Act under section 28(8) or (10) of the 1938 Act (variation or cancellation of registration of registered user) shall be dealt with under the old law and any necessary alteration made to the new register.

10 Pending applications for registration

(1) An application for registration of a mark under the 1938 Act which is pending on the commencement of this Act shall be dealt with under the old law, subject as mentioned below, and if registered the mark shall be treated for the purposes of this Schedule as an existing registered mark.

(2) The power of the Secretary of State under section 78 of this Act to make rules regulating practice and procedure, and as to the matters mentioned in subsection (2) of that section, is exercisable in relation to such an application; and different provision may be made for such applications from that made for other applications.

(3) Section 23 of the 1938 Act (provisions as to associated trade marks) shall be disregarded in dealing after the commencement of this Act with an application for registration.

11 Conversion of pending application

(1) In the case of a pending application for registration which has not been advertised under section 18 of the 1938 Act before the commencement of this Act, the applicant may give notice to the registrar claiming to have the registrability of the mark determined in accordance with the provisions of this Act.

(2) The notice must be in the prescribed form, be accompanied by the appropriate fee and be given no later than six months after the commencement of this Act.

(3) Notice duly given is irrevocable and has the effect that the application shall be treated as if made immediately after the commencement of this Act.

12 Trade marks registered according to old classification

The registrar may exercise the powers conferred by rules under section 65 of this Act (adaptation of entries to new classification) to secure that any existing registered marks which do not conform to the system of classification prescribed under section 34 of this Act are brought to conformity with that system.

This applies, in particular, to existing registered marks classified according to the pre-1938 classification set out in Schedule 3 to the Trade Marks Rules 1986.

13 Claim to priority from overseas application

Section 35 of this Act (claim to priority of Convention application) applies to an application for registration under this Act made after the commencement of this Act notwithstanding that the Convention application was made before commencement.

14

(1) Where before the commencement of this Act a person has duly filed an application for protection of a trade mark in a relevant country within the meaning of section 39A of the 1938 Act which is not a Convention country (a 'relevant overseas application'), he, or his successor in title, has a right to priority, for the purposes of registering the same trade mark under this Act for some or all of the same goods or services, for a period of six months from the date of filing of the relevant overseas application.

(2) If the application for registration under this Act is made within that six-month period –

  (a)   the relevant date for the purposes of establishing which rights take precedence shall be the date of filing of the relevant overseas application, and

  (b)   the registrability of the trade mark shall not be affected by any use of the mark in the United Kingdom in the period between that date and the date of the application under this Act.

(3) Any filing which in a relevant country is equivalent to a regular national filing, under its domestic legislation or an international agreement, shall be treated as giving rise to the right of priority.

A 'regular national filing' means a filing which is adequate to establish the date on which the application was filed in that country, whatever may be the subsequent fate of the application.

(4) A subsequent application concerning the same subject as the relevant overseas application, filed in the same country, shall be considered the relevant overseas application (of which the filing date is the starting date of the period of priority), if at the time of the subsequent application –

  (a)   the previous application has been withdrawn, abandoned or refused, without having been laid open to public inspection and without leaving any rights outstanding, and

  (b)   it has not yet served as a basis for claiming a right of priority.

The previous application may not thereafter serve as a basis for claiming a right of priority.

(5) Provision may be made by rules as to the manner of claiming a right to priority on the basis of a relevant overseas application.

(6) A right to priority arising as a result of a relevant overseas application may be assigned or otherwise transmitted, either with the application or independently.

The reference in sub-paragraph (1) to the applicant's 'successor in title' shall be construed accordingly.

(7) Nothing in this paragraph affects proceedings on an application for registration under the 1938 Act made before the commencement of this Act (see paragraph 10 above).

15 Duration and renewal of registration

(1) Section 42(1) of this Act (duration of original period of registration) applies in relation to the registration of a mark in pursuance of an application made after the commencement of this Act; and the old law applies in any other case.

(2) Sections 42(2) and 43 of this Act (renewal) apply where the renewal falls due on or after the commencement of this Act; and the old law continues to apply in any other case.

(3) In either case it is immaterial when the fee is paid.

16 Pending application for alteration of registered mark

An application under section 35 of the 1938 Act (alteration of registered trade mark) which is pending on the commencement of this Act shall be dealt with under the old law and any necessary alteration made to the new register.

17 Revocation for non-use

(1) An application under section 26 of the 1938 Act (removal from register or imposition of limitation on ground of non-use) which is pending on the commencement of this Act shall be dealt with under the old law and any necessary alteration made to the new register.

(2) An application under section 46(1)(a) or (b) of this Act (revocation for non-use) may be made in relation to an existing registered mark at any time after the commencement of this Act.

Provided that no such application for the revocation of the registration of an existing registered mark registered by virtue of section 27 of the 1938 Act (defensive registration of well-known trade marks) may be made until more than five years after the commencement of this Act.

18 Application for rectificatpion, &c

(1) An application under section 32 or 34 of the 1938 Act (rectification or correction of the register) which is pending on the commencement of this Act shall be dealt with under the old law and any necessary alteration made to the new register.

(2) For the purposes of proceedings under section 47 of this Act (grounds for invalidity of registration) as it applies in relation to an existing registered mark, the provisions of this Act shall be deemed to have been in force at all material times.Provided that no objection to the validity of the registration of an

existing registered mark may be taken on the ground specified in subsection (3) of section 5 of this Act (relative grounds for refusal of registration: conflict with earlier mark registered for different goods or services).

19 Regulations as to use of certification mark

(1) Regulations governing the use of an existing registered certification mark deposited at the Patent Office in pursuance of section 37 of the 1938 Act shall be treated after the commencement of this Act as if filed under paragraph 6 of Schedule 2 to this Act.

(2) Any request for amendment of the regulations which was pending on the commencement of this Act shall be dealt with under the old law.

20 Sheffield marks

(1) For the purposes of this Schedule the Sheffield register kept under Schedule 2 to the 1938 Act shall be treated as part of the register of trade marks kept under that Act.

(2) Applications made to the Cutlers' Company in accordance with that Schedule which are pending on the commencement of this Act shall proceed after commencement as if they had been made to the registrar.

21 Certificate of validity of contested registration

A certificate given before the commencement of this Act under section 47 of the 1938 Act (certificate of validity of contested registration) shall have effect as if given under section 73(1) of this Act.

22 Trade mark agents

(1) Rules in force immediately before the commencement of this Act under section 282 or 283 of the Copyright, Designs and Patents Act 1988 (register of trade mark agents; persons entitled to described themselves as registered) shall continue in force and have effect as if made under section 83 or 85 of this Act.

(2) Rules in force immediately before the commencement of this Act under section 40 of the 1938 Act as to the persons whom the registrar may refuse to recognise as agents for the purposes of business under that Act shall continue in force and have effect as if made under section 88 of this Act.

(3) Rules continued in force under this paragraph may be varied or revoked by further rules made under the relevant provisions of this Act.

Schedule 4
Consequential Amendments

Section 106(1)

1 General adaptation of existing references

(1) References in statutory provisions passed or made before the commencement of this Act to trade marks or registered trade marks within the meaning of the Trade Marks Act 1938 shall, unless the context otherwise requires, be construed after the commencement of this Act as references to trade marks or registered trade marks within the meaning of this Act.

(2) Sub-paragraph (1) applies, in particular, to the references in the following provisions –

Industrial Organisation and Development Act 1947	Schedule 1, paragraph 7
Crown Proceedings Act 1947	section 3(1)(b)
Printer's Imprint Act 1961	section 1(1)(b)
Patents Act 1977	section 19(2)
	section 27(4)
	section 123(7)
Unfair Contract Terms Act 1977	Schedule 1, paragraph 1(c)
Judicature (Northern Ireland) Act 1978	section 94A(5)
State Immunity Act 1978	section 7(a) and (b)
Senior Courts Act 1981	section 72(5)
	Schedule 1, paragraph 1(i)
Civil Jurisdiction and Judgments Act 1982	Schedule 5, paragraph 2 Schedule 8, paragraph 2(14) and 4(2)
Value Added Tax Act 1983	Schedule 3, paragraph 1
Law Reform (Miscellaneous Provisions) (Scotland) Act 1985	section 15(5)
Atomic Energy Authority Act 1986	section 8(2)
Consumer Protection Act 1987	section 2(2)(b)

Consumer Protection (Northern Ireland) Order 1987	article 5(2)(b)
Income and Corporation Taxes Act 1988	section 83(a)
Taxation of Chargeable Gains Act 1992	section 275(h)
Tribunals and Inquiries Act 1992	Schedule 1, paragraph 34.

2 Patents and Designs Act 1907 (c 29)

(1)–(3) (*repealed*)

(4) The repeal by the Patents Act 1949 and the Registered Designs Act 1949 of the whole of the 1907 Act, except certain provisions, shall be deemed not to have extended to the long title, date of enactment or enacting words or to so much of section 99 as provides the Act with its short title.

3–9 (*repealed*)

Amendments–Plant Varieties Act 1997, s 52, Sch 4; Statute Law (Repeals) Act 2004; Northern Ireland Act 1998, s 100(2), Sch 15; Constitutional Reform Act 2005, s 59(5), Sch 11, Pt 1, para 1(2); Companies Act 2006, s 1295, Sch 16; SI 2009/1941, art 2(2), Sch 2; Legal Services Act 2007, s 210, Sch 23.

Schedule 5
Repeals and Revocations

Section 106(2)

Chapter or number	Short title	Extent of repeal or revocation
1891 c 50	Commissioner for Oaths Act 1891.	In section 1, the words 'or the Patents, Designs and Trade Marks Acts, 1883 to 1888,'.
1907 c 29	Patents and Designs Act 1907.	In section 63(2), the words from 'and those salaries' to the end.
1938 c 87	Trade Marks Act 1938	The whole Act
1947 c 44	Crown Proceedings Act 1947.	In section 3(1)(b), the words 'or registered service mark'.

Chapter or number	Short title	Extent of repeal or revocation
1949 c 87	Patents Act 1949	Section 92(2).
1964 c 14	Plant Varieties and Seeds Act 1964	In section 5A(4), the words 'under the Trade Marks Act 1938'.
1967 c 80	Criminal Justice Act 1967	In Schedule 3, in Parts I and IV, the entries relating to the Trade Marks Act 1938
1978 c 23	Judicature (Northern Ireland) Act 1978	In Schedule 5, in Part II, the paragraphs amending the Trade Marks Act 1938.
1984 c 19	Trade Marks (Amendment) Act 1984.	The whole Act.
1984 c 6	Companies Act 1985.	In section 396 –
		(a) in subsection (3A)(a), and
		(b) in subsection (2)(d)(i) as inserted by the Companies Act 1989, the words 'service mark,'
1985 c 12.	Statute Law (Repeals) Act 1986.	In Schedule 2, paragraph 2.
1986 c 39.	Patents, Designs and Marks Act 1986.	Section 2.
		Section 4 (4)
		In Schedule 1, paragraphs 1 and 2
		Schedule 2
SI 1986/1032 (NI 6).	Companies (Northern Ireland) Order 1986.	In article 403

Chapter or number	Short title	Extent of repeal or revocation
		(a) in paragraph (3A)(a), and
		(b) in paragraph (2)(d)(i) as inserted by the Companies (No 2) (Northern Ireland) Order 1990,
		the words 'service mark,'
1987 c 43	Consumer Protection Act 1987.	In section 45
		(a) in subsection (1), the definition of 'mark' and 'trade mark';
		(b) subsection (4).
SI 1987/2049.	Consumer Protection (Northern Ireland) Order 1987.	In article 2 –
		(a) in paragraph (2), the definitions of 'mark' and 'trade mark';
		(b) paragraph (3).
1988 c 1	Income and Corporation Taxes Act 1988	In section 83, the words from 'References in this section' to the end.
1988 c 48	Copyright, Designs and Patents Act 1988	Sections 282 to 284
		In section 286, the definition of 'registered trade mark agent'
		Section 300.

Chapter or number	Short title	Extent of repeal or revocation
1992 c 12.	Taxation of Chargeable Gains Act 1992.	In section 275 (h), the words 'service marks' and 'service mark'.

Appendix 2

TRADE MARKS RULES 2008

SI 2008/1797

Preliminary

1 Citation and commencement

These Rules may be cited as the Trade Marks Rules 2008 and shall come into force on 1st October 2008.

2 Interpretation

(1) In these Rules –

'the Act' means the Trade Marks Act 1994;

'the Journal' means the Trade Marks Journal published in accordance with rule 81;

'the "Nice Agreement" means the Nice Agreement Concerning the International Classification of Goods and Services for the Purposes of the Registration of Marks of 15th June 1957, which was last amended on 28th September 1979;

'the "Nice Classification" means the system of classification under the Nice Agreement;

'the Office' means the Patent Office which operates under the name 'Intellectual Property Office';

'send' includes give;

'specification' means the statement of goods or services in respect of which a trade mark is registered or proposed to be registered;

'transformation application' means an application to register a trade mark under the Act where that mark was the subject of an international registration prior to that registration being cancelled.

(2) In these Rules a reference to a section is a reference to that section in the Act and a reference to a form is a reference to that form as published under rule 3.

(3) In these Rules references to the filing of any application, notice or other document, unless the contrary intention appears, are to be construed as references to its being delivered to the registrar at the Office.

Amendments–SI 2009/2089.

3 Forms and directions of the registrar; section 66

(1) Any forms required by the registrar to be used for the purpose of registration of a trade mark or any other proceedings before the registrar under the Act pursuant to section 66 and any directions with respect to their use shall be published on the Office website and any amendment or modification of a form or of the directions with respect to its use shall also be published on the Office website.

(2) Except in relation to Forms TM6 and TM7A a requirement under this rule to use a form as published is satisfied by the use either of a replica of that form or of a form which is acceptable to the registrar and contains the information required by the form as published and complies with any directions as to the use of such a form

4 Requirement as to fees

(1) The fees to be paid in respect of any application, registration or any other matter under the Act and these Rules shall be those (if any) prescribed in relation to such matter by rules under section 79 (fees).

(2) Any form required to be filed with the registrar in respect of any specified matter shall be subject to the payment of the fee (if any) prescribed in respect of that matter by those rules.

Application for Registration

5 Application for registration; section 32 (Form TM3)

(1) An application for the registration of a trade mark (other than a transformation application, which shall be filed on Form TM4) shall be filed on Form TM3 or, where the application is filed in electronic form using the filing system provided on the Office website, on Form e-TM3.

(1A) Where an application is filed on Form TM3 (a 'standard application') the application shall be subject to the payment of the standard application fee and such class and series fees as may be appropriate.

(1B) Where an application is filed on Form e-TM3 (an 'electronic application') the application shall be subject to the payment of the e-filed application fee and such class and series fees as may be appropriate, which shall be payable at the time the electronic application is made and if they are not so paid the application shall be subject to the payment of the standard application fee referred to in paragraph (1A) and such class and series fees as may be appropriate.

(2) Subject to paragraph (6) where an application is for the registration of a single trade mark, an applicant may request the registrar to undertake an expedited examination of the application.

(3) A request for expedited examination shall be made on Form e-TM3 and shall be subject to payment of the prescribed fee.

(4) Where an applicant makes a request for expedited examination, the application fee and any class fees payable in respect of the application shall be payable at the time the application is made and accordingly rule 13 shall not apply insofar as it relates to the failure of an application to satisfy the requirements of section 32(4).

(5) In this rule and rule 15 a 'request for expedited examination' means a request that, following an examination under section 37, the registrar notify the applicant within a period of ten business days (as specified in a direction given by the registrar under section 80) beginning on the business day after the date of filing of the application for registration whether or not it appears to the registrar that the requirements for registration are met.

(6) Where it appears to the registrar that the period (the 'routine period') within which applicants are routinely notified of the outcome of an examination under section 37 is equal to or less than the period specified in paragraph (5), the registrar may suspend the right of applicants to file a request for expedited examination until such time as the routine period exceeds the period specified in paragraph (5) and the registrar shall, in each case, publish a notice on the Office website to this effect.

Amendments–SI 2009/2089.

6 Claim to priority; sections 35 & 36

(1) Where a right to priority is claimed by reason of an application for protection of a trade mark duly filed in a Convention country under section 35 or in another country or territory in respect of which provision corresponding to that made by section 35 is made under section 36 (an 'overseas application'), the application for registration under rule 5 shall specify –

  (a) the number accorded to the overseas application by the registering or other competent authority of the relevant country;
  (b) the country in which the overseas application was filed; and
  (c) the date of filing.

(2) The registrar may, in any particular case, by notice require the applicant to file, within such period of not less than one month as the notice may specify, such documentary evidence as the registrar may require certifying, or verifying to the satisfaction of the registrar, the date of the filing of the overseas application, the country or registering or competent authority, the representation of the mark and the goods or services covered by the overseas application.

7 Classification of goods and services; section 34

(1) The prescribed system of classification for the purposes of the registration of trade marks is the Nice Classification.

(2) When a trade mark is registered it shall be classified according to the version of the Nice Classification that had effect on the date of application for registration.

8 Application may relate to more than one class and shall specify the class (Form TM3A)

(1) An application may be made in more than one class of the Nice Classification.

(2) Every application shall specify –

    (a)   the class in the Nice Classification to which it relates; and

    (b)   the goods or services which are appropriate to the class and they shall be described in such a way as to indicate clearly the nature of those goods or services and to allow them to be classified in the classes in the Nice Classification.

(3) If the application relates to more than one class in the Nice Classification the specification contained in it shall set out the classes in consecutive numerical order and the specification of the goods or services shall be grouped accordingly.

(4) If the specification contained in the application lists items by reference to a class in the Nice Classification in which they do not fall, the applicant may request, by filing Form TM3A, that the application be amended to include the appropriate class for those items, and upon the payment of such class fee as may be appropriate the registrar shall amend the application accordingly.

9 Determination of classification

(1) Where an application does not satisfy the requirements of rule 8(2) or (3), the registrar shall send notice to the applicant.

(2) A notice sent under paragraph (1) shall specify a period, of not less than one month, within which the applicant must satisfy those requirements.

(3) Where the applicant fails to satisfy the requirements of rule 8(2) before the expiry of the period specified under paragraph (2), the application for registration, insofar as it relates to any goods or services which failed that requirement, shall be treated as abandoned.

(4) Where the applicant fails to satisfy the requirements of rule 8(3) before the expiry of the period specified under paragraph (2), the application for registration shall be treated as abandoned.

10 Prohibition on registration of mark consisting of arms; section 4

Where having regard to matters coming to the notice of the registrar it appears to the registrar that a representation of any arms or insignia as is referred to in section 4(4) appears in a mark, the registrar shall refuse to accept an application for the registration of the mark unless satisfied that the consent of the person entitled to the arms has been obtained.

11 Address for service

(1) For the purposes of any proceedings under the Act or these Rules, an address for service shall be filed by –

(a) an applicant for the registration of a trade mark;

(b) any person who opposes the registration of a trade mark in opposition proceedings;

(c) any person who applies for revocation, a declaration of invalidity or rectification under the Act;

(d) the proprietor of the registered trade mark who opposes such an application.

(2) The proprietor of a registered trade mark, or any person who has registered an interest in a registered trade mark, may file an address for service on Form TM33 or, in the case of an assignment of a registered trade mark, on Form TM16.

(3) Where a person has provided an address for service under paragraph (1) or (2), that person may substitute a new address for service by notifying the registrar on Form TM33.

(4) An address for service filed under this Rule shall be an address in the United Kingdom, another EEA state or the Channel Islands.

(5) (*revoked*)

Amendments–SI 2009/546.

12 Failure to provide an address for service

(1) Where –

(a) a person has failed to file an address for service under rule 11(1); and

(b) the registrar has sufficient information enabling the registrar to contact that person,

the registrar shall direct that person to file an address for service.

(2) Where a direction has been given under paragraph (1), the person directed shall, before the end of the period of one month beginning with the date of the direction, file an address for service.

(3) Paragraph (4) applies where –

(a) a direction was given under paragraph (1) and the period prescribed by paragraph (2) has expired; or

(b) the registrar had insufficient information to give a direction under paragraph (1),

and the person has failed to provide an address for service.

(4) Where this paragraph applies –

(a) in the case of an applicant for registration of a trade mark, the application shall be treated as withdrawn;

(b) in the case of a person opposing the registration of a trade mark, that person's opposition shall be treated as withdrawn;

(c) in the case of a person applying for revocation, a declaration of invalidity or rectification, that person's application shall be treated as withdrawn; and

(d)   in the case of the proprietor opposing such an application, the proprietor shall be deemed to have withdrawn from the proceedings.

(5) In this rule an 'address for service' means an address which complies with the requirements of rule 11(4).

Amendments–SI 2009/546.

13 Deficiencies in application; section 32

(1) Where an application for registration of a trade mark does not satisfy the requirements of section 32(2), (3) or (4) or rule 5(1), the registrar shall send notice to the applicant to remedy the deficiencies or, in the case of section 32(4), the default of payment.

(2) A notice sent under paragraph (1) shall specify a period, of not less than 14 days, within which the applicant must remedy the deficiencies or the default of payment.

(3) Where, before the expiry of the period specified under paragraph (2), the applicant –

(a)   fails to remedy any deficiency notified to the applicant in respect of section 32(2), the application shall be deemed never to have been made; or
(b)   fails to remedy any deficiency notified to the applicant in respect of section 32(3) or rule 5(1) or fails to make payment as required by section 32(4), the application shall be treated as abandoned.

Amendments–SI 2009/2089.

14 Notifying results of search

(1) Where, following any search under article 4 of the Trade Marks (Relative Grounds) Order 2007, it appears to the registrar that the requirements for registration mentioned in section 5 are not met, the registrar shall notify this fact to –

(a)   the applicant; and
(b)   any relevant proprietor.

(2) In paragraph (1), 'relevant proprietor' means –

(a)   the proprietor of a registered trade mark or international trade mark (UK) which is an earlier trade mark in relation to which it appears to the registrar that the conditions set out in section 5(1) or (2) obtain but does not include a proprietor who does not wish to be notified and who has notified the registrar to this effect; and
(b)   the proprietor of a Community trade mark or international trade mark (EC) which is an earlier trade mark in relation to which it appears to the registrar that the conditions set out in section 5(1) or (2) obtain and who has filed a request to be notified in relation to that mark in accordance with paragraph (4) below.

(3) References in paragraph (2) to the proprietor of a trade mark include a person who has applied for registration of a trade mark which, if registered, would be an earlier trade mark by virtue of section 6(1)(a) or (b).

(4) The proprietor of a Community trade mark or international trade mark (EC) may file a request to be notified in relation to that mark of the results of a notifiable search on Form TM6, which shall be filed electronically using the filing system provided on the Office website, or by such other means as the registrar may permit in any particular case, and shall be subject to payment of the prescribed fee.

(5) In paragraph (4) a 'notifiable search' means any search under article 4 of the Trade Marks (Relative Grounds) Order 2007 conducted within the period of three years beginning with the date on which the request was filed.

(6) The filing of any request under paragraph (4) shall be subject to such terms or conditions as the registrar may specify generally by published notice or in any particular case by written notice to the person desiring to file the request otherwise than by electronic means.

(7) Rule 63 shall not apply to any decision made in pursuance of this rule.

(8) No decision made in pursuance of this rule shall be subject to appeal.

15 Compliance with request for expedited examination

Where the registrar receives a request for expedited examination under rule 5, the date on which the registrar shall be deemed to have notified the applicant whether or not it appears to the registrar that the requirements for registration are met shall be the date on which notice is sent to the applicant.

Publication, Observations, Oppositions and Registration

16 Publication of application for registration; section 38(1)

An application which has been accepted for registration shall be published in the Journal.

17 Opposition proceedings: filing of notice of opposition; section 38(2) (Form TM7)

(1) Any notice to the registrar of opposition to the registration, including the statement of the grounds of opposition, shall be filed on Form TM7.

(2) Unless paragraph (3) applies, the time prescribed for the purposes of section 38(2) shall be the period of two months beginning with the date on which the application was published.

(3) This paragraph applies where a request for an extension of time for the filing of Form TM7 has been made on Form TM7A, before the expiry of the period referred to in paragraph (2) and where this paragraph applies, the time prescribed for the purposes of section 38(2) in relation to any person having filed a Form TM7A (or, in the case of a company, any subsidiary or holding

company of that company or any other subsidiary of that holding company) shall be the period of three months beginning with the date on which the application was published.

(4) Where a person makes a request for an extension of time under paragraph (3), Form TM7A shall be filed electronically using the filing system provided on the Office website or by such other means as the registrar may permit.

(5) Where the opposition is based on a trade mark which has been registered, there shall be included in the statement of the grounds of opposition a representation of that mark and –

    (a)   the details of the authority with which the mark is registered;
    (b)   the registration number of that mark;
    (c)   the goods and services in respect of which –
        (i)   that mark is registered, and
        (ii)   the opposition is based; and
    (d)   where the registration procedure for the mark was completed before the start of the period of five years ending with the date of publication, a statement detailing whether during the period referred to in section 6A(3)(a) the mark has been put to genuine use in relation to each of the goods and services in respect of which the opposition is based or whether there are proper reasons for non-use (for the purposes of rule 20 this is the 'statement of use').

(6) Where the opposition is based on a trade mark in respect of which an application for registration has been made, there shall be included in the statement of the grounds of opposition a representation of that mark and those matters set out in paragraph (5)(a) to (c), with references to registration being construed as references to the application for registration.

(7) Where the opposition is based on an unregistered trade mark or other sign which the person opposing the application claims to be protected by virtue of any rule of law (in particular, the law of passing off), there shall be included in the statement of the grounds of opposition a representation of that mark or sign and the goods and services in respect of which such protection is claimed.

(8) The registrar shall send a copy of Form TM7 to the applicant and the date upon which this is sent shall, for the purposes of rule 18, be the 'notification date'.

(9) In this rule 'subsidiary' and 'holding company' have the same meaning as in the Companies Act 2006.

18 Opposition proceedings: filing of counter-statement and cooling off period (Forms TM8, TM9c & TM9t)

(1) The applicant shall, within the relevant period, file a Form TM8, which shall include a counter-statement.

(2) Where the applicant fails to file a Form TM8 or counter-statement within the relevant period, the application for registration, insofar as it relates to the

goods and services in respect of which the opposition is directed, shall, unless the registrar otherwise directs, be treated as abandoned.

(3) Unless either paragraph (4), (5) or (6) applies, the relevant period shall begin on the notification date and end two months after that date.

(4) This paragraph applies where –

(a)   the applicant and the person opposing the registration agree to an extension of time for the filing of Form TM8;

(b)   within the period of two months beginning on the notification date, either party files Form TM9c requesting an extension of time for the filing of Form TM8; and

(c)   during the period beginning on the date Form TM9c was filed and ending nine months after the notification date, no notice to continue on Form TM9t is filed by the person opposing the registration and no request for a further extension of time for the filing of Form TM8 is filed on Form TM9e,

and where this paragraph applies the relevant period shall begin on the notification date and end nine months after that date.

(5) This paragraph applies where –

(a)   a request for an extension of time for the filing of Form TM8 has been filed on Form TM9c in accordance with paragraph (4)(b);

(b)   during the period referred to in paragraph (4)(c), either party files Form TM9e requesting a further extension of time for the filing of Form TM8 which request includes a statement confirming that the parties are seeking to negotiate a settlement of the opposition proceedings; and

(c)   the other party agrees to the further extension of time for the filing of Form TM8,

and where this paragraph applies the relevant period shall begin on the notification date and end eighteen months after that date.

(6) This paragraph applies where –

(a)   a request for an extension of time for the filing of Form TM8 has been filed on Form TM9c in accordance with paragraph (4)(b); and

(b)   the person opposing the registration has filed a notice to continue on Form TM9t,

and where this paragraph applies the relevant period shall begin on the notification date and end one month after the date on which Form TM9t was filed or two months after the notification date, whichever is the later.

(7) The registrar shall send a copy of Form TM8 to the person opposing the registration.

19 Opposition proceedings: preliminary indication (Form TM53)

(1) This rule applies if –

(a)   the opposition or part of it is based on the relative grounds of refusal set out in section 5(1) or (2); and

(b)   the registrar has not indicated to the parties that the registrar thinks that it is inappropriate for this rule to apply.

(2) After considering the statement of the grounds of opposition and the counter-statement the registrar shall send notice to the parties ('the preliminary indication') stating whether it appears to the registrar that –

(a)   registration of the mark should not be refused in respect of all or any of the goods and services listed in the application on the grounds set out in section 5(1) or (2); or

(b)   registration of the mark should be refused in respect of all or any of the goods and services listed in the application on the grounds set out in section 5(1) or (2).

(3) The date upon which the preliminary indication is sent shall be the 'indication date'.

(4) Where it appeared to the registrar under paragraph (2) that registration of the mark should not be refused in respect of all or any of the goods or services listed in the application on the grounds set out in section 5(1) or (2), the person opposing the registration shall, within one month of the indication date, file a notice of intention to proceed with the opposition based on those grounds by filing a Form TM53, otherwise that person's opposition to the registration of the mark in relation to those goods or services on the grounds set in section 5(1) or (2) shall be deemed to have been withdrawn.

(5) Where it appeared to the registrar under paragraph (2) that registration of the mark should be refused in respect of all or any of the goods or services listed in the application on the grounds set out in section 5(1) or (2), the applicant shall, within one month of the indication date, file a notice of intention to proceed on Form TM53, otherwise the applicant shall be deemed to have withdrawn the request to register the mark in respect of the goods or services for which the registrar indicated registration should be refused.

(6) A person who files a Form TM53 shall, at the same time, send a copy to all other parties to the proceedings.

(7) The registrar need not give reasons for the preliminary indication nor shall the preliminary indication be subject to appeal.

20 Opposition proceedings: evidence rounds

(1) Where –

(a)   Form TM53 has been filed by either party;

(b)   the opposition or part of it is based on grounds other than those set out in section 5(1) or (2) and the applicant has filed a Form TM8; or

(c)   the registrar has indicated to the parties that it is inappropriate for rule 19 to apply, the registrar shall specify the periods within which evidence and submissions may be filed by the parties.

(2) Where –

    (a)   the opposition is based on an earlier trade mark of a kind falling within section 6(1)(c); or

    (b)   the opposition or part of it is based on grounds other than those set out in section 5(1) or (2); or

    (c)   the truth of a matter set out in the statement of use is either denied or not admitted by the applicant,

the person opposing the registration ('the opposer') shall file evidence supporting the opposition.

(3) Where the opposer files no evidence under paragraph (2), the opposer shall be deemed to have withdrawn the opposition to the registration to the extent that it is based on –

    (a)   the matters in paragraph (2)(a) or (b); or

    (b)   an earlier trade mark which has been registered and which is the subject of the statement of use referred to in paragraph (2)(c).

(4) The registrar may, at any time, give leave to either party to file evidence upon such terms as the registrar thinks fit.

21 Procedure for intervention

(1) If the opposition or part of it is based on the relative grounds for refusal set out in section 5(1), (2) or (3), any person in paragraph (3) may file an application to the registrar on Form TM27 for leave to intervene and the registrar may, after hearing the parties concerned if so required, refuse such leave or grant leave upon such terms and conditions (including any undertaking as to costs) as the registrar thinks fit.

(2) Any person granted leave to intervene shall, subject to any terms and conditions imposed in respect of the intervention, be treated as a party to the proceedings for the purposes of the application of the provisions of rules 19, 20 and 62 to 73.

(3) The persons referred to in paragraph (1) are –

    (a)   where the opposition is based on an earlier trade mark, a licensee of that mark; and

    (b)   where the opposition is based on an earlier collective mark or certification mark, an authorised user of that mark.

22 Observations on application to be sent to applicant; section 38(3)

The registrar shall send to the applicant a copy of any document containing observations made under section 38(3).

23 Publication of registration; section 40

On the registration of the trade mark the registrar shall publish the registration on the Office website, specifying the date upon which the trade mark was entered in the register.

Amendment of Application

24 Amendment of application; section 39 (Form TM21)

A request for an amendment of an application to correct an error or to change the name or address of the applicant or in respect of any amendment requested after publication of the application shall be made on Form TM21.

25 Amendment of application after publication; section 39 (Form TM7)

(1) Where, pursuant to section 39, a request is made for amendment of an application which has been published in the Journal and the amendment affects the representation of the trade mark or the goods or services covered by the application, the amendment or a statement of the effect of the amendment shall also be published in the Journal.

(2) Any person claiming to be affected by the amendment may, within one month of the date on which the amendment or a statement of the effect of the amendment was published under paragraph (1), give notice to the registrar of objection to the amendment on Form TM7 which shall include a statement of the grounds of objection which shall, in particular, indicate why the amendment would not fall within section 39(2).

(3) The registrar shall send a copy of Form TM7 to the applicant and the procedure in rules 17, 18 and 20 shall apply to the proceedings relating to the objection to the amendment as they apply to proceedings relating to opposition to an application for registration, but with the following modifications –

    (a)   any reference to –
        (i)   an application for registration shall be construed as a reference to a request for amendment of an application,
        (ii)   the person opposing the registration shall be construed as a reference to the person objecting to the amendment of an application,
        (iii)   the opposition shall be construed as a reference to the objection;
    (b)   the relevant period, referred to in rule 18(1), shall for these purposes be the period of two months beginning with the date upon which the registrar sent a copy of Form TM7 to the applicant; and
    (c)   rules 18(3) to (6), 20(2) and (3) shall not apply.

Division, Merger and Series of Marks

26 Division of application; section 41 (Form TM12)

(1) At any time before registration an applicant may send to the registrar a request on Form TM12 to divide the specification of the application for

registration (the original application) into two or more separate applications (divisional applications), indicating for each division the specification of goods or services.

(2) Each divisional application shall be treated as a separate application for registration with the same filing date as the original application.

(3) Where the request to divide an application is sent after publication of the application, any objections in respect of, or opposition to, the original application shall be taken to apply to each divisional application and shall be proceeded with accordingly.

(4) Upon division of an original application in respect of which notice has been given to the registrar of particulars relating to the grant of a licence, or a security interest or any right in or under it, the notice and the particulars shall be deemed to apply in relation to each of the applications into which the original application has been divided.

Amendments–SI 2009/2089.

27 Merger of separate applications or registrations; section 41 (Form TM17)

(1) An applicant who has made separate applications for registration of a mark may, at any time before preparations for the publication of any of the applications have been completed by the Office, request the registrar on Form TM17 to merge the separate applications into a single application.

(2) The registrar shall, if satisfied that all the applications which are the subject of the request for merger –

    (a)   are in respect of the same trade mark;

    (b)   bear the same date of application; and

    (c)   are, at the time of the request, in the name of the same person,

merge them into a single application.

(3) The proprietor of two or more registrations of a trade mark may request the registrar on Form TM17 to merge them into a single registration and the registrar shall, if satisfied that the registrations are in respect of the same trade mark, merge them into a single registration.

(4) Where any registration of a trade mark to be merged under paragraph (3) is subject to a disclaimer or limitation, the merged registration shall also be restricted accordingly.

(5) Where any registration of a trade mark to be merged under paragraph (3) has had registered in relation to it particulars relating to the grant of a licence or a security interest or any right in or under it, or of any memorandum or statement of the effect of a memorandum, the registrar shall enter in the register the same particulars in relation to the merged registration.

(6) The date of registration of the merged registration shall, where the separate registrations bear different dates of registration, be the latest of those dates.

28 Registration of a series of trade marks; section 41 (Form TM12)

(1) An application may be made in accordance with rule 5 for the registration of a series of trade marks in a single registration provided that the series comprises of no more than six trade marks.

(1A) Where an application for registration of a series of trade marks comprises three or more trade marks, the application shall be subject to the payment of the prescribed fee for each trade mark in excess of two trade marks.

(2) Following an application under paragraph (1) the registrar shall, if satisfied that the marks constitute a series, accept the application.

(3) (*revoked*)

(4) (*revoked*)

(5) At any time the applicant for registration of a series of trade marks or the proprietor of a registered series of trade marks may request the deletion of a mark in that series and, following such request, the registrar shall delete the mark accordingly.

(6) Where under paragraph (5) the registrar deletes a trade mark from an application for registration, the application, in so far as it relates to the deleted mark, shall be treated as withdrawn.

(7) (*revoked*)

Amendments-SI 2009/2089.

Collective and Certification Marks

29 Filing of regulations for collective and certification marks; Schedules 1 & 2 (Form TM35)

Where an application for registration of a collective or certification mark is filed, the applicant shall, within such period of not less than three months as the registrar may specify, file Form TM35 accompanied by a copy of the regulations governing the use of the mark.

30 Amendment of regulations of collective and certification marks; Schedule 1 paragraph 10 and Schedule 2 paragraph 11 (Forms TM36 & TM7)

(1) An application for the amendment of the regulations governing the use of a registered collective or certification mark shall be filed on Form TM36.

(2) Where it appears to be expedient to the registrar that the amended regulations should be made available to the public the registrar shall publish a notice in the Journal indicating where copies of the amended regulations may be inspected.

(3) Any person may, within two months of the date of publication of the notice under paragraph (2), make observations to the registrar on the amendments relating to the matters referred to in paragraph 6(1) of Schedule 1

to the Act in relation to a collective mark, or paragraph 7(1) of Schedule 2 to the Act in relation to a certification mark and the registrar shall send a copy of those observations to the proprietor.

(4) Any person may, within two months of the date on which the notice was published under paragraph (2), give notice to the registrar of opposition to the amendment on Form TM7 which shall include a statement of the grounds of opposition indicating why the amended regulations do not comply with the requirements of paragraph 6(1) of Schedule 1 to the Act, or, as the case may be, paragraph 7(1) of Schedule 2 to the Act.

(5) The registrar shall send a copy of Form TM7 to the proprietor and the procedure in rules 18 and 20 shall apply to the proceedings relating to the opposition to the amendment as they apply to proceedings relating to opposition to an application for registration, but with the following modifications –

(a) any reference to –
   (i)   the applicant shall be construed as a reference to the proprietor,
   (ii) an application for registration shall be construed as a reference to an application for the amendment of the regulations,
   (iii) the person opposing the registration shall be construed as a reference to the person opposing the amendment of the regulations;
(b) the relevant period, referred to in rule 18(1), shall for these purposes be the period of two months beginning with the date upon which the registrar sent a copy of Form TM7 to the proprietor;
(c) rules 18(3) to (6), 20(2) and (3) shall not apply.

31 Registration subject to disclaimer or limitation; section 13

Where the applicant for registration of a trade mark or the proprietor by notice in writing sent to the registrar –

(a) disclaims any right to the exclusive use of any specified element of the trade mark; or
(b) agrees that the rights conferred by the registration shall be subject to a specified territorial or other limitation,

the registrar shall make the appropriate entry in the register and publish such disclaimer or limitation.

32 Alteration of registered trade marks; section 44 (Forms TM25 & TM7)

(1) The proprietor of a registered trade mark may request the registrar on Form TM25 for such alteration of the mark as is permitted under section 44 and following such request the registrar may require evidence as to the circumstances in which the application is made.

(2) Where, upon the request of the proprietor, the registrar proposes to allow such alteration, the registrar shall publish the mark as altered in the Journal.

(3) Any person claiming to be affected by the alteration may, within two months of the date on which the mark as altered was published under paragraph (2), give notice to the registrar of objection to the alteration on Form TM7 which shall include a statement of the grounds of objection.

(4) The registrar shall send a copy of Form TM7 to the proprietor and the procedure in rules 18 and 20 shall apply to the proceedings relating to the objection to the alteration as they apply to proceedings relating to opposition to an application for registration, but with the following modifications –

(a) any reference to –
    (i) the applicant shall be construed as a reference to the proprietor,
    (ii) an application for registration shall be construed as a reference to a request for alteration,
    (iii) the person opposing the registration shall be construed as a reference to the person objecting to the alteration,
    (iv) the opposition shall be construed as a reference to the objection;
(b) the relevant period, referred to in rule 18(1), shall for these purposes be the period of two months beginning with the date upon which the registrar sent a copy of Form TM7 to the proprietor;
(c) rules 18(3) to (6), 20(2) and (3) shall not apply.

33 Surrender of registered trade mark; section 45 (Forms TM22 & TM23)

(1) Subject to paragraph (2), the proprietor may surrender a registered trade mark, by sending notice to the registrar –

(a) on Form TM22 in respect of all the goods or services for which it is registered; or
(b) on Form TM23, in respect only of those goods or services specified by the proprietor in the notice.

(2) A notice under paragraph (1) shall be of no effect unless the proprietor in that notice –

(a) gives the name and address of any person having a registered interest in the mark; and
(b) certifies that any such person –
    (i) has been sent not less than three months' notice of the proprietor's intention to surrender the mark, or
    (ii) is not affected or if affected consents to the surrender.

(3) The registrar shall, upon the surrender taking effect, make the appropriate entry in the register and publish the date of surrender on the Office website.

Renewal and Restoration

34 Reminder of renewal of registration; section 43

(1) Subject to paragraph (2) below, at any time not earlier than six months nor later than one month before the expiration of the last registration of a trade mark, the registrar shall (except where renewal has already been affected under rule 35) send to the registered proprietor notice of the approaching expiration

and inform the proprietor at the same time that the registration may be renewed in the manner described in rule 35.

(2) If it appears to the registrar that a trade mark may be registered under section 40 at any time within six months before or at any time on or after the date on which renewal would be due (by reference to the date of application for registration), the registrar shall be taken to have complied with paragraph (1) if the registrar sends to the applicant notice to that effect within one month following the date of actual registration.

35 Renewal of registration; section 43 (Form TM11)

Renewal of registration shall be effected by filing a request for renewal on Form TM11 at any time within the period of six months ending on the date of the expiration of the registration.

36 Delayed renewal and removal of registration; section 43 (Form TM11)

(1) If on the expiration of the last registration of a trade mark the renewal fee has not been paid, the registrar shall publish that fact.

(2) If, within six months from the date of the expiration of the last registration, a request for renewal is filed on Form TM11 accompanied by the appropriate renewal fee and additional renewal fee, the registrar shall renew the registration without removing the mark from the register.

(3) Where no request for renewal is filed, the registrar shall, subject to rule 37, remove the mark from the register.

(4) Where a mark is due to be registered after the date on which it is due for renewal (by reference to the date of application for registration), the request for renewal shall be filed together with the renewal fee and additional renewal fee within six months after the date of actual registration.

(5) The removal of the registration of a trade mark shall be published on the Office website.

37 Restoration of registration; section 43 (Form TM13)

(1) Where the registrar has removed the mark from the register for failure to renew its registration in accordance with rule 36, the registrar may, following receipt of a request filed on Form TM13 within six months of the date of the removal of the mark accompanied by the appropriate renewal fee and appropriate restoration fee –

    (a)   restore the mark to the register; and
    (b)   renew its registration,

if, having regard to the circumstances of the failure to renew, the registrar is satisfied that it is just to do so.

(2) The restoration of the registration, including the date of restoration, shall be published on the Office website.

Revocation, Invalidation and Rectification

38 Application for revocation (on the grounds of non-use); section 46(1)(a) or (b) (Forms TM8(N) & TM26(N))

(1) An application to the registrar for revocation of a trade mark under section 46, on the grounds set out in section 46(1)(a) or (b), shall be made on Form TM26(N).

(2) The registrar shall send a copy of Form TM26(N) to the proprietor.

(3) The proprietor shall, within two months of the date on which he was sent a copy of Form TM26(N) by the registrar, file a Form TM8(N), which shall include a counter-statement.

(4) Where the proprietor fails to file evidence of use of the mark or evidence supporting the reasons for non-use of the mark within the period specified in paragraph (3) above the registrar shall specify a further period of not less than two months within which the evidence shall be filed.

(5) The registrar shall send a copy of Form TM8(N) and any evidence of use, or evidence supporting reasons for non-use, filed by the proprietor to the applicant.

(6) Where the proprietor fails to file a Form TM8(N) within the period specified in paragraph (3) the registration of the mark shall, unless the registrar directs otherwise, be revoked.

(7) Where the proprietor fails to file evidence within the period specified under paragraph (3) or any further period specified under paragraph (4), the registrar may treat the proprietor as not opposing the application and the registration of the mark shall, unless the registrar directs otherwise, be revoked.

(8) The registrar may, at any time, give leave to either party to file evidence upon such terms as the registrar thinks fit.

39 Application for revocation (on grounds other than non-use); section 46(1)(c) or (d) (Forms TM8 & TM26(O))

(1) An application to the registrar for revocation of a trade mark under section 46, on the grounds set out in section 46(1)(c) or (d), shall be made on Form TM26(O) and shall include a statement of the grounds on which the application is made and be accompanied by a statement of truth.

(2) The registrar shall send a copy of Form TM26(O) and the statement of the grounds on which the application is made to the proprietor.

(3) The proprietor shall, within two months of the date on which he was sent a copy of Form TM26(O) and the statement by the registrar, file a Form TM8 which shall include a counter-statement, otherwise the registrar may treat the proprietor as not opposing the application and the registration of the mark shall, unless the registrar directs otherwise, be revoked.

(4) The registrar shall send a copy of Form TM8 to the applicant.

40 Application for revocation (on grounds other than non-use): evidence rounds

(1) Where the proprietor has filed a Form TM8, the registrar shall specify the periods within which further evidence may be filed by the parties.

(2) Where the applicant files no further evidence in support of the application the applicant, shall, unless the registrar otherwise directs, be deemed to have withdrawn the application.

(3) The registrar shall notify the proprietor of any direction given under paragraph (2).

(4) The registrar may, at any time give leave to either party to file evidence upon such terms as the registrar thinks fit.

Amendments–SI 2008/2300.

41 Application for invalidation: filing of application and counter-statement; section 47 (Forms TM8 & TM26(I))

(1) An application to the registrar for a declaration of invalidity under section 47 shall be filed on Form TM26(I) and shall include a statement of the grounds on which the application is made and be accompanied by a statement of truth.

(2) Where the application is based on a trade mark which has been registered, there shall be included in the statement of the grounds on which the application is made a representation of that mark and –

    (a)   the details of the authority with which the mark is registered;
    (b)   the registration number of that mark;
    (c)   the goods and services in respect of which –
        (i)   that mark is registered, and
        (ii)   the application is based; and
    (d)   where neither section 47(2A)(a) nor (b) applies to the mark, a statement detailing whether during the period referred to in section 47(2B)(a) it has been put to genuine use in relation to each of the goods and services in respect of which the application is based or whether there are proper reasons for non-use (for the purposes of rule 42 this is the 'statement of use').

(3) Where the application is based on a trade mark in respect of which an application for registration has been made, there shall be included in the statement of the grounds on which the application is made a representation of that mark and those matters set out in paragraph (2)(a) to (c), with references to registration being construed as references to the application for registration.

(4) Where the application is based on an unregistered trade mark or other sign which the applicant claims to be protected by virtue of any rule of law (in particular, the law of passing off), there shall be included in the statement of the grounds on which the application is made a representation of that mark or sign and the goods and services in respect of which such protection is claimed.

(5) The registrar shall send a copy of Form TM26(I) and the statement of the grounds on which the application is made to the proprietor.

(6) The proprietor shall, within two months of the date on which a copy of Form TM26(I) and the statement was sent by the registrar, file a Form TM8, which shall include a counter-statement, otherwise the registrar may treat the proprietor as not opposing the application and registration of the mark shall, unless the registrar otherwise directs, be declared invalid.

(7) The registrar shall send a copy of Form TM8 to the applicant.

42 Application for invalidation: evidence rounds

(1) Where the proprietor has filed Form TM8, the registrar shall send notice to the applicant inviting the applicant to file evidence in support of the grounds on which the application is made and any submissions and to send a copy to all the other parties.

(2) The registrar shall specify the periods within which evidence and submissions may be filed by the parties.

(3) Where –

    (a)   the application is based on an earlier trade mark of a kind falling within section 6(1)(c); or

    (b)   the application or part of it is based on grounds other than those set out in section 5(1) or (2); or

    (c)   the truth of a matter set out in the statement of use is either denied or not admitted by the proprietor, the applicant shall file evidence supporting the application.

(4) Where the applicant files no evidence under paragraph (3), the applicant shall be deemed to have withdrawn the application to the extent that it is based on –

    (a)   the matters in paragraph (3)(a) or (b); or

    (b)   an earlier trade mark which has been registered and is the subject of the statement of use referred to in paragraph (3)(c).

(5) The registrar may, at any time give leave to either party to file evidence upon such terms as the registrar thinks fit.

43 Setting aside cancellation of application or revocation or invalidation of registration; (Form TM29)

(1) This rule applies where –

    (a)   an application for registration is treated as abandoned under rule 18(2);

    (b)   the registration of a mark is revoked under rule 38(6) or rule 39(3); or

    (c)   the registration of a mark is declared invalid under rule 41(6),

and the applicant or the proprietor (as the case may be) claims that the decision of the registrar to treat the application as abandoned or revoke the registration of the mark or declare the mark invalid (as the case may be) ('the original decision') should be set aside on the grounds set out in paragraph (4).

(2) Where this rule applies, the applicant or the proprietor shall, within a period of six months beginning with the date that the application was refused or the register was amended to reflect the revocation or the declaration of invalidity (as the case may be), file an application on Form TM29 to set aside the decision of the registrar and shall include evidence in support of the application and shall copy the form and the evidence to the other party to the original proceedings under the rules referred to in paragraph (1).

(3) Where the applicant or the proprietor demonstrates to the reasonable satisfaction of the registrar that the failure to file Form TM8 within the period specified in the rules referred to in paragraph (1) was due to a failure to receive Form TM7, Form TM26(N), Form TM26(O) or Form TM26(I) (as the case may be), the original decision may be set aside on such terms and conditions as the registrar thinks fit.

(4) In considering whether to set aside the original decision the matters to which the registrar must have regard include whether the person seeking to set aside the decision made an application to do so promptly upon becoming aware of the original decision and any prejudice which may be caused to the other party to the original proceedings if the original decision were to be set aside.

44 Procedure on application for rectification; section 64 (Form TM26(R))

(1) An application for rectification of an error or omission in the register under section 64(1) shall be made on Form TM26(R) together with:

(a)   a statement of the grounds on which the application is made; and
(b)   any evidence to support those grounds.

(2) Where any application is made under paragraph (1) by a person other than the proprietor of the registered trade mark the registrar –

(a)   shall send a copy of the application and the statement, together with any evidence filed, to the proprietor; and
(b)   may give such direction with regard to the filing of subsequent evidence and upon such terms as the registrar thinks fit.

45 Procedure for intervention

(1) Any person, other than the registered proprietor, claiming to have an interest in proceedings on an application under rule 38, 39, 41 or 44, may file an application to the registrar on Form TM27 for leave to intervene, stating the nature of the person's interest and the registrar may, after hearing the parties concerned if they request a hearing, refuse leave or grant leave upon such terms and conditions (including any undertaking as to costs) as the registrar thinks fit.

(2) Any person granted leave to intervene shall, subject to any terms and conditions imposed in respect of the intervention, be treated as a party to the

proceedings for the purposes of the application of the provisions of rules 38 to 40, 41 and 42 or 44 (as appropriate) and rules 62 to 73.

The Register

46 Form of register; section 63(1)

The register required to be maintained by the registrar under section 63(1) need not be kept in documentary form.

47 Entry in register of particulars of registered trade marks; section 63(2) (Form TM24)

In addition to the entries in the register of registered trade marks required to be made by section 63(2)(a), there shall be entered in the register in respect of each trade mark the following particulars –

(a) the date of registration as determined in accordance with section 40(3) (that is to say, the date of the filing of the application for registration);
(b) the date of completion of the registration procedure;
(c) the priority date (if any) to be accorded pursuant to a claim to a right to priority made under section 35 or 36;
(d) the name and address of the proprietor;
(e) the address for service (if any) filed under rule 11;
(f) any disclaimer or limitation of rights under section 13(1)(a) or (b);
(g) any memorandum or statement of the effect of any memorandum relating to a trade mark of which the registrar has been notified on Form TM24;
(h) the goods or services in respect of which the mark is registered;
(i) where the mark is a collective or certification mark, that fact;
(j) where the mark is registered pursuant to section 5(5) with the consent of the proprietor of an earlier trade mark or other earlier right, that fact;
(k) where the mark is registered pursuant to a transformation application,
    (i) the number of the international registration, and
    (ii) either: –
        (aa) the date accorded to the international registration under Article 3(4), or
        (bb) the date of recordal of the request for extension to the United Kingdom of the international registration under Article 3*ter*,as the case may be, of the Madrid Protocol;

(l) where the mark arises from the conversion of a Community trade mark or an application for a Community trade mark, the number of any other registered trade mark from which the Community trade mark or the application for a Community trade mark claimed seniority and the earliest seniority date.

48 Entry in register of particulars of registrable transactions; section 25

Upon application made to the registrar by such person as is mentioned in section 25(1)(a) or (b) there shall be entered in the register in respect of each trade mark the following particulars of registrable transactions together with the date on which the entry is made –

(a) in the case of an assignment of a registered trade mark or any right in it –
   (i)   the name and address of the assignee,
   (ii)   the date of the assignment, and
   (iii) where the assignment is in respect of any right in the mark, a description of the right assigned;

(b) in the case of the grant of a licence under a registered trade mark –
   (i)   the name and address of the licensee,
   (ii)   where the licence is an exclusive licence, that fact,
   (iii) where the licence is limited, a description of the limitation, and
   (iv)   the duration of the licence if the same is or is ascertainable as a definite period;

(c) in the case of the grant of any security interest over a registered trade mark or any right in or under it –
   (i)   the name and address of the grantee,
   (ii)   the nature of the interest (whether fixed or floating), and
   (iii) the extent of the security and the right in or under the mark secured;

(d) in the case of the making by personal representatives of an assent in relation to a registered trade mark or any right in or under it –
   (i)   the name and address of the person in whom the mark or any right in or under it vests by virtue of the assent, and
   (ii)   the date of the assent;

(e) in the case of a court or other competent authority transferring a registered trade mark or any right in or under it –
   (i)   the name and address of the transferee,
   (ii)   the date of the order, and
   (iii) where the transfer is in respect of a right in the mark, a description of the right transferred; and

(f) in the case of any amendment of the registered particulars relating to a licence under a registered trade mark or a security interest over a registered trade mark or any right in or under it, particulars to reflect such amendment

49 Application to register or give notice of transaction; sections 25 & 27(3) (Form TM16, TM24, TM50 & TM51)

(1) An application to register particulars of a transaction to which section 25 applies or to give notice to the registrar of particulars of a transaction to which section 27(3) applies shall be made –

(a) relating to an assignment or transaction other than a transaction referred to in sub-paragraphs (b) to (d) below, on Form TM16;

(b)   relating to a grant of a licence, on Form TM50;

(c)   relating to an amendment to, or termination of a licence, on Form TM51;

(d)   relating to the grant, amendment or termination of any security interest, on Form TM24; and

(e)   relating to the making by personal representatives of an assent or to an order of a court or other competent authority, on Form TM24.

(2) An application under paragraph (1) shall –

(a)   where the transaction is an assignment, be signed by or on behalf of the parties to the assignment;

(b)   where the transaction falls within sub-paragraphs (b), (c) or (d) of paragraph (1), be signed by or on behalf of the grantor of the licence or security interest,

or be accompanied by such documentary evidence as suffices to establish the transaction.

(3) Where an application to give notice to the registrar has been made of particulars relating to an application for registration of a trade mark, upon registration of the trade mark, the registrar shall enter those particulars in the register.

50 Public inspection of register; section 63(3)

(1) The register shall be open for public inspection at the Office during the hours of business of the Office as published in accordance with rule 80.

(2) Where any portion of the register is kept otherwise than in documentary form, the right of inspection is a right to inspect the material on the register.

51 Supply of certified copies etc; section 63(3) (Form TM31R)

The registrar shall supply a certified copy or extract or uncertified copy or extract, as requested on Form TM31R, of any entry in the register.

52 Request for change of name or address in register; section 64(4) (Form TM21)

The registrar shall, on a request made on Form TM21 by the proprietor of a registered trade mark or a licensee or any person having an interest in or charge on a registered trade mark which has been registered under rule 48 ('the applicant'), enter a change in the applicant's name or address as recorded in the register.

53 Removal of matter from register; sections 25(5)(b) and 64(5) (Form TM7)

(1) Where it appears to the registrar that any matter in the register has ceased to have effect, before removing it from the register –

(a)   the registrar may publish in the Journal the fact that it is intended to remove that matter, and

(b) where any person appears to the registrar to be affected by the removal, notice of the intended removal shall be sent to that person.

(2) Within two months of the date on which the intention to remove the matter is published, or notice of the intended removal is sent, as the case may be –

(a) any person may file notice of opposition to the removal on form TM7; and

(b) the person to whom a notice is sent under paragraph (1)(b) may file in writing their objections, if any, to the removal,

and where such opposition or objections are made, rule 63 shall apply.

(3) If the registrar is satisfied after considering any objections or opposition to the removal that the matter has not ceased to have effect, the registrar shall not remove it.

(4) Where there has been no response to the registrar's notice the registrar may remove the matter and where representations objecting to the removal of the entry have been made the registrar may, if after considering the objections the registrar is of the view that the entry or any part of it has ceased to have effect, remove it or the appropriate part of it.

Change of Classification

54 Change of classification; sections 65(2) & 76(1)

(1) The registrar may at any time amend an entry in the register which relates to the classification of a registered trade mark so that it accords with the version of the Nice Classification that has effect at that time.

(2) Before making any amendment to the register under paragraph (1) the registrar shall give the proprietor of the mark written notice of the proposed amendments and shall at the same time advise the proprietor that –

(a) the proprietor may make written objections to the proposals, within two months of the date of the notice, stating the grounds of those objections; and

(b) if no written objections are received within the period specified the registrar shall publish the proposals and the proprietor shall not be entitled to make any objections to the proposals upon such publication.

(3) If the proprietor makes no written objections within the period specified in paragraph (2)(a) or at any time before the expiration of that period decides not to make any objections and gives the registrar written notice to this effect, the registrar shall as soon as practicable after the expiration of that period or upon receipt of the notice publish the proposals in the Journal.

(4) Where the proprietor makes written objections within the period specified in paragraph (2)(a), the registrar shall, as soon as practicable after having considered the objections, publish the proposals in the Journal or, where the registrar has amended the proposals, publish the proposals as amended in the Journal; and the registrar's decision shall be final and not subject to appeal.

55 Opposition to proposals; sections 65(3), (5) & 76(1) (Form TM7)

(1) Any person may, within two months of the date on which the proposals were published under rule 54, give notice to the registrar of opposition to the proposals on Form TM7 which shall include a statement of the grounds of opposition which shall, in particular, indicate why the proposed amendments would be contrary to section 65(3).

(2) If no notice of opposition under paragraph (1) is filed within the time specified, or where any opposition has been determined, the registrar shall make the amendments as proposed and shall enter in the register the date when they were made; and the registrar's decision shall be final and not subject to appeal.

Request for Information, Inspection of Documents and Confidentiality

56 Request for information; section 67(1) (Form TM31C)

A request for information relating to an application for registration or to a registered trade mark shall be made on Form TM31C.

57 Information available before publication; section 67(2)

(1) Before publication of an application for registration the registrar shall make available for inspection by the public the application and any amendments made to it and any particulars contained in a notice given to the registrar under rule 49.

(2) Nothing in section 67(2) relating to publication of information shall be construed as preventing the publication of decisions on cases relating to trade marks decided by the registrar.

58 Inspection of documents; sections 67 & 76(1)

(1) Subject to paragraphs (2) and (3), the registrar shall permit all documents filed or kept at the Office in relation to a registered mark or, where an application for the registration of a trade mark has been published, in relation to that application, to be inspected.

(2) The registrar shall not be obliged to permit the inspection of any such document as is mentioned in paragraph (1) until the completion of any procedure, or the stage in the procedure which is relevant to the document in question, which the registrar is required or permitted to carry out under the Act or these Rules.

(3) The right of inspection under paragraph (1) does not apply to –

    (a)   any document prepared in the Office solely for its own use;

    (b)   any document sent to the Office, whether at its request or otherwise, for inspection and subsequent return to the sender;

    (c)   any request for information under rule 56;

    (d)   any document received by the Office which the registrar considers should be treated as confidential;

(e)   any document in respect of which the registrar issues directions under rule 59 that it be treated as confidential.

(4) Nothing in paragraph (1) shall be construed as imposing on the registrar any duty of making available for public inspection –

(a)   any document or part of a document which in the registrar's opinion disparages any person in a way likely to cause damage to that person; or

(b)   any document or information filed at or sent to or by the Office before 31st October 1994; or

(c)   any document or information filed at or sent to or by the Office after 31st October 1994 relating to an application for registration of a trade mark under the Trade Marks Act 1938.

(5) No appeal shall lie from a decision of the registrar under paragraph (4) not to make any document or part of a document available for public inspection.

59 Confidential documents

(1) Where a document (other than a form required by the registrar and published in accordance with rule 3) is filed at the Office and the person filing it requests at the time of filing that it or a specified part of it be treated as confidential, giving reasons for the request, the registrar may direct that it or part of it, as the case may be, be treated as confidential, and the document shall not be open to public inspection while the matter is being determined by the registrar.

(2) Where such direction has been given and not withdrawn, nothing in this rule shall be taken to authorise or require any person to be allowed to inspect the document or part of it to which the direction relates except by leave of the registrar.

(3) The registrar shall not withdraw any direction given under this rule without prior consultation with the person at whose request the direction was given, unless the registrar is satisfied that such prior consultation is not reasonably practical.

(4) The registrar may where the registrar considers that any document issued by the Office should be treated as confidential so direct, and upon such direction that document shall not be open to public inspection except by leave of the registrar.

(5) Where a direction is given under this rule for a document to be treated as confidential a record of the fact shall be filed with the document.

Agents

60 Proof of authorisation of agent may be required; section 82 (Form TM33)

(1) Where an agent has been authorised under section 82, the registrar may in a particular case require the personal signature or presence of the agent or the person authorising the agent to act as agent.

(2) Subject to paragraph (3), where a person appoints an agent for the first time or appoints one agent in substitution for another, the newly appointed agent shall file Form TM33.

(3) Where after a person has become a party to proceedings involving a third party before the registrar, the person appoints an agent for the first time or appoints one agent in substitution for another, the newly appointed agent shall file Form TM33P.

(4) Any act required or authorised by the Act in connection with the registration of a trade mark or any procedure relating to a trade mark may not be done by or to the newly appointed agent until on or after the date on which the newly appointed agent files Form TM33 or TM33P as appropriate.

(5) The registrar may by notice in writing require an agent to produce evidence of his authority under section 82.

61 Registrar may refuse to deal with certain agents; section 88

The registrar may refuse to recognise as agent in respect of any business under the Act –

    (a)   a person who has been convicted of an offence under section 84;

    (b)   an individual whose name has been erased from and not restored to, or who is suspended from, the register of trade mark agents on the ground of misconduct;

    (c)   a person who is found by the Secretary of State to have been guilty of such conduct as would, in the case of an individual registered in that register, render that person liable to have their name erased from it on the ground of misconduct;

    (d)   a partnership or body corporate of which one of the partners or directors is a person whom the registrar could refuse to recognise under paragraph (a), (b) or (c).

Proceedings Before and Decision of Registrar, Evidence and Costs

62 General powers of registrar in relation to proceedings

(1) Except where the Act or these Rules otherwise provide, the registrar may give such directions as to the management of any proceedings as the registrar thinks fit, and in particular may –

    (a)   require a document, information or evidence to be filed within such period as the registrar may specify;

    (b)   require a translation of any document;

    (c)   require a party or a party's legal representative to attend a hearing;

    (d)   hold a hearing by telephone or by using any other method of direct oral communication;

    (e)   allow a statement of case to be amended;

    (f)   stay the whole, or any part, of the proceedings either generally or until a specified date or event;

    (g)   consolidate proceedings;

(h)   direct that part of any proceedings be dealt with as separate proceedings;

(i)   exclude any evidence which the registrar considers to be inadmissible.

(2) The registrar may control the evidence by giving directions as to –

(a)   the issues on which evidence is required; and

(b)   the way in which the evidence is to be placed before the registrar.

(3) When the registrar gives directions under any provision of these Rules, the registrar may –

(a)   make them subject to conditions; and

(b)   specify the consequences of failure to comply with the directions or a condition.

(4) The registrar may at any stage of any proceedings direct that the parties to the proceedings attend a case management conference or pre-hearing review.

63 Decisions of registrar to be taken after hearing

(1) Without prejudice to any provisions of the Act or these Rules requiring the registrar to hear any party to proceedings under the Act or these Rules, or to give such party an opportunity to be heard, the registrar shall, before taking any decision on any matter under the Act or these Rules which is or may be adverse to any party to any proceedings, give that party an opportunity to be heard.

(2) The registrar shall give that party at least fourteen days' notice, beginning on the date on which notice is sent, of the time when the party may be heard unless the party consents to shorter notice.

64 Evidence in proceedings before the registrar; section 69

(1) Subject to rule 62(2) and as follows, evidence filed in any proceedings under the Act or these Rules may be given –

(a)   by witness statement, affidavit, statutory declaration; or

(b)   in any other form which would be admissible as evidence in proceedings before the court.

(2) A witness statement may only be given in evidence if it includes a statement of truth.

(3) The general rule is that evidence at hearings is to be by witness statement unless the registrar or any enactment requires otherwise.

(4) For the purposes of these Rules, a statement of truth –

(a)   means a statement that the person making the statement believes that the facts stated in a particular document are true; and

(b)   shall be dated and signed by –

(i)   in the case of a witness statement, the maker of the statement,

(ii)   in any other case, the party or legal representative of such party.

(5) In these Rules, a witness statement is a written statement signed by a person that contains the evidence which that person would be allowed to give orally.

(6) Under these Rules, evidence shall only be considered filed when –

(a)   it has been received by the registrar; and

(b)   it has been sent to all other parties to the proceedings.

65 Registrar to have power of an official referee; section 69

The registrar shall have the powers of an official referee of the Supreme Court as regards –

(a)   the attendance of witnesses and their examination on oath; and

(b)   the discovery and production of documents,

but the registrar shall have no power to punish summarily for contempt.

66 Hearings before registrar to be in public

(1) The hearing before the registrar of any dispute between two or more parties relating to any matter in connection with an application for the registration of a mark or a registered mark shall be in public unless the registrar, after consultation with those parties who appear in person or are represented at the hearing, otherwise directs.

(2) (*revoked*)

Amendments–SI 2008/2683.

67 Costs of proceedings; section 68

The registrar may, in any proceedings under the Act or these Rules, by order award to any party such costs as the registrar may consider reasonable, and direct how and by what parties they are to be paid.

68 Security for costs; section 68

(1) The registrar may require any person who is a party in any proceedings under the Act or these Rules to give security for costs in relation to those proceedings; and may also require security for the costs of any appeal from the registrar's decision.

(2) In default of such security being given, the registrar, in the case of the proceedings before the registrar, or in the case of an appeal, the person appointed under section 76 may treat the party in default as having withdrawn their application, opposition, objection or intervention, as the case may be.

69 Decision of registrar (Form TM5)

(1) The registrar shall send to each party to the proceedings written notice of any decision made in any proceedings before the registrar stating the reasons

for that decision and for the purposes of any appeal against that decision, subject to paragraph (2), the date on which the notice is sent shall be taken to be the date of the decision.

(2) Where a statement of the reasons for the decision is not included in the notice sent under paragraph (1), any party may, within one month of the date on which the notice was sent to that party, request the registrar on Form TM5 to send a statement of the reasons for the decision and upon such request the registrar shall send such a statement, and the date on which that statement is sent shall be deemed to be the date of the registrar's decision for the purpose of any appeal against it.

Appeals

70 Decisions subject to appeal; section 76(1)

(1) Except as otherwise expressly provided by these Rules an appeal lies from any decision of the registrar made under these Rules relating to a dispute between two or more parties in connection with a trade mark, including a decision which terminates the proceedings as regards one of the parties or a decision awarding costs to any party ('a final decision') or a decision which is made at any point in the proceedings prior to a final decision ('an interim decision').

(2) An interim decision (including a decision refusing leave to appeal under this paragraph) may only be appealed against independently of any appeal against a final decision with the leave of the registrar.

71 Appeal to person appointed; section 76

(1) Notice of appeal to the person appointed under section 76 shall be filed on Form TM55 which shall include the appellant's grounds of appeal and his case in support of the appeal.

(2) Such notice shall be filed with the registrar within the period of 28 days beginning with the date of the registrar's decision which is the subject of the appeal ('the original decision').

(3) The registrar shall send the notice and the statement to the person appointed.

(4) Where any person other than the appellant was a party to the proceedings before the registrar in which the original decision was made ('the respondent'), the registrar shall send to the respondent a copy of the notice and the statement and the respondent may, within the period of 21 days beginning with the date on which the notice and statement was sent, file a notice responding to the notice of appeal.

(5) The respondent's notice shall specify any grounds on which the respondent considers the original decision should be maintained where these differ from or are additional to the grounds given by the registrar in the original decision.

(6) The registrar shall send a copy of the respondent's notice to the person appointed and a copy to the appellant.

72 Determination whether appeal should be referred to court; section 76(3)

(1) Within 28 days of the date on which the notice of appeal is sent to the respondent by the registrar under rule 71(4);

    (a)   the registrar; or
    (b)   any person who was a party to the proceedings in which the decision appealed against was made,

may request that the person appointed refer the appeal to the court.

(2) Where the registrar requests that the appeal be referred to the court, the registrar shall send a copy of the request to each party to the proceedings.

(3) A request under paragraph (1)(b) shall be sent to the registrar following which the registrar shall send it to the person appointed and shall send a copy of the request to any other party to the proceedings.

(4) Within 28 days of the date on which a copy of a request is sent by the registrar under paragraph (2) or (3), the person to whom it is sent may make representations as to whether the appeal should be referred to the court.

(5) In any case where it appears to the person appointed that a point of general legal importance is involved in the appeal, the person appointed shall send to the registrar and to every party to the proceedings in which the decision appealed against was made, notice to that effect.

(6) Within 28 days of the date on which a notice is sent under paragraph (5), the person to whom it was sent may make representations as to whether the appeal should be referred to the court.

73 Hearing and determination of appeal; section 76(4)

(1) Where the person appointed does not refer the appeal to the court, the person appointed shall send written notice of the time and place appointed for the oral hearing of the appeal –

    (a)   where no person other than the appellant was a party to the proceedings in which the decision appealed against was made, to the registrar and to the appellant; and
    (b)   in any other case, to the registrar and to each person who was a party to those proceedings.

(2) The person appointed shall send the notice at least fourteen days before the time appointed for the oral hearing.

(3) If all the persons notified under paragraph (1) inform the person appointed that they do not wish to make oral representations then –

    (a)   the person appointed may hear and determine the case on the basis of any written representations; and
    (b)   the time and place appointed for the oral hearing may be vacated.

(4) Rules 62, 65, 67 and 68 shall apply to the person appointed and to proceedings before the person appointed as they apply to the registrar and to proceedings before the registrar.

(5) If there is an oral hearing of the appeal then rule 66 shall apply to the person appointed and to proceedings before the person appointed as it applies to the registrar and to proceedings before the registrar.

(6) A copy of the decision of the appointed person shall be sent, with a statement of the reasons for the decision, to the registrar and to each person who was a party to the appeal.

Correction of Irregularities, Calculation and Extension of Time

74 Correction of irregularities in procedure

(1) Subject to rule 77, the registrar may authorise the rectification of any irregularity in procedure (including the rectification of any document filed) connected with any proceeding or other matter before the registrar or the Office.

(2) Any rectification made under paragraph (1) shall be made –

    (a)   after giving the parties such notice; and
    (b)   subject to such conditions,

as the registrar may direct.

75 Interrupted day

(1) The registrar may certify any day as an interrupted day where –

    (a)   there is an event or circumstance causing an interruption in the normal operation of the Office; or
    (b)   there is a general interruption or subsequent dislocation in the postal services of the United Kingdom.

(2) Any certificate of the registrar made under paragraph (1) shall be displayed in the Office and published on the Office website.

(3) The registrar shall, where the time for doing anything under these Rules expires on an interrupted day, extend that time to the next following day not being an interrupted day (or an excluded day).

(4) In this rule –

    'excluded day' means a day which is not a business day as specified in a direction given by the registrar under section 80; and
    'interrupted day' means a day which has been certified as such under paragraph (1).

76 Delays in communication services

(1) The registrar shall extend any time limit in these Rules where the registrar is satisfied that the failure to do something under these Rules was wholly or mainly attributed to a delay in, or failure of, a communication service.

(2) Any extension under paragraph (1) shall be –

    (a)   made after giving the parties such notice; and
    (b)   subject to such conditions,

as the registrar may direct.

(3) In this rule 'communication service' means a service by which documents may be sent and delivered and includes post, facsimile, email and courier.

77 Alteration of time limits (Form TM9)

(1) Subject to paragraphs (4) and (5), the registrar may, at the request of the person or party concerned or at the registrar's own initiative extend a time or period prescribed by these Rules or a time or period specified by the registrar for doing any act and any extension under this paragraph shall be made subject to such conditions as the registrar may direct.

(2) A request for extension under this rule may be made before or after the time or period in question has expired and shall be made –

    (a)   where the application for registration has not been published and the request for an extension [relates to a time or period other than one specified under rule 13 and] is made before the time or period in question has expired, in writing; and
    (b)   in any other case, on Form TM9.

(3) Where an extension under paragraph (1) is requested in relation to proceedings before the registrar, the party seeking the extension shall send a copy of the request to every other person who is a party to the proceedings.

(4) The registrar shall extend a flexible time limit, except a time or period which applies in relation to proceedings before the registrar or the filing of an appeal to the Appointed Person under rule 71, where –

    (a)   the request for extension is made before the end of the period of two months beginning with the date the relevant time or period expired; and
    (b)   no previous request has been made under this paragraph.

(5) A time limit listed in Schedule 1 (whether it has already expired or not) may be extended under paragraph (1) if, and only if –

    (a)   the irregularity or prospective irregularity is attributable, wholly or in part, to a default, omission or other error by the registrar, the Office or the International Bureau; and
    (b)   it appears to the registrar that the irregularity should be rectified.

(6) In this rule –

'flexible time limit' means –

    (a)   a time or period prescribed by these Rules, except a time or period prescribed by the rules listed in Schedule 1, or

    (b)   a time or period specified by the registrar for doing any act or taking any proceedings; and

'proceedings before the registrar' means any dispute between two or more parties relating to a matter before the registrar in connection with a trade mark.

Amendments–SI 2009/2089.

Filing of Documents, Hours of Business, Trade Marks Journal and Translations

78 Filing of documents by electronic means

The registrar may permit as an alternative to the sending by post or delivery of the application, notice or other document in legible form the filing of the application, notice or other document by electronic means subject to such terms or conditions as the registrar may specify either generally by published notice or in any particular case by written notice to the person desiring to file any such documents by such means.

79 Electronic communications

(1) The delivery using electronic communications to any person by the registrar of any document is deemed to be effected, unless the registrar has otherwise specified, by transmitting an electronic communication containing the document to an address provided or made available to the registrar by that person as an address for the receipt of electronic communications; and unless the contrary is proved such delivery is deemed to be effected immediately upon the transmission of the communication.

(2) In this rule 'electronic communication' has the same meaning as in the Electronic Communications Act 2000.

80 Directions on hours of business; section 80

Any directions given by the registrar under section 80 specifying the hours of business of the Office and business days of the Office shall be published on the Office website.

81 Trade Marks Journal; section 81

The registrar shall publish a journal, entitled 'The Trade Marks Journal' containing such information as is required to be published in the Journal under these Rules and such other information as the registrar thinks fit.

82 Translations

(1) Where any document or part thereof which is in a language other than English is filed or sent to the registrar in pursuance of the Act or these Rules,

the registrar may require that there be furnished a translation into English of the document or that part, verified to the satisfaction of the registrar as corresponding to the original text.

(2) The registrar may refuse to accept any translation which the registrar considers to be inaccurate in which event there shall be furnished another translation of the document in question verified in accordance with paragraph (1).

Transitional Provisions and Revocations

83 Revocation of previous rules and proceedings commenced under previous rules

(1) The instruments set out in Schedule 2 ('the previous rules') are revoked to the extent specified.

(2) Where immediately before these Rules come into force, any time or period prescribed by the previous rules has effect in relation to any act or proceeding and has not expired, the time or period prescribed by the previous rules and not by these Rules shall apply to that act or proceeding.

(3) Except as provided by paragraph (4) where a new step is to be taken on or after 1st October 2008 in relation to any proceedings commenced under the previous rules these Rules shall apply to such proceedings from that date.

(4) Subject to paragraph (5) where prior to the entry into force of these Rules-

    (a)   a Form TM8 and counter-statement have been filed in-
        (i)   opposition proceedings, or
        (ii)   proceedings for the revocation of a trade mark on the grounds set out in section 46(1)(c) or (d); or
        (iii)   invalidation proceedings; or
    (b)   an application for revocation of a trade mark on the grounds set out in section 46(1)(a) or (b) has been filed,

the previous rules shall apply with regard to the filing of any evidence in relation to those proceedings.

(5) Where proceedings as described in paragraph (4) are consolidated with proceedings commenced on or after 1st October 2008 these Rules shall apply with regard to the filing of any evidence in relation to those consolidated proceedings.

Schedule 1
Extension of Time Limits

Rule 77

rule 17(2) (filing notice of opposition)

rule 17(3) (filing notice of opposition: request for extension of time)

rule 18(1) (counter-statement in opposition proceedings)

rule 19(4) (responding to preliminary indication)

rule 25(2) (opposition to amendment after publication)

rule 30(4) (opposition to amendment of regulations of collective and certification marks)

rule 32(3) (opposition to alteration of mark)

rule 35 (renewal of registration)

rule 36(2) (delayed renewal)

rule 37(1) (restoration of registration)

rule 38(3) (counter-statement for revocation on grounds of non-use)

rule 39(3) (counter-statement for revocation on grounds other than non-use)

rule 41(6) (counter-statement for invalidity)

rule 43(2) (setting aside cancellation of application or revocation or invalidation of registration)

rule 53(2) (opposition to removal of matter from register)

rule 5(1) (opposition to proposals for change of classification)

rule 77(4) (period for making a retrospective request to extend a flexible time period).

Schedule 2
Revocations

Rule 83

Rules revoked	References	Extent of Revocation
The Trade Marks Rules 2000	SI 2000/136	The whole rules
The Trade Marks (Amendment) Rules 2001	SI 2001/2832	The whole rules
The Trade Marks (Amendment) Rules 2004	SI 2004/947	The whole rules
The Patents, Trade Marks and Designs (Address for Service and Time Limits etc) Rules 2006	SI 2006/760	Rules 15 to 20

The Trade Marks and Designs (Address for Service)(Amendment) Rules 2006	SI 2006/1029	The whole rules
The Trade Marks (Amendment) Rules 2006	SI 2006/3039	The whole rules
The Trade Marks (Amendment) Rules 2007	SI 2007/2076	The whole rules
The Trade Marks and Trade Marks (Fees) (Amendment) Rules 2008	SI 2008/11	Rules 2 to 4

Appendix 3

COUNCIL DIRECTIVE (EC) NO 2008/95

of 22 October 2008

to approximate the laws of the Member States relating to trade marks

THE EUROPEAN PARLIAMENT AND THE COUNCIL OF THE EUROPEAN UNION,

Having regard to the Treaty establishing the European Community, and in particular Article 95 thereof,

Having regard to the proposal from the Commission,

Having regard to the opinion of the European Economic and Social Committee [1],

Acting in accordance with the procedure laid down in Article 251 of the Treaty [2],

Whereas:

(1) The content of Council Directive 89/104/EEC of 21 December 1988 to approximate the laws of the Member States relating to trade marks [3] has been amended [4]. In the interests of clarity and rationality the said Directive should be codified.

(2) The trade mark laws applicable in the Member States before the entry into force of Directive 89/104/EEC contained disparities which may have impeded the free movement of goods and freedom to provide services and may have distorted competition within the common market. It was therefore necessary to approximate the laws of the Member States in order to ensure the proper functioning of the internal market.

(3) It is important not to disregard the solutions and advantages which the Community trade mark system may afford to undertakings wishing to acquire trade marks.

(4) It does not appear to be necessary to undertake full-scale approximation of the trade mark laws of the Member States. It will be sufficient if approximation is limited to those national provisions of law which most directly affect the functioning of the internal market.

(5) This Directive should not deprive the Member States of the right to continue to protect trade marks acquired through use but should take them into account only in regard to the relationship between them and trade marks acquired by registration.

(6) Member States should also remain free to fix the provisions of procedure concerning the registration, the revocation and the invalidity of trade marks

acquired by registration. They can, for example, determine the form of trade mark registration and invalidity procedures, decide whether earlier rights should be invoked either in the registration procedure or in the invalidity procedure or in both and, if they allow earlier rights to be invoked in the registration procedure, have an opposition procedure or an ex officio examination procedure or both. Member States should remain free to determine the effects of revocation or invalidity of trade marks.

(7) This Directive should not exclude the application to trade marks of provisions of law of the Member States other than trade mark law, such as the provisions relating to unfair competition, civil liability or consumer protection.

(8) Attainment of the objectives at which this approximation of laws is aiming requires that the conditions for obtaining and continuing to hold a registered trade mark be, in general, identical in all Member States. To this end, it is necessary to list examples of signs which may constitute a trade mark, provided that such signs are capable of distinguishing the goods or services of one undertaking from those of other undertakings. The grounds for refusal or invalidity concerning the trade mark itself, for example, the absence of any distinctive character, or concerning conflicts between the trade mark and earlier rights, should be listed in an exhaustive manner, even if some of these grounds are listed as an option for the Member States which should therefore be able to maintain or introduce those grounds in their legislation. Member States should be able to maintain or introduce into their legislation grounds of refusal or invalidity linked to conditions for obtaining and continuing to hold a trade mark for which there is no provision of approximation, concerning, for example, the eligibility for the grant of a trade mark, the renewal of the trade mark or rules on fees, or related to the non-compliance with procedural rules.

(9) In order to reduce the total number of trade marks registered and protected in the Community and, consequently, the number of conflicts which arise between them, it is essential to require that registered trade marks must actually be used or, if not used, be subject to revocation. It is necessary to provide that a trade mark cannot be invalidated on the basis of the existence of a non-used earlier trade mark, while the Member States should remain free to apply the same principle in respect of the registration of a trade mark or to provide that a trade mark may not be successfully invoked in infringement proceedings if it is established as a result of a plea that the trade mark could be revoked. In all these cases it is up to the Member States to establish the applicable rules of procedure.

(10) It is fundamental, in order to facilitate the free movement of goods and services, to ensure that registered trade marks enjoy the same protection under the legal systems of all the Member States. This should not, however, prevent the Member States from granting at their option extensive protection to those trade marks which have a reputation.

(11) The protection afforded by the registered trade mark, the function of which is in particular to guarantee the trade mark as an indication of origin, should be absolute in the case of identity between the mark and the sign and the goods or services. The protection should apply also in the case of similarity

between the mark and the sign and the goods or services. It is indispensable to give an interpretation of the concept of similarity in relation to the likelihood of confusion. The likelihood of confusion, the appreciation of which depends on numerous elements and, in particular, on the recognition of the trade mark on the market, the association which can be made with the used or registered sign, the degree of similarity between the trade mark and the sign and between the goods or services identified, should constitute the specific condition for such protection. The ways in which likelihood of confusion may be established, and in particular the onus of proof, should be a matter for national procedural rules which should not be prejudiced by this Directive.

(12) It is important, for reasons of legal certainty and without inequitably prejudicing the interests of a proprietor of an earlier trade mark, to provide that the latter may no longer request a declaration of invalidity nor may he oppose the use of a trade mark subsequent to his own of which he has knowingly tolerated the use for a substantial length of time, unless the application for the subsequent trade mark was made in bad faith.

(13) All Member States are bound by the Paris Convention for the Protection of Industrial Property. It is necessary that the provisions of this Directive should be entirely consistent with those of the said Convention. The obligations of the Member States resulting from that Convention should not be affected by this Directive. Where appropriate, the second paragraph of Article 307 of the Treaty should apply.

(14) This Directive should be without prejudice to the obligations of the Member States relating to the time limit for transposition into national law of Directive 89/104/EEC set out in Annex I, Part B,

HAVE ADOPTED THIS DIRECTIVE:

Article 1
Scope

This Directive shall apply to every trade mark in respect of goods or services which is the subject of registration or of an application in a Member State for registration as an individual trade mark, a collective mark or a guarantee or certification mark, or which is the subject of a registration or an application for registration in the Benelux Office for Intellectual Property or of an international registration having effect in a Member State.

Article 2
Signs of which a trade mark may consist

A trade mark may consist of any signs capable of being represented graphically, particularly words, including personal names, designs, letters, numerals, the shape of goods or of their packaging, provided that such signs are capable of distinguishing the goods or services of one undertaking from those of other undertakings.

Article 3
Grounds for refusal or invalidity

1. The following shall not be registered or, if registered, shall be liable to be declared invalid:

(a)   signs which cannot constitute a trade mark;

(b)   trade marks which are devoid of any distinctive character;

(c)   trade marks which consist exclusively of signs or indications which may serve, in trade, to designate the kind, quality, quantity, intended purpose, value, geographical origin, or the time of production of the goods or of rendering of the service, or other characteristics of the goods or services;

(d)   trade marks which consist exclusively of signs or indications which have become customary in the current language or in the bona fide and established practices of the trade;

(e)   signs which consist exclusively of:
  (i)   the shape which results from the nature of the goods themselves;
  (ii)   the shape of goods which is necessary to obtain a technical result;
  (iii) the shape which gives substantial value to the goods;

(f)   trade marks which are contrary to public policy or to accepted principles of morality;

(g)   trade marks which are of such a nature as to deceive the public, for instance as to the nature, quality or geographical origin of the goods or service;

(h)   trade marks which have not been authorised by the competent authorities and are to be refused or invalidated pursuant to Article 6 ter of the Paris Convention for the Protection of Industrial Property, hereinafter referred to as the 'Paris Convention'.

2 Any Member State may provide that a trade mark shall not be registered or, if registered, shall be liable to be declared invalid where and to the extent that:

(a)   the use of that trade mark may be prohibited pursuant to provisions of law other than trade mark law of the Member State concerned or of the Community;

(b)   the trade mark covers a sign of high symbolic value, in particular a religious symbol;

(c)   the trade mark includes badges, emblems and escutcheons other than those covered by Article 6 ter of the Paris Convention and which are of public interest, unless the consent of the competent authority to their registration has been given in conformity with the legislation of the Member State;

(d)   the application for registration of the trade mark was made in bad faith by the applicant.

3. A trade mark shall not be refused registration or be declared invalid in accordance with paragraph 1(b), (c) or (d) if, before the date of application for registration and following the use which has been made of it, it has acquired a distinctive character. Any Member State may in addition provide that this

provision shall also apply where the distinctive character was acquired after the date of application for registration or after the date of registration.

4. Any Member State may provide that, by derogation from paragraphs 1, 2 and 3, the grounds of refusal of registration or invalidity in force in that State prior to the date of entry into force of the provisions necessary to comply with Directive 89/104/EEC, shall apply to trade marks for which application has been made prior to that date.

Article 4
Further grounds for refusal or invalidity concerning conflicts with earlier rights

1. A trade mark shall not be registered or, if registered, shall be liable to be declared invalid:

(a) if it is identical with an earlier trade mark, and the goods or services for which the trade mark is applied for or is registered are identical with the goods or services for which the earlier trade mark is protected;

(b) if because of its identity with, or similarity to, the earlier trade mark and the identity or similarity of the goods or services covered by the trade marks, there exists a likelihood of confusion on the part of the public; the likelihood of confusion includes the likelihood of association with the earlier trade mark.

2. 'Earlier trade marks' within the meaning of paragraph 1 means:

(a) trade marks of the following kinds with a date of application for registration which is earlier than the date of application for registration of the trade mark, taking account, where appropriate, of the priorities claimed in respect of those trade marks;
   (i) Community trade marks;
   (ii) trade marks registered in the Member State or, in the case of Belgium, Luxembourg or the Netherlands, at the Benelux Office for Intellectual Property;
   (iii) trade marks registered under international arrangements which have effect in the Member State;

(b) Community trade marks which validly claim seniority, in accordance with Council Regulation (EC) No 40/94 [5] of 20 December 1993 on the Community trade mark, from a trade mark referred to in (a)(ii) and (iii), even when the latter trade mark has been surrendered or allowed to lapse;

(c) applications for the trade marks referred to in points (a) and (b), subject to their registration;

(d) trade marks which, on the date of application for registration of the trade mark, or, where appropriate, of the priority claimed in respect of the application for registration of the trade mark, are well known in a Member State, in the sense in which the words 'well known' are used in Article 6 bis of the Paris Convention.

3. A trade mark shall furthermore not be registered or, if registered, shall be liable to be declared invalid if it is identical with, or similar to, an earlier Community trade mark within the meaning of paragraph 2 and is to be, or has

been, registered for goods or services which are not similar to those for which the earlier Community trade mark is registered, where the earlier Community trade mark has a reputation in the Community and where the use of the later trade mark without due cause would take unfair advantage of, or be detrimental to, the distinctive character or the repute of the earlier Community trade mark.

4. Any Member State may, in addition, provide that a trade mark shall not be registered or, if registered, shall be liable to be declared invalid where, and to the extent that:

(a)   the trade mark is identical with, or similar to, an earlier national trade mark within the meaning of paragraph 2 and is to be, or has been, registered for goods or services which are not similar to those for which the earlier trade mark is registered, where the earlier trade mark has a reputation in the Member State concerned and where the use of the later trade mark without due cause would take unfair advantage of, or be detrimental to, the distinctive character or the repute of the earlier trade mark;

(b)   rights to a non-registered trade mark or to another sign used in the course of trade were acquired prior to the date of application for registration of the subsequent trade mark, or the date of the priority claimed for the application for registration of the subsequent trade mark, and that non-registered trade mark or other sign confers on its proprietor the right to prohibit the use of a subsequent trade mark;

(c)   the use of the trade mark may be prohibited by virtue of an earlier right other than the rights referred to in paragraph 2 and point (b) of this paragraph and in particular:
   (i)   a right to a name;
   (ii)   a right of personal portrayal;
   (iii)   a copyright;
   (iv)   an industrial property right;

(d)   the trade mark is identical with, or similar to, an earlier collective trade mark conferring a right which expired within a period of a maximum of three years preceding application;

(e)   the trade mark is identical with, or similar to, an earlier guarantee or certification mark conferring a right which expired within a period preceding application the length of which is fixed by the Member State;

(f)   the trade mark is identical with, or similar to, an earlier trade mark which was registered for identical or similar goods or services and conferred on them a right which has expired for failure to renew within a period of a maximum of two years preceding application, unless the proprietor of the earlier trade mark gave his agreement for the registration of the later mark or did not use his trade mark;

(g)   the trade mark is liable to be confused with a mark which was in use abroad on the filing date of the application and which is still in use there, provided that at the date of the application the applicant was acting in bad faith.

5. The Member States may permit that in appropriate circumstances registration need not be refused or the trade mark need not be declared invalid where the proprietor of the earlier trade mark or other earlier right consents to the registration of the later trade mark.

6. Any Member State may provide that, by derogation from paragraphs 1 to 5, the grounds for refusal of registration or invalidity in force in that State prior to the date of the entry into force of the provisions necessary to comply with Directive 89/104/EEC, shall apply to trade marks for which application has been made prior to that date.

Article 5
Rights conferred by a trade mark

1. The registered trade mark shall confer on the proprietor exclusive rights therein. The proprietor shall be entitled to prevent all third parties not having his consent from using in the course of trade:

(a) any sign which is identical with the trade mark in relation to goods or services which are identical with those for which the trade mark is registered;

(b) any sign where, because of its identity with, or similarity to, the trade mark and the identity or similarity of the goods or services covered by the trade mark and the sign, there exists a likelihood of confusion on the part of the public; the likelihood of confusion includes the likelihood of association between the sign and the trade mark.

2. Any Member State may also provide that the proprietor shall be entitled to prevent all third parties not having his consent from using in the course of trade any sign which is identical with, or similar to, the trade mark in relation to goods or services which are not similar to those for which the trade mark is registered, where the latter has a reputation in the Member State and where use of that sign without due cause takes unfair advantage of, or is detrimental to, the distinctive character or the repute of the trade mark.

3. The following, inter alia, may be prohibited under paragraphs 1 and 2:

(a) affixing the sign to the goods or to the packaging thereof;

(b) offering the goods, or putting them on the market or stocking them for these purposes under that sign, or offering or supplying services thereunder;

(c) importing or exporting the goods under the sign;

(d) using the sign on business papers and in advertising.

4. Where, under the law of the Member State, the use of a sign under the conditions referred to in paragraph 1(b) or paragraph 2 could not be prohibited before the date of entry into force of the provisions necessary to comply with Directive 89/104/EEC in the Member State concerned, the rights conferred by the trade mark may not be relied on to prevent the continued use of the sign.

5. Paragraphs 1 to 4 shall not affect provisions in any Member State relating to the protection against the use of a sign other than for the purposes of

distinguishing goods or services, where use of that sign without due cause takes unfair advantage of, or is detrimental to, the distinctive character or the repute of the trade mark.

Article 6
Limitation of the effects of a trade mark

1. The trade mark shall not entitle the proprietor to prohibit a third party from using, in the course of trade:

    (a)   his own name or address;

    (b)   indications concerning the kind, quality, quantity, intended purpose, value, geographical origin, the time of production of goods or of rendering of the service, or other characteristics of goods or services;

    (c)   the trade mark where it is necessary to indicate the intended purpose of a product or service, in particular as accessories or spare parts;

provided he uses them in accordance with honest practices in industrial or commercial matters.

2. The trade mark shall not entitle the proprietor to prohibit a third party from using, in the course of trade, an earlier right which only applies in a particular locality if that right is recognised by the laws of the Member State in question and within the limits of the territory in which it is recognised.

Article 7
Exhaustion of the rights conferred by a trade mark

1. The trade mark shall not entitle the proprietor to prohibit its use in relation to goods which have been put on the market in the Community under that trade mark by the proprietor or with his consent.

2. Paragraph 1 shall not apply where there exist legitimate reasons for the proprietor to oppose further commercialisation of the goods, especially where the condition of the goods is changed or impaired after they have been put on the market.

Article 8
Licensing

1. A trade mark may be licensed for some or all of the goods or services for which it is registered and for the whole or part of the Member State concerned. A licence may be exclusive or non-exclusive.

2. The proprietor of a trade mark may invoke the rights conferred by that trade mark against a licensee who contravenes any provision in his licensing contract with regard to:

    (a)   its duration;

    (b)   the form covered by the registration in which the trade mark may be used;

    (c)   the scope of the goods or services for which the licence is granted;

    (d)   the territory in which the trade mark may be affixed; or

(e)   the quality of the goods manufactured or of the services provided by the licensee.

Article 9
Limitation in consequence of acquiescence

1. Where, in a Member State, the proprietor of an earlier trade mark as referred to in Article 4(2) has acquiesced, for a period of five successive years, in the use of a later trade mark registered in that Member State while being aware of such use, he shall no longer be entitled on the basis of the earlier trade mark either to apply for a declaration that the later trade mark is invalid or to oppose the use of the later trade mark in respect of the goods or services for which the later trade mark has been used, unless registration of the later trade mark was applied for in bad faith.

2. Any Member State may provide that paragraph 1 shall apply mutatis mutandis to the proprietor of an earlier trade mark referred to in Article 4(4)(a) or an other earlier right referred to in Article 4(4)(b) or (c).

3. In the cases referred to in paragraphs 1 and 2, the proprietor of a later registered trade mark shall not be entitled to oppose the use of the earlier right, even though that right may no longer be invoked against the later trade mark.

Article 10
Use of trade marks

1. If, within a period of five years following the date of the completion of the registration procedure, the proprietor has not put the trade mark to genuine use in the Member State in connection with the goods or services in respect of which it is registered, or if such use has been suspended during an uninterrupted period of five years, the trade mark shall be subject to the sanctions provided for in this Directive, unless there are proper reasons for non-use.

The following shall also constitute use within the meaning of the first subparagraph:

(a)   use of the trade mark in a form differing in elements which do not alter the distinctive character of the mark in the form in which it was registered;

(b)   affixing of the trade mark to goods or to the packaging thereof in the Member State concerned solely for export purposes.

2. Use of the trade mark with the consent of the proprietor or by any person who has authority to use a collective mark or a guarantee or certification mark shall be deemed to constitute use by the proprietor.

3. In relation to trade marks registered before the date of entry into force in the Member State concerned of the provisions necessary to comply with Directive 89/104/EEC:

(a)   where a provision in force prior to that date attached sanctions to non-use of a trade mark during an uninterrupted period, the relevant period of five years mentioned in the first sub-paragraph of paragraph 1 shall be deemed to have begun to run at the same time as any period of non-use which is already running at that date;

(b)   where there was no use provision in force prior to that date, the periods of five years mentioned in the first subparagraph of paragraph 1 shall be deemed to run from that date at the earliest.

Article 11
Sanctions for non-use of a trade mark in legal or administrative proceedings

1. A trade mark may not be declared invalid on the ground that there is an earlier conflicting trade mark if the latter does not fulfil the requirements of use set out in Article 10(1) and (2), or in Article 10(3), as the case may be.

2. Any Member State may provide that registration of a trade mark may not be refused on the ground that there is an earlier conflicting trade mark if the latter does not fulfil the requirements of use set out in Article 10(1) and (2) or in Article 10(3), as the case may be.

3. Without prejudice to the application of Article 12, where a counter-claim for revocation is made, any Member State may provide that a trade mark may not be successfully invoked in infringement proceedings if it is established as a result of a plea that the trade mark could be revoked pursuant to Article 12(1).

4. If the earlier trade mark has been used in relation to part only of the goods or services for which it is registered, it shall, for purposes of applying paragraphs 1, 2 and 3, be deemed to be registered in respect only of that part of the goods or services.

Article 12
Grounds for revocation

1. A trade mark shall be liable to revocation if, within a continuous period of five years, it has not been put to genuine use in the Member State in connection with the goods or services in respect of which it is registered, and there are no proper reasons for non-use.

However, no person may claim that the proprietor's rights in a trade mark should be revoked where, during the interval between expiry of the five-year period and filing of the application for revocation, genuine use of the trade mark has been started or resumed.

The commencement or resumption of use within a period of three months preceding the filing of the application for revocation which began at the earliest on expiry of the continuous period of five years of non-use shall be disregarded where preparations for the commencement or resumption occur only after the proprietor becomes aware that the application for revocation may be filed.

2. Without prejudice to paragraph 1, a trade mark shall be liable to revocation if, after the date on which it was registered:

(a)   in consequence of acts or inactivity of the proprietor, it has become the common name in the trade for a product or service in respect of which it is registered;

(b)   in consequence of the use made of it by the proprietor of the trade mark or with his consent in respect of the goods or services for which it is registered, it is liable to mislead the public, particularly as to the nature, quality or geographical origin of those goods or services.

Article 13
Grounds for refusal or revocation or invalidity relating to only some of the goods or services

Where grounds for refusal of registration or for revocation or invalidity of a trade mark exist in respect of only some of the goods or services for which that trade mark has been applied for or registered, refusal of registration or revocation or invalidity shall cover those goods or services only.

Article 14
Establishment a posteriori of invalidity or revocation of a trade mark

Where the seniority of an earlier trade mark which has been surrendered or allowed to lapse is claimed for a Community trade mark, the invalidity or revocation of the earlier trade mark may be established a posteriori.

Article 15
Special provisions in respect of collective marks, guarantee marks and certification marks

1. Without prejudice to Article 4, Member States whose laws authorise the registration of collective marks or of guarantee or certification marks may provide that such marks shall not be registered, or shall be revoked or declared invalid, on grounds additional to those specified in Articles 3 and 12 where the function of those marks so requires.

2. By way of derogation from Article 3(1)(c), Member States may provide that signs or indications which may serve, in trade, to designate the geographical origin of the goods or services may constitute collective, guarantee or certification marks. Such a mark does not entitle the proprietor to prohibit a third party from using in the course of trade such signs or indications, provided he uses them in accordance with honest practices in industrial or commercial matters; in particular, such a mark may not be invoked against a third party who is entitled to use a geographical name.

Article 16
Communication

Member States shall communicate to the Commission the text of the main provisions of national law adopted in the field governed by this Directive.

Article 17
Repeal

Directive 89/104/EEC, as amended by the Decision listed in Annex I, Part A, is repealed, without prejudice to the obligations of the Member States relating to the time limit for transposition into national law of that Directive, set out in Annex I, Part B.

References to the repealed Directive shall be construed as references to this Directive and shall be read in accordance with the correlation table in Annex II.

Article 18
Entry into force

This Directive shall enter into force on the 20th day following its publication in the Official Journal of the European Union.

Article 19

Addressees

This Directive is addressed to the Member States.

Done at Strasbourg, 22 October 2008.

For the European Parliament

The President

H.-G. Pöttering

For the Council

The President

J.-P. Jouyet

****

INDEX

References are to paragraph numbers.